The Ottoman Crimean War (1853-1856)

The Ottoman Crimean War (1853-1856)

By
Candan Badem

BRILL

LEIDEN • BOSTON
2012

Library of Congress Cataloging-in-Publication Data

Badem, Candan, 1970–
 The Ottoman Crimean War, 1853–1856 / by Candan Badem.
  p. cm. — (The Ottoman Empire and its heritage ; v. 44)
 Includes bibliographical references and index.
 ISBN 978-90-04-18205-9 (hardback : alk. paper)
 1. Crimean War, 1853–1856—Participation, Turkish. 2. Crimean War, 1853–1856—Diplomatic history. 3. Crimean War, 1853–1856—Campaigns. 4. Crimean War, 1853–1865—Economic aspects—Turkey. 5. Crimean War, 1853–1856—Social aspects—Turkey. 6. Turkey—History—Abdul Mejid, 1839–1861. 7. Crimean War, 1853–1856—Influence. I. Title. II. Series.

 DR567.B334 2010
 947'.073809561—dc22

2010007553

This paperback was originally published in hardback under ISBN 978 90 04 18205 9 as volume 44 in the series *The Ottoman Empire and its Heritage*.

ISBN 978 90 04 22684 5

Copyright 2010 by Koninklijke Brill NV, Leiden, The Netherlands.
Koninklijke Brill NV incorporates the imprints Brill, Global Oriental, Hotei Publishing, IDC Publishers, Martinus Nijhoff Publishers and VSP.

All rights reserved. No part of this publication may be reproduced, translated, stored in a retrieval system, or transmitted in any form or by any means, electronic, mechanical, photocopying, recording or otherwise, without prior written permission from the publisher.

Authorization to photocopy items for internal or personal use is granted by Koninklijke Brill NV provided that the appropriate fees are paid directly to The Copyright Clearance Center, 222 Rosewood Drive, Suite 910, Danvers, MA 01923, USA.
Fees are subject to change.

This book is printed on acid-free paper.

CONTENTS

List of Illustrations and Maps vii
List of Abbreviations ix
List of Geographical Names xi
A Note on Transliteration and Dates xiii
Acknowledgements xv

I. Introduction and Review of the Sources 1
   Introduction 1
   Ottoman and Turkish Sources 5
   Turkish Official Military History 19
   Dissertations and Theses in Turkish 22
   Sources in Russian 25
   Sources in Other Languages 34

II. The Origins of the War 46
   Overview of the Ottoman Empire on the Eve of the War ... 46
   Relations with Britain 58
   Russia between Expansionism and Legitimism 60
   Dispute over the Holy Places 64
   Positions of France, Austria and Other States 65
   The "Sick Man of Europe" 68
   The Mission of Prince Menshikov 71
   The Vienna Note and the "Turkish Ultimatum" 82
   European and Ottoman Public Opinion before the War ... 87

III. Battles and Diplomacy during the War 99
   The Declaration of War 99
   The Danubian Front in 1853 101
   The Battle of Sinop and European Public Opinion 109
   The Caucasian Front in 1853 143
   Relations with Imam Shamil and the Circassians in 1853 ... 149
   The Battle of Şekvetil 154
   The Battles of Ahısha, Bayındır and Başgedikler 156
   The Danubian Front in 1854 and the Declaration of War
      by France and Britain 177

The Caucasian Front in 1854–1855	190
Relations with Shamil and the Circassians in 1854–1855	195
The Campaign of Summer 1854 and the Battle of Kürekdere	212
The Siege and Fall of Kars and Ömer Pasha's Caucasian Campaign in 1855	238
Battles in the Crimea and the Siege of Sevastopol	268
The End of the War and the Treaty of Paris	285
IV. Financing the War	**289**
Ottoman Financial Crisis before the War	289
The Abortive Loan of 1852	294
Ottoman War Expenses	295
Conspicuous Consumption by Palace Women	300
The Mission of Namık Pasha	301
The Mission of Black and Durand and the First Foreign Loan of 1854	316
The *İane-i Harbiye*	319
The Guaranteed Loan of 1855	322
The Loan Control Commission of 1855	324
V. The Impact of the War on Ottoman Social and Political Life	**329**
Contacts with the Europeans	329
The *Islahat Fermanı* and the Question of the Equality of Muslims and Non-Muslims	335
The Prohibition of the Black Sea White Slave Trade	348
Law and Order in the Provinces	359
The Revolt of Yezdanşêr	360
British Interference and the Suppression of the Rebellion	370
Desertions and the *Başıbozuk* Troops as a Source of Disorder	377
Public Opinion and Patriotism	394
Corruption and its Treatment	398
Conclusion	**403**
Bibliography	**413**
Index	**427**

LIST OF ILLUSTRATIONS AND MAPS

Illustrations

1. Ottoman infantry	53
2. Redif soldiers	56
3. Müşir Ömer Lütfi Pasha (1801–1871), the Ottoman Generalissimo (*Serdar-ı Ekrem*) during the war	57
4. Müşir İsmail Pasha, deputy commander of the Rumelian army	104
5. Ferik Ahmed Pasha, commander at Kalafat	105
6. Admiral Sir Adolphus Slade (Mushaver Pasha)	114
7. Patrona (Vice-Admiral) Osman Pasha and Commander Adil Bey, prisoners of war at Sevastopol	127
8. Mushir Selim Pasha, commander of the Ottoman army of Batum	208
9. Prince Mikhail Shervashidze of Abkhazia (Hamid Bey)	209
10. Williams Pasha's house, Kars, 1855	239
11. Sadyk Pasha receiving Cossacks from the Dobrudja at Shumla	241
12. Mushir Kerim Pasha (Baba Kerim), chief of staff of the Anatolian army, 1855	257
13. Surrender of Kars, 1855	258
14. The Turkish contingent for the Crimea	261
15. Council of war, Lord Raglan, Ömer Pasha and Marshal Pélissier	271
16. Ottoman soldiers and Tatar children at Gözleve	281
17. Ferik İsmail Pasha, commander of the Egyptian troops in the Crimea	285
18. Sultan Abdülmecid at British fancy-dress ball, Pera	336
19. Başıbozuks coming into Shumla from Machin	380

Maps

1. The Danubian theatre of war 1853–1854	102
2. Plan of the battle of Sinop	110
3. The Caucasian theatre of war	144

LIST OF ABBREVIATIONS

A. AMD.	Sadaret Amedî Kalemi
A. DVN.	Divan-ı Hümayun
AGKK	*Akten zur Geschichte des Krimkriegs.* Ed. Winfried Baumgart.
AKAK	*Akty, Sobrannye Kavkazskoyu Arkheograficheskoyu Komissieyu.*
A. MKT. MHM.	Sadaret Mektubî Mühimme
A. MKT. NZD.	Sadaret Mektubî Nezair ve Devair
A. MKT. UM.	Sadaret Mektubî Umum Vilâyat
ATASE	Genelkurmay Askeri Tarih Arşivi (Military Historical Archive of the Turkish General Staff), Ankara.
AVPRI	Arkhiv Vneshney Politiki Rossiyskoy Imperii (Archive of the Foreign Policy of the Russian Empire), Moscow.
BOA	Başbakanlık Osmanlı Arşivi (Prime Ministerial Ottoman Archives), Istanbul.
C. AS.	Cevdet Askeriye
CH	*Ceride-i Havadis.* Ottoman semi-official newspaper.
DMA	Deniz Müzesi Arşivi (Archive of the Naval Museum), Istanbul.
DŞA	*Dâr-ı Şûra-yı Askerî* (Military High Court)
enc.	Enclosure
FO	Foreign Office
GARF	Gosudarstvenny Arkhiv Rossiyskoy Federatsii, Moscow.
GPIB	Gosudarstvennaya Publichnaya Istoricheskaya Biblioteka, Moscow.
HR. MKT.	Hariciye Nezareti Mektubî Kalemi
HR. SFR (04)	Hariciye Nezareti Paris Sefareti
HR. SYS.	Hariciye Nezareti Siyasi Kısım
HR. TO.	Hariciye Nezareti Tercüme Odası
ILN	The *Illustrated London News.*
İ. DH.	İrade Dahiliye
İ. HR.	İrade Hariciye
İ. MMS.	İrade Meclis-i Mahsus

LIST OF ABBREVIATIONS

İ. MSM.	İrade Mesail-i Mühimme
İ. MTZ.(05)	İrade Eyalat-i Mümtaze Mısır
İ. MVL.	İrade Meclis-i Vâlâ
MAT	Meclis-i Âli-i Tanzimat (The Supreme Council of Reforms)
MVL	Meclis-i Vâlâ-i Ahkâm-i Adliye, (Meclis-i Vâlâ in short) The Supreme Council for Judiciary Ordinances.
NYDT	*New York Daily Tribune.* Newspaper.
OBKS	*Osmanlı Belgelerinde Kırım Savaşı 1853–1856.* Ankara: BOA Yayın Nu. 84, 2006.
PRMA	*Papers relative to Military Affairs in Asiatic Turkey and the Defence and Capitulation of Kars. Presented to Both Houses of Parliament by Command of Her Majesty.* London: Harrison and Sons, 1856.
RGIA	Rossiyskiy Gosudarstvenny Istoricheskiy Arkhiv, St. Petersburg
RGVIA	Rossiyskiy Gosudarstvenny Voenno-Istoricheskiy Arkhiv (Russian State Military-Histrical Archive), Moscow.
RGVMF	Rossiyskiy Gosudarstvenny Arkhiv Voenno-Morskogo Flota, St. Petersburg
Savaştan Barışa	*Savaştan Barışa: 150. Yıldönümünde Kırım Savaşı ve Paris Antlaşması (1853–1856). 22–23 Mayıs 2006. Bildiriler.* Istanbul: İ. Ü. Ed. Fak. Tarih Araştırma Merkezi, 2007.
TNA	The National Archives, London. (Formerly the Public Records Office, PRO)
TTK	Türk Tarih Kurumu, Ankara. (Turkish Historical Society)

LIST OF GEOGRAPHICAL NAMES

Turkish	Russian (in transcription)	English / French
Ahıska, Ahısha	Akhaltsykh	Akhaltzikh, Akhaltsik
Ahılkelek	Akhalkalaki	Akhalkelek
Akmescit	Simferopol	Simferopol
Sivastopol, Akyar	Sevastopol	Sevastopol
Almalu, Elmalı	Alma	Alma
Anakra	Anakliya, Anakriya	Anakria
Başgedikler	Bashkadyklar	Bashgedikler
Buğdan	Moldava	Moldavia
Cizre	Djezire	Jezireh, Jazira
Çamçıra, Çamşıra	Ochamchire	Shemsherrai, Tchamshirah
Çatana	Chetati	Cetate, Citate
Çürüksu	Churuk-Su, Kobulety	
Eflak	Valakhiya	Wallachia
Erzurum	Erzrum	Erzeroom
Gözleve	Yevpatoriya	Eupatoria
Gümrü	Aleksandropol	Alexandropol
Hocabey	Odessa	Odessa
Halep		Aleppo
İsakçı, İsakça	Isakchi	Isaktschi, Isacchea
Kancaçay	Kacha	Katscha
Kefe	Feodosiya	Feodosia, Kaffa
Kılburun	Kinburn	Kinburn
Megrelistan	Megreliya	Mingrelia
Oltaniçe	Ol'tenitsa	Oltenitza
Or (Ur) Kapusu	Perekop	Perekop
Özi	Ochakov	Ochakof
Rahova	Rassova	Rassova
Rusçuk	Ruschuk	Ruse
Semirzağan	Samurzakan	Samursachan
Sohum, Sohumkale	Sukhumi	Souchoum, Sukhum, Soukoumkale
Süzebolu	Sizopol'	Sizepolis
Şekvetil, Şefketil	Svyaty Nikolai	St. Nicholas
Şumnu	Shumla	Shumla, Schumla
Tırhala		Tricala
Trabzon	Trebizond	Trapezund, Trebizond

Turkish	Russian (in transcription)	English / French
Tutrakan, Totrakan	Turtukai	Turtukai
Üsküdar	Skutari	Scutari
Yergöğü, Yerköy	Zhurzhev	Giurgevo
Ziştovi	Svishtov	Sistov
Zugdidi	Zugdidi	Sugdidi

A NOTE ON TRANSLITERATION AND DATES

All Ottoman-Turkish proper names have been given in their modern Turkish orthography. Thus, instead of Omar (or Omer) Pasha I preferred Ömer Pasha. The final -d in Arabic names has been preserved. Thus, instead of Ahmet, Mehmet and Mahmut, I wrote Ahmed, Mehmed, Mahmud etc. Geographical proper names with a different Turkish version have also been given in the original Turkish version, with their European counterpart provided in the list of geographical names. Thus we have Gözleve instead of Eupatoria and Şekvetil instead of St. Nicholas.

Russian personal Christian names were not anglicized but their original orthography was maintained. Thus, instead of Nicholas I and Alexander II, we have emperors Nikolai I and Aleksandr II. Russian proper names were also transliterated in a phonetic way, closer to their pronunciation. Thus, instead of Evgeny (or Eugene) and Muraviev, I used Yevgeniy and Muravyov, which correspond better both to the pronunciation and spelling of these names. European proper names that appear in Ottoman texts were also duly given in their original spelling as far as possible.

Muslim (*Hicri*) and Julian (*Rumi*) dates were converted to the Western calendar by using the online calendar converter at the website of the TTK (www.ttk.gov.tr). For the sake of brevity, Muslim dates have not been given together with Western dates, unless necessary. However, it must be noted that due to the irregularities of the Muslim calendar, this converter may err by one day in cases when the day of the week is not known. Wherever possible, I have tried to check and compare important dates with Western sources.

ACKNOWLEDGEMENTS

I would like to thank Prof. Hakan Erdem and Prof. Akşin Somel from Sabancı University for their enthusiastic support during the completion of my PhD. I am also thankful to Prof. Suraiya Faroqhi from Bilgi University who has greatly helped me in turning my dissertation into a book. Prof. Winfried Baumgart from the Mainz University read the draft of the dissertation and made some suggestions and comments. Prof. Şevket Pamuk and Prof. Edhem Eldem from the Boğaziçi University have been kind enough to answer my questions about Ottoman finances.

Mehemed Malmisanîj, author of books on Kurdish history, has given valuable information on Kurdish geography, names and history. Karolina Fursewicz brought from Poland for me Michal Czajkowski's (Sadık Pasha's) memoirs in Polish and translated some passages from it. Joanna Błaszkowska has also helped me in the translation of some passages from Czajkowski's work. My friend and colleague Dr. Aysel Danacı Yıldız has helped me in the transcription of some Ottoman texts. Irma Kreiten has generously shared with me the AKAK, which is really hard to find. Charles M. Samaha has sent me copies of the Walpole Papers and some rare books. Sinan Kuneralp gave me the AGKK and made some comments on an earlier version of this book.

I have benefited from conversations with Prof. Andrew Lambert from King's College of the University of London. Prof. Lambert has also kindly sent me some documents on the battle of Sinop from TNA. Oleg Shkedya from the Tavriya University in Simferopol has brought some Russian sources to my attention. Dr. Douglas Austin from the Crimean War Research Society in the UK sent me his publication of the Blunt Papers and many copies and images from the ILN. Dr. Austin and Oliver Perrin have read some chapters and have made very useful suggestions in terms of English style. Prof. Moshe Gammer from Tel Aviv University answered my questions about Sheikh Shamil.

The director of the BOA, Dr. Mustafa Budak and the archive staff have been very helpful. Caroline Shaw from the Rothschild Archive in London has been kind enough to send me free of charge copies of many documents related to the 1855 loan.

Among librarians, I am indebted most to Mehmet Manyas from Sabancı University for his efforts to provide me with books and articles from other national and international libraries. Veronika Lapshina and Yelena Strukova from the GPIB in Moscow have also been kindly helpful. Librarians of the Boğaziçi University were also very kind and helpful. The staff of the library of the Centre for Islamic Studies (ISAM) was also very helpful.

Associazione Europiemonte in Turin financed my participation in the congress on the 150th anniversary of the end of the Crimean War in Turin in November 2006. My friend Kemal Çetinelli has generously financed all the costs of my research trip to Moscow in June 2006. My friend Tarık Tayfun has also supported me in many ways during my studies.

While I thank all for their help, comments and criticism, I alone am responsible for all possible mistakes and omissions.

CHAPTER ONE

INTRODUCTION AND REVIEW OF THE SOURCES

Introduction

This book concerns the Ottoman involvement in the Crimean War of 1853–1856. While a huge literature in the European languages (including Russian) is available on this topic, there hardly exists any modern, up-to-date, comparative, scholarly monograph based on original research in Ottoman sources and focusing on the Ottoman state and society. The main concern of this study is to re-construct the narrative of the war as experienced by the Ottomans, setting the record straight by an up-to-date, comparative study of factual data from primary sources. While doing so, I will also examine the political, economic, social and intellectual impact of the war on the Ottoman state and society. Language barriers, neglect and, indeed, total ignorance of the Ottoman archival material have hitherto prevented Western and Russian historians from paying sufficient attention to the role of the Ottomans in the war.[1] The present study aims to fill this gap in the historiography of this all-European, proto-world war of the long nineteenth century. While a good deal of the Western historiography focuses on the origins of the war and the role of diplomacy, the present study will rather concern itself with the conduct of the war itself and with its implications, results and impact upon the Ottoman state and society.

Interestingly, the Ottoman and Turkish historians themselves have neglected this topic and their references have also come primarily from Western sources. Although recently there have been new studies and some dissertations written in Turkey, the general coverage of the Turkish historiography on the subject is not very impressive. The existing general histories of the nineteenth century give scanty place to the war and the few monographs on the topic confine themselves

---

[1] Prof. David Goldfrank adds "parochialism" to the list of causes. See his article "The Ottoman Empire and the Origin of the Crimean War: Sources and Strategies", in *The Turks* 4, Ankara: Yeni Türkiye, 2002, p. 233.

to making a summary of Western sources, whereas Ottoman archives are open and the subject is waiting for its researchers.

The Crimean War is the only all-European war in the one hundred years between the Napoleonic Wars and the First World War. It is also the only war in the nineteenth century when the Ottomans defeated Russia. Of the ten wars between Russia and the Ottoman Empire from 1678 to 1917, only three ended with victory for the Ottomans. The Crimean War is also the only time when two European great powers, Britain and France fought against the Russians in alliance with the Ottomans. The Crimean War, indeed, proved to be of the utmost importance for the Ottoman Empire in the nineteenth century. It officially introduced the Ottoman Empire into the European state system, the so-called *Concert of Europe*. The Crimean War is an exceptional example of Russian diplomatic isolation due to the personal miscalculations of Nikolai I and to the successful alliance policies of the Porte. Ottoman statesmen, however, later discovered the practical value of being included in the European system or becoming allied with European powers; when, in 1877, their hopes of British or French help against Russia did not materialize. Even the promulgation of the 1876 Constitution did not help the Ottoman Empire to gain European favour. Nevertheless, the doctrine of Turkey's geopolitical strategic importance carried over into the twentieth century.

One of the possible reasons of the relative oblivion concerning this war in Turkish historiography is that it was seen as creating too many problems even though the Ottoman Empire was on the winning side at the end of it. In fact, the Treaty of Paris neutralized the Black Sea for both Russia and the Ottoman Empire. Territorially the Ottoman Empire did not make any significant gain, but it was exhausted economically and morally. Soon after the war, the idea that it was quite a useless and senseless conflict gained popularity in both European and Ottoman public opinion. Public opinion was indeed important during the war: We can argue that the Crimean War was the first war in world history where public opinion did matter. This was in part due to the wonderful effect of the electric telegraph, bringing news from the front almost daily. In 1877, when Russia again attacked the Ottoman Empire, the British government was again influenced by public opinion; on that occasion, however, Britain took Cyprus from the Ottoman Empire as a reward for its support without going into war. That Britain could gain its ends without going to war against Russia also contributed to the common (especially British) notion that the Crimean War was useless. Such a view is very misguided because it does not pay attention to the tensions between Russia and Europe related to influence over the Ottoman Empire. Needless to say, these tensions were based on very material interests and not on personal matters or religious quarrels.

From a wider perspective, the Crimean War divides the long nineteenth century (from 1789 to 1917) into two periods, terminating the reign of peace in Europe after the Napoleonic wars. It starts the age of modern warfare and many military novelties. It gives us a prototype or foretaste of the long trench wars of the First World War. There has been much debate about the naming of this conflict, including the recent studies by Trevor Royle[2] and Winfried Baumgart.[3] They have also pointed to the inadequacy of the term 'Crimean' to describe the war. I maintain that this war comes very close to the definition of a "Proto-World War" or an All-out European War. Some Turkish sources call it simply the '1853–1856 Turco-Russian War', beyond doubt as narrow as the term 'Crimean'. Not surprisingly, there is very little mention of the Baltic, White Sea and Pacific fronts of the war in Turkish historiography.

We can ask a very legitimate question: what is a World War or a European War? How can we define it? Should we define it by the importance and number of belligerent states? That is, by whether all great powers take part in it? Alternatively, should we define it by the extent and proximity to Europe of the war areas? The Crimean War was fought on seven fronts and not just in the Crimea: in the lower Danube, in the Black Sea, in the Baltic, White and Pacific Seas, and in the Caucasus. All major powers either actively fought or, as in the case of Austria, came close to war. Now the only missing party for this war to be called a World War would seem to be the USA. Then, was the USA truly a great power in the middle of the nineteenth century? Did it have a major say in world politics? I rather think it did not. Nevertheless, even the USA came close to breaking its isolationist stand in world politics during the war.

---

[2] Trevor Royle, *Crimea. The Great Crimean War 1854–1856*. London: Little, Brown and Company, 1999. Second edition: London: Abacus, 2000. As is seen from the title, like many other Western narratives of the war, the book starts the war from 1854, when Britain and France joined the war, ignoring the battles of 1853 to a great extent.

[3] Winfried Baumgart, *The Crimean War, 1853–1856*. London: Arnold; New York: Oxford University Press, 1999.

It is also surprising that some Russian sources use the term *vostochnaya voina* (eastern or oriental war). The term was first used in Europe (*guerre d'Orient*) and came to Russia later. Nevertheless, as in some other cases, this intellectual invention proved to be more permanent in Russia than in Europe. Russian historians used the term as if it was an original Russian term. As for Turkish historiography, there is naturally no mention of an "eastern" or "oriental" war. In some cases the war is called the Turco-Russian war of 1853–1856. I think the term *vostochnaya voina* is useful only in that it reminds us of the so-called Eastern Question of the nineteenth century. Apart from that, it is of course rather Eurocentric. What is east of Europe may well be west of Asia. Geographically speaking, for instance, Trans-Caucasus (*Zakavkaz'e* in Russian), is the area *beyond* the Caucasian mountains for Russia, Ukraine and also for Europe, but for someone looking from Turkey, it is the area *in front of* the Caucasian mountains, or it is simply the Caucasus. Nevertheless, such kind of Eurocentrism is so powerful that that we find even some Ottoman and Turkish sources using the literal translation of Trans-Caucasus or *Zakavkaz'e* as *Mavera-i Kafkas* or *Kafkaslar Ötesi*.

One of the problems of the Ottoman-Turkish historiography remains in its limited use of Russian sources. For example, the name of the Russian Extraordinary Ambassador Aleksandr Sergeyevich Menshikov is usually misspelled in Ottoman and Turkish sources as *Mençikof* while the correct form in Turkish would be *Menşikov*. Only in the work of the late historian Akdes Nimet Kurat do we encounter a correct spelling of his name. The confusion probably stems from using French sources instead of Russian or from the influence of the Italian, which was still a popular *lingua franca* between the Ottomans and the Europeans. In the Ottoman archives the name of the Russian Extraordinary Ambassador is mostly spelled as *Mençikof*, although there are instances of the more correct spelling of *Menşikof*. History textbooks of the 1930s use the almost correct form, *Menşikof*. From the 1950s onward we observe a return to the old incorrect form of *Mençikof*. Even recent publications still misspell his name as *Mençikof*. This seemingly insignificant spelling error in fact clearly illustrates the perils of using secondary sources and not checking the orthography of proper names.

What's more, in Turkey, Russian history and Turkish-Russian relations came to be written by émigré intellectuals who fled the Russian revolution and who were very fervently anti-Russian and anti-Soviet.

These historians could not be objective in their studies due to personal affiliations and ideological-political engagements. One of them, the above mentioned Prof. Akdes Nimet Kurat, who came from an *ulema* and *mirza* family, wrote two voluminous books on Russian history and Russo-Turkish relations from just such a perspective. During the Cold War period, it was hard to find unbiased approaches to the questions of Russo-Ottoman relations. Now the ice is broken, there are more and more Turkish researchers willing to learn Russian and study these relations in a more relaxed and objectively detached way.

The method used here is a comparative historical social analysis that aims to present a balanced view of all sides without any nationalist agenda to prove the "heroism" of one side or the "cowardice" of another. This requires a thorough critique of the nationalist, imperialist, state-worshipping and apologetic discourses in the Ottoman, Turkish, Russian and European historiographies.

Ottoman and Turkish Sources

Our survey begins with the primary and secondary sources of the Ottoman-Turkish historiography on the subject.[4] First a few words about the archives. In Turkey, the most important archive is of course the Prime Ministerial Ottoman archive in Istanbul (BOA). It contains the former archive of the Ottoman foreign ministry as well. The other related archives in Turkey are those of the Turkish Naval Museum in Istanbul (DMA) and of the General Staff in Ankara (ATASE). The latter archives are not open to all, those who apply to do research in these archives go through a "security check". I applied to the DMA in January 2006 and only at the end of May 2006 was told that my application was rejected, without citing any reason. Therefore I did not apply to the ATASE. However, I do not think that I have lost much, because, as we will see later, there are two doctoral dissertations related to our subject that have used these two military archives and their results imply that these archives probably do not contain much significant information on our topic.

---

[4] Candan Badem, "The Treatment of the Crimean War in Turkish Historiography", *Vostochnaya (Krymskaya) Voina 1853–1856 godov: Novye materialy i novoe osmyslenie*. Tom 1, Simferopol: Krymskiy Arkhiv, 2005, pp. 24–35.

The Ottoman official chronicler (*vakanüvis*) Ahmet Cevdet Pasha (1822–1895) served in that office from 1855 to 1865 and he wrote his *Tarih-i Cevdet*, a history of the Ottoman Empire from 1774 to 1825. After that he continued to write historical notes or memoranda (*Tezâkir*) about current events of his time for his successor Lütfi Efendi. Cevdet Pasha was a first-hand witness of many of the events he described in his notes. Although he was a protégé of Mustafa Reşid Pasha (1799–1857), he managed to survive under all cabinets, because he was also a well-placed bureaucrat, capable of preserving his position during changes in the government. Cevdet Pasha's observations are sharp and witty. Prof. Cavid Baysun first began publishing the whole of the *Tezâkir* only in 1953.[5] Until then it existed only as a manuscript. Another work of Cevdet Pasha that concerns us is the *Ma'rûzât*, which covers the period from 1839 to 1876.[6] The work was written on the order of Sultan Abdülhamid II (r. 1876–1909) and was published in 1980. Although the subjects of the two works overlap, the *Tezâkir* is the more reliable because it does not try to appeal to Sultan Abdulhamid II. In general, Cevdet Pasha is an influential source for our subject. Some mistakes in the secondary sources originate from his account of the war. Despite that, Cevdet Pasha is a very valuable and indispensable source for understanding the attitudes of the Ottoman bureaucracy towards the war. He was the first Ottoman chronicler to attempt a reform in Ottoman historiography by introducing comparative analysis and social history into it. It is a pity that even those international historians who read Turkish have neglected him.

Ahmed Lütfi Efendi (1816–1907) was the Ottoman official chronicler after Cevdet Pasha. From 1866 until his death Lütfi was responsible for the chronicle of the period 1826–1876. Unfortunately, his work is very insipid, insignificant, scanty and without much analysis. In many cases he copies from the official newspaper *Takvim-i Vekayi* and the *Tezâkir*. Lütfi wrote his chronicle when many participants and statesmen of the time of the Crimean War were still alive, yet in many cases where he gives little information, he simply makes the following comment: "only this much information has been given in the *Takvim-i Vekayi*"! On the question of the actual losses of the Ottoman army

---

[5] Ahmet Cevdet Paşa, *Tezâkir*. Ed. Cavid Baysun. 4 vols. Ankara: TTK, 1991. First Edition 1953.

[6] Ahmet Cevdet Paşa, *Ma'rûzât*. Ed. Yusuf Halaçoğlu. Istanbul: Çağrı Yayınevi, 1980.

during the Crimean War, he writes of his having applied to the war ministry and their inability to give an answer. The new edition of his chronicle by Prof. Münir Aktepe contains some transliteration errors. For example, the French foreign minister Drouyn de Lhuys appears as "Verone (?) de Louis", [question mark by Aktepe], etc. Admittedly, Ottoman script can be very troublesome for some foreign words; in this case, however, the editor does not have an excuse, because it is easy to check out who the French foreign minister was at that time.

The scarcity of Ottoman primary sources may at times be disappointing for the historian of the Ottoman Empire. Although the BOA contains a great wealth of documents, they are by their very nature prosaic and official. The two newspapers in Turkish, the official *Takvim-i Vekayi* and the semi-official *Ruzname-i Ceride-i Havadis* are also very dry and colourless. What is missing are personal narratives and memoirs. As noted by the late James Reid, while many Russian and British officers have written their memoirs, Ottoman officers did not, with very few exceptions.[7] Thus in the absence of Ottoman personal narratives, we have to make do with those of the foreign officers who were temporarily in Ottoman service such as the Hungarian general György Kmety (İsmail Pasha), the Polish general Michal Czajkowski (Mehmed Sadık Pasha) and the British naval adviser Vice-Admiral Adolphus Slade (Mushaver Pasha), General William Fenwick Williams, Colonel Atwell Lake and Doctor Humphry Sandwith. (Their memoirs will be dealt with below). The Ottoman exceptions are those of Zarif Mustafa Pasha (1816–1862),[8] governor of Erzurum in 1853 and commander of the Anatolian army from March to October 1854; Nafiz Efendi,[9] an artillery officer who wrote on the siege of Silistria of 1854, and Major Osman Bey (alias Frederick Millingen), step-son of Grand Vizier Kıbrıslı Mehmed Pasha (1853–1854 and 1859–1861) and aide de camp to Müşir Mustafa Pasha at Batum.

---

[7] James J. Reid, *Crisis of the Ottoman Empire. Prelude to Collapse 1839–1878*, Stuttgart: Franz Steiner Verlag, 2000, pp. 47–51.

[8] Enver Ziya Karal (ed.), "Zarif Paşa'nın Hatıratı 1816-1862", *Belleten* IV, Ankara, 1940, pp. 442–494. These memoirs had not been published anywhere until 1940.

[9] Nafiz Efendi, *Silistre Muhasarası*, Istanbul: Teodor Kasap Matbaası, 1290 [1874]. Hakkı Tarık Us has argued that the book was written by Namık Kemal. Russian translation: "Krepost' Silistriya v 1854 godu", *Voenny Sbornik* 106(12), 1875, pp. 488–502. The editor of the *Voenny Sbornik* remarks that the article is published as a rare example of "Turkish" military literature.

During the war, Osman Bey was an adjutant (aide-de-camp) of *Müşir* (marshal) Mustafa Pasha, commander of the Batum army from August 1854 to August 1855. Osman Bey's article was published in a Russian journal in 1877 and has not been translated into Turkish to the best of my knowledge.[10] In fact there are no references to this article in Turkish literature. Osman Bey seems to have been an eccentric adventurer, as he was characterised by Russian authorities.[11] After serving nine years in the Ottoman army, Osman Bey resigned or was dismissed from the service, then he travelled much in the world. In July 1873, he went to St Petersburg and applied for Russian citizenship. He also wrote some articles for Russian journals, signing his name as Vladimir Andrejevich Osman-Bey. One of these articles is on the "Turkish" army.[12] He converted to Orthodoxy, served in the Russian army in the next war against the Ottoman Empire and took part in the storming of Kars in November 1877, for which he received the order of St. Anne, third class. Like his mother Melek Hanım, Osman Bey is very hostile to Islam and an anti-Semite, but he is not biased against all Muslims; he even shows some sympathy to Muhammed Emin, the *naib* of Sheikh Shamil (1797–1871) in Circassia. He gives us interesting information about his stepfather's relations with Mustafa Pasha and others.

Aşçıdede Halil İbrahim's memoirs are only very slightly relevant to the war: He was appointed *ruznamçeci* (daybook accountant) of the Anatolian army in March 1856 and when he arrived at Erzurum in April 1856, peace had already been declared.[13]

It would be very interesting to read the personal memoirs of Ömer Lütfi Pasha (1806–1871), the commander-in-chief, Müşir Selim Mehmed Pasha and Müşir Mustafa Pasha of the Batum Army, Abdi Pasha, Kerim Pasha and Vasıf Pasha of the Anatolian Army, Vice-Admiral Osman Pasha, commander of the Ottoman squadron at Sinop, etc., if such memoirs existed. Indeed, the memoirs of any Ottoman officer or soldier or bureaucrat would be very valuable. We only have the statements (evidence) of some pashas during their trial at the MVL for

---

[10] Mayor Osman Bey, "Vospominaniya o 1855 gode", *Kavkazskiy Sbornik*, vol. 2, 1877, pp. 143–214.
[11] RGVIA, fond 485, op. 1, d. 575, list 11. Zapiska dlya pamyati.
[12] Osman Bey, "Zametki o Turetskoy armii", *Voenny Sbornik* 6, June 1874, pp. 338–355.
[13] Aşçıdede Halil İbrahim, *Hatıralar*. Istanbul: İstanbul Ansiklopedisi Kütüphanesi, 1960.

their misdeeds in battles and in the administration of the army. Unfortunately for historians, Ottoman statesmen like Mustafa Reşid Pasha, Mehmed Emin Âli Pasha (1815-1871) and Fuad Pasha (1814-1869) have also left no memoirs, except for the unauthenticated political testaments of Âli Pasha and Fuad Pasha.[14]

I have located two Ottoman manuscripts on the Crimean War in Turkish libraries. One is an anonymous *ruzname* (diary) of the war titled *Kırım Harbi Hakkında Ruzname*. Its author must be an official who had access to some official correspondence. This manuscript does not give much important information. The other manuscript is titled *1270 Rus Seferi* (the Russian campaign of 1853-1854) written by a certain Arif Efendi who seems to have been a director of the Public Debt Administration. It does not contain much significant information either.

On the other hand, there is a rich literature in Turkish on the Crimean War, mostly poetry and theatre plays. There are many military marches (*harbiyye*), epic poems (*destan, zafername*) and epic folk songs (*koçaklama*). Some of the *destans* are indeed good sources for information on the war. For example, Salih Hayri's *Hayrabat* is such a work. The editor Necat Birinci informs us that Salih Hayri, also known as *"Türk Hayri"*, was a quarantine officer in Istanbul and a protégé of Âli Pasha. Hayri must have talked to many people and listened to many high officials during the war because he gives much specific information about the war. Unfortunately, this modern Turkish edition of the *Hayrabat* by Necat Birinci is not free from transliteration errors of proper names. Thus Russian generals Muravyov and Brimmer become "Moradif" and "Barimov", the British officer Teesdale becomes *"mir-i tez-dil"*, etc. Necat Birinci refers to Fahrettin Kırzıoğlu's work,[15] but he seems not to have read Kırzıoğlu carefully, because if he had done so, he would probably not have made some mistakes. Birinci has provided some useful biographical notes, but these also include some errors, by confusing the Hungarian-British refugee Hurşid Pasha (Richard Guyon) with another Hurşid Pasha, who was a slave of Yahya Pasha

---

[14] Roderic Davison, *Nineteenth Century Ottoman Diplomacy and Reforms*. Istanbul: Isis Press, 1999, pp. 27-40, 47-64. Also see Engin Akarlı, *Belgelerle Tanzimat: Osmanlı Sadrazamlarından Ali ve Fuad Paşaların Siyasi Vasiyyetnameleri*. Istanbul: Boğaziçi Üniversitesi, 1978.
[15] Fahrettin Kırzıoğlu, *100. Yıldönümü Dolayısıyla 1855 Kars Zaferi*, İstanbul: Işıl Matbaası, 1955, pp. 210-213.

and by confusing Abdi Pasha with a certain Circassian Abbas Pasha. In his biographical footnote for Sheikh Shamil, the editor even argues that Shamil was a "Turkish hero".[16] Shamil was, as is well known, ethnically an Avar from Dagestan. Though he accepted the authority of the Ottoman caliph, he never considered himself a "Turk".

Another important *zafername* or *destan* is Ahmed Rıza Trabzoni's *Manzume-i Sivastopol* that was first printed in 1869.[17] Ahmed Rıza was a trader from Trabzon who had business in the Crimea. He seems to have been in Gözleve, Sevastopol, Kerch and Sohum and talked to Ottoman officers during the war. He has depicted many battles of the war. While his account is not altogether reliable, especially for numbers, it is not entirely without interest either. Occasionally he gives an interesting piece of information or interpretation. Veysel Usta's recent edition is good in general, with some minor biographical errors in dates and persons, by confusing Kerim Pasha with Abdülkerim Nadir Pasha and by giving a totally unrelated Hüseyin Pasha's biography for Riyale Bozcaadalı Hüseyin Pasha who died during the battle of Sinop, and by a few transliteration errors. Usta's introduction also contains a few minor errors such as bringing the French and British troops to the defence of Silistre.

Other known *destans* are Aşık Selimi's *Rus Destanı*, Eflâki's *Şuregel Destanı*, Karslı İbrahim Baba's *72 Kars Destanı*, Gülzâri's *Destan-ı Sivastopol*, Karslı Süleyman Şâdi's *Muzaffername*[18] and Râzi's *Destan-ı Şeyh Şamil*.[19] Apart from these, Bezmi, Yusuf Halis Efendi, Hayali, Cemali, Ervahi, Muhsin and Safderi have also written or composed such epics.[20] Among them Yusuf Halis Efendi, who was an Arabic translator in the Translation Bureau of the Sublime Porte, stands out

---

[16] Salih Hayri, *Kırım Zafernamesi – Hayrabat*. Hazırlayan Necat Birinci. Ankara: Kültür ve Turizm Bakanlığı Yayınları, 1988, p. 96.

[17] Ahmed Rıza Trabzoni, *Manzume-i Sivastopol*. Hazırlayan Veysel Usta. Ankara: Kültür Bakanlığı Yayınları, 2000.

[18] Selahattin Tozlu, "Kırım Harbi'nde Kars'ı Anlatan Kayıp Bir Eser: Muzaffer-Name", *Akademik Araştırmalar* 1(2), Erzurum, Güz 1996, pp. 123–144.

[19] Ömer Faruk Akün, "Eski Bir Şeyh Şamil Destanı", in *Atsız Armağanı*, Erol Güngör et al. (eds.), Istanbul: Ötüken Yayınevi, 1976, pp. 17–59.

[20] Fevziye Abdullah Tansel, "Yardıma Koşan Manevi Ordu ve Kırım Harbi (1853–1856)", *Kubbealtı Akademi Mecmuası* 16(3), Temmuz 1987, pp. 25–41. By the same author, "1853–1856 Kırım Harbi'yle İlgili Destanlar", *X. Türk Tarih Kongresi. Ankara: 22–26 Eylül 1986. Kongreye Sunulan Bildiriler*, V. Cilt, Ankara: TTK, 1994, pp. 1977–2009. Also see Cahit Öztelli. *Uyan Padişahım*. Istanbul: Milliyet Yayınları, 1976, pp. 344–371.

as probably the first Ottoman-Turkish patriotic poet. He wrote many poems in the newspaper *Ceride-i Havadis* during the war and these were published in October 1855 under the title of *Şehname-i Osmani*.[21] These were epic and patriotic poems and marches in plain Turkish that are probably the first of their kind. For example, he used the word *vatan* (*la patrie* or fatherland) in a very European and modern way. Before, the word simply meant one's place of birth or native area. His *Destan-ı Askeri* contains lines closely resembling the Marseillaise of the French.

Namık Kemal, one of the earliest Turkish patriotic poets and by far the most famous in the nineteenth century, wrote the first patriotic Ottoman (and Turkish) theatre play *Vatan yahut Silistre* which took its theme from the siege of Silistria in 1854. Thus the word *vatan* was for the first time used in a theatre play. Indeed the literary legacy of the Crimean war in Turkish literature is interesting and could be a good topic for a separate study. Nevertheless, such literature (with a few exceptions) is of little value for writing the history of the war. It is all the more surprising that despite the old tradition of Ottoman prose writing, we have few narratives of this war other than epic poems.

In his master's thesis Hakkı Yapıcı has transliterated many news articles about the war that appeared in the *Takvim-i Vekayi*. This has saved me time, notwithstanding the fact that he has mistransliterated many foreign proper names, without bothering to find their original spellings.

Hüseyin Hüsnü's *Saika-i Zafer* (Lightning of Victory) and Hayreddin Bey's *1270 Kırım Muharebesinin Tarih-i Siyasisi* (The Political History of the 1270 [1853–1854] Battle of the Crimea) are two monographs that do not offer much insight. The first is a summary account derived from foreign sources and the latter is mainly about the diplomatic history of the question of the "holy places". Hayreddin Bey (Hayreddin Nedim Göçen, 1867–1942) was a high ranking bureaucrat in the ministry of foreign affairs and an instructor of political history at the Ottoman War Academy (*Erkan-ı Harbiye Mektebi*). Although Hayreddin Bey stated that he carried out much research for the book, the result is not satisfactory. He was aware of the existence of Cevdet

---

[21] Yusuf Halis Efendi, *Şehname-i Osmani*. Istanbul: Ceride-i Havadis Matbaası, 1855. For some of these poems, see Fahrettin Kırzıoğlu, op. cit., pp. 53–55 and 214–215. Also see Cahit Öztelli, ibid., pp. 372–373.

Pasha's *Tezâkir*, but he could not obtain it. He also wrote that he went to Paris, but that he could not gain access to the archives of the French Ministry of Foreign Affairs. In the end, one cannot help but feel sympathy to him because he at least tried to do original research.

Ali Fuat Türkgeldi (1867–1935), who served as head secretary (*mabeyn başkatibi*) of Sultan Mehmed Reşad from 1912 to 1920, wrote some important articles which were later published in a book that includes many documents which are not available elsewhere.[22] Among these rare documents is an account of the proceedings of the war council in Istanbul in September 1853, narrated by Rifat Paşazade Rauf Bey (later Rauf Pasha). The three-volume work was only published in 1960 by Bekir Sıtkı Baykal who has also written probably the first research-based article on the question of the Holy Places. A deficiency of this work is its inattention to dates, mixing the Russian old style (Julian calendar) dates with the Gregorian (*Miladi*) calendar.

Ali Haydar Emir published some documents about the naval battles of the war in the naval journal of *Risale-i Mevkute-i Bahriye* (Periodical Naval Pamphlet) in 1916 and 1918.[23] Another naval officer, Ali Rıza Seyfi wrote a series of articles about the Caucasian campaign of Ömer Pasha and the fall of Kars in 1855, drawing largely from Laurence Oliphant's book.[24] These articles were published in the *Donanma Mecmuası* (Journal of the Fleet) in 1912.[25]

The first relevant book from the republican era of Turkey came from Captain Fevzi (Kurtoğlu).[26] Kurtoğlu was a teacher at the Naval School (*Bahriye Mektebi*). He was also the author of many works on Turkish naval battles. His book is a military history of the war focusing on military-naval techniques and technology. However, he did not analyse

---

[22] Ali Fuat Türkgeldi, *Mesâil-i Mühimme-i Siyâsiyye*. 3 vols. Yay. Haz. Bekir Sıtkı Baykal. Ankara: Türk Tarih Kurumu, 1957–60. Second edition 1987.

[23] Ali Haydar Emir [Alpagot], "Kırım Harbinin Safahat-ı Bahriyesine Müteallik Vesaik-ı Resmiye", *Risale-i Mevkute-i Bahriye*, cilt 3, numero 2, Istanbul, Kanun-u Evvel 1332 [December 1916], pp. 49–62, 193–202, cilt 4, numero 11–12, Eylül – Teşrin-i Evvel 1334 [Sept.–Nov. 1918], pp. 481–502, 529–545.

[24] Laurence Oliphant, *The Trans-Caucasian Campaign of the Turkish Army under Omer Pasha. A Personal Narrative*. Edinburgh and London: William Blackwood and Sons, 1856.

[25] Ali Rıza Seyfi, "Serdar-ı Ekrem Ömer Paşa'nın Mavera-i Kafkas Seferi ve Kars Niçün Sükut Etti?", *Donanma Mecmuası*, Istanbul, 1327–1328 [1912], pp. 2017–2022, 139–142.

[26] Yüzbaşı Fevzi [Kurtoğlu], *1853–1855 Türk-Rus Harbi ve Kırım Seferi*, Istanbul: Devlet Matbaası, 1927.

Turkish defeats, devoting too little space to them. One exception is the Sinop naval battle of 30 November 1853, which he described in some detail. However, even here he made some factual mistakes. As captain of the Fazlullah frigate, he cites Kavaklı Mehmed Bey whereas in reality it was is Ali Bey, who was taken prisoner by Russians, and thanks to Russian painter Ivan Aivazovsky, there is even a portrait of him published in Vasiliy Timm's Russkiy Khudozhestvenny Listok in 1854.[27]

Captain A. Tevfik Gürel's book (*1853–55 Türk-Rus ve Müttefiklerin Kırım Savaşı*) was published in 1935. This is a rather superficial military history without serious research and with many factual and even grammatical errors. Thus, almost all foreign and many Turkish proper names have been misspelled, such as Menshikov being spelled as "Minçikof", Bebutov as "Robodof", Gözleve as "Güzelova", Simferopol as "Sahferpol", Sasık Göl as "Sarık" Göl, etc. etc. The author also confuses Mustafa Zarif Pasha, commander of the Anatolian army, with Mustafa Pasha of the Batum army and Müşir Mehmed Selim Pasha of the Batum army with Ferik Selim Pasha of the Bayezid army corps. He also does not realize that General Cannon and Behram Pasha are not two different persons but the latter is simply his new Muslim name. As James Reid has noted, Gürel also mistakenly states that Ahmed Pasha commanded at the battle of Kürekdere, without naming Zarif Pasha.[28] The rare good parts of the book are those passages that are taken directly from the Russian General Andrey Nikolaevich Petrov's book. (Gürel acknowledges Petrov).

Mustafa Zarif Pasha, mentioned above, was the governor of Erzurum at the beginning of the war and commander-in-chief (*müşir*) of the Anatolian army from February to the end of October 1854. His memoirs are very important because they are the only known memoirs of an Ottoman pasha about the Crimean War, except for the court evidences and interrogations of Abdi Pasha, Ahmet Pasha and Ali Rıza Pasha as well about their participation in the war. In fact, part of Zarif Pasha's memoirs is also part of his testimony at the military court in

---

[27] Vasily Timm (Georg Wilhelm), *Russkiy Khudozhestvenny Listok*. St. Petersburg, 1854.
[28] Reid, op. cit., p. 238. Reid mentions some other shortcomings of Gürel's work as well. However, as we will see in Chapter 3, Reid is not entirely right in his critique of Gürel's narrative of the behaviour of the Ottoman troops in the Battle of Balaklava on 25 October 1854 (Gürel's account in general is not correct either).

Istanbul. I have found in the BOA another copy of the second part of Zarif Pasha's memoirs, related to his command of the Anatolian army from February to October 1854, among the documents related to his trial.[29] There are some slight differences between this document and the one published by Karal. Zarif Pasha had written his memoirs in Istanbul towards the end of 1854 while he was under custody for charges of corruption, made by the British military commissioner Colonel Williams. Zarif Pasha had been dismissed after the defeat of the Ottoman army in the Battle of Kürekdere in August 1854 and after the reports from Williams. As Karal noted, Zarif Pasha's memoirs, covering the period from 1829 to 1854, do not give us any information on the great changes of his time beginning with the *Tanzimat,* focusing instead only in his petty affairs like how much money he accumulated, how he bought his wife, etc. These memoirs indeed may serve as an indication of the intellectual, cultural and military horizon of a successful, careerist Ottoman officer of the pre-war years. Nevertheless, Zarif Pasha still makes some valuable observations. For example, he attributes his imprisonment to British ambassador Lord Stratford de Redcliffe's personal grudge against him because of his handling of some affairs of the Christians in Jerusalem in 1847, when he was the governor (*mutasarrıf*) there. Karal transliterated these memoirs and wrote an introduction. He also noted the problem of the lack of memoirs of Ottoman statesmen. On the other hand, Karal made some omissions and errors (as Fahrettin Kırzıoğlu noted, reading *somar* as "*himar*", Ahılkelek as "Ahleklik", etc.). Karal's biographical notes on the officers also contain many mistakes, such as mistaking the Polish refugee officers Arslan Pasha (Bystrzonowski) and Şahin Pasha (Breansky) for some other Ottoman pashas with the same names, mistaking the illiterate chief of staff of the Anatolian army Ahmed Pasha for the Nazır Ahmed Pasha of the Rumeli army, who was one of the first graduates of the *Mekteb-i Harbiye* (War Academy) in 1840's, mistaking the Prussian-Hungarian Ferhad Pasha (Stein) for another Ferhad Pasha, etc. Karal made some useful editorial comments as well, however, he did not take a critical attitude towards his subject and therefore he did not try to answer the most delicate question: Did Zarif Pasha commit embezzlement? The fact that Karal received the memoirs from a grandson of Zarif Pasha must have complicated the matter.

---

[29] BOA. İ. MMS. 5/170 enc. 10.

Enver Ziya Karal devoted thirty five pages to the Crimean War and the 1856 Rescript of Reform in the multi-volume *Osmanlı Tarihi*.[30] His bibliography on the subject includes only four books and two articles. One of those is Hayreddin Bey's book, mentioned above. Karal is of the opinion that the British ambassador Stratford de Redcliffe was happy to see that war had began against Russia. Karal totally omits (or is unaware of) the White Sea and the Pacific fronts of the war and does not mention the battles of Başgedikler, Ahıska, Kürekdere etc. and the Caucasian campaign of Ömer Pasha. He even argues that at the time of the fall of Sevastopol (September 1855), Ömer Pasha defeated the Russians in "Eupatoria", while in reality the battle of Gözleve took place in February 1855 and Ömer Pasha had left the Crimea for Trabzon shortly before the fall of Sevastopol. In short, besides unfounded conclusions and interpretations, Karal's account includes many omissions and material errors in dates, numbers, etc. For example, he gives the number of Ottoman troops landed in September 1854 in the Crimea as 60,000, which was in fact only about 6,000. (The number of Ottoman troops in the Crimea reached 55,000 to 60,000 only in 1855).

Fahrettin Kırzıoğlu (1917–2005), a native of Kars, published in 1955 a book titled *1855 Kars Zaferi* ("1855 Kars Victory") on the centennial anniversary of the Battle of Kars. For him it was victory, despite the fact that one month after this victory the Kars garrison capitulated to the Russian army. In general, Kırzıoğlu's work is very nationalistic and has a strong anti-Russian bias. The relative merits of his work are some good research in the BOA (considering the conditions of work in the archives at that time), use of at least one Russian source (*Blokada Karsa*, Tiflis 1856), although without giving its original title, and the collection of some unknown Turkish local epic folk poetry on the war. He also used the works of the English doctor Humphry Sandwith (whose name he turns into "Sandoviç") and Colonel Atwell Lake (whose name he spells as "Lik"). In 1994, in a symposium on "Kars and Eastern Anatolia in the Recent History of Turkey", Kırzıoğlu stated the Russian casualties (dead and wounded) from the unsuccessful Russian attack on the Kars fortification as more than 20,000, although in his 1955 book he had given a more reliable and accurate figure (around 7,000) depending on reports of the Ottoman commanders. He repeated

---

[30] Enver Ziya Karal, *Osmanlı Tarihi*, vol. V. Ankara: TTK, 1995. First edition in 1947.

Cevdet Pasha to the effect that "this battle was greater than the battle of Silistria" and "Kars victory was greater than Sevastopol victory".

In 1957 Emin Ali Çavlı published a superficial treatise written for the occasion of the centennial anniversary of the Treaty of Paris.[31] Like Gürel, Çavlı changed Gözleve into Güzelova, which means "beautiful plain"; being unaware that Gözleve itself is a Turkic (Tatar) word, which means a hunters' hut. He also uses the spelling of "Menchikov" for *Menşikov*. As James Reid has also noted, Çavlı failed to consider even the basic issues of the war.

Professor Akdes Nimet Kurat's book[32] on Russo-Turkish relations is much biased against Russia. Kurat seems to have read Temperley and Tarle (in fact he cites only three sources on the Crimean War, including these two authors). He also seems to have visited the Ottoman, Austrian, British, French, German and even Swedish archives, but his account of the war is surprisingly very superficial and contains several blunders. First of all, he really confines the Crimean War to the battles in the Crimea and for him the war begins in 1854 (instead of 1853), as for many European historians. In his narrative, Prince Menshikov's mission to Istanbul, then the Russian occupation of the Danubian principalities and the battle of Sinop all happen in 1854, whereas all three of these events happened in 1853. He does not mention the Danubian front at all and, for the Caucasian front, he only mentions briefly at the end that Kars had been captured by the Russians. Kurat considers that the theatre of war was transferred from Wallachia and Moldavia to the Crimea, whereas the principalities were involved in the war only tangentially, most of the battles being fought along the Danube or south of it, as in the case of the siege of Silistria. Then he claims that the "Ottoman-Turkish" forces in the Crimea raided Russian positions, while in fact it was the Russians who attacked the Ottoman forces in Gözleve, although they were repulsed. He then argues that Emperor Nikolai I died of grief when he received the news of the defeat of the Russian army in Gözleve, which is rather an exaggeration. All of this gives the impression that he did not read Tarle carefully.

---

[31] Emin Ali Çavlı, *Kırım Harbi (Paris Muahedesi 1956)*. Istanbul: Hilmi Kitabevi, 1957.

[32] Akdes Nimet Kurat, *Türkiye ve Rusya: XVIII. Yüzyıl Sonundan Kurtuluş Savaşına Kadar Türk-Rus İlişikleri (1798–1919)*. Ankara: Ankara Üniversitesi Dil ve Tarih-Coğrafya Fakültesi Yayınları, 1970.

Ahmet Nuri Sinaplı's biography[33] of Mehmed Namık Pasha gives some important information on the then Minister of Commerce and Public Works Mehmed Namık Pasha's (1804–1892) loan mission to Paris and London in 1853–1854. Sinaplı, who claims to be a relative of Namık Pasha, provides some correspondence of Namık Pasha from the BOA. However, as in many other cases, this information is intertwined with misinformation and one has to be careful. Sinaplı shows the attitude which is so characteristic of so many traditional Turkish Ottomanists: an uncritical narrative of the events and simple juxtaposition of the documents. He unquestioningly accepts whatever Namık Pasha says. Finally his work is really amateurish and full of transliteration mistakes, such as reading the name of Kostaki Musurus, the Ottoman ambassador in London, as "Mösyö Roz".

In the 1990's and after, Besim Özcan wrote several articles on some aspects of the Crimean War. His doctoral dissertation was about the Battle of Sinop. He has also written a book on the financial situation and the war "policy" of the Ottoman subjects during the war.[34] There he published long lists of contributions to the so called "*iane-i harbiye*" (war assistance), which was in fact a war tax. In Özcan's view, these were only voluntary donations showing the willingness of the population in their support of their government's war effort against Russia. However, there are many documents in the BOA showing that the *iane-i harbiye* was for all practical purposes a tax, euphemistically not named as such, the amount of which was strictly determined beforehand based on everyone's material wealth. Moreover, if this were a donation and not a tax, then distant governors would not have paid exactly the same amounts.

Professor Fahir Armaoğlu has devoted more than thirty pages to the Crimean War and the *Islahat Fermanı* in his political history of the nineteenth century.[35] Armaoğlu's account is based largely on Karal, Temperley, Kurat, A. Debidour and Edouard Driault. Therefore he has repeated some of their mistakes. For example, he has quoted from Karal that "60,000 Turkish troops" were landed on the Crimea

---

[33] Ahmet Nuri Sinaplı, *Şeyhül Vüzera Serasker Mehmet Namık Paşa*, Istanbul: Yenilik Basımevi, 1987.
[34] Besim Özcan, *Kırım Savaşı'nda Mali Durum ve Teb'anın Harb Siyaseti (1853-1856)*. Erzurum: Atatürk Üniversitesi Yayınları, 1997.
[35] Fahir Armaoğlu, *19. Yüzyıl Siyasî Tarihi (1789-1914)*. Ankara: TTK, 1999, pp. 227–260.

on 20 September 1854.[36] This is, as we have seen above, incorrect. Armaoğlu gives at first three alternative spellings for Menshikov including the correct one (as Mençikof, Menchikov and Menshikov) but then sticks to the usual wrong one (*Mençikof*) throughout the text.

Fuat and Süphan Andıç's recent book[37] is mainly a short diplomatic history, written from secondary sources in a popular style without bibliographical footnotes and marred by hero-worshipping of the Grand Vizier Âli Pasha, whom the authors called "the last of the Ottoman grandees" in another book. The narrative has some minor factual, chronological and logical errors and gaps.

Şevket K. Akar and Hüseyin Al's thin monograph[38] on the Ottoman foreign loans and loan control commissions of 1854–1856 is the most up-to-date and factually most correct work in Turkish on the subject. Akar and Al have done quite a good job, with only a few minor errors. However, their work is too technical and lacks comparative analysis. The authors have not searched all the relevant correspondence of Namık Pasha available in the BOA, or even the work of Ahmet Sinaplı, whom they do not mention at all. Furthermore they also subscribe to Olive Anderson's thesis of Namık Pasha's "amateurishness" as the reason of his failure to contract the loan. I have shown in Chapter 4 that the causes were more complex.

Thanks to the happy coincidence of the round-number (150th) anniversary of the war, there have been conferences, symposia, exhibitions and publications in Turkey as well as in Russia, Ukraine (the Crimea), UK, France and Italy from 2003 to 2006. The BOA has published a collection of documents[39] for the 150th anniversary of the war and of the Treaty of Paris. The book includes a total of 126 documents under six headings: Diplomatic Relations, Reforms, Military Activities, War and Economy, Immigrants and Settlement, and Awards and Promotions. To the best of my knowledge, only three of the 126 documents have been published before. As such, this is a useful collection of documents for researchers. However, its use is limited due to several reasons. Firstly, while we must admit the difficulty of selecting

---

[36] Armaoğlu, op. cit., p. 244.
[37] Fuat Andıç; Süphan Andıç, *Kırım Savaşı. Âli Paşa ve Paris Antlaşması*. İstanbul: Eren Yayıncılık, 2002.
[38] Şevket K. Akar; Hüseyin Al, *Osmanlı Dış Borçları ve Gözetim Komisyonları 1854–1856*. Istanbul: Osmanlı Bankası Arşiv ve Araştırma Merkezi, 2003.
[39] *Osmanlı Belgelerinde Kırım Savaşı 1853–1856*. Ankara: BOA Yayın Nu. 84, 2006 (hereafter OBKS).

INTRODUCTION AND REVIEW OF THE SOURCES 19

126 documents from among thousands of documents, the selection of documents nevertheless leaves much to be desired. In particular, the section on reforms is rather weak while other sections are also fragmentary. Secondly, there are almost no editorial notes, the documents are simply transliterated. This makes the selection useful only for historians and specialists on the period. For example, Document 56 is presented as a document on the Ottoman loan, whereas it is only a fictitious (estimated) calculation of loan repayments over assumed rates. However, since there are no explanatory notes, the reader might conclude that these calculations refer to an actual, executed loan agreement.[40] The collection also includes some errors in the transliteration of proper nouns, such as "Paul" instead of Buol, "Edgar Duplier" instead of Argiropulo, "Brock" instead of Brück, "Brany" instead of Pisani, "Chiffer" instead of Schefer, etc.

Istanbul University in collaboration with Marmara University organized its annual seminar on 22–23 May 2006 around the theme of the 150th anniversary of the Crimean War and of the Treaty of Paris. The papers presented in this symposium were published in May 2007. The collection includes many interesting papers.[41]

The Sadberk Hanım Museum in Büyükdere, Istanbul held an exhibition on the 150th Anniversary of the Crimean War from 9 December 2006 until 25 February 2007. The museum also published a fully-coloured, large-size catalogue of the exhibition, including some articles.[42]

Turkish Official Military History

The Turkish General Staff has published a multi-volume history of the Turkish Armed Forces and three monographs on the Crimean War. Retired Full Captain Saim Besbelli of the Turkish Navy has provided a naval history of the war.[43] The book is written in the form of a text-

---

[40] OBKS, pp. 209–211. For a review of the book, see my article in *Toplumsal Tarih* 160, Istanbul, April 2007, pp. 92–94.

[41] *Savaştan Barışa: 150. Yıldönümünde Kırım Savaşı ve Paris Antlaşması (1853-1856). 22-23 Mayıs 2006. Bildiriler*. Istanbul: İ. Ü. Ed. Fak. Tarih Araştırma Merkezi, 2007.

[42] *Kırım Savaşı'nın 150nci Yılı / 150th Anniversary of the Crimean War*, Istanbul: Vehbi Koç Vakfı Sadberk Hanım Müzesi, December 2006.

[43] Saim Besbelli [Retired Naval Colonel], *1853-1856 Osmanlı-Rus ve Kırım Savaşı (Deniz Harekâtı)*. Ankara: Genelkurmay Harp Tarihi Yayınları, 1977.

book from secondary sources (among which Adolphus Slade's book *Turkey and the Crimean War* is prominent) without any references to archival documents and without any footnotes, except a few for explanation. Besbelli argues that the Russian fleet was equal to the Allies in terms of battleships and guns and also that it was a mistake of the Russian command to sink its own fleet in order to blockade the entry of the Sevastopol harbour. We know that the Battle of Sinop was the first major international demonstration of the destructive power of explosive shells against wooden ships. Interestingly this point is not clearly understood and sufficiently explained by Turkish historians, even the military historians including Besbelli. He also asserts that while the "Turkish" forces fought on the Danube, Caucasus, the Crimea and Anatolia, the allies fought only in the Crimea. He is simply unaware of the Baltic, White Sea and Pacific (Kamchatka) fronts of the war.

Part 5 of the volume III of the *Türk Silahlı Kuvvetleri Tarihi* (History of the Turkish Armed Forces), published by the general staff in 1978, includes only seventeen pages devoted to the Crimean War.[44] In 1981 the general staff published another book (with a long title) including an article on the Caucasian front of the Crimean War. The following quotation from the conclusion of this article is very characteristic of the perspective of the works of the Turkish general staff on the Crimean War:

> During the time of the Crimean War Turkey had almost no real friends in the outside world. Those who seemed friendly were not real friends either... Turkey in this war lost its treasury. For the first time it became indebted to Europe. What is worse, by participating in this war with allies, thousands of foreign soldiers and civilians were allowed to see closely the most secret places and shortcomings of Turkey... Even some friendly opponents [sic, "*dost muhalifler*"] characterised as perfidy the indifferent attitude and foot-dragging of the allies for a long time in the participation in the war. Another negative impact of this war was that some semi-intellectual circles of Turkish society came to admire Western fashions and values, losing their identity. While Turkish people showed their traditional hospitality and opened their seaside mansions to Allied commanders, their soldiers did not show respect to Turkish people and Turkish graves. Furthermore, they prevented Turkish troops from landing on the shores of the Caucasus for months because this was against their political aims and national interests. While the great

---

[44] Genelkurmay Harp Tarihi Başkanlığı, *Türk Silahlı Kuvvetleri Tarihi. III. Cilt. 5. Kısım. 1793–1908.* Ankara: Genelkurmay Basımevi, 1978, pp. 450–466.

city of Istanbul with its hospitals, schools and military buildings was laid at the discretion of the Allied commanders, they caused such historical army headquarters as Davutpasha, Harbiye and Varna to catch fire due to their carelessness... While Turkish soldiers showed every sign of selflessness and shed their blood on the fronts, the Allies took all the honours of the war to themselves. Likewise some historians came under the influence of this propaganda and neglected the role of the Turks in this war, despite the fact that Turkish casualties in this war amounted to 120,000.[45] [My abridged translation]

The Caucasian front of the Crimean War was covered in another book by the general staff. The book *1853–1856 Osmanlı-Rus Kırım Harbi Kafkas Cephesi* (1986) written by Retired Brigadier General (Air Commodore) Hikmet Süer is about the Caucasian (Anatolian) theatre of the war. Süer seems to have written the article quoted above in addition, because the conclusions of the article and of this book are very similar.

Many of Süer's arguments in his conclusion come from Slade's book. In fact many of his sentences are simply translations of Slade's sentences without, however, due references. For example, the idea that the Ottomans should have better accepted the "Vienna Note" comes from Slade. By this, Slade argued and Süer repeated, the Porte would have avoided war, that Rumanian independence (meaning union of the Danubian principalities that later formed Romania) would perhaps not have occurred and that Syria would not have been occupied by the French. Süer also argues that the Caucasian people who fought for thirty years against Russia for independence were "Caucasian Turks" and "they originated from the Turkish race". He also describes the Laz, Ajarian and Avar peoples as Turks. The reason for including Avars among "Turks" must be to turkify Sheikh Shamil, who was an ethnic Avar.[46] As for Georgians and Circassians, Süer does not go so far as to make them Turks as well, but still makes them originate from Central Asia. The fallacy of these arguments is too obvious to demand any refutation here.

---

[45] Genelkurmay Askeri Tarih ve Stratejik Etüt Başkanlığı, *Selçuklular Döneminde Anadolu'ya Yapılan Akınlar – 1799–1802 Osmanlı-Fransız Harbinde Akka Kalesi Savunması – 1853–1856 Osmanlı – Rus Kırım Harbi Kafkas Cephesi*. Ankara: Kültür Bakanlığı Yayınları, 1981, pp. 84–86.

[46] Süer, op. cit., pp. 2, 30, 176 ("*30 yıldır vatanları için savaşan 500,000 Kafkas Türkü*", "*Türk ırkından gelen yarım milyon Kafkasyalı halkı*", "*Acara ve Laz dediğimiz Türk türleri*", "*Avar Türkleri*").

Both military historians of the Turkish general staff (Süer and Besbelli) do not mention Karl Marx and Friedrich Engels's articles on the Crimean War, even those articles written from a military strategic point of view. As we shall see below, those articles were translated into Turkish and published in 1966, 1974 and 1977. Despite the manifestly pro-Turkish stand of Marx and Engels, the military historians have ignored them, probably because of the cold war mentality or simply out of ignorance.

Dissertations and Theses in Turkish

Finally, a review of the doctoral dissertations and master's theses in Turkish will not be out of place here. I will make here only very short comments on some of their strengths and weaknesses.

Among these dissertations and theses on our subject, Mustafa Budak's doctoral dissertation about the Caucasian front of the war (*1853–1856 Kırım Savaşı'nda Kafkas Cephesi*, Istanbul University, 1993) stands out. Budak has made good use of the BOA, the ATASE and some use of TNA. The dissertation focuses on military history and covers only the Ottoman side, without use of the Russian sources, therefore it does not address the questions of how the Russians organized their efforts and how Georgians, Armenians and other Caucasian peoples reacted to the war. It has also little analysis over the causes of Ottoman defeats in battles and in the war in general. The question of the slave trade that was conducted by some Ottoman officers is omitted as well. I must add that this omission is general to all dissertations and theses.

Besim Özcan's doctoral dissertation (*Rus Donanmasının Sinop Baskını (30 Kasım 1853)*, Atatürk University, 1990) is about the battle of Sinop and is based upon archival research in the BOA (except for the HR SYS and HR MKT collections which were not included in the BOA at that time and were probably not open to researchers), DMA and ATASE; yet it is one-sided, because it does not tell the Russian story. Özcan states that it was difficult to get Russian sources. He still refers to some secondary and general reference sources in Russian, but these are superficial sources and there are translation mistakes and even transcription mistakes in these references. Özcan also refers to some articles in the NYDT but he fails to indicate Karl Marx as the author of those articles, for example, of the leading article on

27 December 1853. In one place, Özcan quotes approvingly an openly racist comment on the Russians from an unimportant article, stating that the Russians exhibited "the savagery that is characteristic of their race".[47] Such expressions are of course not scholarly. I have given a more comprehensive, comparative, analytical and unbiased account of the Battle of Sinop in Chapter 3, using new archival material from the BOA as well as Russian and British sources.

The topic of Cezmi Karasu's doctoral dissertation (*Kırım Savaşı Sırasında Osmanlı Diplomasisi (1853–1856)*, Ankara University, 1998) is the Ottoman diplomacy during the war. It is a pity that the dissertation did not benefit from the archive of the political section and translation bureau of the Ottoman foreign ministry (BOA. HR. SYS and HR. TO) because these sections were not open at that time. Karasu argues that the handling of this war was the greatest success of Ottoman diplomacy in all its history. He uses the incorrect and abridged Turkish translation of Stanley Lane-Poole's biography of Stratford de Redcliffe. Like Besim Özcan, Karasu also presents the *iane-i harbiye* as donations. Repeating Sait Açba's mistake, who himself repeated A. du Velay's mistake, Karasu sends Lord Hobart instead of Edmund Hornby to Istanbul as the British commissioner for the Turkish loan in 1855. Like most Turkish historians, Karasu uses the incorrect spelling of the name of the Russian ambassador *Menşikov* as *Mençikof*.

Mehmet Yıldız's doctoral dissertation (*1856 Islahat Fermanının Tatbiki ve Tepkiler*, Istanbul University, 2003) concerns the 1856 Reform Edict, its application and reactions to it. Yıldız has made good use of the Ottoman archive (except for the political section of the foreign ministry (HR SYS) which should have been used more fully). Some important documents are published for the first time, but there is almost no use of works in languages other than Turkish. This reliance on translations is dangerous as shown above in the case of the translation of Lane-Poole's biography of Stratford de Redcliffe. Yıldız argues that the *ulema* did not strongly oppose reform. Apart from that, the dissertation does not contain original arguments. He is also one-sided in his conclusion as to why non-Muslims were not accepted into military service, with a pro-Muslim bias.

---

[47] Özcan, op. cit. (1990), p. 119.

Hasan Şahin's doctoral dissertation carries the title *1855 Erzurum Harekatı* (Atatürk University, 1995). That title is a misnomer, for it was Kars, and not Erzurum, that was involved to a greater degree in all the operations of 1855 (and indeed in the whole war on the Caucasian front). Şahin has a definite anti-Russian bias, as if Russia was the only power that wanted to subdue the Ottoman Empire. The dissertation includes no references to sources in Russian; it includes some references to English sources like the works of Lake, Sandwith and Allen-Muratoff, but no reference to the PRMA. There is a lack of critical attitude towards sources such as Zarifi Mustafa Pasha's memoirs. Nor is there any evaluation of the charges against him. Moreover, Şahin misunderstands the "Turkish Contingent" as a "reform" in the Anatolian army, while in reality it had nothing to do with the Anatolian army or with reform. Şahin also confuses the identity of some persons, turning the Circassian Sefer Pasha into a Georgian notable (*eşraf*), the Polish refugee officer Arslan Pasha (Bystrzonowski) into a brother of İzzet Bey of Göle, the Polish officer Şahin Pasha (Breanski) into a refugee from Dagestan. Like Budak, Şahin makes no mention of the question of the slave trade. Problems of spelling include the typical case of *Menşikov* given as *Mençikof*, General Dannenberg as "Donneberg", General Lüders as "Lüdens", etc.

Figen Taşkın's doctoral dissertation (*Kırım Savaşı'nın Osmanlı İmparatorluğu'na Ekonomik Etkileri ve İaşe Sorunu*, Istanbul University, 2007) is on the economic impact of the war and the question of provisions. However, half of the text is rather general history, not related to the title, and the other half is not well-organized. The best section is on the export bans. Fatih Akyüz's MA thesis (*Kırım Savaşı'nın Lojistiğinde İstanbul'un Yeri*, Marmara University, 2006) is also on the logistics of the war. Both Taşkın and Akyüz have used the BOA well; however, both have become victims of their unquestioning use of the faulty Turkish translation of Slade's book.[48] Taşkın (op. cit., p. 117) has quoted from this Turkish edition the cost of the transport of Ottoman troops from Varna to Gözleve as 250 pounds sterling, whereas it is given as 250,000 pounds in the original text in English. As for Akyüz, he has also quoted (op. cit., p. 86) the equivalent of 20 million

---

[48] *Türkiye ve Kırım Harbi*. Translated by Ali Rıza Seyfi. Istanbul: Genelkurmay X. Şube, 1943. This edition contains both translation and typing errors.

piastres as 1,000 pounds, whereas in the original this amount is given as 180,000 pounds.

Caner Türk has written his MA thesis on the Ottoman-Iranian relations and secret Russo-Iranian treaty during the war: *1853–56 Kırım Harbi Sırasında Osmanlı-İran İlişkileri, Osmanlı Devletine Karşı Rus-İran Gizli Antlaşması* (Atatürk University, 2000). His supervisor was Hasan Şahin. Türk has committed many errors of transliteration, translation and spelling. Thus Dolgorukov, the Russian ambassador to Tehran, becomes first "Dolgorki" and then "Dolgorkof"; Russian foreign minister Nesselrode is transformed into "Neseldorf", "Neseldrof" and "Neseldroft", the word *züvvar* (visitors) has been turned into *zevar*, etc. To Türk's credit must be mentioned his references to the AKAK. Şenol Kantarcı's MA thesis deals with the building of the earthworks or bastions of Kars: *Kars Tabyalarının İnşası* (Atatürk University, 1997).

Finally, my own PhD dissertation (*The Ottomans and the Crimean War*, Sabancı University, 2007) lies at the basis of this book.

Sources in Russian

The international literature on our subject is very large and, for the purposes of this study, the focus will be more on Ottoman and Russian sources rather than on British, French and other European sources, because the emphasis here is to fill the gaps in the narrative of the war with less-used Ottoman and Russian sources. Although the literature in Russian is probably larger than that in other European languages, it is almost totally unknown in Turkey and little known in Europe. A fine bibliography lists 242 memoirs (books and articles) of the participants alone of the war.[49] Therefore it is not possible here to mention even all the major works. Indeed the Crimean War is a well-researched and well-discussed topic in Russian and Soviet historiography.[50] Here, I will introduce only some of these sources. Attention will be given

---

[49] Pyotr Andreyevich Zayonchkovskiy (ed.), *Istoriya Dorevolyutsionnoy Rossii v dnevnikakh i vospominaniyakh*. T. 2. Ch. 1. *1801–1856*. Moscow: Izdatel'stvo "Kniga", 1977. See section "Krymskaya (Vostochnaya) voina 1853–1856 gg.", pp. 307–347. This is a well annotated bibliography of diaries and memoirs. The author is the son of the tsarist military historian Andrey Medardovich Zayonchkovskiy.

[50] Badem, "Rus ve Sovyet Tarih Yazımında Kırım Savaşı", *Toplumsal Tarih* 155, Istanbul, November 2006, pp. 16–23.

especially to those works that are more or less related to the involvement of the Ottomans in the war.

In Moscow, the two relevant archives are the RGVIA and the AVPRI. The two other important Russian archives for our research are located in St. Petersburg: The RGIA and the RGVMF. I was able to use only the most important one, the RGVIA. As for libraries in Moscow, the GPIB is a very rich, specialized library for historians. It contains many rare books and periodicals of the nineteenth century. The former Lenin library (now Russian State Library) is also very helpful. Its manuscripts section includes some documents related to the Crimean War.

Imperial Russia published many documents related to the war. Among these the AKAK is a very impressive mass of documents relating to many aspects of the Caucasian wars and affairs. Then there are many articles in the journals *Kavkazskiy Sbornik*, *Russkaya Starina*, *Russkiy Arkhiv*, *Russkiy Invalid* and *Voenny Sbornik* as well as newspapers like *Kavkaz*. Nikolai Putilov has published 33 volumes of documents from 1854 to 1957.[51]

In 1856 a diary of events during the siege of Kars was published in Tiflis: *Blokada Karsa* (Blockade of Kars).[52] Although the book is about letters by witnesses of the campaign in Asiatic Turkey, all these "letters" seem to have been written by an officer from the general staff of the commander in chief (General Muravyov) from the Çivilikaya camp near Kars, most probably after the war, on the basis of notes or diaries, because the senders are not identified, the letters are too well-informed to have been written by ordinary soldiers, and, finally, their literary style is the same throughout. The unsuccessful attack on Kars and the defeat of the Russian army on 29 September 1855 is narrated very briefly, in an understatement of the Russian defeat, without citing exact details of the Russian and Ottoman losses, while in all other battles and skirmishes won by the Russians, losses are given in detail. The news of the fall of Sevastopol during the siege of Kars is not mentioned. Except for these two gaps, the narrative is interesting and seems to be realistic.

---

[51] Nikolay Putilov (ed.), *Sbornik izvestiy, otnosyashchikhsya do nastoyashchey voiny, izdavaemy s Vysochayshego soizvoleniya N. Putilovym*. 33 vols. St. Petersburg: Tip. E. Veymara, 1854–1857.

[52] *Blokada Karsa. Pis'ma ochevidtsev o pokhode 1855 goda v Aziatskuyu Turtsiyu*. Tiflis: Tipografiya kantselyarii namestnika Kavkazskago, 1856.

Many of the Russian generals who took part in the war also wrote their memoirs. Although all these works were published under censorship, they are full of details of events and comments. As it is to be expected, tsarist writers and historians in their analyses tried to justify the policies of Nikolai I and Aleksandr II. Nevertheless, they made important contributions to the historiography of the war. Thus, when General Nikolai Nikolayevich Muravyov-Karsskiy, conqueror of Kars, wrote in his memoirs that "the Turks do not write anything", he was very right in his complaint.[53] It was the Russians, the British and the French who continued the discussion in writing, while the Turks wrote only patriotic theatre plays (Namık Kemal, the patriotic "Young Ottoman") and verses about the war. Some of the other Russian officers who wrote their memoirs are Pyotr Alabin, A. S. Korsakov, Colonel Mikhail Lihutin, General Yakov Baklanov, General Yegor Kovalevskiy, Prince Aleksandr Dondukov-Korsakov, General Nikolai Ushakov, etc.

The Russian novelist, publicist and revolutionary democrat Nikolai Chernyshevskiy (1828–1889) published in his journal *Sovremennik* in 1863 a partial translation of the British historian Alexander Kinglake's book *The Invasion of the Crimea* and wrote a preface to the translation.[54] Chernyshevskiy commented that although politically Kinglake was just a Tory (whom Chernyshevskiy did not like), he had fulfilled the duty of a historian conscientiously.

Typical tsarist military historians Modest Ivanovich Bogdanovich (1805–1882) and Andrey Medardovich Zayonchkovskiy (1862–1926) have also produced histories of the Crimean War.[55] The latter gave the most developed classical tsarist account of the war, rich in detail and amply documented. Staff Colonel Zayonchkovskiy was commissioned by the Russian general staff to write this history in 1900, with all archives opened to him. For this work he was paid 2,000 roubles

---

[53] Nikolay Nikolayevich Muravyov, *Voina za Kavkazom v 1855 godu*. 2 vols. St. Petersburg: Tipografiya tovarischestva "Obschestvennaya pol'za", 1877.

[54] N. G. Chernyshevskiy, "Rasskaz o Krymskoi Voyne (po Kingleku)", *Polnoe sobranie sochineniy*, tom X, Moscow: Gospolitizdat, 1951, pp. 193–440.

[55] Modest Ivanovich Bogdanovich, *Vostochnaya Voina 1853–1856 godov*. St. Petersburg: Tip. M. Stasiulievicha, 1877. Andrey Medardovich Zayonchkovskiy. *Vostochnaya Voina 1853–1856 gg v svyazi s sovremennoy ey politicheskoy obstanovkoy*. Tom I–II. St. Petersburg, 1908–1912. St. Petersburg: Poligon, 2002. 2 vols., vol II in two parts. Simferopol: Krymskiy Arkhiv, 2005. 2 vols.

per year.⁵⁶ He had the opportunity to read Prince Menshikov's diary as well. (Nevertheless the diary was not published in the appendices of his work.) The colonel finished his work in 1904 but the Russo-Japanese war delayed its publication until 1908. The two-volume book (bound in four), which amounted to more than three thousand pages, was dedicated to Emperor Nikolai II. Unfortunately for researchers, the new edition of 2002 has omitted many appendices (actually more than half) from volume one. Among these are many important documents like the instructions to Menshikov and Nikolai's letter to Sultan Abdülmecid (*prilozheniya* no. 105–112).

Staff Captain (later General) Pyotr Ivanovich Averyanov (1867–1937) was a Russian military agent who worked some time at the Russian consulate-general in Erzurum. His book on the Kurds in Russian-Persian and Russian-Ottoman wars includes a chapter on the Crimean War and covers the revolt of Yezdanşêr at some length.⁵⁷ Depending on Russian sources, Averyanov gives important information on the relations of the Kurdish tribes with the Russian army. Nevertheless, he mistakes Yezdanşêr as brother of Bedirhan Bey, while in reality Yezdanşêr was the grandson of Bedirhan's uncle. The book has been translated into Turkish as well. I have not yet seen the 1926 translation, which is out of print now. The new edition of 1995 is actually a transliteration into modern Turkish of an earlier translation from Russian into Ottoman Turkish.⁵⁸ Due in part to the inconvenience of Arabic letters, almost all Russian proper names, beginning with that of the author, have been mistransliterated. The author's name is given as Avyarov. There are translation errors as well. For example, the Ottoman word *kese*, which means a purse of 500 piastres, has been turned into *çuval* (sack). Thus we read 400 *çuvals* of money, which does not make sense. The anonymous Kurdish editor has provided some footnotes, correcting some mistakes and arguing with the author from a Kurdish nationalist position. Nevertheless, the editorial quality of this translation in general is very low, there is no information on the author and even his first name is not given.

---

⁵⁶ RGVIA, fond 481 "Voyna 1853–1856 gg", op. 1, d. 65, ll. 240–280. Materialy o sostavlenii polkovnikom gen. shtaba Zayonchkovskim istorii voiny 1853–1856 gg.

⁵⁷ P. I. Averyanov, *Kurdy v voinakh Rossii s Persiey i Turtsiey v techenie XIX stoletiya*. Tiflis: Tipografiya Shtaba Kavkazskago voennago okruga, 1900.

⁵⁸ Avyarov [sic], *Osmanlı-Rus ve İran Savaşları'nda Kürtler 1801–1900*. Osmanlıcadan tercüme eden: Muhammed (Hoko) Varlı (Xani). Ankara: Sipan Yayıncılık, 1995.

A common characteristic of the tsarist apologist military historians was their inclination to neglect socio-economical processes in their explanations of the reasons for the war, to give too much emphasis to individuals and individual mistakes in their explanations of the defeat of Russia, and to try to put all the blame on the French and British cabinets. Since these historians could not criticise Nikolai's despotic regime and Russia's relative economic backwardness, they explained Russia's defeat by the blunders of certain commanders and by the "tactical superiority" of the allies.

The Soviet era of the Russian historiography of the Crimean War began even before the October revolution of 1917, with an article by the Bolshevik historian Mikhail Pokrovskiy, published in 1908. There he made an attempt to explain Russia's defeat in the war by its economic and political backwardness. His characterization of Nikolai I is brilliant. He explains Nikolai's inability to understand the social-class essence of politics as follows:

> The Emperor believed naively that all over the world, politics were determined by the personal tastes and sympathies of those who led it. For this reason, it always remained an enigma for him why Wellington or Aberdeen, sincere and profound conservatives, who were personally well-disposed towards him, could not prevent Britain's involvement in various "revolutionary" conspiracies against Russia.[59] [My translation]

Pokrovskiy became very influential in the foundation of the Soviet historical school in the 1920's. Pokrovskiy's articles can be considered the first attempts of a Russian Marxist historian to give a Marxist account of the war. He was later criticised for being too uncritical about the cabinets of Napoleon III and Palmerston in comparison with tsarism and for exaggerating the victories of the allies, while not giving enough attention to the "heroic defence of the Russian people". He also came under criticism for his treatment of Sheikh Shamil's movement as an anti-colonial freedom struggle against tsarism, because the new trend in Soviet historiography on the eve of the World War II was rather pro-Russian. After Pokrovskiy, we see a more moderate attitude in the Soviet historiography in the 1940's towards imperial Russian policies. Yet Pokrovskiy had also politicized history too much, even arguing

---

[59] Mikhail N. Pokrovskiy, *Diplomatiya i Voiny Tsarskoy Rossii v XIX stoletii. Sbornik statey*, Moscow: Krasnaya Nov', 1923, p. 110. Reprinted in *Istoriya Rossii v XIX veke. Epokha Reform*. Moscow: Tsentrpoligraf, 2001, p. 9.

that history is simply politics turned towards the past (*istoriya yest' politika, oprokinutaya v proshloe*).

On the eve of and during the World War II, interest towards the Crimean War among Soviet historians had risen considerably. Many new monographs began to appear. The naval battle of Sinop was the subject of several monographs. Two collections of documents about the admirals Nakhimov and Kornilov were also published during this period. Without doubt, the single most important monograph from this period is Yevgeniy Tarle's two-volume classical diplomatic history, the *Krymskaya Voina*, which has since set the standard in the Soviet historiography of the Crimean War. Tarle in his work subjected all the warring states and their diplomacies to a thorough critique. He also criticised some tendencies of the Russian *intelligentsia*. He wrote that the contradiction of the Slavophiles consisted of the fact that they did not wish to admit for a long time that Nikolai I was as concerned about the freedom of the Slavs as Palmerston and Napoleon were about the independence of "Turkey".[60]

Tarle shows good command of the Russian archives and of the European sources, with only a deficiency in Ottoman/Turkish sources. Considering that the Ottoman archives were not open to all at that time and that the published sources in Turkish were insignificant, this was not so important a gap at that time. However, Tarle in general gives too great a role to Stratford and almost no role to individual Ottomans. His Ottoman terminology is also somewhat old fashioned, for example, he calls the Ottoman foreign minister *Reis Efendi*, a title which was already out of use at that time, replaced by *Hariciye Nazırı*.

Tarle also made an analysis of the economic relations among the warring states, trying to show the importance of the Ottoman markets for Britain. However, he also warned against the vulgarised Marxist conception of history that might reduce the reasons for the war to no more than economic rivalry. Tarle is incorrect in the details of the Ottoman foreign loans. He writes that Namık Pasha contracted a loan in Paris and London in 1853, while in fact Namık Pasha had failed in contracting a loan and the task was completed by others in 1854.[61] Tarle's characterization of the Ottoman ministers is also somewhat

---

[60] Yevgeny V. Tarle, *Krymskaya Voina*, vol. 1, Moscow: Eksmo, 2003, p. 17.
[61] Tarle, op. cit., p. 61.

simplistic and superficial, suffering from the wide-spread tendency among so many Western writers to create a permanent dichotomy between pacifist and warlike or between conservative and reformist Ottoman statesmen. Thus Tarle wrote that there were two tendencies among the Ottoman ministers. Some of them, headed by Reşid Pasha and Grand Vizier Mehmed Ali Pasha (*Damad*, a brother-in-law of the Sultan) were trying to solve the dispute by diplomatic negotiations, while others headed by Ömer Pasha and Fuad Efendi firmly believed that it was time for revenge for the peace of Edirne.[62] However, as we will see in Chapter 2, this view may be misleading, because the differences of policy among Ottoman ministers did not as a rule originate from ideas, they originated rather from personal rivalry. Those who had lost their office and were yet unemployed simply tried to replace those in office. In other words, their policies depended upon whether they were in office or not. For example, Mehmed Ali Pasha, after being dismissed or forced to resign from the office of grand vizier in May 1853, immediately became much belligerent. Finally, we must note that Tarle's work, written during WWII, bears a certain tone of Russian nationalism.

In the 1940's and 1950's, there was an acute discussion among Soviet historians about the role of the movement of Sheikh Shamil in the nineteenth century. While the movement was until then seen as a progressive, anti-colonial independence movement, now the emphasis was on the reactionary side of the movement, the so called "*muridism*". E. Adamov and L. Kutakov's article in the *Voprosy Istorii*, the prestigious journal of the historical section of the Academy of Sciences, contains fifteen documents from the AVPR, showing relations among British agents, Circassians and the Ottomans.[63] The article represents one of the turning points in Soviet historiography on the question of the historical role of Shamil and his movement. At that time, it was considered reactionary. Another collection of documents about Shamil's movement was published in Tiflis 1953: *Shamil' - Stavlennik Sultanskoy Turtsii i Angliyskikh Kolonizatorov. Sbornik dokumental'nykh materialov* (Shamil - Agent of the Sultan's Turkey and of British Colonizers. Collection of documentary materials).

---

[62] Tarle, op. cit., p. 165.
[63] E. Adamov; L. Kutakov. "Iz istorii proiskov inostrannoy agentury vo vremya Kavkazskikh voyn", *Voprosy Istorii* 11, Moscow, November 1950, pp. 101–125.

As the title clearly indicates, it was intended to prove that Shamil waged a reactionary war and not a national liberation war, and that he was an agent of the Turkish Sultan and British imperialism. This collection showed the anti-Shamil atmosphere of the Soviet post-WWII years.

After 1956 this policy was abandoned under Khrushchev and once again Shamil became an anti-colonial freedom fighter. Shamil had indeed rendered invaluable service to the Ottoman army by distracting a large portion of the Russian Caucasus army (see Chapter 3). Recently Khalat Omarov from the Dagestan branch of the Russian Academy of Sciences has translated and edited a collection of one hundred letters by Shamil, written in Arabic. These letters have also been translated into Turkish by Fikret Efe. However, Omarov's name has not been mentioned at all by Efe or the publisher. In this form the translation represents a case of plagiarism.[64]

After Tarle's work, the Soviet historiography of the Crimean War was mainly engaged in filling the gaps in his work in one way or another. Igor Vasilyevich Bestuzhev concentrated on military technology in his book.[65] Three important contributions complemented the work of Tarle on the Caucasian front. These are the dissertations and books of the Georgian Yermolai Burchuladze, the Armenian A. M. Pogosyan and the Azerbaijanian (of ethnic Circassian origins) Khadji Murat Ibragimbeyli (1924–1999). Burchuladze's and Pogosyan's contributions were on the Georgian and Armenian participation in the Crimean War respectively. But their books were published in their native languages only, thus reaching a limited public. (Burchuladze wrote two articles in Russian as well). On the other hand, Ibragimbeyli wrote two books on the contributions of the Caucasian peoples to the war effort of Russia, based on his doctoral dissertation.[66] He described Sheikh Shamil as the spiritual and military leader of the national liberation movement of the mountain peoples of Dagestan, Chechnya

---

[64] Khalat A. Omarov (ed.), *100 pisem Shamilya*. Mahachkala: Dagestanskiy Nauchny Tsentr Rossiyskoi Akademii Nauk, 1997. *Şeyh Şamil'in 100 Mektubu*. Mektuplar ve açıklama notları: DAM RBA [sic]. Çeviren: Dr. Fikret Efe. İstanbul: Şule Yayınları, Mayıs 2002. "DAM RBA" probably stands for Dagestan Center of the Russian Academy of Sciences.

[65] Igor V. Bestuzhev, *Krymskaya Voina 1853–1856*. Moscow: Izdatel'stvo AN SSSR, 1956.

[66] Khadji Murat Ibragimbeyli, *Stranitsy Istorii Boevogo Sodruzhestva Russkogo i Kavkazskikh Narodov (1853–1856 gg)*. Baku: Azerbaidjanskoe gosudarstvennoe izdatel'stvo, 1970. *Kavkaz v Krymskoi Voine 1853–1856 gg. i Mezhdunarodnye Otnosheniya*. Moscow: Nauka, 1971.

and the North Caucasus against tsarism. He made good use of Russian archives, in addition to European, Turkish and Iranian sources. However, Ibragimbeyli's work, ostensibly Marxist, does not give in fact a non-biased, non-nationalist, materialistic explanation of the Russian defeats and victories on the Caucasian front. His main concern is to stress the contribution of the Caucasian peoples in the war against "Turkish" aggressors. He explains Russian victories simply by the heroism and patriotism of the Russian army (including local militias), not attempting to describe what problems (political, social, strategical, tactical, logistics, etc.) the other side had had. It is also remarkable that Ibragimbeyli showed himself as an ardent anti-Communist and a Muslim Circassian nationalist politician and publicist after the fall of the Soviet Union.

In the 1970's Vitaliy Ivanovich Sheremet has written several articles on the Crimean War and the Ottoman Empire. One of them (co-author L. S. Semenov), is on the foreign economic ties of the Ottoman Empire in the era of the Crimean War.[67] Another article, written together with Khadji Murat Ibragimbeyli, is a review or survey of the modern Turkish historiography of the Crimean War. The authors are in general highly objectively critical, except for the fact that they have omitted some historians and have most notoriously undervalued (or simply not understood) Cevdet Pasha's *Tezâkir*. This may probably stem from their inability to understand the text of the *Tezâkir* written in the rather bookish style of the Ottoman Turkish.[68] Sheremet also dealt with the question of the Crimean War and Ottoman-West European relations in his book published in 1986.

V. E. Bagdasaryan and S. G. Tolstoy, two academicians from Moscow, have written a recent book on the historical lessons of the Crimean War.[69] This is an anti-Western, anti-Soviet, anti-liberal, nationalist Russian historiographical account that tries to analyse the lessons of the Crimean War for today, arguing that the West is still a threat to Russia's security. The authors also make comparisons between Nikolai I and Stalin and between Nesselrode and Molotov.

---

[67] V. I. Sheremet; L. S. Semenov, "Vneshneekonomicheskie svyazi Turtsii epokhi Krymskoi voiny", *Vestnik Leningradskogo Universiteta* 14, vypusk 3, 1973, pp. 44-49.

[68] "Sovremennaya Turetskaya Istoriografiya Vostochnoy (Krymskoi) Voiny", *Voprosy Istorii* 4, Moscow, April 1977, pp. 45-57.

[69] V. E. Bagdasaryan; S. G. Tolstoy, *Russkaya Voina: Stoletniy istoricheskiy opyt osmysleniya Krymskoi kampanii*. Moscow: Izdatel'stvo MGOU, 2002.

Sources in Other Languages

A great work has already been done by Prof. Winfried Baumgart by publishing the Austrian, British, French and Prussian documents in a twelve-volume series called AGKK. These are well-edited, well-annotated, invaluable primary sources. They almost eliminate the need to go in person to those archives.

Besides the AGKK, an important source of published documents lies in the British parliamentary papers, the PRMA. These documents cover the correspondence among the British cabinet in London, ambassador Stratford de Redcliffe in Istanbul, Her Majesty's military commissioner Colonel (General) Williams in Kars and the British commander in chief Lord Raglan in Sevastopol in the period from 2 August 1854 to 18 March 1856.

Karl Marx and Friedrich Engels contributed many articles to the NYDT during the war. Those articles sometimes appeared as anonymous leaders. Engels' articles also appeared under the name of Marx. Marx and Engels saw tsarist Russia as the stronghold of monarchy and reaction against the forces of democracy and revolution. Therefore they had a clear anti-Russian and pro-Turkish attitude. Although they wrote from London and Manchester, they provided astonishingly sound analysis and good foresight into military affairs. Especially the anonymous articles of Engels were written with an expert knowledge of military strategy. These articles are among the best reportage of the war. They were published in a volume by Marx's daughter and son in law in 1897.[70] There are two Turkish translations as well.

The *Times* correspondent William Howard Russell's despatches from the Crimea and his book *The British Expedition to the Crimea* are among the important first-hand eyewitness narratives.[71] But eyewitnesses can be misleading. Russell's despatches and book, together with Lord Raglan's nephew and aide-de-camp Colonel Somerset Calthorpe's book[72] formed the basis of the false reports on the "cowardice"

---

[70] Karl Marx, *The Eastern Question. A Reprint of Letters Written 1853–1856 Dealing with the Events of the Crimean War*. Edited by Eleanor Marx Aveling and Edward Aveling. London, 1897. New York: B. Franklin, 1968. London: Frank Cass, 1969.

[71] William Howard Russell, *The British Expedition to the Crimea*. Revised Edition. London: G. Routledge & Co., 1858. *Despatches from the Crimea 1854–1856*. London: Deutsch, 1966.

[72] [Colonel Somerset Calthorpe], *Letters from Head-Quarters, or the Realities of the War in the Crimea. By an Officer on the Staff*. Two vols. Vol. I. London: John Murray, 1856.

of some Ottoman troops defending the redoubts on the hills of Balaklava on the day of the famous (for the British) battle of Balaklava on 25 October 1854. However, it was again some British historians and researchers who set the record straight on this question and not Ottoman or Turkish historians, who have been quite disinterested in general and in the battles fought in the Crimea in particular. Especially welcome was the publication by Dr Douglas Austin of the reminiscences of John Elijah Blunt, civilian interpreter and unofficial aide de camp to Lt General Lord Lucan (see Chapter 3).

Alexander W. Kinglake's six-volume work was the first major history of the war in English, based chiefly on Lord Raglan's papers.[73] While the book is not altogether useless, Raglan's apologist is strongly anti-Napoleon III and anti-Stratford. Kinglake's study is interesting but it does not cover much material related to the Ottoman involvement.

There are also a number of memoirs of British officers, doctors and journalists who served in the Anatolian front. Colonel Atwell Lake wrote two books on the defence of Kars. The second book includes letters from General Williams (the British military commissioner at Kars), Captain Thompson and Major Teesdale.[74] Doctor Humphry Sandwith also wrote his memoirs.[75] Lake and Sandwith are too pro-Williams, failing to point out any deficiencies on the part of their superior officer. Surprisingly, Sandwith even asserted that Williams arrived with the rank of General, while in fact Williams had come to Istanbul as a lieutenant-colonel; in December 1854 the Sultan conferred upon him the Ottoman rank of *ferik* (general of division) and after the battle of Kars on 29 September 1855, he was promoted to the rank of *müşir* (marshal or general of army). Nevertheless, these memoirs contain very valuable, lively observations, especially on Ottoman rule in the province of Erzurum, on the influence of European consuls and the situation of Christians in the Ottoman Empire.

The *Morning Chronicle* correspondent Charles Duncan's two-volume memoirs of the Anatolian campaign give interesting details of

---

[73] Alexander W. Kinglake, *The Invasion of the Crimea: Its Origin, and an Account of its Progress Down to the Death of Lord Raglan*. 6 vols. New York, London: Harper, 1863–87.

[74] Colonel Henry Atwell Lake, *Kars and Our Captivity in Russia*. London: Richard Bentley, 1856. *A Narrative of the Defence of Kars*. London: Richard Bentley, 1857.

[75] Humphry Sandwith, *A Narrative of the Siege of Kars*. London: John Murray, 1856.

the Ottoman army and of the people of Kars.[76] While Duncan is not altogether unbiased, his account is very useful. Duncan gives a detailed description of the battle of Kürekdere (he even gives a wonderfully correct spelling of "Kürekdere", just as in modern Turkish). Interestingly, Duncan includes the despatch of General Bebutov on this battle as well. However, he does not disclose his source of that despatch. In addition to the testimonies of Abdi Pasha, Ahmed Pasha and Ali Rıza Pasha before the court, Duncan's narrative is a useful counterbalance to Russian eye-witness accounts of the battles around Kars in 1854.

The eccentric English journalist and writer Laurence Oliphant participated in the Caucasian campaign of Ömer Pasha during the fall of 1855 as correspondent of the *Times* newspaper and published his memoirs. Oliphant is critical of both the British and the French governments for delaying the campaign. Like almost all foreigners, he has a high opinion of the "gallantry" of the Ottoman ("Turkish") soldiers and a very low opinion of the Ottoman officers, of whom, he argues, "the less said the better". He has in general a low opinion of both Russia and the Ottoman Empire, considering them "the two most barbarous nations in Europe".[77] Nevertheless, he gives many details on the battle of Ingur and on the Circassians and Georgians.

Lady Emilia Bithynia Hornby, wife of Sir Edmund Grimani Hornby, arrived at Constantinople on 8 September 1855 with her husband. Lady Hornby wrote her memoirs of their stay in Istanbul firstly under the title *In and Around Stamboul* (London, 1858) and then in an enlarged and illustrated version in 1863. It has been translated into Turkish.[78] The book takes the form of letters sent by Lady Hornby from Constantinople to England from September 1855 to September 1856. They are generally superficial, but contain some insights into Turkish daily life. Especially valuable is the description of the balls at the British and French embassies in February 1856, when for the first time an Ottoman Sultan visited a ball at an embassy.

Another lady who wrote her memoirs of Istanbul after the Crimean War was Marie de Melfort, a relative of Edouard Thouvenel, the

---

[76] Charles Duncan, *A Campaign with the Turks in Asia*. London: Smith, Elder and Co., 1855.

[77] Oliphant, op. cit., p. 48.

[78] Lady Hornby [Emelia Bithynia Maceroni Hornby], *Constantinople during the Crimean War*. London: Richard Bentley, 1863. Turkish translation: *Kırım Savaşı Sırasında İstanbul*. Istanbul: Kitap Yayınevi, 2007. Translated by Kerem Işık.

French ambassador to Istanbul. But that book was published much later in 1902 under her new marital name, La Baronne Durand de Fontmagne. These memoirs include some important accounts of Ottoman statesmen such as Fuad Pasha and some details of social life such as women wearing corsets! The rest is the usual orientalist banalities so characteristic of the European travel literature of the nineteenth century. The book has also been translated into Turkish.[79]

Sir Edmund Grimani Hornby (1825-1896) was appointed as the British commissioner for the "Turkish Loan" of 1855. His duty was to control the spending of the loan money of more than five million pounds sterling strictly on the needs of the Ottoman army. In his *Autobiography*, written most probably after the "Bulgarian horrors" of 1870s, he argues against Britain's fighting for "Turkey", because of her misgovernment of the Christian subjects. He also argues that without the threat from the Russians, "the Turks" did not consent to reforms in the long run. His words are indeed quite indicative of the mentality of many British gentlemen of the time. They are worth quoting here because of their unusual openness:

> I have never been able to understand any adequate cause for the Crimean War, or why England took any prominent part in it. It began by a squabble between the European Powers about the "Holy Places". We had absolutely nothing to do with that quarrel...the Treaty of Paris (1856) was a huge diplomatic blunder. It freed Turkey from the fear of Russia and left her to misgovern her Christian subjects as she pleased, which she forthwith proceeded to do. I know that although during the war, and immediately after it, neither Lord Stratford nor myself acting under his orders felt much difficulty in getting the Turks to consent to reforms, especially in their courts of law, in provincial administration, and in the management of their prisons; yet within eighteen months of the treaty it was impossible to do anything with them.[80]

Another Englishman who took part in the war and has written his memoirs is the naval officer Adolphus Slade (1804-1877) whom the Ottomans called Mushaver (Adviser) Pasha. Slade had come to the

---

[79] La Baronne Durand de Fontmagne, *Un séjour à l'ambassade de France à Constantinople sous le second empire*. Paris: Plon-Nourrit, 1902. Turkish translation: *Kırım Harbi Sonrasında İstanbul*. Istanbul: Tercüman 1001 Temel Eser, 1977. Translated by Gülçiçek Soytürk.

[80] Sir Edmund Hornby, *An Autobiography*. London: Constable and Co. Ltd, 1929, pp. 80-81.

Ottoman Empire first in 1829–1831 and wrote his reminiscences in 1833.[81] In 1849, Captain Slade was selected by the British government to be sent as an adviser to the Ottoman navy, where his rank was promoted to Mirliva (Rear-Admiral). Together with another British officer his main duty was to train the Ottoman sailors. Slade's account of the war[82] is more interesting than those of other European observers, because he had more knowledge about the Ottoman bureaucracy and people in general, and because he was in the unique position of acting as intermediary between the Ottoman and Allied navies. His attitude is also very pro-Ottoman and anti-Stratford. He also takes issue with General Williams. In many cases he speaks up for the Ottomans. Indeed, to a certain extent he fills the void in the literature caused by the lack of Ottoman accounts of the war. The fact that Slade published his book in 1867, when he had already retired from Ottoman service[83] and returned to Britain, gives more credibility to his words because he was no longer an Ottoman official and in principle he could be more objective. Nevertheless, as for all sources, a critical attitude is necessary towards him as well. We must also admit that memoirs are more valuable when they are written not long after the events described in them.

Another delayed reminiscence is Dr. Thomas Buzzard's book.[84] Dr. Buzzard was a member of the British medical staff and he was for some time attached to the headquarters' staff of Ömer Pasha in the Crimea and the Caucasus.

Georges Kmety (Ismail Pasha) was a Hungarian revolutionary émigré officer who served in the Ottoman Anatolian army. He left a narrative of the defence of Kars, but I have been unable to locate that book.[85]

---

[81] Adolphus Slade, *Records of Travels in Turkey, Greece, etc. and of A Cruise in the Black Sea, with the Capitan Pasha, in the Years 1829, 1830, and 1831*. 2 vols. London: Saunders and Otley, 1833.

[82] Rear-Admiral Sir Adolphus Slade (Mushaver Pasha), *Turkey and the Crimean War. A Narrative of Historical Events*. London: Smith, Elder and Co., 1867.

[83] Mushaver Pasha retired from Ottoman service at the rank of *ferik* (vice-admiral) in May 1866. His final British rank was also Vice Admiral. See BOA. A. MKT. MHM. 356/30.

[84] Thomas Buzzard, *With the Turkish Army in the Crimea and Asia Minor. A Personal Narrative*. London, 1915.

[85] [Georges Kmety (Ismail Pasha)], *A Narrative of the Defence of Kars*. London, 1856.

The Polish refugee Michal Czajkowski (1804–1886), who accepted Islam and took the Muslim name of Mehmed Sadık (Mehmed Sadyk in English and Polish) also left important memoirs of the year 1854.[86] Sadık Pasha was the commander of the first Turkish Cossack regiment in the Balkans. His memoirs seem to contain important information and remarks about many Ottoman officers and statesmen. Although I have received help from native speakers in translating some passages from this book, I could not make full use of it. (My Russian was of little help in understanding Polish fully). I think this important book must be translated into Turkish, Russian and English. Fortunately, Czajkowski also left some autobiographical notes which were translated into Russian and published in the journal *Russkaya Starina* with intervals from 1895 until 1904. They contain important comments on Stratford de Redcliffe's attitude towards the issue of Christian or non-Muslim military service in the Ottoman army (see Chapter 5).

Stanley Lane-Poole's biography[87] of the British ambassador in Istanbul, Lord Stratford de Redcliffe is useful but the biographer exaggerates the role of his hero. This is not an objective biography but rather a eulogy of the "Great Elchi". Lane-Poole also exaggerates the role of the British military officers-advisers in the Ottoman army to an extent that sometimes becomes ridiculous, as in the following passage:

> Perhaps with merely Ottoman commanders the garrison might have surrendered; but it happened that two young English officers, Butler and Nasmyth, had thrown themselves into the beleaguered city and had inspired the defenders with a zeal and enthusiasm that no skill of Russian engineers could quench. Silistria was saved...[88]

Nevertheless, the author had the private and official papers and memoirs of Canning at his disposal and this gives some interest and value to his work.

From 1932 to 1936, English historian Harold Temperley wrote four long articles and a book on the Crimean War. In his articles and in his book he made good use of the British, Austrian, French, and remarkably of the Dutch archives. He has indeed shown that Stratford was not "the human agency which caused the Crimean War" and that he

---

[86] Michal Czajkowski (Mehmed Sadyk Pasza), *Moje Wspomnienia o Wojnie 1854 Roku.* Warsaw: Wydawnictwo Ministerstwa Obrony Narodowej, 1962.
[87] Stanley Lane-Poole, *The Life of the Right Honourable Stratford Canning: Viscount Stratford de Redcliffe.* London: Longmans, Green and Co., 1888.
[88] Lane-Poole, op. cit., vol. II, p. 367.

was not "animated throughout by personal feeling against Tsar Nicholas". Nevertheless, despite his achievements in setting some points right in the record, Temperley basically followed a British imperialist, Orientalist and pro-Stratford view of the British policy in the Ottoman Empire. The following quotation provides ample proof of his Orientalist and hero-worshipping approach:

> Stratford had set out to drive orientals along new roads, a task to baffle the most expert of drovers. There seem to be two ways of moving orientals in new directions. One way is to imitate them, to yield to them to pretend to be theirs. Then they follow you as a flock of sheep the bellwether. That was Lawrence's way with the Arabs... There is another way, and one by which an Englishman may preserve his faith and yet instruct orientals in reality. It is 'to stand against them, to persuade himself of a mission, to batter and to twist into something which they, of their own accord, would not have done'. That is to drive, not to lead, and it was Stratford's way with the Turks.[89]

The American historian Vernon John Puryear, on the other hand, criticized this pro-Stratford view. In 1931 he published an article ("New Light on the Origins of the Crimean War") and a book: *England, Russia, and the Straits Question, 1844–1856*.[90] This book was based on his doctoral dissertation at the University of California, Berkeley, in 1929. He was very critical of Stratford de Redcliffe. The book included a chapter on the "commercial preliminaries" of the war, where an interesting economic analysis of the importance of the Black Sea trade was made. In 1935 he published another book, where he developed his economic analysis in full. Puryear was probably the first Western historian who argued that "the causes of the Crimean War, although several in number, were in great part economic in nature".[91]

Olive Anderson has written several articles on the Crimean War and the best is, in my opinion, the one on the beginnings of Ottoman

---

[89] Harold Temperley, *England and the Near East: The Crimea*. London: Longmans, Green and Co. Ltd., 1936. Reprinted: London: Frank Cass, 1964, pp. 242–243.

[90] Vernon John Puryear, *England, Russia, and the Straits Question, 1844–1856*. Berkeley: University of California Publications in History, 1931. Reprinted, Hamden: Archon Books, 1965.

[91] Puryear, *International Economics and Diplomacy in the Near East: A Study of British Commercial Policy in the Levant, 1834–1853*. Stanford University Press; London: H. Milford, Oxford University Press, 1935. Reprinted, Hamden: Archon Books, 1969.

public debt.⁹² This is probably the only research-based article (although based only on the British archives) in English on the "Turkish" loans of 1854 and 1855. Nevertheless, the article includes several minor factual errors. Furthermore, its general attitude is pro-British, it puts the blame too easily on Namık Pasha for his unsuccessful efforts to contract a loan, taking Lord Clarendon's words for granted that Namık Pasha abided by unrealistic instructions. We will see in the chapter on finances that this claim does not reflect the whole picture.

English scholar, Foreign Service officer, politician and businessman William Edward David Allen's book, *Caucasian Battlefields*, written together with Paul Muratoff and first published in 1953, includes two chapters (45 pages) on the Caucasian battles of the Crimean War.⁹³ The authors give a clear and understandable account of these battles, based upon English and Russian sources. Although they also refer to some works in Turkish, it is highly doubtful that they could read Turkish. The book includes a few minor errors like giving in one passage the commander of the Batum army as Ahmet Pasha (instead of Selim Pasha) and turning the Abkhazian prince Mikhail Sharvashidze's name into Iskander Sharvashidze. The book was translated into Turkish and published by the Turkish general staff in 1966, but I have not located this translation.

Ann Pottinger Saab's book is one of the first Western revisionist and pro-Ottoman accounts of the war, trying to understand the views of the Ottomans from their sources.⁹⁴ Saab makes some use of Ottoman archive sources. However, very surprisingly, she makes no mention of Cevdet Pasha. This is all the more surprising, because she acknowledges help from Stanford Shaw and other Ottomanists.

Robert Edgerton's book was among the first to try to revise the Western notions of the role of the Ottoman soldiers and officers in this war.⁹⁵ The book has a chapter titled "Pride and Prejudice: the Turks at War". There he shows that at the battle of Balaklava, 500 "ethnic

---

[92] Olive Anderson, "Great Britain and the Beginnings of the Ottoman Public Debt, 1854–55", *The Historical Journal* 7(1), 1964, pp. 47–63.

[93] W. E. D. Allen; Paul Muratoff, *Caucasian Battlefields. A History of the Wars on the Turco-Caucasian Border, 1828–1921*. Cambridge: Cambridge University Press, 1953. Nashville: The Battery Press, 1999.

[94] Saab, *The Origins of the Crimean Alliance*. Charlottesville: University Press of Virginia, 1977.

[95] Robert B. Edgerton, *Death or Glory: The Legacy of the Crimean War*. Boulder, CO: Westview Press, 1999.

Turks" in the first gun positions were attacked by 6,000 Russians with superior artillery and despite these "overwhelming odds" they did not leave their position for an hour while losing 170 men. Finally they broke and retreated and from then on the British and the French troops held the "Turks" in contempt. Before Edgerton and later other authors, researchers and historians also tried to set the record right and thus the "Turks" at the battle of Balaklava were rehabilitated by many British historians.[96]

Professor Winfried Baumgart's book *The Crimean War 1853–1856* is up to date and shows good command of Russian and Western sources. It also covers the battles in the Danubian front remarkably better than any other Western study that I have seen. However, it contains little information on the Ottoman army, a fact admitted by the author himself.

The late James J. Reid's above-mentioned book includes a substantial coverage of the Crimean War. He also made a review of Ottoman and Turkish sources in his introduction, giving concise and correct evaluations. However, like Saab, he has very strangely omitted Ahmet Cevdet Pasha's *Tezâkir* and *Ma'rûzât*. This is all the more surprising, because Reid made some marginal references to the *Tezâkir* elsewhere in his book, which means that he was at least aware of its existence. Nevertheless, Reid was unaware of other Turkish works such as those of Yüzbaşı Fevzi Kurtoğlu and the military historians Hikmet Süer and Saim Besbelli, not to mention dissertations in Turkish. Despite that, Reid's study addresses some important issues and suggests some interesting explanations as well. He also attempted to introduce elements of psycho-historical inquiry and analysis of cultural mentality into the study of the Ottoman nineteenth century. I think one of the major contributions of Reid's study is its ability to show the hazards of the Ottoman outmoded strategy of the "scattered" (or "piecemeal" or "detached" or "dispersed") deployment of troops. As Reid stated,

---

[96] These are Michael Hargreave Mawson and Major Colin Robbins of the Crimean War Research Society, Dr Feroz Yasamee of the University of Manchester and the "Battlefield Detectives" of the Channel Five in the UK. See Mawson, *The True Heroes of Balaclava*, Kent, Bedford, London: Crimean War Research Society Publications, spiral-bound printout, 1996. Yasamee maintained that these troops were from Tunis. See David Wason, *Battlefield Detectives: What Really Happened on the World's Most Famous Battlefields*, London: Granada Television Production, 2003, pp. 150–179.

Rather than concentrate armies to build greater force, Ottoman generals feared the loss of even a small territory to invasion or rebellion, and attempted to deploy forces everywhere to hold everything. Part of their problem was the factional strife in the officer corps and in the Ottoman government. Such factional conflicts made it difficult for a general staff to operate in unity and placed a commanding officer in jeopardy for failing to defend any part of the empire from loss.[97]

Therefore I shall refer to some of its positive achievements as well as errors in Chapters 3 and 5. The basic problem with Reid's book is that it is almost exclusively based on Western sources, with few references to Russian, Ottoman or Turkish sources and with no reference to Ottoman archive material. Reid even made a very strange statement on the Ottoman archives:

> Ottoman documents relating to the period 1853 to 1862 exist outside the Ottoman archive in Istanbul. In addition to former Ottoman provinces [now independent states where one can find Ottoman archival remnants] the following archival sources exist.[98] [Brackets in the quotation are from the original].

The author mentions the Walpole Papers, the Fraser Papers and Ottoman *salnames* (almanacs) after this statement. The above statement is indeed vague at best: Did the author really mean that Ottoman documents relating to the period 1853 to 1862 exist in those former provinces? If so, that is incorrect. Alternatively, did he mean that there are some Ottoman documents outside the BOA *as well*? But then, what about the documents in the BOA? Did he ever attempt to do research in the BOA? In reality, these documents do exist in the BOA. There are tens of thousands of them for the period in question. Reid's statement betrays a complete ignorance of the contents of the BOA. Indeed, the statement is especially surprising, because Reid claimed that the place of his book in modern scholarship on the Crimean War was "to give a uniquely Ottoman perspective on the conduct of that war". After such a claim, we had a right to expect from the author some serious research in the BOA. Furthermore, referring to some authors, Reid chooses not their relevant works but some rather irrelevant works. For example, he does not mention at all Adolphus Slade's very important book on the Crimean War (*Turkey and the Crimean War*). Instead he

---

[97] Reid, op. cit., p. 257.
[98] Reid, op. cit., p. 38.

44   CHAPTER ONE

refers to another book by Slade, published in 1833, which is an important source on the Ottoman Empire, but is obviously not related to the Crimean War. I think that any study of the Ottoman involvement in the Crimean War without reference to Slade's book will suffer from a serious deficiency. Again, Reid refers to the Turkish historian Fahrettin Kırzıoğlu's book on the history of Kars (*Kars Tarihi*, vol. I), but not to that book of Kırzıoğlu which is directly related to the Crimean War (*1855 Kars Zaferi*).[99] These omissions also show that the author did not conduct a thorough research of the Turkish historiography on the Crimean War.

Referring to Helmut von Moltke, Reid spells the name of the Kurdish rebel chief Bedirhan Bey as "Vede Khân Bey". Then in the section on the insurrection of "Yazdân Shîr" (Yezdanşêr, a relative of Bedirhan and another Kurdish rebel chief), Reid mentions the Kurdish chief "Bedir Khân Bey", this time referring to a contemporary Kurdish writer.[100] One can of course use different spellings, but "Vede Khan" is simply wrong and Reid should have indicated its correct form(s). Still, the main problem here is that Reid did not realize that "Vede Khan" and Bedirhan were the same person. For this reason, Reid's index too gives Vede Khan and Bedir Khan separately without any cross references.

While Reid's critical attitude towards the efficiency of Ottoman reforms in general in the nineteenth century and military reforms in particular is welcome, it is not possible to say that he has provided an objective and balanced account throughout his analysis. In many cases he relies upon a single Western source without referring to others. For example, in his interpretation of the conduct of the Ottoman troops in the Battle of Balaklava, Reid does not rise about the traditional cliché view of Russell and (to a lesser degree) Kinglake that has lately been challenged by new research (see Chapter 3).

To sum up, Reid's book has some aims and claims similar to those of this book; however, the result is fragmentary. Reid also wrote an interesting article based upon Dr Humphry Sandwith's article on the roots of the Armenian question in the Crimean War.[101] In particular, Reid has been able to show the impact on the Armenian question of

---

[99] Reid, op. cit., p. 239.
[100] See Reid, op. cit., p. 79 and p. 299.
[101] Reid, "'How the Turks Rule Armenia'", in Richard G. Hovannisian (ed.), *Armenian Karin / Erzerum*, Costa Mesa, CA: Mazda Publishers, 2003, pp. 147–187.

the disorders resulting from the abuse of the Ottoman irregular troops by Ottoman pashas.

Tobias Heinzelmann's work[102] on military conscription in the Ottoman Empire in 1826–1856 has some relevance for our study, though it has very few references to the Crimean War.

Recently, Clive Ponting published a book with a provocative subtitle: *The Truth Behind the Myth*. Unfortunately, this book does not tell the Ottoman story either.[103] Most recently Virginia Aksan has published an extensive book on Ottoman wars from 1700 to 1869.[104] She has devoted some 45 pages to the Crimean War. While the book in general is good, the section on the Crimean War is not based on original research. Like Saab and many other Westerners, Aksan has ignored Cevdet Pasha.

---

[102] Tobias Heinzelmann, *Heiliger Kampf oder Landesvertedigung? Die Diskussion um die Einführung der allgemeinen Militärpflicht im Osmanischen Reich 1826–1856*. Frankfurt am Main: Peter Lang, 2004.

[103] Clive Ponting, *The Crimean War. The Truth Behind the Myth*. London: Chatto & Windus, 2004. London: Pimlico, 2005.

[104] Virginia H. Aksan, *Ottoman Wars 1700–1870: An Empire Besieged*. London, New York: Pearson Longman, 2007.

CHAPTER TWO

THE ORIGINS OF THE WAR

Overview of the Ottoman Empire on the Eve of the War

At the beginning of 1853, the Ottoman Empire was no longer a great power, despite contrary claims by Ottoman officialdom. Its very existence depended on the balance of power prevailing in Europe. Constant wars with Russia since 1768 and revolts throughout the empire from Serbia, Greece, and Egypt to Kurdistan had weakened the Ottoman state. By this time, however, the Ottoman Empire had become an important market for European great powers and had to be defended against its main adversary, Russia. The Ottoman Empire had not taken part in the post-Napoleonic Vienna conferences; it was not a member of the Concert of Europe and did not play a role in European politics as such. It had become the object of the so called "Eastern Question". Its participation in the 1841 Straits Convention did not make it a member of the European state system either, but rather the empire became subordinate to the European system.[1] In fact, European diplomacy had long forgotten when the Ottoman Empire had last taken any initiative in European politics. One notable exception was during the crisis concerning Hungarian refugees in 1849, when Grand Vizier Mustafa Reşid Pasha (1800–1858), supported by Britain and France, refused to hand over Hungarian revolutionaries to Austria and Russia. This decision was to prove very beneficial indeed for the standing of the Ottoman Empire in European public opinion, which exerted considerable influence during the Crimean War thanks to war reporting and telegraph communication.

For many of his contemporaries, Sultan Abdülmecid (r. 1839–1861) appeared as a weak and indecisive person, with a "melancholic" face. The weakness and indecision of Abdülmecid meant that every movement

---

[1] This was clear from the form of address of the Padishah as "His Highness", while European protocol demanded "His Majesty". The Ottoman Sultan or Padishah became "His Majesty" in the Treaty of Paris of 1856, but still he was not an equal party to the system. See J. C. Hurewitz, "Ottoman Diplomacy and the European State System", *Middle East Journal* XV, 1961, p. 151.

to reform was applied half-heartedly and then compromised, in the interests of the "Old Turkish" party, the enemies of reforms. In contrast, Butrus Abu-Manneh portrays a different Abdülmecid:

> Through his tutor on the one hand and his mother on the other, it is believed that Sultan Abdülmecid at a young age was exposed to Naqshbandi-Mujaddidi belief and that orthodox Islamic ideals formed the foundation of his convictions and socio-political outlook, which naturally after his rise and for some years to come continued to reflect itself in his actions.[2]

However, such a strictly orthodox Islamic outlook is not compatible with his way of life, characterised by attraction to women and heavy drinking, and by his benevolent attitude toward Western customs and methods.

On the other hand, it is not easy to establish a permanent dichotomy of "old Turkish" and "reformist" parties within the bureaucracy; in most cases the real reason for opposition or support within the Ottoman elite regarding any particular reform or measure was not a matter of principle, but rather a question of personal intrigues and petty interests. The same person who followed a policy of reforms could oppose those very reforms when out of office. The classic example is the best-known reformer himself, that is, Reşid Pasha, whose jealousy of Âli Pasha, one of his protégés, made him oppose the recognition of equal political rights for non-Muslim subjects of the Empire.

Grand viziers, ministers and governors did not stay long in their office because the Sultan would yield to the influence first of one party, then another, reshuffling the ministries and military positions all the time. These reshuffles were also due to the rival influences of the great powers. Abdülmecid knew some French and liked to talk about politics and life with ambassadors such as the British ambassador Stratford Canning, who had great influence in Istanbul. Promoted to the peerage as Viscount Stratford de Redcliffe in 1852, he was destined to play an important role before and during the war. However, his overbearing character turned many people against him, and in the 1850s he also began to lose faith in his main protégé within the Ottoman

---

[2] Butrus Abu-Manneh, *Studies on Islam and the Ottoman Empire in the 19th Century (1826–1876)*, Istanbul: The Isis Press, 2001, p. 83. Abu-Manneh (op. cit., p. 84) has also argued that "when Sultan Abdülmecid rose to the Sultanate, both the Palace and the Porte appear to have been motivated by the ideals of Orthodox Islam, perhaps more than at any time before".

bureaucracy, Reşid Pasha, who had become less enthusiastic about reforms. Nevertheless, Lord Stratford considered him the best man in the Ottoman Empire to carry out reforms.[3]

Starting from the 1830s, the office of the foreign ministry had become prominent among the various Ottoman institutions due to the need for the Ottoman Empire to balance the great powers against each other in order to survive. The *Tercüme Odası* (Translation Bureau) prepared many prominent statesmen, among whom Mustafa Reşid Pasha was the foremost. The Ottomans were now more dependent on diplomacy and the crucial necessity to treat the Europeans as equals was becoming increasingly clear. Mustafa Reşid Pasha attempted to modernize diplomacy in the Ottoman Empire along European lines.[4] Reşid Pasha first became grand vizier (*sadrazam*) in 1845 and his office lasted until 1851 with two short interruptions. In May 1853, during the final stage of the Menshikov crisis in Istanbul, he became foreign minister, actually controlling the Sublime Porte, and again *sadrazam* in 1854. Nevertheless, he did not remain in office long enough to see the end of the war and to participate in the peace negotiations in Paris. His relations with his former protégés Âli and Fuad Pashas had already deteriorated in 1853, and after the *Islahat Fermanı* of 1856, Reşid Pasha's criticism of their policy increased[5] (see Chapter 5).

Reşid Pasha resigned in May 1855 when Sultan Abdülmecid forgave his brother-in-law (Damad) Mehmed Ali Pasha, whom he had recently exiled to Kastamonu, following charges of embezzlement. Mehmed Ali owed his return from exile to the quarrel and rivalry between Stratford de Redcliffe and his French colleague Edouard Thouvenel, who, in the absence of Lord Stratford in August 1855, managed to get his protégé Mehmed Ali back into government as *Kapudan Pasha* (Lord High Admiral). As the Ottoman statesman and chronicler Cevdet Pasha admitted, the state had lost its power and its ministers their honour and dignity, each one seeking protection from the embassy of this or that great power. Therefore, interference by the great powers in the internal affairs of the Ottoman Empire were now conducted

---

[3] "Among the ministers, whether in office or expectant, Reshid Pasha was the one who in sentiment and policy sympathized most with me. The Sultan seemed to be jealous of our intimacy". Stanley Lane-Poole, op. cit., vol. II, p. 104.

[4] Cevdet Pasha even argues that Reşid Pasha instituted the method of diplomacy in the Ottoman Empire. See Cevdet Paşa, *Tezâkir 1–12*, p. 7.

[5] Op. cit., p. 16.

openly.⁶ The Sublime State (*Devlet-i Aliyye*), as the Ottoman Empire called itself, was truly in a pitiable situation.

Despite his great enthusiasm and efforts, Sultan Mahmud II (r. 1808–1839) had been only partially successful in setting up a new modern army. The biggest problem was finding European officers of high reputation to drill and train the army. Mehmet Ali Pasha of Egypt was more successful and effective in bringing out a modern army on the European model. He was willing to pay 17,500 piastres monthly to his French instructor Colonel Joseph Sève (Süleyman or Soliman Pasha, 1788–1860) who trained his troops, while Mahmud II would not give more than 2,000 piastres in salary to any foreign advisor.⁷ Sultan Mahmud II did not greatly approve of foreign advisors and he asked Mehmed Ali Pasha of Egypt to send him some Muslim advisors. In fact, Mehmed Ali had much more impact on Mahmud II than anyone else.

Although Abdülmecid was more fortunate with foreign military advisers, the army and the navy were still not professional in any modern European sense. As the Russian commander in chief of the Danube army General Prince Mikhail Dmitrievich Gorchakov (1793–1861) reported in his "Instructions for Battle against the Turks", submitted to Emperor Nikolai I on 30 June 1853, the Ottomans had destroyed the old army, but they had not built a new regular army in a European sense.⁸ The Ottoman army was not professional in a strict sense, because high ranks (as a rule) were still distributed by favouritism and not by merit. There was also marked rivalry and hatred between the uneducated "old Turks" and those officers who received some education in Europe. For example, in the Anatolian army the commander in chief Abdi Pasha represented the latter, while his chief of staff Ahmet Pasha belonged to the former group. There was marked distrust between them. The Rumeli army under the command of Ömer Lütfi Pasha (1806–1871) was better officered and better trained, yet still not a match for the Russian army, despite some successes in battle. Ömer Pasha was born a Croat (his original name was Mihaylo Latas) and

---

⁶ Cevdet Pasha, *Tezâkir 13-20*, p. 15.
⁷ Avigdor Levy, "The Officer Corps in Sultan Mahmud II's New Ottoman Army, 1826-39", *International Journal of Middle East Studies* 2, 1971, p. 24.
⁸ "Rukovodstvo dlya boya protiv turok, sostavlennoe knyazem Gorchakovym", quoted in Andrey M. Zayonchkovskiy, *Vostochnaya Voina 1853-1856*, vol. II, part two, St. Petersburg: Poligon, 2002, p. 560.

received military education at an Austrian school. Later he fled from Austria, came to Istanbul and converted to Islam. By luck and ability, he rose quickly in the Ottoman army. Lower ranks had few incentives to work hard for promotion because without links to the court elite or without some good fortune they had few chances of being promoted, while those with the right connections rose rapidly.

Recruitment for the Ottoman army was through levies among the Muslim male population at the age of 20 to 25 by lots (*kur'a*). Draftees could send a substitute for themselves. Military service in the Ottoman army lasted six years in active service and then seven years in reserve (*redif*). Non-Muslims did not serve in the army, paying a poll-tax (*cizye*, after 1855 called *iane-i askeriye*) instead. Nevertheless, patriotic feelings seem to have spread among Ottoman non-Muslims at the beginning of the war. 3,000 Bulgarians from notable families applied voluntarily for service in the Ottoman army, according to the *Berliner Zeitung* on 1 September 1853.[9] They were not accepted. Likewise, some patriotic Ottoman Armenians and Greeks from Saruhan and İzmir applied to the Porte to serve in the army; they were courteously rejected.[10] Thus the Ottoman Empire, with an estimated population of around 35 millions, that is, roughly half of Russia's population, had still fewer human resources to fill up the ranks of its armies, because it depended only on its Muslim subjects, while Russia could levy troops from a much larger (approximately four times larger) population base.

Muslims could rise to high ranks in the Russian army, whereas non-Muslims were not accepted in the Ottoman army as officers, NCOs or privates, except for the two Cossack regiments recruited from the Dobruca Cossacks, the Old Believers (*starovertsy*), especially the Nekrasovites (*Nekrasovtsy*), also known as Ignat-Cossacks, and Polish refugees under the command of the Polish officers Mehmed Sadık Pasha (Michał Czajkowski) and Count Wladislaw Zamoyski.[11] In November 1853, 799 democratic Polish emigrants in France headed

---

[9] Mustafa Gencer, "Alman Basınında Kırım Savaşı", in *Savaştan Barışa*, 2007, p. 168.
[10] BOA. HR. SYS. 1346/52, 10 January 1854, OBKS, pp. 104–106.
[11] Fikret Adanır, "Der Krimkrieg von 1853–1856", in *Handbuch der Geschichte Russlands*, Band 2, Stuttgart: Anton Hiersemann Verlag, 2001, pp. 1196–1197. Also see Czajkowski, op. cit. (1962), pp. 11, 50–66, 80–100, 202–211, 232–255; and Ivan Lysiak Rudnytsky, "Michał Czajkowski's Cossack Project During the Crimean War: An Analysis of Ideas", in P. L. Rudnytsky (ed.), *Essays in Modern Ukrainian History*, Edmonton, Alberta: Canadian Institute of Ukrainian Studies, 1987, pp. 173–186.

by General Josef Wysocki signed a petition to Sultan Abdülmecid to form a "*Légion Polonaise*" in the Ottoman Empire. Their request was not satisfied mainly due to the disapproval of the French government.[12] However, during the war, Adam Czartoryski, leader of the monarchist Polish emigrants in France, sent many Polish officers to the Porte.[13] Czartoryski's son Vitol also served as colonel in the second Cossack regiment.[14] The Porte was careful not to describe these regiments as Polish, preferring instead the name of Cossack regiments. It was also careful not to employ these Polish and Hungarian officers near the Austrian border, because it had previously given guarantees on this issue to Austria.[15] Ottoman Greeks from Macedonia and other places were recruited for the navy and the naval arsenal (*Tersane-i Amire*) for some time, but this practise was abandoned.[16]

We must not forget that Russia had a far longer border to defend and only a fraction of the Russian army did actually fight in the Crimea, Caucasus and other places, while the rest guarded the borders, awaiting attacks from hostile neighbours. For example, the Russians had to employ most of the Caucasus army against Shamil and the Circassians while the remainder had to fight against the Ottoman army. Russia also had to post large armies on the Swedish, Prussian, and Austrian borders. A recent Russian study has argued that during the war only 15 per cent of the Russian army was engaged in actual war.[17]

Almost all Russian and European military observers of the time coincide in the opinion that the Ottoman soldiers were good fighters while the quality of the Ottoman officers was low. In terms of military art, the Ottoman officer class as a whole lacked the ability to manoeuvre in the open field with a coordinated use of cavalry, infantry and artillery. The once formidable Ottoman cavalry that had threatened all of Europe was now the worst part of the Ottoman army, while artillery was the best developed. However, the ability (or even desire?) of these three groups to help each other in battle was again very limited. Cavalry and infantry relied heavily upon artillery, but if the enemy were not disrupted by bombardment, the cavalry and infantry did

---

[12] BOA. HR. SYS. 1194/1 and 1345/46.
[13] BOA. HR. SYS. 1336/18.
[14] Sultan's *irade*, 3 May 1855. BOA. İ. HR. 120/5904 enc. 5.
[15] Grand vizier Kıbrıslı Mehmed Emin Pasha's *tezkire* to Sultan Abdülmecid, 27 October 1854. BOA. İ. MMS. 2/88 enc. 2.
[16] Heinzelmann, op. cit., pp. 269-279, 305-310.
[17] Bagdasaryan and Tolstoy, op. cit., preface.

not show much discipline. In many cases, especially on the Caucasian front, some of the Ottoman officers left their troops unguided in the battlefield. The irregular cavalry, the so-called *başıbozuk* troops, were more of a nuisance than a resource. They were also inclined towards plundering villages and their own army quarters, when they did not receive their pay and rations. In fact, for most of them, hope of plunder was the ultimate reason for joining the war (more will be said on this subject in Chapters 3 and 5).

The upper ranks systematically robbed the poor soldiers of their rations, uniforms and pay (this will also be discussed further in Chapter 3). The differences in pay between upper and lower ranks were also much greater than those in European and Russian armies. For example, infantry privates in the Ottoman army received 20 piastres (*kuruş*) per month, corporals 30 piastres, captains 270 piastres, majors 900 to 1200 piastres, colonels 1,800 piastres, brigadier generals 7,500 piastres, and lieutenant generals 15,000 piastres, while the full general or field marshal (*müşir*) earned 70,000 piastres.[18] Navy men and officers received the same amounts for corresponding ranks, while the cavalry earned slightly more. Indeed, the salary for privates (20 piastres for infantry and 24 piastres for cavalry) had not changed at least since the abolition of the Janissaries in 1826, despite inflation.[19] It would be raised to 30 piastres only two years after the Crimean War, on 10 April 1858.[20] Furthermore, while the privates and lower ranks received food rations that were barely adequate, the upper ranks again received much better pay and greater food and fodder allowances.

---

[18] Russian military agent Count Osten Sacken's report to the Russian minister of war, June 1852. RGVIA, fond 450, op. 1, d. 45. Also available at fond 846, op. 16, d. 5414, list 14. Also see *Troops in Turkey. Returns of the Pay and Allowances... War Department*, London, April 1856, Turkish Contingent, p. 11. Cf. Hikmet Süer, op. cit., p. 160. The pay of the men and officers of the "Turkish Contingent" was by treaty equal to those in the Ottoman army. On the other hand, Süer's table of salaries and rations, with fewer differences among ranks, seems rather more egalitarian than the British and Russian accounts given here. For example, Süer gives 30 piastres to the private, 400 piastres to the captain, 3,000 piastres to the colonel and 10,000 piastres to the ferik, without mentioning the müşir's salary at all. However, Süer does not give any references for his table, therefore, we cannot take it for granted. It may also belong to a later period.

[19] See Avigdor Levy, op. cit. (1982), pp. 496–497.

[20] Cevdet Pasha, *Tezâkir 13–20*, p. 48.

Illus. 1   Ottoman infantry. *ILN*, 26 Nov. 1853.

In comparison, the differences in pay among Russian officers were much smaller. For example, a Russian captain received about 36 silver roubles per month, equivalent to 6 pounds sterling or 750 piastres, including salary (*zhalovanye*) and house rent money (*kvartirnye*), but excluding rations, while a full general received about 420 roubles or 70 pounds or 8,750 piastres (including pay, rent and *stolovye*). Thus a Russian general earned about 12 times as much as a Russian captain, while in the Ottoman army, as calculated from the above numbers, a divisional general (*ferik*) earned 55 times as much as a captain.[21] (If we equate the Russian full general to the Ottoman *müşir* and not to the *ferik*, and if we also take the rations into account, then the difference is even greater). Furthermore, we see that while the Ottoman captain earned only 270 piastres, his Russian colleague earned about 750 piastres in equivalent, thus 2.77 times as much! If we go higher in rank, then the situation differs in the opposite direction. The Ottoman *ferik* earns 1.7 times as much as the Russian full general and the *müşir* earns nearly 8 times as much as the Russian general! However, we must note that the Ottoman pashas had to care for a large household of servants, slaves, wives and concubines.

When we compare the rank and file, then the situation is at first sight favourable to the Ottoman soldier: he earns 4 times as much as his Russian colleague, who receives only 2.7 roubles per year, that is, about 5 piastres per month, assuming food rations to be more or less equal. Thus the Ottoman soldier was in theory better paid than the Russian soldier, but in practice the Ottoman soldier did not receive his salary for months and years during the war, while the Russian soldier could even receive money rewards after victories. For example, after the battle of Başgedikler (1 December 1853), the rank and file received 2 roubles each.[22]

The well-known Russian diplomat, military agent, traveller, geographer, geologist, botanist, zoologist and palaeontologist, Pyotr Aleksandrovich Chikhachev (1808–1890), who had made many journeys in Asia Minor and published many works on the geography and palaeontology of the region, had also reported on the disproportion between the pay of higher and lower ranks in the Ottoman army while

---

[21] Zayonchkovskiy, op. cit., vol. I, p. 442.
[22] Zayonchkovskiy, op. cit., vol. II, part 1, p. 416.

he worked at the Russian embassy in Istanbul in 1849.[23] He seems to have written these remarks in the first volume of his monumental 8-volume work *L'Asie Mineure*, which was published in France in 1853. Chikhachev wrote that the yearly cost of the Ottoman ("Turkish") infantry soldier consisted of 12.5 silver roubles (equivalent of 120 piastres) for salary and 6.25 roubles for rations and clothing, thus a total of 18.75 silver roubles, whereas a Russian infantry soldier cost 31.25 roubles, a British infantry soldier 134 roubles, an Austrian soldier 53 roubles, a Prussian soldier 60 roubles and a French soldier cost 85 roubles.[24] The Ottoman officer, however, received more than his European colleagues. In the case of the *müşir*, he wrote that only 25 per cent of his pay went to the expenses of his *konak* (household) and the rest to his pocket.

As recognized by many Russian and European observers, the Ottoman regular soldier in general, excluding the irregulars and the *redif*, fought bravely despite these deprivations. These poor soldiers could not even hope for any promotion or reward, except for bringing in living prisoners.[25] On the other hand, the Ottoman officer class had all the opportunities for promotion and rewards during the war, but few of them, especially among the high command, showed themselves worthy of praise. For these and other reasons, the Ottoman army was not fit for an attack in the open field but was very firm in defending a fortified place.

It is necessary to note here that Emperor Nikolai had well-founded information on the condition of the Ottoman army through the reports of the Russian military agents in Istanbul and other cities. Before the war, the military agent in Istanbul, Staff Colonel Count Osten-Sacken (not to be confused with the other Osten-Sacken, governor of Odessa) regularly sent reports to the war minister General Prince Vasiliy Andreyevich Dolgorukov (1804–1868). On all these reports there is

---

[23] "Donesenie kamer-yunkera Chikhacheva iz Konstantinopolya o sostoyanii turetskoi armii i Bosforskikh i Dardanellskikh ukrepleniy". 1849 g. RGVIA. Fond 450, opis 1, delo 33.

[24] "Iz sochineniya l'Asie Mineure izvestnago russkago puteshestvennika P. A. Chikhacheva", *Kavkaz*, [Russian official newspaper of the viceroyalty of the Caucasus], No. 45, Tiflis, 20 June (2 July) 1853, Saturday.

[25] In a letter from the grand vizier to the *serasker*, dated 25 February 1854, it was said that a reward of 100 piastres would be given to those who brought a live prisoner of war. See BOA. A. MKT. NZD. 111/79. But this reward was abused as some soldiers caught civilians instead of soldiers.

Illus. 2 Redif soldiers. *ILN*, 24 Sep. 1853.

Illus. 3   Müşir Ömer Lütfi Pasha (1801–1871), the Ottoman Generalissimo (*Serdar-ı Ekrem*) during the war. Photo by Roger Fenton, Crimea, 1855.

the note "His Majesty has read". In his reports, Count Osten-Sacken tried to give complete information on the Ottoman army and navy, in detail for all corps, including their material and moral conditions. He also characterised all the leading commanders in the Ottoman army. For example, in his report on the "general review of the condition of the Turkish military forces in the year 1852", he described Ömer Pasha the commander of the Rumelian army as "more suitable for *small war*, than *command of an army*, although the Turkish government *expects much from him* in this latter respect" [My translation, italics underlined in the original].²⁶ Osten-Sacken listed only a handful of Ottoman commanders worthy of notice for their military training or knowledge. Nikolai's overconfidence may have partly stemmed from these reports. While the Ottoman army included many foreign military advisers and émigré officers who had knowledge of modern warfare, their effectiveness was limited by jealousy and bickering among themselves. The Anatolian army at Kars for example had many foreign (Polish, Hungarian, French, British, etc.) officers in all of the operations, but they were divided among themselves as to what to do. Even if they offered sound advice, its application by the lower ranks was problematic.

Relations with Britain

It has long been argued that the Anglo-Ottoman commercial treaty of 1838 was an important turning point in the process of the commercialization of the Ottoman agriculture and the peripheralization or semi-colonization of the Ottoman Empire within the capitalist world system. Ever since the appearance of David Urquhart's book *Turkey and Its Resources* in 1833, the importance of Ottoman markets for British industry has been researched well.²⁷ A brief look at the figures of Britain's foreign trade with the Ottoman Empire shows a large expansion of exports and imports especially from 1845 onward. These figures show clearly that the Ottoman Empire was an important exporter of raw materials such as madder root, raw silk, raisins, wool, wheat and valonia (acorns used in tanning and dying) to Britain and a significant importer of British manufactured goods such as cotton cloth, refined sugar, iron and steel, woollens, hardware and cutlery.²⁸ According to data published by the *The London Economist*, British

---

²⁶ RGVIA, fond 846 (VUA), op. 16, d. 5414, l. 19. "Obshchiy obzor sostoyaniya turetskikh voennykh sil v 1852 godu". Also available at RGVIA, fond 450 (Turtsiya), op. 1, d. 45.
²⁷ See for example, Puryear, op. cit. (1935), Şevket Pamuk, *Osmanlı Ekonomisi ve Dünya Kapitalizmi (1820–1913)*. Ankara: Yurt Yayınları, 1984. Revised edition: *Osmanlı Ekonomisinde Bağımlılık ve Büyüme 1820–1913*. Istanbul: Tarih Vakfı Yurt Yayınları, 1994.
²⁸ See Frank Edgar Bailey, "The Economics of British Foreign Policy, 1825–50", *The Journal of Modern History* XII/4, December 1940, pp. 462–476. Also see Bailey, *British Policy and the Turkish Reform Movement*, Cambridge, MA, and London: Harvard University Press, 1942, chapters II and III.

exports to the Ottoman Empire, including Egypt and the Danubian principalities, increased nearly threefold from 1840 to 1851.[29]

Recent studies have shown that not all Ottoman industries declined after the opening of Ottoman markets to British goods and some sectors adapted themselves to new conditions.[30] But these are just slight modifications in the whole picture. The fact remains that Britain dominated Ottoman imports and exports. Increasing competition from other European powers made Britain ever watchful for new markets for its fast-growing manufactures. It is also well known to the students of nineteenth century Ottoman economic history that the Ottomans gave little thought to maintaining the trade balance or a protective system of tariffs. The Ottomans levied 3 per cent customs duty on imports and 12 per cent on exports, doing exactly the opposite of other states that tried to protect their industries and their domestic market. Thus it was very important, from the financial point of view, for Britain to prevent the Ottoman Empire from falling into other hands.

Before and during the war, when the Porte or its dominions (Wallachia or Egypt) tried to increase the export duty on grain or to prohibit the export of grain in order to secure enough grain for themselves, the British ambassador strongly protested such practices as a breach of the treaty of 1838. For example, in June 1853, when Wallachia wanted to increase its export duty on grain, Lord Stratford de Redcliffe sent the following note to the Sublime Porte:

> It being generally understood that the Government of Wallachia intended to increase the duty on grain destined for exportation to a degree which would contravene the Commercial Treaty of 1838, the Undersigned received Instructions from his Government to enter his Protest against any such departure from the engagements subsisting between the Two Governments.
>
> In execution of those instructions the undersigned now protests in the customary form against this supposed infraction of Treaty, and holds the Porte responsible for any losses which may accrue therefrom to any subject or subjects of Her Britannic Majesty.[31]

---

[29] Quoted by [Friedrich Engels], in Marx, op. cit., p. 16.

[30] See Donald Quataert, *Ottoman Manufacturing in the Age of the Industrial Revolution*, Cambridge & New York: Cambridge University Press, 1993. Also see by the same author, "Manufacturing", in Halil İnalcık and Donald Quataert (eds.), *An Economic and Social History of the Ottoman Empire*, vol. II, Cambridge: Cambridge University Press, 1997, pp. 888–933. Also see Pamuk, op. cit. (1994), p. 21.

[31] Stratford to the Ottoman foreign ministry, dated 4 June 1853. BOA. HR. SYS. 1192/1 enc. 11.

Even in time of war, Britain did not want to restrict its foreign trade. Thus when in July 1854 the pasha of Egypt tried to restrict the export of grain, Stratford protested again, arguing that, "as the supplies usually drawn from Russia, are now interrupted, it is extremely desirable that the trade should be unfettered in all other quarters".[32]

Two months later, Stratford sent another note when the Porte tried to restrict the export of grain:

> ...The Commercial Treaty stipulates for unrestricted liberty of commerce in articles of Turkish produce, as well for exportation as for internal trade. The occasional restrictions which have been submitted to with respect to grain were justified by urgent necessity. In the present instance no such necessity exists. There is an abundant harvest, and the armies no longer look to Constantinople for their supplies....[33]

Russia between Expansionism and Legitimism

Emperor Nikolai I[34] had witnessed the revolt of the Decembrist (*Dekabrist*) officers during his accession in December 1825. From then on he vowed to suppress any revolutionary disorder in Russia and Europe and to be the defender of law and order. Russia, on the other hand, was the main antagonist of the Ottoman Empire in the Balkans, the Black Sea and the Caucasus. From his accession until the Crimean War, Nikolai had seen two major wars, one with Iran in 1826–1828 and the other with the Ottoman Empire in 1828–1829. In both cases, Russia continued its expansion, gaining Nahçivan and Erivan from Iran by the Treaty of Türkmençay in 1828 and Ahıska, Ahılkelek and the Caucasian coast of the Black Sea from the Ottomans by the Treaty of Edirne in 1829. Nikolai ruthlessly suppressed the Polish insurrection during the upsurge of revolutions in Europe in 1830. Marshal Ivan Fyodorovich Paskevich, conqueror of Warsaw and afterwards Prince of Warsaw, ruled Poland in a military manner as Nikolai's viceroy. In 1833, Nikolai helped Sultan Mahmud II against Mehmed Ali Pasha of Egypt. The Treaty of Hünkâr İskelesi, signed on 8 July 1833, made Russia and the Porte allies for a period of eight years.

---

[32] BOA. HR. SYS. 1192/1 enc. 36, dated 10 July 1854.
[33] BOA. HR. SYS. 1192/1 enc. 31, 7 September 1854.
[34] Interestingly, Nikolai calls himself "Nicolas Premier" in his own letters written in French, as if knowing for sure that there will be a second Nikolai. See for example BOA. İ. HR. 327/21182, Nikolai's letter, dated 27 January 1853.

At the end of its term, this treaty was altered to the advantage of the European great powers by the Straits Convention of 13 July 1841. In 1848 Emperor Nikolai helped Austria to crush the revolt of the Hungarians. This earned him the title of the "gendarme of Europe". Nikolai's notion of legitimism did not allow any revolutionary disorders or nationalist insurrections against the "lawful" sovereign of a state. This, however, had not deterred him from supporting the Greek War of Independence in 1827. In fact, he pursued policies of autocratic rule and police control in internal matters and of reactionary conservatism in international matters. At home, all liberties were suppressed, the press and universities brought under strict supervision and a special third division of the imperial chancellery was organised as the secret police. Consequently, many talented officers, civil servants, artists were arrested, exiled or removed from their duties.[35]

In 1853, Emperor Nikolai I was probably the most powerful monarch in the world. He commanded the biggest land army of Europe. The army was indeed Nikolai's favourite agency, yet he "stressed unthinking obedience and parade ground evolutions rather than combat training".[36] He had surrounded himself with military men, filling most of the ministries with generals. Thus, by 1840, ten of the thirteen ministers were generals aide-de-camp.[37] His army was not up to date because of incapacity at the top, inflexibility, corruption[38] and technical backwardness. The soldiers were supplied with outdated weapons and had little training, if any. Dmitriy Alekseevich Milyutin (1816–1912),

---

[35] George Vernadsky, *A History of Russia*, Yale: Yale University Press, 1969, pp. 212–213. Nicholas Riasanovsky has described the regime of Nikolai in similar terms, yet he has also insisted that Nikolai I "retained the earmarks of his basic belief in legitimism" in his attitude toward the Ottoman Empire. See Riasanovsky, *A History of Russia*, Oxford: Oxford University Press, 2000, p. 337. Seventh edition, with Mark Steinberg, vol. I, 2005, p. 314.

[36] John Shelton Curtiss, "The Army of Nicholas I. Its Role and Character", *The American Historical Review* 63(4), July 1958, p. 886.

[37] Albert Seaton, *The Crimean War. A Russian Chronicle*, London: B. T. Batsford Ltd, 1977, p. 22.

[38] On corruption in the administration of the Russian army, see Curtiss, *The Russian Army under Nicholas I, 1825–1855*, Durham, NC: Duke University Press, 1965, pp. 212–232. British consul James Henry Skene also writes that the embezzlement of rations was an old and common practise in the Russian army. Marshall Diebich's army in 1829 drew rations and drugs for 2,400 men per regiment while their effective strength was 400. See Skene, *With Lord Stratford in the Crimean War*, London: Richard Bentley and Son, 1883, p. 261.

War Minister from 1861 to 1881 under Nikolai's successor, Aleksandr II, writes the following in his notes:

> Speaking frankly, like most of the contemporary young generation, I also had no sympathy for the regime at that time, which was built on administrative arbitrariness, police repression and strict formalism. In most of the state affairs, undertaken during the reign of Emperor Nikolai, a police point of view prevailed, that is to say, a concern about the maintenance of order and discipline. From here originated the suppression of personality and the extreme tightening of freedom in all spheres of life, in science, arts, speech, and press. Even in the military affairs, in which the Emperor took a passionate interest, the same concern about order and discipline prevailed; not the substantial well-being of the army, not the adaptation of it to military tasks were pursued, but only orderliness in appearance, bright outlooks in parades, pedantic observation of countless small formalities were sought after, blunting one's judgement and killing genuine military spirit.[39] [My translation]

Friedrich Engels, in one of his anonymous leading articles in the NYDT had also written in 1854 that Nikolai

> limited promotion to mere parade martinets, whose principal merit consists in stolid obedience and ready servility, added to accuracy of eyesight in detecting a fault in the buttons and button-holes of the uniform – constantly preferring such sticks to men of real military ability and intellectual superiority.[40]

The exception to the rule in Nikolai's armies was the Caucasus army that had been waging an irregular war against the Caucasian mountaineers for many years. Many talented but politically unreliable officers had also been sent to the Caucasus as a punishment. They in turn enhanced the capacity of the Caucasian army through constant war with the guerrilla forces of Caucasian mountaineers. Thus during the war, Russia was to gain its great victories in the Caucasus front.

Russia's weak point was the navy, where Britain and France had the advantage. Russia had a strong naval base at Sevastopol but its Black Sea fleet was no match for either the British or French fleet, let alone their combined power. In a one-to-one fight Nikolai had no doubt of beating the Ottoman armies and navy, but he knew very well that the

---

[39] Yevgeniy Viktorovich Tarle, *Krymskaya Voina*, vol. 1, Moscow: Eksmo, 2003, pp. 69–70.
[40] "The Russian Failure", Leader, NYDT, 11 July 1854, quoted in Karl Marx, op. cit., p. 397.

other powers would not let him gain control of the Turkish Straits or even control of the mouth of the Danube. The fact that he occupied part of the Ottoman Empire without gaining the consent of the great powers is a clear indication that he had lost some sense of reality by this time. Long before then, he had already discussed with the British ambassador Seymour his plans on the partition of the "sick man of Europe".

Economically, Russia and the Ottoman Empire were rivals, both of them exporting wheat to Europe. Grain exports represented 35 per cent of the total value of Russian exports in 1855.[41] Russia was also fostering its own industries. The Russian port of Odessa was in competition with the Danubian principalities that had been freed from the obligation to sell their grain only to Istanbul at fixed prices and given the right of export of their produce by the Treaty of Edirne of 1829, confirmed by the Anglo-Ottoman Commercial Treaty of 1838. After 1830 Moldavia and Wallachia increased their wheat exports from the ports of Galatz and Brailov on Austrian and British commercial ships to customers who had previously purchased wheat from Russia. Nevertheless, Russian exports continued to increase. For the period from 1832 to 1840, the Russian grain trade increased by 56 per cent annually on average.[42] Russian industry was weak and could not compete with that of Britain with its cheap prices and better quality. An economic alliance of Russia and the Ottoman Empire was not possible.

On the other hand, Russia's trade with Britain in 1851 accounted for around one-third of its total foreign trade.[43] But the relative importance of Russia for the British economy had fallen in comparison with the Ottoman Empire. As a customer of British goods Russia had fallen behind the Ottoman Empire. While in 1827 British exports to Russia were three times more than the exports to the Ottoman Empire, this ratio had changed significantly by 1849, when the Ottoman Empire (including the Danubian principalities) bought far more British goods than Russia. The principalities alone imported more goods from Britain than Russia did.[44] This was largely the effect of the 1838 Commercial Treaty. The Turkish Straits had become important channels for both the Black Sea and the Indian trade, which now reached Trabzon

---

[41] Riasanovsky and Steinberg, op. cit. (2005), p. 320.
[42] Vernon John Puryear, op. cit. (1965), p. 88.
[43] Tarle, op. cit., vol. 1, p. 51.
[44] Puryear, op. cit. (1969), p. 109.

via Iran. Caravans reached Trabzon from Turkistan, Mesopotamia and Persia. Thus the spices of India, the grain, wool and hides of Hungary, Poland, and Ukraine, the carpets of Iran, etc., all travelled through the Turkish Straits.

Dispute over the Holy Places

The Holy Places were the Church of the Nativity and several other significant early Christianity sites in Jerusalem and its vicinity. Both Latin (Catholic) and Greek (Orthodox) churches endeavoured to gain supremacy in controlling these places. The dispute over holy places revolved around such seemingly trivial issues as whether Latin or Greek clergy would possess the key to the Great Church of Bethlehem and which of them would have the priority of holding services in the Church of the Holy Sepulchre in Jerusalem. The Ottomans on their part were happy to control both churches but Ottoman bureaucracy, stressed from both sides, was hard pressed to satisfy both sides. The French justified their demands based on firmans dating from the time of Süleyman the Magnificent.

Russia, on the other hand, claimed the right of remonstration on behalf of the Orthodox subjects of the Porte by a broad interpretation of the Treaty of Küçük Kaynarca of 1774, reaffirmed by the treaties of Bucharest in 1812, Akkerman in 1826, Edirne in 1829 and Hünkar Iskelesi in 1833.[45] The Orthodox subjects of the Porte were by far more numerous than the Catholics; their number reached 13.5 million, almost equal to the total European Ottoman population. In Jerusalem as well they were far more numerous than the Catholics. In 1850, when these problems erupted, the Catholic population of Jerusalem was less than six per cent and Catholic pilgrims constituted a negligible percentage of the total visitors of Jerusalem.[46]

From a legal point of view, the position of France was more powerful since it was based upon capitulations, the last of which dated from 1740. Yet from then on the Latins had not fulfilled their responsibilities and the Greeks were given special firmans. Thus in practice the

---

[45] For more information see Roderic Davison, *Essays in Ottoman and Turkish History, 1774–1923: The Impact of the West*, London: Saqi Books, 1990, pp. 29–59.

[46] Brison D. Gooch, "A Century of Historiography on the Origins of the Crimean War", *The American Historical Review* 62(1), October 1956, p. 35.

Greeks had more rights.[47] In this quarrel, France took the initiative by officially demanding from the Porte the return of certain places to the Latin Church. The Sultan was vexed by this Christian dispute and finally tried to solve the problem in February 1852 by issuing two firmans, giving the keys to the Latins and assuring the Greeks that their rights would remain unchanged. Russia lost no time in protesting. Thus began a diplomatic war in Istanbul in which the Ottomans were caught between France and Russia, unable to find a solution acceptable to both. Commissions were set up and all of the documents were examined, yet it was difficult to satisfy both sides.

At present most historians (except for the new Russian Orthodox nationalists) accept that the question of the holy places was no more than a pretext for the Crimean War. That the issue of the holy places was a fabrication to conceal the imperialist aims of tsarist Russia, or that the defence of the Ottoman Empire by Britain and France was simply because of imperialist rivalry, is a commonplace in contemporary Turkish historiography. While these factors appear true, one has to be consistent and apply the same scepticism to the actions of the Ottoman Empire as well. Many Turkish historians like to perceive the Ottoman state as simply a victim of the great powers, without itself having any imperialist or expansionist aims or practices and in other cases even as the "last island of humanity".[48]

Positions of France, Austria and Other States

In France, Louis-Napoleon Bonaparte was first elected president in 1849 and then, through a coup d'état in 1852, proclaimed himself as Emperor of the French under the name of Napoleon III – in a clear association with his famous uncle. Searching some cause to reassert the greatness of France, Napoleon III willingly took up the issue of the Holy Places against Russia. France being the protector of Catholics in the Ottoman Empire, Napoleon III made strong representations at the Porte in defence of the Latin Church in Jerusalem. He

---

[47] For a detailed account, see Bekir Sıtkı Baykal, "Makamat-ı Mübareke Meselesi ve Babıali", *Belleten* XXIII (90), Ankara, April 1959, pp. 240–266. In English, see David Goldfrank, *The Origins of the Crimean War*, London and NY: Longman, 1994, pp. 75–90.

[48] Mustafa Armağan, *Osmanlı: İnsanlığın Son Adası*, Istanbul: Ufuk Kitapları, 2003.

owed much to his Catholic followers for their assistance in his rise to power. Thus, contrary to most Turkish histories, it was Bonapartist France and not Tsarist Russia that first raised the question of the holy places. France had always been interested in the maintenance of the Nativity Church (*Kamame Kilisesi*) and other Christian holy places in Jerusalem. Reşid Pasha had held many negotiations on this issue with the French authorities in the 1840s.[49]

Napoleon III also had a personal grudge against Nikolai I because Nikolai had not addressed him as "my brother" in the usual form between monarchs, but merely as his "good friend" (*bon ami*). Emperor Nikolai thought only those monarchs who, like himself, came to rule "by the grace of God", were worthy of being addressed as a brother, whereas Napoleon had only been elected by the people.[50] Napoleon III could not help but feel slighted. Furthermore, at that time he found it necessary to draw the attention of the French people away from domestic problems towards an international, religious problem. In European politics, ever since the 1815 restoration, France had wished to end the policy of containment maintained by the other great powers, especially by Britain against France. Although France was a member of the Concert of Europe, it had been excluded for a short time in 1840–1841. An alliance with Britain was essential for France to break its isolation.

Austria's position was troublesome during the war, torn between Russia and the Allies. Nikolai had saved the Austrian Empire by suppressing the Hungarian revolution in 1848. In the eyes of the absolutist Austrian aristocracy, he was a true monarch who ruled with an iron hand against all kinds of revolutionaries and democrats. In their recent dispute over Montenegro with the Porte, Austria had again depended on Russian support. Count Leiningen's mission to Istanbul on the Montenegrin question had ended successfully a few days before or on very day of Menshikov's arrival in Istanbul, with the Porte acceding to Austrian demands.[51] While thus owing gratitude towards Russia, Austria's interests dictated otherwise.

No longer facing any revolutionary threats, Austria did not want war, nor could it allow Russia's control over the mouth of Danube or over the Balkans in general. Austria's large Slavic population made it

---

[49] Reşat Kaynar, *Mustafa Reşit Paşa ve Tanzimat*, Ankara: TTK, 1991, pp. 582–587.
[50] Mikhail Nikolayevich Pokrovskiy, "Krymskaya Voyna", in *Istoriya Rossii v XIX veke*, Moscow: Tsentrpoligraf, 2001, p. 18 (first published in 1908).
[51] Goldfrank, op. cit. (1994), pp. 120–123. Cezmi Karasu, op. cit. (1998), pp. 44–50.

highly sensitive to any moves that would unite Balkan Slavs or show them an example of insurrection, even against the Ottoman Empire, because, once begun, an insurrection of Slavic peoples would certainly affect the Austrian Slavs (Serbs, for example) as well. Furthermore, Austria could not afford to be on hostile terms with Napoleon III, because of the problems of Venetia and Lombardy, claimed by the Italians. While Nikolai could not help Austria against France in Italy, France could help and was willing to help Austria on the Danube. Thus the Austrian foreign minister Karl Ferdinand Graf von Buol-Schauenstein, Count Buol (1797–1865) tried to strike a compromise between the final Ottoman and Russian notes. But he was unsuccessful, Reşid Pasha refused to compromise further. In the end, Austria's ultimatum to Russia at the end of December 1855 contributed much to the making of peace. Austria was certainly among the losers at the end of the war, for it had gained Russia's hate, yet without gaining France and Britain's sympathy.

Iran had had a basically stable frontier with the Porte since the signing of the Treaty of Kasr-ı Şirin in 1639, despite occasional wars. Border violations by nomadic Kurdish tribes remained a continuing issue of controversy between Iran and the Porte. In 1847 a commission had re-adjusted the Ottoman-Iranian border. Despite that, the *nahiye* of Kotur in Van province was captured by Iran and the Porte demanded it back. The Tehran-Tabriz-Trabzon caravan road was an important outlet for Iran's foreign trade. Iran had always had designs upon the Ottoman province of Baghdad province because of the importance of the holy places there (such as Kerbela) for the Shiite sect. For these reasons, Iran and the Porte had never made an alliance even against such a Christian power as Russia that threatened both of them. Consequently, Russia had successively defeated Iran and the Porte between 1826 and 1829. The present war presented a good opportunity for Iran to capture Baghdad, but Britain served as a deterrent. During the war Iran signed a secret agreement with Russia on 29 September 1854. Iran promised not to give any assistance (including exports of military items) to the enemies of Russia. Russia promised to cancel Iran's remaining debt of 500,000 *tümens* at the end of the war.[52] Iran moved

---

[52] İ. Caner Türk, op. cit. (2000), pp. 43–44. Also see Mustafa Aydın, "Kırım Harbi Esnasında Osmanlı-İran İran-Rus İlişkileri (1853-1855)", in *Savaştan Barışa*, pp. 131-150; Ibragimbeyli, op. cit., pp. 232-244.

some troops towards the Ottoman border and its attitude remained a serious uncertainty for the Porte and the allies.

The young state of Greece under King Otho was the most ready client for Nikolai's propaganda. At the beginning of the war, the Greek government secretly supported the Ottoman Greek insurgents in Thessaly and Epirus. A number of Greek officers including Lieutenant-General Hatzi-Petros, an aide-de-camp of King Otho, crossed the border with troops to join the insurgents.[53] The Porte suppressed the revolt and the allies blockaded Greece from the sea in May 1854. Austria and Prussia also did not wish the Greek revolt to spread into the Balkans. Therefore soon Greece had to give up its policy of support for insurgence.

The "Sick Man of Europe"

Emperor Nikolai had first announced "Turkey" sick just two months after the Treaty of Hünkâr İskelesi in September 1833 during his meetings in Münchengrätz with Prince Metternich of Austria. Metternich avoided discussion on this point according to his words.[54] In 1844, the Russian Tsar visited England and this time talked with the British ministers about the "Eastern Question" (at that time the foreign secretary was Lord Aberdeen). The fall of the Ottoman Empire was not, however, a requirement of British policy in the East. A weak Ottoman state best suited British interests. Therefore, the British ministers did not make any pledge to Nikolai. The two parties agreed to maintain the Ottoman Empire as long as possible, but in case of its dissolution they would come together for an understanding on its partitioning. The results of the negotiations were summarised by the Russian foreign minister Count Nesselrode in a memorandum, which the British government accepted as accurate.[55] The British considered the memorandum as a secret exchange of opinions and not as a binding agreement, while Nikolai thought of it more seriously.

On 9 January 1853, Emperor Nikolai once again approached the British ambassador Sir Hamilton Seymour (1797–1880) in St. Petersburg and repeated his famous words about the Ottoman Empire:

---

[53] Clive Ponting, op. cit. (2005), p. 59.
[54] Vitztum von Eckstaedt, *St.-Petersbourg and London in the Years 1852–1864*, London 1887, pp. 29–30, quoted by Tarle, op. cit., p. 89.
[55] Nicholas V. Riasanovsky, op. cit. (2000), p. 336; (2005), p. 313.

"*Nous avons sur les bras un homme malade – un homme gravement malade*". Nikolai added that "Turkey" seemed to be falling into pieces and that it was important that England and Russia should come to an understanding as to what was to happen in the event of the sudden downfall of "Turkey".[56] A few days later (on 14 January) Nikolai held a long conversation with Seymour, this time being more definite. He said he did not want to expand at the cost of "Turkey", but there were several millions of Christians in the Ottoman Empire whose interests he was called upon to watch over, and he was making "moderate and sparing" use of his right to do so. While he avowedly did not wish for the downfall of the "sick man", if the Ottoman state were to collapse they would find themselves obliged to deal with the situation, and in that case he would not allow any other power to occupy Istanbul; neither would he himself do so. Therefore he wanted to reach a preliminary agreement with Britain for such an event.

Nikolai supposed that the alliance of the strongest European land power (Russia) with the strongest naval power (Britain) would be enough to decide the fate of the Ottoman Empire and he openly said that he did not care what others would think in case of such an alliance. Seymour on his part said that, in his opinion, "Her Majesty's Government will be indisposed to make certain arrangements connected with the downfall of Turkey, but it is possible that they be ready to pledge themselves against certain arrangements which might, in that event, be attempted". Then, on the question of the holy places, Nikolai seemed quite content with the Sultan's firman of February 1852 and believed that his objects would be attained by negotiation. However, as Vernon Puryear has pointed out, Seymour was not shocked by Nikolai's frank comments. In his report to Lord John Russell, the British Secretary of State for Foreign Affairs, he seemed to endorse the plan:

> A noble triumph would be obtained by the civilization of the nineteenth century if the void left by the extincion of Mohammedan rule in Europe could be filled up without an interruption of the general peace, in consequence of the precautions adopted by the two principal governments the most interested in the destinies of Turkey.[57]

---

[56] Bilal Şimşir, "Kırım Savaşı Arifesinde Mustafa Reşid Paşa'nın Yazışmaları (91 belge ile birlikte)", in *Mustafa Reşid Paşa ve Dönemi Semineri. Bildiriler*. Ankara: TTK, 1987, Ek No. 1.
[57] Puryear, op. cit., p. 214.

In reply to the report of Ambassador Seymour's conversations with Nikolai I, Lord John Russell reflected that Her Majesty's Government saw no actual crisis, "which renders necessary a solution of this vast European problem". It was also uncertain when the event was going to happen. In twenty, fifty or a hundred years? "In these circumstances", it was said, "it would hardly be consistent with the friendly feelings towards the Sultan which animate the Emperor of Russia, no less than the Queen of Great Britain, to dispose beforehand of the provinces under his dominion".[58] Furthermore it was noted that such an agreement between England and Russia could not be kept secret and "European conflict would arise from the very means taken to prevent it". It is also worth noting here that Russell characterizes the attitude of the Ottoman Sultan and his government as "inert" and "supine". Nevertheless, it is clear from Russell's reply that those inert and supine Turks should be allowed to rule in Istanbul, simply because there was no better replacement without causing a European war.

Emperor Nikolai I and Sir Hamilton met again on 20 and 21 February 1853. Seymour read the above reply of Russell to Nikolai. Nikolai repeated that the catastrophe was "impending" on "Turkey" ("the bear is dying") and "it might be brought about at any moment, either by an external war, or by a feud between the "old Turkish party" and that of the "new superficial French reforms", or again, by an uprising of the Christians, already known to be very impatient to shake off the Mussulman "yoke".[59] Nikolai wanted a 'gentleman's agreement' with the British cabinet as to what to do in the event of the fall of the Ottoman Empire. Did he really believe that the end of the Ottoman Empire was so close? If so, on what grounds? Those are interesting, yet not easily answerable questions. In any case, he did not, nor could he, show any compelling evidence of the "sick man's" or the "bear's" dying, and he certainly failed to convince the British.

---

[58] Şimşir, op. cit., ek no. 2. Also see M. S. Anderson, *The Great Powers and the Near East 1774–1923*, London: Edward Arnold Publishers Ltd., 1970, pp. 73–74.

[59] Şimşir, op. cit., ek no. 4–5. We must add that these secret conversations did not remain so for long, being published in the Blue Books, i.e. the British parliamentary papers, within one year. See Karl Marx, "The Secret Diplomatic Correspondence", NYDT, 11 April 1854, also available in *The Eastern Question* (London 1969), pp. 298–313.

On the other hand, Nicholas Riasanovsky has argued that

> Even his [Nikolai's] ultimate decision to partition the Turkish Empire can be construed as a result of the conviction that the Porte could not survive in the modern world, and that therefore the leading European states had to arrange for a proper redistribution of possessions and power in the Balkans and the Near East in order to avoid anarchy, revolution, and war.[60]

The Mission of Prince Menshikov

In the meantime Nikolai sent to Istanbul a mission headed by Prince Aleksandr Sergeyevich Menshikov (1787–1869) as ambassador extraordinary and plenipotentiary in order to press upon the Porte to arrange for a solution of the holy places and to receive formal guarantees for the future. Prince Menshikov, who bore the titles of Governor General of Finland, General-Adjutant, Admiral and Marine Minister was not a good choice for a diplomat. He was a rather sarcastic, conceited and vainglorious person. As such, he had a high appreciation of his own abilities and little respect for the opinions of others.[61]

Count Karl Robert Vasilyevich Nesselrode (1780–1862), the Russian minister of foreign affairs (1822–1856) and chancellor (1845–1862), had recommended, instead of Menshikov, such experienced diplomats as General Prince Aleksey Fyodorovich Orlov (1786–1861), the Russian representative at the Treaty of Edirne (1829) and of Hünkar İskelesi (1833), or Count Nikolai Dmitrievich Kiselev (1802–1869), the Russian ambassador in Paris, or his brother Pavel D. Kiselev. Either they all declined the mission (because they did not believe in its success), or Nikolai did not accept them. In any case, Nikolai wanted not only a diplomat but also a military-naval commander who could take immediate and direct military decisions if need be. Furthermore, Menshikov possessed at least one virtue, which was rare among the ministers and officials of the Russian emperor: He was rich and he did not steal from the state treasury. For this reason he was a favourite of the emperor.[62]

---

[60] Riasanovsky, op. cit., pp. 337–338. Seventh edition, 2005, p. 314.
[61] Zayonchkovskiy, op. cit., vol. I, p. 349. Tarle is of the same opinion. See Tarle, op. cit., p. 160.
[62] Tarle, op. cit., vol. I, p. 161.

Menshikov received oral instructions from Nikolai and some written instructions (in French) from Count Nesselrode, the foreign minister. These instructions described in detail how and what he should demand from the Porte, and if the demands were not accepted, how to leave Istanbul.[63] Menshikov had also received the outline of a treaty and a secret defence agreement with the Sublime Porte, whereby the Tsar offered military aid to Turkey in case of any attack. Nikolai also gave Menshikov a personal letter to Abdülmecid, dated 24 January 1853, where he wrote in friendly terms – as though it was not himself who had discussed the partition of the Ottoman Empire with the British ambassador. Another letter dated 27 January 1853 simply advised Prince Menshikov's appointment as ambassador extraordinary and plenipotentiary, citing all the titles of Nikolai and all the orders worn by Menshikov.[64] The emperor also instructed Menshikov to threaten the "Turks", if necessary, with recognition of the independence of the Danubian principalities.

The tasks for Menshikov and his staff included a military reconnaissance of the defences of the Bosphorus, because Nikolai's plans included a possible lightning attack on Istanbul and the Dardanelles. While talking to Seymour and sending letters to Abdülmecid, on 19 January 1853 Nikolai had also signed off a plan of attack on the Turkish Straits. For this purpose he detached the 13th division from Sevastopol and the 14th division from Odessa. On 28 March Menshikov sent him a report on the weakness of the Ottoman fleet and the fortifications of the Straits, naming the most suitable places for landing Russian troops.[65]

On his way to Istanbul, Prince Menshikov conducted two conspicuous inspections, undertaken to make an impression: he visited first the 5th army corps in Kishinev (capital of Bessarabia, north of Moldavia), and then the Black Sea Fleet in Sevastopol. General Nepokoychitskiy, chief of staff of the fifth army corps and Vice-Admiral Vladimir Alek-

---

[63] Zayonchkovskiy, op. cit. (1908), *Prilozheniya* no. 105–109. Also see Anderson, op. cit., pp. 70–71.

[64] BOA. İ. HR. 327/21182. The French translation of this second introductory letter and its Ottoman (Turkish) translation were submitted on 2 March 1853 to the grand vizier and through him to the Sultan. It is interesting to note that the Turkish translation renders "Votre Majesté" in various terms, among which "Hazret-i Hilafetpenahileri" is significant because the title Caliph seems to be seldom used in contexts related to the Crimean War.

[65] Baumgart, op. cit., p. 67.

seyevich Kornilov (1806-1854), chief of staff of the Black Sea Fleet, joined his mission. Thus Menshikov, with a large and impressive retinue, arrived at Istanbul on 28 February 1853 on the steam frigate *Gromonosets* (which means *The Thunderer*).[66] The Russian military and naval officers had come to observe the defences of the straits and of Istanbul and the opportunities for a sudden attack on the city. They were also enjoined to mobilize Russian land and naval forces in case of necessity. In Istanbul a crowd of Greeks, other Orthodox subjects and Russians welcomed the mission with cheerful applause.[67]

On 2 March, Menshikov, dressed in an overcoat instead of in full uniform,[68] went to the Porte to visit the grand vizier Mehmed Ali Pasha, to whom he declared flatly that he did not trust Fuad Efendi, the foreign minister, on the question under negotiation, and demanded that someone else be appointed for negotiations. Then, as he wrote in his diary,

> My declaration disturbed the vizier, and on leaving him, wishing to confirm my words with actions and to show how little I value Fuad Efendi, I did not pay him the usual courtesy visit. This made a big impression and aroused the Porte's displeasure, and Fuad resigned.[69] [My translation]

---

[66] See Zayonchkovskiy, op. cit. (2002), vol. I, p. 354. Nicolae Jorga gives the name of this steamship as "Donnerer" only in German translation. See his *Osmanlı İmparatorluğu Tarihi* 5, Istanbul: Yeditepe Yayınevi, 2005, p. 375. Fevzi Kurtoğlu (op. cit., p. 14) has read it as Gromonec. Alan Palmer turns it into Gromovnik. See Alan Palmer, *1853-1856 Kırım Savaşı ve Modern Avrupa'nın Doğuşu*, Istanbul: Sabah Kitapçılık, 1999, p. 23. Trevor Royle (op. cit., p. 33) also calls it Gromovnik. These names are wrong. Naval captain Dr Celalettin Yavuz, referring to Retired Admiral Afif Büyüktuğrul, writes that Menshikov arrived at Büyükdere on board "the biggest galleon of the Russian fleet" on "15 March" 1853, which is not true. See *Osmanlı Bahriyesi'nde Yabancı Misyonlar*, Kasımpaşa, İstanbul: İst. Dz. İk. Grp. K.'lığı Basımevi Müdürlüğü, [2000?], p. 71.

[67] See Zayonchkovskiy, op. cit., vol. 1, p. 354. Tarle, op. cit., vol. 1, p. 166. Zayonchkovskiy writes that Menshikov arrived at Büyükdere, while Tarle gives Tophane. Türkgeldi (op. cit., vol. 1, p. 13) does not mention the applauding Greeks and others, but he writes that Menshikov arrived "with unprecedented pomp and splendour".

[68] While Tarle and most European historians wrote that Menshikov did not wear an official uniform, Zayonchkovskiy argued that Menshikov wore his overcoat over the uniform, and on entering the first cabinet he could not find time to take off his overcoat when he was met by the grand vizier. He also argued that European newspapers reported this as if Menshikov appeared before the Sultan without uniform. See Zayonchkovskiy, ibid., vol. I (2002), p. 392, footnote 18.

[69] Zayonchkovskiy, ibid., p. 354. The author claimed to have read Menshikov's diary and quotes from it from time to time, but the diary does not seem to be deposited in an archive.

Fuad Efendi was not liked by the Russian emperor for Fuad's conduct during the 1849 crisis with the Hungarian refugees and he was known to be pro-French. Having heard of the concentration of the Russian fourth and fifth army corps in Bessarabia, the Sultan was alarmed. Rifat Pasha was appointed as the new foreign minister and he took office on 6 March.[70] Thus Menshikov had dealt his first blow to the pride of the Porte.

At that time the French and British ambassadors were not present and the two great powers were represented at the level of chargé d'affaires. The British chargé d'affaires was Colonel Hugh Rose (1801–1885), his French colleague was their first secretary Vincent Benedetti (1817–1900), who became chargé d'affaires from 20 May 1854 onwards. Rose recommended to the Porte to temporize until the return of Stratford de Redcliffe, who had resigned the ambassadorship in January 1853, but had been reappointed by the new government of Lord George Aberdeen (1784–1860) in February. Rose had become so alarmed by Menshikov's words and actions that he also ordered Vice-Admiral Sir James Whitley Deans Dundas (1785–1862), commanding the British Mediterranean squadron at Malta, to bring his fleet up to Urla near Izmir. However, Dundas refused to move without confirmation from the government. Colonel Rose was informed on 23 March that the British government did not approve of his order and the fleet remained at Malta.[71] On 19 March, however, Napoleon III had already ordered the dispatch of a squadron from Toulon to the island of Salamis (near Athens and Piraeus).[72]

Menshikov was granted an audience on 8 March and only then did he submit Emperor Nikolai's letter to the Sultan (written in French, dated 24 January). That letter contained both proposals of friendship and a threat. Nikolai put the blame for the crisis on the "inexperienced and ill-advised" ministers of the Sultan, who had not well informed him of the consequences of non-compliance with the firman already issued by the Sultan one year before. The Tsar added that in the case of another state insisting that the Sultan should not fulfil his promises towards Russia, or threatening the Ottoman Empire, Russia was

---

[70] BOA. İ. DH. 17578.
[71] Harold Temperley, "Stratford de Redcliffe and the Origins of the Crimean War", Part I, *The English Historical Review* 48 (192), October 1933, p. 605.
[72] Baumgart, op. cit., p. 93.

ready to offer assistance.[73] Menshikov also submitted to the Sultan the proposed secret defence agreement. In short, the tsar wanted to establish an exclusive agreement with the Ottoman Empire by adding an article to the Treaty of Küçük Kaynarca, giving a formal guarantee of the rights and privileges of the Greek Church in the Ottoman Empire under the protectorate of Russia, in return for a military alliance, implicitly against France. These demands by far exceeded the question as to the custody of some religious places.

The new foreign minister Rifat Pasha was authorized to negotiate with Menshikov. After the courtesy visits of Menshikov and Rifat Pasha, the first serious negotiation took place on 16 March 1853 at the pasha's house and lasted for six hours.[74] According to the minutes of the meeting, Menshikov did not follow a gradual opening of demands but set out his demands and offers at once. He stated that he was specifically authorized to negotiate the question of revision of the Treaty of Küçük Kaynarca and that unless Rifat also had the authority to negotiate the whole question, there was no point in negotiations.[75]

Rifat Pasha, by a skilful diplomatic tactic, separated the question of holy places from the question of protection of the Greek Church and said that they must begin by resolving the first question. Menshikov warned Rifat Pasha not to reveal the Russian proposals to the British embassy; otherwise he would cut off diplomatic relations. Nevertheless, grand vizier Mehmet Ali Pasha passed on the essence of the Russian intentions to Colonel Rose on 1 April. He added that "nothing whatever should be added to the Treaty of Kaynarji; that he would ask to retire from office rather than agree to either of the two propositions

---

[73] The original of this letter and two different translations of it are available at BOA. A. AMD. 50/56. One of the translations is done in the style of Ottoman official correspondence, while the other is remarkable as a literal translation. In the first instance, *Votre Majesté* is rendered, among other forms, "*canib-i hilafetpenahileri*" as well, (referring to caliphate), and the address "*très haut et très puissant Ami*" is not translated at all (because the caliph is too exalted to be a friend of a Christian monarch?) whereas in the latter, everything is translated literally. It is not a less curious fact that Menshikov appears as "Mençikof" in the first translation and as "*Menşikof*" in the second. This confusion of the spelling of Menshikov's name seems to have started right from the beginning and continues to this day. It is also an interesting question whether the second translator was ordered to make a literal translation or it was his decision to do so. Most probably he was ordered to; otherwise there would not be a second translation at all.
[74] Cezmi Karasu, op. cit., p. 54.
[75] Ali Fuat Türkgeldi, op. cit., vol. 1, Zeyl 5, pp. 257–264.

made by Prince Menshikov, which would be fatal to Turkey".[76] As Lane-Poole pointed out, this shows that the Ottoman ministers were resolved to resist Menshikov's demands before Lord Stratford's arrival, which took place on 5 April 1853.

Lord Stratford had an interview with the grand vizier and the foreign minister on the day after his arrival. He advised them "to keep the affair of the Holy Places separate from the ulterior proposals, whatever they may be, of Russia".[77] He also advised them that the rights and privileges of Christians should be guaranteed by direct sovereign authority and not by any instrument addressed exclusively to Russia. For Protestant Britain, a religious quarrel between Catholic France and Orthodox Russia was indeed not important in itself, she did not care what privileges they obtained within the religious sphere. However, any real increase of authority of one of them over the Ottoman Empire that could tilt the European balance of power was not to be tolerated. Yet what was clear to Stratford was also clear to the Ottoman ministers; the difficulty was that Menshikov would not accept anything less than a formally binding treaty or a *sened* (convention). The demands of Russia stipulated that all the Orthodox subjects of the Ottoman Empire would be under Russian protection, that the patriarchate would be lifelong and that no patriarchs would be dismissed, that a new Russian church and hospital would be built in Jerusalem and put under the protection of the Russian consulate and that a new firman would point out clearly all the rights of the Orthodox in the holy places in Palestine. On the other hand, in his conversations with Lord Stratford and the French ambassador Edmond de la Cour, Menshikov told them that if the Porte did not agree with his proposals, this would at most result in a break-up of relations but not war. Yet these assurances proved to be false. Lord Stratford pleased Menshikov by justifying the demands concerning the holy places, but avoided any discussion of the broader question of a Russian protectorate for the Greek Church in the Ottoman Empire.

On 19 April Menshikov sent another note to Rifat Pasha urging a decision. The note included accusations and threats. The Ottoman extended council of ministers (*Meclis-i Mahsus*) convened on 23 April to discuss the demands made by Menshikov. It found the demands on

---

[76] Stanley Lane-Poole, op. cit., vol. II, p. 248.
[77] Lane-Poole, op. cit., pp. 248–249.

the holy places negotiable but the question of the privileges and rights of the Orthodox subjects was not to be negotiated.[78]

On 5 May Menshikov gave an ultimatum with a period of five days for an answer. This time he informed the Porte that if the *sened* was not signed, he would cut off diplomatic relations and leave Istanbul.[79] At this stage, Lord Stratford entered the scene. On 8 May he pointed out to Menshikov that his demand "was an innovation altogether disproportionate to the question which is the chief cause of your Embassy, and as being little in accordance with the spirit of legality recorded by common consent in the Treaty of 1841".[80] From then on their intercourse practically ended.

On the next day Stratford visited the Sultan and found him full of "weakness and melancholy" and "ready to die", because his mother had just died. The British ambassador informed Abdülmecid that in case of danger he "was instructed to request the commander of her Majesty's forces in the Mediterranean to hold his squadron in readiness".[81] Emboldened by this information, the Ottoman cabinet rejected Menshikov's demands at the end of the ultimatum period, on 10 May. In his official reply, Rifat Pasha used very careful and conciliatory language, stressing that the Porte would continue as always to respect the rights and privileges of the Greek Church, and maintain friendly relations with Russia, but such a convention with another state would harm its independence and would be against international law.[82] Upon this Menshikov sent still another ultimatum on 11 May, demanding an answer before 14 May. In this note Menshikov was still describing Nikolai as an ally of the Sultan.[83] The Ottoman foreign ministry (Reşid Pasha), however, did not consider Russia an ally of the Porte, but talked rather of "friendly relations" between the two states.[84]

---

[78] Karasu, op. cit., p. 57.

[79] This note, together with other diplomatic correspondence, was published in the British Parliamentary Papers (known as the Blue Books) and quoted by the *Times*. See "The Turkish Blue-Books. The Menschikoff Note", *The Times*, London, 4 February 1854.

[80] Harold Temperley, op. cit., p. 609.

[81] Lane-Poole, op. cit., p. 266.

[82] BOA. HR. SYS. 1188/7, 11 May 1853. The text is given by Türkgeldi, op. cit., pp. 270-272.

[83] For the text of Menshikov's ultimatum see Türkgeldi, op. cit., pp. 272-274. Türkgeldi however, gives the date of the note as 21 May, which must be a typing error, as understood from the contents of the note itself. Cf. Karasu, op. cit., p. 60.

[84] Reşid Pasha to Menshikov. BOA. HR. SYS. 1188/8, dated 16 May 1853.

Meanwhile Stratford and Reşid Pasha probably agreed to act together and decided to send Nikolaos Aristarchi (1799–1866), the Greek patriarchal logothete and representative of Wallachia (*Eflak kapı kethüdası*) to Menshikov. Reşid told the logothete that the problem under negotiation should not be exaggerated and could be solved.[85] The logothete (*Logofet Bey*) told Menshikov that Reşid Pasha would be more amenable. Menshikov thought he might have a chance of success if he could get Reşid Pasha appointed, so he requested Abdülmecid to appoint Reşid as foreign minister. Abdülmecid should not have received him, but he did, although, according to Lane-Poole, he referred Menshikov back to his ministers.[86] On 13 May, the indignant grand vizier resigned and a reshuffle of ministers took place. Grand vizier Mehmed Ali Pasha became the new minister of war (*serasker*), Mustafa Naili Pasha, president of the MVL, took the office of the grand vizier and Reşid Pasha replaced Rifat Pasha in the foreign ministry. The latter took the presidency of the MVL. Yet the prospects for Menshikov did not improve thereby; the new government was not pro-Russian at all. Menshikov had in fact made a serious mistake by replacing a less skilful opponent with a more skilled one.

The new foreign minister had only one day left for a response to Menshikov's ultimatum. He therefore asked Menshikov for five or six days more to prepare "an arrangement, conveying assurances satisfactory to both parties" on a matter of such delicacy as this one concerning religious privileges.[87] On that day he had received the dispatch of the Ottoman ambassador in London, Kostaki Musurus. Musurus wrote that in his interview with the British secretary of state for foreign affairs, George Villiers, 4th Earl of Clarendon (1800–1870), he received assurances of Britain's guarantees for the independence and sovereign rights of the Ottoman Empire.[88] This news of course made Reşid bolder. The Ottoman ambassador in Paris Veli Pasha had also reported the adverse French reactions to Menshikov's conduct.[89] The

---

[85] Faik Memduh Paşa, *Mir'at-ı Şuunat*, pp. 19–20, quoted by Cavit Baysun, "Mustafa Reşit Paşa", in *Tanzimat 2*, Istanbul: MEB Yayınları, 1999, pp. 741–42.
[86] Lane-Poole, ibid., p. 267.
[87] Reşid Pasha to Menshikov. BOA. HR. SYS. 1188/8, 16 May 1853. Cf. Şimşir, op. cit., document 15.
[88] Musurus to Reşid Pasha, 13 May 1853. BOA. A. AMD. 44/81.
[89] BOA. İ. HR. 327/21188, 9 April 1853.

Berlin charge d'affaires Ali Rıza Efendi reported that Prussian policy was not necessarily pro-Russian.[90]

On 15 May Menshikov received a note from the Porte and on the evening of the same day replied that he had cut off official relations with the Porte but would wait a few days more in Istanbul. Storms in the Black Sea were delaying his departure. Finally, on 21 May, Menshikov with his suit departed from Büyükdere towards Odessa on board his steamer. The Russian coat of arms was taken down from the palace of the embassy. On his departure, Menshikov wrote a non-official, personal letter to Reşid Pasha from the *Gromonosets* at the harbour of Büyükdere.[91] He even attached a draft of an official note to his letter hoping for a last minute solution. He must have been disappointed by Reşid Pasha, whom he himself had suggested to the post of foreign minister. Now that the crisis reached a high point, Reşid Pasha decided to convene a general assembly (*Meclis-i Umumi*) of 46 persons from the bureaucracy, including former ministers and sadrazams, undersecretaries and the *ulema*. There, Reşid's rival Mehmet Ali carried the day and a majority of 43 persons against 3 voted down the Russian demands.[92]

Menshikov had started by demanding a treaty, then a *sened*, finally he was content with a ministerial note – but the essence of his demands had not changed. He had not shown himself capable of the skills of a great diplomat. On 26 May, the Russian chargé d'affaires Ozerov also departed with the rest of the embassy personnel. Only a secretary and the head dragoman Argyropoulo remained in Istanbul. In the meantime, the French and British fleets had arrived at Beşike Bay, which is at the entrance of the Dardanelles.

By this time Nikolai had decided what to do if the Porte did not comply with his demands. In his instructions to Baron Peter von Meyendorff, the Russian ambassador in Vienna, dated 29 May 1853, he ordered four successive consequences: 1) to demand that the Porte sign the treaty, otherwise the immediate occupation of the Danubian principalities would follow, 2) If "Turkey" continued to resist, then

---

[90] BOA. A. AMD. 44/82.
[91] Menshikov to Reshid Pasha, Büyükdere, "le 3/15 Mai 11 h. du soir". BOA. HR. TO. 286/12. Menshikov to Reshid Pasha from the *Gromonosets*, 6/18 May 1853. Türkgeldi, op. cit., vol. I, pp. 291–293.
[92] For the minutes and resolution (*mazbata*) of this meeting see Türkgeldi, op. cit., pp. 274–291.

a blockade of the Bosphorus and *the recognition of the independence of the principalities* would follow, 3) If "Turkey" remained obstinate, then *recognition of the independence of Serbia* would follow and 4) the Austrian emperor would be invited to provide moral support.[93] [Italics underlined by Nikolai. It seems that, after his plans to reach an agreement with Britain on the partitioning of the Ottoman Empire had failed, Nikolai began a serious approach to Austria.

After Menshikov's departure and the interruption of diplomatic relations, the Russian foreign minister Count Nesselrode confirmed Menshikov's demands in his note of 31 May and Reşid Pasha responded on 16 June.[94] Reşid Pasha in his reply stressed that the rejection of the demanded *sened* on grounds of its violation of the sovereignty of the state did not mean an insult to the Tsar. He added that if it were to be approved, an extraordinary envoy could be sent to St. Petersburg to resume negotiations. Reşid Pasha also informed the embassies of the four signatories of the 1841 Straits Convention (Great Britain, France, Austria and Prussia) in Istanbul with a note on 27 May 1853.[95] Reşid Pasha advised them informed them that, while the question of the holy places was solved in a way to please all sides, an agreement was not reached on the question of the rights and privileges of the Greek confession and their clergy. On the same day he also wrote to Lord Stratford explaining that Menshikov's demands were not acceptable to an independent government.[96]

Meanwhile, the Porte was working on a new firman to please its Christian and also its Jewish subjects and to leave no excuses for Russian complaints. On 7 June an imperial firman was issued to the Greek patriarchate, reassuring the Orthodox subjects of the Porte of their rights and privileges *ab antiquo*.[97] Similar firmans were addressed to

---

[93] Tarle, op. cit., vol. I, p. 243.

[94] For Nesselrode's note and Reşid's response, see ibid., pp. 297–301. Türkgeldi gives these dates as 19 May and 4 June respectively, which correspond to the Orthodox calendar. Cezmi Karasu's thesis reproduces this confusion, giving the latter date as 4 June. See Karasu, op. cit., p. 65.

[95] BOA. HR. SYS. 1188/9, 27 May 1853. For the French translation of this note sent to the British embassy, see TNA. FO 424/8, no. 388/I published by Bilal Şimşir, op. cit., document no. 22, where the date is set as 26 Mai, which is wrong.

[96] For the French translation of this letter see Şimşir, op. cit., document no. 23. I could not find the original of this letter in the BOA.

[97] Şimşir, op. cit., document 25.

other religious communities. Stratford in a letter to his wife claims that he "put two good sentences into them".⁹⁸

Towards the end of June, Nikolai ordered the two Russian armies in Bessarabia to occupy the Ottoman tribute-paying principalities of Moldavia and Wallachia. The Porte, for its part, sent orders to the commander of the Rumeli army – Ömer Pasha – to strengthen the fortifications along the Danube and to be ready for defence. It also sent orders to the Ottoman dominions of Egypt and Tunis to send troops. According to a report dated 24 June from the British consulate in Alexandria, 10,000 to 15,000 Egyptian troops had already received their salaries in arrears for the past 15 months and an advance of six months pay before sailing off to Istanbul.⁹⁹ Salih Hayri in his *Hayrabad* writes that the governor of Egypt Abbas Pasha sent 17 battalions and the governor of Tunis Ahmed Pasha sent three regiments under Ferik Reşid Pasha.¹⁰⁰ Süleyman Kızıltoprak gives the number of Egyptian troops as 20,000–22,000.¹⁰¹ Ahmed Pasha of Tunis in fact sent 7,000 regular troops with 12 cannons and more than 700 horses.¹⁰²

On 2 July the Russian armies commanded by General Gorchakov crossed the river Pruth, forming the border between Russia and Moldavia. The news reached the Porte on 7 July. This was an obvious *casus belli* for the Sultan, but he did not declare war. Nor did the Tsar declare war, arguing that this action was simply intended to put pressure on the Ottoman Empire to protect the rights of the Orthodox. The Russian consulate in Bucharest also warned the principalities to interrupt all relations with the Porte and not to send off the tribute. The Porte then requested the Hospodar of Wallachia Prince Stirbey and the Hospodar of Moldavia Prince Ghyka to quit the principalities but they declined this request saying that they were needed by their people. The Serbian prince Aleksandr declared his loyalty to the Porte.¹⁰³

---

⁹⁸ Lane-Poole, op. cit., vol. II, p. 274.
⁹⁹ BOA. İ. MTZ (05) 16/548.
¹⁰⁰ Salih Hayri, op. cit., pp. 32, 146, 284.
¹⁰¹ Süleyman Kızıltoprak, "Egyptian troops in the Crimean War (1853–1856)", in *Vostochnaya (Krymskaya) Voina 1853–1856 godov: Novye materialy i novoe osmyslenie*. Tom 1, Simferopol: Krymskiy Arkhiv, 2005, p. 49.
¹⁰² Ahmed Pasha to the grand vizir. BOA. İ. DH. 306/19403, 28 June 1854.
¹⁰³ Cezmi Karasu, op. cit., p. 68.

On 15 July the Porte issued its official note of protest against the occupation of the principalities by Russia.[104] It also reminded the four signatories of the 1841 Treaty of their obligations, and declared that it would not accept the occupation of any part of its territory and that, though it did not intend to start a war, it would be prepared for one.[105] Meanwhile, a dense traffic of plans and projects of notes, coming and going in all directions, had already begun among the great powers. It seemed that none of them wanted war and that all sought a peaceful solution. Several offers and plans were presented to Reşid Pasha by different powers. Vienna became the centre of diplomatic communication between Russia and the Ottoman Empire, thanks to Austria's neutral and interested position. Austria was both politically and geographically in the middle of Europe and was the natural candidate for an intermediary because it had good relations with both Russia and the allies. While it was grateful to Russia for the suppression of the Hungarian revolution in 1848, it could not allow Russian possession or influence in the Principalities and around the mouth of the Danube. Several notes were sent from the Porte to Russia via Vienna. In fact there occurred a "revolution" in international diplomacy. Never before had so many diplomatic efforts, by so many parties, been made in attempts to prevent war. Nevertheless, these efforts were complicated by the distances involved, so that many of them became obsolete before reaching their destinations. Istanbul had not yet been connected to European centres by electric telegraph.

The Vienna Note and the "Turkish Ultimatum"

When Reşid Pasha's note (known as the "Turkish Ultimatum") reached Vienna, it was not seen as sufficiently conciliatory and it was not sent on to St. Petersburg. The Austrians did not want to irritate Russia. Instead, on 27 July, the Austrian foreign minister Count Buol, in collaboration with the British and French ministers, prepared another proposal, which came to be known as the Vienna Note, and sent it to Istanbul and St. Petersburg. The proposal contained demands similar to those made by Russia but differed in that it extended the role of guarantor to all the great powers. This time the Tsar accepted the note

---

[104] Şimşir, op. cit., document 34.
[105] BOA. A. AMD. 46/100.

but the Ottoman *Meclis-i Umumi* convened on 14 August 1853 did not approve of it as it stood and subjected it to some modification.[106] The embassies of the four great powers in Istanbul tried in vain to persuade the Ottoman ministers. Reşid Pasha was now bitter at his European friends who had at first supported him against Russian demands and now seemed to be forcing him into accepting those demands. "It would have been better for Turkey, he said, to have yielded at the first, than after so much support from the Powers to be now unseasonably abandoned".[107] The questions of whether Lord Stratford did all in his power to support the Vienna Note or not, and whether he informally encouraged the Ottoman statesmen to resist or not, belong to the disputed areas of the diplomatic history of the Crimean War. Adolphus Slade claims that while officially advising acceptance of the note in accordance with his instructions, Lord Stratford confidentially advised its rejection. According to Slade, Lord Stratford did this when he met Serasker Mehmed Ali Pasha, "the representative of the war party" at a ball at the French embassy, and he "entered into conversation with him through a chance interpreter – an unusual condescension – and alluding to the 'Vienna note', just then arrived, said that in his opinion, speaking in his individual capacity, it was unacceptable."[108] This is possible and very interesting, but it is not supported by other sources.

Meanwhile, Reşid Pasha talked with the French ambassador Edmond de la Cour but received no support from him. In any case the Ottoman council accepted the Vienna Note only with modifications. Those modifications stressed the sovereignty of the Ottoman Empire and the fact that the rights and privileges accorded to Orthodox subjects were granted by the will of the Ottoman Sultan rather than as a result of any treaty, and were not subject to Russian enforcement.[109] On 7 September, Russia totally rejected the Ottoman modifications.[110] All the diplomatic efforts up to this time now seemed to have been fruitless. War was impending. The questions raised were now a matter of interest for the whole of Europe.

---

[106] Türkgeldi, op. cit., p. 25.
[107] Lane-Poole, op. cit., vol. II, p. 293. Lane-Poole's remark that Reşid Pasha "kissed the ambassador's hand and implored him with tears" is highly improbable and does not coincide even with his own narrative where he also writes that the Turks were obstinate at that time.
[108] Slade, op. cit., p. 110.
[109] Türkgeldi, op. cit., p. 311.
[110] Tarle, op. cit., vol. 1, p. 327.

In the capital of the Ottoman Empire signs of warlike enthusiasm appeared among part of the population or at least the most conservative sections of society. *Medrese* (theological schools) students or *softas* demonstrated in favour of war against the "infidel". A placard was posted on the walls of mosques, calling the Padishah to holy war. Its style and language leaves no doubt as to its being written by the *ulema* or the *softas*:

> O Glorious Padishah! All your subjects are ready to sacrifice their lives, property and children for the sake of your majesty. You too have now incurred the duty of unsheathing the sword of Muhammad with which you girded yourself in the mosque of Eyyub-i Ansari like your grandfathers and predecessors. The hesitations of your ministers on this question stem from their addiction to the disease of vanity and this situation has the potential (God forbid) to lead us all into a great danger. Therefore your victorious soldiers and your praying servants want war for the defence of their clear rights, O My Padishah![111] [My translation]

Lord Stratford at this point still tried to gain time for a peaceful solution. It was now the British cabinet that actually instructed him to bring the navy to Istanbul. On 3 October, Lord Clarendon wrote privately to Stratford:

> We should have been glad if the fleets were now in Constantinople... great care must be taken that they don't give too much encouragement to the Turks nor assume an aggressive position towards Russia, with whom, however much we may be displeased with her for her conduct to Turkey, we have as yet no quarrel.[112]

From the beginning of the dispute over the holy places, Ottoman diplomacy reflected an anxious desire to appease the Tsar without compromising the independence of the state. Essentially, the tsar wanted to treat the whole Ottoman Empire like the Danubian principalities. No sovereign body could accept another state's protection over a significant part of its subjects. Indeed Bolshevik (Soviet) historian Mikhail Nikolayevich Pokrovskiy was probably the first Russian historian to express the absurdity of Nikolai's demands:

> In order to evaluate this demand correctly, it is enough to imagine the Kazan Tatars receiving the right to complain of the Russian Emperor to

---

[111] Cevdet Pasha, *Tezakir 1–12*, p. 24.
[112] Harold Temperley, "Stratford de Redcliffe and the Origins of the Crimean War", Part II, *The English Historical Review* 49 (194), April 1934, p. 288.

the Turkish Sultan, whose representations the Emperor would have to take into consideration and even to satisfy.[113] [My translation]

Curiously, however, Ottoman diplomacy made no use of a 'human factor' that could have countermanded the demands of Russia: the Sunni Muslims (Tatars, Kuban Nogays, Circassians and Dagestanis) of the Russian Empire. If Russia were to interfere on behalf of the Orthodox Christians of the Ottoman Empire, then the Ottomans could also interfere on behalf of the Sunni Muslims of Russia. While there is no doubt that by the 19th century the Ottomans were not in a position to seek a protectorate over the Muslims of Russia, they could nevertheless make that the subject of diplomatic rhetoric. But why did the Ottomans never raise any such questions with the Russians? Were they simply too frightened take up this issue with Russia or did they think that they had nothing effective to say? It is really difficult to find an answer. In fact, it seems that the Ottomans had no plan, even for the future of the Crimean Tatars after the war was transferred to the Crimea. The Ottomans did not try to make use of the Girays, descendants of the Crimean khans who lived around Şumnu and other parts of Bulgaria. One of them, Mesud Giray, approached Marshal Saint Arnaud in Varna and went to Gözleve with him. The Porte, on the other hand, had no interest in him. When Mesud Giray applied later for a Mecidiye order for himself, the sadrazam asked the serasker whether Giray had rendered any services worthy of an order.[114] However, we do not know of the serasker's answer. The Ottoman army did form a Tatar cavalry regiment in Gözleve in the Crimea, however, this was only at the request of the Tatars and after the French had already accepted 150 Tatars into their cavalry.[115]

It is indeed one of the peculiarities of the Crimean War that diplomatic efforts never ceased during more than two years of war. War and diplomacy went in parallel. Numerous notes, conventions, and declarations were prepared in Vienna, Paris, Istanbul, and London and were then sent in all directions. The Prussians also tried to make Berlin a venue for the negotiations. Sweden and Denmark maintained a policy of alert neutrality. Sardinia-Piedmont (early in 1855) joined

---

[113] Pokrovskiy, op. cit., p. 19.
[114] BOA. A. MKT. MHM. 64/66, 19 January 1855.
[115] Hakan Kırımlı, "The Crimean Tatar Units in the Ottoman Army during the Crimean War", unpublished symposium paper presented at the French Institute of Anatolian Studies (IFEA) in Istanbul on 27 November 2004.

the war on the side of the Allies in the hope of gaining further support for Italian unification. Iran vacillated between Russia and the Ottomans, and had it not been for the efforts of Britain and France, she might have joined the war on Russia's side. This war had the full potential of turning into an all-out European war. All the powers of Europe, in one way or another, were involved in it. Diplomacy in this war proved almost as important as military action. There were many occasions when it seemed that a solution satisfactory to all parties had been found, yet all these efforts were fruitless until the capture of Sevastopol by the Allies and of Kars by the Russians towards the end of 1855. Yet this was an unfinished war, and the peace that ended this war was also to prove unstable.

Cevdet Pasha's remarks seem sober and realistic:

> At the beginning of this matter, naïve people of the time acted quite belligerently and ambitious with vain hopes of going as far as Moscow and maybe Petersburg or at least conquering the Crimea. As for the Western-minded, they claimed that in case of war Russia would come as near as Edirne. Both parties had wrong opinions. That our forces are not equal to those of Russia is unquestionable. Nevertheless, it was also known to well-informed people that the regular and reserve forces mustered by our state could for a long time engage and halt the Russian forces. Events too have proved this fact. His Majesty Abdülmecid Han did not like shedding blood and Reşid Pasha too was trying to solve the matter with the pen. Diplomats like Âli Pasha and Fuad Efendi who were raised in his school were also of the same opinion with him. The military people, on the other hand, especially Mehmed Ali Pasha, cunningly appeared as supporters of war. Even those of them who at heart were for the maintenance of peace, were dreaming of saying: 'Let the diplomats forbid war, then we will be able to say that we could do this and that, alas, this and that person prevented war'.[116] [My translation]

The Ottoman Empire had become an arena of contest among the great powers. While these powers competed among themselves for more influence over the Porte, Ottoman sovereignty suffered more and more. The Ottoman Empire had to answer even for matters totally alien to it. A good example is the affair of the Hungarian revolutionary refugee Martin Koszta, who had taken refuge in the Ottoman Empire and lived for a while in Kütahya. Koszta was then released and he went to America. After a while he came back to Izmir, where he was

---

[116] Cevdet Pasha, *Tezâkir 1–12*, p. 23.

arrested by the Austrian consulate and imprisoned in an Austrian ship in the harbour. Since he was under American protection when he was arrested, an American corvette had forced the Austrian brig in İzmir harbour to return Koszta to the Americans. Some Italians had also attacked three officers of the Austrian ship in a café, killing one of them and injuring another. Yet the newly appointed Austrian envoy (the internuncio) in Istanbul, Baron Karl Ludwig von Brück, protested and demanded the dismissal of the governor of Izmir Âli Pasha, (the former foreign minister) and the appointment of a new governor who would be capable of restoring the security of the Europeans in Izmir. This was in June 1853, when the crisis with Russia was ripening. The Porte did not want a quarrel with Austria as well and was obliged to satisfy her demand. It was first decided that Âli Pasha and the governor of the province of *Cezayir-i Bahr-i Sefid* (Aegean islands) would be interchanged. However, Brück did not accept this solution and therefore Âli Pasha was simply removed from office. Just as in many other cases, an Ottoman official had been forced to resign because of a dispute between rival great powers.[117]

European and Ottoman Public Opinion before the War

In the summer of 1853, European public opinion was definitely pro-Ottoman, because Russia was seen as the aggressor and the Ottoman Empire as the victim. As mentioned by Prof. Winfried Baumgart, since the 1830s (especially after the Treaty of Hünkâr İskelesi in 1833) a strong Russophobia had developed in Britain. Russian southward expansion against the Porte and Iran had heightened such fears. Among the chief representatives of Russo-phobia, we can cite Lord Palmerston and David Urquhart. Russian suppression of the struggles of the Poles (1831) and Hungarians (1849) had also made Russia the stronghold of autocracy and reaction in the eyes of liberal and socialist European public opinion. An increase of Russian influence on the Ottoman Empire was not in the interests of the European bourgeoisie who controlled most of the newspapers. Almost all British and many

---

[117] İbnülemin Mahmut Kemal İnal gives the text of the *tezkire-i maruza* of the grand vizier. But he does not mention the release of Koszta by the American ship. See his *Son Sadrazamlar*. 1. Cilt. Istanbul: Dergah Yayınları, 1981?, pp. 10–11.

French newspapers were full of pro-Ottoman and anti-Russian sentiments. Even the neutral Prussian newspapers noted that anti-Russian sentiments had increased among the general European public.[118]

There is no doubt that the Ottoman cabinet knew what was written in these newspapers. The Ottoman ambassador in London Kostaki Musurus, especially, sent home clippings of newspaper articles on the Russo-Ottoman conflict. Thus we have many of them in the BOA and we shall now review some of them. Upon the news of the passage of the river Pruth by 12,000 Russian troops and the occupation of Jassy, capital of Moldavia, British newspapers in general were much excited against this act of aggression. For example, the *Observer* wrote on 3 July 1853 that "the present and late conduct of the Czar, in his insolent aggressions upon his weak Neighbour and Ally, and his contempt for the opinion of his best friends in Europe have left him without an apologist in England…"[119]

The Sun on the other hand, reflecting the voice of the British bourgeoisie, declared on 4 July 1853, that Britain had nothing to lose from a loss of trade with Russia,

> We have nothing to fear from Nicholas; and Russia is not so profitable a customer that we need care for the suspension of commercial intercourse. In 1851 our export trade to Russia amounted to less than 1,300,000*l.*, while we have admitted her raw produce, her hides and hemp, and tallow to an enormous account, on the most favourable terms. Her magnates will regret the loss of our custom far more than we shall theirs.

The Daily News, a Liberal paper, wrote on 4 July 1853: "It seems the die is cast, and Russia has at length resolved to put to proof the value of Europe's diplomatic declarations that the faith of treaties and the integrity of the weaker states must be maintained". *The Standard* on 4 July 1853 also declared that "the conquest of Turkey by Russia would seriously damage the commerce of England, if it should not threaten her Eastern empire". The Tory newspaper *The Morning Herald* argued that "the honour and safety of Europe both demand that the act of

---

[118] See Gencer, op. cit., p. 161.
[119] The Ottoman ambassador in London Kostaki Musurus sent these newspaper clippings attached to his despatches to Istanbul. They are available at BOA. İ. HR. 329/21224.

invasion cannot be passed over unnoticed" (4 July 1853). *The Morning Chronicle*, another Liberal, Peelite paper, played the same tune on 4 July 1853:

> Russia wages war upon Turkey, not to redress any wrong, nor to avenge any affront, but to wring from a weaker Power an acknowledgement of the sovereign rights of the EMPEROR over a large portion of its subjects; and, so far as the Porte is concerned, the attack is as wanton and unprovoked as if he believed that the moment had arrived when he might with impunity overrun and subdue what he probably regards as a falling empire...

Tory newspaper *The Morning Advertiser* advised firm action against the tsar on 5 July 1853. Even the conservative *Times* could find no apologies for Russia on 4 July 1853:

> The utter insufficiency of the alleged causes of resentment against Turkey, especially after satisfaction had been obtained on the only tangible grievances complained of, suggests that other and deeper motives must be at work... the concentration of armies on the frontier, the review at Odessa, the demeanour of the Envoy and his reception at Constantinople, awakened other suspicions. He seems to have been sent not so much to obtain a treaty as to pick a quarrel...

After 7 July, when Nikolai's manifesto was published and reached Britain, the newspapers increased their criticism. For example, the *Daily News*, on 6 July 1853 wrote that the Russian emperor had declared a new crusade:

> The Manifesto of the Emperor Nicholas, which we this day publish with less surprise than regret, affects to proclaim against the Ottoman Empire a religious war... it is the summons to a new crusade. It is an appeal, direct and undisguised, to the fanaticism of a bigoted priesthood and an ignorant population...

The Morning Herald, went so far as to accuse some members of the British cabinet of being pro-Russian:

> There is no use in concealing the disastrous truth. There is a Russian party in the Cabinet – that is, Russian as far as their feeble blundering permits them to have any settled foreign policy at all. We care not by what foreign influence this party is backed; it is high time that England should know to what extent they have sacrificed – to what greater extent they are prepared to sacrifice – English honour and English interests. (7 July 1853)

The Morning Advertiser wrote on 6 July 1853:

> By force of arms the Czar will endeavour to impose upon Turkish subjects a protection which they hold in such horror, that they will brave death to escape it... the moment a Russian soldier has crossed the Pruth for hostile purposes, that moment Turkey is at war, and the Dardanelles are, by treaty, open, with permission of the Sultan, to the ships of war of all nations. The right, then, of the fleets to advance is undisputed.

The Morning Advertiser on the next day wrote that "the Autocrat of all the Russias has thrown down the glove to public opinion and to Europe. The opinion he despises, the Europe he defies can never hesitate to take it up". *The Globe* defended Reşid Pasha's and the Sultan's "temperate and dignified" stand on 5 July 1853:

> The text of the note addressed by Redschid Pacha, in reply to the note of Count Nesselrode, is now before the public, and it will be found to support the temperate and dignified position of the Turkish Government... The Sultan has newly confirmed the privileges, rights and immunities of the Greek Church as they have existed *ab antiquo*...

The Morning Herald, 28 July 1853, even threatened the British ministers:

> Once it comes to this, that the Cabinet are avowedly ready to prostrate British honour and British faith before the ambition of Russia, we venture to promise that the British people will make very short work of the Ministers.

Reading these newspapers, one may consider that British public opinion was both very strongly pro-Ottoman and belligerent. But this was all the more misleading for the Ottoman ministers, because they did not really understand that newspapers do not necessarily reflect the views of their governments. A more or less free press was not quite conceivable to them. Therefore they mistook the tone of the newspapers for proof of real support from their respective governments in the case of Ottoman war against Russia. Adolphus Slade argues that the "prime councillor" of the Porte (London Ambassador Kostaki Musurus?) contributed to its indecision about the inevitability of war by sending the minister for foreign affairs articles extracted from the Western press, eulogizing "Turkey" and depreciating Russia. Thus,

> Unused to free discussion, their own newspapers being strictly censored, the Turkish ministers were unable to discriminate justly between the government and the press. Innately suspicious, they may readily have

fancied collusion. The warlike articles of sundry English and French journals weakened the effect of foreign offices' pacific despatches. They were decidedly more palatable. The latter alluded to social aberrations and rayas' [non-Muslims'] rights; whereas the former made no allusion in that day to such delicate topics.[120]

By beginning of September 1853, the anti-Russian spirit in Istanbul had reached a peak. The conciliatory approach of the government was also much criticised. This was largely the result of the pressure of Ottoman public opinion that favoured war against Russia. This public mood was mainly expressed by the professors and students of religious schools (*medreses*), the ulema and the *softas*. Some of the ministers like Damad Mehmed Ali Pasha and part of the military also backed them. They were easily organised in the mosques.

Ann Pottinger Saab has asserted that the reactions of the ulema and the *softas* were based largely on their own deteriorating material conditions. The new secular schools had largely diminished their career prospects, opening the way instead to the graduates of the new schools. The expropriation of the *waqf* (pious foundations) property had also deprived them of some of their traditional revenues. Therefore as a social group they were discontented. Referring to Kovalevsky, Saab gives the number of *softa*s in Istanbul as around 45,000, which seems to be rather an overestimate.[121] Şerif Mardin has also argued that the destruction of the Ottoman industries had created new unemployment and had increased the number of medrese students, as well as their disobedience.[122] However, the *medrese* students were still numerically stronger than those attending the new Western style *rüşdiye* schools. According to Stanford Shaw and Ezel Kural Shaw, at the beginning of the Crimean War there were only 60 *rüşdiye* schools in the entire empire with 3,371 male students, whereas *medrese*s in Istanbul alone had 16,752 students, all male. However, the numbers for *rüşdiye*

---

[120] Slade, op. cit., p. 99. Ali Rıza Seyfi, the translator into Turkish of Slade's book, has totally misunderstood this passage. Cf. Adolphus Slade, *Türkiye ve Kırım Harbi*, Istanbul: Askeri Matbaa, 1943, p. 63.

[121] Saab, op. cit., pp. 81-82 and 84. According to a study by Mübahat Kütükoğlu, there were 5,769 students and instructors in the medreses of Istanbul in 1869. See Kütükoğlu, *XX. Asra Erişen İstanbul Medreseleri*, Ankara: TTK, 2000, pp. 345-352.

[122] Şerif Mardin, *Yeni Osmanlı Düşüncesinin Doğuşu*, Istanbul: İletişim Yayınları, 1998, p. 189.

schools and *medrese* students seem exaggerated.¹²³ Cevdet Pasha was of the opinion that Damad Mehmed Ali Pasha provoked the softas in order to secure the dismissal of Reşid Pasha.¹²⁴

On 10 September 1853, some 36 or 35 members of the ulema submitted a petition to the MVL, citing verses from the Koran and the prophet Muhammad's words (*hadis*) that the *imam* of the true believers must fulfil his duty of proclaiming jihad.¹²⁵ The *Times* newspaper in London gave the news as follows:

> ...The petition was principally composed of numerous quotations from the Koran, enjoining war on the enemies of Islam, and contained covert threats of disturbance were it not listened to and complied with. The tone of the petition is exceedingly bold, and bordering on the insolent. Some of the principal Ministers endeavoured to reason with those who presented it, but the answers they obtained were short and to the point. The spokesman observed – 'Here are the words of the Koran: if you are Mussulmans you are bound to obey. You are now listening to foreign and infidel ambassadors who are the enemies of the Faith; we are the children of the Prophet; we have an army and that army cries out with us for war, to avenge the insults which the Giaours have heaped upon us.' It is said that on each attempt to reason with these fanatics, the Ministers were met by the answer 'These are the words of the Koran.' The present Ministers are undoubtedly in a state of alarm, since they look upon the present circumstance (a very unusual event in Turkey) as but the commencement of a revolution, and fear to be forced at the present inopportune juncture into a war. It seems that three petitions have been presented by these softas, one to the Sultan, one to Mehemet Ali, the Seraskier or Commander-in-Chief, and one to the Council. The party of Redschid Pacha believe the affair to have been instigated by Mehemet Ali, who has been from the first openly and avowedly in favour of war...Should a popular movement urge the Ministry to declare war, the peaceful and reasonable policy of Redschid Pacha would of course be at an end, and so would his services, while Mehmet Ali would become

---

¹²³ Shaw and Shaw, *History of the Ottoman Empire and Modern Turkey*, Vol. II, Cambridge, UK: Cambridge University Press, 1977, p. 107. The authors refer to the *Salnâme-i Devlet-i Aliyye* of 1268 (1852–1853). However, this *salnâme* and others for the following five years do not contain such information. It seems doubtful that the number of *rüşdiye* schools had reached 60, for the *salnâmes* of these years mention only a few of them in Istanbul. Necdet Sakaoğlu and Nuri Akbayar (op. cit., p. 301) on the other hand, wrote that in 1860 the number of high schools (meaning *rüşdiye* schools) in all the Ottoman Empire had reached 60 with 3,920 students. The authors, however, as usual for them, do not cite any reference.

¹²⁴ Cevdet Pasha, *Tezâkir 1–12*, p. 23.

¹²⁵ BOA. İ. MVL. 26350 enc. 1, 12 September 1853. There are 35 seals on the petition and one place is left unsealed.

practically the chief man in the Empire; whereas should these unhappy questions with Russia be settled by the acceptation by the Emperor of the note of Redschid Pacha, the latter would acquire thereby immense influence and consolidation of power, with the confusion of all his rivals... The Ministry is much puzzled in its endeavours to ascertain how far the body of the nation agrees with the sentiments expressed in the petition – whether, in short, public opinion supports the movement of these softas, or whether their bold address has originated entirely within the walls of their mosques and tékés.[126]

On the next day a special council of eleven ministers and high officials convened in the seaside mansion of the grand vizier Mustafa Naili Pasha to discuss the petition. According to the protocol or minutes (*mazbata*) of the council, the reason for not proclaiming war against Russia until then was the insufficiency of the military preparations. To the questions on this issue, Ömer Pasha, the commander of the Rumeli army, had replied that the Rumelian army needed 40,000 regular troops in addition to its current forces as well as several months for the preparation of bridges and fortifications. The Anatolian army was in a similar situation, as confirmed by the *serasker*. While the Porte kept trying to find a political solution, it was obvious that if a political solution were not found, then war was inevitable.[127]

The ministers further argued that since the decisions had been taken unanimously and since seeking the assistance of other states was approved by the *şeriat*, and since the *şeyhülislam* had not yet sanctioned the formal proclamation of war, then the protest of some *hoca efendis* was very improper and contrary to law. Therefore they should be reprimanded and punished. The ministers observed that "the real issue to be regretted here was the audacity and insolence of the common people to interfere with state affairs". Such things had caused a lot of trouble in ancient times and had been unseen for a long time "by the will of God and thanks to his Imperial Majesty's firm rule". Therefore it was very urgent to prevent such insolence. Here we see a really interesting development as regards Ottoman public opinion. It

---

[126] "Turkey (From Our Own Correspondent). Constantinople, Sept. 12", *The Times*, Issue 21544, London, 27 September 1853, p. 7.

[127] BOA. İ. MVL. 26350 enc. 2, 11 September 1853. The *mazbata* is sealed by Şevket Bey, Mehmed Arif Efendi, Mehmed (?), Mahmud Pasha, Rifat Pasha, Ali Fethi Pasha, Mehmed Ali Pasha, Mustafa Reşid Pasha, Rauf Bey, Esseyyid Ahmed Arif Efendi and Mustafa Naili Pasha (the grand vizier).

seems that the Ottoman public had started to take a genuine and active interest in "state affairs".

The *mazbata* added that, according to the news from Vienna, the modifications made by the Porte to the Vienna Note had been approved by the ambassadors in Vienna and sent to St. Petersburg. The answer from Petersburg was expected in eight to ten days. If the answer turned out to be negative then the Porte would not yield. Finally the council decided to summon prominent members of the ulema and receive from them written approvals of government policy. Thus the excitement and agitation of the people would also be diminished. In any case the petition was not signed by well-known *hoca efendis* but only by the lesser ones. Vidinli [Mustafa] Hoca Efendi was inclined to sign the petition but after a reprimand from the şeyhülislam he had abstained from putting his seal. It was also observed that while the petition was prepared and circulated for signature over a period of several days, the police had not duly informed the authorities and had not taken measures to prevent it. Such indifference by the police force,[128] in such a delicate time when it should have been more vigilant than ever was really regrettable. Therefore the *zabtiye müşiri* should be strongly admonished to be on the alert. On the next day, the grand vizier submitted the *mazbata* together with the *arzuhal* to the Sultan, who approved the decision of the ministers.[129] On the other hand, the *Berliner Zeitung* wrote that the ulema and the *medrese* students had collected 60,000 signatures from Istanbul and its vicinity for war against Russia.[130] That number seems decidedly exaggerated.

The disturbances caused by the softas worried some of the European diplomats, who feared a fanatical wave of Christian massacres. The French ambassador Edmond de La Cour sent this alarming news to his government, and the French foreign minister Edouard Drouyn de Lhuys (1805–1881) telegraphed the news to London as well. Lord Clarendon, without waiting for despatches from Lord Stratford, instructed him "to send for the British fleet to Constantinople" on 23 September. Then the Russian ambassador in London, Baron Filipp Ivanovich

---

[128] Interestingly the *mazbata* uses exactly the word *polis* for the police (*polis memurları*), while officially the police were called the *zabtiye*, their chief being the *zabtiye müşiri*. I have not come across the word *polis* elsewhere in those documents for this period that I have seen in the BOA.

[129] BOA. İ. MVL. 26350 enc. 3, submitted on 11 September 1853 and approved on the next day.

[130] Gencer, op. cit., p. 168.

Brunnov (1797-1875) declared that the call to the fleet was a violation of the Treaty of the Straits of 1841, which banned the passage of warships through the straits in peacetime. To this protest, Clarendon's reply was that the Porte "had ceased to be at peace from the moment when the first Russian soldier entered the Danubian Principalities".[131]

Lord Stratford, however, was not aroused so much. He simply ignored the order, as if the summons to the fleet had been left to his discretion. But still he called for two or three steamships to Istanbul as a precaution. The French ambassador also called in some steamships. Stratford in his despatch wrote: "Fortunately there is no necessity whatever for calling up the squadron... I wished to save Her Majesty's Government from any embarrassments likely to accrue from a premature passage of the Dardanelles".[132] Thus it seems that Stratford probably did not have belligerent aims, contrary to the allegations of some historians, especially the Russian historians who consider him to have been a great enemy of Russia and one of the chief causes of the war. On the contrary, he seems here to have been careful not to provoke Russia while still defending British interests. Nevertheless, the question of the role of Stratford de Redcliffe is a complicated and still controversial point among historians. Some documents published by Prof. Baumgart in AGKK show that even such British statesmen as Lord Clarendon, Sir James Graham (1792-1861), First Lord of the Admiralty, and Baron Henry Cowley (1804-1884), British ambassador to France, saw Stratford as "bent on war", "resolved to embroil matters at home and abroad in the hope of obtaining a triumph for his own morbid vanity and implacable antipathies", his tendencies being "clearly more for war than for peace".[133]

On 26 and 27 September 1853, another grand council (*Meclis-i Umumi*) of 163 high-level official dignitaries was convened to discuss the question of war against Russia. The council consisted of the three distinct groups of the Ottoman bureaucracy: the *mülkiye*, that is, ministers, ex-ministers and other officials, the *seyfiye*, i.e. the military, and the *ulema*, i.e. the religious establishment. According to the testimony of Rauf Bey, who was present at the meeting, first the *hoca efendis* were asked to give their opinion. Hoca Yahya Efendi answered that the

---

[131] Lane-Poole, op. cit., vol. II, p. 307.
[132] Lane-Poole, op. cit., vol. II, p. 308.
[133] Winfried Baumgart, "Einleitung", AGKK, III/1, Munich, 2005, pp. 46-47.

ministers (*vükela*) knew better and they should be asked. Finally Vidinli Mustafa Hoca Efendi asked why the war had not yet begun.[134]

At this point Reşid Pasha the foreign minister interfered and told the council that the state was not prepared militarily at that time. He added that although the ambassadors of the great powers advised against a declaration of war until the European opinion was clarified, the Sublime State was free to make its own decisions. Therefore she could either accept the advice or declare war. Everybody should speak up, he remarked. Then some of the *ulema* asked: "If we begin war, will the great powers be against us or not?". To this question Reşid Pasha replied that they were not expected to be against war, but that their fleets might withdraw, although they would perhaps remain. It was up to the Porte to endeavour to keep them nearby, or not. Some of the *ulema* then asked how Christian allies could be useful, referring to them as one nation of infidels (*el küfrü milletün vahide*). Then Reşid Pasha explained that although their religion was one, they also had conflicts among them like the one between Iran and the Ottoman Empire.

The ulema then turned to Serasker Mehmed Ali Pasha to learn whether the Ottoman Empire had enough military strength to fight against Russia. The serasker pasha gave an account of the military strength of the empire but avoided any definite answer as to whether this power was sufficient for a war against Russia. Edhem Pasha discussed the population and the military power of Russia and concluded that war against them would be a difficult undertaking, even such a great conqueror as Napoleon I had been unsuccessful against them.

Rauf Bey writes that at this point the majority of the ulema attacked these words and made "unbecoming" remarks about Edhem Pasha as if he were an infidel. Former grand vizier İzzet Pasha also read a paper, saying that war should not be started without proper preparations. Another former grand vizier Âli Pasha also recommended caution. Former foreign minister Fuad Efendi said that "the Ottoman Empire cannot make another treaty like the Treaty of Edirne. The matter must be considered well. Furthermore, the question of war finances should also be taken into consideration". Rauf Bey goes on to remark here

---

[134] Rauf Bey was a son of Rifat Pasha, the president of the MVL. For the text of his minutes of the meeting, see Türkgeldi, op. cit., vol. I, pp. 315–320. However, we do not know when he wrote these minutes, immediately after or much later? Their historical value would increase certainly if they had been written immediately.

that some *hoca efendis* said "we will seize the wealth of the enemy by the force of the sword and recover our expenses"; therefore, the question of money, which was the essence of the matter, was not properly discussed but instead irrelevant and meaningless words were uttered.

Rifat Pasha, the president of the MVL said that the real point to be looked to in this matter was the alliance of the naval powers with the Ottoman Empire and, internally, the unanimity of the officials of the state. After some discussion, Rıfat Pasha asked the opinion of the high ranking ulema. Then the *mufti* of the MVL Arif Efendi (the future *şeyhülislam*) referred the question to the office of the *fetva*. To this the *fetva emini* from the office of the *şeyhülislam* replied that if the commander of the Muslim armies says that there are enough forces to go against the enemy then it is necessary to go to war. Arif Efendi also complained about the rumours about himself spread by the *softas* because he had participated in the negotiations of Rıfat Pasha with Menshikov. After that he asked the serasker to report whether the state had enough force at its disposal. The serasker again stated the number of the imperial troops but said that he was not sure whether this amount was sufficient for a war against Russia. Rauf Bey remarks that the serasker did not give a certain answer to the repeated question, because he did not want to be held responsible if the result of the war turned out to be unfavourable. When some lieutenant-generals (*feriks*) from the DŞA were asked, they gave vague answers. Then Reşid Pasha asked the opinion of the Kapudan Pasha, the grand admiral. Mahmud Pasha replied, "if the great powers do not send fleets to the Mediterranean and attack the Ottoman Empire, then the imperial fleet could certainly be a match for the Russian fleet in the Black Sea. But if later we will be held responsible for these words then I will not accept it". These words surprised everyone and a total silence fell in the hall.

Reşid Pasha broke the silence and said that "It is better to die with arms in hand than to die with tied hands. God willing, we will be victorious and destroy the harmful treaties as well". Reşid Pasha seems to have carried the day and determined the outcome.

Thus after two days of discussions, war was decided unanimously and the resolution was sent to the Sultan for approval. The resolution of the council was written by Mustafa Reşid Pasha immediately during the night of the second day of the negotiations.[135] It was stated that

---

[135] The text of this *mazbata* can be seen at Türkgeldi, op. cit., vol. I, pp. 320–321. A better transliteration is provided by OBKS, pp. 126–127.

Russia had not accepted the modifications made by the Porte to the proposals in the Vienna Note. While the four great powers had asked the Porte to accept the note without alterations and offered some guarantees against the risks it contained, this was not sufficient from the point of view of honour even if it had any legal benefit. Acceptance of the note without alterations would mean taking a "killing poison". Therefore it was decided unanimously to declare war. It was emphasised that the war was declared on the Russian state and that the Christian subjects of the Ottoman Empire should not in any way be offended; on the contrary, more care and protection than before should now be exercised with regard to them in order not to cause any hostility from other states because of their ill treatment. Sheikhulislam Arif Hikmet Bey Efendi issued a *fetva* sanctioning the declaration of a holy war (*cihad ve kıtal*) and on 30 September Sultan Abdülmecid approved the resolution.[136]

If we can rely on the accuracy of the account of Rauf Bey, then an interesting picture emerges. Serasker Mehmed Ali Pasha, whom some sources like to assign to the war party, seems to have maintained a very low profile at the meeting. Reşid Pasha on the other hand, who is seen as a proponent of a diplomatic solution, seems to have played the role of war-hawk. It is also important to observe that the seemingly more Western-oriented Reşid Pasha was rather in accord with the ulema as regards support for the war effort. While we cannot make sweeping generalizations on the basis of this account alone, it is certain that there were no clear-cut dichotomies based on 'reformers versus conservatives' or 'pacifists versus belligerents' among the Ottoman statesmen.

---

[136] See OBKS, pp. 126–128.

CHAPTER THREE

BATTLES AND DIPLOMACY DURING THE WAR

The Declaration of War

In this chapter I will dwell on the battles of the war to the extent that Ottomans were involved in them, using Ottoman, Russian and European sources in a comparative and critical manner. I will focus on those battles, events and aspects of the war that I see as most important. One of the aims of this chapter is to examine the extent of reforms in the Ottoman army, how it fought, how it was led, organized and supplied. I will also analyse how the Porte carried out its diplomacy in this period, considering the efforts of the great powers and the Porte from the declaration of war in October 1853 until the Treaty of Paris at the end of March 1856.

On 4 October 1853, the Porte's declaration of war was published in the official newspaper *Takvim-i Vekayi*. On the same day official notes were sent to the embassies of the four great powers in Istanbul (France, Britain, Austria and Prussia).[1] The next day a leaflet was published in French, bearing the title *"Manifeste de la Sublime Porte"*.[2]

The declaration was still mild and conciliatory in style. It stated that the Sublime Porte was forced to declare war since Russia had occupied Ottoman territory and had not evacuated it despite various diplomatic efforts. It also announced that, as a last sign of the peaceful intentions of the Porte, the commander of the Rumelian army Ömer Pasha was instructed to allow a period of 15 days for General Mikhail Gorchakov (the Russian commander of the Danubian armies) to evacuate the principalities. Ömer Pasha sent the ultimatum on 8 October 1853, stating that if he received a negative answer or no answer, then hostilities would begin. General Gorchakov replied on 10 October that he was not authorised to remove his armies. Thus from the legal point of view, war was fully declared on the day when General Gorchakov rejected

---

[1] BOA. HR. SYS. 1189/4. Also see CH, nr. 648, 6 Muharrem 1270 (9 October 1853).
[2] BOA. HR. SYS. 907/5, 5 October 1853.

the ultimatum of Ömer Pasha.³ This point is important because later Nikolai I and some Russian sources claimed that the Porte did not wait until its own ultimatum expired, when Ottoman artillery opened fire on Russian ships on the Danube on 21 October.

Meanwhile Reşid Pasha was afraid that a sudden Russian attack on Istanbul might take place before the end of the ultimatum period. Therefore he requested the French and the British embassies on 8 October⁴ to bring some part of their fleets from the Dardanelles to Istanbul. He knew that the ambassadors were instructed and authorised by their governments to bring their fleets to Istanbul in case of necessity to protect the Sultan. Despite this, the ambassadors did not hasten to answer. Their notes came only on 16 October. The French note was positive and clear. It stated that Russia had violated Ottoman territorial integrity and the Porte was now by treaty entitled to freedom of action concerning the Straits. It also indicated that the French fleet was ready to come as a sign of friendship.⁵ Further, it stated that due to weather conditions, it was in any case desirable that the fleet enter the Straits. The British response was also positive, though less enthusiastic than that of the French.⁶

On 20 October 1853, the "Emperor and Autocrat of All-Russias" Nikolai I issued his proclamation, finally declaring war on the Porte.⁷ Nikolai distorted the facts in this statement to such an extent that it was as though he assumed his subjects had no source of information other than the document itself. He argued that the Porte had declared

---

³ Mustafa Budak writes that the Russians rejected the proposal on 17 October, referring to an ATASE document, the contents of which he does not explain. See Budak, op. cit. (1993), p. 41.

⁴ This date is given by Lane-Poole (op. cit., p. 309). I could not find Reşid Pasha's note in the BOA; therefore its date is not certain, although I found the replies of the two ambassadors to it.

⁵ Translation of the French note to the Ottoman foreign ministry. Edmond de la Cour to Reşid Pasha, 16 October 1853. BOA. HR. SYS. 1193/2 enc. 9. I could not find the original of this note.

⁶ Translation of the British note to the Ottoman foreign ministry. Stratford to Reşid, 16 October 1853. BOA. HR. SYS. 1193/2 enc. 8. I could not find the original of this note.

⁷ For the Russian original, see Zayonchkovskiy, op. cit., vol. II, part two, p. 531. This proclamation was translated into Bulgarian as well and distributed in Bulgaria. The *kocabaşı* of Rusçuk (Ruse) sent it to the governor of Silistria, who forwarded it to Ömer Pasha and to the Porte. The proclamation in Bulgarian, its translation into Ottoman Turkish and the letter of the governor of Silistria Mehmed Said Pasha to the grand vizier, dated 18 March 1854 can be found at BOA. A. AMD. 51/1.

war despite the peaceful efforts of Europe and his enduring patience, pretending that Europe supported him. He added that the Porte had accepted revolutionaries from all countries into its army and initiated military operations on the Danube. He declared Russia now had to defend its sacred cause of protecting the Orthodox faith by arms. But it seems that he had lost his confidence and initiative. Now it was not he who guided events but events that began to direct him. He did not give definite orders to the Danubian army as to what to do against the Ottoman army, other than to act in self-defence. Although war had been declared by both sides, both remained as yet on the defensive. There were still hopes of a diplomatic solution. Emperor Nikolai on his part was still assuring the European powers that his actions would be defensive. Meanwhile, Sultan Abdülmecid assumed the title of *Ghazi* on 3 November 1853.[8]

On 30 October, General Louis-Achille Baraguey d'Hilliers (1795–1878) was appointed to replace Ambassador Edmond de la Cour at the French embassy in Istanbul. The general, who had distinguished himself in Algeria, like so many other French generals, was chosen by Napoleon III to balance the influence of Stratford de Redcliffe on the Porte. The new French ambassador arrived at Istanbul in mid November and served here until 4 May 1854.

The Danubian Front in 1853

Now that war was declared, the Ottoman side was expected to initiate actual hostilities first, because it was Ottoman territory that had been occupied. Actual hostilities between Russia and the Ottoman Empire broke out at the mouth of the Danube, near İsakçı on 21 October 1853. Ottoman shore batteries opened fire on two Russian steamships with eight barges going to Galatz. However, this was only a small skirmish and neither side was as yet ready for a great confrontation. In some of the Russian studies, the Ottomans are accused of beginning the war without waiting for the end of their own ultimatum. However, as mentioned above, this view is not confirmed by the existing documents.

---

[8] BOA. HR. MKT. 68/4, 6 December 1853. Also see Lütfi Efendi. *Vak'a-nüvis Ahmed Lütfi Efendi Tarihi. C. IX.* Yayınlayan Prof. Dr. Münir Aktepe. Istanbul: İstanbul Üniversitesi Edebiyat Fakültesi Yayınları, 1984, p. 91.

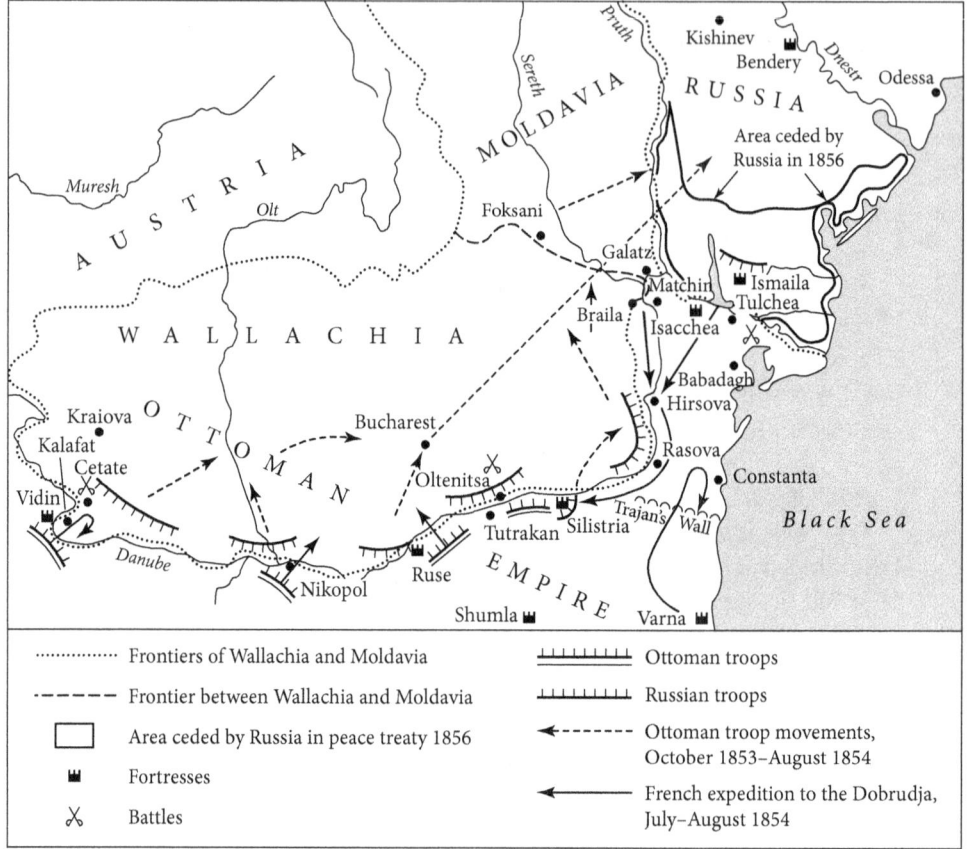

Map 1   The Danubian theatre of war 1853–1854.

The Ottoman Rumelian army was commanded by Müşir Ömer Pasha. The conqueror of revolts in Bosnia, Kurdistan and Arabia, he was at the height of his career and full of energy. He spoke several European languages in addition to Turkish and was considered by both the British and the French as the most talented officer in the Ottoman army. Nevertheless, as described in the previous chapter, Russian military reports sent before the war about his capabilities did not express so complimentary a view. Marshal Saint-Arnaud, the French Commander-in-Chief, evaluated him as a good general but needing guidance. Saint-Arnaud also commented that the Ottoman army had a high command and soldiers, but "no officers and even fewer NCO's".[9]

---

[9] David B. Ralston, *Importing the European Army*, Chicago & London: The University of Chicago Press, 1990, p. 62.

Ömer Pasha's chief of staff in the Rumelian army and later (from December 1854 on) deputy [*kaimmakam*] was Ferik Çerkez İsmail Pasha (1815?–1861)[10] and another chief of staff was Nazır Ahmed Pasha (?–1860).[11] It seems that they did not like each other. According to Hüseyin Avni Pasha, who was a staff officer in the Rumelian army during the war, Ömer Pasha saw İsmail Pasha as a rival and tried to undermine him, while Ahmed Pasha also did not help İsmail Pasha in the battle of Çatana.[12]

On the staff of Ömer Pasha, there were also some Polish and Hungarian refugee officers, veterans of the Polish uprising of 1831 and of the Hungarian uprising of 1848–1849. In November 1853, the Polish émigré Michal Czajkowski, who had converted to Islam and taken the name of Mehmed Sadık Efendi, was promoted to the rank of *mirmiran* and appointed to recruit and command a Cossack (*Kazak* or *Kozak*) regiment from Polish emigrants and the Ignat-Cossacks.[13] For the Russians, Czajkowski was a "renegade" like any Christian who converted to Islam. About one year later a second regiment was formed under the command of Count Wladislaw Zamoyski, as described in Chapter Two.

The Rumelian army was the best Ottoman army in terms of discipline, training, and quality of officers, arms and provisions. Its supplies of arms and provisions were not inferior to that of the Russian army. The number of troops under Ömer Pasha's command was about 145 to 178 thousand.[14] These troops were stationed along the Danube, from

---

[10] According to Mehmed Süreyya's *Sicill-i Osmani* (Istanbul: Tarih Vakfı, 1996, p. 830) he was a Circassian slave of İzzet Mehmed Pasha. He became a mirliva in 1838 in Nizip. He was made a vizier in March 1854 after his success at the battle of Çatana. Michal Czajkowski calls him Satan İsmail Pasha ("Szajtan Izmaił Pasza"), which is rather a doubtful and informal nickname. See Czajkowski, op. cit., p. 44 and the editorial note on p. 292. Veysel Usta gives İsmail Pasha's birth year as 1805. See Ahmed Rıza Trabzoni, op. cit., p. 95.

[11] From the documents it is not clear of which army or corps he was a chief of staff. Ahmed Pasha was one of the first graduates of the war academy (*Mekteb-i Harbiye*). He became a *ferik* and the superintendent (*nazır*) of the *Mekteb-i Harbiye* in 1848. He was made a vizier in November 1854 and commander of the Ottoman forces in the Crimea in September 1855. See Mehmed Süreyya, op. cit., pp. 216–217. Ahmed Pasha was sentenced to death by Fuad Pasha for his involvement in the massacres of Christians in Damascus in 1860. See Cevdet Pasha, *Tezâkir 13–20*, p. 111.

[12] See Cevdet Pasha, ibid.

[13] Abdülmecid's *irade*, dated 7 November 1853. BOA. İ. DH. 282/17740.

[14] There are different numbers for the strength of the Rumeli army. While Tarle gives 145 thousand troops excluding the *başıbozuk*, (op. cit., vol. I, p. 264), Captain Fevzi (Kurtoğlu) gives 178 thousand with 12 thousand başıbozuk troops and thus 166 thousand without the *başıbozuk*. See Yüzbaşı Fevzi Kurtoğlu, *1853–1855 Türk-Rus Harbi ve Kırım Seferi*, İstanbul: Devlet Matbaası, 1927, p. 8.

Illus. 4 Müşir İsmail Pasha, deputy commander of the Rumelian army. *ILN*, 6 May 1854.

Vidin to Varna, mainly in Şumnu, Vidin, Kalafat, Tutrakan, Rusçuk, Zistovi, Silistria and Varna. Ömer Pasha's headquarters was in Şumnu with about 40,000 troops.

Field Marshal Ivan Fyodorovich Paskevich (1782–1856), the Count of Erivan, Prince of Warsaw, the conqueror of the Persians in 1826–1828, of Erzurum in 1828–1829, of Warsaw in 1831 and of the Hungarian insurrection in 1848–1849, was at that time commanding three Russian armies in Europe from his headquarters in Warsaw. He still held much prestige and authority in the eyes of Emperor Nikolai I, who called him "father-commander" (*otets-komandir*). Yet Paskevich, at the age of 72, had lost initiative and deep in his heart he opposed the war, though he could not say so openly. According to Tarle, he did not use his influence on the emperor.[15] His hesitations and contradic-

---

[15] Tarle, op. cit., vol. I, p. 255.

Illus. 5   Ferik Ahmed Pasha, commander at Kalafat. *ILN*, 11 Feb. 1854.

tions were to have a negative impact on the Russian war efforts along the Danube. Afraid of ruining his reputation by an unlucky defeat, he behaved with too much caution, although he did not think that the Ottoman army could fight well against the Russian army. In his report to Nikolai, dated 23 September 1853, he wrote that

> As is known, the Turks are strong in fortresses, but they cannot hold out against our troops on the field. It is necessary to manoeuvre in such a way as to lure them out of their fortresses and smash them... I do not share the idea that the Turks could dream of causing us great damage from the Asian side. The Turkish cavalry, the Kurds, have always been beaten by our Muslims and line troops... As regards their regular troops, they are not frightening in Europe and even less in Asia.[16] [My translation]

---

[16] Paskevich to Nikolai, 11 (23) September 1853, Zayonchkovskiy, op. cit. (1912), vol. 2, pp. 105–107.

However, on 6 October 1853, Paskevich recommended to Nikolai that he take a defensive position without crossing the Danube.[17] Then, in contradiction to this defensive posture, he added that Russia had a powerful weapon against the Ottoman Empire in its influence on Ottoman Christians. Therefore Russia could take advantage of a Christian revolt against the "Mussulman yoke". Paskevich, knowing well Nikolai's dislike of any revolutionary movements against any "legitimate" monarch, added that this was not a "revolutionary" call to insubordination to a sovereign, but a rightful cause, because Russia could not remain indifferent to the suffering of Orthodox Christians under Ottoman rule. Thus, while the Russian armies would remain behind the Danube, an Ottoman Christian revolt against the Sultan was expected to happen in some fashion, despite the obvious hostility of Austria toward any such revolt.

Did Paskevich really believe what he recommended to Nikolai? It seems doubtful. Paskevich might have simply wanted to please Nikolai I, who heretofore had not been well-disposed towards Slavophiles at all, but now thought that the Slavs could be of use. Paskevich also did not want to move his second army corps from Poland – neither to the Danube nor later to the Crimea – observing the danger of an intervention by Austria. One month later, Paskevich developed his cautious attitude further and recommended maintaining defences in "Europe" to avoid angering the great powers. He argued that even if Russia were to take Edirne, the great powers would interfere and would not permit them to benefit from their conquests. The Russians would suffer many losses from disease and not gain much even if they were victorious. According to him, time was on the side of Russia; it was necessary to wait. Thus he recommended a defensive position on the Danube, but an offensive one in the Caucasus. He suggested that with 16 battalions now in the Russian Caucasus army, it was possible to act offensively, because there the great powers could not interfere and the Russian army could easily beat the Ottoman army when it stood alone.[18]

The Russian occupation army in the Danubian principalities numbered about 88,000 in October 1853. The headquarters of this army was

---

[17] "Vsepoddanneyshaya zapiska knyazya Paskevicha", Warsaw, 24 September (6 October) 1853, *Russkaya Starina*, August 1876, pp. 698–702. Also see Tarle, op. cit., pp. 262–263.

[18] Paskevich to Nikolai, 24 September (6 November) 1853, Zayonchkovskiy, op. cit. (1912), vol. 2, Prilozhenie 41, pp. 108–111.

in Bucharest. The Commander-in-Chief General Prince Mikhail Dmitrievich Gorchakov, having served twenty-two years as Paskevich's chief of staff in Warsaw, was used to receiving orders and was not noted for resolution and initiative. According to Tarle, from Gorchakov's army only a small portion (about 10,000 men under the command of General Count Anrep) was given the vanguard position to guard against the Ottoman forces until February 1854.[19]

Taking the events of the 1828–1829 Russo-Ottoman War into consideration, Ömer Pasha had concentrated a considerable force around Vidin, the westernmost fortress on the Danube. The importance of Vidin also derived from its proximity to Serbia. However, Russia wished to avoid arousing the suspicions of Austria by being too close to the Serbians, and hence did not concentrate troops there.

On 28 October, Ferik İsmail Pasha's forces crossed the Danube from Vidin and occupied the small town of Kalafat with a force of 12,000. The small Russian force in Kalafat retreated. On 30 October Ömer Pasha himself came to Tutrakan, in the middle of the Danube front. An Ottoman infantry battalion with six guns under the command of Kaimmakam Hüseyin Bey crossed the Danube on 2 November and occupied the quarantine house of Wallachia at the village of Oltenitsa. These forces were reinforced by another battalion the next day and some earthworks were built there.[20]

On the Russian side, Gorchakov's characteristic indecision had passed from him to his generals in command of various positions on the Danube. Thus General Pyotr Dannenberg, commanding the forces in Little Wallachia, had given orders to his forces to the effect that if the "Turks" crossed the Danube, they should not engage in battle with them but should definitely not let them proceed farther. General Pavlov at Oltenitsa, on the left hand (north) side of the Danube was at a loss to understand this order. How could he not engage in war and at the same time not let them pass? When the Ottomans started crossing the Danube at the beginning of November, Dannenberg at first did not believe that it was a serious affair. He was soon proved wrong.[21]

---

[19] Tarle, ibid., p. 274.
[20] See Ömer Pasha's report in Lütfi, op. cit., p. 205. Also see Yüzbaşı Fevzi Kurtoğlu, op. cit., p. 17. Kurtoğlu gives the date as 1 November.
[21] Tarle, op. cit., vol. 1, p. 280.

On Friday, 4 November 1853[22] Russian forces commanded by General Pavlov attacked the fortified Ottoman positions in Oltenitsa. The Russian forces were met with a powerful cannonade from the Ottoman positions. Russian and Ottoman sources give different numbers for the strength of both sides, each side arguing that the enemy troops were more numerous. Ömer Pasha's report after the battle and the official chronicler Lütfi Efendi maintain that a few Ottoman battalions fought against 20 infantry battalions and 4 cavalry regiments. Ömer Pasha's report states that, at the quarantine house, the Ottoman forces consisted of 3 companies of infantry, 2 companies of rifles or chasseurs (*şeşhaneci*), 150 cavalrymen and 6 guns, while the Russians attacked with 20 battalions of infantry, 4 battalions of cavalry and 32 guns.[23] On the other hand, the Russian generals Petrov and Kovalevskiy, participants in the Danubian campaign and the Soviet historian Tarle argue that only one Russian brigade (2 infantry regiments consisting of 4 battalions each and 9 cavalry squadrons) attacked the Ottoman forces, which in turn amounted to 8,000 men with 20 cannons.[24]

In any case, on that day the Ottomans had their first serious victory on the Danube. The Russian force retreated. E. H. Nolan stated that the Cossacks "suffered considerably from the rifle carbine of the Turks, a weapon superior to any which their assailants used".[25] However, the Ottoman army did not pursue the enemy. Ömer Pasha was content with having won the battle. According to him, Russian losses were more than 2,000, while the Ottomans lost 30 dead and 150 wounded. Lütfi Efendi, however, writes that the Russians lost about 1,000 dead and twice as much wounded, while the Ottomans lost 18 dead and 83 wounded. Nevertheless, Lütfi then writes that this battle is called the battle of Çatana. He has probably confused the battle of Oltenitsa with the battle of Çatana. Ömer Pasha had remained in Tutrakan during

---

[22] *Takvim-i Vekayi*, 14 Safer 1270 (15 November 1853), transliterated by Hakkı Yapıcı, op. cit., p. 13. For Ömer Pasha's report on the battle see Lütfi, op. cit., pp. 205–207. Kurtoğlu gives the date as 17 November.

[23] Lütfi, op. cit., p. 206. I could not find Ömer Pasha's report after the battle in the BOA, but I found the draft of the *tezkire-i samiye* of the grand vizier, which refers to it and confirms the above numbers. See BOA. A. AMD. 50/5. As for the Ottoman forces, Lütfi mentions a few battalions with some guns and adds that during the battle another Ottoman battalion was sent from Tutrakan. See Lütfi, op. cit., pp. 89–90.

[24] See Eg. Kowalewski, *Der Krieg Russlands mit der Türkei in den Jahren 1853 und 1854 und der Bruch mit den Westmächten*. Leipzig: Verlag von Bernard Schlicke, 1869, pp. 74–79. Tarle, op. cit., p. 281.

[25] Quoted by James Reid, op. cit., p. 244.

the battle, together with some foreign officers including the Spanish General Prim.

According to General Yegor Petrovich Kovalevskiy (1809–1868), Russian losses amounted to 236 dead and 734 wounded.[26] Russian sources in general argue that the defeat was due to the untimely or unnecessary order of retreat given by General Dannenberg to General Pavlov. However, General Gorchakov endorsed the decision of Dannenberg, for which he too has been criticised.[27] Although this battle was not important from a military-technical point of view, the European press exaggerated it as a great "Turkish" success. However small a battle it might have been, Russian pride was certainly stung and Ottoman confidence increased.

The Battle of Sinop and European Public Opinion

The event that started the war in earnest and turned the Russo-Ottoman war into a European one was the naval battle of Sinop on 30 November 1853. The battles on the Danube front until then had not created such a great sensation in Europe.

The Ottoman navy had never recovered its strength after its crushing defeat at the battle of Navarino on 20 October 1827. Not only the fleet but also a whole generation of the best mariners was lost in that battle, when the combined fleet of Britain, France and Russia had destroyed the combined Ottoman and Egyptian fleet during the Greek war of independence. Mahmud II had in 1829 appointed as *Kapudan-ı Derya* or the Kapudan Pasha (marine minister and grand admiral) a certain Pabuççu Ahmed Pasha (?–1830), who was a shipyard sergeant during the revolt of the janissaries in 1826. From 1827 to 1853 little improvement had been achieved.[28]

In April 1851, Adolphus Slade reported to Lord Stratford on the condition of the Ottoman navy.[29] According to Slade, the navy consisted

---

[26] Kowalewski, op. cit., p. 79. Kowalewski is simply the German version of Kovalevskiy.

[27] General Andrey Nikolayevich Petrov, *Voina Rossii s Turtsiey. Dunayskaya kampaniya 1853 i 1854 gg*. St. Petersburg, 1890, vol. I, pp. 142–144. Also see Tarle, op. cit., vol. I, pp. 283–284.

[28] Besbelli, op. cit., pp. 18–25. Süer, *Türk Silahlı Kuvvetleri Tarihi. Osmanlı devri. Osmanlı-Rus Kırım Harbi Kafkas Cephesi Harekatı (1853-1856)*. Ankara: Genelkurmay Askeri Tarih ve Stratejik Etüt Başkanlığı Yayınları, 1986, p. 40.

[29] Bernard Lewis, "Slade on the Turkish Navy", *Journal of Turkish Studies / Türklük Bilgisi Araştırmaları* 11, Harvard University, 1987, pp. 6–7.

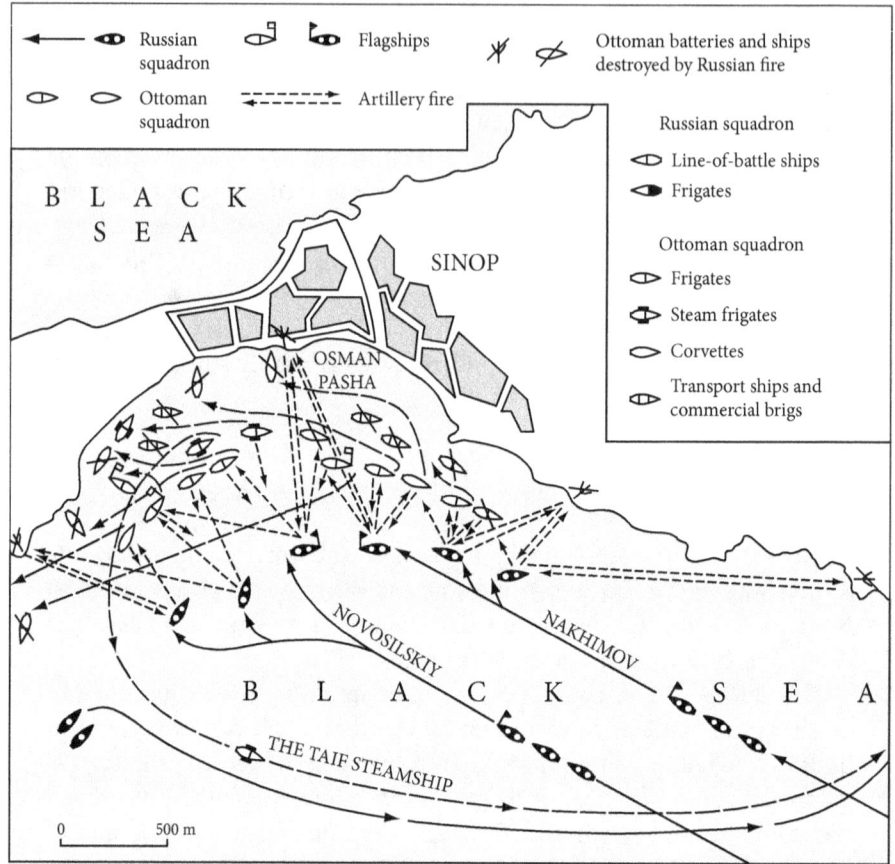

Map 2   Plan of the battle of Sinop.

of about 15,000 men and 68 vessels in more or less good condition. The naval hospital was in good order. The biggest problem was the poverty of the naval chest. The budget of the navy was £400,000, while the cost of coal for a single year was £55,000. The navy was in debt like all the institutions of the Porte. It can be safely assumed that from 1851 to 1853 there was no substantial improvement, because the financial crisis of the Porte had not been resolved (see Chapter 4).

Therefore in 1853, the Ottoman navy, although probably the fourth or fifth naval power in the world, was not a match for the Russian Black Sea fleet in terms of training and fire power. Most of the Ottoman sailors (the rank and file) were untrained novices. From September 1852 Kapudan Pasha was Mahmud Pasha, a man who had no naval training or education. He was a protégé of Damad Mehmed Ali Pasha, who had been promoted to the office of the grand vizier from the admiralty. The officers of the navy, like those of the army, were divided into the educated and the uneducated, with many of the latter in high positions. Both groups had their deficiencies in theory and practice. The system of promotion like everywhere else was not professional. While the uniforms of the sailors had been changed, corresponding changes in mentality had not kept pace.[30]

After the declaration of war by the Porte on 4 October 1853, some necessary defensive measures were taken by the naval authorities. Russian commercial ships were not to be arrested but rather were requested to quit Ottoman waters within 15 days or more in some specific cases. Orders were also given that commercial ships were not to be allowed to lay anchor near Ottoman men-of-war for fear of fire, explosion or sabotage.[31] Indeed this measure should have been taken immediately after the suspension of relations with Russia, because, as Slade points out, any commercial ship (i.e., a Greek ship) could transform itself into a fire-ship and then anchor among the wooden ships of the Ottoman fleet at Büyükdere. However, the Ottoman captains were helpless against foreign commercial ships, because the Ottoman captains were unable to apply the right of keeping clear water around them (exercised by all other navies), for fear of the representations of consulates and embassies. Even the allies did not respect this right of the Ottoman navy. Thus Slade observed that "notwithstanding repeated representations the co-operation of the European legations could not be obtained to make their respective merchant vessels anchor clear of the lines of the Turkish fleet".[32]

Meanwhile the French and British fleets had anchored at Beykoz on 23 October. The French fleet commanded by Vice-Admiral Ferdinand Alphonse Hamelin consisted of three line-of-battle ships, seven two-deckers (*kapak*), three brigs and three steamers. The British fleet under the command of Vice-Admiral Dundas included two line-of-battle ships, four two-deckers, one frigate and ten steamers. Their combined power was more than sufficient to keep the Russian navy at bay. Thus their presence in the Bosphorus gave the Porte much confidence

---

[30] Rear-Admiral Sir Adolphus Slade, op. cit. (1867), p. 129.
[31] Özcan, op. cit. (1990), pp. 49–52.
[32] Slade, op. cit., p. 96.

that the Russian fleet would not dare leave its port to cruise the Black Sea. Furthermore, the Egyptian fleet consisting of two galleons, three frigates, one corvette, one brig and two steamers under Patrona Halil Pasha had also joined the Ottoman fleet.[33] Egypt's total contribution of troops during the war reached 23,931 men towards the end of 1855.[34] Those troops were mainly collected by force from among veterans who had fought in the Greek war of independence and in the army of Ibrahim Pasha against the Porte in the 1830's.

The Ottoman fleet was divided into four squadrons. The commander of the fleet *Bahriye Feriki* (Vice-Admiral) Kayserili Ahmed Pasha (1796–1878) commanded the patrolling ships charged with protecting the merchant ships of the Ottoman Empire, as well as allied and neutral ships. The Egyptian Mirliva Hasan Pasha's squadron was to carry troops to Varna and to patrol the shores of Rumelia. The Egyptian squadron landed the Egyptian troops in Varna and returned to Istanbul on 13 November 1853. A third group, composed of four paddle steamers (*Saik-i Şadi, Feyz-i Bari, Taif* and *Ereğli*)[35] under the command of Ferik İngiliz[36] Mustafa Pasha was tasked with patrolling the north-eastern coasts of Anatolia and those of Georgia and Çerkezistan (Circassia). He was required to call on the harbours of Trabzon, Batum, Çürüksu, Sohum and Soğucak (Novorossiysk), gathering information, landing ammunition for the Circassian insurgents against Russia and communicating with Hassa Müşiri Haseki Selim Mehmed Pasha (?–1872), the commander of the Ottoman army in Batum. Mustafa Pasha's flotilla had on board Çerkes İsmail Bey, who carried letters to the emissary (*naib*) of Sheikh Shamil in Circassia.[37]

---

[33] Saim Besbelli, op. cit., p. 35.
[34] Report of the Ottoman finance ministry to the loan control commission, *Le Moniteur Universelle*, Paris, 8 January 1856. See BOA. HR. SYS. 1355/3.
[35] BOA. İ. HR. 106/5182 enc. 7, not dated, end of December 1853 or beginning of January 1854, cited by Özcan, op. cit., p. 90. To the four steamers in this squadron, Özcan adds the steamer *Mecidiye* and the frigate *Muhbir-i Sürur*. See Özcan, op. cit., p. 81. However, Mustafa Pasha does not mention these two ships in his own statement referred to above. Besbelli also includes the frigate *Muhbir-i Sürur*. See Besbelli, op. cit., Kuruluş 5, p. 44ff.
[36] Because he had been to England and knew English.
[37] Özcan, op. cit., p. 82. Kapudan-ı Derya Mahmud Pasha to the grand vizier before his dismissal on 17 December 1853. BOA. İ. HR. 106/5182 enc. 4, written between 4 and 17 December 1853. Özcan mentions this document elsewhere but he does not quote from it.

Sheikh Shamil (1797–1871), the Muslim leader of North Caucasus, had been waging a war of independence against the Russians in Chechnya and Dagestan since 1834. His deputy (*naib*) in Circassia (Muhammed Emin) was also active among the Circassians trying to organize their resistance to the Russian army. This was not an easy task, neither for Shamil nor for the Porte and its allies, as we shall see later.

The fourth group of ships was sent to cruise the shores of north-western Anatolia from Amasra to Sinop under Patrona (Vice-Admiral) Osman Pasha (1798–1860) and Riyale (or *Mirliva*, Rear-Admiral) Hüseyin Pasha on 5 November. In the event of coming across Russian ships, their instruction was to engage in battle only if they were certain of winning.[38] This order seems at some variance with the order given to Slade, in which he was instructed to abstain from firing first. These differences stemmed from the contradictory orders of the Porte, hesitating to engage in outright war, yet having declared it, unable to prevent drifting into it. The Porte was also under the influence of the French and British embassies and their admirals, as far as naval affairs were concerned. The Porte also asked the French and the British embassies to bring the rest of their fleets from the Dardanelles to the Bosphorus.

At this time a Russian squadron of three line-of-battle ships,[39] two frigates and a steamer was reported to be cruising the north-western coasts of Anatolia, 120 miles away from Istanbul. Having heard this news, Mahmud Pasha gave orders to reinforce the light squadron of Osman Pasha, consisting of frigates and corvettes, with another frigate from the fleet at Büyükdere. Slade (alias the Mirliva Mushaver Pasha), reminded him of the superiority of the Russians in nominal force and the dangers of sending a squadron of unequal strength against the enemy. Mahmud Pasha said he could not discuss orders with the Porte but promised to send the second squadron intended to winter at Sinop to be made up of line-of-battle ships and frigates instead of frigates and corvettes. The Kapudan Pasha also gave a written order to abstain from firing first in case of meeting the enemy. "Are we not at war?" asked Mushaver Pasha. "We are, but such is the Porte's order" replied the Ottoman grand admiral. When Mushaver Pasha protested

---

[38] Kapudan Pasha's instructions to Patrona Osman Pasha and Mirliva Hüseyin Pasha, 17 November 1853. BOA. İ. HR. 106/5182 enc. 6. Cf. Özcan, op. cit., pp. 74–75, 85.

[39] A line-of-battle ship was a two or three-deck ship with at least 70 guns.

Illus. 6   Admiral Sir Adolphus Slade (Mushaver Pasha). From *Donanma Dergisi*, October 1952.

that the first broadside fire from a ship in position might be decisive, Mahmud Pasha was indifferent: "I have given you the order and that suffices me".[40]

---

[40] Slade, op. cit., p. 132.

The Porte decided to send line-of-battle ships to the Black Sea, but when the ships were ready to sail, the order was cancelled. The grand admiral said it was the desire of the British ambassador. It was indeed the desire of the British and French ambassadors, both of whom sent their dragomans to the Porte on 4 November, warning the Porte of the danger of sending the fleet into the Black Sea in the face of the superior Russian fleet, until their vessels had fully gathered in the Bosphorus and even after that. The French ambassador, in his written instructions to his dragoman, stated to Reşid Pasha his readiness to bring the rest of the French fleet to the Bosphorus. But the ambassador also expressed his surprise at the decision of the Porte to send the Ottoman fleet to the Black Sea. He wrote that this measure seemed untimely to him, because he expected the Kapudan Pasha to concert his activities with the admirals of the allied fleets, before taking action.[41]

Lord Stratford de Redcliffe, on the same day, also expressed his readiness to bring the rest of the British fleet to the Bosphorus, as it was decided together with M. de la Cour. He wrote that they were impressed by the *"courage et de l'esprit de patriotisme"* manifested by the Ottoman ministers by sending their fleet into the Black Sea, except for the three-deckers. However, he observed that the opinions of both the French and British experts were against this enterprise because of the advanced season and the great danger from the large Russian fleet in Sevastopol. It would be imprudent to risk such a large part of the Ottoman fleet, and a failure at this moment would cause a number of problems for the Porte. He argued that in any case it would be *"une folie"* to send the Ottoman fleet before the allied fleets arrived in full in the Bosphorus. He further commented that according to the opinion of the allied admirals, even after the arrival of the allied fleets, three or four big steamships should be sent instead of sailing ships of the line. He concluded that if the Porte decided to send sail or steam ships to the Black Sea, it should wait until the appearance of the full moon that would diminish the navigational hazards of the Black Sea in November.[42]

---

[41] Instructions of the French ambassador Edmond de la Cour to head dragoman Charles Schefer, 4 November 1853. BOA. HR. SYS. 1193/2 enc. 17 (translation into Ottoman Turkish in enc. 16).

[42] Stratford de Redcliffe's instructions to head dragoman Etienne Pisani, 4 November 1853. BOA. HR. SYS. 1193/2 enc. 15. See enc. 14 for the official translation into Ottoman Turkish. This translation, however, has rendered the expression of "sail ships of the line" (in the original *"vaisseaux de ligne a voile"*) into *"birtakım bayağı kapak-*

On 5 November, the date of departure of the light squadron of Osman Pasha and Hüseyin Pasha, the French ambassador sent another warning to the Porte of the serious disadvantages of sending the fleet and advised the Porte to defer it.[43] On the same day Lord Stratford de Redcliffe wrote to Lord Clarendon that he had "succeeded in dissuading the Porte from sending a detachment of line-of-battle ships and frigates into the Black Sea at this moment".[44]

Sometime later, when the parliamentary papers (the Blue Books) were published, Slade asked the ambassador why he had prevented the sending of line-of-battle ships to Sinop. Stratford replied that he had depended on the advice of Admiral Hamelin of the French fleet and Admiral Dundas of the British fleet. Slade further asked why he had relied on the opinion of men unacquainted with the local conditions; he said that their rank and position given by their governments left him no choice. Lord Clarendon from London on 21 November also approved the decision of Admiral Dundas and his Excellency the ambassador, adding that the Porte would do better by relying on the authority of the British and French admirals.[45]

Five years later, in a letter to the grand vizier Âli Pasha, Slade wrote that at the beginning of the war, when Mahmud Pasha ordered him to cruise with a squadron in the Black Sea, Lord Stratford had ordered him on behalf of the Queen to remain in the Bosphorus. Because Britain was at peace with Russia, his presence in the Black Sea could compromise her. Slade replied that the Ottoman navy relied on the cooperation of Britain and if he did not go, this might have an inappropriate meaning. According to Slade, "His Excellency then threatened to submit a complaint against me to the British government: that he did". Slade also wrote that "on other occasions during the war my views of my duty to the Sublime Porte led me to opposition to the allies".[46] [My translation]

---

lar", which means "certain ordinary two-deckers". It seems that either the concept of the line-of-battle ship was not used by the Ottomans at that time or simply that the translator was unaware of it.

[43] Edmond de la Cour to head dragoman Charles Schefer, 5 November 1853. BOA. HR. SYS. 1193/2 enc. 19.

[44] Lord Stratford de Redcliffe to the Secretary of State for Foreign Affairs. Therapia, Nov. 5, 1853, quoted by Slade, op. cit., p. 136.

[45] Slade, op. cit., pp. 136–137.

[46] Slade to Âli Pasha. Arsenal imperial, le 31 mars 1858. BOA. HR. TO. 429/22 enc. 3.

Stratford de Redcliffe's motives are open to a double interpretation. Those who believe that he wanted to accelerate the war suggest that he deliberately left the Ottoman squadron to destruction in order to involve Britain in the war against Russia. Those who are of the opinion that he had most peaceful intentions can argue that he wanted to prevent a possible collision between the Ottoman and Russian fleets. As an alternative to these views, we can argue that he simply followed the advice of the admirals, without a hidden agenda. But in any case it is difficult to understand the logic of not sending line-of-battle ships in this case. If the danger presented by the Russian fleet was real, it would seem that despatching a light fleet consisting only of frigates and corvettes, rather than a fleet consisting of line-of-battle ships and frigates, would only increase what was at risk. Would it not make more sense to advise not sending any ships at all, or instead to send stronger support? Did Stratford and the admirals think that since the Porte was so determined, and destruction was in any case imminent, then at least line-of-battle ships should be saved? It is hard to come to a conclusion.

That the prevention of line-of-battle ships being sent to the Black Sea was the expressed desire of the allied admirals is also confirmed by Mahmud Pasha in his evidence at his trial after the disaster of Sinop and his dismissal from his post.[47]

In mid-November, Bahriye Feriki Mustafa Pasha with his flotilla returned from Batum and saw the position of Patrona Osman Pasha and Riyale Hüseyin Pasha's flotilla at Sinop, which is closer to Sevastopol than to Istanbul. The Ottoman squadron in Sinop consisted of seven frigates (*Avnillah* (Osman Pasha's flagship, 50 guns), *Nizamiye* (second flag, commanded by Riyale (Mirliva) Hüseyin Pasha, 64 guns), *Nesim-i Zafer* (48 guns), *Fazlullah* (the former Russian frigate *Rafail*, captured in 1829, 48 guns), *Navek-i Bahri* (42 guns), *Dimyat* (42 guns) and *Kaid-i Zafer* (22 guns), three corvettes (*Necm-i Efşan*, *Fevz-i Mâbud* and *Gül-i Sefid*, 22 guns each) and two transports.[48] They had encountered gales in transit and lost each other, only arriving at the

---

[47] BOA. İ. HR. 106/5182 enc. 4, written between 4 and 18 December 1853.
[48] Fevzi Kurtoğlu, op. cit., pp. 26–27. Besbelli, op. cit., p. 44f. Slade, on the other hand, in his report to Stratford de Redcliffe, dated HMS *Retribution*, Bay of Sinop, 7 December 1853, gives the following numbers of guns for these ships: *Avnillah* (36), *Nizamiye* (60), *Nesim-i Zafer* (32), *Fazlullah* (38), *Navek-i Bahri* (52), *Dimyat* (54) and *Kaid-i Zafer* (50), *Necm-i Efşan* (24), *Fevz-i Mâbud* (22) and *Gül-i Sefid* (24). See TNA. FO 195/309.

Sinop harbour with great difficulty. Mustafa Pasha also saw the danger of this flotilla being exposed to a Russian attack, but he did not take any measures to prevent it. He left a further two steamers (the *Taif* and the *Ereğli*) at Sinop and on 24 November came to Istanbul, where he reported the vulnerable position of the squadron and the insufficiency of the shore batteries of Sinop. Adolphus Slade interprets his conduct as a result of caution and fear of reprobation from the authorities and enemies or rivals in Istanbul in case the Russians did not attack. It is true that every pasha had enemies in Istanbul, ready to agitate against him at the first opportunity. While at that time many of the Ottoman pashas in general had more cunning than merit, it was also true that working under a weak government open to all kinds of influence was not an easy task either. This uncertainty prevented them from taking any initiative.

On the Russian side, Prince Menshikov was still the Minister of Marine and was now also the Commander-in-Chief of all the land and naval forces in the Crimea. At the beginning of the war, the Russian Black Sea fleet was divided into two squadrons or divisions, commanded by two talented and prominent admirals, Chief of Staff Vice-Admiral Vladimir Alekseyevich Kornilov (1806–1854) and Vice-Admiral Pavel Stepanovich Nakhimov (1802–1855), both of them pupils of Admiral Lazarev (1788–1851). Nakhimov cruised the eastern part of the Black Sea from Sinop to Sohum and Kornilov cruised the western part of it. Nakhimov's first duty was to transport the Russian 13th division (16,393 persons, 824 horses and their load) from Sevastopol to Fort Anakra at the mouth of the river Ingur, and he completed it successfully in September 1853.[49]

Kornilov for his part came as close as the northern mouth of the Bosphorus at the beginning of November. Menshikov had given him instructions to engage in battle with any Ottoman warships. Kornilov cruised the western coasts of the Black Sea from Balchik, Varna, and Sizepol to Burgaz and he did not meet Ottoman battle ships. Finally he sent back most of his squadron to Sevastopol and himself remained on the steam frigate *Vladimir*. At that time the Ottoman-Egyptian steamer *Pervaz-ı Bahri* was sent to Ereğli for coal. On its way it fell in with the *Vladimir* on 17 November 1853. In the battle that followed, the *Vladimir* captured the *Pervaz-ı Bahri*, which lost 22 dead including the

---

[49] Yevgeny Viktorovich Tarle, op. cit., vol. 1, p. 294 and p. 371.

Egyptian captain Said Pasha and 18 wounded men and officers. The Russians lost two dead and two wounded; one of the dead was Lieutenant Zheleznov, Kornilov's aide-de-camp.[50] The Russians returned to Sevastopol with their booty, which was renamed *Kornilov*. This small affair can be considered as the first battle in history between steamships.

From 23 November onwards Osman Pasha knew that a Russian squadron of three line-of-battle ships (three-deckers), two brigs and one steamer was nearby. However, he did not choose to accept battle in the open sea and remained instead in port. According to the report of Captain Yahya Bey and other officers of the *Taif*, submitted after it escaped the enemy and came to Istanbul, the Patrona Pasha gave the following instructions to all the captains:

> The enemy's ships are at sea and we cannot cope with them. If we put out to sea we will be lost; the best thing is to fight them, if they come, so long as we have a gun left. If there be any danger of their capturing you, slip your cable, run your ships on shore and let fire to them.[51]

As this squadron was not particularly powerful, Osman Pasha could have engaged it, or at least attempted a running fight towards Istanbul. However, he instead sent an alarming report on 24 November to Istanbul asking for immediate help. Meanwhile Admiral Nakhimov sent for reinforcement from Sevastopol. Prince Menshikov sent out another squadron of three galleons and two frigates under the command of Rear-Admiral Fyodor Mihailovich Novosilskiy. Reşid Pasha in Istanbul informed the British and French embassies on 29 and 30 November, just before and on the day of the fateful battle, that a Russian squadron was cruising the waters of Sinop, Amasra and Bartın.[52] The ambassa-

---

[50] V. Timm, *Russkiy Khudozhestvenny Listok*, no. 3, 20 January (1 February) 1854. In an anonymous report written in Rumanian from Bucharest, dated 16 (28) November 1853, it is stated that Menshikov had reported to the Commander-in-Chief of the (Russian) imperial troops that the *Vladimir* had returned to Sevastopol on 7 (19) November with two ships. One of them was a passenger ship loaded with iron, the other was the Egyptian 10-gun steamer *Pervaz-ı Bahri*, which was taken only after a "strong resistance". The report must be the work of Ottoman spies in Bucharest. See BOA. A. AMD. 51/1.

[51] "Deposition of the Captain & Officers of the Turkish Steamer 'Tayf' [sic], concerning the action at Sinope on Wednesday the 30 November, Constantinople, Dec. 6. 1853. Translation". TNA. FO 195/309. The original Ottoman document, dated 3 December 1853, has been published in OBKS, pp. 138–141.

[52] Official note to the British and French embassies. BOA. HR. SYS. 1189/54, 30 November 1853.

dors consulted their respective admirals in the Bosphorus and decided that it would not be recommended to send their fleets into the Black Sea. In any case, they did not hurry to answer. The Ottoman Admiralty had also sent some warnings to Osman Pasha just prior to the fateful battle. We shall review these letters after the battle, together with the case against Mahmud Pasha.

On 27 November the squadron of Novosilskiy joined Nakhimov's squadron. Now Nakhimov's power was more than sufficient to destroy the Ottoman squadron, which was still at anchor at the bay of Sinop. On the morning of 30 November Nakhimov gave the order of attack to his squadron consisting now of six battleships: *Imperatritsa Mariya* (flag ship, 84 guns), *Parizh*, (2nd flag, 120) *Tri Svyatitelya* (120), *Velikiy Knyaz Konstantin* (120), *Rostislav* (84), *Chesma* (84), two frigates *Kagul* and *Kulevchi* and three steamers (*Odessa, Krym* and *Khersones*). These ships were certainly equipped with more guns of greater calibre than those possessed by the Ottomans.[53] The largest Ottoman guns were 24-pounders, while the Russians had 68-pounders. Furthermore the Russian ships had 38 Paixhans guns that used explosive shells.[54] These shells penetrated deep inside the wooden planking of the Ottoman ships, exploding there and igniting the hulls. Although Paixhans guns had been used before, hitherto they were clumsy and dangerous to use on board ships. The Russian navy had developed an advanced design with a far greater explosive capacity and destructive force than previously available, which were used to sink almost all the ships in the bay of Sinop. Cannon fire had sunk ships before, but the staggering effect of the explosive shells now surprised the entire world.

Although the Ottoman forces could make use of the shore batteries as well, the position of the Ottoman squadron did not allow a full use

---

[53] The exact number of guns of the two sides is difficult to establish. Zayonchkovskiy gives 344 to 237 guns on one side for Russian and Ottoman ships respectively (plus 26 Ottoman shore batteries), Tarle gives 358 to 236 (Saab quotes from him), Besbelli gives 327 to 199 guns, Özcan gives 337 to 196. Slade gives only the number of Ottoman guns as 430, that is, 215 on one side. In any case, if we consider the calibre of the guns as well, Russian firepower was three times greater. Prof. Winfried Baumgart writes that the "Turks" had more guns (about 500 as against 359 guns) because there were a number of batteries on the shore, without however, reference to any source. See Winfried Baumgart, *The Crimean War, 1853–1856*, London: Arnold; New York: Oxford University Press, 1999, p. 97.

[54] Lawrence Sondhaus, *Naval Warfare, 1815–1914*, London & New York: Routledge, 2001, p. 58. Sondhaus describes Ottoman guns at maximum 32 pounds. Besbelli and Özcan give 24 pounds. Cf. Besbelli, op. cit., p. 44, Özcan, op. cit., p. 110.

of them because, owing to short-sighted disposition, the field of fire of some of the batteries was blocked by the squadron. In any case these batteries were of small calibre, firing shots of 14 to 19 pounds.[55] It is also not clear why Osman Pasha did not use the guns on the other side of his ships (which could not be brought to bear on the attackers) as shore batteries. Zayonchkovskiy also argues that the Ottoman squadron could have shown better resistance if it had taken up a position not near the city but to the south. Taking into consideration that Osman Pasha was an experienced sailor and a good admiral, Zayonchkovskiy can find no explanation for his carelessness other than senility or the effects of the British delusion that the Russians could not attack fortified positions.[56]

Osman Pasha's squadron was lying in crescent form in the bay. The Russian squadron entered in two columns and demanded the surrender of the Ottoman squadron. Osman Pasha refused to surrender but vacillated about firing first. The Russian ships anchored at some 900 meters from the Ottoman squadron. The signal of *Navek-i Bahri* for leave to fire was disregarded. Then the *Nizamiye* first opened fire and the others followed it.[57] There began a devastating combat or rather cannonade between unequal forces. At first the Ottoman guns inflicted severe damage on the Russian ships during their manoeuvring. However soon the Russian ships took position and after a while started to make good hits. Then the destructive effects of the explosive shells from the 68-pound guns became clear. The Ottoman ships were burnt and blown up in a few hours (estimates range from one to six hours).

Adolphus Slade, the Mushaver Pasha was on board the *Taif*. At the approach of the Russian ships, he took advantage of the high speed of this steamship and fled the battle scene. Nakhimov had already ordered the *Kagul* and the *Kulevchi* to look after the *Taif*, but they could not overtake it. The *Taif* fired some shots and then turned first towards Gerze to the east, then set course for Istanbul.

At this time Admiral Kornilov had arrived with his reinforcements and, seeing the escape attempt of the *Taif*, he tried to capture it, but it

---

[55] Besbelli, ibid.
[56] Zayonchkovskiy, op. cit., p. 275. Osman Pasha, like Nakhimov, had participated in the battle of Navarino in 1827. He had served 21 years in the Egyptian navy and during the last ten years in the Ottoman navy.
[57] Ahmed Rıza Trabzoni (op. cit., p. 77) confirms that the first fire was from Hüseyin Pasha's frigate.

managed to get away thanks to its superior speed. Kornilov was late; Nakhimov had already devastated the whole squadron except the *Taif*. However, Nakhimov did not cease fire even after all the ships were burning. The Muslim quarters of the city were also set ablaze and since the governor and the Muslim population had fled, there was no one to extinguish the fires. Because of this conduct Nakhimov was later criticised for hitting civilian targets; he defended himself by claiming this was a result of the Ottoman fleet's position. After the bombardment stopped, Nakhimov sent an envoy to the city but the envoy found no authorities or consuls. The only resident consul, the Austrian consul, had also fled. The envoy gave to the consulate Nakhimov's explanations that he did not intend to harm the city but had come to destroy the Ottoman squadron which carried ammunition to Circassian insurgents.

According to Slade, Ottoman losses were about 2,700 dead out of the 4,200 personnel of the squadron. However, this figure seems rather exaggerated for the capacity of the eleven ships that were present. According to the written statement of naval commander (Miralay) Mehmed Bey, who was a secretary of the commander at that time, given in a report in 1891 to the chronicler Lütfi Efendi, the number of naval personnel in Sinop was 2,989 men and the dead included Bozcaadalı Riyale Hüseyin Pasha, together with 56 officers and more than 1,000 men, while Patrona Osman Pasha together with 4 officers and some men was taken prisoner.[58] Out of this number (2,989), only 958 men and officers turned up in Istanbul after the battle.[59] More sailors from the Egyptian frigates had survived, probably because they swam well, while those sailors recruited from Anatolia did not.[60]

---

[58] Miralay Mehmed Bey's *varaka*, 12 August 1891. Lütfi, op. cit., p. 210.

[59] BOA. İ. DH. 18095, 23 January 1854, quoted by Özcan, op. cit., p. 126. Özcan gives the number of Ottoman prisoners as 125. Zayonchkovskiy (op. cit., 2002, vol. II, part one, p. 287) gives the number of Ottoman prisoners of war as more than 200 and the Russian loss as one officer and 36 sailors. Tarle (op. cit., p. 379) argues that the "Turks" considered that about 3,000 were dead. Slade (op. cit., pp. 144, 148) gives the Ottoman dead at 2,700, with five officers and about 150 men prisoners and 110 wounded.

[60] Captain Fevzi Kurtoğlu (op. cit., p. 28, footnote 1), referring to some unidentified documents, writes that three *kaimmakams* (lieutenant-colonels or navy commanders), one *binbaşı* (navy commander), three *kol ağası*, 20 captains (*yüzbaşı*), four lieutenants and 186 men from the Egyptian frigate *Dimyat* had reached Istanbul. Cf. Slade, op. cit., p. 144; Özcan, op. cit., p. 116.

According to the report of Patrona Osman Pasha, whom the Russians returned to the Porte towards October 1855 together with four other Ottoman officers from his squadron, 156 Ottoman prisoners of war (sailors) were still held by the Russians.[61] If we add this number to the number above, then we get 1,114 survivors or rather those survivors who turned up, without counting the deserters. Thus the total number of Ottoman losses becomes 1,875. Patrona Osman Pasha was wounded in the foot and taken prisoner. Riyale Bozcaadalı Hüseyin Pasha was among the dead. Ali Bey, the commander of *Navek-i Bahri* had blown up his frigate with himself on board. Apart from Osman Pasha, the commanders of two frigates, Miralay Ali Mahir Bey (1820–?), commander of the frigate *Fazlullah* and Kaimmakam Ethem Bey, commander of the frigate *Feyz-i Bari*, the commander of one of the three corvettes, Binbaşı Yalovalı Hasan Bey (1814–?) and Mülazım Halil Efendi, together with at least 156 sailors (as explained above) were taken prisoners.[62] The Russians lost one officer and 33 to 36 sailors.

At this point a question arises naturally: Did Slade receive explicit orders from Osman Pasha "to get out to sea and carry to Constantinople the news of the imminent danger which menaced the Turkish squadron"?[63] Alternatively, did he leave the battle scene at his own discretion? Slade himself is not clear on this question in his book.[64] Saab argues that the *Taif* "had been ordered to leave the harbour before the fighting commenced", but she does not rely on any authority.[65] Ottoman and Turkish historians do not even ask this question. For them,

---

[61] Kapudan Pasha to the Grand vizier. BOA. HR. SYS. 1354/6, 29 October 1855. These 156 sailors were from the following ships: 28 men from the *Avnillah*, 100 men from the *Nesim-i Zafer*, 22 men from the *Fazlullah* frigates and six men from the *Necm-i Feşan* corvette. In his petition the grand admiral asks these men to be exchanged with the 20 Russian prisoners of war at the *Tersane-i Amire*.

[62] "Kontrol'naya kniga razmena russkikh i turetskikh voenno-plennykh", RGVIA, *fond* 481, *opis* 1, *delo* 695, 13 December 1856, Odessa. This register contains the names of 8,030 Ottoman prisoners of war, including Patrona Osman Pasha, Hasan Bey, Ali Bey and Ethem Bey from Sinop and Abdülkerim Pasha, Abdurrahman Pasha and Hafız Pasha from Kars together with their ages, seals and signatures. The above Russian register shows Ali Bey as a colonel, whereas Özcan (op. cit., pp. 121, 166–167) describes him as a *kaimmakam* (lieutenant-colonel), referring to a document from the DMA. Ali Bey's title is *miralay* (colonel) in another document. BOA. A. DVN. 109/40, 10 November 1855. Özcan does not cite Kaimmakam Ethem Bey among the prisoners, apparently because his documents from the DMA do not give his name.

[63] "The State of the Continent. Russia and Turkey", *The Times*, Issue 21616, London, 20 Dec. 1853, p. 9.

[64] Slade, op. cit., p. 146.

[65] Saab, op. cit., p. 116.

it seems a very normal action. Enver Ziya Karal, for example, writes that the *Taif* was sent to Istanbul by Osman Pasha. But he does not give any reference on this point. He simply repeats the Western secondary literature on this question, as he has done throughout his narrative of the Crimean War.[66]

Russian historians, on the other hand, openly accuse Slade of abandoning his commander at the time of battle and running away. They suggest that had he chosen to do so, the *Taif* could have caused significant damage to the Russian squadron thanks to its high speed and greater capacity for manoeuvring. Tarle even argues that had Slade been a "Turk" instead of a British subject, he would certainly have been hung from a ship's mast. Then he further insists that the other Ottoman steamer, the *Ereğli* could also have escaped, but it did not do so, because it was commanded by a "Turk".[67] However, Ahmed Rıza Trabzoni writes that the "other steamer" could not escape because its engine was not ready due to lack of steam.[68] Considering the certainty of destruction in the face of a powerful enemy, the question of whether the *Taif* received orders from the commander or not or whether it should have remained and fought with the enemy might seem to be rather a technical detail for some, while others may insist that it should have remained and fought. These interesting questions are difficult to answer.

Nevertheless, the problem of punishment still exists. During the entire war, no Ottoman high ranking (above the rank of colonel, to be precise) officer seems to have been punished seriously, whatever the charges may have been against him. The most received was a temporary exile or a short dismissal, which was usually followed by restoration to his former office or appointment to another office. As we will see, the commanders of the Anatolian army are good examples. In the case of Sinop, Yahya Bey, the captain of the *Taif*, was dismissed from the service but apparently this was not because of his retreat from battle. He had argued in Trabzon at a heated discussion that the employees of the foreign merchant steamers were informing the Russians.[69] The

---

[66] Karal, *Osmanlı Tarihi V*, Ankara: TTK, 1995, p. 235.
[67] See Tarle, op. cit., p. 377 and 379; Zayonchkovskiy, op. cit., p. 277; R. N. Mordvinov, *Sinopskiy Boy*, Leningrad: Obshchestvo po rasprostraneniyu politicheskikh i nauchnykh znaniy, 1953, p. 17.
[68] Trabzoni, op. cit., p. 87.
[69] Ali Haydar Emir. "Kırım Harbinin Safahat-ı Bahriyesine Müteallik Vesaik-ı Resmiye", *Risale-i Mevkute-i Bahriye* 4 (11–12), Eylül – Teşrin-i Evvel 1334 [Sept. –

question of the discipline of the Ottoman army and navy is itself an important question, but we shall take up this issue later.

A contemporary critic, Friedrich Engels, in an anonymous leading article published in the NYDT, argued that the battle of Sinop resulted from such an unparalleled series of blunders on the part of "the Turks, that the whole affair can only be explained by the mischievous interference of Western diplomacy or by the collusion with the Russians of some parties in Constantinople connected with the French and English embassies". Engels then asked the obvious questions:

> How it happened that a squadron of some three hundred guns, mostly of inferior calibre, was thus abandoned to the tender mercies of a fleet of three times its force and weight of metal, at that point of the Turkish shore which from its proximity to Sebastopol is most exposed to a Russian attack, while the main fleet was enjoying the tranquil ripple of the Bosphorus, we have yet to learn... How then it came to pass that the Turkish batteries were in such a bad trim, when a couple of days' labour might have done a great deal towards their repair? How did it happen that the Turkish vessels were at anchor in places where they obstructed the fire of the batteries, and were not shifted to moorings more fit to meet the threatened danger? There was time enough for all this...[70]

However, Engels also argued that according to the report of the steamer *Taif*, "the Turks" were taken by surprise, which is not correct, as we have already seen that Osman Pasha knew the danger. Engels then like a naval expert suggested that

> Considering the clumsiness of Russian naval manoeuvres, the bad position of the Turkish fleet in front, and in the line of fire, of their own batteries, and above all the *absolute certainty of destruction*, it would have perhaps been better if the whole Turkish squadron had got under weigh and borne down as far as the wind permitted upon the enemy. The ruin of some, which could by no means be avoided, might have saved at least a portion of the squadron. Of course the direction of the wind must have decided as to such a manoeuvre, but it seems doubtful whether Osman Pasha ever thought of such a step at all.[71] [Italics in the original]

Nov. 1918], p. 530. Despite this information, Besim Özcan, referring to the same article, argues (op. cit., p. 118) that Yahya Bey was dismissed because of not fighting in the battle.

[70] "Progress of the Turkish War", Leader, *NYDT*, January 9, 1854. See Karl Marx. *The Eastern Question. A reprint of letters written 1853–1856 dealing with the events of the Crimean War*. London: Frank Cass, 1969, pp. 194–196.

[71] Marx, op. cit., p. 197.

Engels concluded that the victory of Sinop "has no glory for the Russians, while the Turks fought with almost unheard-of bravery, not a single ship having struck its flag during the whole action". The defeat was entirely due to the "good offices" of Western diplomacy, "which prevented the Turkish fleet from standing out and protecting and fetching home the Sinope squadron".

From a military-technical point of view, the battle of Sinop did not reflect gloriously on the Russian fleet. A squadron consisting of line-of-battle ships with two to three times greater fire power against a squadron of frigates anchored in the bay was sure to win the battle. Had the Ottoman squadron not fired first, the Russian squadron could have been accused of breaching a naval point of honour that held it despicable to attack frigates with first-raters. There were almost no naval manoeuvres during the battle, so it was more like a siege bombardment. The Ottoman shore batteries were few, small and inefficiently positioned. Yet the battle lasted about two hours during which the Ottoman squadron was still active and the Russian squadron also received serious damage. A more efficient fleet (for example the British fleet) in the place of the Russian fleet in such a situation could have won the battle in much less time. Many historians admit that the Paixhans naval guns and explosive shells used by the Russian ships were very effective against the shot fire of the Ottoman squadron. Nevertheless, with such a superiority of fire power, the Russian squadron could easily have won the battle even with shot fire instead of the explosive shells.[72]

The Ottoman squadron had fallen into a situation similar to that of the French fleet, which was destroyed by Admiral Nelson at the bay of Abukir on 1 August 1798. Napoleon III took heed of lessons apparent in the battle of Sinop; he understood that wooden ships were vulnerable against such shells and thus ordered armour-plated floating wooden batteries for the French fleet. These floating batteries were used in October 1855 in the seizure of Fort Kılburun (Kinburn), guarding the mouths of the rivers the Bug and the Dnieper in the Black Sea.

Ivan Konstantinovich Aivazovskiy (Hovhannes Aivazian, 1817–1900), the famous Crimean Russian Armenian naval painter of the nineteenth century, went to Sevastopol to talk to the Ottoman POWs

---

[72] Andrew Lambert, *The Crimean War: British Grand Strategy against Russia, 1853–56*. Manchester: Manchester University Press, 1991, p. 60.

Illus. 7 Patrona (Vice-Admiral) Osman Pasha and Commander Adil Bey, prisoners of war at Sevastopol. Pencil drawing by Aivasovsky, *RHL*, 1854.

Osman Pasha and Ali Bey and made pencil portraits of them as well. When Aivazovskiy asked Osman Pasha why he did not take line-of-battle ships to Sinop, Osman Pasha replied: "With our sailors it would be the same".[73] Poor Osman Pasha had enough cause to deplore his mariners, he was badly injured in his foot during the battle and had been robbed by his own crew while lying unconscious. He might have been justified in not depending on his sailors for open sea operations, because at the beginning of October his experienced crew was given to Bahriye Feriki Mustafa Pasha, while he received newly-recruited peasant boys from Anatolia. They had become seasick on their first voyage.

The *Taif* reached Istanbul on 2 December and delivered the news of the catastrophe. Mahmud Pasha at once reproached the French and British governments for their questionable attitude. "They bade us arm", he said, "and resist Russia, and now in the hour of our need their fleets look calmly on!"[74] It was necessary to go to Sinop and to check the situation there, but the naval pashas seemed unwilling to undertake the mission. From the office of the Kapudan Pasha, Mushaver Pasha went to the French embassy where the two ambassadors were in conference with their admirals Dundas and Hamelin. The French ambassador Baraguey d'Hilliers saw the event as a normal war incident. Stratford de Redcliffe and the admirals professed they had been ignorant of an Ottoman squadron's presence out in the Black Sea until only a few days before the event. At this point Adolphus Slade bitterly observed that the squadron had sailed from Büyükdere in full view of Therapia and Beykoz, where Stratford and the admirals resided. The ambassadors objected to sending Ottoman steamers alone to Sinop for fear of further disaster, and they also objected to their accompanying the French and British steamers, because they thought that might compromise their governments. Nevertheless, they declared that two steamers, one British and one French, were ready to go to Sinop alone.[75]

---

[73] "Otryvok pis'ma iz Simferopolya, ot 24-go Dekabrya", Vasiliy Timm, *Russkiy Khudozhestvenny Listok* 3, 20-go Yanvarya 1854 goda.
[74] Slade, op. cit., p. 146.
[75] Baraguey d'Hilliers to Reşid Pasha, 3 December 1853. BOA. HR. SYS. 1193/2 enc. 13.

The news of Sinop was received by Emperor Nikolai with joy. He wrote to Prince Menshikov that he was happy to see that the Çeşme naval victory (of 1770) was not forgotten in the Russian navy.[76]

On 4 December, Reşid Pasha again applied to the British and French embassies, giving the news and this time asking the allied fleets to join the Ottoman fleet to go into the Black Sea.[77] Although unaware of the full consequences of the battle, he rightly guessed that the defeat was probably severe. Reminding the ambassadors that the reason for the presence of their fleets in the Bosphorus was to protect the coasts of the Sublime State, he now called them to the task. It was indeed now a direct challenge by Russia and a task for the naval great powers to undertake. The war had now definitely gone beyond a collision between Russia and the Porte. On that day the British steamship *Retribution* with Slade on board and the French steamship *Mogador* departed for Sinop.

At Sinop they found disorder and confusion everywhere, with more than one hundred suffering wounded men scattered in cafes. Six days had passed without proper treatment for the wounded. The governor (*kaimmakam*) of Sinop and the population who had defected at the beginning of the battle had now returned to the city. There were 10 officers, 3 doctors and about 120 seamen in town.[78] Many officers and about 1000 men had gone into the interior of the country. The governor tried to excuse his defection but to no avail. The steamers took 110 wounded with them and returned to Istanbul. At Tophane they were required to delay the landing of the wounded until evening so that they might not be seen.

Summoned to the Porte the next day to relate the details of the battle, Slade found the Ottoman ministers completely unaffected by the incident:

> Their cheerful cushioned apartment and sleek fur-robed persons deepened in imagination, by the force of contrast, the gloom of the dingy cafes of Sinope with their writhing occupants. They listened, apparently unconcerned, to the woful [sic] tale; they regarded composedly a panoramic

---

[76] Nikolai to Menshikov, 29 November (11 December) 1853. RGVIA. Fond 481, op. 1, d. 8, list 7.
[77] Official note, 4 December 1853. BOA. HR. SYS. 1189/55 and BOA. A. AMD. 50/30.
[78] Adolphus Slade to Viscount Stratford de Redcliffe, H.M.S. *Retribution*, Bay of Sinope, 7 December 1853. TNA. FO 195/309.

view of the Bay of Sinope, taken a few days after the action by Lieutenant O'Reilly of the *Retribution*. A stranger, ignorant of the *nil admirari* of Ottomans, would have fancied them listening to an account and looking at a picture of a disaster in Chinese waters. The mention, however, of the flight of the Pasha of Sinope elicited a spark of the old Turkish spirit. Redshid Pasha, in whose household he had formerly served, attempted to excuse his conduct: 'He could not,' he naively remarked, 'be expected to remain in the way of cannon balls.' On which Kiridli Mustafa Pasha gave him a scowl pregnant with meaning.[79]

On 11 December the grand vizier Giritli Mustafa Naili Pasha submitted to Sultan Abdülmecid the results of the investigations into the Sinop affair and the remedies proposed.[80] By this time he had received the reports of the Mushaver Pasha, the *kaimmakam* of Sinop and the *vali* of the province of Kastamonu with a *mazbata* from the *meclis* of the province. The grand vizier informed the Sultan of the declaration of the Russian admiral given to the Austrian consulate in Sinop as explained above. However, he wrote that this was only a trick to appease France and Britain. In any case, this ruse could not long be credited in the face of informed European public opinion. He observed that if the European states sent cash donations to the victims of the burning of the town who were left without shelter, this would entail harmful effects for the Sublime State (the Porte). Therefore the governor should immediately set out to determine the fire victims and to make appropriate payments to them. He indicated that the governor should also attend to the wounded.

The grand vizier further stated that the Sublime State should be able to protect its shores without aid from others, and that while this could be done in the long run, for the time being it needed to strengthen its navy by purchasing two two-deckers (*kapak*) and three frigates from the Americans or other sources and to pay off the debt owing for the steamship still under construction in London. He pointed out that in a few weeks Namık Pasha in London was expected to contract the loan and then the steamer's cost could be paid. The Sultan approved the petition (*tezkire*) of the grand vizier after two days.

---

[79] Slade, op. cit., pp. 152–153. Slade also writes that some weeks after this scornful glance, Reşid Pasha replaced Giritli Mustafa Naili Pasha as grand vizier. However, his memory fails him utterly, for Giritli was only replaced in May 1854 by Kıbrıslı Mehmet Ali Pasha.

[80] BOA. İ. HR. 105/5133 enc. 5, 11 December 1853. The draft of this report is at BOA. A. AMD. 50/31.

Meanwhile a struggle was going on between the Kapudan Pasha and his officers. The Kapudan Pasha accused Ferik Ahmed Pasha and Ferik Mustafa Pasha as well as other officers of not taking necessary measures and avoiding their duty. The two *ferik* pashas for their part forgot their animosities temporarily and united against the Kapudan Pasha. As Slade remarked, the Kapudan Pasha seems to have made the mistake of uniting his enemies against himself. In the end, most of the officers sided with the *ferik* pashas. Kapudan Mahmud Pasha was dismissed from the admiralty on 18 December 1853 and later exiled to Bolu.[81] He was replaced first by the former *serasker* Hasan Rıza Pasha (1809–1877), and then by Kıbrıslı Mehmed Emin Pasha (1813–1871) in February 1854. The *kaimmakam* of Sinop Hüseyin Pasha was also dismissed from office, but according to Slade, he was reappointed to a "more lucrative" location the next year.[82] Mahmud Pasha was also pardoned in 1857 and returned to Istanbul, where he died soon thereafter.[83]

Although Mahmud Pasha was apparently not fit as Navy minister, the fault did not entirely lie with him. He seems rather to have been chosen as a scapegoat. In his testimony before the MVL during his trial after his dismissal, he showed his instructions to Osman and Hüseyin Pashas dated 26 and 27 November, wherein he had ordered them to leave Sinop immediately with all the ships and to come to the vicinity of the Bosphorus.[84] At that time Mustafa Pasha had returned to Istanbul and reported the situation of the squadron of Osman Pasha in Sinop. Nevertheless, these orders probably never reached their destination. In any case the carelessness of Osman Pasha and Hüseyin Pasha must bear the greater part of the blame.

There are two documents written by Mahmud Pasha in his defence. One is a letter to the grand vizier some time before his dismissal on 18 December, the other is a report or formal statement (*layiha*) submitted

---

[81] Abdülmecid. *Beyaz üzerine hatt-ı hümayun*. BOA. İ. DH. 17914, 18 December 1853. Slade (op. cit., p. 158) has turned Bolu into "Borloz". Besim Özcan (op. cit., p. 153) gives the date of Mahmud Pasha's exile to Bolu as 3 Rebiyülevvel 1271 (24 November 1853), referring to a document from the BOA. Most probably he misread the month of Rebiyülahir as Rebiyülevvel. Furthermore, he seems unaware of the obvious contradiction of sending Mahmud Pasha to exile before the disaster happened!

[82] Özcan, op. cit., p. 154. Slade, op. cit., p.

[83] Mehmed Süreyya, op. cit., vol. 3, p. 924.

[84] Kapudan Pasha to Patrona Osman and Mirliva Hüseyin Pashas, 27 and 28 November 1853. BOA. İ. HR. 106/5182 enc. 5, paragraph two and three.

to the *Meclis-i Mahsus*. However, both documents have been neglected even by those Turkish historians, who have done archival research on this topic and who must have seen them. Thus the voice of Mahmud Pasha, after being suppressed for more than 150 years, will echo here for the first time. Mahmud Pasha's defence statements show the tensions and rivalries within the Ottoman navy. He accuses Ferik Ahmed Pasha and Ferik Mustafa Pasha of long having hostile intentions against him and the desire to replace him. He argues that the two feriks had earlier complained of each other many times but now they had united against him, temporarily forgetting old quarrels between themselves. This account is in line with Adolphus Slade's observations.[85]

In his letter to the grand vizier, Mahmud Pasha writes that following reports of Russian ships being seen around Amasra, it was first decided to send the galleons to the Black Sea against the Russian ships. However, the French and British admirals prevented such ships from being sent, proposing instead the sending of the frigates. After that, Mahmud Pasha gathered his commanders on the galleon *Mahmudiye*, in their presence instructing Osman and Hüseyin Pashas to patrol the waters of Amasra and Ereğli in two separate squadrons but to keep close to each other. If they met Russian ships they would judge their chances of success and if they thought they could win, they should fight them. Otherwise they were to take care of themselves. They were authorised to return to the Bosphorus in case of bad weather or the presence of a superior enemy.

Mahmud Pasha then comments on the task of Mustafa Pasha's squadron. Mustafa Pasha had not visited Sokhumi as planned, excusing himself on grounds of bad weather. However, Mahmud Pasha had learned from captains that the weather was good and Mustafa Pasha acted rather timidly, not venturing to go as far as Sokhumi. He had returned to Sinop but had not taken any measures other than leaving two steamers there. When Mahmud Pasha criticised Mustafa Pasha on his return to Istanbul for leaving those ships open to danger in such an unprotected place, Mustafa Pasha replied that the place was not open to danger and in any case he had strongly recommended that they return to Istanbul.

---

[85] "The naval captains, seeing him [Mahmud Pasha] the doomed scapegoat, sided with the admirals [Ahmed and Mustafa pashas]. Accordingly, the forms of inquiry having been complied with, Mahmoud Pasha was dismissed…" Slade, ibid.

Mahmud Pasha then directs his criticism to Ferik Ahmed Pasha, who allegedly avoided going to Sinop with a squadron of five or six steamers to save the sailing ships there from Russian attack. Ahmed Pasha reportedly replied to him: "You sent Mustafa Pasha and he returned without doing anything. Now you are sending me into danger". To this Mahmud Pasha retorts:

> You will go on board the steamers. If you perceive such a danger any time then you can return. Why do you speak like this, are you not ashamed? If you cannot go, then give me an official answer and I will go to the Porte and report the situation. Then God willing I shall go myself tomorrow on board the imperial steamships.[86]

Ahmed Pasha, sensing that now things would go badly for him, stated that he did not object to going to Sinop absolutely, but the matter should be discussed with naval commanders in the naval council (*Meclis-i Bahriye*). Mahmud Pasha, again according to his own statement, criticised Ahmed Pasha for trying to evade the task. "Are you going to take instructions from the commanders? Did you always ask their instructions before going out on an expedition?" Nevertheless, Ahmed Pasha insisted on the meeting of the council and the next day the council was convened.

At the council, Mahmud Pasha addressed all the officers as follows:

> Hitherto there have been many conquests in Rumelia and Anatolia thanks to the prophet and the imperial majesty. But we as the navy have not yet achieved anything. I cannot go to visit any person and even if I go, I do not know what to do because of my embarrassment. Isn't this a disgrace? By imperial grace we received these ranks and orders but we have done nothing and whenever we want to send any of you on a mission, you present certain fallacies and demagogueries. I officially state to you that if you won't be able to go and if you are afraid, then tell me, let me go to the Sublime Porte and express these circumstances. Tomorrow I will take from among you the *Reis* Pasha or another and go on board the imperial steamers.[87]

In reply to this reprimand, the officers expressed their apprehensions. They stated that going out with steamers alone would not provide an adequate force against the many enemy ships. The galleons on the other hand would prove difficult to navigate in winter conditions. They

---

[86] Mahmud Pasha to the Grand Vizier. BOA. İ. HR. 106/5182 enc. 4, between 4 and 17 December 1853.
[87] Ibid.

also said that the allied admirals were of the same opinion. Even those frigates that went out previously (the frigates of Osman Pasha and Hüseyin Pasha) met harsh weather and took shelter in the harbour of Sinop and they could not get out of the harbour. Now it was difficult to go back to Istanbul after passing the waters off Amasra. True, the Russians were out cruising, but sailing from Sevastopol to Sinop and going back to Sevastopol or to Batum and Sohum was much easier than sailing from Istanbul to Sinop and coming back. Russian harbours were closer to those places. Nevertheless, the Russians could not bring their big ships near the Bosphorus. Because in the event of adverse weather, they would be unable to return and would be forced to enter the Bosphorus.

Mahmud Pasha then argued that these officers were not reliable and it was necessary to make them sign their instructions every time, because they would distort his words after a while. He also argued that they always tried to blame their superiors and dreamed of receiving the post of *kapudan* pasha for themselves. They were now spreading rumours among common people and servants that the events at Sinop were due to the Kapudan Pasha.

The other document is Mahmud Pasha's statement (*layiha*) submitted to the *Meclis-i Mahsus* after his dismissal from office. At the beginning of his statement, Mahmud Pasha writes that when he was appointed to the office of the Kapudan Pasha, both the Padishah and the ministers knew that he was not well versed in the naval art.[88] Thus by his own admission Mahmud Pasha confirms Abdülmecid's appointment of high officials without consideration of their capabilities. In this case Abdülmecid had been under the influence of his brother-in-law Damad Mehmed Ali Pasha or Mustafa Reşid Pasha.[89]

Mahmud Pasha further argues that since he was already dismissed, but the *feriks* remained at their posts, the officers of the navy and the shipyard (*Tersane-i Amire*) were unwilling to testify against the evidence of the *ferik* pashas for fear of the consequences. If these two pashas had also been removed from their posts, the officers would probably find

---

[88] BOA. İ. HR. 106/5182 enc. 1, not dated. Mücteba İlgürel and Besim Özcan must have seen this and the fourth enclosure, because they refer to the same folder (*gömlek*) in the *İrade Hariciye* collection of the BOA. However, they have not made any references to these documents.

[89] Lütfi (op. cit., p. 113) writes that the reason for Mahmud Pasha's appointment to the post of kapudan pasha was that his elder brother was the kethüda of Mustafa Reşid Pasha.

the courage to tell the truth, he added. The ex-Kapudan Pasha then accuses Mustafa Pasha of not visiting all the places on the Circassian coast. Judging from the information he gathered from the captains of the flotilla, Mahmud Pasha argues that although the weather was fine, Mustafa Pasha did not visit Sohum and did not capture a small Russian ship that he met. In fact, according to the *Kapudan-ı Derya*, the duty of Mustafa Pasha was to circumnavigate the whole Black Sea, patrolling the Crimean shores as well and returning to Istanbul from the Rumelian shores. Then Mustafa Pasha is accused of seeing the squadron of Osman Pasha undefended in Sinop and, without taking any measures, slipping away to Istanbul. Mahmud Pasha asserts that he had not given any orders to lie at the bay of Sinop; instead he had given permission to return to the Bosphorus in the face of bad weather or superior enemy force.[90]

Against the accusations of Mahmud Pasha, Mustafa Pasha defended himself with a *layiha* that was sealed by six other naval officers as well.[91] He argued that although it was known that Sinop was not a safe harbour, Mahmud Pasha had ordered Osman and Hüseyin Pashas to patrol the coasts of Amasra, Ereğli and Sinop on 4 November 1853. In case of bad weather or going short of drinking water, they were not to return to Istanbul, but to go to Sinop. When Mustafa Pasha together with Ahmed Pasha expressed their concerns for this trip and volunteered instead to go themselves, the Kapudan Pasha rejected this offer, saying that it was not necessary for them to go.

Five days later, Mustafa Pasha was ordered to deliver ammunition to the Circassians with four steamers (*Feyz-i Bari, Saik-i Şadi, Taif* and *Ereğli*). According to Mustafa Pasha, his only duty was to deliver the ammunition and he was not authorised to give any commands to the squadrons of Osman Pasha and Hüseyin Pasha if he met them on his way. At Sinop, he took coal for his steamers and inspected the fortifications and shore batteries there. Having found them insufficient, he wrote to the Kapudan Pasha on their condition and also informed him that he would send the *Ereğli* back to Istanbul from Trabzon with some news, because it was not in good order and might

---

[90] BOA. İ. HR. 106/5182 enc. 1.
[91] BOA. İ. HR. 106/5182 enc. 17, not dated, around January 1854. Other seals are those of Mehmed Emin, İsmail, Ahmed (?), Mehmed Pir and two other unidentified officers.

hamper his movement. Mustafa Pasha then refers to the secretary of the *Tersane-i Amire* as witness to the fact that his petition had really reached Kapudan Pasha. After Sinop, he cruised the coasts of Trabzon, Batum and Çürüksu, and on his return to Sinop found Osman Pasha lying in the bay with five ships. He saw an order from the Kapudan Pasha to Osman Pasha to keep the *Ereğli* with himself on its return from Trabzon. He advised Osman Pasha to sail into open sea since the harbour was not safe. On his departure from Sinop, the squadron of Hüseyin Pasha also entered the bay. Hüseyin Pasha informed him that the Russian squadron had returned to Sevastopol due to bad weather. Mustafa Pasha advised him as well to keep away from Sinop harbour. At Hüseyin Pasha's request, he left the steamer *Taif* with him and returned to Istanbul, where he begged the Kapudan Pasha to call back the ships from Sinop. Mahmud Pasha, however, did not heed his cautionary advice. Two days later, Mustafa Pasha repeated his request and this time Mahmud Pasha accepted it. Nevertheless, at that time, the *Taif* brought the bad news about Sinop. Now it was too late.

Both Mahmud Pasha's and Mustafa Pasha's statements seem to contain some falsehoods and some calculated uncertainties. For example, since Hüseyin Pasha was dead and Osman Pasha a prisoner of the Russians, it was not possible to check what Mustafa Pasha really told them. It is not possible either to put the whole blame on one person. In any case, these documents provide us with important information.

The Ottoman foreign minister Reşid Pasha in his notes to the French and British embassies dated 29 and 30 November and 4 December 1853 had expressed his hopes of assistance from their fleets lying in the Bosphorus. Lord Stratford in his reply to Reşid Pasha dated 11 December 1853 informs him that "with sentiments of deep affliction" he learnt "the full extent of loss sustained by the Porte's flotilla in its late unfortunate conflict with a Russian force of disproportioned magnitude". Stratford then argues that the destruction might, to all appearance, have been avoided, "if earlier attention had been paid either to the dangers of their position or to the means of protecting them by effective batteries on shore". However he recommends not sending the Ottoman fleet and the allied fleets into the Black Sea:

> It can hardly be necessary either for me or for the French Ambassador to assure Your Highness that such measures will be taken by the respective Admirals as the season may permit, and as circumstances may require for giving effect to the instructions, under which they are called upon to act. Their principal object is the protection of the Turkish territory

against any direct aggression, but in the performance of that defensive duty they can not be expected to lose sight of those considerations which are prescribed by the earnest desire of both Governments to render their operations as much as possible conducive to the restoration of peace as well as to the maintenance of the Sultan's rights.[92]

It is remarkable that Stratford was still talking of "restoration of peace". At that time the four great powers were preparing a note to Russia and the Porte for a ceasefire and peace.

One day later the French ambassador General Baraguey d'Hilliers also replied to Reşid Pasha's note officially.[93] General d'Hilliers expressed his regret over the incident but added that he would not accept any responsibility, as they had earlier warned of the dangers of sailing into the Black Sea with the Ottoman fleet given its material and military condition. These dangers stemmed from the severity of the weather and the possibility of meeting a numerically more powerful enemy squadron. The French ambassador then argued that apart from the political meaning of the presence of the allied fleets in Büyükdere, it also meant a moral assistance in so far as hopes for a peaceful solution were not exhausted. Finally the ambassador stated that they would defend the Bosphorus in case of a Russian attack but did not specify how and when they might go into the Black Sea.

Kostaki Musurus, the Ottoman ambassador in London, wrote to Reşid Pasha that he found Lord Clarendon "*très affecté*":

> The news of the deplorable event at Sinope, received by a telegram from Vienna, produced here a most painful impression, a universal sadness and one can say an indignation against the inaction imposed on the fleets moored in the Bosphorus. This feeling of national self-esteem is shared by the Cabinet itself, whatever his efforts for the maintenance of peace....
>
> I pointed out to him [to Clarendon] what he had said to me on one occasion regarding the assistance that the two fleets would lend to the Sublime Porte, which would limit itself to help in the event of aggressive attacks on behalf of Russia, but by no means in an offensive war on our part. Together with His Lordship I remarked that it was certainly in consequence of this promise of assistance that the Sublime Porte had not

---

[92] Stratford to Reşid. BOA. HR. SYS. 903/2 enc. 55–57, 11 December 1853. Translation of the note into Turkish is in HR. SYS. 1193/2 enc. 24.
[93] BOA. HR. SYS. 1193/2 enc. 25, 12 December 1853. This is the translation of the French note. I could not find the original in the BOA. Nor is it to be found in AGKK, IV/1.

sent, or perhaps had been advised not to send all its fleet into the Black Sea, convinced that such a promise would not have been given without a preliminary engagement of Russia towards the Powers in this respect.[94]
[My translation]

Lord Stratford, in his despatch to the British Secretary of State for Foreign Affairs, dated 17 December 1853, again put the blame on the Porte and its advisers. "They alone, or their professional advisers", he wrote, "were cognizant of the miserable state of the land defences of Sinope". They alone were answerable "for the obvious imprudence of leaving so long in helpless danger a squadron exposed to attacks from hostile ships of far superior force". To these accusations, which certainly touched him as well, Slade replied with a proverb common to both Turkish and English:

> His Excellency did not think of his own glass-house while throwing those stones. The French and English fleets were more or less under the direction of their ambassadors at Constantinople; and it has not appeared that *previous* to the battle of Sinope a wish had been expressed by them for any French or English ships to enter the Black Sea. The state of the defences, not only at Sinope but in every part of the empire, ought to have been familiar to men who claimed the right to dictate to the Porte its war operations, deeming it superfluous to counsel preliminarily with any of its military or naval officers; and who, with consuls at outports and contingent service money, had ready means for obtaining special information. The Capitan Pasha, the Porte's professional adviser, had recommended sending line-of-battle ships into the Black Sea, to obviate the exposure of a squadron of frigates and corvettes 'to attacks from hostile ships of far superior force;' and his recommendation, approved by the Porte, had been overruled.[95]

The foreign office in London on the same date was instructing Lord Stratford to order the fleet into the Black Sea. However, there was a difference of opinion between the British and French admirals on the question of sailing to the Black Sea. They were quite reluctant to leave their picturesque anchorage at Beykoz.

On 18 and 19 December the Ottoman grand council convened again, this time to consider the conditions for peace offered by the great powers on the basis of a modified Vienna note. The council voted for peace based on the evacuation of the Danubian principalities, recognition of

---

[94] Musurus à Son Altesse Rechid Pacha, le 15 Décembre 1853. BOA. İ. HR. 105/5151 enc. 37.
[95] Slade, op. cit., p. 159.

the sovereign rights of the Porte and a guarantee from the four powers.[96] Reşid Pasha however had some difficulty in persuading the *ulema*. The *softas* again demonstrated against peace. On 21 December they started a boycott of classes, closing down mosques and preventing the call to prayers (*ezan*) from the minarets. "If you want peace now, why did you declare war two months ago?" was their question. The government published a statement in the semi-official *Ceride-i Havadis* newspaper on 22 December 1853. Here is its translation published in the *Times*:

> His powerful allies have made known to the Sublime Porte the pacific intentions which the Court of Russia never ceases to testify, and, also, in impelling the Imperial Government in that path, they have demanded what its intentions were on the subject. In consequence, on the 17th and 18th of the present month, the affair was submitted to the deliberations of the Grand Council, convoked immediately for that purpose, and composed of all the Ministers, Viziers, Ulemas, military Pashas of the army and navy, and other dignitaries of the empire. It unanimously decided on replying that, since the Sublime Porte has commenced hostilities to protect its rights and the integrity of its states [sic], it will not reject a peace calculated to guarantee them both for the present and the future. A *fetva* confirmative of this decision has just been drawn up by the Sheik-ul-Islam, and an Imperial order has been published to that effect. Communication of what precedes has been made to the representatives of the four Powers. The affair at this moment only rests on a simple question and answer. The question is not now of peace, and even an armistice has not been declared. The state of war continues, and despatches announcing what has just taken place have been sent to the Pashas, and to the Generals of the armies of Rumelia and Anatolia, in order that the course of the military movements may not be interfered with...
>
> The above-mentioned decision having been come to unanimously, conformably to the glorious provisions of the fetva, emanating from the sacred law, any one who shall allow himself to speak against the foregoing shall be considered to have spoken against a decision come to unanimously, and be immediately subjected to the penalties which he will have incurred for this act.[97]

Meanwhile rumours of a massacre of the Christians were spread in Istanbul. A wave of fanaticism was expected and feared, causing some panic and confusion in the European quarters of the city, that is, Galata, Beyoğlu and Therapia. Lord Stratford invited all diplomats and their families to the British Palace. On behalf of the whole *corps diplo-*

---

[96] *Mazbata* of the *Meclis-i Umumi*. BOA. İ. HR. 21334 enc. 1, 21 December 1853.
[97] "The State of the Continent", *The Times*, London, 7 January 1854, Issue 21632, p. 7.

matique Stratford wrote to Reşid Pasha to stand firm against the *softas*.⁹⁸ The capital was menaced by *une insurrection immédiate* and Stratford believed that "the government will not hesitate, undoubtedly, to take the measures necessary to maintain order". However, Reşid Pasha, who was not known for personal courage, had resigned and was hiding in his son's house at Beşiktaş. Stratford could not reach him. On 22 December Stratford finally found Reşid, but Reşid Pasha did not promise firmness, even saying that the Sultan was indifferent.

Stratford then went to see Abdülmecid and insisted on firm measures. Abdülmecid accepted the proposal and some steamers were brought from Beykoz near the Porte. Then the Sultan told the grand vizier Mehmed Ali Pasha and the sheikhulislam that he would hold a council meeting at the Porte. Mehmed Ali got alarmed and tried to calm down the *softas*. However, they demanded the release of those imprisoned in the seraskeriat. The government this time did stand firm and about 170 *softas* were arrested.⁹⁹ When they were asked to go to the battlefront if they were so warlike, they replied that their duty was to preach, not to fight. Then they were shipped to Crete.¹⁰⁰ The resistance was thus broken. Two days after Stratford's letter, Reşid Pasha replied that the softas were exiled and order was restored in the capital.¹⁰¹

On 26 December the grand vizier submitted the *mazbata* of the Kastamonu *meclis* on the details of the material damages and human losses in the city, dated 14 December and the letter of the *vali* Hamdi Pasha, dated 16 December.¹⁰² According to these documents, from the civilians, five Muslims became martyrs (*şehid*) and sixteen non-Muslims simply died (*fevt*). Seven *mescids*, two schools, 247 houses and 170 shops belonging to Muslims were destroyed and burnt, while the losses of the non-Muslims were 50 shops and 40 to 50 houses. The *mazbata* was signed by the two non-Muslim members (*kocabaşı*) of the *meclis* as well.

The Battle of Sinop disturbed the European balance of power. It was a flagrant denial of Nikolai's assurances of his non-aggressive intentions, despite war being declared on both sides. However, from a military

---

⁹⁸ Lord Stratford to Reşid Pasha. Pera, 21 December 1853. BOA. HR. SYS. 1346/38.
⁹⁹ Lane-Poole, op. cit., vol. II, pp. 333–335.
¹⁰⁰ BOA. İ. DH. 285/17944, 25 December 1853. These *softas* were to be assigned salaries of 30 piastres per month and bread rations during their stay in Crete.
¹⁰¹ Reşid Pasha to Lord Stratford, 23 December 1853. BOA. HR. SYS. 905/1 enc. 70.
¹⁰² BOA. İ. DH. 17947, the *irade* is dated 27 December 1853.

point of view, it was a brilliant operation of the Russian navy against a military target. From a legal point of view, it was a legitimate act of war except for its excessive bombardment and the civilian losses. For Britain and France, the most objectionable aspect of the affair was that it was a direct defiance to their fleets anchored in the Bosphorus. The Russians had destroyed a Turkish flotilla lying at anchor almost under the eyes of the great naval powers. This was too much indeed. Thus Admiral Nakhimov by his very victory at Sinop had prepared the ruin of the Russian Black Sea fleet, which was later sunk by the Russians themselves to block the entrance to Sevastopol.

The repercussions of the battle of Sinop were different in Britain and France. While the British public opinion reacted to the event with much excitement, the French public opinion was in general calm. On the other hand, while Napoleon III was "determined to make an issue out of the incident", the British cabinet took it as a matter of course.[103] British newspapers in general described the battle of Sinop as a "massacre". Especially the damage to the city and its civilian inhabitants caused anger. The number of the dead was given as 4,000. Even the conservative, cautious and pacifist *Times* now turned belligerent. On 13 December 1853 it described a new phase in the war:

> The war, hitherto confined to the occupation of the Danubian Principalities and to a few partial encounters of the hostile armies, appears to have assumed on the Black Sea the character of direct aggression, and the Emperor of RUSSIA has thrown down the gauntlet to the maritime Powers precisely on that element on which they are best prepared to meet him. We have thought it our duty to uphold and defend the cause of peace, as long as peace was compatible with the honour and dignity of the country, and we feel no regret that to the very last we have adhered to a course of policy which a just concern for the best interests of England and of the civilized world prescribed. But we have never concealed our opinion that the events occurring in the East might ere long compel us to meet by more resolute measures a sterner alternative; and we have repeatedly urged upon the Governments of England and France the necessity of being prepared with a plan of operations adapted to such an emergency.

In many British cities and towns like London, Manchester, Derby, Hanley, Sheffield, Leicester, Paisley, Newcastle upon Tyne, Rochdale, Southampton and Stafford, meetings were held in the city halls in sup-

---

[103] Saab, op. cit., p. 126.

port of the Ottoman Empire. The well-known anti-Russian publicist David Urquhart participated in some of them. In Paisley he spoke two hours and a quarter and ended his words by declaring that "what the people of England have now to do is, to call on their Sovereign to require that either war shall be proclaimed against Russia, or the British squadron withdrawn from the Turkish waters".[104] Memorials likewise from many cities were being sent to the Queen, asking for a more active British policy. These memorials were usually published in the newspapers such as the *Times* and Kostaki Musurus sent such articles with his despatches to the foreign ministry.[105]

Napoleon III wanted to use the incident both to develop his alliance with Britain and to turn the attention of the French public towards foreign issues and away from domestic problems. Therefore he proposed to the British that the two fleets enter the Black Sea and force the Russian navy back to its base. The French foreign minister even declared that if Britain did not enter, France would go alone. This declaration and the agitated British public opinion forced the British cabinet to agree to send the fleet into the Black Sea. The Home Secretary Lord Palmerston, the symbol of the anti-Russian spirit and known for his support of the "Turks", resigned briefly in December 1853, but soon returned to office. The British public opinion was further excited by rumours of Prince Albert's being in league with the tsar. The allied fleets were ordered to enter the Black Sea towards the end of December 1853 but they could weigh anchor only on 4 January 1854. However, after a short cruise along the Black Sea coast the allied fleets returned to Büyükdere.

The coverage of the defeat of Sinop was, as could be expected, minimal in the official newspaper *Takvim-i Vekayi*. On 8 December 1853, it announced that a Russian squadron of two three-deckers, four two-deckers, three frigates, three steamers and one *navi* had entered the Sinop bay in a foggy weather and signalled the Ottoman squadron of seven frigates, three corvettes and two steamers for surrender. It was stated that, although the magnitude of the Russian squadron was such that resistance was not possible, the imperial navy did not surrender

---

[104] See BOA. İ. HR. 105/5151 enc. 36 for the article of the *Times* (December 1853, date not visible) on the meeting in the town of Paisley.

[105] See for example BOA. HR. SYS. 905/1, İ. HR. 108/5293 enc. 37, HR. SYS. 907/18 and İ. HR. 105/5151 enc. 39–40. The last is about a public meeting in Newcastle, published in *The Newcastle Guardian* on Saturday, December 17, 1853.

and entered into battle by virtue of its religious patriotism (*hamiyyet-i diniyye*) and bravery. The *Takvim-i Vekayi* further argued that although the Ottoman ships were destroyed, the Russian squadron was also severely damaged and had lost a lot of men. While there was no mention of the number of Ottoman losses, it was stated that 110 wounded were brought to Istanbul.

Müşir Selim Pasha, the commander of the Batum army, reported to the *serasker* that for the needs of current politics they would spread the news that the Russian ships were repulsed in defeat from Sinop.[106]

We must mention here that in the Ottoman official correspondence the disaster or defeat of Sinop is mentioned usually as the "regrettable" or "sorrowful" event of Sinop (*Sinop vaka-i müteellimesi* or *mükeddiresi*).[107] (The same adjectives were later used for the fall of Kars). But we do not see any equivalent of the expression of "the massacre of Sinop" which was much used in the European press, especially the British press. It seems that the Ottoman bureaucracy did not see it as a "massacre", but something like a natural disaster or something that regularly accompanied war.

The Caucasian Front in 1853

The Ottoman Anatolian army was in a much neglected state in comparison with the Rumelian army. The Anatolian army was under the command of Müşir Abdülkerim Nadir Pasha (better known as Çırpanlı Abdi Pasha, 1807–1883) and this army was deployed in Erzurum, Kars, Ardahan and Bayezid. Abdi Pasha's chief of staff was Ferik Tacirli Ahmed Pasha (?–1883)[108] and their relations were not good.

---

[106] Selim Pasha to the *serasker*, 22 December 1853. BOA. İ. HR. 106/5181.
[107] See for example BOA. A. AMD. 50/38, A. MKT. NZD. 110/78, İ. MMS. 3/93.
[108] Necat Birinci in his biographical footnotes on Abdi Pasha and Ahmed Pasha in Salih Hayri's *Hayrabad* gives completely incorrect information. He mistakes Abdi Pasha for a certain Abbas Pasha and Ahmed Pasha for the other (Nazır) Ahmed Pasha of the Rumeli army. Thus he writes that Ahmed Pasha was executed in 1860 (op. cit., p. 100). See Sinan Kuneralp, *Son Dönem Osmanlı Erkan ve Ricali (1839-1922)*, Istanbul: The Isis Press, 1999, p. 39. Birinci also writes that Ahmed Pasha became a pasha after the victory of Çatana, which is illogical and impossible because Ahmed Pasha could not have been both in Kars and in Çatana (on the Danube) simultaneously. Apparently he mixes the two different Ahmed Pashas of the Anatolian and the Rumelian armies. But he is wrong even for the other, Nazır Ahmed Pasha, because that Ahmed Pasha became a *müşir* and not a pasha after the battle of Çatana. Mehmed Süreyya and S. Kuneralp record Ahmed Pasha's death as being in 1883. See Mehmed Süreyya,

Map 3 The Caucasian theatre of war.

There was one division in Ardahan under the command of infantry division commander Ferik Ali Rıza Pasha, and another division under the command of cavalry division commander Ferik Selim Pasha in Bayezid.[109] Another army under Müşir Haseki Mehmed Selim Pasha

---

Sicill-i Osmani, vol. 1, Istanbul: Tarih Vakfı Yayınları, 1996, p. 203 and Kuneralp, op. cit., p. 60.

[109] Russian military agent in Istanbul, Colonel Count Osten Saken had described Ali Rıza Pasha and Selim Pasha in his report on 24 March (5 April) 1852 as follows: "Ferik Ali Rıza Pasha: Been to St. Petersburg with Ahmed Fethi Pasha. Served in the navy and then appointed at once lieutenant-general to the Anatolian army. Diligent but not

(who held the command of the *Hassa* army as well) was deployed in Batum. The usual dispersed deployment of troops and especially the separation of these two armies would prove to be detrimental to Ottoman war efforts. The headquarters of the Anatolian army was at first in Erzurum, and then it was moved to Kars.

The fortress of Kars was an important stronghold but in the previous war of 1829 the Russians had captured it and had taken Erzurum as well. Therefore those memories were still fresh in the minds of both sides. For the Russians it meant confidence that they could conquer the area again. As for the Ottoman officers, their initial optimism was soon replaced by a lack of confidence, bordering on defeatism, after the first setbacks. However, at the beginning of the war, great hopes were entertained by the Kars army, as expressed so well by the British doctor Humphrey Sandwith, who served in Kars:

> "Here", it was said, "you have the Turks posted on their own soil in the midst of a Mussulman population. At the summons of the fiery crescent thousands of warlike tribes will rush to the standard of Islam. It will be a holy war, and the enthusiasm of religious zeal will rouse the whole population, and amply atone for any deficiencies in tactics or military science".[110]

Events, however, proved that "tactics or military science" were not to be overruled by any "religious zeal".

The weakness of the Ottoman army was not expressed in numbers of men or weapons, at least at the beginning of the war. The Ottoman Anatolian army in 1853 and 1854 had a definite superiority in size against the Russian army located along the Russo-Ottoman border, because the Russians had to maintain a large portion of their army against the forces of Sheikh Shamil. Thus at the beginning of the war the Russians could raise against the Ottoman army only 20,000 to

---

talented. Ferik Selim Pasha: Originally an Armenian from Georgia, who converted to Islam. Islamist. Not talented, not remarkable. Passed all ranks in the Anatolian army from private to major-general. Promoted to lieutenant-general last year for his success in that year's recruitment". [My translation] See "Donesenie russkogo voennogo agenta v Konstantinopole polkovnika Osten-Sakena o sostave i kvartirnom raspolozhenii IV-go Anatoliyskogo korpusa turetskoy armii." RGVIA. Fond 450, *opis* 1, *delo* 44.

[110] Humphrey Sandwith, *A Narrative of the Siege of Kars*, London: John Murray, 1856, p. 91. Sandwith had lived in Istanbul since 1849. During the war he served first on the Danube and in October 1854 was appointed to the staff of Colonel (General) Williams in Kars. He spoke Turkish as well.

30,000 men.¹¹¹ The Anatolian army or the fourth army received reinforcements from other parts of the Ottoman Empire, from the Arabistan and Iraq armies. Although we do not have exact numbers, we can safely say that at the beginning of the war, there were at least about 30,000 men in Kars, 6,000 in Ardahan, 25,000 in Erzurum, 10,000 in Bayezid and 16,000 in Batum, altogether making 87,000 men.¹¹² Nevertheless, with only a few exceptions, the officers' corps, from the Commander-in-Chief downwards, did not show themselves equal to the task. They did not have a war plan, nor were they supplied with one by the war ministry.

Furthermore, there was much animosity and jealousy between the educated and uneducated officers within the army. The Commander-in-Chief Müşir Abdi Pasha, who had received education in Vienna from 1835 to 1840, belonged to the former group, while his chief of staff Ferik Ahmed Pasha belonged to the latter. During his trial at the end of 1854 in Istanbul, Abdi Pasha stated that he had to give oral instructions to Ahmed Pasha because Ahmed Pasha was illiterate and secret written messages had to be read to him by others.¹¹³ The illiteracy of Ahmed Pasha is confirmed by many other sources as well.¹¹⁴ Thus factional strife among officers started from the top, to a much greater extent than in the Rumelian army. Ahmed Rıza Trabzoni also mentions this rivalry in his *destan*.¹¹⁵ In any case, the fact that an illiterate pasha had become the chief of staff of the second biggest Ottoman army during wartime tells us much about the quality of officers in the Ottoman high command.

---

¹¹¹ Süer, op. cit., p. 42.

¹¹² See Süer, op. cit., p. 38. However, having given these numbers, the author somehow makes a total of 95,000 troops, instead of the mathematically correct sum of 87,000. Cevdet Pasha, on the other hand, mentions the figure of 70,000 men for the Anatolian army, but it is not clear which year he has in mind. See Cevdet Pasha, op. cit., p. 100.

¹¹³ BOA. İ. MMS. 3/107 enc. 5, page 2.

¹¹⁴ General Klapka describes Ahmed Pasha as "a rough and ignorant Kurd". See Klapka, *The War in the East: From the Year 1853 till July 1855*. London: Chapman and Hall, 1855, p. 43. Mehmed Süreyya (op. cit., p. 203) records him as "illiterate, simple-minded, brave, fierce and harsh". The Russian military agent in Istanbul, Colonel Count Osten Saken in his report on the Anatolian army in 1852 also described the chief of staff Ahmed Pasha as illiterate and having bad relations with the mushir [Gözlüklü] Reşid Pasha, the predecessor of Abdi Pasha, who was also well-educated and well-read. See RGVIA. Fond 450, opis 1, delo 44, list 2.

¹¹⁵ Ahmed Rıza, op. cit., p. 61.

There were many foreign officers in the service of the Padishah as well. In fact from the summer of 1853 many military adventurers had come to Istanbul to offer their services. The Serasker Damad Mehmed Ali Pasha at first believed the testimonials of the applicants in good faith and bestowed commissions liberally. But when the new foreign officers began to apply for money for their preparations, he got alarmed. Hasan Rıza Pasha, who was considered as a French protégé, succeeded him in February 1854. While he was averse to the employment of foreign officers, much harm had already been done, because many worthless first-comer officers were employed and some really good late-comer officers were turned away.

Apart from these adventurers, the Porte had a more reliable source of foreign officers. Many of the Hungarian and Polish officers who had sought refuge in the Ottoman Empire after Russia crushed the Hungarian revolution of 1848 were now serving in the Anatolian army and to a lesser extent in the Rumelian army. The Hungarians and Poles as a rule were not appointed to the Rumelian army to avoid problems with Austria.[116] There were a few exceptions such as the Polish officers Michal Czajkowski (Mehmed Sadık Pasha) and Count Antoni Ilinski (Iskender Bey). In fact there could have been a Polish "Legion", because 799 Polish Democrat emigrants living in France had signed a petition authorizing General Wysocki to act as their representative to the Sultan in requesting the formation of a "*Legion Polonaise*".[117] This proposal was not accepted.

Some of the foreign officers serving in the Ottoman armies were well-trained officers, but others had little or no training and some also engaged in intrigues. Though few of them had accepted Islam, they were given Muslim names and the Ottoman soldiers were led to believe that these officers were Muslims. Nevertheless, except for the Hungarian general György Kmety (İsmail Pasha, 1813–1865), the commander of the *başıbozuks* at Kars, they were not given command posi-

---

[116] İlber Ortaylı has written that General Bem (Murat Pasha) was appointed commander of the forces on the right bank [south] of the Danube. See Ortaylı, *İmparatorluğun En Uzun Yüzyılı*, Istanbul: İletişim Yayınları, 2001, p. 245. Ortaylı repeated the same claim in an article in 2006 published in Mehmet Seyitdanlıoğlu, Halil İnalcık (eds.), *Tanzimat*, Ankara: Phoenix, 2006, p. 295. In reality, Bem was not appointed and might not have been appointed anywhere near the Danube due to Austrian and Russian pressures. Accordingly, he was sent to Aleppo, where he died in 1850.
[117] BOA. HR. SYS. 1194/1 enc. 1, 5 November 1853.

tions, but employed rather as staff officers. Among such staff officers were Colonel Kollman (Feyzi Bey), the two Polish generals Feliks Klemens Breanski (Şahin Pasha, 1794–1884) and Ludwik Bystrzonowski (Arslan Pasha, 1797–1878), Polish colonels Gościmiński (Tufan Bey), Paczek (Yıldırım Bey), Zarzycki (Osman Bey), majors Grotowski (Sahil Bey), Jagmin, Antoni Wieruski (1804–1870), and the Belgian Baron Schwarzenberg (Emir Bey). The Hungarian (Prussian?) general Maximilian Stein (Ferhad Pasha, 1811–1860) was sent as an inspector to the Anatolian army, but was recalled soon after. Another Hungarian general George (György) Klapka (1820–1892) wrote that the foreign officers, instead of living together on amicable terms, and setting a good example to the men, "seemed to have no higher idea of their mission than the carrying on a constant war of intrigue against each other". Ferhad Pasha, "the most able amongst them, who from his influence with the Turks might have given a favourable turn to the ensuing operations, was, in consequence of some calumny, recalled soon after his appointment."[118] There were even two American officers, Major Bonfanti (Nevris Bey) and Major Tevis. Although these foreign officers were capable of giving good counsel, there were too many of them and conflicts frequently arose among them. At one time there were 23 staff officers in the Kars army. Therefore their total impact was not altogether healthy or constructive. More will be said later on this point.

The Russian viceroy or vicegerent of the Caucasus (*Namestnik na Kavkaze*, in Turkish *Tiflis Serdarı*), General Prince Mikhail Semyonovich Vorontsov (1782–1856) was old and ill. He had already requested his removal from his post at the beginning of 1853 because of his health conditions and also because he was worried that he had few forces available to deploy against the Ottomans. He constantly demanded reinforcements and even after receiving the 13th division from the Crimea in September 1853, he was still worried. However, Nikolai I did not share his worries and at the beginning of October 1853 wrote to him that he should now take Kars and Ardahan.[119] Vorontsov was a cunning administrator, from 1844 onwards in his fight against Imam Shamil he had pursued a subtle policy of gaining the support of the local feudal class, introducing Caucasian elites into tsarist service,

---

[118] Klapka, op. cit., pp. 44–45.
[119] Tarle, op. cit., vol. I, pp. 292–294.

paying attention to indigenous traditions, while supporting the growth of education, literature, and journalism in the native languages.[120] His deputy was General Nikolai Andreyevich Read (1792–1855). As we have seen in the previous chapter, there were very competent officers in the Russian Caucasian army. Thus we can say that both the Ottoman and the Russian commander-in-chief on the Caucasian front were cautious and did not have offensive plans. Events soon led to both being dismissed from their posts.

Relations with Imam Shamil and the Circassians in 1853

Imam Shamil or Shamuil[121] (1797–1871), the third *imam* and leader of the anti-Russian resistance of Dagestan and Chechnia, had been waging a guerrilla war against the occupying Russian army since 1834. Since he had no chance of winning the war without the assistance of the Ottoman Empire, he appealed to the caliph several times beginning from 1839. However, circumstances did not favour his entreaties. By the Treaty of Edirne of 1829, the Ottoman Empire had relinquished all its claims to Circassia and Georgia in favour of Russia. Russia had supported the Porte against Mehmed Ali of Egypt in 1833 and by the Treaty of Hünkar İskelesi the two states had become allies, albeit a half-hearted one in the case of the Porte. Therefore the Porte, now at peace with the court of St. Petersburg, did not want to irritate it by helping Shamil. Furthermore, Shamil's relations with Mehmed Ali of Egypt, with the Halidi sheikhs in Kurdistan and with other local notables who were opponents of the *Tanzimat*, as well as the activity of his messengers on the sensitive north-eastern frontier made Shamil suspect in the eyes of the Sublime Porte.[122] When Shamil sent his mes-

---

[120] Khadji Murat Ibragimbeyli writes that Vorontsov followed a "consistent policy of colonial Russification". See Ibragimbeyli, *Kavkaz v Krymskoi Voine 1853–1856 gg. i Mezhdunarodnye Otnosheniya*, Moscow: Nauka, 1971, p. 120.

[121] Shamil himself always wrote his name as Shamuil in Arabic letters. His signature in his hand-written letters and in his seal is read clearly as Shamuil. In official correspondence in the BOA both versions are used. For his letters, see Khalat Omarov, *100 pisem Shamilya*, Mahachkale: Dagestanskiy Nauchny Tsentr Rossiyskoi Akademii Nauk, 1997. A Turkish translation (without mentioning Omarov's name!) was published by Dr. Fikret Efe. *Şeyh Şamil'in 100 Mektubu*. İstanbul: Şule Yayınları, 2002. James Reid (op. cit., p. 140) has misread Shamuil, claiming that it is "spelled Shamvîl in documents".

[122] Moshe Gammer, "Shamil and the Ottomans: A Preliminary Overview", V. *Milletlerarası Türkiye Sosyal ve İktisat Tarihi Kongresi. Tebliğler. İstanbul 21–25 Ağustos 1989*. Ankara: TTK, 1990, pp. 387–394.

senger Hasan Hasbi to the region of Acara (Ajaria, Muslim Georgia in the vicinity of Batum and Çürüksu) to recruit volunteers in 1845, the Russian embassy protested and the Porte exiled eight of the local notables, collaborators of Hasan Hasbi, to Salonica. Hasan Hasbi himself escaped.[123]

With the deterioration of relations with Russia in 1853, the Porte had to modify its view of Shamil. The war with Russia could be very helpful for Shamil as well, because he had been lately pressed by the Russian army. He now had an opportunity to receive help from the Ottomans. A joint operation against the Russian army in the Caucasus would obviously pose a real threat to Russian dominance in the Caucasus. Shamil had already written a letter to Sultan Abdülmecid (as the Caliph) in March 1853, asking for help and informing him that they were now producing "cannons, gun powder and Congreve rockets".[124] He must have corresponded with the Anatolian army in Erzurum and with the governor of Erzurum, although contacts between Shamil and the Porte were neither steady nor secure, as many messages were being intercepted by the Russians, including the letter mentioned above.

Zarif Mustafa Pasha (1816–1862), the governor of the province of Erzurum (which included Ardahan, Kars and Bayezid) sent a letter to the grand vizier on 12 June 1853, stating that imperial decorations (commissions) and orders should be sent to Sheikh Shamil to ease his co-operation with the Ottoman army. However, the grand vizier Mustafa Naili Pasha, in his petition to Abdülmecid on 9 August 1853, did not approve of sending such orders to "such outside parties as that of Sheikh Shamil" due to some previously mentioned obstacles. We do not know these obstacles or drawbacks, but we can guess that they arose from the hopes of a diplomatic solution to the problem with Russia. The grand vizier wrote that in the future it might be reconsidered

---

[123] BOA. İ. MSM. 26/728, 729 and 739, dated 21 October, 29 November and 27 August 1845, respectively.

[124] *Shamil' – Stavlennik Sultanskoy Turtsii i Angliyskikh Kolonizatorov. Sbornik dokumental'nykh materialov*. Tbilisi: Gosizdat Gruzinskoi SSR, 1953, p. 367. Moshe Gammer quotes part of this letter, but he does not mention the production of cannons, etc. See Moshe Gammer, *Muslim Resistance to the Tsar: Shamil and the Conquest of Chechnia and Daghestan*, London: Frank Cass, 1994, p. 267.

in accordance with the situation. Abdülmecid, as usual, approved the decision of the grand vizier.¹²⁵

In a document from July 1853, it is reported that Shamil had mustered a significant force and had come to a place called Çar Kalesi. Shamil had seized Russian mail on 16 July 1853 on the road to Gence and confiscated a large sum of money.¹²⁶

On 5 September 1853, without waiting for a reply to his letter, Shamil appeared around Zakataly, close to Tiflis, with 10,000 men and 4 guns. However, he was too early, for the Ottomans had not yet declared war and therefore he did not hold too long, retreating to Dagestan. His deputy (*naib*) in Circassia Muhammed Emin also started to recruit volunteers from the Circassians and Abkhazians. Muhammed Emin made his intention to advance from Circassia, in the event of the beginning of war operations by the Ottomans, known to the *mutasarrıf* of Lazistan, who reported to his superior, the governor of Trabzon. The governor of Trabzon then reported to the Porte on the situation, but the reply was that the army of Batum under the command of Müşir Selim Pasha did not yet have sufficient strength and it would be reinforced by two battalions.¹²⁷ A complimentary letter was sent to Muhammed Emin.¹²⁸

After the declaration of war by the Porte on 4 October 1853, the Porte at last decided to send a firman to Shamil. Abdülmecid called him to holy war for the defence of Islam, without however using the word *jihad*. The firman was conveyed through Halil and Ibrahim Beys, notables of Dagestan, Kolağası Hacı Hüseyin Bey and Mülazım Kasım. Russia's "obstinacy and persistence" in its demands was said to be "a kind of malevolence and insult" to the *millet* of Islam. Shamil was instructed to subdue the *khans* and *ümera* of Şeki, Kuban, Şirvan, Karabağ, Derbend, Şemhal etc and to attack the Russian armies. He was also instructed to enter into correspondence and coordination with the commander of the Anatolian army Abdi Pasha. Shamil was

---

¹²⁵ These documents have been published by Mustafa Budak. See Budak, "1853-1856 Kırım Harbi Başlarında Doğu Anadolu-Kafkas Cephesi ve Şeyh Şamil", *Kafkas Araştırmaları* 1, 1988, pp. 52-58, transcriptions pp. 132-137, document photocopies pp. 236-243.
¹²⁶ BOA. A. DVN. 90/15, 23 July 1853. The signature is not readable.
¹²⁷ Masayuki Yamauchi, "Sheikh Shamil and the Ottoman Empire in the Period of the Crimean War. Enlightened by the ATASE Archives in Ankara", *Orient* XXII, Tokio, 1986, pp. 144-145.
¹²⁸ BOA. A. MKT. NZD. 96/38, 24 October 1853.

also informed that all those who fought with good faith for the cause of Islam would be rewarded by the Sultan according to their rank and deeds.[129]

On 17 October 1853, James Brant, the British consul in Erzurum, reported to the British foreign minister that Shamil sent "messengers to assure the Turks that they may depend on his cooperation and that as soon as he learns (that) they are prepared to attack the Russians, he will fall upon them on his side".[130] According to a news article in the *Journal de Constantinople*, Shamil had expressed to Abdi Pasha that he was ready with 20,000 men to fight against the Russians.[131]

Meanwhile Sefer Bey Zanuko (in Turkish Zanoğlu or Zanzade, "Zan's son"), a Circassian noble from Anapa who had fought in the Ottoman-Russian war of 1828–29 and had been subject to living in Edirne after the Treaty of Edirne in 1829, was now recalled to Istanbul together with Abdullah Ağa from his retinue in September 1853. For many years Sefer Bey had supplied reference letters for British diplomats and agents going to Circassia, such as David Urquhart, Captain Lyon, Mr Longworth, Mr Bell and others.

In November, Sefer Bey and Behcet Efendi, also a Circassian from the Bureau of Translation, were given the rank of *mirmiran* with the title of pasha and appointed by the Porte to the task of organizing the Circassians and smuggling arms and ammunition to them. A certain Circassian İsmail Bey, a former timariot officer, was also given the rank of *ıstabl-ı amire müdiri* and included in the group. Ostensibly they would be appointed to the Rumeli, Anatolian and Batum armies but in reality they would have a special mission to Circassia.[132] Sefer Pasha sent two of his agents, Mehmet Efendi and Ahmed Ağa to Trabzon to cross into Circassia. The governor of Trabzon and the commander of

---

[129] BOA. İ. DH. 17605 and C. HR. 5454, 9 October 1853. See Budak, op. cit. (1988), pp. 132–133, for the text of the firman. Halil Bey seems to have been made a pasha, for in an undated document he is addressed as "*mir-i ümera Dağıstani Halil Paşa*". See BOA. A. MKT. NZD. 117/53, October? 1853. In April 1854 he was definitely a pasha.

[130] Gammer, op. cit. (1990), p. 390.

[131] *Journal de Constantinople*, nr. 476, 19 October 1853, quoted by Ömer Faruk Akün, *Atsız Armağanı*, Erol Güngör et al. (eds.), Istanbul: Ötüken Yayınevi, 1976, p. 34.

[132] The *serasker* to the grand vizier and the grand vizier to the Sultan. BOA. HR. SYS. 1345/94, Sultan's *irade* is dated 24 November 1853. Sefer and Behcet Pashas were also assigned a salary of 12,500 piastres each with the rations of a brigadier general and 50,000 piastres each for travel expenses. İsmail Bey would receive a salary of 5,000 piastres and the same rations.

the Batum army Müşir Selim Pasha were given instructions to assist them.[133]

Shamil sent a letter to Abdi Pasha on 13 December 1853 apparently in reply to Abdi Pasha's letter. He seems to be unaware of the battle of Başgedikler of 1 December, which had ended with defeat for the Ottomans. In his letter Shamil writes that he heard that the Ottoman[134] army had besieged the fortresses of Gümrü, Erivan and Üç Kilise (Echmiadzin) of the infidel. He further informs Abdi Pasha that he had come to Georgia with his Dagestani army and entered the "country of the tsar" after a violent battle. Nevertheless, rain and snow fell on the mountains and he was forced to retreat to Dagestan. Then Shamil warns of the deception of the Russians, who might offer peace.[135]

This letter from Shamil was only sent to Serasker Hasan Rıza Pasha on 5 May 1854 by the new commander of the Anatolian army Mustafa Zarif Pasha, a protégé of the *serasker*.[136] Probably it was lost somewhere and found by chance. The *serasker* sent the letter to the grand vizier on 3 July 1854 and finally it was submitted to the sultan on 9 July 1854. This delay in correspondence is interesting in itself, but we do not know what caused it. What is more interesting is the fact that the commander of the Anatolian army, the *serasker* and the grand vizier all wrote in their letters as though there were no unusual delays and they do not offer any explanations. This may also be a result of their indifference to Shamil and to the Caucasus in general.

---

[133] Yamauchi, op. cit., pp. 146–148. However, Yamauchi gives the date of the letter of governor of Trabzon as 27 Muharrem (30 October). Either this date is wrong or Sefer Bey had already sent his agent before his official appointment. Also see Mustafa Budak, "1853–1856 Kırım Savaşı'nda Osmanlı Devleti ile Şeyh Şamil Arasındaki İlişkiler", *Tarih Boyunca Balkanlardan Kafkaslara Türk Dünyası Semineri, 29-31 Mayıs 1995. Bildiriler*, Istanbul: İ. Ü. Edebiyat Fakültesi Basımevi, 1996, p. 90.

[134] Budak writes (op. cit., 1988, p. 56) that the Russians had besieged these fortresses, as if they would besiege their own fortresses! This mistake is repeated in his PhD thesis (op. cit., 1993) and in his symposium paper/article, published eight years later (op. cit., 1996, p. 85).

[135] The Imam of Dagestan, El Gazi Shamuil to Abdi Pasha, commander of the Anatolian army, 13 December 1853. BOA. İ. DH. 19277 enc. 3.

[136] Budak writes that it was sent by Abdi Pasha (op. cit., 1988, p. 56). However, at that time Abdi Pasha and his successor Ahmed Pasha had already been dismissed and Mustafa Zarif Pasha had become the new commander. See BOA. İ. DH. 19277 enc. 2, Zarif Pasha to the *serasker*, 5 May 1854.

The Battle of Şekvetil

Selim Pasha, the *müşir* of the *Hassa* army (the imperial guards in Istanbul) and also the newly appointed commander of the Ottoman army in Batum, made a plan to capture the Russian fortress of Şekvetil located north of Batum. This small fortress was defended only by a small Russian garrison.[137] Selim Pasha's superior forces, three or five battalions including the *başıbozuks*, commanded by Hasan and Ali Beys and Dede Ağa, natives of Çürüksu, captured the post after a pitched battle on 25 October 1853.[138] According to Selim Pasha, more than one thousand Cossack cavalrymen were killed and 80 men were taken prisoner in this battle.[139] Ottoman losses were 32 dead and 59 wounded. It seems that Selim Pasha has rather exaggerated the number of the Russian dead in his letter to Ali Rıza Pasha in Ardahan. If we accept that, only two Russian cavalry companies and two or three guns were there, then their number cannot be more than one thousand. Prince Menshikov in his report to the tsar stated that the *başıbozuks* had committed grave atrocities, killing and torturing civilians, women and children.[140] These başıbozuks and even some of the regular men and officers also took many boys and girls into slavery from the neighbouring Georgian villages. It was also alleged that even Selim Pasha did not consider it beneath his dignity to retain some of these slaves for himself, probably as bribes to be sent to Istanbul.[141]

These acts naturally turned the Georgian population against the Porte, including even those Muslim Georgians who were at first well disposed. In February 1854, Lord Stratford reported to Lord Claren-

---

[137] General Hikmer Süer (op. cit., p. 72) writes that Şekvetil was defended by a Russian force of two battalions of infantry, three companies of Cossack cavalry and one artillery battery. Tarle (op. cit., vol. I, p. 294) on the other hand, argues that the Russian forces consisted only of two incomplete companies and two guns. Allen and Muratoff (op. cit., 1999, p. 60, footnote 2) also write that the fort was held by two companies of infantry.

[138] This Ali Bey must be a Georgian Christian apostate. Georgian Soviet historian Yermolay Burchuladze calls him "Ali Bey Kobuletskiy (Tavdgiridze)". See Burchuladze, "Krushenie Anglo-Turetskikh Zakhvatnicheskikh Planov v Gruzii v 1855–1856 godakh", *Voprosy Istorii* 4, Moscow, 1952, p. 14.

[139] Müşir Selim Pasha to Ferik Ali Rıza Pasha in Ardahan, 27 October 1853 and the *kaimmakam* of Çıldır to the grand vizier, 4 November 1853. BOA. HR. SYS. 1345/53. Reply of the grand vizier at BOA. A. MKT. UM. 1963/63. Tarle gives the date of the battle as 28 October.

[140] Yevgeny Tarle, op. cit., vol. 1, p. 294.

[141] General George Klapka, op. cit., p. 50.

don that the "desultory forces" (the irregulars) "have made the Turkish name odious among the Georgians, who at first gave a cordial welcome to the Sultan's troops."[142] Ferhad Pasha (General Stein) wrote in June 1854 that the Georgians hated Circassians for their pillaging, the Ottomans for the behaviour of their *başıbozuks* and the British for their treatment of the Circassians as their reserve forces. Instead he recommended that French troops join the Batum army.[143] When Selim Pasha summoned all the Georgian notables to submit to Ottoman power, only one of them came to his headquarters. This was Demetrius, who stated the true feelings of the Georgians. Selim Pasha however, charged him with treachery and had him put to death. When the Porte, around one year later, urged by the allies, tried to regain the sympathy of the Georgians by returning the enslaved boys and girls, it was too late. The Georgians had become staunch allies of Russia. We will dwell more on the Black Sea slave trade in Chapter 5. We must record here the fact that this issue has not been dealt with in the Turkish or other histories of the Crimean War.

After the capture of Şekvetil by the Ottomans, the Russian forces in Ozurgeti tried to recapture it but they were defeated and forced back. Meanwhile Selim Pasha reinforced the fortress with the Tunisian contingent, consisting of 7,000 infantry, 2,000 cavalry and 1,000 artillery men.[144] The marshy coast of Batum and Çürüksu was fertile ground for many diseases and Salih Hayri writes that 4,200 Tunisian troops had died of disease in Batum.

The Russians again attacked the fortress from the sea using four frigates on 18 November, but this attack was also repulsed, as were other attempts by the Russians. Thus the fortress became a formidable stronghold and remained in the hands of the Batum army until the end of the war. The Ottomans could not make any efficient use of it to reach out to the Circassians. The Russians for their part started to evacuate the whole coast line from Şekvetil to Anapa.

---

[142] Stratford to Clarendon, 3 February 1854. AGKK III/2, pp. 195–196.
[143] Hamiyet Sezer, "Ferhat Paşa'nın Kırım Savaşı Sırasında Kafkas Cephesindeki Osmanlı Ordusuna Dair Düşünceleri", *Sekizinci Askeri Tarih Semineri Bildirileri*, I, Ankara: Genelkurmay Basımevi, 2003, p. 79. Sezer is unaware that this Ferhad Pasha was the Prussian general Maximilian Stein. Instead she uses the *Sicill-i Osmani* biography of another Ferhad Pasha, who was one of the slaves of Hüsrev Pasha.
[144] Slade, op. cit., p. 176. As we have seen, Kızıltoprak (op. cit., p. 49), writes that 7,000–8,000 troops came from Tunis. Salih Hayri (op. cit., p. 146) writes that Ahmed Pasha the govenor of Tunis sent three regiments.

The Battles of Ahısha, Bayındır and Başgedikler

After the capture of Şekvetil, the Ottoman forces in Kars and Ardahan decided to move toward Ahılkelek, Ahısha and Gümrü. Nevertheless, there was no harmony among the high officers and officials such as Müşir Abdi Pasha, the governor Zarif Pasha, Ferik Ahmed Pasha, Ferik Ali Rıza Pasha and the *müsteşar* (paymaster general) of the Anatolian army Rıza Efendi. From the accounts of Zarif Pasha's memoirs and other pashas' testimonies during their trials, it is understood that the *müsteşar efendi* was an influential figure; he interfered in military decisions and independently sent reports to the Porte regarding military affairs and containing his views on the pashas as well. While Abdi Pasha was cautious the others favoured an engagement with the Russians. Hurşid Pasha and other European officers had not yet come to serve in the staff of the Anatolian army by the autumn of 1853.

The Ottoman forces in Ardahan included 8 battalions of infantry, one regiment of cavalry, 12 cannons and the *başıbozuks* of Çıldır.[145] Captain Fevzi gives this force as 10,000 *redif* and 2,000 *nizamiyye* infantry with 13 cannons, one regiment of cavalry and about 6,000 *başıbozuks*.[146] There were two brigadier-generals under Ferik Ali Rıza Pasha: Mirliva Ali Pasha and Mirliva Mustafa Pasha. The fact that the majority of the forces in Ardahan were *redif* troops was to prove fatal for the Ottoman forces. Ferik Ali Rıza Pasha would later complain that he had asked Abdi Pasha for more *nizamiye* troops but he was not given such troops. To this accusation Abdi Pasha would reply that those *redif* troops were the best of the *redif* from Taşköprü and also that it was not possible to send more *nizamiye* troops to Ardahan because they were necessary elsewhere. Ali Rıza Pasha had also asked for an artillery major with war experience, but the *müşir* had not given him such an officer. To this complaint, Abdi Pasha replied that the military *meclis* in Erzurum had sent Captain Şakir Ağa, promoting him to major. All other officers were stationed elsewhere.[147]

---

[145] BOA. İ. MMS. 3/107 enc. 5.

[146] Kurtoğlu, op. cit., p. 100. Kurtoğlu calls the redif *"muavine askeri"* and gives the number of guns as 3. According to Ibragimbeyli (op. cit., p. 193) there were 8,000 infantry, 3,000 cavalry with 13 guns and 7,000 irregulars. Allen and Muratoff (op. cit., p. 61) write that there were about 18,000 men in Ardahan, half of whom were Laz and other irregular formations.

[147] Ali Rıza Pasha's statement at the military court in Istanbul. BOA. İ. MMS. 3/107 enc. 4.

The Ottoman forces defeated the small Russian forces around Ahılkelek and Ahısha, capturing many villages of the region from 5 November to 25 November.[148] The governor of Erzurum Zarif Pasha, who had come to Kars from Erzurum with 2,000 *başıbozuks*, went to Ardahan together with these irregulars to encourage the troops and organize provisions.[149] According to Abdi Pasha, Zarif Pasha and Müsteşar Rıza Efendi had urged the high ranking officers in Kars to attack the Russians. However, Abdi Pasha thought that winter had come and the war season was over, therefore no offensive operations could be made. Furthermore, the aim was to join forces with Sheikh Shamil and at this season this was impossible. Abdi Pasha also stressed in his statement to the military court that since he had received military education, he based all his actions on the "military sciences of strategy and tactics". Thereby he implied that his chief of staff Ahmed Pasha did not possess such education, mentioning at the same time Ahmed Pasha was illiterate.

The newly appointed *müsteşar* Rıza Efendi had interfered in military matters by giving instructions to Ferik Abdülkerim or Kerim Pasha (?–1863), whom he met in Yeniköy (between Kars and Erzurum) while he was travelling to Kars. Rıza Efendi had asked Ferik Kerim Pasha not to go to Erzurum but to wait in Yeniköy because Rıza Efendi would have him summoned back to Kars. Arriving at Kars, the *müsteşar* started urging the officers for action, arguing that there had been successive victories in Rumeli and the Anatolian army was lagging behind. Abdi Pasha stressed that although the *müsteşar* was kind, honest and hardworking, he was like a foolish friend in military questions because he was unversed in military science and therefore the *müsteşar* interpreted Abdi Pasha's caution as cowardice. According to Ahmed Pasha, Zarif Pasha had reprimanded him (Ahmed Pasha) in front of other officers for not going to war, to which Ahmed Pasha answered that he had his superior commander, meaning the commander Abdi Pasha. Rıza Efendi had even told Abdi Pasha that if Abdi Pasha did not move against the enemy, he would summon the population using town criers and go himself. Upon this declaration Abdi Pasha asked the *müsteşar*: "If things go bad, will your word save me?" Rıza Efendi replied yes,

---

[148] Budak, op. cit. (1993), pp. 51–53.
[149] Zarif Pasha's memoirs, see Karal, op. cit. (1940), pp. 477–478. Cf. Budak, op. cit. (1993), p. 53.

but Abdi Pasha was not satisfied. Abdi Pasha added that even those officers who thought that the war season was over could not say so openly for fear of being considered cowards. Later during the interrogation of the pashas in Istanbul by a military commission at the war ministry, Abdi Pasha complained that Rıza Efendi had "changed the minds of everybody" in favour of battle, while it became apparent from a letter of Rıza Efendi dated 27 November 1853 that Rıza Efendi had charged Abdi Pasha with "laxity and hesitancy".[150] Finally the warlike attitude affected the rank and file as well and Abdi Pasha was forced to take some action. Meanwhile the weather also improved a bit and Abdi Pasha decided to engage in what he called *petit guerre*, using the original French term.[151]

Ferik Veli Pasha was posted as *avant garde* in the Subatan village to the east of Kars with 5 battalions of infantry, one regiment of cavalry and a sufficient number of irregular cavalry. Abdi Pasha sent his chief of staff Ferik Ahmed Pasha with 6 battalions of infantry, one regiment of cavalry and the remaining *asakir-i muvazzafa* together with the forces under Veli Pasha to Baş Şüregel (15 km from Gümrü), which was opposite the Bayındır (Bayandur) village (10 km from Gümrü). Mirliva Mustafa Pasha from the Arabistan army was sent to Baş Şüregel with 4 infantry battalions, 5 cavalry squadrons and 4 guns. *Başıbozuk* troops stationed in the villages of the *kaza*s of Şüregel and Zarşat were also ordered to come to Baş Şüregel. According to Abdi Pasha, Ahmed Pasha's task was to deploy the regular troops behind the hill there and to drive away the Russian irregular cavalry in Bayındır with his own irregular cavalry. Ahmed Pasha was allegedly instructed not to cross the river Arpaçay that formed the border with Russia. However, Ahmed Pasha stated that the instructions given him did not mention the hill or the ban on crossing the Arpaçay. According to him, Abdi Pasha had just instructed him to go to fight in order to silence the population clamouring for war.

Thus Ahmed Pasha came to Bayındır on 13 November and easily captured the village, driving away the Russian Karapapak irregular cavalry (more than 2,000 men) under the command of Taştimur.[152] Although

---

[150] BOA. İ. MMS. 3/107 enc. 6.

[151] Abdi Pasha's statement and answers to questions together with Ahmed Pasha and Ali Rıza Pasha. BOA. İ. MMS. 3/107 enc. 5.

[152] Ahmed Pasha's statement, BOA. İ. MMS. 3/107 enc. 2. Budak (op. cit., 1993, pp. 56–57) has named this skirmish as the "Battle of Bayındır", and the battle next day as

Ahmed Pasha also stated that his *başıbozuks* chased the enemy as far as Gümrü and also defeated a Russian cavalry regiment there and forced them to enter the fortress of Gümrü, this seems doubtful. In the opinion of Abdi Pasha, removing a small Russian unit had emboldened Ahmed Pasha. Some 1,000 *başıbozuks* under the command of Meded Bey the *müdir* of the *kaza* of Şüregel were sent to the Russian village of Tuhaber (or Tukaber?) where some 300 Cossack cavalry were reported. These *başıbozuks* later returned with 20 prisoners.

Meanwhile the Russian Armenian commander in Gümrü, General-Lieutenant Prince Vasiliy Osipovich Bebutov (1791–1858) had sent a force of 7 battalions of infantry, 4 squadrons[153] of cavalry with 28 guns and more than 1,000 Muslim Azerbaijani (or Karapapak) irregular cavalry under the command of General-Major Prince Iliko (Ilya) Orbeliani towards Bayındır on reconnaissance and for the protection of Armenian villages from the Kurds and other *başıbozuks*.[154] Ahmed Pasha, however, argued that the enemy had 10 battalions of infantry, 2 regiments of cavalry with 40 guns and more than 2,000 Karapapak irregular cavalry on the battle field.[155] Orbeliani's forces were met by surprising fire from the Ottoman guns deployed on the heights of the village of Bayındır (Bayandur) on 14 November 1853.[156] Orbeliani had fallen into a dangerous position: He could neither attack the strong Ottoman positions nor retreat without risk of being attacked by the Ottoman cavalry and the *başıbozuks*. Orbeliani lost about 1,000 men but Ahmed Pasha did not take any further initiative. Ottoman losses included 23 dead, 47 wounded among the regular troops and an approximately equal number from the *başıbozuks*, according to Ahmed Pasha.

---

the "Battle of Gümrü". However, I agree with those Russian historians who accept only the second as the Battle of Bayındır.

[153] Usually 6 squadrons make up a cavalry regiment.

[154] Zayonchkovskiy, op. cit., vol. II, part I, p. 390. Ibragimbeyli (op. cit., p. 112) does not mention Orbeliani's guns and the 4 squadrons.

[155] Ahmed Pasha's statement, BOA. İ. MMS. 3/107 enc. 2.

[156] The *serasker* to the grand vizier. BOA. İ. DH. 285/17910, 1 December 1853. Arif Efendi, *1270 Rus Seferi*, manuscript, pp. 16–17. The *Takvim-i Vekayi* of 7 Rebiyülevvel 1270 (8 December 1853) and other Ottoman sources also give the date of the battle as Monday, 13 Safer 1270, which might correspond to 14 or 15 November 1853. Since it is a Monday, it must be 14 November. However, many modern Turkish historians have mistaken this date for 15 November. See, for example, Budak, op. cit. (1993), p. 57. Hikmet Süer (op. cit., p. 78) also gives the date as 13 Safer 1270 but converts it even farther into 16 November. Also see Zayonchkovskiy, ibid. Tarle, op. cit., vol. I, p. 295.

Towards evening Prince Bebutov came to help Orbeliani from Gümrü with the remains of the Russian army there (3 battalions of infantry, 6 squadrons of dragoons and 12 guns).[157] Abdi Pasha had also come as far as Baş Şüregel with 6 battalions of infantry, one regiment of cavalry and 12 guns to help Ahmed Pasha. Although Abdi Pasha argues that his forces went into battle, it is not certain to what extent they participated. Ahmed Pasha argues that Abdi Pasha did not immediately send help to him and did not encourage the troops by appearing on the battlefield. Both sides retreated after sunset. In any case, the Ottoman army (as usual) did not follow up its gains against the defeated enemy, being content with the initial success of the artillery only. In fact artillery was the only efficient Ottoman class of arms. W. E. D. Allen and Paul Muratoff justly observe that

> Bebutov had been lucky in extricating the ineffectual Orbeliani from a very dangerous situation, and Abdi Pasha had missed the opportunity of destroying the principal Russian field force in Transcaucasia at one blow in the first week of the campaign. Never was the inadequacy of the Turkish high command at this period more dramatically demonstrated.[158]

Prince Vorontsov reported the battle of Bayındır as a victory to Nikolai I and the Russian emperor even conferred the Order of Stanislav First Class upon General Orbeliani.[159]

After the battle, Abdi Pasha did not retreat because he feared that the Russians, as a "technically well-informed enemy", might guess that his army had run out of ammunition and follow him up. Therefore he waited in Bayındır for 12 days building fortifications and he asked for ammunition from Kars. Meanwhile one battalion and two guns came from Subatan, three battalions of *redif* and one battalion of *nizamiye* under the command of Mirliva Hafız Pasha also joined the forces in Bayındır. On 21 November the *şeşhane* battalion of the Hassa army came to Bayındır. Thus according to Ahmed Pasha, their forces in Bayındır reached 22 infantry battalions, two and a half regiments of cavalry, 800 artillery men with 38 guns and more than 3,000 irregular cavalry. Abdi Pasha also states that the Ottoman army in Bayındır (including his forces) consisted of 22 or 23 infantry battalions, 3 cavalry

---

[157] Zayonchkovskiy, op. cit., vol. II, part I, p. 390–391. Ibragimbeyli, op. cit., p. 114.
[158] Allen and Muratoff, op. cit., p. 63.
[159] Ibragimbeyli, op. cit., p. 115.

regiments and more than 30 guns.[160] During the 12 days in Bayındır, Ahmed Pasha urged Abdi Pasha concerning three different options of actions against the Russians in Gümrü or Ahısha, but Abdi Pasha did not accept any of them. Abdi Pasha accepts this and even adds that more than three variants were discussed but that in the end none of them seemed useful.[161]

Since the Russian army did not appear during these twelve days, Abdi Pasha decided to retreat towards Kars because in his opinion he did not have enough troops, provisions, ammunition and means of transport for an offensive. He moved to the village of Başgedikler on 25 November while Veli Pasha with his forces was posted again to the village of Subatan as *avant garde*.[162]

Meanwhile the Ottoman forces were experiencing minor victories against small Russian forces near Ahısha and Ahılkelek and took positions in the villages near Ahısha. Miralay (Colonel) Hasan Bey was sent as *avant garde* with two squadrons of regular cavalry and about 2,000 irregular cavalry (*asakir-i muvazzafa*). These *başıbozuks* had taken some prisoners and decapitated five to ten persons. Ali Rıza Pasha states that since the orders not to cut off heads and ears had not yet reached them, he sent the decapitated heads and ears together with the prisoners of war to the müşir.[163] While Ali Rıza Pasha does not state whether he rewarded these *başıbozuks* for the heads and ears brought to him, most probably he did so, because this was the custom.

Since Ali Rıza Pasha did not have siege artillery to attack the fortress of Ahıska, he asked for two battalions of infantry and some guns from Abdi Pasha but Abdi Pasha sent them very late. On 26 November 1853 the Russian forces of the Ahısha fortress received a reinforcement of 5 battalions of infantry, one squadron of cavalry and 7 guns from the 13th division in Ozurgeti under the command of Lieutenant-General Prince Ivan Malkhazovich Andronikov or Ivane Andronikashvili (1798–1868).[164] General Andronikov attacked the forces of Mirliva Ali

---

[160] Abdi Pasha, ibid. Zayonchkovskiy (op. cit., vol. II, part I, p. 391) and Ibragim-beyli (op. cit., p. 113) describe the strength of the Ottoman army in Bayındır as 30,000 men with 40 guns. However, after a few pages (p. 115) Ibragimbeyli gives this number as 40,000 men. This must be a typing mistake.

[161] Ahmed Pasha's statement. BOA. İ. MMS. 3/107 enc. 2.

[162] Abdi Pasha's statement. BOA. İ. MMS. 3/107 enc. 5.

[163] Ali Rıza Pasha's testimony at the MVL in Istanbul. BOA. İ. MMS. 3/107 enc. 4.

[164] Ibragimbeyli (op. cit., p. 195) wrote (like some other Soviet sources) that General Andronikashvili was an ethnic Georgian. An article in the *Times*, however, reports

Pasha around the village of Suflis with a force of 7 and a half battalions of infantry with 14 guns, 9 Cossack squadrons and about 2,000 Georgian and Ossetian irregular cavalry early in the morning on 27 November 1853.[165] Mirliva Mustafa Pasha commanded the Ottoman right wing in the village of Ab (or Abashi) including 3 infantry battalions with 5 guns and more than 1,000 *başıbozuks* and Mirliva Ali Pasha commanded the left wing in Suflis, consisting of 3 infantry battalions with 7 guns and one cavalry regiment. Two infantry battalions and about 2,000 *başıbozuks* were deployed in neighbouring villages around Suflis at a distance of a quarter of an hour. Ferik Ali Rıza Pasha remained behind in the village of Bamık (Yemak?) somewhere in the middle at the distance of one quarter hour. This traditional scattered deployment of troops contributed to the Ottoman defeat in this battle. The distance of a quarter of an hour among these villages seems to be an understatement even without any knowledge of the territory, because Ali Rıza Pasha tries to justify his deployment of troops and argues that they were not dispersed. In fact, the military *meclis* in Erzurum in reply to Inspector Hayreddin Pasha's questions stated this distance as half an hour to three quarters.[166] Furthermore, during his trial together with Ahmed Pasha, Zarif Pasha and Ali Rıza Pasha at the MVL and the DŞA, Müşir Abdi Pasha also stated that Ali Rıza Pasha had dispersed his forces in villages contrary to the rules of warfare.[167] Abdi Pasha added that although Ali Rıza Pasha acted against his orders and against the warnings of Zarif Pasha, he (Abdi Pasha) could not have foreseen such a disaster because according to his intelligence the Russians had only 5 battalions there, while Ali Rıza Pasha had 8 battalions of infantry, one regiment of cavalry and the irregular cavalry of Çıldır and those with Zarif Pasha, so that his available forces far exceeded those available to the Russians. To this comment Ali Rıza Pasha replied that although his forces were distributed among villages

---

that the Greeks took pride in his being a Greek from Odessa, "who has changed the final "kos" of his name into "koff". See *The Times*, London, 19 August 1854, Issue 21824, p. 8. The Crimean Armenian historian V. E. Grigoryants, on the other hand, argues that Andronikov was of Armenian origins from a princely family at the court of the last Georgian king. See Grigoryants, "Vostochnaya (Krymskaya) voina i armyane", *Istoricheskoe Nasledie Kryma* 6–7, Simferopol, 2004, p. 136.

[165] Ali Rıza Pasha, ibid. Ibragimbeyli, op. cit., p. 195. Ibragimbeyli gives the date of the battle as 14 November, which corresponds to 26 November according to the Western calendar.

[166] BOA. İ. MMS. 3/107 enc. 3, page 3.

[167] Abdi Pasha's statement. BOA. İ. MMS. 3/107 enc. 5.

they all came together when the battle began. He also argued that he made all his moves with the approval of Abdi Pasha and he did not receive any help from Zarif Pasha.

According to Ali Rıza Pasha's own statement, the Ottoman forces on the battlefield included 6 battalions of infantry and one regiment of cavalry with 7 guns. In addition, 2 battalions of infantry and 5 guns remained on the reserve. The cannonade of the two sides lasted for four hours.[168] Then they attacked each other. While the Russians shouted *"Ura!"* the Ottomans shouted *"Padişahım çok yaşa!"* (Long live the Padishah!). The *redif* battalions and the *başıbozuks* in the army of Ali Rıza Pasha could not resist the massive attack of the Russian regular troops and only the Ottoman artillery fought to the end. Ali Rıza Pasha also stated that he saw some of the *redif* troops from Harput retreating. He ordered their retreat to be prevented, but the officers were unable to stop it. Then he ordered to beat the signal to rally. Nevertheless, the officers were again unable to gather the troops. He shouted at those *redif* soldiers a hundred steps away from him fleeing towards a mountain: "You have read the law. Why are you fleeing? Come back!". However, the soldiers did not listen to him. Ali Rıza Pasha shouted at the *başıbozuks* as well: "You have come voluntarily and why do you flee now? You have also affected the (regular) troops, I will shoot you!". He then fired a shot towards them and said: "If you do not return, I will let the artillery fire on you". However, the *başıbozuks* did not listen to him either. Then he was informed that Mirliva Ali Pasha was wounded. Ali Rıza Pasha took Ali Pasha to the village of Bamık (Yemak?) in order to conceal him from the view of the troops and then returned to the battlefield.

However, by this statement alone, Ali Rıza Pasha puts himself under suspicion: Why should he himself go with the wounded Ali Pasha and leave the troops without command at the most crucial moment of the battle? However, no such questions (which seem obvious) are recorded in the interrogations. Ali Rıza Pasha then states that he rejects the accusations from Hurşid Pasha that he fled at the beginning of the battle. However, there are other sources that do accuse Ali Rıza Pasha of fleeing the battlefield.

According to a report from the French consulate in Erzurum to the French embassy in Istanbul, Ferik Ali Rıza Pasha had retreated from

---

[168] Ali Rıza Pasha's testimony, ibid.

the battle on 27 November with five battalions, instead of coming to the assistance of Hüseyin Bey who commanded three battalions of regular infantry and the *başıbozuk*. The French consul stated that Ali Rıza Pasha not only gave the order to retreat but he himself deserted, leaving the troops alone. When it was heard that the commander had gone, the soldiers retreated in panic and disorder.[169] The French consul added that although Mirliva Veli Pasha had fought bravely and tried to resist, he had been unable to control the troops and he was also forced to retreat. However, he seems to have confused the battle of Başgedikler with the battle of Ahısha, because Veli Pasha was in Kars. The report also stated that the Ottoman troops had abandoned not only 14 guns, but also all provisions and other supplies in order to run away as fast as possible. Consequently, it was stated that the Russian force, consisting of 6 battalions of infantry and one regiment of cavalry, had completely routed the Ottoman army corps of 15,000 men (regular and irregular together) within two hours. Ardahan and its villages were now left to the mercy of the enemy.

Furthermore, the report described another of Ferik Ali Pasha's deeds. He had sent his servants together with the treasury of the army to the village of Badele and joined them two hours before the defeat of the Ottoman troops. Some soldiers came to the said village and when he asked them why they had come, they answered that they hastened together with other troops to catch up with their ferik. Upon this answer, Ferik Ali Pasha took out his pistols and fired at them, killing two and severely wounding five of them. In another village near Badele, a *müdir* of a *kaza* came up to him and asked him to take measures to protect the Ottoman villages on the border from the Russians. Ali Pasha however answered that this was not possible and he should go to the army headquarters. The *müdir* then said that it was not appropriate to abandon one's religious brethren in Islam. This answer angered the pasha, who again took out his pistol and shot the *müdir* in the chest. The report then stated that Zarif Pasha had come to Erzurum on the date of the report with about 2,000 troops that he could collect in Ardahan. The sadness of the soldiers affected the people of Erzurum

---

[169] Translation of a report from the French consulate in Erzurum to the French embassy in Istanbul, dated 10 Kanun-ı Evvel 1853 (10 December? ▪▪1853), forwarded to the Ottoman foreign ministry on 30 December 1853. BOA. HR. SYS. 1190/32 enc. 14.

as well. The report also covered the battle of Başgedikler which we will consider below.

In any case, the defeat of the Ottoman forces was so decisive that the event was called the "Ahıska rout" (*Ahısha bozgunu*).[170] Ottoman losses included 1,500 dead, 2,000 wounded and 120 prisoners with 11 guns and ammunition, while the Russians lost one officer and 51 men dead, 311 wounded.[171]

The anonymous military analyst of the *NYDT* (Friedrich Engels), wrote the following on the Russian victory in Ahısha in the same article where he discussed the battle of Sinop:

> The Russians declare that with about 10,000 men they have routed 18,000 Turks. Of course we cannot rely upon such statements, but must confess that the great number of irregulars in the Turkish Anatolian army and the almost total absence of European officers, particularly in the higher commands and on the staff, must make them but a poor match for an equal number of Russians... [The Russians] confess they have made only 120 prisoners. This amounts to a confession that they have massacred almost all the wounded on the field of battle, they being necessarily left in their hands. Besides, they prove that their measures for pursuit and intercepting the retreat of at least part of the enemy, must have been wretchedly planned. They had plenty of cavalry; a bold charge in the midst of the fugitives would have cut off whole battalions...[172]

Khadji Murat Ibragimbeyli refers to the same article of Engels, but he quotes only the last two sentences from the passage above. Although he is very critical of the tsarist policies in general and particularly in the Caucasus, he does not quote from Engels that which is not good for the reputation of the Russian army. This is a rather typical attitude among Soviet historians after Pokrovskiy. We may assume that if the Russians massacred the wounded Ottoman soldiers, most likely it was the work of the Georgian *başıbozuks*, the militia or the *druzhina*, who must have been particularly enraged by the acts of the Ottoman *başıbozuks* in Şekvetil and their kidnapping of Georgian children into slavery from Georgian villages. As Ibragimbeyli tells us, there were

---

[170] Kırzıoğlu, op. cit., p. 70.
[171] Ibragimbeyli, op. cit., p. 196. Allen and Muratoff (op. cit., 1999, p. 62) give similar numbers. Mustafa Budak, who had access to the ATASE, also refers to Allen and Muratoff on this question in his PhD dissertation (p. 55). There are references to some detailed tables of Ottoman losses in the evidences of Abdi, Ahmed and Ali Rıza Pashas, however, I could not find these tables in the BOA.
[172] Engels, article cited above. See also Marx, op. cit., p. 199.

about 2,000 sabres of Georgian and Ossetian cavalry *druzhina* and 900 Cossacks in the army of General Andronikashvili.[173]

At Bayındır, towards the end of November, Abdi Pasha heard that the Russians were coming. He sent Miralay İsmail Bey for reconnaissance and that colonel brought the information that a Russian army of 12 battalions of infantry, 2 regiments of cavalry and some irregular troops had passed the Arpaçay and was coming closer. Abdi Pasha then states that the advent of Russians in such a composition was a rare opportunity for them and he took preparations to meet them. Veli Pasha and Kerim Pasha's forces were also summoned. However, the Russian forces did not appear. Meanwhile on 29 November, Abdi Pasha received the news of the defeat of Ali Rıza Pasha in Ahıska. He had also heard that Rıza Efendi had written to the Porte citing Abdi Pasha's retreat from Bayındır as a cause of the disaster in Ahıska. According to Ahmed Pasha, Abdi Pasha told him:

> We left Bayındır on Friday [25 November] and the defeat of Ahısha is reported to happen on Saturday. How could it be possible that the Russians in Ahısha learnt so quickly of our departure from Bayındır that the defeat might be attributed to it?[174] [My translation]

At this point Abdi Pasha argues that Ahmed Pasha urged him to go to Kars because he was needed there and also assured him that he (Ahmed Pasha) would inform him immediately if anything happened. Abdi Pasha consequently asserts that he went to Kars, instructing Ahmed Pasha to bring the army to Subatan in a few days after him. Ahmed Pasha, on the contrary, argues that he told Abdi Pasha that the enemy was there, had remained in its position and that Abdi Pasha should not leave the army. Ahmed Pasha then produces some letters from *başıbozuk* commanders (*sergerdes*) about the presence of the Russian army in the vicinity as well as a letter from Abdi Pasha sent on Tuesday instructing him to wait until Thursday. Abdi Pasha does not answer these arguments and it seems that Ahmed Pasha was correct on this point. In any case, Abdi Pasha decided to go to Kars. In his statement he also asserts that he had instructed Ahmed Pasha to send him news four times a day under normal circumstances and immediately in the case of a noteworthy event. According to Abdi Pasha, Ahmed Pasha did not send him news when the Russians were seen coming,

---

[173] Ibragimbeyli, op. cit., p. 197.
[174] BOA. İ. MMS. 3/107 enc. 5.

because Ahmed Pasha wanted to prove his worthiness by gaining a victory under his own command.

As we saw above, the Ottoman army corps at Başgedikler and around it included 22 infantry battalions, two and a half cavalry regiments, 800 artillerists with 38 guns and more than 3,000 irregular cavalry in neighbouring villages.[175] However, not all of these troops and guns were actually used in the battle, because some of them were in the neighbouring villages. Most of the *başıbozuk*s had fled towards Kars before the battle even started. Ahmed Pasha detached 3 infantry battalions with 6 guns under the command of Mirliva Hafız Pasha as reserve troops. Then he detached 5 infantry battalions (including 2 companies of chasseurs), one regiment of cavalry, 6 guns and 500 irregular cavalry under the command of Veli Pasha to the neighbouring village on the left to protect his flank. Five battalions (including 6 companies of chasseurs) out of the remaining 13 battalions, together with one regiment of cavalry with 8 guns and the irregular cavalry of Hasan Yazıcı, were detached on his right flank under the command of Mirliva Hüseyin Pasha. Finally, 5 battalions (including 6 companies of chasseurs) with 8 guns, commanded by Mirliva Mustafa Pasha, were deployed somewhat to the right of centre. Alltogether there were 32 guns on the battle field. Ahmed Pasha also states that because staff officers had gone to Kars, he could not receive help from them and so deployed the guns in a hurry. In response, Abdi Pasha observed that in any case there was only one staff officer in the army who was qualified to deal with this (Faik Bey) and he did not know where Faik Bey was at that time. Ahmed Pasha in turn replied that Faik Bey had gone to Kars.

In any case, however, the Ottoman army exceeded the Russian army in numbers, even though Abdi Pasha would later argue that he had only 17,000–18,000 troops, regular and irregular, when he was asked why he did not send two battalions and some guns to Ali Rıza Pasha in

---

[175] Allen and Muratoff (op. cit., p. 63) give the total number as 36,000 men, including 20,000 regular infantry and one brigade of cavalry, the rest being "başıbozuks and Kurds of doubtful value". Cf. Budak, op. cit. (1993), p. 58. General Bebutov reported after the battle to Prince Vorontsov that the Ottoman forces included 20,000 infantry, 4,000 regular cavalry with 42–46 guns and more than 12,000 Kurdish and other "militia". See Tarle, op. cit., vol. I, p. 297. Ibragimbeyli (op. cit., p. 198) cites 27 battalions of regular infantry. Averyanov (op. cit., 1900, pp. 87–88; op. cit., 1995, p. 52) mentions 20,000 regular infantry, 3,000 regular cavalry with 46 guns and 14,000 irregulars, including 4,000 Kurds.

Ardahan.¹⁷⁶ The irregulars were the *başıbozuks* under the command of Hasan Yazıcı of Damascus and the nomadic Kurds under the command of their tribal chiefs, who were more interested in pillaging Armenian villages than in the war. The number of these *başıbozuks* seems to have been exaggerated by Russian sources. Ahmed Pasha states that when he asked Hasan Yazıcı how many cavalry he had, Hasan Yazıcı answered he had 2,000 men. Upon a close view of them, however, Ahmed Pasha found out that there were only about 800 horsemen, of which more than half were youngsters and riff raff.¹⁷⁷ It is certain that these *sergerdes* as well as the pashas were engaged in muster roll fraud, receiving pay and rations for more troops than were actually employed. We will see more on this matter.

On the Russian side, upon the news of the success of Andronikov, Bebutov decided to attack the Ottoman army, even though his force consisted only of 10 and a half battalions of infantry (7,000 bayonets), 10 squadrons of cavalry and 15 irregular cavalry hundreds (*sotnya*) (together 2,800 sabres) together with 32 guns.¹⁷⁸ Ahmed Pasha, however, during his trial in Istanbul, gave much exaggerated figures for the Russian army at Başgedikler: 24 battalions of infantry, 6 regiments of cavalry, about 3,000 irregular cavalry and 60 guns. Of these, he further argued, 6 battalions had remained in the rear near their wagons, the rest having taken up a position in front of the Ottoman army, with one regiment of cavalry and 4 guns opposite Veli Pasha. Abdi Pasha on the other hand stated that he heard the Russians had 12 battalions.¹⁷⁹

On 1 December 1853, when the Russians advanced from Şüregel towards Başgedikler, Ahmed Pasha also decided to attack them, relying upon his numerical superiority, notwithstanding his later understatement of his forces and overstatement of Russian forces. The problem was that an open field battle requiring high manoeuvrability and tight coordination of infantry, cavalry and artillery was apparently beyond

---

¹⁷⁶ In the interrogation of Abdi Pasha, Ali Rıza Pasha and Ahmed Pasha, the *müsteşar* of the Anatolian army produces a document where the forces before Gümrü are described as more than 40,000 men including both regulars and irregulars. Abdi Pasha, however, argues that he had only 17,000 to 18,000 men and he even argues that the number of troops at that time around Gümrü can be found in the reports to the office of the *serasker*. Budak has used the ATASE archive extensively, but he does not mention any such reports or Abdi Pasha's claim. See BOA. İ. MMS. 3/107 enc. 6, 17 December 1854. Cf. Budak, ibid.
¹⁷⁷ BOA. İ. MMS. 3/107 enc. 2.
¹⁷⁸ Zayonchkovskiy, op. cit. (2002), vol. II, part I, p. 404. Tarle, op. cit., vol. I, p. 297.
¹⁷⁹ Ahmed Pasha's statement. BOA. İ. MMS. 3/107 enc. 2.

the competence of the Ottoman army. Furthermore, Ahmed Pasha did not have a battle plan, therefore the officers under his command did not receive any orders as to how to begin the battle, what to do and where to retreat if the enemy should prove stronger and retreat become necessary.[180] The military *meclis* in Erzurum also stated that Ahmed Pasha had hidden behind a rock during the battle and had not issued proper commands. Many soldiers were absent from the battalions, because they had been sent after barley, hay and tezek and for washing clothes. Thus even the 19 infantry battalions and 10 cavalry squadrons that actually participated in the battle were not complete and they were formed into one line without the second line and the reserve. Ahmed Pasha in fact confesses that he did not give specific instructions to his troops. He himself states that he had collected the pashas and told them: "Here is the enemy in front of you. It is high time to serve our religion and community. Let everybody act accordingly and take care of his own command!".[181] Ahmed Pasha did not accept the other charges and claimed that he found it harmful to announce beforehand where to retreat in case of defeat because this would have discouraged the troops.

In this battle the Ottoman army was routed and collapsed into a disorderly retreat towards Kars, with heavy losses. Ahmed Pasha reports that at one point there were no Ottoman officers on the field above the rank of captain. Hafız Pasha and his reserve battalions and guns also fled. The Ottomans lost 24 guns and a total of 6,000 (8,000?) men, of whom about 1,500 men including 8 officers were killed and the rest were wounded or taken prisoner. Russian losses amounted to about 1,300 men, including 9 officers killed.[182] General-Major Iliko Orbe-

---

[180] BOA. İ. MMS. 3/107 enc. 3, page 3, answers to question [13]. Budak briefly mentions this document, but does not quote from it. Cf. Budak, op. cit. (1993), p. 58. In fact, Budak has devoted, somewhat surprisingly, very meagre space (one and a half pages) to this battle, in comparison with his coverage of other less important battles.

[181] BOA. İ. MMS. 3/107 enc. 3, page 3, answers to question [13].

[182] Despite his research in the ATASE and the BOA, Budak (op. cit., 1993, p. 59) does not provide Ottoman figures for losses in this battle. Instead he quotes from John Curtiss. Thus he claims that Ottoman losses included 26 guns and 8,000 dead, while the Russian commander Bebutov reported Ottoman losses as 24 guns and more than 6,000 men. See Tarle, ibid. Although there is reference to certain detailed tables of losses in the interrogation of Abdi and Ahmed Pashas, I could not find them in the BOA. Zayonchkovskiy (op. cit., vol. II, part I, p. 414) gives total Ottoman losses as 8,000 men, including more than 1,500 dead in the field, including a certain Ibrahim Pasha, 2 regimental and 5 battalion commanders.

liani died of his wounds soon after the battle.[183] According to Ahmed Pasha, Ottoman losses included more than 500 dead, more than 700 wounded and 7 prisoners, while the Russians lost about 3,000 dead (of which 120 were officers from lieutenant to general), more than 4,000 wounded and 5 prisoners. Obviously these figures have nothing to do with reality: One can hardly believe that the Russians drove away the Ottoman army and captured 24 guns although they suffered about 6 times more losses! The Kurdish *başıbozuks* plundered the Ottoman headquarters during their retreat and dispersed to their homes. On the relations of Kurds with the Russians, more will be said in Chapter 5 on the revolt of Yezdanşêr. The *başıbozuks* of Hasan Yazıcı also did not participate in the battle.[184]

According to the French consul in Erzurum, wounded soldiers from the battle of Başgedikler who had been brought to Erzurum stated that there were about 1,200 wounded in the hospitals of Kars. It was also reported that the Russian army had captured 28 guns and 500 to 600 prisoners. It had occupied the villages between Kars and Arpaçay. The troops of the Anatolian army had been demoralized and they were deserting every day in groups. The consul added that Zarif Pasha had returned to Erzurum and asked him to request the French ambassador to help dismiss the current army commander and to find an able person for the job. Zarif Pasha even said that since it was difficult to save the Anatolian army without the help of the French, it was desirable that the French emperor appoint a general or at least a few high-ranking officers to the Anatolian army.[185]

On the day following the destruction of the Ottoman squadron at Sinop, the Ottoman army had now suffered a great defeat on land as well. These Russian victories more than compensated for early Ottoman victories on the Danubian and the Caucasian fronts. According to Russian military reports, the Ottoman army had shown some progress in comparison with previous wars, especially the artillery was worthy of praise. Artillery officers and soldiers did their duty very well. The infantry also showed signs of being well trained in movements but in

---

[183] Ibragimbeyli, op. cit. (1971), p. 200.
[184] Salih Hayri, op. cit., pp. 102–103. Salih Hayri gives the Ottoman losses in this battle as 1,200 dead and wounded with 24 guns and provisions. He blames Ahmed Pasha for the defeat. Ahmed Rıza Trabzoni (op. cit., pp. 59–60) also blames the commanders of the army.
[185] BOA. HR. SYS. 1190/32 enc. 14.

the open field it was not steady. The cavalry was the worst part of the Ottoman army.[186]

The news of Sinop, Ahısha and Başgedikler quickly changed the first impressions of the capabilities of the Ottoman army. Now France and Britain were definitely convinced that the Porte needed help, otherwise it would be defeated. The Russians had now gained the initiative in the Caucasian theatre of war. The Ottoman army had lost much confidence and had become demoralised. From this point on, desertions from the army in Kars increased. The *müşir* and his *feriks* accused each other. Ahmed Pasha was indeed in a difficult situation, because he had disobeyed his commanding officer and had been defeated. However, Ahmed Pasha had enough money to bribe the authorities in Istanbul. He sent his agents to Istanbul with a great deal of money and became the winner of this struggle.[187] Abdi Pasha was recalled to Istanbul and Ahmed Pasha took his place, with Ali Pasha as chief of staff. Meanwhile the commander of the Rumelian army Ömer Pasha proposed his chief of staff Ferik İsmail Pasha to be appointed as commander of the Anatolian army. He also suggested as chief of staff to the same army Ferhad Pasha (General Stein) who was residing in Aleppo.[188]

Ahmed Pasha's command was probably the worst that the Anatolian army had ever seen during this war. He was also probably the most corrupt and venal of the pashas at that post. Doctor Sandwith has the following to say of him:

> The fate of the miserable army under Ahmed Pasha is among the darkest records of war. His whole faculties were bent upon making money. He had in the first place to recover the sums he had already expended in bribes at Constantinople, and he had, besides, to make his fortune. I could not exaggerate the horrors the poor men suffered under his com-

---

[186] See Zayonchkovskiy, op. cit., vol. II, part I, p. 415. One year later, the British Vice-Consul in Trabzon would also report of the inferiority of the Ottoman cavalry in his report on the Battle of Kürekdere. See Vice-Consul Stevens to Lord Stratford de Redcliffe, Trebizond, August 12, 1854. PRMA, p. 6.

[187] Sandwith, op. cit., pp. 93–94. Mehmed Süreyya (op. cit., vol. 1, p. 202) in his biographic entry on Ahmed Pasha interestingly notes that he had become a *mirliva* (brigadier general) in a short time and also earned a lot of money in Tripolis (Libya) before 1846. He does not specify how he earned so much money, but in any case it must be certain that he was rich. Doctor Sandwith (op. cit., p. 93) also writes that Ahmed Pasha had formerly enriched himself by plunder in the Kurdish campaign. This is possible and probable, because Ahmed Pasha was appointed to the Anatolian army in 1846, at the time of the insurrection of the Kurdish Bedirhan Bey.

[188] Ömer Pasha to the *serasker*, Şumnu, 22 January 1854. BOA. HR. SYS. 904/1 enc. 58.

mand, for no chief can plunder without allowing a considerable license to his subordinates, so that the poor soldier was fleeced by every officer higher than the Major.[189]

Ahmed Pasha's intrigues and corruption are confirmed by Russian sources as well. Ibragimbeyli, referring to some documents in the Georgian archives, writes that Ahmed Pasha made intrigues against Abdi Pasha in Istanbul to receive the command and that he robbed the army to such an extent that it was ruined by misery, hunger and mass diseases.[190] The British consul in Erzurum James Brant also reported to Stratford de Redcliffe on Ahmed Pasha's rule. Stratford forwarded this report to Lord Clarendon, who in turn wrote a strong worded letter to Lord Stratford, intended for the consumption of Reşid Pasha. Clarendon made it clear that the "rapacity, ignorance and neglect of Ahmed Pasha" were not to be tolerated, adding that

> If the Turkish government has not the will or the the [sic] power to punish this man, and to make him refund the wealth which he has amassed by defrauding the soldiers, others will follow his criminal example, and the Allied Armies will look in vain for that support from the Turkish Troops that they have a right to expect while engaged in defending the Sultan's cause.[191]

Abdi Pasha's evidence in Istanbul also worked against Ahmed Pasha and, in February 1854, Ahmed Pasha was replaced in his post by Zarif Mustafa Pasha, the governor of Erzurum.[192] Zarif Pasha arrived at Kars to take over the command of the army on 6 March 1854.[193] Abdi Pasha and Ahmed Pasha's trials in Istanbul began only at the end of 1854 following pressure from Lord Stratford. Abdi Pasha was finally acquitted in 1855. Ahmed Pasha was found guilty and first exiled to Cyprus in 1855. However, like so many other Ottoman pashas, he was pardoned after conviction and a period of unemployment. Thus we see that in December 1859, he was made the *mutasarrıf* of Adana with the rank of *mirmiran*. His last office is recorded as governorship of Yemen from 1867 to 1869.[194]

---

[189] Sandwith, op. cit., p. 94.
[190] Ibragimbeyli, op. cit., p. 202.
[191] Clarendon to Statford de Redcliffe, 11 April 1854. BOA. HR. TO. 222/27.
[192] Karal, op. cit. (1940), p. 484.
[193] Hayreddin Pasha to the *serasker*, 8 March 1854. BOA. İ. DH. 298/18801 enc. 2.
[194] Mehmed Süreyya, op. cit., vol. 1, pp. 202–203. Kuneralp, op. cit., p. 60.

Karl Marx's article in the NYDT, published on 15 November 1853, had described the future prospects of the Anatolian army prophetically:

> A short time ago it might have been believed that the Turks, if weaker in Europe, enjoyed a decided superiority in Asia. Abdi Pasha, who commands the Asiatic army, was said to have collected 60,000 or 80,000, nay 120,000 men, and swarms of Bedouins, Kurds, and other warlike irregulars were reported to flock daily to his standard. Arms and ammunitions were said to be in store for the Caucasian insurgents; and as soon as war was declared, an advance was to be made into the very heart of these centres of resistance to Russia. It may, however, be as well to observe that Abdi Pasha cannot possibly have more than about 30,000 regular troops, and that before the Caucasus is reached, with these, and with these alone, he will have to encounter the stubborn resistance of Russian battalions. His Bedouins and Kurdish horsemen may be capital for mountain warfare, for forcing the Russians to detach largely and to weaken their main body; they may do a great deal of damage to the Georgian and Colonist villages in the Russian Territory, and even open some sort of an underhand communication with the Caucasian mountaineers. But unless Abdi Pasha's regulars are capable of blocking up the road from Batum to Erzurum, and can defeat whatever nucleus of an active army the Russians may be enabled to bring together, the success of the irregulars will be of a very ephemeral nature... In 1829 the Russian forces in Asia amounted, before Erzerum, to 18,000 men only, and considering the improve-ments that have since then taken place in the Turkish army (although that of Asia has least participated in them), we should say the Russians would have a fair chance of success if they could unite 30,000 men in a body before the same place now.[195]

Indeed the Russian army did take Kars again when its number reached this figure. By then the Ottoman army had fallen behind in numbers.

Thus the year 1853 ended on the Caucasian front with a Russian superiority. The Ottoman army had suffered a powerful blow to its self-confidence at the battles of Ahıska and Başgedikler. Disorganised and demoralised, its high command no longer thought of any attack or advance. The need for a remedy in the Anatolian army was obvious for the allies as well. The British embassy had been urging the Porte to send the Hungarian refugee general of British origin Richard Debaufre Guyon (1813–1856), who lived under his new Ottoman name Hurşid Pasha in Damascus. In fact, Hurşid Pasha himself had already applied to the Porte to serve in the Rumelian or Anatolian army even before

---

[195] "The Holy War", NYDT, Leader, November 15, 1853. See Karl Marx, op. cit., pp. 155–156.

the declaration of war and he was ordered to go to Erzurum soon after the declaration of war.[196] (As was said before, the Porte did not want to send Hungarian refugee officers to the Danubian front due to Austrian pressure.) The order of appointment of Hurşid Pasha to the Anatolian army did not, however, specify his position. From the wording of the *tezkire*, it seems that he was meant to serve on the staff of the army in Erzurum.

Hurşid Pasha arrived at Erzurum in early December. According to a British consular report from Erzurum, dated 23 December 1853, Hurşid Pasha had reportedly said to the *müşir* and to the members of the *meclis* of the city, that he had an imperial order to take up matters in the Anatolian army and if his advice went unheeded, he would at once return to Istanbul and report accordingly to the Porte. Thereupon the governor and the *meclis* assured him that his advice would be listened to. Again according to this report, he inspected the fortifications of the city and ordered new ones to be built. He also inspected the military hospitals, provisions and the troops. He found that the salaries of the soldiers were 12 to 18 months in arrears, while the pashas were usually one month or in some cases 3 months in arrears of pay. Then he reproached the pashas for not caring for the men under their command while protecting their own comfort very well. He told them that they could have given up their salaries for one year instead of leaving the soldiers without salary and this would not be a great burden for them. Then he ordered the payment of two months' salaries to the soldiers. The consular report also states that Hurşid Pasha had thus gained much popularity among the soldiers and they pledged to follow him to the last step.[197] This is interesting information, but unfortunately we do not have a confirmation from another source, preferably an Ottoman source. If the contents of this report are true, then we can safely assume that the seeds of dissension between Hurşid Pasha and some other pashas had already been sown by this act. Indeed, we will see later that Hurşid Pasha did not get along well with Zarif Pasha, the former governor and the new Commander-in-Chief of the Anatolian army beginning from March 1854.

---

[196] Sultan's *irade*, 13 October 1853. See BOA. İ. DH. 281/17617. Also see instructions (*tezkire*) from the grand vizier to the *serasker*, 16 October 1853. BOA. A. MKT. NZD. 95 /82.

[197] Translation of an extract from a report from the British consulate in Erzurum to the British embassy. BOA. HR. TO. 219/84, 23 December 1853.

According to Hurşid Pasha's own letter from Kars, dated 27 December 1853, he departed from Damascus and arrived at Kars on 9 December 1853.[198] In this letter, he does not mention Erzurum at all. Hurşid Pasha writes that he could have arrived earlier had he not been kept waiting for two weeks to receive his travel money. He was soon appointed chief of staff of the Anatolian army, but from his first letter from Kars it is clear that he did not yet know his exact position in the army. The tone of this letter does not coincide with the consular report mentioned above, where he boldly states to all pashas and other officials in Erzurum that he holds an imperial order and his advice should be heeded. Stratford de Redcliffe wanted him to practically command the army. Nevertheless, Hurşid Pasha was to face the opposition of both the Ottoman and the Polish parties in the Anatolian army.

In his letter Hurşid Pasha stated his opinion on the causes of the defeats of the Anatolian army. First, he wrote that the artillery had ammunition enough for only 200 shots for each cannon whereas it had been 400 shots previously. Secondly, he argued, two corps had been detached from the Kars army to Ahısha and Bayezid; as those places were far away from Kars, they did not receive help from Kars and they were uselessly placed in danger. Thirdly, it was a mistake to march with 28,000 men upon such a well-fortified fortress as Gümrü. The army should instead march upon Tiflis. Furthermore, he argued that, at the battle of Bayındır, the Russian army was half the size of the Ottoman army and thus it provided a good opportunity for the Ottoman army. Although the Russians suffered big losses, the battle consisted only of 4.5 hours of cannonade and neither the Ottoman cavalry nor the infantry were sent against the enemy, even the retreat route of the enemy towards the fortress (of Gümrü) was not blocked. Fourth, in the battle of Ahısha, the Russian forces were equal to Ottoman forces in number but the Ottoman battalions were separated from each other, therefore the compact Russian forces were superior to the Ottoman battalions. Furthermore, the commander Ferik Ali Pasha had himself "retreated" from the battle scene, leaving the troops to disorder and total defeat with the loss of 14 cannons. Fifth, in the battle of Başgedikler, the *Reis*

---

[198] Translation of Ferik Hurşid Pasha's letter from Kars to the foreign minister Reşid Pasha, dated 27 December 1853. BOA. HR. SYS. 904/1 enc. 49 and BOA. HR. MKT. 68/42. (The second document is not a full translation). This translation gives the date of Hurşid Pasha's arrival at Kars as 9 *Kanun-ı Evvel*, which by the Julian calendar corresponds to 21 December. However, it might mean 9 December as well.

(Chief of Staff) Ahmed Pasha should have retreated in orderly fashion towards Kars, waiting for the 8 battalions of infantry, 18 cannons and 3 regiments of cavalry from the Arabistan army in Kars, then the Ottoman forces would have had a definite superiority against the Russians. Hurşid Pasha asserted that the Ottoman losses in this battle were not only 26 cannons but also demoralisation of the army, which variously retreated in confusion, deserted, or showed signs of distrust towards its commanders.

Hurşid Pasha suggested that by the next spring the number of the Anatolian army should be increased to 50 or 60 thousand and the number of cannons up to 100 or 130. Then the army should leave a corps around Gümrü and march against Tiflis, trying to urge the Russian Muslims to insurgence and to meet with the forces of "Shamil Bey", meaning Sheikh Shamil, the Imam of Dagestan. Hurşid Pasha also observed that the Anatolian army did not have any proper maps of the region. He suggested that the French ministry of war had a good map of the Caucasus in Paris, the grand vizier might ask the French for a copy. Hurşid Pasha wanted more money allowance for spies and better administration of the provisions.

Hurşid Pasha considered Abdi Pasha to be the most competent officer in the Anatolian army but he wrote that Abdi Pasha shared his authority with Ahmed Pasha, who was totally unfit for large scale army operations and unexperienced in commanding an army. However, in his report from Kars to the British embassy, dated 17 January 1854, Hurşid Pasha wrote that he got on very well with Ahmed Pasha and he hoped to get on better when his firman arrived. On the other hand, the mushir was trying to get things out of his hands "by forming a medjlis for the wants and operations of the army". Hurşid Pasha also wrote that Staff Colonel Faik Bey was intriguing against him. Having heard that Ferhad Pasha was coming to the Kars army, Hurşid Pasha was vehemently against Ferhad Pasha. "With stupidity on one side, and treachery on the other, I shall have a nice berth of it"[199] Hurşid Pasha also wrote that the goverment owed the troops 11 million (piastres) in salaries.

---

[199] Extract. Kars, 17 January 1854. BOA. HR. SYS. 904/1 enc. 55. Translation into Ottoman Turkish is in enc. 54. Although this extract of a letter is not signed, its form and contents leave no doubt on its authorship.

The Danubian Front in 1854 and the Declaration of War by France and Britain

The year 1854 opened with another Ottoman victory on the Danubian front. The commander of the Ottoman forces in Kalafat (opposite Vidin), Ferik Çerkes İsmail Pasha attacked the Russian forces near the village of Çatana to the north of Kalafat on 31 December with a few thousand cavalry and infantry. The attack was repulsed, but on 6 January, the Orthodox Christmas day, a large Ottoman force of about 18,000 men attacked a smaller Russian force under the command of Colonel Aleksandr Baumgarten near Çatana. A second small Russian force was in a nearby village under the command of Brigadier General Belgard. Thus the total number of these two units (according to Tarle and other Russian sources) was about 7,000.[200] On the other hand, according to the report of the Ottoman Commander-in-Chief Müşir Ömer Lütfi Pasha, the Ottoman force that took part in this battle consisted of 11 infantry battalions, 4 batteries (24 guns) and 3 cavalry regiments, while the Russian forces included 15 infantry battalions, 24 guns and 3 cavalry regiments, that is to say, the Russians had 4 battalions more of infantry.[201]

These Russian units were under the command of General Anrep, who stayed in Boloeshti, not far from Çatana. In this battle, the Russians lost about 2,300 men and officers, killed and wounded, according to Tarle.[202] According to Ömer Pasha, Ottoman losses were 300 dead and 700 wounded, while the Russians lost about 4,000 dead and many wounded. He also wrote that the Ottoman soldiers had bayoneted many Russian prisoners of war in their rage and anger, bringing only a few of them alive to Kalafat.[203]

Serasker Mehmed Ali Pasha, however, in his report to Grand Vizier Mustafa Naili Pasha, wrote that, although it was reported that this bayoneting of live prisoners was a result of the soldiers' rage, and while it was understood that they were reprimanded for this act, this was not in fact an act of spontaneous fury as stated by Ömer Pasha, but the result of the soldiers' awareness of Russian atrocities during the battle

---

[200] Tarle, op. cit., vol. 1, p. 289.
[201] Ömer Pasha to the *serasker*, Şumnu, 13 January 1854. BOA. İ. HR. 114/5554–09 enc. 1.
[202] Tarle, ibid.
[203] Ömer Pasha, ibid.

of Sinop, when the Russians had continued to shell the Ottoman sailors who had jumped into the sea trying to reach the shore, and had fired about one thousand cannon shots on the corpses on the shore. Thus, the *serasker* continued, he had heard that the Ottoman soldiers had intentionally killed the prisoners and the wounded. He acknowledged that this act was indeed illegitimate and was in itself a harmful thing, being also contrary to earlier directions, and it was necessary to announce and to confirm once again that such actions were not to be repeated.[204]

At the battle of Çatana, the Russians had captured two cannons from the Ottomans due to the desertion of some squadrons from the 4th cavalry regiment. For this reason, Lieutenant-Colonel Sadık Bey and Major Ahmed Bey of the said 4th cavalry regiment were later found guilty of desertion and expelled from the army by decision of the DŞA.[205] However, Ömer Pasha does not mention this fact in his first report above, nor does he seem to have reported it in his three other reports submitted during January 1854.[206] In any case, this is just another example showing that the regular cavalry, like the irregular cavalry, was one of the least efficient components of the Ottoman army.

On the Russian side, most Russian sources (both tsarist military historians and Soviet historians) accuse General Anrep of not coming to the assistance of his units, although the cannonade could clearly be heard in Boloeshti. They also argue that due to the incompetence of General Gorchakov, the small Russian forces in Little Walachia were sacrificed to the Ottoman army.[207]

Thus the Ottomans closed the winter campaign on the Danube with victory. In his report dated 14 January 1854, Ömer Pasha informed the Serasker that Cetate would indeed remain as the most significant battle on the Danube front. However, the Ottomans did not follow the enemy and retreated to Kalafat. In both cases they had luck on their side,

---

[204] Serasker Pasha to the grand vizier, 22 January 1854. BOA. İ. DH. 18116. However, the grand vizier in his petition (*arz tezkiresi*) does not relate this event to the Sultan. The *serasker* pasha mentions three attached letters from Ömer Pasha dated January 1854. However, these letters are not found in this file.
[205] BOA. İ. DH. 21265, 31 August 1855.
[206] BOA. İ. DH. 18116.
[207] For example, see Tarle, op. cit., vol. I, pp. 284–290. Also see Modest Ivanovich Bogdanovich, *Vostochnaya Voina 1853–1856 godov*. St. Petersburg: Tip. M. Stasiulievicha, 1877, Glava VII. Winfried Baumgart (op. cit., p. 96) gives the Russian losses as 831 dead and 1,190 wounded.

while the Russian command was inefficient. Overall, like many battles of the Crimean War, this was an unfinished and indecisive battle.

The rest of January and February was quiet on the Danubian front. Sultan Abdülmecid conferred on Mushir Ömer Pasha the title of *Serdar-ı Ekrem* (generalissimo) on 15 February 1854. Ömer Pasha also retained his post of the commander of the Rumeli army.[208]

While these battles took place, diplomatic missions continued their work. During this time, both Russian and Western diplomacy focused on winning Austria and Prussia as allies. Towards the end of January, Nikolai sent Count Aleksey Orlov to the young Austrian Emperor Franz Joseph (1830-1916), whom he saw as a son and almost like a vassal. Orlov was one of the favourites of Nikolai and unlike Menshikov, had the reputation of being a good diplomat. Although he was the brother of Mikhail Orlov, one of the leaders of the Decembrist revolt in 1825, his behaviour as the commander of a cavalry regiment during the revolt had made him a favourite of the tsar. According to Tarle, Orlov did not believe that he could come to an agreement with Franz Joseph and his foreign minister Count Ferdinand Buol.[209] However, he could not object to Nikolai's request, so he went to Vienna. His task was to convince Franz Joseph to be neutral for the moment, but to enter the war on the side of Russia if France and Britain declared war against Russia. In return he was promised Russian help against all enemies and internal revolutions, and Russia also promised not to make any decision regarding the fate of the Ottoman Empire without agreement from Austria. In Vienna however, the pro-Russian party had lost ground. Franz Joseph and Buol did not want to commit themselves to the policy of Nikolai. Thus Orlov's mission of was unsuccessful.[210]

Towards the end of January 1854 Napoleon III wrote a letter to Nikolai I, which was published in the French official newspaper *Le Moniteur Universel* and the *St Peterburgskie Vedomosti* together with Nikolai's reply on 9 February. The French emperor stated that *"Notre attitude vis avis de la Turquie était protective mais passive"*.[211] Napoleon proposed the withdrawal of the French and British fleets from the Black

---

[208] BOA. İ. DH. 18072. Also see Lütfi, op. cit., pp. 211-212.
[209] Tarle, op. cit., vol. I, p. 409.
[210] The details of this mission are to be found in Tarle, "Missiya grafa Alekseya Orlova k Frantsu-Iosifu i pozitsiya Avstrii pered perekhodom russkikh voysk cherez Dunai", op. cit., vol. I, pp. 405-428.
[211] A copy of this letter is at BOA. HR. SYS. 905/1 enc. 82.

Sea and the withdrawal of Russian troops from Moldavia and Wallachia. Nikolai in return proposed that the Franco-British fleets should only prevent the Ottomans from carrying weapons and ammunition to Russian coasts and that the Porte should send its representative to St Petersburg for negotiations on the basis of these conditions. Diplomatic relations between Russia and France and Britain were severed in February 1854. The Russian ambassadors (Count Kiselev in Paris and Brunnov in London) left for Russia. The British and French ambassadors in St. Petersburg also returned home.[212]

Towards the end of February 1854, Britain and France gave an ultimatum to Emperor Nikolai to withdraw from the principalities. Nikolai did not give an official answer and unofficially made it known that he would not reply to such an ultimatum. Therefore Britain and France concluded an agreement of alliance with the Porte on 12 March 1854. On 27 March, France and Britain finally declared war on Russia. On 31 March the first French and then British troops landed in Gallipoli. By this time Lord Aberdeen had dealt another blow to Nikolai: He approved of the publication of Sir Hamilton Seymour's conversations with Nikolai in January-February 1853. The publication of these conversations was especially harmful for Russo-Austrian relations, because Franz Joseph and Count Buol were indignant at Nikolai's disrespect and patronizing attitude towards Austria in his talks with the British envoy, when Nikolai had made it clear that he felt Austria need not be considered as an independent actor, and had taken Austrian consent for granted. The Russian government's objections were published in Russian newspapers, stating that Seymour had misunderstood Nikolai. "The Emperor has never thought of any partition, he directed attention to the future and not to the present, he had in mind only future possibilities", it was announced.[213] But these excuses were, of course, not convincing in the eyes of European diplomats or the public.

It would be interesting to know whether the Porte knew of the Nikolai–Seymour conversations before their publication. It seems that it did not. Kostaki Musurus's despatch dated 17 March 1854 mentions the intention of the British cabinet to disclose these conversations, but very interestingly he argues that the Petersburg cabinet itself had dis-

---

[212] Paris Ambassador Veli Pasha to the foreign minister, 10 February 1854. BOA. HR. SYS. 905/1 enc. 97.
[213] Tarle, op. cit., vol. 1, p. 494.

closed in a Petersburg newspaper the offers of Nikolai I to the Queen regarding the partition of Ottoman Empire with the purpose of setting France and Britain against each other.[214]

Thus the efforts of the Russian ambassador in Vienna (Baron Peter von Meyendorff) to gain Austria as an ally came to nothing. The French and British ambassadors in Vienna finally managed to sign a protocol of four points with Count Buol.[215] This protocol came to be known as the "four points". The first point stated that the Russian protectorate over Serbia, Wallachia and Moldavia should be ended and these principalities should be placed under the guarantee of the great powers. Secondly, the mouths of the Danube should be free for navigation. The third and probably the most important (but also the vaguest) point stipulated that the Straits Treaty of 1841 should be revised "in the interest of the European balance of power". The fourth was the only point related to the immediate cause of the war: Russia should abandon its claim to protect the Orthodox population of the Ottoman Empire and the Christians of the Ottoman Empire should be placed under the protection of the great powers, without violating the sovereign rights of the Sultan. A secret fifth point, agreed between France and Britain only, clarified the third point to some extent: Russia should give up its "preponderance" in the Black Sea, by reducing its navy to four ships of war and by demolishing and not re-establishing the Sevastopol naval base.[216]

Meyendorff, who was a brother-in-law of Buol, tried to obtain the text of this protocol but he was rejected. He then almost threatened Count Buol: "Remember that Russia has a 700,000-strong army and it should not be approached as a second-rate state".[217] Nevertheless he had gained some unofficial and vague information about the protocol. According to what he heard, the agreement concerned maintaining the integrity of the Ottoman Empire, evacuation of the principalities by Russia and improving the status of Christians in the Ottoman Empire.

---

[214] Translation of Kostaki Bey's despatch to Reşid Pasha, dated 17 March 1854. BOA. HR. TO. 52/59.

[215] Gavin Henderson has called this event and the consequent alienation of Austria from Russia as a diplomatic revolution in the Concert of Europe. However, he claimed that the four points came into being in July 1854. See Henderson, "The Diplomatic Revolution of 1854: I The Four Points", *The American Historical Review* 43(1), October 1937, p. 27.

[216] Baumgart, op. cit., p. 19.

[217] Zayonchkovskiy, op. cit., vol. II, part one, p. 511.

It seems that he did not manage to learn the full contents of all the four points. He also observed that prices in the Vienna stock exchange had risen. He felt that the stock exchange fluctuations reflected the opinion that the greater the number of enemies of Russia, the greater the chances for a peace. On 20 April, Austria also signed a "defensive and offensive" agreement with Prussia.[218]

Meanwhile the first clash between the allies and Russia happened at Odessa. On 9 April the British frigate *Furious* came to Odessa to take onboard the British consul there. A sloop was detached from the frigate with a white flag. The port authorities then told the officer in the sloop that the consul had already left, and the sloop then returned to the *Furious*. At that time, or some time before, the Russian port battery fired a few shots which were not aimed at the sloop or the frigate. The Russian authorities later claimed it was intended as a warning only. They argued that the frigate had come too close to the shore. In any case no damage was done. As Adolphus Slade remarked, a boat flying a truce flag should wait at a distance, until another boat came to meet it from the shore.[219] The allied admirals took offence and sent a squadron of sail ships of the line and steamers to demand the release of neutrals and the surrender of all British, French and Russian ships at anchor in the port as reparation for the breach of international law. The governor of Odessa, Count Osten-Sacken released the neutral ships but refused to give up the Russian ships. Then the allied fleet on 22 April bombarded the harbour and its facilities. Although they claimed that they did not aim at the city and the civilians, the city was also damaged. Slade is very critical of such acts, arguing that "war is never aided by needless severity or destruction of domestic property".[220] Though this was a skirmish, the allied navies had now sent a clear message that they were the masters in the Black Sea.

Austria continued its armed neutrality; mobilizing its army and effectively becoming more and more anti-Russian. It even informed Russia that if Russian troops crossed the Danube then Austria would respond with force. For fear of a Serbian uprising that would upset its own Serbs, Austria concentrated troops on the Serbian frontier. Emperor Nikolai I was still undaunted; he thought he could

---

[218] Zayonchkovskiy, op. cit., vol. II, part one, pp. 510–511.
[219] Slade, op. cit., p. 215.
[220] Slade, op. cit., p. 218.

still go on with his plans without Austria. The Greeks had revolted in Thessaly and Epirus. Nikolai now harboured the illusion that the Serbs and Bulgarians would also rise against the "Turkish yoke". The Greek government secretly supported the insurgents, while the Greek newspapers openly called for an uprising. However, in April and May the Greek insurrection was suppressed by the Ottoman army under the command of Fuad Efendi, with the help of the allied fleets threatening Athens and Piraeus.[221]

Nikolai's plans for the spring campaign included crossing the Danube to Vidin, Rusçuk and Silistria and the siege of these cities together with Galatz and Brailov in the north. Russian troops, in accordance with this plan, occupied the whole Dobruca region during 23 to 29 March. The Russian army across the Danube numbered 45,000 men under the command of General Aleksandr Lüders.[222] For Nikolai, Silistria was to be the stronghold from which to attack the allied expeditionary force which he assumed would be landed at Varna. Indeed his assumption was proven to be correct.

In Silistria there was an Ottoman force of 12,000 men under the command of Ferik Musa Hulusi Pasha (?–1854). There were also about six British officers in Silistria, among whom Captain James Butler and Lieutenant Charles Nasmyth are best remembered.[223] In the Russo-Ottoman war of 1828–1829, the Ottoman army in Silistria had held out against Russia for six months. The fortress there had subsequently been strengthened by the addition of outer fortifications. Russia laid siege on 5 April. The commander of the siege forces was the aged General Karl Andreyevich Schilder (1785–1854), who had taken Silistria in 1829 by mining operations. One of his aides was military engineer Lieutenant-Colonel Eduard Ivanovich Totleben (1818–1884) responsible for fortification and sapper works. Later, Totleben was to undertake the fortification of Sevastopol. Meanwhile, Field Marshal Paskevich came

---

[221] See Cevdet Pasha, *Tezâkir 40-Tetimme*, pp. 67–68. Interestingly, Fuad Efendi signs a letter to Cevdet Pasha as "*Ceneral-i orduy-ı Yanya ve Narda*". This is probably because he had become temporarily a general but not a pasha. Also see Besbelli, op. cit., p. 59, Reid, op. cit., pp. 248–253.

[222] Baumgart, op. cit., p. 99.

[223] Both had served in the East India Company army. Butler has left a "journal". These six British officers received the Mecidiye order. See BOA. İ. DH. 19455, 14 August 1854. However, as we have seen in the introductory chapter, Lane-Poole has quite exaggerated their role, arguing that without them "the garrison might have surrendered".

from Warsaw to Bucharest to take direct command of the occupation army. Paskevich arrived at Bucharest on 22 April. Ottoman reinforcements also began to arrive at Silistria. By May, the garrison muster-roll rose to 18,000 troops of all types.[224]

Paskevich had only grown more sceptical of the Danubian campaign. He was worried by the concentration of Austrian troops (said to have reached 280,000 men) along the borders of Wallachia and Moldavia.[225] They posed a real threat as Austria had already warned Russia not to cross the Danube. Paskevich now tried to convince Nikolai to evacuate the principalities. He said that the Bulgarians and the Serbians were not to be expected to rise. By the evacuation of the principalities, Paskevich argued, Russia would gain time, which would work against the allies. Meanwhile Russia could reinforce its armies. But Nikolai did not heed his advice.[226] Retaining Paskevich, who simply did not believe in his plans, was indeed one of Nikolai's biggest mistakes.

By May 1854, the Russian forces around Silistria had reached 90,000 men with 266 cannons.[227] This was, at the time, the single largest Russian siege force ever deployed against an Ottoman fortress. It soon started siege works around the fortress and the Russian bombardment of Silistria began in the middle of May.[228] But Paskevich hesitated to make a decisive assault on the fortifications and Ferik Musa Pasha energetically continued to improve the fortifications. On 4 May, Paskevich wrote a second letter to Nikolai, this time more clearly proposing to retreat. He wrote that, surrounded by the French and the "Turks" from the front, and by Austria from the rear, they did not have a chance. On receipt of this letter on 11 May, Nikolai felt offended and angry. After all their efforts, losses and expenses, now his Commander-in-Chief was proposing to leave the principalities with shame! On the next day he wrote his reply, stating that he had received the letter with "extreme grief and no less astonishment" and he would not accept his

---

[224] Reid, op. cit., p. 256.
[225] Baumgart, ibid.
[226] Tarle, op. cit., vol. 1, pp. 486–487.
[227] Zayonchkovskiy, op. cit., vol. II, part 2, p. 272. Tarle gives 210 cannons. Cf. Tarle, op. cit., vol. 1, p. 500.
[228] Captain Nafiz Efendi, who was an Ottoman artillery sergeant-major at that time, gives the date of the beginning of the siege as 12 May 1854. M. Bogdanovich (editor of the article), however, remarks that the bombardment began on the night of 17–18 May. See Nafiz Efendi, "Krepost' Silistriya v 1854 godu", *Voenny Sbornik* 106(12), 1875, p. 502. Captain Butler on the other hand, as quoted by Reid, wrote in his journal that the Russian bombardment began on 16 May. See Reid, op. cit., p. 256.

proposals because they were "shameful" for him. He emphasized that Austria could not enter the war against Russia, and that there was no reason to be afraid of the allies.[229]

Meanwhile on 18 May, the allied commanders Marshal Armand-Jacques Leroy de Saint Arnaud (1801–1854) and General Fitzroy James Henry Somerset, Lord Raglan (1788–1855) together with Serasker Hasan Rıza Pasha came to Varna from Istanbul and on 19 May they held a war council with Ömer Pasha who had come from Şumnu. Ömer Pasha was very worried about the Russian siege and offensive. His hopes lay with the allied troops. The allied commanders agreed with Ömer Pasha's request to bring their troops to Varna as soon as possible. St. Arnaud promised to send 55,000 troops. However, these troops would not arrive at Varna before June and before they were ready to help, the Russians raised the siege of Silistria.[230]

Ömer Pasha remained in Şumnu with 40,000 to 45,000 troops, but he hesitated to come to the rescue of Silistria or to make a diversionary operation. In fact he did not want any open field encounter with a large Russian army. All he did was to send the Cossack regiment of Sadık Pasha and 5,000 irregulars from Razgrad to take positions at some distance around the Russian forces. He also allowed Behram Pasha (General Cannon) to make a manoeuvre before the city with a brigade of infantry.[231]

On 28 May the Russians made an assault on the Arab Tabia in Silistria, but they were repulsed, losing 22 officers (dead and wounded) and 315 dead and 596 wounded rank and file.[232] General Selvan was among the dead. Ottoman losses were about 68 dead, 121 wounded.[233] On 2 June Musa Pasha was killed by shrapnel while preparing for prayers. His heroic death further increased the spirit of the defenders.[234] Hüseyin Rifat Pasha came from Şumnu to take the command of the defence. He also brought from Ömer Pasha the news that Silistria

---

[229] Tarle, op. cit., vol. 1, pp. 488–489.
[230] Baumgart, op. cit., p. 109. Also see General Andrey N. Petrov, op. cit., as quoted by Staff Captain A. Tevfik Gürel, *1853-55 Türk-Rus ve Müttefiklerin Kırım Savaşı*. Istanbul: Askeri Matbaa, 1935, p. 56. Also see Tarle, op. cit., vol. 1, p. 502.
[231] Gürel (op. cit., p. 66) has taken General "Kannon" and "General Behram" for two different persons.
[232] See Tarle, op. cit., vol. 1, p. 505.
[233] Bogdanovich, op. cit., vol. II, glava XIII, footnote 17.
[234] See Yüzbaşı (Captain) Fevzi, op. cit., p. 43. Captain Fevzi Kurtoğlu writes that Musa Pasha was killed when he got out of his room to perform ablution before the noon prayers and while he was talking with an officer. However, Slade (op. cit.,

should not expect relief for about two weeks, until the allies arrived.[235] Meanwhile the provisions of the city were almost at their end. The Russians made a few further indecisive attacks without result. Paskevich in his reports to Nikolai stated that the Ottomans were defending the city with much energy and good strategic knowledge, assisted by foreign officers. However, he could just as well have been concealing his own indecision and vacillation.[236] The French General Pierre F. J. Bosquet also found it strange and wrote that he did not understand what paralysed the Russian army: "This is strange and I feel reluctant to explain it by the impotence of the Russians. There is another thing, like a demoralization, a concern, I do not know what, which paralyses this army" [my translation].[237]

On 9 June Paskevich suffered a real (or pretended) contusion and left the command of operations again to Gorchakov, himself returning to Jassy. On 13 June General Schilder was severely wounded and died shortly afterwards. On 21 June the Russian army was prepared to storm the main fortress. At this point, hours before the commencement of storming, Gorchakov received an order from Paskevich to raise the siege and retreat to the left of the Danube. Thus the Russian army retreated but the Ottoman army, as usual, did not follow.[238] The reason for Paskevich's order of retreat was Austria's menacing position and the concentration of allied forces in Varna. On 3 June Austria demanded that Russia evacuate the principalities otherwise it would join the allies to force Russia out.[239]

On 14 June, the Porte and Austria signed the convention of Boyacıköy, whereby Austria received the right to occupy the principalities temporarily.[240] Alarmed, Nikolai decided to retreat. Nesselrode finally responded to the Austrian demand for a retreat on 29 June when the Russians began to evacuate Dobrudja. There were skirmishes between Russian and Ottoman forces at Yergöğü on 5–7 July, but the Russians continued to retreat. In order to save face Russia called its retreat a strategic withdrawal. On 1 August the Russian army left Bucharest.

---

p. 251) argues that Musa Pasha was killed while he was stepping on to his *seccade* (small carpet) for the evening prayers.

[235] Captain Butler's journal, quoted by Reid, op. cit., p. 257.
[236] Baumgart, op. cit., pp. 99–100.
[237] Zayonchkovskiy, op. cit., vol. II, part 2, p. 290.
[238] Tarle, op. cit., vol. 1, pp. 515–516.
[239] Baumgart, op. cit., p. 101.
[240] BOA. İ. HR. 111/5445.

The Ottoman army entered Bucharest on 8 August under the command of Halim Pasha and on 22 August Ömer Pasha came to the city.[241] The Austrians and the Ottomans started to occupy the principalities. The Austrians were careful not to meet the retreating Russians and on 7 September the principalities were completely evacuated by the Russian army.

At the beginning of July the allies decided to embark their armies for the Crimea. They wanted to destroy the Russian navy at Sevastopol. According to Slade, Austria sent a military envoy to Varna to urge the allied generals to a joint campaign in Bessarabia, while Cevdet Pasha, on the contrary, argues that the allies later admitted their mistake and said that they were misled by the Austrians. Cevdet Pasha also writes that the proposal for a campaign in Bessarabia came from Ömer Pasha.[242] In any case, France and Britain, too confident of their military might and not wanting to share their victory with anybody, even with the Ottoman Empire, started preparations for embarkation from Varna on 14 August. They relied on their steam frigates and screw-propelled line-of-battle ships to defy distance, facilitate logistic support and destroy the Russian fleet. They had planned to finish the Crimean campaign by Christmas.

The allied fleets had come to Varna and anchored off Balçık. They did not want the Ottoman fleet to have any active role in the Black Sea. Rather, they wanted it to protect the Bosphorus and cruise between Varna and Istanbul. While the Ottomans and the allies could not or did not want to conquer Bessarabia, a brave Russian war steamer called the *Bessarabia* left Sevastopol on 19 July and steamed among enemy shipping across the Black Sea up to the north-western cost of Anatolia, capturing two Ottoman merchant vessels, one off Kerempe, the other off Amasra, laden with maize and coal. The *Bessarabia* then took the coal, burned the vessels and disembarked their crew at Ereğli, retaining only their captains and scribes as evidence. She then returned to Sevastopol. When the *kaimmakam* of Ereğli reported the situation to Istanbul, he was met with suspicion. The Russian navy had once again showed its contempt for the allied fleets.[243]

---

[241] Baumgart, op. cit., p. 104.
[242] Slade, op. cit., p. 253. Cf. Cevdet Pasha, op. cit., p. 28.
[243] Besbelli, op. cit., p. 66. Özcan (op. cit., 1990, p. 93) mentions only one merchant vessel, *Medar-ı Ticaret* and states that the steamer *Şehper* was attacked off Kerempe by Russian pirates but managed to come to the harbour of Sinop intact.

Varna had become a hub of activity, brimming with ships, troops, stores of provisions and ammunition. The best houses and private shops had been occupied by the allies without any payment to the owners. A year later these owners, Muslim and non-Muslim, were sending petitions to the Porte, complaining that they had not received any rent.[244] Foreign residents alone were exempt from this free quartering. The inhabitants were also irritated by the drunkenness of the allied soldiers. On one occasion, French soldiers went to a Muslim café and demanded wine. When they were told wine was not sold there, a quarrel ensued and consequently one person was killed and several wounded. On 10 August a fire broke out and lasted six hours burning many wooden houses, the bazaar and military stores. Slade then remarks: "As on other occasions when honour or loot was to be obtained, the Turkish soldiers and sailors were not invited to join: they neither robbed nor rioted".[245]

The city *meclis* held a stormy meeting after the fire. Many notables were angry with the allies, even comparing them unfavourably with the Russians who had besieged Varna in 1828. "The Muscovites", they said,

> came to Varna after the irritation of a double siege; they remained there two years, gave nobody reason to lament their conduct, and left the town better than they had found it. The Franks have scarcely been at Varna three months; they have taken our dwellings and store-houses compulsorily, have covered us with opprobrium, and now the place is ruined by their carelessness.[246]

The governor of Varna and the military commandant said that they had warned the allies of the danger of fire. They also complained that the allied generals were like sultans; it was difficult to obtain an audience with them. They did not answer their letters either.

Meanwhile cholera had started to ravage the allied troops and fleets, from the beginning of July 1854. For this reason the embarkation was constantly delayed. The French made an incursion into Dobrudja in

---

[244] BOA. HR. SYS. 1353/12 enc. 1–8, June–July 1855. Osman Nuri Bey, head of the "Varna commission", also reported to the Porte several times on this point. See BOA. HR. SYS. 1356/8, 31 March 1855, HR. SYS. 1353/73, 5 September 1855 and HR. SYS. 1354/46 enc. 4, 5 November 1855.

[245] Slade, op. cit., pp. 258–259, 261.

[246] Slade, op. cit., p. 262. Tarle (op. cit., vol. 2, p. 27) has quoted this passage apparently with much pleasure.

August, but they lost nearly 7,000 men from cholera, fever, drought and heat. The British also lost about 700 men from diseases. Furthermore 12,000 to 15,000 French and about 1,900 British troops were hospitalized. Sanitary and logistics problems now made themselves strongly felt and they did not cease to be felt during the war. At last the departure for the Crimea was set for 2 September, but it was again delayed until 7 September. The formidable armada consisted of 350 ships carrying 30,000 (24,000?) French, 25,000 (27,000?) British and about 5,000 or 6,000 Ottoman troops (10 infantry battalions).[247] Another 11,000 French troops were to follow later. Among the Ottoman troops, 8 battalions were selected from the *esnan*, that is, new recruits that were 20 to 25 years of age and the remaining two battalions from the *redif*, that is, the reserve, middle-aged soldiers with families to be worried about. The *esnan* had received only three months of drilling in Üsküdar. They had with them only three weeks of provisions, after which the Allies were to feed them. The Ottoman commander chosen for the expedition, Mirliva Süleyman Pasha, was not a distinguished officer; he had spent the last 12 years of his life as the superintendent of Beykoz tannery. To encourage him for the mission, he had been promoted from colonel to the rank of mirliva. Other officers had shunned the mission, expecting neglect from the Allies.[248] Events proved that they were right to have been wary.

While the allied forces left for the Crimea, Ömer Pasha was contented with himself in Bucarest and was not in a hurry to go forward. In October 1843, he wrote to Istanbul that the time was late for a forward movement. There were problems of provisions. Therefore he had postponed his forward march towards Pruth until early spring. A telegram from Vienna (from the Ottoman embassy or Austrian government?) gave him freedom of movement in the direction of Braila and Galatz, but he had to negotiate with the Austrian General Coronini for any movement beyond the Pruth. In practise, Ömer Pasha had spent ten days corresponding with General Coronini even for establishing

---

[247] Calthorpe, op. cit., vol. I, pp. 122–123. Calthorpe gives the number of Ottoman troops as 6,000. While Slade argues (op. cit., p. 273) that the Ottoman force consisted of 10 battalions of more or less 800 men each, totaling 8,000 men, Besbelli (op. cit., p. 71) gives the number as 5,000. The grand vizier had written to the *serasker* that 10,000 regular troops should be given to Marshal St. Arnaud and Lord Raglan by 15 August 1854. See BOA. İ. MMS. 2/61, 3 August 1854.

[248] Slade, op. cit., p. 274.

a sentry station near Galatz.²⁴⁹ Seeing that there was little to do in Bucharest, Ömer Pasha asked for a leave to come to Istanbul. Like most Ottoman pashas, he wanted to spend the winter in Istanbul. The grand vizier however, reminded him of the existence of still some Russian forces near Tolçı, İsakçı and Maçin and of the scattered deployment of the Danubian army and Ömer Pasha gave up the idea of coming to Istanbul on leave.²⁵⁰

The Caucasian Front in 1854–1855

After the defeat of Başgedikler, the Porte sent the minister of the police (*Zaptiye Müşiri*) Mehmed Hayreddin Pasha (?–1869) in January 1854 to inspect the Anatolian and Batum armies and to enquire into the deeds of Abdi Pasha and Ahmed Pasha. Upon arrival at Erzurum and then at Kars, Hayreddin Pasha reported the guilt of both pashas in robbing the soldiers and they were recalled to Istanbul for trial.²⁵¹

The Ottoman armies in Kars, Erzurum and Batum spent the winter of 1853–1854 in very unhealthy conditions. They were scarcely fed and badly clothed, quartered in poorly heated, unventilated, filthy, crowded inns (*khans*) or houses in conditions ripe for the spread of contagious diseases like typhus. Therefore 18,000 to 20,000 soldiers died from diseases and malnutrition.²⁵² Zarif Pasha confirms this situation and states that when he took over the command of the Anatolian army in March 1854, there were 17,000 troops in Kars, of which 11,000 were in the hospitals.²⁵³ On the day of his arrival at Kars, 50 soldiers died of diseases. When he asked the doctors what was to be done, they wanted some of the troops to be sent to villages to leave more room for others, opening holes in the barracks for better ventilation and supplying the hospitals with clothing, beds and linen. He writes that the daily

---

[249] Ömer Pasha to the grand vizier, Bucharest, 22 October 1854. BOA. HR. SYS. 1336/24 enc. 14.
[250] Ömer Pasha to the grand vizier, Bucharest, 19 November 1854. BOA. HR. SYS. 1336/24 enc. 17.
[251] Duncan, op. cit., vol. I, p. 111.
[252] Clarendon to Redcliffe, 29 November 1854, PRMA, p. 51.
[253] See Zarif Pasha's memoirs, Karal, op. cit. (1940), p. 485. Also see Zarif Pasha's answers to questions in the MVL. BOA. İ. MMS. 5/170 enc. 9, paragraph 2. The second part of Zarif Pasha's memoirs, related to the period of his command of the Anatolian army is also available at BOA. İ. MMS. 5/170 enc. 10. Zarif Pasha had submitted it as part of his evidence during his trial.

death-toll fell by half afterwards. The Batum army was also reduced to a few thousands. However, reinforcements began to be sent as early as February 1854. Two steamers under the command of Bahriye Feriki Mustafa Pasha, escorted by an allied squadron, brought 5,000 troops to Trabzon (for the Anatolian army) on 10 February and 3,000 men to Batum on 11 February 1854.[254] Although the Russian fleet still patrolled the coasts, it did not dare to confront the allied fleet.

Likewise, Doctor Humphrey Sandwith writes that during the winter of 1853–1854, some 20,000 men had died of disease and hunger, being deprived of proper food and clothing, and "crowded into the dark, ill-ventilated hovels" of Kars. The great mortalities from diseases were not reported in the muster-rolls sent to Istanbul, "for the pay, food and appointments of dead men went to fill the coffers of the Pasha and his myrmidons".[255] Sandwith also writes that Abdi Pasha was a "poor and honest man", but then he tells of a curious story related to Abdi Pasha's journey from Kars to Istanbul, when he was removed from his post and called back to Istanbul. According to the story, on the road between Erzurum and Trabzon, when one of the mules of Abdi Pasha's large-train of heavily-laden baggage-mules slipped and fell over a precipice, the load was smashed and a treasure of gold and silver rolled out, which was plundered by the muleteers and the peasantry.[256]

At the beginning of 1854, Damad Mehmed Ali Pasha lost the office of the *serasker* and Hasan Rıza Pasha replaced him. The new *serasker* did not like the existence of so many foreign officers in the Ottoman armies. He controlled the appointment of the new commander of the Anatolian army. Thus with Hasan Rıza Pasha's backing, the governor of Erzurum, Mustafa Zarif Pasha, was appointed the *müşir* of the Anatolian army in February 1854. This was to prove the second most unfortunate appointment after that of Ahmed Pasha. Although Zarif Pasha had been successful as the governor of Erzurum, he was unfit for the post of the Commander-in-Chief, because he had never commanded an army or even a regiment. As seen from his memoirs, his army life had been spent chiefly in the capacity of a regimental secretary.

---

[254] *Tezkire* of *Kapudan-ı Derya*, 21 February 1854, BOA. İ. DH. 18414 enc. 1, quoted by Budak, op. cit. (1993), p. 68. Budak writes that the *tezkire* belonged to Kapudan-ı Derya Mahmud Pasha. However, Mahmud Pasha was at that time dismissed. Kıbrıslı Mehmed Emin Pasha had become the grand admiral. See Cevdet Pasha, *Tezâkir 40–Tetimme*, p. 67.
[255] Sandwith, op. cit., p. 48.
[256] Sandwith, op. cit., p. 47 and p. 49.

Actually Zarif Pasha had already sensed the possibility of this post being offered to him as early as December 1853, when he reported on the incompetence of Abdi Pasha.[257] In his letter to the grand vizier he had asked to be saved from such responsibility, and he was saved by the appointment of Ahmed Pasha. However this time he could not evade the appointment. He also writes in his memoirs that he had not wanted to be appointed mushir.

The post of the governor of Erzurum was given to the *kaimmakam* of Çıldır, Zaim Feyzullah Pasha. Lütfi Efendi, the official chronicler, makes one of his rare criticisms in his chronicle on these three appointments. About Ahmed Pasha he writes that he knows little, but he says that Ahmed is famous for his bravery. However, he argues, bravery alone is not enough for a commander. As for Zarif Pasha, he has no compliments and sees him as incompetent while he cannot conceal his contempt for Feyzullah Pasha, and altogether he considers their appointments in such a delicate time as matters of curious business.[258] But Lütfi might better have recorded whether any prominent pashas were willing to take the governorship of Erzurum upon themselves. We must note that poor Feyzullah worked more energetically in his post than his predecessors.

Zarif Pasha was indeed a typical non-slave[259] origin Ottoman pasha and governor of the mid-nineteenth century. Since he has left his memoirs, albeit very scanty, we have more information about him than about many of his contemporaries. Therefore we can dwell at some length on his memoirs to understand the mentality and world-view of the pashas. Problems arise immediately; Zarif Pasha in his memoirs, written for his children and not for publication, does not comment

---

[257] Mustafa Zarif Pasha to the grand vizier, 11 December 1853. BOA. HR. MKT. 68/46.

[258] Lütfi, op. cit., p. 93. While Lütfi calls Feyzullah an *ağa*, he is called a pasha in the documents. For example Zarif Pasha calls him pasha in his memoirs: See Enver Ziya Karal, "Zarif Paşa'nın Hatıratı", *Belleten* IV, 1940, pp. 480–481. The grand vizier in a letter dated 25 November 1853 to the *serasker* also calls him a pasha. See BOA. A. MKT. NZD. 104/28.

[259] Charles Duncan, the British war correspondent for the newspaper *Morning Chronicle* in the Kars army, argues that Zarif Pasha "passed in early youth through that imperial road to success in Turkey – the slave market". Duncan seems to have taken a stereotype for granted. See *A Campaign with the Turks in Asia*, vol. I, London: Smith, Elder and Co., 1855, p. 180. He must have read Captain Charles White's book *Three Years in Constantinople* (1846). Nevertheless, there were other pashas of slave origins, such as Vasıf Pasha, who became the commander of the Anatolian army in 1855.

on the political and social events of his time, which was indeed the interesting period of the *Tanzimat* reforms. These memoirs are a great disappointment, as pointed out by Enver Ziya Karal, their editor. They are full of personal details, with a lot of information on how much money he earned and where he put his money. Thus, as the Ottoman saying goes, he describes his peculation as if it was an accomplishment or an act of bravery (*Şecaat arzederken merd-i Kıpti sirkatin söyler*).

Zarif Mustafa was given by his father to an accounting office in the ministry of finance as a scribe at the age of twelve. Two years later, at fourteen, he became by chance the secretary to a regiment in lieu of the son of an accountant, Hamdi Bey, who had just been promoted from a secretary to the rank of major in the army. From Zarif's account, it appears that this Hamdi Bey received his brevet rank out of the blue, without military training or education. Then Zarif himself became both a secretary and a lieutenant, and even a deputy captain at the age of sixteen. He was also received by Sultan Mahmud II. This is interesting because it shows both the degree of Mahmud II's interest in his new army, and also the degree of liberty in the distribution of military ranks. Afterwards Mustafa Zarif was appointed to many campaigns as regimental secretary and quickly rose in rank. His accounts of the behaviour of his colonels reveal much ignorance and gambling on their part. However, some of them "give" a lot of money to our Zarif (for what?) and he mentions them with gratitude, while a certain Şerif Pasha still owes him forty to fifty thousand piastres (again for what?).

Mustafa Zarif became a *ferik* (division general) in 1845 at the age of 29 without commanding any units in battle. He worked first at the head of some military production then in the military tribunal. At all steps he records his salary and his side earnings. Thus we learn that as a *ferik*, he received a salary of 25,000 piastres, which is more than the usual salary of this rank (15,000 piastres). Then in 1847 he was appointed *mutasarrıf* of Jerusalem, with a salary of 27,500 piastres. A British doctor there was beaten by some Arabs for entering the great mosque. When the British authorities insisted on the punishment of the culprits, Zarif Pasha temporized with them, eventually returning to Istanbul under pressure. At that time also Stratford Canning was the British ambassador in Istanbul. (Thus when Zarif Pasha was arrested in 1854 for his misconduct in the Anatolian army, he saw this as the work of the British ambassador.) In 1852 Zarif Mustafa Pasha was appointed governor of Erzurum.

Mustafa Zarif Pasha in his memoirs tries to relate all his services as governor and as commander of the army. He claims that in the present war he spent 2,000 purses[260] from his own pocket for the sake of the state. But then the question arises naturally: Where did he get this money from? (2,000 purses were equal to 40 months of a *ferik*'s pay). During his interrogation at the MVL, Zarif Pasha again says that he gave more than 100,000 piastres (200 purses) as *bahşiş* to soldiers who worked in the construction of fortifications.[261] Salih Hayri in his *zafername* states that Zarif Pasha had "hoarded" much money for his own benefit.[262] Likewise, Charles Duncan argues that Zarif Pasha had appropriated 15,000 purses when he was still a *bey* in the civil administration of an army.[263] Thus, according to Charles Duncan, at that time Zarif Pasha had been removed from his post for this act. He had also repaid some portion of the embezzled money. However, the current Serasker Hazan Rıza Pasha protected him and soon he returned to state service.[264] While we do not know the accuracy of this specific information, it is entirely possible, because many corrupt pashas, even those convicted, eventually returned to their posts. Damad Mehmed Ali Pasha is the best-known example of this.

While the new campaign season approached, the Porte tried to reinforce its armies, including the Anatolian army, which had been greatly reduced during the winter by deaths from disease and desertions (especially by the *başıbozuk* and the *redif*). New forces of recruits, *redifs*, and *başıbozuks* were pouring in from Arabistan and Anatolia to Erzurum. Provisions and ammunition were being sent from Istanbul to the port of Trabzon, but from then onwards it was a very difficult journey on mules and camels. The Russian army was also receiving reinforcements since the allied fleets had not yet blockaded the Black Sea.

---

[260] See Karal, op. cit. (1940), p. 472. 2,000 purses make 10,000 Ottoman pounds, equal to about 8,000 pounds sterling at that time, which is approximately 480,000 pounds sterling at current prices. The *Sicill-i Osmani* records Zarif Mustafa Pasha as "possessor of great wealth". See Mehmed Süreyya, op. cit., vol. 5, p. 1706.
[261] Zarif Mustafa Pasha's answers to questions in the MVL. February 1855. BOA. İ. MMS. 5/170 enc. 9.
[262] Salih Hayri, op. cit., p. 150.
[263] Duncan, op. cit., p. 182.
[264] In April 1857 Zarif Pasha was entitled to a salary of unemployment of 15,000 piastres. See BOA. İ. HR. 375/24803, 21 April 1857 and BOA. A. MKT. NZD. 223/65, 3 May 1857. Then, in October 1857, he became president of the DŞA. See Mehmed Süreyya, ibid.

The allied fleets finally entered the eastern part of the Black Sea in April. The Russians had evacuated all the coastline from Anapa down to Redutkale, because they knew that they stood no chance against the combined allied fleets. Towards the end of May, the commander of the British fleet Admiral Dundas informed his Ottoman colleague Ahmed Pasha that "from Kertch to Batoum the only fortresses in the possession of Russia are Anapa and Soujak".[265] Soon those two fortresses were also captured by the allies.

While the Porte wanted to attack Russia in the Caucasus, the allies showed little interest. Both Britain and France had as primary objectives the destruction of the Russian Black Sea fleet and the naval base at Sevastopol. Any other targets were secondary for them. Nevertheless they had sent officers to Batum, Circassia, Trabzon, Erzurum and Kars. The prospects of a combined Ottoman-Circassian-Shamil offensive did not look bright to them. As we have seen above, the Ottoman armies had experienced a harsh winter and nearly half of the troops in Kars and Batum had died of diseases like typhus and malaria. The Circassians were divided among themselves and the *murids* of Shamil were easily kept at bay by the Russians. The Christian population of most of Georgia was united under the Russian command.[266]

Relations with Shamil and the Circassians in 1854–1855

By the beginning of the 1854 campaign season, Shamil had accomplished the task given to him by the caliph, namely the task of uniting and subduing most of the khans and *ümera* of the Caucasus in the name of the Ottoman cause. According to the testimony of Mahmud Efendi, who had been sent to Shamil by the former Serasker Damad Mehmed Ali Pasha and returned to Istanbul in April 1854, Shamil stated that he had secured the loyalty of many Caucasian Muslim khans to the Porte. They were Major-General Cemedi (?) Khan, General Ebuselim Shemkhal Khan, General Ağalar Khan, General Yusuf Khan, General Hasay Khan and General Danyal Sultan. These khans, who were all given the rank of general by Russia, all stated their loyalty to the caliph and

---

[265] Vice-Admiral Dundas to Vice-Admiral Ahmed Pasha, the *Britannia* off Baljik [Balçık], 25 May 1854. BOA. HR. SYS. 1348/73 enc. 1.
[266] Ibragimbeyli, op. cit., pp. 353–354. Tarle, op. cit., vol 1, p. 292. Budak (op. cit., 1993, p. 80) also writes that not all Georgians were committed to the Ottoman state.

readiness for joint action against Russia. However, unless the Anatolian army attacked and took the fortress of Gümrü, they would not feel safe and would not openly declare their support for the Porte. Therefore they had not yet declared their support of the Porte and they were waiting for action from the Ottoman army. Otherwise they would be vulnerable to Russian vengeance if the Ottoman army did not move against Gümrü and Tiflis.[267]

Meanwhile Halil Pasha of Dagestan had also returned from Dagestan. He suggested conferring rank upon these khans of Dagestan. Consequently, a provisional council (*Meclis-i Muvakkat*) convened on 15 May 1854 and proposed to give the following ranks and titles: Sheikh Shamuil Efendi would receive the rank of vizier and the title of *Dağıstan Serdar-ı Ekremi* (Commander-in-Chief of Dagestan), his son Gazi Muhammed would be *Mirliva* (Brigadier-General), Ebu Selim Shemkhal Khan the rank of *Ferik* (Lieutenant-General), Cemed (?) Khan, Hasay (?) Khan, Danyal Sultan and İsmail Pasha would also become *Mirliva*s. These appointments were to be kept secret for the time being. The grand vizier then submitted the decision to the Sultan on 24 May 1854 and the appointments were approved on the next day.[268]

Nevertheless, apart from distributing ranks and titles to Circassian and Dagestani notables, the Porte did very little. Shamil's naib in Circassia, Muhammed Emin, in a letter written in Arabic, dated 21 May 1854, complained that six months had passed since receiving some gunpowder but that nothing had come from the sea (that is, from the Porte).[269] He had received orders from "Shamuil"[270] to march towards Georgia with the forces of the Abzeh tribe. Shamil had informed him that he would also march in that direction and they would meet if possible. Muhammed Emin also complained of not receiving instructions from the Porte:

---

[267] See Budak, op. cit. (1988), pp. 56–57, transcription of the document is at p. 134. However, the transcription contains several errors, for example, reading "*taraf-ı mugayir*" instead of "*turuk ve meabir*". The date of the document is also mistransliterated as 22 Cemaziyelevvel 1270, whereas it should be 22 Receb 1270, therefore it corresponds to 20 April 1854, and not to 20 February 1854.

[268] BOA. İ. DH. 19040. Budak, op. cit., 1988, pp. 134–135.

[269] BOA. İ. DH. 19234, 21 May 1854. For the text of the translation of this letter, see Budak, op. cit. (1988), pp. 135–137. The date of the letter, however, is mistransliterated as 23 Ramazan 1270 (19 June 1854).

[270] In the original Arabic letter, the name is Shamuil, but the translator has turned it into Shamil.

We need to know the aim of the Sublime State and also what to do and how to be here and what news to send to Sheikh Shamuil. However no orders have appeared from your grand vizirial Excellency except for only conferment of rewards and favours and expressions of affection. When I contemplate the situation I wish the Sublime State had at least sent some troops here. Then I thought in my inadequate mind that a great victory would have been gained. Because, although there is a distance of one month between Anapa and Temürkapu from the mountains, it is less by way of the plains. Since the population of the mountains is from old times brave and warlike, if they had seen some regular imperial troops with us, then the population of the places under Russian rule would hasten to submit to our rule. Thanks to the majority of the Circassian population, the affairs of the mountains would have been completed and the Russians' road to Tiflis would be cut in the vicinity of the Abzeh tribe. Then the Russians would leave Tiflis by their own will, or it would be attacked from all sides by the mountain population down to children. They would not know what to do since they would have to deal with both the Danube and the mountains and then they could not have found enough troops to cope with all.[271] [My slightly simplified translation]

The allied fleets sent a steam squadron to the Circassian coasts in May 1854. The Ottoman fleet (including the Egyptian squadron) with Sefer and Behcet Pashas and many Circassian notables with their families as well as gifts from the Sultan for Circassian chiefs also wanted to join the allies off Sevastopol and go to Circassia. The fleet would make Sohum a base for its operations and embark 4,000 troops at Batum to transfer to the Circassian coast. The Kapudan Pasha had already informed the allied admirals verbally and by letter of the departure of the Ottoman squadron to the same destination. The appearance of the Ottoman fleet and troops was intended to encourage the Circassians to rise against the Russians. The fleet was commanded by Ferik Kayserili Ahmed Pasha, and included 12 European officers to instruct the Circassian militia, artillery officers, ammunition and small arms. Thus it was composed of 8 line-of-battle ships, 3 frigates, 4 corvettes and brigs, 5 steam frigates and 3 steam corvettes mounting 1,100 guns. It sailed from the Bosphorus on 6 May 1854.

The Ottoman fleet went to Varna, where it found a rather offensive letter from Vice-Admiral Dundas to Ahmed Pasha, in which Admiral Dundas informed Ahmed Pasha that he had received Kapudan Pasha's letter, but his and Admiral Hamelin's opinion was that the Ottoman

---

[271] BOA. İ. DH. 19234 enc. 2. Cf. Budak, op. cit., 1988, pp. 135–137.

fleet should "cruise along the coasts of Bulgaria and Roumelia, between the Danube and the Bosphorus, until the return of Rear-Admiral Lyons from the coast of Circassia and the arrival of the combined squadrons at Varna".[272] Thus the British admiral slighted Kapudan Pasha and gave directions to the Ottoman fleet without even consulting him! Mushaver Pasha bitterly observed that, if Ahmed Pasha had any sense of dignity, he would have given an appropriate answer and steered for Batum without the company of the allied fleet. But Ahmed Pasha did not want to offend the allied admirals. He feared that the Porte would not support him in case of complaints about his conduct. We must note that he was right in his prediction. Thus he acted like a typical career-building Ottoman pasha. The Ottoman system promoted people like him, who thought of their selfish interests and career more than any concerns of dignity.

As a way out, Ahmed Pasha requested that Mushaver Pasha go to Sevastopol to negotiate with the allied admirals. Mushaver Pasha found the allied fleet off Sevastopol on 11 May. He had noted down a memorandum for the admirals, explaining the importance of the mission. His memorandum read in part as follows:

> With orders to proceed to the coast of Circassia, after consultation with the allied admirals, the Turkish fleet has left the Bosphorus. Sefer Pasha and Behchet Pasha with 300 of their countrymen, and several European officers to act as *talimgis* (instructors), are embarked in it. Those pashas bear the Sultan's firman, empowering them to act in his name, and are carrying *nishans* of merit and *berats* of rank to influential chieftains. In their opinion, unless the Caucasians operate timely in concert and with strategy, the Russian advance in Asia will be certain. There are embarked in the fleet a battery complete with artillery officers and 300 rounds for each gun, 500 barrels of gunpowder, 500 cases of musket cartridges, 400 cases of muskets, 2,000 pistols, 20 cases of cutlasses, 10,000 moulds of lead...It is anticipated that with the aid of 4,000 regular troops, the marines of the fleet, European military instructors, field-pieces, and other named munitions of war, the Circassians will be able to act offensively on the enemy's territory.[273]

Mushaver Pasha added that the Circassians were already expecting the Ottoman fleet as the signal for their gathering and if it did not soon appear off their coast, then doubts would arise in their minds

---

[272] Slade, op. cit., pp. 224–225.
[273] Slade, op. cit., pp. 228–229.

of the Porte's sincerity. However, Admiral Dundas met this proposal very coldly. He was astonished that his directions to the Ottoman fleet had been disregarded because he said that fleet had been placed under his orders. Mushaver Pasha then visited Admiral Hamelin. Hamelin admitted the importance of the Circassian mission but he was worried that the Russian fleet might pursue the Ottoman fleet and that another disaster might happen. Mushaver Pasha said that if the Russian fleet dared to move from Sevastopol then it would be all the worse for it and a good opportunity for the allied fleets. The Ottoman fleet was also in a much better position now. Yet Admiral Hamelin was of the opinion that if the Ottoman fleet went to Circassia then the allies should remain off Sevastopol, which was out of the question. He also said that he had already been blamed for the Sinop disaster and now did not want to risk a repetition. Two days later, Admiral Dundas gave his and Admiral Hamelin's joint answer in an insulting message to Ahmed Pasha. The admirals simply repeated their opinion briefly and added that future communications should be made in writing, "as verbal messages may lead to serious inconveniences and mistakes".[274] The allied admirals had treated the Commander of the Ottoman fleet with contempt and described a mission entrusted by him to a flag officer as a verbal message. Furthermore, they themselves had given a verbal message indicating that the Ottoman fleet should leave Balçık exclusively for the anchorage of the allied fleets.

When Mushaver Pasha brought the news to Varna the Circassian pashas were desperate. Ahmed Pasha, however, did not take much offence. After several days of counselling, he finally signed a letter to the allied admirals, in which he tried to reemphasise the importance of the mission and the reasons for sending Mushaver Pasha to them.[275] He also wrote that, in compliance with their wish, he had anchored at Kavarna, leaving Balçık for the allies. The allied fleets came to Balçık after a week. As they passed Kavarna, the Ottoman fleet saluted them and showed all signs of respect. The admirals informed Ahmed Pasha that next time he should come to visit them without Mushaver Pasha, thus showing their anger with him. They even conspicuously failed to

---

[274] Slade, op. cit., p. 235.
[275] The letter is given by Slade in its original French together with an English translation. Ahmed Pasha in his letter also mentions the *envoyé* of Shamil among the passengers. However, as we have seen from the above letter of Muhammed Emin, dated 21 May 1854, this cannot be Muhammed Emin. See Slade, op. cit., pp. 446–448.

invite Mushaver Pasha to an official dinner on 24 May in honour of the Queen's birthday, while inviting all the pashas and one *bey* from the Ottoman fleet. Ironically, it was a British officer who defended Ottoman interests to the extent of bringing upon himself the scorn of the allied admirals, while the Ottoman commander complied obediently with all the wishes of the allies.

Meanwhile the French steamer *Mogador* brought the first news from the Circassian expedition of the Anglo-French squadron. The Russians had evacuated the coast from Anapa to Redutkale. Sohumkale was in the hands of Circassians. The allied squadron had embarked an Ottoman battalion from Batum to occupy Redutkale, which was then being evacuated by the Russians. The allied admirals then ordered the Ottoman pashas, whom they had invited to dinner, to hastily transfer their passengers and ammunition intended for Circassia to an English screw line-of-battle ship (the *Sans Pareil*) and two Ottoman steam frigates to depart that very evening for Sohumkale and Redutkale. The Ottoman sail ships were to remain in Kavarna. The Ottomans proposed to take four steam frigates to tow four line-of-battle ships, but the admirals would not hear of it. Thus they wanted to turn the Ottoman expedition to Circassia into a consignment. Instead of an Ottoman squadron appearing at the Circassian coast with all due pomp and ceremony, disembarking its envoys with dignity, the Ottoman Circassian pashas with their retinue, families and goods would be cast into the coast of Circassia like ordinary passengers or adventurers from crowded transports. As Slade observes, this could not fail to diminish the importance of the Porte in the eyes of the Circassians. The allied admirals did not even accept a delay until the next forenoon. Thus the Ottoman pashas returned to their ships without dinner. They had again obeyed an insulting order. Pashas, military instructors, traders, women, children, field-pieces, small arms, gunpowder, provisions etc were transferred in five hours from a dozen vessels into three steamers with much natural confusion and damage. The European instructors swore loudly at the admirals.[276]

Four days after the *Mogador*, the British Rear-Admiral Sir Edmund Lyons also arrived from the coast of Circassia. Sir Edmund reported that the Circassians were divided among themselves and requesting

---

[276] Slade, op. cit., p. 242.

troops for action against the Russians.[277] But he was opposed to the expedition of the Ottoman fleet to Circassian coasts. Thus the allied admirals now totally disapproved of an Ottoman expedition. Then they asked Ahmed Pasha to write to the Serasker to request troops to be sent to Circassia. The Serasker Hasan Rıza Pasha replied that they sent the fleet with orders to take 4,000 troops from Batum and the Allies' admirals had detained it at Kavarna. The reason for the allied admirals' desire to keep the Ottoman fleet idle nearby was, as Slade remarks, to prevent its activity on the Circassian coast, as compared to their own inactivity at Balçık, being subject to criticism by the public.

Then these "gallant admirals" spent all the summer lying at Balçık until September, from time to time sending a few steamers to inspect Sevastopol. While this was of course not an effective blockade, the formidable reputation of the British fleet was enough to keep the Russian fleet bottled up in the harbour of Sevastopol. If the Russians had become aware of this allied inactivity, they could have done much harm. But in this war such blunders and such lost opportunities were numerous on all sides. The allied fleets did not do much and in any case did not allow the Ottomans do anything with regard to Circassia. They apparently did not want the Ottomans to be strong in Circassia.

About the middle of June, the Ottoman fleet was allowed to come to Balçık. When the Ottomans proposed to cruise the Anatolian coasts, the allies were again opposed to this idea, being fearful of letting the Ottoman fleet out of their reach, for it might go to Circassia. When they ordered it to go and lie up at Varna, the Ottoman admirals finally lost patience and gathered enough courage to ask kindly why they were being held idle at Varna. The allies replied that they were waiting for an answer from their embassies. Finally the Porte decided to recall its fleet (except for two line-of-battle ships) to Istanbul, because there was no sense in keeping it at Varna if it was not to do anything. The Ottoman fleet anchored in the Bosphorus on 3 July 1854.[278]

Marshal St. Arnaud was of the opinion that the efforts of the Porte to bring Circassia under Ottoman suzerainty fostered the fragmentation of the Circassians and impeded military planning. In a letter dated 27 July 1854 from Varna to the French chargé d'affaires in Istanbul Vincent Benedetti, he wrote that while Shamil sent his naib to unite the

---

[277] Op. cit., p. 244. Besbelli, op. cit., p. 63.
[278] Besbelli, op. cit., p. 65.

Circassians, the Porte "sends emissaries who act in the opposite direction by engaging the tribes to place themselves under the suzerainty of the Ottoman government that will protect them in need".[279]

Thus the allies had prevented the Ottoman expedition to Circassia. But why did the Ottoman admirals not simply go to Circassia on their own? Was it not obvious that the Russian fleet would not dare to move from Sevastopol, when the allied fleets were concentrated in force nearby? The only reasonable explanation seems to lie in the lack of leadership combined with the atmosphere of distrust in the Porte. Nobody wanted to take responsibility for anything, always trying to defer to the authority of some other body.

Sefer Pasha, Behcet Pasha and other Circassians of rank, landing in this way on the shore, without honours from an Ottoman fleet, did not (of course) produce any great impression on the Circassians; they had returned like refugees. Furthermore the presents remained in the hands of those who brought them. Behcet Pasha was involved in his personal affairs and Sefer Pasha could not regain his old influence. The military instructors were left unguided and unattended to. The Circassians felt betrayed by the Porte, because they had expected the Ottoman fleet to come with Ottoman troops.[280]

In mid-July 1854, Shamil made his second attack on the Russian positions in Georgia, his last attempt during the war, in an effort to reach the Ottoman army. With a force of about 15,000 cavalry and infantry, he advanced towards Tiflis, coming as near as Shildi 60 kilometres north-east of Tiflis. While Shamil camped on Mount Pakhalis-Tavi, he sent a force of 10,000 infantry and cavalry into the Alazan valley under the command of his son Gazi Muhammed and Danyal Sultan (or Daniel Bek?). They came quite close to breaking the Russian line but the native Georgian population, the Kakhetians, resisted his forces with determination. After three days of fighting in the Alazan valley, Russian reinforcements under the command of Prince David Chavchavadze arrived and dispersed the *murid* force. Shamil retreated to Dagestan on 22 July.[281] Meanwhile, a detachment commanded by

---

[279] AGKK, IV/2, p. 356.
[280] Slade, op. cit., p. 243. Besbelli, op. cit., p. 63.
[281] Major Prince Baratov, "Opisanie nashestviya skopisch' Shamilya na Kakhetiyu v 1854 godu", *Kavkavskiy Sbornik*, tom I, Tiflis, 1876, pp. 237–267. Budak (op. cit., 1993, pp. 88–90) also gives Shamil's force as 15,000 men, referring to the newspaper CH and Gammer's unpublished dissertation of 1989. Gammer (op. cit., 1994, p. 270), however,

his son Gazi Muhammed raided Prince Chavchavadze's summer house in Tsinondali and brought back many prisoners and much booty. Among the prisoners were Princess Anna, the wife of Prince David Chavchavadze and Princess Varvara, the widow of Prince Iliko Orbeliani (granddaughters of the last Georgian king) with their children and their French governess Madame Anne Drancy. Shamil hoped to exchange them for his son Jemaleddin who was a captive in the court of St. Petersburg.[282]

However, the news of the capture of these women caused quite a sensation.[283] The French embassy demanded that an order to be given to Mustafa Pasha, the commander of the Batum army, to search in cooperation with M. Steyert (the French consul in Batum) for Madame Drancy, a daughter of the French postal employee M. Lemaire.[284] Accordingly an order was sent to Mustafa Pasha.[285] For Lord Stratford it was also an outrage, because the information he received was that two young ladies and their French governess were murdered. Therefore he urged the Porte to apply to the Sultan to write to Shamil or cause a letter to be written to him to release the surviving women and children, while strongly condemning the murder and kidnap of women and children. On 23 September 1854 Stratford gave instructions to his head dragoman to be conveyed to Reşid Pasha:

> I brought verbally under Reshid Pasha's notice some days ago an occurrence which has been stated in the public prints. It appears from the published statement, to which I allude, that an act of barbarous atrocity has been committed in Georgia by a party of soldiers, – it may be presumed, irregulars, detached from Sheik Shamyl's army. These practical marauders are described as having attacked the country house of some person of wealth and official distinction in Georgia. The owner was absent. No resistance was made. Two young ladies and their French governess were, nevertheless, murdered by them in the house.

---

gives Shamil's force as consisting of 7,000 cavalry and 5,000 infantry. Cf. Baumgart, op. cit., pp. 178–179.

[282] For a romanticized story of their captivity, see Lesley Blanch. *The Sabres of Paradise*. New York: Carroll & Graf Publishers, 1995.

[283] See *Journal de Constantinople*, nr. 536, 29 Aout 1854, nr. 537, 4 Septembre 1854, *Ceride-i Havadis*, nr. 704, 9 Zilhicce 1270 (2 September 1854). Budak argues that one of the results of this event was that it caused Britain and France to seek connections with Shamil for the independence of Circassia, without mentioning any negative effects for Shamil (op. cit., 1993, p. 90).

[284] BOA. HR. SYS. 907/16, dated 20 August 1854, but this date is not included in the text of the note, so it is probably a later date than the actual submission of the note.

[285] BOA. HR. MKT. 91/14.

> The proprietor's wife, a lady of rank and education, was carried off to the mountains with several female friends, her guests at the time. I need not remark to you that these are circumstances which shock every feeling of humanity. They are not the acts of soldiers, but of assassins. Honorable war rejects them, and honorable men can have no sympathy with the perpetrators.[286]

Stratford stated that an officer from the Kars army together with a British officer should be detached to present the letter to Shamil and bring the ladies back. "No expense need be incurred by the Porte for the object of benevolence", wrote Stratford, adding insult to injury. It is interesting that the wording of Stratford's note is much more severe than the French note.

Sadrazam Kıbrıslı Mehmed Emin Pasha applied to the Sultan on 12 October 1854, stating that some *başıbozuks* from the army of Shamil had perpetrated atrocities, killing two young ladies and their governess and kidnapping women of from a notable family.[287] Thus the grand vizier repeated the incorrect information concerning the murder of women. He asked for a letter of advice and warning to be sent to Shamil, advising him to punish the culprits and prevent such events in the future. The letter was to be sent with Dagestani Enis Efendi from the Bureau of Translation. He would be given verbal instructions as well. His travel allowance would also be given. The draft of the letter was attached. The Sultan approved it.

The letter to Shamil first began with praising him for his brave war for the cause of Islam. Then followed the news of the murder and kidnapping of women. It was stated that a groups of *başıbozuks* had attacked innocent children and women. Although it was certain that Shamil as a pious man would punish such an act contrary to the shariat, it was necessary to carry out the punishment of those responsible for this deplorable act because Shamil's name could otherwise be defamed. Therefore Shamil was required to punish the culprits and to return the women to their families. Furthermore, Russian prisoners of war should be kept well according to international rules. In general the

---

[286] Stratford de Redcliffe's instructions to head dragoman Stephen Pisani, Therapia, 23 September 1854. BOA. HR. TO. 220/48. Translation into Ottoman Turkish is in BOA. İ. HR. 114/5577.
[287] BOA. İ. HR. 114/5577 enc. 5.

tone of the letter was not offensive, but certainly it would not please Shamil.[288]

Stratford had also written to the British military commissioner in the Anatolian army Colonel William Fenwick Williams (1800–1883) in Kars, requesting him to exercise his influence with Sheikh Shamil to get the women released. Williams wrote a letter to Shamil, but the letter seems to have reached Shamil rather late, after Shamil exchanged the ladies for his son Jemaleddin and 40,000 silver roubles on 22 March 1855.[289] Shamil's reply to Williams, dated 12 Receb 1271 (31 March 1855), written in Arabic and translated by Williams' secretary for Ottoman, Henry Churchill, reads in part as follows:

> We thank you for the notice you take of our dignity and honour, and for giving us a place amongst worthy men; and though we may not be that in truth and reality, God forbid that we should do anything which might be considered disgraceful by the Mohammedan laws or by the exalted government [the Sublime Porte?]. We had liberated the women before the arrival of your letter, and had you been acquainted with the true circumstances you would not have found fault with us; for everybody knows that we are always humane; that we expend our breath in reciting the holy words of the Lord of the Creation, and scorn the enmity of the infidels our foes.[290]

A Russian account from 1860, when Shamil was already in captivity in Kaluga, gives his narrative of this event:

> At the very beginning of the war he [Shamil] received an offer to prepare to meet the allied forces at Imereti. Expressing his agreement Shamil immediately took steps to carry out his plan…In the spring of 1854 he marched towards the district of Chartalah…He intended to march on Tiflis, but in order to act more freely, he sent to inform the Ottoman commanders in Kars and in Abkhazeti of his intentions. Awaiting an answer, he sent his son with all the cavalry and some infantry into Kakheti, while he himself with the rest of his force camped near one of our forts…Soon he received an answer, the contents of which were extremely insulting. Instead of being grateful for his expressed readiness to cooperate with the plans of the allies and for the speed with which he

---

[288] Letter to Shamil. BOA. İ. HR. 114/5577 enc. 2 and HR. SYS. 1354/60 enc. 1.
[289] Gammer, op. cit., 1994, p. 272.
[290] See Colonel Atwell Lake, *Kars and Our Captivity in Russia*, London: Richard Bentley, 1856, pp. 340–341. The letter was addressed as "From the slave of God, Shemouil, to the illustrious and honourable Colonel Williams" and sealed "Shemouil" according to Mr Churchill.

had carried out his promise, he was reproached and told off as a common subject.[291]

After this event, Shamil remained on the defence. In any case he and his followers must have felt great disappointment from the Ottoman defeats by the Russians. Nevertheless he continued to seek the favour of the caliph and use this favour to enhance his political standing.

Shamil's naib in Circassia Muhammed Emin was made a pasha with the rank of *mirmiran* in May 1854.[292] He came to Istanbul with seventy notables of Circassia in July 1854 for negotiations. In August Ferik Alyanak Mustafa Pasha (?–1884) from the Rumelian army, although unsuccessful against the Russians in the Babadağ region, was promoted to the rank of *müşir* and sent to Batum to replace Mehmed Selim Pasha as the commander of the Batum army. Alyanak Mustafa Pasha was apparently chosen because of his Circassian origins. Ömer Pasha had also recommended him.[293] On the request of Mustafa Pasha, Muhammed Emin and his notables received monetary rewards before leaving Istanbul.[294] We do not know, however, what instructions he received.

Müşir Alyanak Mustafa Pasha in Batum tried to gain the sympathy of the Circassian, Abkhazian and Georgian notables. He sent them gifts and letters inviting them to join the Ottoman side. Especially he tried to win the Abkhazian Prince Hamid (or Abdülhamid) Bey, whose Russian or Christian name was Mikhail Shervashidze. Mikhail Georgievich Shervashidze (r. 1822–1864) was the last Prince (*Vladetel*) of Abkhazia. His title in Abkhazian was *Chachba*. He was given the rank of lieutenant-general by Nikolai I in 1848. In a letter to Hamid Bey, dated 4 October 1854, Mustafa Pasha promised him on behalf of the Sultan all the titles, ranks and rewards that Russia had given him. He argued that all states had now joined the Ottoman Empire and that Russia was soon going to collapse. The Porte would no longer leave those territories and its population to Russia. Therefore Mustafa Pasha had now been appointed as the commander of the Batum army and *muhafız* of all Abkhazia and Circassia with plentiful troops and provisions. He continued his message as follows:

---

[291] Gammer, op. cit., p. 393.
[292] Budak, op. cit. (1993), p. 77.
[293] BOA. İ. MMS. 2/40, 12 June 1854.
[294] BOA. İ. MMS. 2/70, 14 September 1853. Muhammed Emin Pasha received 10,000 piastres, others from 2,500 to 1,500 according to their ranks.

Long ago, you passed over to the Russian side and remained there, leaving your country, land and state. However, since you belong to a great dynasty here and since you are an outstanding, intelligent *bey*, I do not believe that you would leave this place and prefer our enemies the Muscovites. I have even heard when I came to Sohum that you intended to join the Sublime State and serve it. Therefore I presume that the reason for your remaining there is that perhaps you are with us in spirit and Russian only in appearance and that your real intention is to understand the conditions and weakness of the Russians? For nothing is impossible in the world...Did some improper people come to you and stir your mind with some lies? Or did they do something to offend you, hitherto being unable to tell you properly how kind and affectionate the Sublime State will be to such worthy *bey*s as you? Your stay there is no doubt for one of these reasons. In any case, such things are possible.[295] [My translation]

Mustafa Pasha then invited him to the Ottoman side with all honours, addressing him as "fellow countryman" since Mustafa Pasha was from Anapa.

Hamid Bey was now in a difficult situation. He had to choose between Russia and the Ottoman Empire with its allies. Yet the Porte did not inspire much confidence and the allies were not clear in their intentions for Abkhazia and Circassia. Did they plan an independent Abkhazia and Circassia? Did they want to annex these countries to the Ottoman Empire? What protection did they offer against Russia after the war? Naturally, he was afraid of being left in Russian hands if he sided with the allies and if the allies were not permanent in Circassia. So he chose a way between, trying to appease both sides, although by July 1855 Mustafa Pasha seems to have reported Hamid's acceptance of Ottoman suzerainty.[296] Meanwhile Mustafa Pasha had been authorized by the sultan to distribute salaries and ranks from lieutenant to *ferik* to influential and willing notables.[297]

---

[295] Müşir Mustafa Pasha to Hamid Bey (Mikhail Shervashidze), 4 October 1854. BOA. A. MKT. UM. 1970/19 enc. 14. This letter is written in astonishingly simple, clear, plain Turkish expressions, a rare sight in Ottoman official parlance.

[296] BOA. A. AMD. 54/91, 13 July 1855.

[297] BOA. İ. MMS. 3/97 enc. 3, 12–13 November 1854, cited by Budak, op. cit. (1993), p. 88. Budak states that "Abdülhamid Bey" was given a salary of 2,000 piastres and the rank of *mirmiran*. However, the document mentions not him but a certain "Mağan Kasi" to be rewarded with this rank and salary. This person was the Abkhazian notable Katsi Marganiya from Samurzakan, who held the rank of lieutenant-general in the Russian army. See K. Borozdin, *Omer Pasha v Mingrelii*, St Petersburg, 1873, p. 29.

Illus. 8 Mushir Selim Pasha, Commander of the Ottoman Army of Batum. *ILN*, 19 Aug. 1854.

In 1855, the allies, instead of depending on the expertise of the Porte in relations with the Circassians, quite independently sent their agents to Circassia to organize the Circassian tribes.[298] The British sent John Longworth as "civil commissioner" and the French sent Charles Champoiseau as consul to Redutkale.[299] Lord Stratford asked the Porte to

---

[298] Lord Redcliffe's instructions to head dragoman Pisani, 27 May 1855. BOA. İ. MMS. 5/166, cited by Budak, op. cit. (1993), p. 148. Budak gives the name of the French official as "Champassaur".

[299] John Augustus Longworth (?–1875) was one of David Urquhart's agents to Circassia in the 1840s and British consul in Monastir in 1851–60. From April 1855 he was sent with special mission to Circassia. Charles François Noël Champoiseau (1830–1909) was French vice consul in Redutkale in 1855–1857. Müşir Mustafa Pasha wrote to the Porte on 20 May 1855 on Champoiseau's mission to Redutkale. See BOA. HR. SYS. 1352/54. It seems that both of them were in Sohum at the time of Ömer Pasha's campaign. Laurence Oliphant writes that "during my stay at Souchoum I was hospitably entertained by Mons. Champoiseau, the French consul". This was in the first week of October 1855. Oliphant notes that Mr Longworth was also there. See Oliphant, op. cit., pp. 58–59.

Illus. 9   Prince Mikhail Shervashidze of Abkhazia (Hamid Bey). Drawn by Herr Zuther, in Laurence Oliphant's book *The Trans-Caucasian Campaign of the Turkish Army under Omer Pasha*, 1856.

issue orders to Mustafa Pasha at Batum to assist these agents in every way.[300] There is no doubt that the orders were issued. These agents, however, achieved very little. Furthermore the allies tried to check and

---

[300] Stratford's instructions to Pisani, to be read to Fuad Pasha, 27 May 1855. BOA. HR. SYS. 1352/64.

supervise all operations of the Porte by attaching military commissioners to its armies.

The British former Secretary of State for War, the Duke of Newcastle made a six-week tour of Circassia and the northern part of Georgia in the autumn of 1855. There he saw Sefer Pasha and Muhammed Emin as well. His impressions and his opinions in his letter to the British foreign minister reflect the opinion of at least part of the British government:

> I had most unusually good opportunities of seeing the two principal Mahometan Magnates of Circassia – Sefer Pacha and the Naib – indeed as regards the latter very remarkable man I doubt if anybody has seen so much. Sefer is an effete old rogue and robber – just the man whom you might expect to find as deriving his authority from the Sultan and of course thwarting every English view of policy. He must be recalled by the Porte but nobody ought to be sent in his stead – anybody she so sent will be just as bad and the Porte has no right to send anybody. Turkey never had any real possession of the Country – her rights in Anapa were just like ours in Gibraltar and whatever rights she had she resigned by the treaty of Adrianople. She has not recovered them by conquest. English & French Arms have set free the littoral of Circassia, and it is monstrous to see the Turkish flag flying in every deserted Russian fort & to witness attempts to establish Turkish government in the Country. Omer Pacha quite concurs in this view and he has removed some of the scoundrels whom he found feathering their nests at Soukoum Kaleh, Bathum, and other places, – but even he can hardly make head against this system of complicated iniquity.[301]

Newcastle added that Ömer Pasha was now aware of the dangers of sending a Muslim army into a Christian country. Newcastle also wrote that Ömer Pasha told him that an English or French army ought to be where he is and he ought to be on the Kuban. Newcastle reminded Clarendon that Britain ought to declare to the Circassians and the Georgians their future plans for their country and give guarantees for their liberty after they make peace with Russia. Finally Newcastle told Clarendon that his agent in Circassia (Mr Longworth) was unfit for the job.

The power struggle between Sefer Pasha and Muhammed Emin in Circassia finally resulted in an armed conflict between them. A letter from Muhammed Emin, dated 30 December 1855, informs the grand vizier that Sefer Pasha had attacked Muhammed Emin's men and him-

---

[301] Newcastle to Clarendon, Sinop, 3 November 1855. AGKK, III/4, (1988), p. 284.

self while he was residing at the courthouse built with the approval of Serdar-ı Ekrem Ömer Pasha and Sefer Pasha in Şapsuğ region.[302] Muhammed Emin writes that Sefer Pasha's attack was repulsed but that he gathered some regular troops with three guns and some bandits and attacked from Anapa into Abkhazia, plundering Muslim property. They again fought and Sefer Pasha retreated. The naib pasha adds that cavalry Brigadier-General (Mirliva) Ali Pasha has also organized conspiracies among the Circassians against him. Finally he expressed his concerns on the fate of Islam in the region.

There are basically two approaches in Ottoman and Turkish historiography to Shamil's role in the Crimean War. The first one is represented by Cevdet Pasha, who accused Shamil of remaining silent as if he had made an agreement with the Russians. His evaluation of the attitudes of Shamil and the Circassians to the war is interesting and worth quoting at some length here:

> Unfortunately, Sheikh Shamil of Dagestan, having grappled with the Russians in Dagestan for so many years, did not show the action expected of him during the Crimean War. He retreated to an onlooker's position as if he had concluded an armistice with Russia and while the coasts from Batum to Anapa were captured by the allied states, the Abkhazian and Circassian tribes also remained as though neutral. Actually the cold attitude of the Circassians was also caused by the errors of this [our] side because those sent by the Sublime State to summon these tribes were of slave origins. But the Circassians did not trust the slaves whom they had sold. They did not esteem at all the titles and addresses of pasha and *bey* which we had given. The British for their part, as soon as they approached those coasts, advised first the prohibition of the sale of male and female slaves. But if the Circassians were to abandon their old customs and habits, then for them there was no difference between the Russians and the English. In short, the reasons and means used by both the Sublime Porte and the Europeans to gain the tribes of the Caucasus caused their hate and therefore the desired aims were not attained.[303] [My translation]

The second approach is to accuse the Ottoman Empire for not having rendered enough assistance to the Caucasian peoples. The propo-

---

[302] Translation of an Arabic letter from Muhammed Emin to the grand vizier, dated 30 December 1855. BOA. HR. TO. 424/37 enc. 2.
[303] Cevdet Pasha, op. cit., p. 90. Cf. Hakan Erdem, *Slavery in the Ottoman Empire and Its Demise, 1800–1909*, London: Macmillan Press, 1996, p. 106. Lütfi Efendi (op. cit., p. 91) also wrote that the Circassians did not esteem people who are not noble and free by birth.

nents of this approach are usually the Caucasian Ottomans or Turkish citizens of Caucasian origins.[304] However, we have seen that the allies intentionally prevented any meaningful assistance being rendered by the Ottomans to the Circassians. By his presence alone and by his two raids towards Tiflis, Shamil had already rendered invaluable service to the Porte, because he had kept a significant number of Russian troops away from the Russo-Ottoman front. The Porte, however, weak and dependent upon the allies with different aims, could not give a strong assurance to the Circassians and the Dagestanis, because rumours of peace were always present during the war, and the Circassians were rightly afraid of Russia's vengeance in case of their commitment and the abandonment of the Porte and its allies.[305]

The Campaign of Summer 1854 and the Battle of Kürekdere

In the Caucasus, the campaign season of 1854 opened somewhat late in June. The Russian army was now on the offensive. General Prince Andronikov's forces in Guria, around Kutaisi consisted of two infantry regiments, one Cossack regiment, two battalions and the Gurian and Imeretian *militia*, making up approximately 9,000 men and 10 guns. On 8 June, a Russian force under the command of Colonel Prince Eristov was attacked by the Laz *başıbozuks* under the command of Hasan Bey. The Laz were repulsed and lost 200 men. On 15 June, General Andronikov attacked Selim Pasha's forces along the river Çolok between Ozurgeti and Çürüksu (Kobuleti or Kapulet). Selim Pasha lost 4,000 men and all his guns, and retired to Batum. The Russians lost 1,500 men.[306]

---

[304] See, for example, İsmail Berkok, *Tarihte Kafkasya*, Istanbul: İstanbul Matbaası, 1958 and Aytek Kundukh, *Kafkasya Müridizmi: Gazavat Tarihi*, Haz. Tarık Cemal Kutlu, Istanbul: Gözde Kitaplar Yayınevi, 1987.

[305] Budak argues that both positions are wrong. See Mustafa Budak, "1853–1856 Kırım Savaşı'nda Osmanlı Devleti ile Şeyh Şamil Arasındaki İlişkiler", *Tarih Boyunca Balkanlardan Kafkaslara Türk Dünyası Semineri, 29–31 Mayıs 1995. Bildiriler*, Istanbul: İ. Ü. Edebiyat Fakültesi Basımevi, 1996, pp. 79–92. He finds the policy of the Porte simply cautious.

[306] Tarle, op. cit., vol. 1, p. 516. Cf. Budak, op. cit. (1993), pp. 81–82. Budak, referring to CH, gives quite different numbers in favour of the Ottoman army, but adds that "although the Ottoman side claimed victory in this battle, General Andronikov brought his main forces to Ozurgeti on 15 June 1854".

At the end of June 1854, Lieutenant-General Baron K. K. Vrangel's forces, consisting of 5,000 men with 12 guns, advanced towards the Çengel pass near Karabulak village between Iğdır and Bayezid. The pass was occupied by Ferik Selim Pasha's forces consisting of approximately 8,000 regular infantry with 8 guns and 7,000 to 10,000 *başıbozuks*, half of whom were Kurdish.[307] In mid-July, Vrangel, reinforced with 5,000 more troops, attacked this force and dispersed it. The Ottomans lost about 2,000 men dead and wounded with 370 taken prisoner and 4 guns captured, while the Russian losses were 400.[308] The Kurdish başıbozuks fled to their villages, while Selim Pasha retreated towards Van.[309] On 31 July Vrangel occupied Bayezid without battle, where he captured significant provisions. Bayezid was on the commercial road from Tehran to Trabzon, thus the Russians were now in a position to control the caravan trade from Iran to Trabzon, which was as important for Britain as it was for the Ottoman Empire. According to Colonel Mikhail Likhutin of the Erivan corps, Selim Pasha had blamed his chief of staff, a Polish émigré and a "renegade", for the decision to accept battle with the Russians. Consequently, the chief of staff was recalled to Istanbul. But Ferik Selim Pasha was also recalled to Istanbul at the end of 1854.[310]

While these battles took place on the left and right flanks of the front, the decisive battle of the 1854 campaign would be in the middle of the front, between Kars and Gümrü, near a village called Kürekdere, where the main forces confronted each other in an open field battle. On the Ottoman side, Mustafa Zarif Pasha had reinforced his forces to compensate for winter losses and now commanded an army of 44,046 regular and 17,625 irregular troops, as of 13 July 1854, according

---

[307] General-Mayor Mikhail Likhutin, *Russkie v Aziatskoy Turtsii v 1854 i 1855 godakh*, St. Petersburg: Tipografiya tovarischestva "Obschestvennaya Pol'za", 1863, p. 76. Budak, op. cit. (1993), p. 96.

[308] Budak, op. cit., p. 96. Cf. Ibragimbeyli (op. cit., p. 224) also gives the number of Ottoman forces around Bayezid as 18,000 men. According to Ibragimbeyli, Vrangel's forces included about 1,000 Azerbaijanian, 150 Armenian and 150 Kurdish irregular cavalry.

[309] Budak, quoting from Yüzbaşı Fevzi Kurtoğlu, argues that Selim Pasha of Batum had come to help. However, Müşir Selim Pasha did not and could not come to help from as far as Batum to Bayezid, while even those nearer Ottoman forces at Kars, Erzurum and Van did not come. Kurtoğlu is simply unaware of the second Selim Pasha other than the one at Batum, namely Ferik Selim Pasha at Bayezid. Gürel (op. cit., p. 111) makes the same mistake.

[310] Likhutin, op. cit., p. 188.

to his own report to the Ottoman minister of war.³¹¹ However, these numbers may have been inflated in order to draw more rations from the treasury. The Ottoman ministers had told the British ambassador and the French chargé d'affaires (Benedetti) on 1 June 1854 that the army at Kars (including the new *redif*) amounted to 35 thousand men and about 10 thousand irregulars.³¹² According to Zarif Pasha's report, the troops were stationed as follows: At the village of Subatan near Kars, there were 10,431 irregulars (*başıbozuks* and volunteers) of which 8,830 cavalry men and 1,601 infantry, under the command of *mirmirans* Resul Pasha, Edhem Pasha, *mirülümera* Hacı Halil Pasha, *sergerde* Kane (?) and others. Although it is not stated in the report, these irregular troops were all under the command of General Kmety (İsmail Pasha).

The main bulk of the Anatolian regular army (including *redif* troops) was stationed in two divisions at the village of Hacı Veli near Kars. The first division consisted of 18,533 men: 14,672 infantry, 2,871 cavalry and 990 artillery men with 36 cannons. The division was commanded by Ferik Kerim Pasha (called Baba Kerim, that is, "Father Kerim" by soldiers), while Ferik Hacı Rıza Pasha and the *mirliva* pashas Mustafa, Ahmed, Mehmed, (another) Ahmed and Hüseyin were serving under his command.

The second division consisted of 17,010 men: 13,162 infantry, 2,157 cavalry, 220 sappers and 1,471 artillery men with 48 cannons. The division was commanded by Ferik Veli Pasha, while Ferik Raşid Pasha and artillery commander Mirliva Tahir Pasha were serving under his command. 3,104 *redif* infantry men with 41 cannons were stationed in the city of Kars and in the redoubts around it under the command of the *mirliva* pashas Şükrü, Hafız and Salih. It must be noted that Mirliva Abdurrahman Pasha is somehow not listed in this report, whereas he was to play a notorious role in the battle of Kürekdere.

At Bayezid, there were 3,878 regular troops (3,587 infantry, 119 cavalry, 172 artillery men) and 7,194 irregular troops (nearly half of which cavalry) under the command of Ferik Selim Pasha. Finally there were 1,521 men and 18 cannons in Erzurum.

The best regiments in the Kars army were from the Arabistan army, but this had nothing to do with their being from Arabia; it was simply

---

³¹¹ BOA. İ. DH. 305/19393 enc. 3.
³¹² Strtatford to Clarendon, Constantinople, June 2, 1854. AGKK III/2, p. 436.

the result of good command, namely able colonels like Çerkes Hüseyin Bey, in whom the soldiers had confidence. Thus the soldiers fully displayed their military capacity.[313] There were more than twenty Ottoman pashas and also more than twenty European staff officers, with Hurşid Pasha (General Guyon) as their chief, some of them being generals of repute from the Hungarian revolution of 1848, as we have seen above. Colonel Count Charles de Meffray, an envoy of the French emperor, joined them in June 1854 as first aide-de-camp to the *mushir*.[314]

Relations between Hurşid Pasha and the *mushir* and among these staff officers were restrained and full of intricacies. Mustafa Zarif Pasha did not like Hurşid Pasha and favoured instead Miralay Feyzi Bey (Colonel Kollman), who had converted to Islam and spoke Turkish well. Zarif Pasha considered him the best in terms of military and engineering talents. He also praised the Polish generals Mirliva Arslan Pasha (Bystrzonowski) and Şahin Pasha (Breanski) and the Hungarian İsmail Pasha (General Kmety). At the beginning of June 1854, Zarif Pasha wrote to the *serasker* that Hurşid Pasha was a short-tempered person, who did not respect other people's opinions and who did not possess enough knowledge of the area and of military science.[315] In another letter of the same date, he recommended Feyzi Bey be promoted to the rank of *mirliva* and appointed chief of staff. He also added that when Feyzi Bey was a colonel in the Hungarian army, Hurşid Pasha was at that time a major under him.[316] Zarif Pasha's preference for Fevzi Bey was shared by Ferhad Pasha (General Stein), who in his report to the *serasker* dated 26 June 1854 also praised Fevzi Bey and recommended that he be appointed as chief of staff.[317] Ferhad Pasha also noted that though every day new staff officers came to the army headquarters at Kars, very few of them were competent and knew Turkish. Many of them were bad examples for the troops and with their high ranks they were only a burden on the state budget. Therefore they should be sent

---

[313] Duncan, op. cit., p. 188. Russian sources confirm the distinguished character of these Arabistan regiments and the *hassa* or Dersaadet regiments. See for example *Blokada Karsa. Pis'ma ochevidtsev o pokhode 1855 goda v Aziatskuyu Turtsiyu*. Tiflis: Tipografiya kantselyarii namestnika Kavkazskago, 1856, p. 113.

[314] Karal, op. cit. (1940), p. 486 and p. 491. Zayonchkovskiy, op. cit., p. 460. AGKK, IV/2, p. 440.

[315] Zarif Pasha to Serasker Hasan Rıza Pasha, 2 June 1854. BOA. İ. MMS. 2/52 enc. 7.

[316] Zarif Pasha to Serasker Hasan Rıza Pasha, 2 June 1854. BOA. İ. MMS. 2/52 enc. 8.

[317] Sezer, op. cit., p. 82. Ferhad Pasha's report in French and its translation into Ottoman Turkish are at BOA. HR. MKT. 80/51.

back. Two Polish officers were examples. Arslan Pasha, who was there to form a company from Polish deserters from the Russian army, was useless. Şahin Pasha had resigned as second chief of staff. He wore a Sardinian colonel's uniform although he received his salary from the Porte. While these two Polish officers claimed that they were on a special mission from Emperor Napoleon III, Ferhad Pasha argued that they only wanted to avoid being under the command of the chief of staff Hurşid Pasha.

Infantry Brigadier-General (Mirliva) Mustafa Raşid Pasha from his station at the village of Hacı Veli near Kars had also reported to Zarif Pasha that Hurşid Pasha had said that Silistria had been captured by the Russians, despite official news to the contrary.[318] It seems very unlikely that Hurşid Pasha would spread such rumours when there was no need or basis for it. Why should he do so? Although Hurşid Pasha was of British origin, the support of the British government and the British ambassador was not clear. In July, Lord Clarendon wrote that Britain did not have special sympathies for Hurşid Pasha, but objected to leaving the command of the Kars army in incompetent hands.[319] Hurşid Pasha himself, in a letter to an unidentified Ottoman grandee who seems to be out of Istanbul at that time, complained of Zarif Pasha, saying that although he was gentle and elegant as his name suggested, he did not know how to command and did not listen to advice either. Thus Hurşid Pasha was afraid of his honour being harmed in the end. He wrote that in his situation he should quit the army, but he wanted first to seek advice from his addressee. He did not know to whom write. The *serasker* was a friend of the *müşir* and the *sadrazam* was unpredictable. Should he write to the British ambassador? He added that if his advice had been heeded, no Russians would have remained there until that time.[320] One year later, when Hurşid Pasha was unemployed in Istanbul, Lord Clarendon and Lord Palmerston requested an active command for Hurşid Pasha in the Ottoman army in Europe or in Asia.[321]

---

[318] BOA. İ. MMS. 2/52 enc. 11, 16 June 1854. Raşid Pasha was probably promoted to *ferik* in July 1854.
[319] Translation of an extract from Lord Clarendon's letter, dated 11 July 1854. BOA. HR. SYS. 1349/47.
[320] BOA. İ. MMS. 2/65 enc. 6, 23 July 1854.
[321] Musurus to Fuad Pasha the foreign minister, London, 13 October 1855. BOA. HR. SYS. 1354/11.

Polish officers in general did not like Hurşid Pasha. In fact, Bystrzonowski and Breanski soon resigned from their posts. On 7 August 1854 they wrote to the serasker that they had learned from a letter from Count Zamoyski that Lord Stratford was accusing them of plotting against Hurşid Pasha. They were rather indignant of "*cette accusation calomnieuse*" and did not want to serve under him.[322] While British sources in general praise Hurşid Pasha as a good officer, Sadık Pasha is highly critical of him, calling him an "emptier of bottles". Since Sadık Pasha was in Rumelia, he must have gained his opinion of Hurşid Pasha from those Polish staff officers who served under Hurşid Pasha. Sadık Pasha describes Zarif Pasha as a "talented administrator and officer, although better as administrator, than commander". This characterization also seems to come from the Polish officers whom Zarif Pasha favoured, as we have seen. Sadık Pasha was also very critical of Stratford de Redcliffe, whom he called "Little Sultan" and argued that Stratford wanted Hurşid Pasha to have practical and Zarif Pasha only nominal command.

Sadık Pasha writes that Hurşid Pasha gave "Lew" Pasha the task of reading newspapers and taking notes, appointed "Potop" Bey master of bakery and "Piorun" Bey master of trumpets as examples of his contempt for the Polish officers.[323] Sadık Pasha argues that although "among Polish officers there was disorder, disagreement, jealousy, intrigues and gossip", there were also talented and brave officers among them such as Breanski, Bystrzonowski, Zarzycki, Grotowski, Jagmin and Wieruski, who were "a hundred times better than the English and Italian officers".[324] This is in sharp contrast to the characterizations of the Polish officers in the memoirs of the British officers, doctors and journalists who have been with the Anatolian army, such as Atwell Lake, Humphrey Sandwith and Charles Duncan. After the battle of Kürekdere, Colonel de Meffray reported to St. Arnaud that Bystrzonowski must be dismissed.[325]

---

[322] BOA. İ. MMS. 5/170 enc. 12–13, 7 August 1854.
[323] Michal Czajkowski (Mehmed Sadyk Pasza), op. cit., 1962, p. 75. Interestingly, Czajkowski calls the Polish officers by the Polish equivalents of their Ottoman-Turkish names. Thus he writes Lew Pasha instead of Arslan Pasha, Potop Bey instead of Tufan Bey, Piorun Bey instead of Yıldırım Bey and Sokol Pasha instead of Şahin Pasha.
[324] Czajkowski, op. cit., p. 77.
[325] Zayonchkovskiy, ibid.

On the Russian side, Prince Bebutov had about 13,000 infantry, 3,000 regular cavalry and 4,000 irregular cavalry with 68 to 76 guns.[326] According to Zarif Pasha, the Russians had 76 guns while the Ottomans had 84 guns. The Ottoman army was stronger numerically as well.[327] The Russians, being numerically inferior, however, had a weighty counterbalance: the 8 grenadier battalions and 16 squadrons of the dragoon brigade were superior in quality to any of the Ottoman troops, perhaps even the best regiments from the Arabistan army or the rifle (*şeşhaneci*) battalions. This army included formations of irregular cavalry from Azerbaijan, Kabardia, Georgia, and Karabakh. It was under the command of Colonel Mikhail Tarielovich Loris-Melikov, Colonel Andronikashvili and Lieutenant-Colonel Kundukhov. Both Ottoman and Russian commanders were wary however, and limited themselves to observation until August. At the beginning of August, Bebutov took a position between the Kürekdere and Paldırvan villages. After receiving the news of the Russian victory in Bayezid, Bebutov planned an attack on 5 August.[328]

The Anatolian army had taken a position near Hacı Veli Köy. By his own account, Zarif Pasha was not enthusiastic about an attack, referring to orders from the *serasker* to be defensive. However, he maintained that Hurşid Pasha and the European staff officers all wanted to engage the enemy. The *başıbozuks* and the *ulema* among them had also started grumbling: why did we gather here if we are not going to fight? The regular soldiers and officers also wanted to engage. In these conditions, Zarif Pasha writes that, in order to both deceive and appease them, he suggested plans for all kinds of operations while continuing to temporize with them.[329] When he received the news of the defeat at Bayezid on 3 August, Zarif Pasha wanted to send some troops there. But Hurşid Pasha opposed this plan and instead proposed first to attack Bebutov immediately at dawn on 4 August, while he was relatively weak, and then to attack Vrangel's forces that were advancing towards Erzurum. Most of the officers supported this plan. As for the orders to be on the defensive, the war council decided that since they were operating on Ottoman territory and trying to drive the enemy away from Ottoman

---

[326] Zayonchkovskiy, op. cit., p. 465, Ibragimbeyli, op. cit., p. 252.
[327] Zarif Pasha's evidence, BOA. İ. MMS. 5/170 enc. 9, answer 5.
[328] Ibragimbeyli, op. cit., p. 253.
[329] See Karal, op. cit. (1940), p. 492. Cf. Zarif Pasha's evidence, BOA. İ. MMS. 5/170 enc. 9.

territory, they should be considered as acting defensively.[330] Hurşid Pasha's plan was accepted, but according to the *Times* correspondent, who was present at the battle, Zarif Pasha said that the fourth and fifth days were unlucky days so the attack was delayed until 6 August.[331] Meanwhile Bebutov learned of the attack from spies and accordingly he also gathered all his forces together in preparation.

According to Ferik Raşid Pasha, although Hurşid Pasha's plan was accepted, Zarif Pasha did not execute it properly. When the army was to march early in the morning, Hurşid Pasha urged Zarif Pasha to go but Zarif Pasha replied him: "I am the *müşir*. I know when to set out".[332] Thus they quarrelled and the march began only after evening in the dark. Then the second division set out late and came to the battle field very late. Raşid Pasha added that due to lack of water on the battlefield, the Ottoman troops suffered from thirst.

According to Staff Lieutenant-Colonel İskender Bey's report written after the battle, there were two opposing views among officers in the Kars army. Zarif Pasha the *müşir*, Ferik Veli Pasha, Şahin Pasha as well as İskender Bey argued for defensive tactics, while Hurşid Pasha and Colonel Meffray wanted to attack the Russians. In the end, Hurşid Pasha's plan was accepted. Hurşid Pasha divided the Ottoman army into three parts, namely two wings and the reserve. Only five battalions under the command of Hafız Pasha were left in Kars. Ferik Kerim Pasha with Feyzi Bey commanded the right wing or the first division that consisted of 24 battalions of infantry, 2 regiments of cavalry and 30 cannons. Ferik Veli Pasha with Ferik Raşid Pasha and General Kmety[333] (İsmail Pasha) commanded the left wing, while Zarif Pasha with Hurşid Pasha was in the centre or in the left wing which was larger than the right one. The reserve troops were in the middle and consisted of 8 battalions of infantry and one regiment of *redif* cavalry with 6 cannons under the command of Mirliva Hasan Pasha. The *başıbozuks* were on both wings and their duty was to encircle the enemy. On the right side Mirliva Abdurrahman Pasha commanded the *başıbozuks* of Hacı

---

[330] Interrogation of Zarif Pasha. BOA. İ. MMS. 5/170 enc. 9, paragraph (answer) 5.
[331] Quoted by Sandwith, op. cit., p. 101 or p. 53 in the abridged edition.
[332] *Mazbata* of the MVL on the trial of Zarif and Hurşid pashas, 11 April 1855. BOA. İ. MMS. 5/170 enc. 2.
[333] Allen and Muratoff (op. cit., p. 76) call him Colonel Kmety, on account of his former rank in the Hungarian army. Kmety now had he rank of *mirliva*, that is, brigadier-general. Budak (op. cit., 1993, p. 99) repeats this mistake by quoting from them. Furthermore, Allen and Muratoff do not mention Veli Pasha in this battle.

Timur Ağa and Reşid Ağa, reinforced with one battalion of infantry and 4 field cannons. Their duty was to capture the Karadağ hill. On the left side Ferik Mustafa Pasha commanded the *başıbozuks* reinforced with 4 cavalry regiments.[334]

Hurşid Pasha's plan, though well-prepared, required a well-trained army capable of skilful manoeuvring and coordination in order to execute it. The Ottoman army lacked such qualities. It was divided into three widely-separated groups, therefore, before one group came into action the other faced the whole Russian force. İskender Bey argued that the left wing came to the battlefield two hours after the right wing began to fight with the Russian army, because there was some confusion when Hurşid Pasha joined the left wing and it began marching late. İskender Bey also argued that Hurşid Pasha sent Colonel Schwarzenberg to post the reserve troops at the rear of the left wing, therefore they were too far from the right wing to come to its aid.[335] However, since İskender Bey had not supported Hurşid Pasha's plan, he might have a certain bias against Hurşid Pasha. In any case, there was the problem of jealousy among the officers. Hurşid had his enemies as well, both European and Ottoman, whereas he was only the chief of staff and did not command any units; thus at critical moments, commanders of divisions or regiments were at liberty not to obey his orders without confirmation from the *müşir*, who was not to be found during the battle.[336]

On Saturday, 5 August 1854, the two armies met at Kürekdere. The battle lasted from four to seven hours. The Ottoman regular cavalry proved utterly useless. Artillery and part of the infantry fought well. The *başıbozuks* were also useless. However, thanks to its size the Ottoman army could still have won the battle had it not been for the lack of proper (or any) leadership and the inefficiency of some of the officers. Thus the Ottoman army was defeated by an army half or a third of its size. According to Ottoman reports, Ottoman losses included 2,448 dead, 1,009 wounded and 25 guns. The number of regular troops

---

[334] Report of Staff Lieutenant-Colonel İskender Bey, BOA. İ. MMS. 2/65 enc. 7. Cf. Interrogation of Zarif Pasha. BOA. İ. MMS. 5/170 enc. 9, answer 7.

[335] İskender Bey's report, BOA. İ. MMS. 2/65 enc. 7. Allen and Muratoff, op. cit., p. 77.

[336] "The War in Asia. (From Our Own Correspondent). Kars, Aug. 7", *The Times*, Issue 21844, London, 12 September 1854, p. 9. Cf. Sandwith, op. cit., p. 105. Sandwith writes that the *Times* correspondent was an eye-witness of the battle.

that gathered in Kars after the battle was reported to be 28,782.[337] The *başıbozuks* dispersed to villages. Mirliva Hasan Pasha was among the dead. Salih Hayri maintains that there were more than 50,000 Ottoman troops and the Russians were half that number. He also argues that the Ottoman army was defeated due to lack of command.[338] According to Ibragimbeyli, Ottomans lost 2,820 dead, about 2,000 wounded and 86 officers and 1,932 soldiers taken prisoner.[339] The Russian loss included 21 officers and 568 soldiers dead, more than 2,000 wounded.[340] While the Ottoman army retreated in disorder towards Kars, the Russian army did not chase it.[341] Bebutov's caution played a significant role here. If he had followed the Ottoman army, the Ottoman losses would have been much higher and Kars might have been captured.

The *Times* correspondent was a witness of the battle and wrote a lengthy article about it, blaming the Ottoman officers:

> With a vivid impression of the whole engagement, from the first cannon-shot to the last straggling discharges of musketry, I can use no language too strong to express my reprobation of the conduct of nearly four-fifths of the Turkish officers present. In accounting for the defeat of an army numbering nearly 40,000 men of all arms by a hostile force of less than one-half that number, it is not sufficient to say that the management of the whole battle on the side of the Turks was a series of blunders from first to last; strategical errors might have protracted the engagement, and have added to the cost of a victory, but downright cowardice alone – which no generalship could have redeemed – gave the day to the Russians. One arm, and one only, behaved well – the artillery – which with its commander, Tahir Pasha, acted worthily of any army in Europe. Of the whole 40 battalions of infantry two regiments – the 5th Anatolian and 4th Desardet [Dersaadet] – alone stood their ground and resisted cavalry. Three successive times did three squadrons of Russian dragoons bear down upon these exceptionally brave regiments with a force before which many better disciplined troops would have yielded... Than the conduct of the rest of the infantry, nothing could well be worse, except that of the entire cavalry, which would have disgraced the rawest Bashi-

---

[337] BOA. İ. MMS. 2/65 enc. 5.
[338] Salih Hayri, op. cit., p. 153.
[339] Ibragimbeyli, op. cit., p. 259.
[340] Tarle writes that according to Bebutov's report, Russian dead and wounded numbered 3,054, which more or less coincides with the above account. See Tarle, op. cit., vol. 2, p. 517.
[341] Consul Brant to Lord Stratford de Redcliffe, Erzeroom, August 10, 1854. PRMA, p. 7. Tarle (op. cit., vol. 2, p. 517) writes that the Russian cavalry under the command of General Baggovut chased the Ottoman army almost to the walls of Kars, which is not confirmed by other sources.

Bazouks. If such, however, was the conduct of the men, that, as I have said, of the great majority of the superior officers was still more infamous. An hour after the action began, there was hardly a Bunbashi [binbaşı] (major) or Murallai [miralay] (colonel) to be seen; almost to a man they had deserted their regiments, and fled back to the camp to secure their baggage and send it off to Kars.[342] [Corrections in brackets are mine]

The *Times* correspondent further wrote that after the battle, Zarif Pasha collected his pashas and secured their seals to a petition to the *serasker* that it was Hurşid Pasha's fault alone to have hazarded an engagement. He added that the returns represented the losses as 1,200 killed, 1,800 wounded and 8,000 missing (of which last 2,000 were prisoners and the rest deserters, chiefly *redif*).

Indeed, the day after the battle, Zarif Pasha wrote two letters to the *serasker* about the battles at Bayezid and Kürekdere. He claimed that on Hurşid Pasha's insistence he had accepted battle witht the Russian army and because of him they could not win the battle although all troops fought well. Zarif Pasha claimed that although they had sustained some losses, the Russian loss was three or four times greater.[343] He also gathered his pashas in Kars and obtained a statement of accusation against Hurşid Pasha sealed by the *ferik* pashas Mehmed Rıza, Veli, Mehmed Raşid and Abdülkerim, as well as by the governer of Kars Mehmed Sırrı Pasha. The pashas wrote that when they received the news of the defeat at Bayezid, they all agreed with the mushir to send reinforcements to Bayezid and to be on the defensive. However, they argued, Hurşid Pasha strongly objected to this and instead proposed to attack the Russian army. Colonel Meffray also supported him. Thus, although they were reluctant, in order not to seem to be avoiding battle out of cowardice, they also agreed with him. Although all the Ottoman officers and soldiers fought very well, they could not win the battle because of Hurşid Pasha's wrong plans and because he did not listen to anyone's opinion, they claimed. They also accused Hurşid Pasha of mistreating them and of being unaware of military art.[344]

There is however a witness against Zarif Pasha as well. This is (Mirliva?) Şükrü Pasha, whose letter from 8 August 1854 is in the same folder with the reports of Zarif Pasha, İskender Bey and other pashas who supported Zarif Pasha. Şükrü Pasha wrote that it is well known

---

[342] *The Times*, ibid. Cf. Sandwith, op. cit., pp. 107–108.
[343] BOA. İ. MMS. 2/65 enc. 2 and 3, 6 August 1854.
[344] BOA. İ. MMS. 2/65 enc. 4, 6 August 1854.

by everyone that the Ottoman army numbered 70 thousand men in total, while the Russians counted overall 30 thousand men. At Bayezid, there were 1,500 regular troops with 4 cannons and 2,400 *başıbozuks*. The Russians reinforced their forces in front of Bayezid with 8 thousand more troops from Erivan and conquered Bayezid. When it was learnt the Russians were about to march upon Erzurum, it was decided to destroy first the Russian forces in front of Kars and then the force marching from Bayezid towards Erzurum. Şükrü Pasha then wrote that the *müşir* let the 70-thousand-strong Ottoman army be defeated by a 30-thousand-strong Russian army. Şükrü Pasha then used even very strong and abusive expressions against Zarif Pasha, calling him a "Yezid" and a "donkey", and arguing that because he had been busy "with women and boys and with theft", any soldier was better informed than him.[345]

The Sublime Porte decided to recall both Zarif Pasha and Hurşid Pasha to stand trial in Istanbul.[346] When Zarif Pasha was later arrested and tried at the MVL, he blamed Mirliva Abdurrahman Pasha, who did not come to the help of his comrades, keeping five battalions and one battery (six guns) out of battle. Ferik Raşid Pasha confirmed Zarif Pasha in this matter, stating that the said pasha with his five battalions, six guns and 3,000 başıbozuks did not come to help although Kerim Pasha, commander of the first division twice sent orders to him.[347] Raşid Pasha, however, also maintained that the retreat was not in an orderly manner as claimed by Zarif Pasha, since there was confusion and Zarif Pasha could not have counted enemy losses. Of the battle's result in general, Zarif Pasha gave quite a different account, as if he had not been defeated. He even argued that the result of the battle was useful for the Ottoman Empire and discouraging for the Russian army.[348] This had, of course, nothing to do with the truth.

Hurşid Pasha, for his part, told the MVL that originally he was not a supporter of an offensive action. Instead he had proposed to strengthen the fortifications in Kars and the village of Hacı Veli. He had even experienced some tension resulting from this with Zarif Pasha before

---

[345] BOA. İ. MMS. 2/65 enc. 8, 8 August 1854.
[346] BOA. İ. MMS. 2/65 enc. 11, 21 August 1854.
[347] *Mazbata* of the MVL on the trial of Zarif and Hurşid pashas, 11 April 1855. BOA. İ. MMS. 5/170 enc. 2.
[348] See Karal, op. cit. (1940), p. 494. The archival version has a slightly different wording with the same meaning. Cf. İ. MMS. 5/170 enc. 10.

departing for reconnaissance. When he returned the army was moving towards the village of Vezin. When he asked Zarif Pasha the reasons for this move, Zarif Pasha gave him a peremptory answer: "I am the mushir". However, at Subatan, Zarif Pasha asked his opinion on going to battle with the Russians. Although his original opinion was against such a move, taking into consideration the present deployment of troops and the intelligence on the numerical inferiority of the Russian army, he said if the intention was to do battle, then it was just the right time, therefore, immediate action was necessary before the Russians could receive reinforcement. However, Zarif Pasha did not think it was a lucky time because the moon was in the sign of Scorpio.[349] Thus Hurşid Pasha argued that many days passed there uselessly.

The British and French consuls in Erzurum and Trabzon sent reports to Istanbul about the battle of Kürekdere. Extracts from the British reports were given by the British embassy to the Porte as well. These reports contained some details of the battle and even a "list of the well and ill-behaved officers at the battle of Kuruckdereh" and a list of "Ottoman officers accused of being addicted to drinking". Another list included the above Abdurrahman Pasha of the Arabistan army, together with Vanlı Mehmed Pasha, as the officers "whose conduct is most reprehensible in refusing to charge when ordered". It was also noted that Vanlı Mehmed Pasha "purchased his rank for 60,000 piastres from the Mushir".[350]

Although Zarif Pasha did not blame Colonel Meffray in any way, Marshal St. Arnaud complained about him to the French minister of war Marshal Vaillant after the battle of Kürekdere. St. Arnaud wrote that he had not recommended Meffray to the *serasker*. According to St Arnaud, Meffray had prepared some offensive plans for the Anatolian army and although St Arnaud had not approved these plans, but responded politely and vaguely, Meffray had presented St Arnaud's letter to the *serasker* as if it were an approval. Thus Meffray had succeeded in getting appointed as aide de camp to the commander of the Anatolian army. On 24 July 1854, St. Arnaud had written to Serasker

---

[349] Hurşid Pasha's evidence is in harmony with the account of the *Times* correspondent. The only difference is that the *Times* correspondent gives the unlucky sign as the Ram (Aries) or the Crab (Cancer). See Sandwith, op. cit., p. 101.

[350] BOA. HR. SYS. 1191/1 enc. 73–76. These lists are anonymous and undated. Most probably they were written either by Colonel Williams or another British officer at Kars.

Rıza Pasha that they had sent a "non-military Frenchman" to the army of Kars. After the battle of Kürekdere, St. Arnaud even seems to place the blame for the defeat on Meffray's offensive plans.[351]

The battle of Kürekdere had clearly demonstrated the ability of the Russian army to hold the Caucasus. Shamil and the Circassians were further disappointed by the Porte's military inability. Thus the Caucasus front remained quiet until the next campaign season. Meanwhile, in the words of Clarendon, "a foreign general of distinction and said to possess great military talent" was on the spot and willing to take the command of Kars. By the "foreign general of distinction", Clarendon meant General Klapka. His appointment was recommended by the allied commanders-in-chief, by the British ambassador and by all the Ottoman ministers except Reşid Pasha the Grand Vizier. The British foreign minister protested this "disregard of the Sultan's interests", and the fact that "against all this weight of authority his [the Grand Vizier's] decision is allowed to prevail". Clarendon further directed Lord Stratford to request that Reşid Pasha instruct the newly appointed İsmail Pasha "to defer to the advice of Colonel Williams, who is thoroughly acquainted with the people and the country, and who ought to have a high Turkish rank given to him in order to insure respect for his authority".[352] On 27 September, Clarendon wrote to Lord Stratford:

> I have to state to your Excellency that Her Majesty's Government have little doubt that a deep rooted jealousy of foreigners is, as you suppose, the main cause of the neglect of the army in Asia; but the suicidal indulgence of that feeling ill becomes a Government whose very existence depends upon the support of foreigners.[353]

Clarendon also required Stratford to give a copy of his despatch to Reşid Pasha.

The allies recommended that all foreign officers at Kars be recalled and the command of the army be entrusted to General Klapka. However, the Porte did not accept the appointment of General Klapka. Zayonchkovskiy claims that Serasker Rıza Pasha did not like Lord Stratford and therefore declined his nomination of General Klapka, while Klapka

---

[351] St. Arnaud to Vaillant, Varna, 29 August 1854. AGKK, IV/2, pp. 440–441.

[352] The Earl of Clarendon to Lord Stratford de Redcliffe. Foreign Office, Sept. 22, 1854. PRMA, p. 10.

[353] Clarendon to Stratford, 27 September 1854. BOA. HR. SYS. 1191/1 enc. 54, Turkish translation at enc. 55. The PRMA (No. 13, p. 10) gives a smaller extract from this despatch.

himself wrote that the Porte thought it wiser to decline the services of a foreign general from a fear of giving offence to Austria.[354] Klapka also claimed that Ömer Pasha advised the Porte to employ that foreign general (implying himself). Instead the Porte suggested that the Anatolian army be divided into two divisions separately commanded by a French and a British general.[355] However, such a divided command was not acceptable to the allies. Eventually İsmail Pasha, the chief of staff of the Rumelian army was appointed to take the command of the Anatolian army at Kars in September 1854, but he did not go to Kars for alleged reasons of health.

While Klapka himself does not explicitly mention any visit of him to Kars, a letter from Rıza Pasha to Zarif Mustafa Pasha, dated 12 July 1854, informs the latter that the British general Klapka, together with Major Proti (?), Captains Kozlowski and Bertolati (?), two interpreters and four servants, as well as General Staff Major Hamdi Bey were sent to them to see the state of things there and to contact Sheikh Shamuil (Shamil). Rıza Pasha added that although Klapka's mission was not official, he should be treated politely and given all the information and assistance he needed.[356]

The British consul in Erzurum (James Brant) sent reports on the disorganized state of the Anatolian army. The British cabinet decided to send a military commissioner there to get information on the real state of affairs in the army. Three days before the battle of Kürekdere, Lieutenant-Colonel William Fenwick Williams of the Royal Artillery was informed by Lord Clarendon that he had been selected as the officer to attend, as Her Majesty's Commissioner, the head-quarters of the "Turkish" army in Asia, under the orders of Lord Raglan.[357] Williams was chosen for his knowledge of Eastern Anatolia, where he had served as the British representative in the international border commission on

---

[354] Klapka, op. cit., p. 45. Zayonchkovskiy, op. cit. (2002), vol. II, part 2, p. 472. Zayonchkovskiy refers to correspondence in the military archive at Paris, conducted among the French minister of war Marshal Vaillant, Marshal St. Arnaud, chargé d'affaires Vincent Benedetti and Serasker Rıza Pasha.

[355] Grand vizier to the *serasker*, 3 August 1854. BOA. HR. MKT. 82/38.

[356] BOA. HR. MKT. 81/42 enc. 3. An anonymous note in French from the British embassy is also in this file (enc. 4). The note says that General Klapka should be sent immediately via Trabzon to Kars and that all foreign officers at Kars, except General Guyon, should be recalled.

[357] The Earl of Clarendon to Lieutenant-Colonel Williams. Foreign Office, August 2, 1854. PRMA, p. 1.

the Ottoman-Iranian border from 1842 to 1852.[358] Williams arrived at Istanbul in August 1854 and after visiting Lord Stratford there and the Commander-in-Chief Lord Raglan in Varna, he departed for Trabzon on 31 August 1854, from there reaching Bayburt on 10 September and Erzurum on 14 September. He was received with high honours by the governor-general of the province, İsmail Pasha. After two days in Erzurum, Williams headed for Kars.[359]

Williams was promoted to the rank of *ferik* (lieutenant-general, his British rank was brigadier-general) by the Porte at the request of the British ambassador in December 1854 within three months of his arrival in Erzurum and Kars. From Governor of Erzurum Ismail Pasha's letter to the grand vizier we learn that the British consul in Erzurum James Brant had already informed İsmail Pasha that Williams held the rank of *ferik* even at the time of his arrival at Erzurum. Governor İsmail Pasha also states that he honoured Williams and allowed him to visit the army barracks and hospitals in accordance with the advice of the British consul although Williams did not produce an order from the grand vizier or the *serasker*.[360]

Eventually General Williams played a role greater than any other officer in the Anatolian army, Ottoman or foreigner. This role however was not altogether positive or helpful for the Ottoman war effort. Because of his temperament, Williams mixed into his behaviour and reports the most justified complaints on frauds and on corruption together with the most fanciful and vainglorious claims of alleged disrespect towards himself. Therefore one needs to distinguish in his reports between the real and the imagined items. As noted by James Reid, "Victorian British commentators might have made harsh judgments about Ottoman corruption, but they addressed certain realities that impartial observers cannot deny".[361] The fact that a certain European observer shows some prejudices against the Ottomans does not necessarily mean that all his claims are based on fiction. This is especially true in the case of

---

[358] See Robert Curzon, *Armenia: A Year at Erzeroom, and on the Frontiers of Russia, Turkey, and Persia*, New York: Harper & Brothers, 1854, pp. VII–VIII. The author was at that time private secretary to the British ambassador Sir Stratford Canning and also served in this commission until 1847.

[359] Colonel Williams to İsmail Pasha the Governor of Erzurum, 16 September 1854. BOA. HR. MKT. 94/56 enc. 6. Cf. PRMA, p. 21.

[360] Governor İsmail Pasha to the grand vizier, 26 September 1854. BOA. HR. MKT. 94/56 enc. 3.

[361] Reid, op. cit. (2000), p. 89.

General Williams, who made very detailed and concrete accusations and revelations of corruption and schemes of embezzlement, based upon his rigorous investigations. We will see some of these.

In his first reports from Erzurum, Colonel Williams found the winter-quarters of the army satisfactory but needing repair, the military hospitals clean but the apothecary's department in need of surgical instruments and medicine. As we have already mentioned, he wrote that during the previous winter 18,000 soldiers had died due to insufficient housing and care.[362] A week later, Williams reported from Kars that during the last winter, owing to the want of medicines, food, fuel, bedding and light, nearly 12,000 men perished in the hospitals of Kars.[363] The troops in Erzurum were 15 to 19 months in arrears of pay. They had received only one month's pay before the last "*bairam*" (Ramadan). Although 10,000 purses (*kese*) had been sent lately, nearly two-thirds of it was in paper. More money in specie was needed. Winter clothing had not been sent yet.[364]

In his reply to the representations of Lord Stratford, Reşid Pasha reported that supplies were being sent to Erzurum. As regards the payment of the arrears, he said that this point could not be settled until the "financial" (loan) commission sits, and "the sooner they meet the better". Meanwhile 5,000 purses (2,500,000 piastres, about 20,000 pounds) in specie were being prepared for transmission to Erzurum for the pay of the soldiers. Reşid Pasha also asked Lord Stratford to give the name of the British commissioner in the financial commission for the purpose of setting the commission to work at once.[365] However, even in the case of money in specie (gold and silver) being sent from Istanbul to the army, it is unlikely that it reached the soldiers because the müşir, pashas, the *müsteşar* (paymaster-general) and the *defterdar* (accountant-general) kept the specie to themselves and distributed paper money to the colonels, other officers and soldiers. The colonels in turn, receiving paper money that circulated only with a 20 per cent discount, were reduced to inflating the returns of their regiments to get

---

[362] Colonel Williams to İsmail Pasha Governor of Erzurum, 16 September 1854. BOA. HR. MKT. 94/56 enc. 6. The same letter is available at PRMA, p. 21.
[363] Colonel Williams to the Earl of Clarendon, Camp near Kars, September 24, 1854. PRMA, No. 28, p. 26.
[364] Stratford's instructions to Pisani to be read to Reshid Pasha. Therapia, October 1, 1854. PRMA, p. 13.
[365] Pisani to Lord Stratford de Redcliffe. Pera, October 3, 1854. PRMA, Inclosure 2 in No. 17, p. 14.

some extra rations. They would then resell these rations (food items, etc) to the army.³⁶⁶ The soldiers, if they got paid at all, could change their money notes to buy tobacco and coffee, for example, only at the discount of 20 per cent.³⁶⁷

Meanwhile, as we have seen, the Russians had occupied the town of Bayezid which stood on the great commercial road between Persia and the Black Sea port of Trabzon. This was alarming news from a military and commercial point of view because this occupation also threatened the trade of the British manufacturers with Persia. Ferik Selim Pasha had fled at the approach of the Russian army. Some *başıbozuk* and *redif* troops from the Kars army fought the Russians but could not stop them. The Russians, however, in order to strengthen the Erivan army, withdrew from Bayezid towards Erivan in November 1854, taking the Armenians with them. 600 Karapapaks of Şuregel and 300 Kurds under Kasım Ağa had also joined the Russians.³⁶⁸

In Kars, Colonel Williams was received with military honours and attention by Zarif Mustafa Pasha. Together with his aide-de-camp Lieutenant Teesdale and Doctor Sandwith, Williams inspected the troops. The soldiers were in need of many things, such as clothing and provisions, yet their healthy and soldier-like mien impressed Williams. The great portion of the infantry was armed with flint firelocks, but three battalions of chasseurs (*şeşhaneci*) were armed with the Minié rifle (which the Russian army did not have) and seven battalions of infantry had muskets.³⁶⁹ However, the sabres of the cavalry were too

---

³⁶⁶ Sandwith, op. cit., p. 125.
³⁶⁷ PRMA, Inclosure in No. 48, September-October 1854, p. 46. Duncan, op. cit., vol. II, p. 11. Edouard Engelhardt, *Türkiye ve Tanzimat Hareketleri*, Istanbul: Milliyet Yayınları, 1976, p. 83.
³⁶⁸ Lieutenant Teesdale to Colonel Williams. Kars, November 26, 1854. PRMA, p. 73.
³⁶⁹ Colonel Williams to the Earl of Clarendon. Camp near Kars, September 26, 1854. PRMA, p. 29. The dictionary of Ferit Devellioğlu, under the second meaning of *meniyye* (first meaning "death" in Arabic) gives the information that the *meniyye* rifles were introduced into the Ottoman army under Sultan Abdülaziz. (*Osmanlıca-Türkçe Ansiklopedik Lugat*, Ankara, 2002, p. 615). However, Minié has nothing to do with *meniyye*, it is the surname of the French officer who invented these rifles and bullets before 1850. Secondly, as seen above, Minié rifles were already being used in the Ottoman armies during the Crimean War. See PRMA, pp. 102, 333, 335. Laurence Oliphant (op. cit., pp. 100, 205) records their use by Ömer Pasha's army during his Caucasian campaign as well in the autumn of 1855, which is confirmed by Borozdin (op. cit., p. 29). Adolphus Slade also confirms the exclusive possession of Minié rifles by the allies. See Slade, op. cit., p. 99.

short. (After Williams's report, new sabres were imported from Britain). Cavalry was indeed the worst part of the Ottoman army, while the artillery was the best.

In general, the Ottoman army was not armed worse than the Russian army, which did not have Minié rifles at all. But the management of the Ottoman army was very corrupt and subjected the soldiers to terrible abuse. Williams soon discovered huge discrepancies between the actual counted number of troops and the muster-rolls, thus revealing embezzlement by the mushir and his subordinates, who pocketed the pay and rations of the missing soldiers. The army at Kars, that was supposed to be 40,000-strong, actually consisted altogether of 18,340 men including infantry, cavalry, artillery and some irregulars. The *başıbozuks* were also stated as amounting to 10,000 in the muster-rolls, when in reality there were not more than 6,000 of them.[370] Even after Williams' count of the troops, Zarif Mustafa Pasha reported the muster-roll tally to Istanbul as totalling 27,538 effective of all arms, whereas in Williams' opinion only 14,000 effective men were present.[371] Williams also learnt from the "Vakeel" (deputy) of the *defterdar* that rations for 33,000 men were being issued daily.[372]

It is certain that this practise of muster-roll fraud was known and tolerated by the Porte, because it was the widespread and usual practise. An irrefutable proof for this is found in the words of the grand vizier himself. In November 1854 the army of Batum was weakened due to deaths from diseases and desertions and it needed reinforcements. It was decided to send the Tunis army and to levy 1,000 *asakir-i muvazzafa* from the *sancak* of Lazistan. The grand vizier Kıbrıslı Mehmed Emin Pasha wrote that the Porte allowed the levy of 1,000 men, however, he warned that this levy should not be conducted as it usually was in most places by officers, that is, by registering for example 100 men but employing only 60 or 70 of them, and then taking the pay and

---

[370] Report of the Military Board to the *serasker* on the Corps d'Armée of Kars in September and October, 1854. (Translation). PRMA, p. 116. Budak (op. cit. (1993), p. 105) gives these last numbers about the *başıbozuks*, and other similar cases, referring to another British archival document.

[371] Colonel Williams to the Earl of Clarendon. Camp near Kars, October 11, 1854. PRMA, p. 39.

[372] Colonel Williams to the Earl of Clarendon. Camp near Kars, October 25, 1854. PRMA, p. 47.

rations of the remaining men.[373] The grand vizier also warned the local authorities that measures must be taken to prevent these recruits from oppressing anyone. From these words and from the whole of the *tezkire*, it is certain that the grand vizier was trying to prevent the customary practise of fraud because of the demands of the war.

Another proof of the fact that the Porte knew of and tolerated the muster-roll fraud is the complete absence of any direct questions on this matter addressed to the three successive commanders of the Anatolian army (Abdi, Ahmed and Zarif Pashas) during their trial in Istanbul from November 1854 to June 1855. Despite the many reports by Williams on concrete cases of fraud that were forwarded to the Porte by the British embassy, none of these pashas was asked directly about the muster-roll fraud or invited to prove that the numbers of troops conformed with reality. The questions about corruption in the administration of the army were too general, as if corruption were only a rumour. It is also remarkable that while Abdi Pasha and Ahmed Pasha argue against each other and accuse each other regarding many military issues, they never accuse each other of corruption. On the contrary, they firmly confirm each other on that matter.[374]

According to the reports of Colonel Williams and the narratives of Doctor Sandwith, Colonel Lake and the *Morning Chronicle* correspondent Charles Duncan, apart from the muster-roll fraud, the governors, pashas and colonels used every opportunity for peculation and did many other disreputable things. They bought wheat and barley from producers and then sold it to the army at inflated prices, instead of allowing the producers to bring their produce to the army quartermasters for payment. Pashas took bribes for all kinds of purchases for the army, or simply embezzled the money without making any purchases at all. For example, they did not give the soldiers their ration of rice twice a week. This theft alone brought them £30,000. The pashas and colonels also dealt in *kaimes* (paper money). They collaborated with greedy contractors who sold low quality goods and provisions to the army at enormous profits. For example, a Greek baker named Kozma mixed the flour with hay, barley and other things and gave very coarse, hardly edible crumbs at the price of best quality loaves of wheat-flour.

---

[373] Grand Vizier Kıbrıslı Mehmed Emin Pasha to the Sultan, 12 November 1854. BOA. İ. MMS. 3/97 enc. 3.
[374] For the interrogation and statements of these pashas, see BOA. İ. MMS. 3/107 and 5/170.

Kozma was protected by Ahmed Pasha.³⁷⁵ In another instance, pashas and colonels bought old horses worth 3 to 6 pounds each for the cavalry and charged the government 10 to 12 pounds for each horse, thus pocketing the difference. They made the soldiers work for commercial purposes. In general, the pashas lived in luxury together with their large *harems* and did not care for the well-being of the soldiers at all. For example, some of the pashas appropriated houses with accommodation sufficient for 250 men, while the soldiers were packed tightly into overcrowded rooms. When soldiers were quartered in any place, the pashas took bribes from the rich not to use their houses while the poor were forced to evacuate their homes. Thus it was the poorest villages of Erzurum and Kars that were forced to billet soldiers in their houses. Many pashas added drunkenness to their vices.

Another problem was the hostility of the uneducated old officers towards young officers brought up in the military schools of the Sultan or in Europe. Williams reported:

> Several months ago fourteen of these young men, after completing their studies at the Galata Serai, were sent to this army; they found themselves exposed to every description of insult and degradation; not one of them received a paid appointment in the Etat-Major, and several have, in consequence, disappeared altogether from this army; I believe only four remain, and those subsist on the bounty of such superior officers as may find it to their own interest to employ them: in short, the officers at present in command, as well as those in subordinate posts, will always endeavour to keep the young cadets out of employ in order that their own promotion may secure for them those illicit sources of peculation on which they at present fatten, at the expense of the unfed and badly-clothed soldier.³⁷⁶

Sandwith is also of the opinion that especially against these young, educated "Turkish" officers, "a system of persecution" was pursued:

---

³⁷⁵ Duncan writes that the inspector Hayreddin Pasha had made "Kosmo" eat the "bread" of his bakery as a punishment at the beginning of 1854. However, it seems that Kozma continued with his practise with the consent of Müşir Ahmed Pasha, because Duncan also writes that the *müşir* [Zarif Mustafa Pasha] himself bastinadoed Kozma for the same crime in May 1854. See Duncan, op. cit., vol. 1, p. 115 and vol. 2, p. 12. During his trial in Istanbul, Zarif Pasha was asked about Kozma as well and he admitted that he had beaten him or had him beaten and that afterwards he began to perform his duties better. However, Zarif Pasha also argued that other bakers could not provide bread at the same price as Kozma, who had great capital and long experience in this business. BOA. İ. MMS. 5/170 enc. 9, question 15.

³⁷⁶ Colonel Williams to the Earl of Clarendon. Camp near Kars, October 23, 1854. PRMA, No. 46, p. 41.

This mean and spiteful conduct towards these unfortunate young Turks was observable in all their superior officers, from the mushir downwards, and was shown in a variety of ways. No tents, pay or rations were given them, and they prowled about the camp in rags, fed by the charity of those who pitied their sad condition.[377]

The new mushir of the Anatolian army İsmail Pasha was in no hurry to proceed from Istanbul to Erzurum, because of an eye infection which threatened his sight. Whether this was a real problem or an excuse not to spend the winter in Erzurum is open to question. Meanwhile Kerim Pasha acted as his deputy for a short time but then Şükrü Pasha from the Rumeli army was appointed as the acting Commander-in-Chief. His chief of staff was Hüseyin Pasha. Şükrü Pasha arrived at Erzurum toward the end of October. Before Şükrü Pasha arrived at Kars on 12 November, General Williams had already received from the British consul Brant in Erzurum the information that at an evening meeting Zarif Pasha had excited Şükrü Pasha against Williams and Şükrü Pasha had said that Williams should not be allowed to interfere in the affairs of the army.[378] Williams quickly reported the situation to Stratford de Redcliffe and to Lord Clarendon. Williams also reported happily that the new chief of staff Hüseyin Pasha had "taken the young staff-students under his special protection, provided them quarters, claimed their long arrears of pay".[379]

Meanwhile Zarif Pasha came to Istanbul in November 1854 and he was soon arrested[380] in December 1854 after strong demands from Lord Stratford, who gave an official note to the Ottoman foreign minister Âli Pasha on 28 November 1854, demanding the punishment of Zarif Pasha together with his two predecessors Müşir Ahmed Pasha and Ferik Ali Rıza Pasha.[381] In fact even Abdi Pasha, the predecessor

---

[377] Sandwith, op. cit., p. 122, or p. 69 in the abridged edition of the book in the same year.

[378] Consul Brant to Colonel Williams, Erzeroom, November 2, 1854. PRMA, p. 53. Cf. Budak, op. cit. (1993), p. 106. Budak writes that the Porte dismissed Zarif Pasha and appointed instead Şükrü Pasha, omitting the appointment of İsmail Pasha.

[379] Colonel Williams to Lord Stratford de Redcliffe, Camp near Kars, November 4, 1854. PRMA, p. 52.

[380] BOA. İ. MMS. 3/107 enc. 7, 17 December 1854. The *irade* called for an acceleration of the trial of Abdi, Ahmed and Ferik Ali (Rıza) pashas as well as Zarif Pasha.

[381] Lord Stratford de Redcliffe to Aali Pasha, November 28, 1854. PRMA, p. 56. For the official Ottoman translation of this official note, see BOA. İ. MMS. 3/107 enc. 1. Budak (ibid.), refers to the same original document in English, however, he writes that Stratford wanted Kerim and Veli Pashas together with Zarif Pasha to be punished.

of Ahmed Pasha had not yet been tried. The trial of the three successive commanders of the Anatolian army, Abdi, Ahmed and Zarif Pashas, together with Ferik Ali Rıza Pasha, is, however, very important as an indicator of the attitude of the Ottoman elite toward charges of corruption against high officials, as in the case of Kapudan Mahmud Pasha. The difference is that in this case the allies, especially the British, pressed for the punishment of Zarif Pasha and others.

There were two basic charges against Zarif Pasha. The first was strictly military in character: He was accused of taking offensive action in the battle of Kürekdere (and thereby playing into the hand of the Russians) when his orders were to be on the defensive. The second charge concerned corruption in the administration of the Anatolian army. On the first charge the DŞA decided that since the battle took place on Ottoman territory it should be seen as a defensive operation.[382] This decision was approved by the MVL and the Council of Ministers (*Meclis-i Vükela*) as well. On the second charge, Zarif Pasha said that he had no knowledge of this and it must be directed to the *müsteşar*, the *defterdar* and other officials. On the question of the exchange of coins for paper money, he first pretended not to know. When he was asked again, he said that it was perpetrated by the *veznedar* (teller) sent by the treasury and he had sent the *veznedar* to the former *müsteşar* Rıza Efendi. However, Rıza Efendi had only imprisoned the culprit for a short time. Raşid Pasha and Hurşid Pasha said that they had heard of some acts like stealing from the cavalry fodder and buying grain at increased prices but they were not able to prove them.[383] Then the MVL reached the conclusion that there had not been as much corruption in purchases and expenditures under Zarif Pasha as under his predecessors, and that rations to the army had been allocated properly. While it was not denied that some local officials had committed embezzlement, it was not possible to investigate these cases from Istanbul, therefore, Vasıf Pasha and his *defterdar* Vehab Efendi should be questioned.

Consequently, Zarif Pasha's arrest and unemployment did not last long, as was the rule among the Ottoman elite at that time. His trial lasted until June 1855, when he was finally acquitted and released in

---

[382] *Mazbata* of the DŞA, 7 May 1855. BOA. İ. MMS. 5/170 enc. 1.
[383] *Mazbata* of the MVL on the trial of Zarif and Hurşid pashas. BOA. İ. MMS. 5/170 enc. 2, 11 April 1855.

July.³⁸⁴ Within two years, at the end of 1856, Hasan Rıza Pasha was again appointed *serasker* and he again managed to take Zarif Pasha into state service, this time as president of the DŞA.³⁸⁵ As we have seen, only Ahmed Pasha from the Anatolian army was found guilty and exiled to Cyprus for five years.

On 8 December 1854, Colonel Williams complained to Lord Stratford that he had not received any correspondence from him since 23 September. He was disappointed that his demands were not being complied with. Williams observed, among other things, that in such a case, he would fail to preserve the power which he had "seized unaided".³⁸⁶ Meanwhile, at the request of the British cabinet, the Porte agreed to confer upon Colonel Williams the rank of *ferik* (division general or lieutenant-general) towards the end of December 1854. This was his "local" rank, while in the British army, the new rank of Colonel Williams was Brigadier-General.

Lord Stratford in his despatch to Clarendon regarding the complaints of Colonel Williams remarked that Williams had decided in a hasty manner that he was neglected by the British ambassador. "Winter, distance, roads scarcely passable, want of funds, the extent of evil to be cured, the scarcity of trustworthy officers, the greater interest of operations elsewhere, the illness of Ismail Pasha" were to blame. He also blamed the "corruption, ignorance, prejudice, want of public spirit and the instincts of selfishness" of the "Turkish" ministers. But then he added remarkably:

> Has England itself been always without a taint? Have we never heard of Bacon, or of Marlborough? Have we forgotten the Memoirs of Pepys, the profligacies of his day and the one claim of an exiled Sovereign to the gratitude of his country? Are not the denunciations of Burke still ringing in our ears? Place, time, and circumstances vary altogether; but the disease differs only in degree. In Turkey it has reached the stage of extreme virulence; in Christendom, generally, it is in abeyance, or shows itself only under mild forms; in Russia it mingles with the system of administration, and would no doubt fulfil its mission there as elsewhere,

---

[384] Grand vizier's petition and the Sultan's *irade*, 1–2 July 1855. BOA. İ. MMS. 5/170 enc. 14.
[385] Cevdet Pasha, *Tezâkir 13–20*, Ankara: TTK, 1991, p. 37. BOA. İ. MMS. 5/170 enc. 1.
[386] Colonel Williams to Lord Stratford de Redcliffe, Erzeroom, December 8, 1854. PRMA, p. 65.

if the power and energy of Government did not maintain a counteracting vitality.[387]

Lord Stratford also wrote that he had learnt from a "Turkish" minister, on whom he could rely in this instance, that the real cause of the poverty of the Asian army last year was the jealousy of Mehmed Ali Pasha, grand vizier and then *serasker*, towards Mehmed Rüşdi Pasha, then the mushir of the *hassa* army, who seemed to be his rival. Furthermore, the present *serasker* (Hasan Rıza Pasha) and Ömer Pasha had long been at variance with each other. While the *serasker* asserted that he had sent ample supplies to the army in Rumeli, the Generalissimo complained of being neglected.

To those historical allusions concerning England, forwarded by Stratford to Williams as well, the response of Williams is also worth mentioning here:

> although the crimes of Bacon, Pepys, and Marlborough were parallel and identical with those which now brand the characters of the greatest and least of the public men in Turkey, the circumstances which relate to the repression and punishment of them are by no means so; for, if we take the last and greatest of these guilty Englishmen above-mentioned, we find his glory and his avarice associated with the history and fortunes of the greatest nation upon earth. England was not then supported in the arms, as it were, of France and Turkey, and could not have been peremptorily called by great patrons and allies to put her house in order and repress corruption, as Turkey now is by France and England; and had this warning voice been heard, and responded to, we should have been spared this desperate struggle.[388]

Williams added that those "base" (implying Şükrü Pasha), "despicable" (referring to many of the commanding officers), and "drunken" (openly accusing Liva Ahmed Pasha) Ottoman officers were still at the head of various departments and corps of the Anatolian army.

On the other hand, Stratford was pressing the Porte for the trial and punishment of Abdi, Ahmed and Ali Rıza Pashas from the Anatolian army for the corruption and other charges. In December 1854, an important change in office made things easier for Stratford: Reşid Pasha once again became grand vizier. Nevertheless, Reşid Pasha was

---

[387] Lord Stratford to the Earl of Clarendon. Constantinople, December 28, 1854. PRMA, p. 78.
[388] Brigadier-General Williams to the Earl of Clarendon. Erzeroom, January 25, 1855. PRMA, p. 133.

no longer the champion of reform, and even if he were so, his office did not mean everything, the whims of the Sultan and the intrigues of rivals had also to be taken into account. Lord Stratford was growing weary of the complaints of Williams and the constant pressure of Clarendon. Williams had sent the cover of a letter addressed to him by Şükrü (Shukri) Pasha as an instance of the disrespect shown him by the Ottoman authorities. Yet upon an exact translation of the superscription in question, Lord Stratford found that its terms, "far from being disrespectful, rather err on the side of compliment". Lord Stratford observed that the "Queen's Ambassador and personal representative" had no higher titles.[389]

Indeed this despatch of Lord Stratford to Lord Clarendon, dated 21 January 1855, revealed a very curious and important fact: Stratford admitted that there existed no record of his having applied in writing for a formal recognition of Colonel Williams as Her Majesty's Commissioner to the army of Kars. Stratford was "really at a loss to discover how it happened" that he omitted "so obvious a formality". As he noted, "the very facilities" of his "position with respect to the Turkish ministers" had betrayed him into an inadvertency, but this was of so little practical importance since Williams's own correspondence had shown the honours and attentions with which he was received in Erzurum and Kars. Therefore, Stratford very rightly observed that, "surely there are no symptoms here of any disrespect to Her Majesty's Commissioner, who at that time in military rank was a simple Lieutenant-Colonel". Ottoman authorities had in fact shown undue respect to a British lieutenant-colonel without proper documents testifying his appointment and they had even allowed him to search into almost all the details of the Kars army.

---

[389] Lord Stratford de Redcliffe to the Earl of Clarendon. Constantinople, January 21, 1855. PRMA, p. 91. The translation of this address read as follows: "To the most noble presence of the possessor of rank and nobility, his Excellency Williams Bey, a Military Chief Commander of the exalted Government of England, residing at Erzurum". Ibid., p. 93. Later, *The Times* of 7 April 1856, (issue 22335, p. 11) also published a news article on this question, giving a more elaborate translation and comments from Mr. R. W. Redhouse. Redhouse was also of the opinion that the terms of address were polite.

The Siege and Fall of Kars and Ömer Pasha's Caucasian Campaign in 1855

In January 1855, Mehmed Vasıf Pasha (?–1865), the former commander of the Arabistan army, was appointed as the provisional commander-in-chief of the Anatolian army until İsmail Pasha could take over his responsibilities. İsmail Pasha himself was sent to the Danube to replace Ömer Pasha, who was now sent to the Crimea. Vasıf Pasha was known to be an honest commander; since he had independent means, he was not engaged in peculation.[390] Therefore he was chosen to command the Anatolian army. Vasıf Pasha was given instructions from the *serasker* Rıza Pasha and the grand vizier Reşid Pasha. The *serasker* instructed Vasıf Pasha to be on the defensive against the Russians, and in the case of a Russian attack he should consult with Ferik Williams Pasha and other commanders to repel the enemy. Reşid Pasha's instructions placed more emphasis on the need to fight corruption and to follow the advice of Ferik Williams Pasha.[391] According to Sadık Pasha, Redcliffe told Vasıf Pasha that he demanded "absolute obedience" to Colonel Williams, in which case Vasıf could count on Redcliffe's support. Sadık Pasha even claims that Vasıf Pasha kissed the coat of Redcliffe, which no "Turk" had done before. He adds that Vasıf Pasha was no "Turk", but a Georgian of slave origin.[392]

Meanwhile the *firman* conferring on Williams the rank of *ferik* was read in Erzurum on 25 January 1855 in the presence of military and civil authorities. This ceremony was a novelty in that it was probably the first time such a high rank was bestowed upon a Christian, without changing his name to a Muslim one. As Williams noted, this innovation was calculated to do much good, "for, hitherto, the Turks have forced Europeans to take an Osmanli designation and the soldier was made to believe that the officer in question had embraced his religion

---

[390] General Nikolay Nikolayevich Muravyov in his memoirs wrote that Vasıf was a Georgian from the Guria region, village Chokhlati, surname Gudjabidze, and that he was sold as a slave at the age of 12 to the well-known Reşid Pasha in Istanbul. See Muravyov, *Voina za Kavkazom v 1855 godu*, vol. 1, St. Petersburg: Tipografiya tovarischestva "Obschestvennaya pol'za", 1877, p. 41. Mehmed Süreyya also records his Georgian origin. He had become a *ferik* in 1830–31. He had also been governor of Niş, Salonica, Vidin and Trabzon.

[391] Instructions to be delivered to Vassif Pasha, dated January 28, 1855 (translation). The Grand Vizier's addition to the Instructions to Vassif Pasha (translation). PRMA, pp. 107–110.

[392] Czajkowski, op. cit., p. 77.

Illus. 10 Williams Pasha's house, Kars, 1855. From General Nikolay Muravyov's book *Voina za Kavkazom v 1855 godu*, 1877.

also; and this inferred that no Christian was worthy of holding high rank in the armies of the Sultan".[393]

By February 1855, Lord Stratford came into conflict with the demands of Brigadier-General Williams, and this time he complained to the Earl of Clarendon. Even Stratford did not approve of Williams's tone towards the Ottoman command. Finally Lord Stratford asked the question which the Ottoman pashas in Erzurum and Kars should have asked from the beginning: What exactly are the position and powers of Williams? That he was assuming the powers of a Commander-in-Chief was clear from his demands and even Stratford was not prepared to press upon the Porte for all Williams' demands. Therefore Stratford wrote that "he should be made acquainted with the extent of his powers on the spot, with the degree to which he is independent of the Commander-in-chief". He further remarked:

> It appears that the Commissioner asserts in practise a right of being obeyed without hesitation, whether the object of his suggestion be the punishment or removal of an officer accused by him, the correction of an abuse, the introduction of an improvement, or the direction of a military operation. If such are his powers I know not in what he differs from a Commander-in-chief, except that he is not charged with taking the field in person, and directing the whole of the operations on his single responsibility. The Porte most certainly does not put this construction on the authority with which he is invested, nor have I so read my instructions as to ask for more on his behalf than a fair reliance on his judgement in matters affecting the administration of an army, a respectful attention to his advice and suggestions for the promotion of its efficiency, and that amount of confidence as to military movements and plans which ought to be inspired by the intimate relations subsisting between the respective Governments.
>
> Observing in your Lordship's instruction to General Williams that he is directed to maintain the most friendly relations with the Turkish officers, I venture to ask whether the tone which he has assumed towards them, the abruptness of his charges, the violence of his threats, the dictatorial spirit which, according to his own account, has generally characterized his proceedings, can be said to correspond with that intention, or to favour those dispositions to reform which it is our object to produce no less at Kars than throughout the Turkish Empire.

---

[393] Brigadier-General Williams to Lord Stratford. Erzeroom, January 26, 1855. PRMA, pp. 133–134.

Illus. 11 Sadyk Pasha receiving Cossacks from the Dobrudja at Shumla. *ILN*, 6 May 1854.

> We should be inconsistent with ourselves if we sought to trample down what remains of Turkish independence...[394]

Stratford then pointed out the inconsistency of Williams' pretensions to such a high position due to his "ignorance of the native languages, and of practical experience in the field".

Adolphus Slade is also critical of the conduct of General Williams, arguing that his unfavourable estimate of the Turks, formed while employed in delimiting the Ottoman-Iranian border, was

> the inevitable consequence of his dependence on interpreters, drawn from classes prone from infancy to exaggerate in disfavour of the ruling class, and who when conflicting opinions respecting them are deducible, invariably deduce the least flattering. He had seen the Turks with their rayas' eyes, he had heard about them from their rayas' lips, and had passed judgement accordingly. As well might an Algerine's sketch of the French, or a Hindoo's colouring of the English, be accepted as genuine representation.
>
> Thus impressed, the commissioner, face to face with proud susceptible men, unconsciously passed the faint line of demarcation between counsel and dictation...he fancied, in the professional jealousy excited by his visitorial character, disrespect for his position: – singular hallucination, in days when the humblest individual in French or English uniform was caressed![395]

An author by the pen name of S. de Zaklitschine, who seems to have been a well-informed French staff officer (in the Kars army?) published a book in 1856 in response to the British "blue book" (the PRMA). There he wrote that

> the reports of Lieutenant-Colonel Williams on the battle of İncedere testify, if not to his credulity, at least to his premeditated tendency to denigrate everything that had been done in Anatolia prior to his arrival. They do not speak in favour of his calm and cold judgement, neither of his view as a man of war nor of his impartiality as a critic.[396] [My translation]

---

[394] Lord Stratford to the Earl of Clarendon. Constantinople, February 19, 1855. PRMA, pp. 129–130.

[395] Slade, op. cit., p. 411.

[396] S. de Zaklitschine, *Kars et le Général Williams. Réponse au Livre Bleu*, Malta, 1856, p. 19.

Sadık Pasha in his turn, wrote that Colonel Williams, "like most of the English officers who bought their ranks and did not earn them by service and merit, treated his officers like Negroes".[397]

In February 1855, Vasıf Pasha became the mushir of the Anatolian army. He was given clear instructions to follow the advice of General Williams. Ferik Halim Pasha was also appointed to his staff. The chronicler Lütfi went to his house before his departure from Istanbul. Vasıf Pasha was sitting with Ferik Halim Pasha, who was complaining that having changed the old muskets with capsule (cartridge) rifles, what would they do if the French do not give them the cartridges and if they did not have money for the cartridges. Vasıf Pasha kept silent, smoking his *nargile* and pretending not to hear.[398]

Meanwhile General Nikolai Nikolayevich Muravyov (1794–1866), appointed at the end of 1854, came to Tiflis at the beginning of March as the new viceroy of the Caucasus. He was not known and he did not belong to the tsar's circle of favourites, but he was an energetic and able officer. His appointment must have appeared as a surprise to generals like Bebutov, Baryatinskiy and Baklanov, who may have felt some jealousy towards him. Muravyov had been to Istanbul and Egypt in 1833 during the Russian assistance to the Porte against Mehmed Ali Pasha of Egypt. He spoke Russian, French, English, German and Turkish fluently.[399]

At the beginning of June 1855, Muravyov advanced towards the front with 21,200 infantry, 6,000 Cossack and Dragoon cavalry, 88 guns and some militia.[400] His plan was to besiege Kars from all sides, cutting all communication with Erzurum and other centres and thus forcing the fortress to surrender. Vasıf and Williams Pashas on the other hand, knowing very well the hazards of an open field battle with the Russian army, committed all their energy to fortifying the city. Fortunately, Colonel Lake of Williams's staff was an expert on fortification.

Cossack cavalry General Yakov Petrovich Baklanov (1808–1873) crossed the border at the end of May for reconnaissance. Towards the end of June he recommended to Muravyov that Kars be stormed, but Muravyov was hesitant. General Muravyov wrote to the Russian war minister that if he had an additional 15,000 troops, he could storm

---

[397] Czajkowski, op. cit., p. 78.
[398] Lütfi, op. cit., p. 108.
[399] Sandwith, op. cit., p. 303. Vernadsky, op. cit., p. 212.
[400] Tarle, op. cit., vol. 2, p. 520.

the city.⁴⁰¹ Instead he strengthened the blockade of Kars, seizing or destroying all sources of provision for the army at Kars. Soon Kars was suffering from hunger. An Ottoman force under Ali Pasha, sent from Erzurum, was defeated by General Pyotr Petrovich Kovalevskiy (1808–1855) at Penek on 31 August. Ali Pasha himself was taken prisoner.

The peasants around Kars were now forced to submit their grain tithe to the Russian army. Nevertheless, Muravyov in his memoirs writes that for livestock bought from the population, he ordered that they be paid in gold, not with dubious promissory notes, as was the practice of the Ottoman army.⁴⁰² Muravyov issued an appeal to the population of Kars on 28 June. The leaflet was also translated into Ottoman Turkish and distributed. The appeal proclaimed that the Russian army was now encamped near their villages but that "not one ear of their harvest" had been trodden upon by Russian horses, while Istanbul had showered them with taxes, violence and unpaid transport services. It is worth quoting more from this proclamation which illustrates the arguments of Russian propaganda (using the word "propaganda" in a neutral sense):

> When 22 years ago Mehmed Ali Pasha betrayed the Sultan and your present friends England and France sacrificed Istanbul to Mehmed Ali, while Turkey was being ruined and everybody watched cold heartedly, who gave you the hand of help? The late Emperor Nikolai, enemy of rebellion and malice. He ordered his army to cross the sea and shield Istanbul by breast. At that time our troops were in the Bosphorus and Nikolai could have demanded any reward from Turkey. But the Great Sovereign did not make trade on his friendship. He saved his ally and withdrew his army after the danger was past. Did Turkey have a right not to trust Nikolai's word? But Sultan Mahmud died and around Sultan Abdülmecid there appeared men who valued their personal interests more than the peace of the nation. Now the English and the French give orders...while the executors of these orders are Muslims...When a French captain appears beside a pasha at the head of his army, who gives the orders? The French captain! Foreigners have occupied your country, there are foreign troops even in the palace. Open your eyes and know well who is your real friend and who is your enemy!⁴⁰³ [My translation]

---

⁴⁰¹ Tarle, op. cit., vol. 2, p. 523.
⁴⁰² Muravyov, op. cit., vol. I, p. 210.
⁴⁰³ *Vozzvanie Gen. Muravyova k poddannym Turtsii, ot 16-go iyunya 1855 goda* [General Muravyov's appeal to the subjects of Turkey, 28 June 1855]. AKAK, vol. XI, no. 65, p. 79. For the Ottoman Turkish version, see BOA. İ. DH. 331/21600 enc. 1.

Meanwhile, the situation in Kars had become unbearable for the soldiers and for the civilians. Müşir Vasıf Pasha was sending letter after letter to the Porte reporting that the Russians were about to attack the city and asking for reinforcements. In his letter on 20 June 1855, he wrote that a Russian army of 40,000 to 50,000 men had come to the south of Kars preparing for an attack. Vasıf Pasha added that it would be difficult to oppose this Russian force because most of the troops in Kars were *redif* troops and they had been demoralized by earlier defeats.[404] Every day many soldiers were dying and many of them deserting. Some civilians helped these deserters and some civilians, both Muslim and Christian (mainly Armenian), spied for the Russians. Vasıf and Williams had to resort to executions to stop the desertions and spying but even that was insufficient to put an end to them.[405]

While Kars was thus under siege, the Porte and its allies were discussing various plans for relief for the Kars army. While the allies' top priority was the conquest of Sevastopol, the Porte was naturally more interested in Kars. Brigadier-General Mansfield had come from Britain as Stratford's military advisor. There were in general two plans: either landing an army at Trabzon and advancing towards Erzurum and Kars or landing the army at Redutkale and advancing towards Kutaisi and Tiflis.[406] Both plans had their advantages and disadvantages but the Porte favoured the latter. Towards the end of June 1855, a meeting was held in Sadrazam Âli Pasha's *konak* on the Bosphorus with the participation of Foreign Minister Fuad Pasha, Serasker Mehmed Rüşdi Pasha (1811–1882), Lord Stratford, General W. R. Mansfield and Dragoman Stephen Pisani. We do not know why the French did not participate in this meeting. Were they uninvited or uninterested? The second alternative seems more likely.

After conferring with the *serasker*, General Mansfield prepared a memorandum for a landing at Redutkale. It was proposed that command of the campaign be given to Lieutenant-General R. J. H. Vivian, the commander of the "Turkish Contingent". Vivian's contingent (20,000 men, half of which was in Istanbul) was to be reinforced with

---

[404] Müşir Mehmed Vasıf Pasha to the Grand Vizier, 20 June 1855. BOA. İ. MMS. 5/171 enc. 3.
[405] Budak, op. cit. (1993), p. 138. Budak, however, mentions only Armenian spies. Cf. Tobias Heinzelmann, op. cit., p. 245.
[406] Lord Stratford to the Earl of Clarendon, 30 June 1855. See PRMA, p. 221. Stratford mentions "three possible modes of acting", but the third one is not clear. Probably it is a variant of the second plan.

forces from Batum and Rumelia, Egypt and Tunis, reaching a total of about 43,400 troops.[407] Nevertheless, Vivian was not enthusiastic about the plan, stating that the "Turkish Contingent" was not fit for this service, that he must have exact details, and then demanding a long list of facilities of transport and supplies. The list included, among other items, 170 transport ships and 15,000 horses for a proposed corps of 25,000 men.[408]

The decisions, of course, had to be taken by the British government and the Porte. Stratford immediately despatched the plan to Clarendon asking whether a diversion operation from Redutkale was approved by the government. On 14 July, Clarendon replied by telegraph that the plan had not been approved, adding that "Trebizond ought to be the base of operations".[409] The British Secretary of State for War, Fox Maule-Ramsay, Lord Panmure (1801–1874), agreed with Lord Clarendon and warned General Vivian about undertaking "any expedition of a nature so wild and ill-digested as that contemplated by the Porte" and "risking the honour of the British name and your own reputation".[410] Thus began a long series of discussions which delayed the proposed campaign and did much harm to its results. With the French generals and admirals hostile to the plan and the British hesitant, it was left to Ömer Pasha.

Starting from 23 June, Ömer Pasha warned the allied commanders about the situation of the army in Kars and of the necessity of a diversionary operation from Redutkale. On 7 July he sent a memorandum to the British and French generals and admirals in chief, wherein he stated that the Kars army "to the number of 10,000 men, blockaded in the entrenched camp of Kars by a superior Russian force", might capitulate because of hunger if not from some other cause. The commander of the Kars army, finding that his communications with Erzurum were cut off, had requested, on 23 June, reinforcements and a powerful diversion on the side of Redutkale. Then Ömer Pasha added:

---

[407] PRMA, pp. 221–225. Cf. Budak, op. cit., pp. 150–153. Budak has translated the "Turkish Contingent" as "*Türk alayı*", that is, "Turkish regiment". However, General Mansfield's report (which Budak translates) tells that the "Turkish Contingent" would form "a division" of the force that would be sent to save Kars.
[408] Vivian to Redcliffe, 2 July 1855. PRMA, pp. 227–228.
[409] The Earl of Clarendon to Lord Stratford de Redcliffe, July 14, 1855. PRMA, p. 226. Clarendon's detailed dispatch was sent on 13 July. See PRMA, p. 225.
[410] Lord Panmure to Lieutenant-General Vivian. War Department, July 14, 1855. PRMA, pp. 234–235.

The proposal which I wish to make is, that I should throw myself, with the part of my army which is here and at Kertch, 25,000 Infantry, 3,000 Cavalry from Eupatoria, and a proportion of Artillery, upon some point of the coast of Circassia, and by menacing from thence the communication of the Russians, oblige them to abandon the siege of Kars.[411]

Ömer Pasha added that this force and that under Mustafa Pasha at Batum was enough for the operation and he only required assistance in the transport of his troops. He wished a war council to convene to decide upon the operation.

The conference of the generals and admirals took place on 14 July with the participation of the French Commander-in-Chief General Aimable Jean Jacques Pélissier (1794–1864), the British Commander-in-Chief General James Simpson (1792–1868), the Sardinian Commander-in-Chief General Alfonso Ferrero La Marmora (1804–1878), the Commander of the French Fleet in the Black Sea Vice-Admiral Armand Joseph Bruat (1796–19 November 1855), the Commander of the British Fleet in the Black Sea Vice-Admiral Sir Edmund Lyons and Rear-Admiral Houston Stewart (1791–1875). Ömer Pasha told the assembled officers that a superior Russian force of 48,000 men, of whom 10,000 were cavalry, had advanced upon Kars, with other Russian forces taking Bayezid and Toprak Kale on the way to Erzurum. The generals said they could offer no opinion without information from their embassies. Thereupon, Ömer Pasha informed the conference that he would go to Istanbul for a few days to confer with his government and the next day he left for Istanbul on board the British steamer *Valorous*. Regarding General Vivian's contingent, Ömer Pasha had informed the General Simpson that sending General Vivian's contingent would be risky, as the men were not yet acquainted with their officers, the officers did not speak their language, and the contingent was too small for this operation. He argued that he was well-known in Asia (where he had conducted several campaigns) and possessed the confidence of the "Turks" and therefore was "more likely to gain the sympathies and assistance of the inhabitants in provisioning, in gaining information, etc".[412]

---

[411] PRMA, translation of the Inclosure 3 in no. 270, p. 251.
[412] Lieutenant-Colonel Simmons to Lieutenant-General Simpson, camp near Kamara, July 12, 1855. PRMA, p. 247. Simmons was attached to the headquarters of Ömer Pasha.

Ömer Pasha arrived at Istanbul on 17 July 1855 and visited the Serasker and then Sultan Abdülmecid. He complained of neglect by the allies, saying that they were keeping the best Ottoman troops in the Crimea uselessly and did not care for Kars at all. This made him for a while the hero of Istanbul. All resources were placed at his disposal. He chose his officers. The Sultan gave him an estate from the inheritance of Hüsrev Pasha, who had died in the previous year at the age of 97. He was also invested with the Order of the Bath by the British ambassador.[413]

Ömer Pasha was definitely in favour of a landing at Redutkale instead of Trabzon. According to Slade, he argued that

> From Trebizond to Erzeroom the movement would be of long duration, and difficult, from the distance and the mountainous nature of the country; which is only traversed by mule roads, rendering the passage of artillery a work of great labour and of slow process.[414]

Probably what gave more weight to Ömer Pasha's plan was a metaphor most likely originating with Serasker Mehmed Rüşdi Pasha, as the Ottomans liked to use figurative language. Thus he said that the operation was like striking the snake at its tail in order to turn its head to the rear. When Ömer Pasha's campaign finally ended in failure, Rifat Pasha the former president of the MVL remarked "we have given Kars for the sake of a metaphor".[415]

Colonel Simmons and Colonel Vico had come to Istanbul with Ömer Pasha. The latter had brought General Simpson's letter to Lord Stratford. Simpson informed the ambassador that Ömer Pasha's arguments had failed to convince the members of the conference, "who all, without exception, entertain the strongest objection to the withdrawal of any troops from the Crimea".[416] Therefore, Simpson begged Lord Stratford to use his "powerful influence" with the Porte to prevent the acceptance of Ömer Pasha's proposal. On 19 July, Stratford wrote to Clarendon on the sudden arrival of Ömer Pasha and his proposal, having learnt everything from General Simpson and Colonel Simmons.

---

[413] Slade argues that Ömer Pasha went from his ship immediately to the palace and accused the Porte to the Sultan of negligence and incapacity in regard of military matters. See Slade, op. cit., p. 426.

[414] Slade, ibid.

[415] Cevdet Pasha, op. cit., p. 61.

[416] General Simpson to Lord Stratford de Redcliffe, before Sevastopol, July 16, 1855. PRMA, p. 249. As Simpson wrote, this letter was brought by Colonel Vico, who was on the same ship with Ömer Pasha, ostensibly for the purpose of restoring his health.

Stratford wrote that, through Pisani, he had learnt that the arrival of the Generalissimo without orders from the government had created "some feelings of dissatisfaction" and that he had explained his conduct by referring to "the perilous nature of the emergency, and the inutility, as he thought, of his presence near Sebastopol under present circumstances".[417]

Stratford and Clarendon were not categorically against the plan. Their objection was rather to the use of the "Turkish Contingent". Meanwhile Ömer Pasha was received well by the Sultan. He was also on very good terms with the new Serasker Mehmed Rüşdi Pasha, unlike the former Hasan Rıza Pasha, with whom he had been at odds. On 2 August 1855, the Porte delivered an official note to the British embassy, asserting that the best way to save Kars was to march with a 45,000-strong army from Redutkale toward Tiflis via Kutais. Since the British had objected to the use of the "Turkish Contingent" in this operation, the Porte instead proposed, as Ömer Pasha had said, to send the Contingent to the Crimea and to take 20,000 Ottoman troops from there. The remaining troops for the operation would be taken from Rumeli and Batum. The note also argued that a march from Trabzon to Erzurum with cannons and ammunition could take three to four months, by which time Kars would be gone; whereas the road from Redutkale to Tiflis via Kutais was easier and convenient for the transport of cannons.[418] By this time, the French government had also accepted the plan provided that the numbers of Ottoman troops before Sevastopol were not diminished. The shortfall could be filled by the "Turkish Contingent". On 9 August, Clarendon informed Stratford by telegraph that General Vivian's contingent was to go immediately to Gözleve and the Ottoman troops there, 10,000 or 12,000, were to go with Ömer Pasha to Redutkale. The Ottoman troops at Balaklava and Kerch were also not to be diminished in number.[419]

Ömer Pasha spent too much time in Istanbul apparently for preparations but certainly having some leisure time and as in the words of Slade, "enjoying a long ovation".[420] He departed for Sevastopol only on

---

[417] Lord Stratford de Redcliffe to the Earl of Clarendon, Therapia, 19 July 1855. PRMA, pp. 248–249.
[418] OBKS, No. 49, pp. 161–165.
[419] The Earl of Clarendon to Lord Stratford de Redcliffe, 9 August 1855. PRMA, p. 255.
[420] Slade, op. cit., p. 426.

1 September 1855, calling briefly on Süzebolu on the Bulgarian coast.[421] In Süzebolu he met Abdi Pasha the former commander of the Anatolian army and talked with him about the campaign.

Ömer Pasha and Ferik Ahmed Pasha arrived on 4 September at the bay of Kamiesh, south of Sevastopol, where the French fleet was anchored. Ömer Pasha now had to struggle with the allied commanders to get his troops. The admirals said they had sent all the transport ships to France to bring troops and that they could only be provided if approved by the Commander-in-Chief when they returned. However, Ömer Pasha noticed signs of desperation in the admirals. Next he visited General Pelissier and General Simpson and felt the same mood in them as well. On 6 September 1855 a meeting of the generals and admirals was held. The meeting rejected the idea of any troops leaving Sevastopol. General Pelissier was especially opposed to Ömer Pasha's plan, saying that Kars was not important at all and that the campaign season had already passed.[422] Meanwhile they were executing the sixth bombardment of the city that started on 5 September and they were planning an assault on the Malakoff bastion, which was the main bastion defending the city. They asked Ömer Pasha to participate in the assault. However, Ömer Pasha did not believe in the success of the assault and declined the honour by saying that he had urgent duties to perform. He left Sevastopol on board the steamer *Şehper* for Trabzon on 6 September, two days before the fall of the Malakoff.[423] Ferik Ahmed Pasha and Osman Pasha remained in Sevastopol to organise the transfer of 10 Ottoman infantry battalions under the orders of the allies. According to Slade, Ömer Pasha forbade the Ottoman troops investing Sevastopol to take part in the assault.[424]

In the end, after so many efforts, Ömer Pasha neither joined in the conquest of Sevastopol nor did he succeed in his diversionary operation against the Russian army at Kars. But at that moment he still had some time left to come to the relief of the Kars army. He arrived at

---

[421] Ahmed Pasha to Serasker Mehmed Rüşdi Pasha, Gözleve, 10 September 1855. BOA. İ. MMS. 6/196 enc. 4. Slade, op. cit., p. 428. Budak assigns the Bulgarian port of Süzebolu (Sizepolis) to the Crimea (op. cit., 1993, p. 167).

[422] Ömer Pasha to Serasker Mehmed Rüşdi Pasha, Trabzon, 11 September 1855. BOA. İ. MMS. 6/196 enc. 3, quoted by Budak, op. cit., p. 169.

[423] "The Turkish Army in the Crimea", Camp of the Allied Armies on the Tchernaya, Sept. 7, The *Times*, London, 21 September 1855, Issue 22165, p. 8. Also see Oliphant, op. cit., p. 32; Budak, op. cit., p. 169.

[424] Budak, op. cit., pp. 169–170. Cf. Slade, op. cit., p. 428.

Trabzon on 11 September after being delayed by a gale. From Trabzon he wrote to Serasker Mehmed Rüşdi Pasha and advised him of his arrival and plans. The next day he proceeded to Batum. After the fall of Sevastopol, General Pelissier softened his position and allowed 3 battalions of chasseurs with Minié rifles under the command of Colonel Archibald Ballard to go to Batum.[425] But still more troops were needed and these were at last sent by mid-October 1855.

Meanwhile Muravyov was restless before Kars. He had a very effective blockade in place and the city was on the verge of capitulation, but Sevastopol had fallen and Ömer Pasha was about to advance into Georgia. Russia needed an urgent victory to compensate for Sevastopol. Therefore Muravyov wanted to storm and take Kars before Ömer Pasha's forces made any advance. This time General Baklanov was against a frontal assault but Muravyov did not listen to him.[426] Thus on the morning of 29 September 1855 the Russian forces made an all-out attack on the bastions of Kars, mainly on the Tahmasb redoubt. The Ottoman army, although much-weakened by hunger and diseases, fought very well behind their fortifications. General Kmety had sensed the Russian assault beforehand and therefore it was not a surprise attack. The Ottoman artillery was very effective. The Russian army lost about 7,500 to 8,000 men dead and wounded on this day, including General Pyotr Kovalevskiy among the dead.[427] Ottoman losses were insignificant, less than 1,000, including about 100 to 150 civilians from Kars.[428] However, the Ottoman army had no cavalry available to harass the retreating Russians.[429]

The news of the victory at Kars created great pleasure in Istanbul. Ferik Williams Pasha and Ferik Kerim Pasha were promoted to the

---

[425] Budak, op. cit., p. 171.
[426] Tarle, op. cit., vol. II, pp. 525, 528.
[427] According to the official report of General Muravyov after the battle, Russian losses (dead and wounded) totaled 252 officers and 7,274 men. See Bogdanovich, op. cit., vol. 4, pp. 345–346. Tarle (op. cit., vol. 2, p. 528) also quoting from Muravyov, gives the same figure for officers but a slightly different figure for men: 7,226. The Ottoman semi-official newpaper CH had increased the Russian loss up to 15,000 men and 300 officers. See Budak, op. cit. (1993), p. 131. Budak, however, also takes for granted the news from the CH, that Russian generals "Berimerof" (Brimmer) and "Baklonof" (Baklanov) were among the dead (p. 131). In reality, among Russian Generals only Kovalevskiy died of wounds from this battle. See Bogdanovich and Tarle, above.
[428] See Budak, op. cit. (1993), pp. 130–133. Budak gives various numbers related to losses from various sources.
[429] Sandwith, op. cit., p. 284.

rank of *müşir* and decorated with the order of *Mecidiye*. A medal of Kars was struck and distributed. The population of Kars was exempted from taxes for three years.[430]

Muravyov had now suffered a terrible defeat. But he had still enough forces to continue with the blockade and he made a very correct decision after his ill-considered attack: He simply continued the siege without moving from his position, though many had expected him to withdraw to Tiflis. Hunger reached such a pitch that many Ottoman soldiers deserted daily. These deserters were usually captured by Russian patrols surrounding the city. Vasıf Pasha and Williams announced the death penalty for deserters but even this did not stop them. The civilian population of Kars was also suffering from starvation. Women were bringing their children to General Williams's house and leaving them there. Without horses, the army could not make a sortie either. In fact on the orders of Williams, the horses were secretly being slaughtered and their meat given to the hospital kitchen. The Russian troops, on the other hand, were comfortably billeted in huts and well-supplied.[431]

The former commander of the Batum army, Hassa Müşiri Mehmed Selim Pasha had now become the commander of the forces in Erzurum. However, he did not advance beyond Köprüköy in the direction of Kars and soon it became clear that no help or diversion would come from his side. It should be mentioned here that the British consul in Erzurum (James Brant) had a very low opinion of Selim Pasha, accusing him of cowardice in his despatches to Lord Clarendon and Lord Stratford. (Tired of pressure and threats from the British consul and British officers, Selim Pasha finally sent a petition to the Porte in February 1856 to be removed from Erzurum to another place).[432] Meanwhile the army in Kars was again under heavy siege and had no hope other than Ömer Pasha's advance. Yet Ömer Pasha was too slow.

Ömer Pasha changed his mind, probably at Batum, and instead of Redutkale, now chose Sohum as the port of landing. However, since Sohum was to the north of Redutkale, this only further delayed the advance towards Kutaisi. It is indeed hard to explain why Ömer Pasha chose Sohum, if he had in mind the urgent liberation of Kars. Perhaps

---

[430] Kırzıoğlu, op. cit., pp. 174–196. Budak, op. cit., p. 133.
[431] Brigadier-General Williams to Consul Brant, Kars, November 19, 1855. PRMA, p. 330.
[432] Selim Pasha to the grand vizier, 12 February 1856. BOA. HR. SYS. 1355/28.

he thought that his incursion into Georgia would be enough to force Muravyov to abandon the siege of Kars and rush to the assistance of Tiflis. Another reason is suggested by Allen and Muratoff, who argue that Ömer Pasha had no cavalry except for some (less than 1,000) Polish refugees and Ottoman Cossacks and he hoped to find plenty of irregular cavalry among the Circassians. As Allen and Muratoff pointed out, his hopes proved to be unrealistic.[433]

Ömer Pasha also wrote to the Serasker that the Circassians wanted an Ottoman officer in Circassia and therefore he would send them Mustafa Pasha, the commander of the Batum army. Grand vizier Âli Pasha, however, wrote to Serasker Mehmed Pasha that the status of Circassia was under negotiation with the embassies of the allied states and for the time being Mustafa Pasha should not be sent.[434]

Ömer Pasha started his march from Sohum in the middle of October 1855. His army numbered about 40,000, which included three well-trained rifle (şeşhaneci) battalions armed with Minié rifles (about 2,000 men) commanded by Colonel Ballard.[435] Ömer Pasha's chief of staff was Ferhad Pasha (Stein). Abdi Pasha (the former commander of the Anatolian army?) and a certain Osman Pasha also commanded infantry brigades. But half of the army was stationed at Sohum, Çamçıra and then at Zugdidi, leaving only 20,000 for the advance.[436] Some Abkhazian and Circassian irregular cavalry accompanied Ömer Pasha's army. The territory was indeed marshy and densely forested. Laurence Oliphant, the British journalist who accompanied Ömer Pasha's army, noted that "everything was paid for regularly, and the property of the country-people in Abkhasia was scrupulously respected by the Turkish army during its onward progress through the country".[437]

From Sohum, Ömer Pasha reached the river Ingur at the beginning of November covering approximately 75 kilometres in 16 days.[438] On 6 November Ömer Pasha defeated the Russian forces and the local militia commanded by General Prince Ivane Konstantinovich Bagration-

---

[433] Allen and Muratoff, op. cit., pp. 95–96.
[434] Grand Vizier Âli Pasha to Serasker Mehmed Rüşdi Pasha, 7 October 1855. BOA. İ. DH. 21447, quoted by Budak, op. cit., 1993, p. 172.
[435] Oliphant, op. cit., pp. 83–84.
[436] Bogdanovich, op. cit., vol. II, p. 346. Cf. Ibragimbeyli, op. cit., p. 326.
[437] Oliphant, op. cit., p. 83.
[438] Burchuladze, op. cit., p. 16. Burchuladze gives the distance in versts. Allen and Muratoff (op. cit., p. 97), however, argue that Ömer Pasha covered 50 miles (which is close to 75 km) in 20 days.

Mukhranskiy on the banks of the river Ingur.[439] From the Ottoman side, 16 battalions of infantry and 3 battalions of rifles took part in the battle. General Bagration-Mukhranskiy on the other hand had a total of 9,000 regular infantry, 700 Cossacks and about 10,000 irregular infantry and cavalry (*militsiya*).[440] Russian prisoners of war reported that 8 infantry battalions (about 5,000 men) with 8 guns, 3,000 Georgian militia and 7,000 volunteers had participated in the battle, but that the volunteers had deserted just after the first firing. Oliphant gives the Russian losses as about 1,200 killed and wounded and the Ottoman losses as less than 400. He also writes that "it is impossible to speak too highly of the gallantry which the Turkish soldiers displayed throughout the action".[441] On losses, Burchuladze claims the opposite, that the Russians lost more than 500 but the Ottoman losses were "several times bigger".[442] Tarle gives the Russian losses as 450 men. Ibragimbeyli, on the other hand, describes the battle as if it ended indecisively, claiming that the Russians "firmly resisted the onslaught of the numerically overwhelming enemy", and not mentioning losses at all.[443] After the battle of Ingur, the Russian forces retreated to the left bank of the river Tskhenis-tskhali (or Skeniskal, River "Horse"), leaving Mingrelia and Guria. On 9 November, Ömer Pasha came to Zugdidi (capital of Mingrelia) and spent five days there. He behaved as if he was in no hurry. According to Laurence Oliphant, the local population was in general in terror and was hostile to the Ottoman army. Despite Ömer Pasha's efforts to prevent pillage and to reassure the local people, the Abkhazian irregular cavalry in particular (about 200 men) started pillaging villages and kidnapping children to sell as slaves.[444] Ömer Pasha then sent the Abkhazian militia back to their homes. Towards the end of November it started to rain heavily for days. Under such rains it became extremely difficult to advance. On 8 December, after receiving the news of the fall of Kars on 27 November, Ömer Pasha gave the order to retreat. The retreat was however conducted in a disorderly

---

[439] Op. cit., pp. 97–113.
[440] Burchuladze, op. cit., p. 16. Ibragimbeyli's numbers are almost identical (op. cit., p. 329). Tarle (op. cit., vol. II, p. 531) writes that the Russian forces numbered 18,500 men with 28 guns.
[441] Oliphant, op. cit., pp. 112–113.
[442] Burchuladze, op. cit., p. 17.
[443] Tarle, op. cit., vol. II, p. 531. Ibragimbeyli, op. cit., pp. 330–331.
[444] Oliphant, op. cit., pp. 121–122, 125, 146. Cf. Burchuladze, op. cit., p. 19.

fashion. The Ottoman army was demoralized and the Georgian militia emboldened. Oliphant writes that Ömer Pasha said that

> he had good reason to know that the country-people were assisting the enemy by every means in their power, and expressed his determination to deal with them accordingly. He seemed, not unnaturally, in low spirits at the unfortunate issue of the campaign, in which his usual luck seemed to have deserted him.[445]

Slade has very aptly expressed Ömer Pasha's failure: "Too often in the East, administration sacrifices a general: this time the general failed the administration".[446] Tarle has also argued that Ömer Pasha, being an average general, had gained an undeserved reputation on the Danube under favourable conditions and by self-advertisement and now, when he had a superior army, he did not use the results of this victory at the battle of Ingur and did not do anything to save Kars.[447]

On Ömer Pasha's far-fetched campaign, Ahmed Rıza Trabzoni makes an interesting point in his *destan*. Trabzoni writes that he went to Kerch and talked to some Ottoman officers. There Ahmed Rıza asked a major why Kars was left to starvation and why Ömer Pasha landed at Sohum, which is far away and full of marshes difficult to cross. The officer answered him that the intention was to give Kars to the Russians so as to make a peace. The fall of Kars would be an opportunity for peace.[448] While we cannot of course take this information for granted, it does not seem to be altogether illogical. At least it means that there were such rumours among officers. Indeed, after the fall of Sevastopol, Russia badly needed to gain something, in order to save face and thus be willing to make peace.

While Ömer Pasha lost precious time in Mingrelia and Müşir Mehmed Selim Pasha did not move from Erzurum, Kars was finally forced to capitulate on 27 November 1855. With the approval of Müşir Vasıf Pasha, General Williams sent his aide-de-camp Major Teesdale to General Muravyov on 24 November to negotiate the terms of surrender. Muravyov treated him well. Meanwhile General Kmety and General Kollman, having been formally sentenced to death by the Austrian government, did not expect mercy at the hands of the Russians.

---

[445] Oliphant, op. cit., pp. 182–183.
[446] Slade, op. cit., p. 439.
[447] Tarle, op. cit., vol. II, p. 531.
[448] Ahmed Rıza Trabzoni, op. cit., pp. 254–255.

Therefore they requested General Williams to accept their resignations. Williams accepted and they escaped the siege by night and reached Erzurum.

According to the terms of surrender, agreed between Williams and Muravyov, the fortress of Kars would be delivered up intact. The Garrison of Kars would march out and become prisoners. Muravyov appreciated the gallantry of the officers and allowed them to retain their swords. The *redif, başıbozuk,* Laz soldiers and the non-combatants (doctors, secretaries etc) would be allowed to return to their homes. General Williams would provide a list of certain Hungarian and European officers, who would also be allowed to return to their homes. Private property, public buildings and monuments would be respected. Thus about 5,000 to 8,000 regular (*nizam*) troops became prisoners while about 6,000 irregulars marched towards their homes.[449]

Immediately after the surrender, General Muravyov sent provisions to the city population. He talked with Vasıf Pasha and reminded him that they had met in Istanbul in 1833, when Muravyov had come with the Russian military mission. At that time Vasıf Pasha was a division general, Kerim Pasha was a lieutenant-colonel in the guards (Hassa?) cavalry regiment of Avni Bey and Ömer Pasha (the Generalissimo) was then appointed by the *serasker* as interpreter to Muravyov.[450] Kerim Pasha is said to have told the Russian officer Daniil Aryutinov that if Ömer Pasha was defeated, he deserved it because he contemplated manoeuvring instead of urgent help to Kars, and now they had to surrender because of him.[451]

---

[449] Trabzoni (op. cit., p. 256) gives the number as "five to six thousand", while Salih Hayri (op. cit., p. 245) gives as small a number as four thousand. On the testimony of Captain Thomson's Hungarian interpreter, who returned to Erzurum after the surrender, the *Times* correspondent in Erzurum gives the number of *nizam* soldiers at Kars taken prisoner by the Russians as 5,000. See "The Surrender of Kars. Erzeroum Dec. 11", *The Times*, London, 3 January 1856, Issue 22254, p. 8. This might be true, but if we add up the number of deserters who had fallen into Russian hands, then the number is again about 8,000. *Blokada Karsa* (p. 114) gives the number of deserters as 3,000. At the end of the war there were about 7,800 prisoners of war from Kars in Russian hands. The list of Ottoman prisoners of war in Odessa, as of the end of 1856, numbered 8030, with only about 200 from Sinop and other places and the rest from Kars. See "Kontrol'naya kniga razmena russkikh i turetskikh voenno-plennykh", RGVIA, fond 481, op. 1, d. 695. This notebook contains the names of all the Ottoman prisoners of war.
[450] *Blokada Karsa*, pp. 113, 118.
[451] *Blokada Karsa*, p. 109.

Illus. 12   Mushir Kerim Pasha (Baba Kerim), chief of staff of the Anatolian army, 1855. Vasiliy Timm, *RHL*, 1855.

The "Turkish Contingent", the "Osmanli Irregular Cavalry" and the "Spahis d'Orient".

The so-called "Turkish Contingent" and the *başıbozuk* formations under the command of the British and the French are among the interesting and little known subjects of the Crimean War, especially in the Turkish historiography.[452] The fact that they were left to oblivion is understandable because many Ottomans did not like to remember them. The "Turkish Contingent" was an army of 20,000 Ottoman soldiers hired by the British, to be paid, fed, clothed and officered by the British and returned to the Porte at the end of the war. In Turkish it

---

[452] To the best of my knowledge, the only article in Turkish on this topic is by Cezmi Karasu, "Kırım Savaşı'nda Kontenjan Askeri", *Yedinci Askeri Tarih Semineri Bildirileri I*, Ankara: Genelkurmay ATASE Yayınları, 2000, pp. 15–27. This article is rather superficial and contains some major and many minor errors, beginning with the first sentence, which states that the Crimean War happened in 1854–1855!

258 CHAPTER THREE

Illus. 13 Surrender of Kars, 1855. From General Nikolay Muravyov's book *Voina za Kavkazom v 1855 godu*, 1877.

was called *kontenjan askeri* or simply designated as Ottoman troops under the order of the British army. Although the Turkish general staff's *History of the Turkish Armed Forces* calls it *Türk-İngiliz Mukavemet Ordusu*, that is, "Turkish-English Resistance Army",[453] I have not come across this expression or anything remotely like it anywhere in the BOA. Whatever name we give it, it truly represents a turning point in the entire history of the Ottoman Empire, for it consisted of Muslim soldiers fighting under Christian officers in the pay of a Christian state, albeit an ally. One is hard-pressed to find a similar example in military history. For that reason it is discussed here in some detail, although, from a military point of view, it did not play any significant role in the outcome of the war (or rather had no opportunity to do so).

As usual in such cases, the demand for the "Turkish Contingent" arose from dire necessity. The number of British soldiers in the Crimea was small in comparison with those of the French army. At the beginning of 1855, the number of British troops in the Crimea was around 13,000, while the French had almost 70,000 troops. Because of this disparity between the two armies, British commanders could not take the initiative in matters of strategy and tactics in the Crimea. This could not help but be reflected in their influence over the Porte as well.

Lord Stratford was also anxious because his own influence with the Porte had deteriorated. Something had to be done by the British to redress the balance. According to Stratford's biographer,

> It galled his national pride to see the French outnumbering the British troops in the proportion of at least four to one. Not only was the disparity injurious to the success of the siege, inasmuch as our men were numerically incapable of working and holding the wide extent of front which was allotted to them, without undue and consequently injurious physical strain; but the comparative insignificance of the British army brought the credit and prestige of England so low that her commanders found themselves compelled to give way to the superior influence of the French, even when there was no doubt that the latter were in the wrong.[454]

Thus it was probably first in the mind of Stratford that the idea of forming a separate large regular army from hired Ottoman soldiers

---

[453] See TC Genelkurmay Harp Tarihi Başkanlığı, *Türk Silahlı Kuvvetleri Tarihi, III. Cilt, 5. Kısım*, Ankara: Genelkurmay Basımevi, 1978, p. 463. The book gives no references to any source on this point.

[454] Lane-Poole, op. cit., vol. II, p. 408.

occurred. Unable to feed its own armies, the Porte accepted the proposal. Stratford obtained the Sultan's approval in December 1854 and an agreement was signed on 3 February 1855 in Istanbul.[455]

The agreement contained nine articles. The first article stated that Her Britannic Majesty agreed to take into her service a body of "Turkish" regular troops, to consist of twenty thousand men of all arms. Fifteen thousand of these men were to be detached from the regular troops serving in the armies of the Sultan and the remaining five thousand were to be taken from the *redifs*, either serving or in the reserve. All officers above the rank of sergeant were to be British, while the appointment of subaltern officers was left to the Ottoman government, with a few drill sergeants reserved for nomination by the British commanders.[456] Major-General Robert John Vivian, a British East India Company officer, was selected to command the contingent.[457]

The troops designated for the contingent would be handed over with their arms and ammunition. The men and officers in the contingent would receive the same pay and rations as they did in the Ottoman army. However, this rule seems to have been violated and higher salaries were offered, as will be shown below. The troops were to be free to perform their religious rites and ceremonies.

Adolphus Slade argued that the Porte at first thought that the troops to be furnished were intended for immediate active service and only reluctantly accepted the demand. Then the Porte regretted that it had accepted, but it did not have the firmness to state its reasons. As Slade observed, raising an army after the Indian model was not easy in the Ottoman Empire. Slade argued that the officers chosen for the contingent from India were not fit for the service because "Indian officers, accustomed to rule haughtily a subject race, were not the men (with few exceptions) to act judiciously with a dominant race, imbued with traditions of military renown". Those selected came with exclusive ideas "fostered by brevet rank, high expectations and a double pay".[458]

---

[455] BOA. HR. SYS. 1192/2 enc. 2–8, 3 February 1855. The agreement is in French, with English and Turkish translations. The original text in French uses the term "*un corps de troupes régulières turques*". See enc. 3. The Ottoman Turkish text, however, does not use the word "Turkish".

[456] Stratford's memorandum to the Porte, 3 February 1855. BOA. HR. SYS. 1192/2 enc. 9.

[457] The ILN described him as "an able East Indian officer" and "the scion of an old military house". See "The Turkish Contingent", *ILN*, 23 June 1855, p. 630.

[458] Slade, op. cit., p. 380.

Illus. 14   The Turkish contingent for the Crimea. *ILN*, 23 June 1855.

As for the *başıbozuk* formations, they were inspired by the colonial army models of the British in India and of the French in Algeria. Both France and Britain used local irregular cavalry in their colonies. The French Commander-in Chief Marshal St. Arnaud gave the task of forming an Ottoman irregular cavalry corps to General Yusuf, who was renowned for his *spahis* (*sipahi*, the old Persian/Ottoman word for light horseman) in Algeria. While Lord Raglan did not much like such irregular troops, Lord Stratford had introduced Lt Colonel William F. Beatson (1804–1872) to Lord Raglan and Ömer Pasha as early as January 1854. Thus even before the "Turkish Contingent" began to form, the first move of the British was to propose the formation of an irregular (*başıbozuk*) cavalry division under the command of Colonel Beatson.[459] Like many officers of the "Turkish Contingent", Colonel Beatson

---

[459] Stratford to Clarendon, 3 February 1854, AGKK, III/2, p. 196. Also see BOA. HR. SYS. 1192/2 enc. 1, 7 November 1854. This is a translation of the note of the British embassy.

had made his career in India, where he had formed a similar irregular cavalry unit (the Bundelkund Legion) from Indian natives.[460] Beatson had offered his services to Lord Clarendon and he was accepted. Promoted to the rank of general and accordingly made a pasha in the Ottoman army, Beatson was to form an irregular cavalry division of about 4,000 men in Bulgaria (called the "Osmanli irregular cavalry" or in short form "Beatson's Horse"). The formation of this unit was accepted in 1854, but its realization coincided with that of the "Turkish Contingent". The irregular cavalry was at first under the orders of the Foreign Office and Lord Stratford, that is, it was not attached to Lord Raglan. However, in September 1855, it was attached to the "Turkish Contingent". According to Captain Edward Money, who served in this irregular cavalry from July 1855 until July 1856, only about 1,500 of the proposed 5,000 men (8 regiments) had been recruited by August 1855.[461] These troops were stationed in Çanakkale (Dardanelles). We will review the problems they created in Chapter 5.

On the date of the signing of the agreement forming the "Turkish Contingent", Lord Stratford delivered another note demanding that proper steps be taken for raising the separate "Ottoman Irregular Cavalry" (in official translation *başıbozuk süvari askeri*) with necessary orders being issued to provincial authorities. Stratford warned that the orders should contain necessary information especially as regards the pay and rations of the soldiers:

> The success of this important experiment depends so much upon the manner and spirit in which it is begun that the undersigned in addressing Aali Pasha on the subject cannot too strongly impress His Highness with the necessity of having the Vizirial letters, which he solicits, drawn up in the clearest and most stringent terms. It is, in particular, desirable that the men to be enrolled should know from the outset that in point of military service, pay, and rations they are to stand in direct connection with British officers and the Queen's Government. It is also essential that strict precautions should be taken to secure the peaceable inhabitants from any acts of plunder or violence in which the volunteers, if left entirely to themselves, might be tempted to indulge, while passing from their respective homes to the place of their destination.[462]

---

[460] See [Calthorpe], op. cit., p. 47 and Reid, op. cit., p. 271.
[461] Edward Money, *Twelve Months with the Bashi-Bazouks*, London: Chapman and Hall, 1857, p. 32.
[462] Stratford's memorandum to the Porte, 3 February 1855. BOA. HR. SYS. 1192/2 enc. 10.

Accordingly, orders were sent to all Ottoman provinces from Vidin to Damascus. The commander of the Osmanli irregular cavalry General Beatson sent Colonel Frederick Walpole and Colonel Bruce to Syria to recruit troops in March 1855. Colonel Walpole (major in the British army) arrived at Damascus in March.[463] Other officers were also sent to Anatolia and Rumelia. As Captain Money noted, the recruits were offered pay and rations at a "most liberal rate".[464] Captain Money gives the rates of pay for officers and troopers and these rates are indeed much higher than in the Ottoman regular and irregular troops. The *nefer* (private or trooper) received 24 piastres per month plus rations and forage in the regular Turkish cavalry, while the irregular cavalrymen were paid 70 piastres per month, including rations and forage. On the other hand, the British now paid the *nefer*s 1 pound 13 shillings 4 pence per month (equal to about 200 piastres) as well as rations of bread and forage for horses.[465] However, in some places these regular and irregular levies perpetrated the same kind of atrocities and disorders as the *başıbozuks* of the Ottoman armies. We will see more of this in Chapter 5.

The Porte's dissatifaction and unwillingness is confirmed by its slowness in the collection of troops for the Contingent. In the middle of April, General Vivian came to Istanbul and at once made inquiries to the Porte about the forces to be placed under his command. However, very little had been done. Stratford de Redcliffe gave a note dated 19 April 1855 to Saffet Efendi the acting foreign minister. The British ambassador expressed his regret that "so very imperfect a preparation" was observed for that purpose at Constantinople, "notwithstanding the representations addressed repeatedly by him to the proper authorities, and the specific assurances received in reply". Then he requested that

---

[463] Reid (op. cit., p. 275) argues that these officers began their activities there in August 1855. However, this is refuted by the letters of Mehmed İzzet Pasha and İsmail Rahmi Pasha from Damascus, dated May 1855. See Chief of staff of the Arabistan army Mehmed İzzet Pasha to the Serasker, Damascus, 17 May 1855. BOA. HR. SYS. 1352/51.

[464] Captain Money, op. cit., p. 31.

[465] Money, op. cit., pp. 31 and 49. Money claimed that the troops in the regular Ottoman army received 18 piastres or two shillings. However, this is not true, as we have seen, infantry troops received 20 piastres and cavalry 24 piastres. On the other hand, at the rate of pound sterling to piastres which was prevalent at that time, 18 piastres would make slightly less than 3 shillings.

the Troops, which are to compose the Corps in question may be collected, and that such part of them as are at Constantinople, may be at once detached from the remainder of the Garrison, and reviewed in presence of the British General, to the amount of at least six thousand infantry, with two regiments of Cavalry and two or three batteries of Field Artillery. The season for operations in the field is rapidly coming on, and it is most desirable that the Turkish Corps in the Queen of England's pay should be prepared, with all practicable expedition and good effect, for taking part in them.

The Undersigned must remind the Ottoman Secretary of State that he is entitled to expect the number of troops agreed upon from the several places already designated by the Porte, namely, the Danube, Constantinople and Bosnia, or in failure of the required numbers in those quarters from other more convenient sources. He begs to observe at the same time, that according to his advices from the Crimea, there is no probability of any portion of the force in question being sent by Omer Pasha, since it appears beyond a doubt, that His Highness is not in a condition to weaken his army with any degree of prudence, and that he is employing the troops commanded by him, in strict agreement with the Commanders in Chief of the Allied Forces.[466]

The governor of Aleppo, İsmail Rahmi Pasha in his letter dated 20 May 1855 informs the Porte that at present 430 soldiers of cavalry out of the desired 500 have already been recruited and the rest will soon be found.[467] He adds that although there was great enthusiasm at the beginning, the recruitment had slowed down somewhat. He also anticipates that the "Kolonel Bey", meaning the British colonel (Walpole or Bruce?) charged with the task, being a stranger to local affairs, might express some complaints because of the delays, but the troops must be recruited by encouragement rather than through conscription.

It seems that the province of Baghdad was also charged to recruit 500 or more cavalry. Towards the end of June 1855, Mehmed Reşid Pasha, governor of Baghdad and commander of the Iraq army, sent a complaint to the Porte. He wrote that Hilmi Pasha the *mutasarrıf* of Mosul had informed him that the British consul in Mosul was recruiting cavalry troops with a monthly pay of 150 piastres *excluding* rations and forage under the command of Sergerde Laz Osman Ağa and several officers, who had come from the Anatolian army. It was said that the British authorities would recruit troops from Baghdad as well.

---

[466] Stratford de Redcliffe to Saffet Efendi. Pera, 19 April 1855. BOA. HR. SYS. 1192/2 enc. 15–16.
[467] İsmail Rahmi Pasha to the Porte, 20 May 1855. BOA. HR. SYS. 1352/56.

Mehmed Reşid Pasha wrote that while the purpose of this act was fair and beneficent, it was also well-known to the grand vizier that this area was not like Rumelia and Anatolia in that it was not possible to employ local troops there. The troops there had been brought with much difficulty from Anatolia and Rumelia and up to then they were given a monthly salary of 70 piastres *including* rations and forage. Mehmed Reşid Pasha then warned that if now they were offered twice and three times more pay with the prospect of being sent to the side of "*Rum*", towards their own country, then no Turkish soldiers would remain in Baghdad, leaving the area open to danger from the Russians and Iranians.[468]

It is remarkable that the governor used exactly the words "Turkish soldiers" for soldiers from Anatolia and Rumeli to distinguish them from local (Arabic, Kurdish, etc.) soldiers; because Ottoman documents at that time very rarely used the term "Turkish". Sending exclusively Anatolian or Rumelian recruits to the Arabic provinces was indeed a time-honoured practice of the Porte. The logic behind this measure was that local troops would be ineffective against their kinsmen, while the Anatolian or Rumelian recruits would not feel sympathy for the local people. Experience had confirmed the prudence of this practice. Even the Russian consul in Beirut had noticed this fact about the Arabistan army in Damascus.[469]

On the other hand, the situation of the Kars army in the summer of 1855 forced the Porte to try recruiting irregular infantry and cavalry from Anatolia at somewhat raised rates of pay. Müşir Vasıf Pasha asked for 3,000 cavalry and 2,000 infantry to be sent urgently to Kars. Thus infantry troops were offered 70 piastres per month plus rations and cavalry troops were offered 100 piastres per month plus rations and forage. Nevertheless, it was not possible to obtain so many soldiers.[470]

On 28 August 1855, General Vivian (already promoted to the rank of Lieutenant-General) submitted to the Ottoman *serasker* a nominal roll of officers of the Contingent, recommended for "Turkish" rank, which Lord Stratford de Redcliffe had approved in consultation with his military adviser General Mansfield. The "Turkish" rank for British officers usually meant the promotion of one or two or even more steps

---

[468] BOA. HR. SYS. 1353/15 enc. 2, 29 June 1855.
[469] "Doneseniye russkogo voennogo agenta v Konstantinopole generalnogo shtaba grafa Osten-Sakena. 4/16 fevralya 1852". RGVIA. Fond 450, op. 1, d. 47, list 16.
[470] Budak, op. cit., 1993, p. 110.

up in rank with regard to the Ottoman officers, thus a British captain would correspond to an Ottoman major or colonel, and so on. The memorandum from Lord Stratford stressed the fact that these officers would continue to be in the pay of the British government and receive no salaries or rations from the Porte. Their pay and rations would be the same as in the Ottoman army.

General Vivian was first made a *ferik*, but Lord Stratford seems to have been dissatisfied with this promotion and demanded the rank of mushir for him. Accordingly General Vivian was made mushir (full general or marshal), 5 officers were given the rank of *ferik* (division general or lieutenant-general), 8 officers received the rank of *mirliva* (brigadier general), 9 officers became *miralay* (colonel) and finally there were 42 *kaimmakams* (lieutenant-colonels).[471] The commander was given the authority to make provisional appointments to fill possible vacancies during the war, subject to later approval from the Porte. If the commander wanted to promote an Ottoman *binbaşı* (major) to the rank of *kaimakam*, then the Ottoman officer would receive from the British government the pay given to this rank in the Ottoman army.

The "Turkish Contingent" was to be sent to Gözleve to replace the Ottoman troops to be detached for the Caucasian campaign of Ömer Pasha, intended to save Kars from the siege of the Russian army. Indeed, at first, the command of the projected 45,000-strong relief army to be gathered in Redutkale was offered to Lieutenant-General Vivian on 1 July 1855, as described in Chapter 3. In his report to Lord Stratford, Vivian stated that there were a number of material questions that had to be settled before he could give this proposal serious consideration. He had concerns as regarded the sea and land transport of the troops and animals, and the supply of ordinance and commissariat (provisions) on enemy territory. Finally, he required "authority to act independently" together with a guaranteed flow of money for the operations. "Unless all these points can be satisfactorily arranged", asserted Vivian, "I think it would be useless to discuss the measure".[472]

On 11 July, General Mansfield sent a letter to General Vivian, forwarding him the minutes of his conversation with the Ottoman ministers on the matter. Lord Stratford had asked for Vivian's views. Vivian

---

[471] BOA. İ. HR. 123/6166, 5 September 1855.
[472] Vivian to Lord Stratford, Turkish Contingent Head-Quarters, Büyükdere, July 2, 1855. Supplementary PRMA, Inclosure in No. 2, pp. 2–3.

again pointed out a number of deficiencies, being quite unwilling to undertake the campaign. Transport was insufficient and in any case temporary, so the army landed at Redutkale would be left "without shipping to fall back upon in case of a reverse". Vivian further ventured to give his opinion that "as the interests of France and England are centered in Sebastopol, all our means should be directed to that quarter". He pointed out that the officers of the Contingent had to employ interpreters to talk to the soldiers and if these interpreters deserted in action great confusion would ensue and this would damage the prestige of the "English" officers. Vivian then expressed his suspicions as follows:

> Thirty thousand English troops, with all the appliances of money and shipping, with the whole aid of England, were unsupplied before Sebastopol. What would it be with a Turkish army of 40,000, in an enemy's country, some 50 or 100 miles from the sea, its base of operation being an open roadstead?[473]

Vivian then suggested that, for the relief of Kars, Batum might be chosen as the base of landing and operations might be directed against Ahıska.

The "Turkish Contingent" went from Büyükdere to Varna and from there to the Crimea in September. General Vivian, *commandant du Contingent Turc* met the Sultan together with his retinue before going to the Crimea.[474]

After so much preparation, the "Turkish Contingent" with its privileged officers and soldiers was wanted neither by Ömer Pasha, nor by Williams in Kars. Finally it was decided to send them to Kerch. After the fall of Sevastopol to the allies and Kars to the Russians, peace talks started again in the winter of 1855. Stratford was not happy with the abrupt end of the war and the "premature" peace negotiations, because, among other reasons, the "Turkish Contingent" had not yet shown its quality in battle. He wrote in his memoirs:

> The war came to so early a close that the troops in our pay had no opportunity of shewing their prowess, but neither did they afford any grounds of complaint. Even the irregulars submitted with good will to the command of Christian officers and to a degree of discipline which they had

---

[473] Vivian to Lord Stratford, Büyükdere, July 14, 1855. Supplementary PRMA, No. 3, p. 4.
[474] BOA. İ. HR. 123/6184, 11 September 1855.

not previously undergone. On returning to their respective provinces they expressed so much satisfaction with the good treatment they had experienced in our service that when the Indian mutiny broke out it would have been easy to raise an auxiliary force from among the population of their creed.[475]

Our trader and *destan* writer Ahmed Rıza had been to Kerch at that time and he gives the number of Ottoman troops under British command in Kertch as 30,000, obviously with some exaggeration.[476]

Battles in the Crimea and the Siege of Sevastopol

The battles in the Crimea and the siege of Sevastopol are exhaustively-discussed components of the Western and Russian historiography of the Crimean War. Here we will deal only briefly with these events, focusing as always on the Ottoman side.

On 4 September 1854, Nikolai wrote to Menshikov that he had at his disposal 52 battalions, 16 squadrons, 8 infantry and 2 cavalry batteries and 3 Cossack regiments, besides the fleet and the local garrison. He added that he considered these forces enough to repulse the enemy.[477] According to Albert Seaton, Menshikov had 38,000 troops and 18,000 seamen plus 12,000 troops between Kefe (Feodosia) and Kertch, which more or less corresponds with those figures.[478]

The allies landed at Eskihisar (Old Fort), between Alma and Gözleve in the Crimea on 13 September 1854. Prince Menshikov had not taken measures to prevent the allied landing. However, it must be admitted that he could not know where the landing would take place and even if he did know, he could not be certain whether it might be a decoy while the real landing would take place at another location. Then the allies advanced towards Alma on their way to Sevastopol.

The first battle between the allies and the Russian forces took place at the river Alma on 20 September 1854. On that day a Russian army of 33,000 to 40,000 met the allied army of about 60,000 men. Mirliva Süleyman Pasha's forces were incorporated into the division of the French

---

[475] Lane-Poole, op. cit., vol. II, p. 410.
[476] Trabzoni, op. cit., p. 198.
[477] Nikolai to Menshikov, 23 August (2 September) 1854. RGVIA. Fond 481, op. 1, d. 8, list 28.
[478] Albert Seaton. *The Crimean War: A Russian Chronicle*. New York, London: St. Martin's Press, 1977, pp. 50–59.

General Bosquet. The French had the advantage of their Minié rifles. The Russian army was forced to retreat, but the allies did not pursue it. If they had, they could well have taken Sevastopol by the end of the month. The Russians lost about 1,800 killed, 3,900 wounded and missing. The French casualties included 140 to 250 killed and 1,200 to 1,400 wounded. The British loss is put at 362 killed and more than 1,500 wounded.[479] There is no indication of the Ottoman losses in the existing literature. Most probably they are included among the French casualties. The Ottoman commander Mirliva Süleyman Pasha did not report on his casualties in his letter to the Porte.[480]

The allies restarted marching towards Sevastopol on 23 September. Meanwhile the Russians scuttled seven of their ships to block to entrance to the bay of Sevastopol. The allies then made the decision not to attack Sevastopol from the northwest side, but to attack instead from the southeast. However, this was another blunder by the allies, because on the northwest side the city was poorly fortified and defended by only some 5,000 men. Menshikov with his army had gone out of the city to take the road to Bahçesaray and the city was left to the local garrison and the sailors. We must note that both the Russians and the Allies lacked proper reconnaissance services. Meanwhile Marshal St Arnaud died and General François Certain Canrobert (1809–1895) took the French command.

The allied commanders did not want to risk attacking the city before reinforcements from Varna arrived. This was still another blunder. In October the numbers of French forces reached 42,000 and the British 23,000, while the Ottoman forces before Sevastopol remained the same.[481] The Ottoman contingent was kept as reserve. Thus, while the allies lost precious time, the Russians improved their fortifications under the supervision of Colonel Totleben and the admirals Nakhimov, Kornilov and others. Some of Menshikov's army also entered the city, raising the total number of defenders to 25,000.

On 17 October, the allies began the first bombardment of Sevastopol. During the bombardment they caused extensive damage to the

---

[479] See Winfried Baumgart, op. cit., p. 120.

[480] Serasker Hasan Rıza Pasha to the grand vizier, 6 October 1854. BOA. İ. DH. 19668. The *serasker* wrote that the casualty figures were not reported and therefore would be requested. Alma was mentioned as Almalu or Elmalu.

[481] Baumgart, op. cit., p. 126. Baumgart gives the number of the Ottoman troops as 5,000. Captain Saim Besbelli gives the same number. See Besbelli, op. cit., p. 76. According to Slade, however, this number must be about 6,000 to 7,000.

defences but they did not proceed to a direct assault. Thus they missed another opportunity. The bombardment was also undertaken from the sea side. The Ottoman fleet with its line-of-battle ships, including the *Mahmudiye* and the *Teşrifiye*, also took part in this action but the wooden ships proved useless against stone fortifications. The allied ships were badly damaged and casualties were high while the effect on the Russian positions was limited. 12 sailors from the *Mahmudiye* were also wounded. The *Mahmudiye* and three ships from the Egyptian squadron had to be sent to Istanbul for repairs. On their way, two Egyptian ships went aground after a gale and about 1,000 sailors were drowned, including the commander of the Egyptian division (squadron) Hasan Pasha.[482] The failed bombardment of Sevastopol from the sea was a lesson which led to the later construction of ironclad ships. The bombardment continued until 25 October and achieved nothing, although Admiral Kornilov died on the first day of the bombardment. Thus began the 349 days of siege and trench warfare at Sevastopol.

Menshikov, with his army reinforced to 65,000, decided to attack the British supply port at Balaklava on 25 October 1854. Part of the Ottoman contingent, consisting of little-trained *redif* or *esnan* troops (about 1,000 to 1,400 men with 10 guns), was deployed in a line of four lightly constructed artillery earthworks or redoubts to the north of Balaklava. According to Fortescue, Lord Raglan did not wish his soldiers mix up with the "Turkish" soldiers, and his army did not wish it either, because, "in Bulgaria the men had observed how the Bulgarian peasants, who sold them provisions, were insolently waylaid and robbed by the Turks of the money that had been paid to them; and they were very indignant".[483]

Lt General Pavel Petrovich Liprandi (1796–1864), with a force of 25,000 men, made a surprise attack on this line early at dawn on 25 October. The Ottoman troops, overwhelmed by the far superior enemy, after a resistance of more than one hour (during which 170 of them were killed), retreated in disorder. John Blunt, civilian interpreter and unofficial aide-de-camp to Lt General Lord Lucan, wrote in his reminiscences that the Ottoman commander Rüstem Pasha told him after the battle that some of the ammunition supplied to those

---

[482] Besbelli, op. cit., pp. 74–75.
[483] John W. Fortescue, *A History of the British Army*. Vol. XIII (1852–1870). London: Naval & Military Press, 2004, p. 89. Cf. Austin, op. cit., p. 51.

Illus. 15   Council of war, Lord Raglan, Ömer Pasha and Marshal Pélissier. Photo by Roger Fenton, 1855.

redoubts did not fit the bores of the guns. Blunt wrote the following about those in Redoubt No. 1:

> The Turks, although greatly outnumbered, made a gallant stand, and both Lord Lucan and Sir Colin Campbell manifested their approval! The former called out to me 'Blunt, those Turks are doing well!' but, having lost fully one-third of their number, and, expecting no support, they retired leaving their three guns, their killed and a few prisoners, most of them wounded, in the enemy's hands.[484]

---

[484] *"Blunt Speaking". The Crimean War Reminiscences of John Elijah Blunt, Civilian Interpreter*, ed. Dr Douglas Austin, UK: Crimean War Research Society Special

Blunt was then sent to the *binbashi* (major) of the retreating troops to order them to form behind the Highlanders (93rd Regiment). One of the men, bleeding from a wound in his breast, asked "why no troops were sent to our support". Another declared that "the guns in their redoubt were too small and ill-supplied with ammunition, and could not be properly served". A third complained that during the last two days they had nothing to eat but biscuits and very little water to drink. After the first redoubt was captured by the Russians, those in the other three redoubts, about 800 men, "seeing large bodies of Russian cavalry and infantry rapidly advancing in their direction and expecting no support, made but little resistance and fled towards Balaklava".

The *Takvim-i Vekayi* wrote that the Ottoman troops in the first *tabya* (redoubt) were attacked by 8 Russian battalions with 12 guns and that their resistance lasted two hours.[485] Adolphus Slade depicted the situation as follows:

> This exposed and dangerous post, above 2,000 yards away from any support, requiring the staunchest troops of the army to hold, if worth holding, was entrusted to men under depressing influences; men not long enrolled, and never in action. Ignorant and suspicious, in a strange army, they may have fancied themselves placed there by the "infidel" to be sacrificed.[486]

According to the *Times* correspondent William Howard Russell,

> For some mysterious reason or other the Turkish government sent instead of the veterans who fought under Omar Pasha, a body of soldiers of only two years' service, the latest levies of the Porte, many belonging to the non-belligerent class of barbers, tailors, and small shopkeepers. Still they were patient, hardy, and strong…[487]

Publication 33, 2007, pp. 23–24. Dr Austin remarks that shortly after the event itself, however, Major General Sir Colin Campbell was "scathing in his adverse comments on the Turks". Austin further comments that "clearly, Campbell did not then realise how well they had held out".

[485] See Yapıcı, op. cit., p. 65.
[486] Slade, op. cit., p. 327.
[487] Russell, *The British Expedition to the Crimea*, Rev. Ed., London: G. Routledge & Co., 1858, p. 175. Tarle also gives the number of troops in each redoubt at 250. See Tarle, op. cit., vol. 2, p. 169. According to the *Takvim-i Vekayi*, each of these four *tabyas* had half a battalion Ottoman troops. The *esnan* battalions usually numbered about 500. See *Takvim-i Vekayi*, 27 Safer 1261 (19 November 1854). Also see Yapıcı, op. cit., p. 65. Balaklava is here depicted as Balıklı.

It is not surprising that the Ottoman commander did not send his best troops, when Lord Raglan wanted some Ottoman troops to dig and hold earthworks for the defence of British troops. Why should he give his best troops for such a task? Apparently Russell arrived together with Lord Raglan about 8 o'clock. Russell then writes that

> It was soon evident that no reliance was to be placed on the Turkish infantry or artillerymen. All the stories we had heard about their bravery behind stone walls and earthworks proved how differently the same or similar people fight under different circumstances. When the Russians advanced, the Turks fired a few rounds at them, got frightened at the distance of their supports in the rear, looked round, received a few shots and shell, then "bolted," and fled with an agility quite at variance with common-place notions of Oriental deportment on the battle-field... Meantime the enemy advanced his cavalry rapidly. To our inexpressible disgust we saw the Turks in redoubt No. 2 fly at their approach...[488]

Lord Raglan's nephew and aide-de-camp Colonel Somerset Calthorpe wrote in the same vein as Russell:

> A few moments after our arrival the Russians established a battery of field artillery...and opened fire on No. 1 Redoubt; at the same time a column of infantry (some 1,200) men advanced up to it, the Turkish garrison firing on them in a desultory sort of way with small arms, but without attempting to serve their heavy guns. To our intense disgust, in a few moments we saw a little stream of men issue from the rear of the redoubt and run down the hill side towards our lines...[489]

Yet Russell and Calthorpe do not mention the fact that these few Ottoman troops had been under artillery fire for almost two hours before the arrival of the British command staff at their observation point. The vastly superior Russian forces (three columns, commanded by Major Generals Levutskiy, Semyakin and Gribbe) had stormed Redoubt No. 1 towards 8 o'clock after a strong and concentrated cannonade, although the "Turks" fought "very stubbornly" and left 170 dead.[490] Lord Raglan came to observe the battlefield very shortly before 8 a.m. General Can-

---

[488] Russell, op. cit., pp. 184–185. Relying upon the depiction of this battle by Russell and Kinglake and distrusting George Buchanan's observations, Reid (op. cit., p. 268) uses the same argument with the same phrase ("the Ottoman troops bolted and fled"). Reid even argues that the Ottoman "battalions" fled "even before shots were fired by either side".

[489] [Colonel Somerset Calthorpe], op. cit., pp. 302–303.

[490] Nikolai F. Dubrovin, *Istoriya Krymskoi voiny i oborony Sevastopolya*, Vol. II, St. Petersburg: Tip. tov. "Obschestvennaya Pol'za", 1900, pp. 127–130.

robert came thereafter. When he looked from the Chersonese Plateau, Raglan saw only the retreating Ottoman troops. As Michael Hargreave Mawson observed on Calthorpe's narrative:

> The evidence in this passage is most unreliable; the author writing not only from a viewpoint nearly three miles from the action, but also with the specific intention of defending the memory of a beloved commander and uncle – Raglan. The fact that Raglan was two hours or more late for the battle has been carefully glossed over with the claim that the Russian Artillery only opened fire once Raglan and the staff were watching, and that the infantry charge was simultaneous. It is contrary to the usages of war to shell a position whilst your own infantry is attempting to capture it. The figure of 1,200 Russian infantry can be taken as deliberately under-estimated.[491]

From that day onwards, the French and the British officers and soldiers in the Crimea began to treat the Ottoman soldiers ("the Turks") as despicable cowards. On the other hand, according to Oleg Shkedya, the evaluations of Russian researchers and participants in the war concerning the Ottoman troops in this battle were more balanced. The "Turks" had defended the first redoubt as long as possible, and although it was taken by the Russians they were not to be blamed. Shkedya also wrote that Russian sources in general were of the opinion that the allies commanded everything and that the Ottoman generals were in an unenviable position.[492]

James Reid's interpretation of the conduct of the Ottoman troops in this battle is one-sided and biased, due to his reliance on Russell and Kinglake only. He wrote that

> All optimism about the Ottoman reformed army evaporated with the disgraceful performance of the Ottoman battalions at the battle of Balaklava. Here, Ottoman infantry battalions stationed on hill redoubts in the advance of the entire allied army broke and ran, even before shots were fired by either side. The sight of massive Russian cavalry formations bearing down upon them in their isolated forward positions provoked such fear and panic, that to a man, the Ottoman troops bolted and fled.[493]

---

[491] Michael Hargreave Mawson, *The True Heroes of Balaclava*, Kent, Bedford, London: Crimean War Research Society Publications, spiral-bound printout, 1996, p. 13.
[492] Oleg P. Shkedya, "Turetskaya armiya v Krymskoi kampanii", *Vostochnaya (Krymskaya) Voina 1853–1856 godov: Novye materialy i novoe osmyslenie*, vol. 1, Simferopol: Krymskiy Arkhiv, 2005, p. 80.
[493] Reid, op. cit., p. 268.

Had Reid read other sources as well, such as Adolphus Slade, he could have formed a more balanced view. First, he would see that these were *esnan* and *redif* troops. Second, he would understand that these troops did not "bolt" immediately, but resisted a much stronger enemy for almost two hours. Reid's treatment of this episode gives the impression that he has not tried to understand what really took place. Instead, he only attempted to find support for what he already "knows" about what happened. On the other hand, this is not to say that the Ottoman soldiers would not "bolt" in any situation. They might have fled, as they did in several cases, like soldiers in any other army. However, one need not distort historical facts to prove that the Ottoman army was not reformed. There are other ways of showing the extent (or limits) of the effects of reform in the Ottoman army. The point here is to try to understand first what actually happened and then why it happened that way.

After the capture of the redoubts by the Russians, a cavalry battle ensued, with the famous "charge of the light brigade" by the British upon Russian fortified positions, which is still a major point of discussion in the British historiography. We will not go into the details of this battle. The British lost from the light cavalry brigade from 118 to 134 killed and more than 200 wounded. The Russian loss was 550, of which 238 were killed.[494] The *Takvim-i Vekayi* described the folly of the British charge of the light brigade as a "demonstration of bravery at the extreme level".

The battle's results were insignificant from a military point of view, but the Ottoman troops from then on were subjected to all kinds of misery and humiliation. Blunt witnessed and described in detail their deprivations and ill-treatment by the allied troops, who "unjustly accused the Turks of cowardice and in consequence treated them contemptuously". Blunt also argues that Russell later withdrew his imputation of cowardice against them on learning from Lord Lucan and others about their "brave stand".[495] As Robert Edgerton states, the Ottoman soldiers were "cursed at, spat upon, kicked, and slapped, their only duties to carry

---

[494] Baumgart, op. cit., p. 130. These are, I think, the most up-to-date numbers. However, there are various numbers on this account. Dubrovin (op. cit., p. 141) gives the British loss as 400 dead, 60 wounded and 22 prisoners. According to the *Takvim-i Vekayi*, Russian casualties were more than 1,500; Ottomans lost 150 and the British 400 in dead and wounded. See Yapıcı, op. cit., p. 65.

[495] Blunt, op. cit., pp. 54–57.

supplies, maintain roads, and stay out of sight".[496] According to Tarle, the allied officers would not even sit at the table for dinner with the Ottoman officers.[497] Depending on the allies for their food, the Ottoman troops were also left to starvation. They then started stealing food, for which they were flogged.

Soon the Ottoman soldiers started dying from cold, hunger, filth and disease. According to the Russian military historian Nikolai Dubrovin, old and torn tents did not protect the Ottoman soldiers from the cold and sometimes up to 300 men died in one day.[498] They were deprived of all necessities: poorly fed, clothed, and sheltered, without bed and linen, morally depressed, disdained and insulted. They had no money either. Furthermore, they had no press, no Ottoman correspondents to write about their plight. Everyday they buried their comrades and the dogs dug up the dead bodies and devoured them. There was a "hospital", a building or a hovel where Russian prisoners had previously been kept. After they all died of cholera, the building was given over to the Ottomans, but the dirt had never been cleaned away. Up to 400 men were strewn on the damp mud floors of its rooms, the doors and windows closed to keep out the cold air.[499] The Ottoman surgeon in charge of the "hospital", who had been trained in London, told the British war correspondent N. A. Woods: "The deadly fetid air which issued from this charnel-house made me involuntarily shrink back from the door with loathing". He further commented: "None of those poor fellows will come out alive. I have not saved a single man who entered that fatal building".[500] When Woods asked whether he had enough medicine, the surgeon said he had plenty, but medicine was useless against hunger.

Mushaver Pasha took a steamer to transport the Ottoman sick to Istanbul and 75 out of the 158 invalids died on the way. He then wrote to the naval council in Istanbul for two hospital ships to be sent to Balaklava and Kamış. A frigate was then converted into a hospital with all the personnel and equipment and sent to Kamış in February.

---

[496] Robert B. Edgerton, *Death or Glory: The Legacy of the Crimean War*, Boulder, CO: Westview Press, 1999, p. 169.

[497] Tarle, vol. 2, op. cit., p. 169.

[498] Dubrovin, op. cit., vol. II, p. 381. Blunt (op. cit., p. 55) wrote that an adjutant on Rüstem Pasha's staff showed him a report in which it was stated that nearly half of the "Turkish" troops in Balaklava had died.

[499] Slade, op. cit., p. 331. Also see Blunt, op. cit., pp. 56–57; Dubrovin, op. cit., p. 382.

[500] Quoted by Edgerton, op. cit., p. 170.

But the British fleet could not find a place for it: "the hospital frigate remained ten days in the offing of Kamiesh, waiting the pleasure of the British authorities, and was then sent back to Constantinople by order of the naval commander-in-chief, on the plea of want of room for her either at Kamiesh or Balaclava. Large vessels were then lying in those harbours for the accommodation of a few officers." Mushaver Pasha was also an eye-witness to the deprivations of the Ottoman army in the Crimea:

> One day the pasha in command at Kadykeuy spoke to the author about the slender rations issued to his troops: each man he said, received a daily allowance only of biscuit and rice, without butter to cook the latter into pilaf, and fresh meat about once a week. Had he represented the case in the right quarter, I asked. He had not: he declined doing so; and the tenor of his remarks showed an indisposition, in common with other pashas serving the Allies, to say or do aught likely, in his opinion, to make him seem troublesome. The loss of a thousand men was not to be named in the same breath with the loss of the English general's smile.[501]

Once again, as in the army of Anatolia, we see that the Ottoman officers took little interest in the condition of their troops. The problem was that the Muslim soldiers did not accept pork and rum and for this they were issued only an additional half pound of biscuit. As Slade observes, the Ottoman soldiers in the Crimea were theoretically equal with the British soldiers, but not in practice. Interestingly, as Slade observes, the Muslims were not cunning enough to accept the pork and rum and then sell or give it to their European comrades, who might then have treated them with more respect.

> Tea, coffee, sugar, etc. – appropriate articles – always abounding in store, were never regularly issued to the Turks; who were more dependent, with their pay in arrears, than others with silver in their pockets, on the commissariat for comforts. The hucksters in the Crimea, unlike the *bakkals* of Constantinople, gave no credit. Whence arose this indifference about the Turks is difficult to say; unless one might trace it to the habitual bearing of Anglo-Saxons towards an "inferior race".[502]

James Henry Skene, the British consul at the Dardanelles also wrote that the Ottoman troops in the Crimea were so badly paid, and so

---

[501] Slade, op. cit., p. 334.
[502] Slade, op. cit., p. 335.

irregularly, that they begged the British and French soldiers for scraps of food. Skene further described their misery:

> When English sailors went from their ships to the Naval Brigade at the front, they would capture three Turkish soldiers apiece, ride on the shoulders of one, and drive the others before them with a long whip, to relieve the first when he should get tired. The poor Turks would then get a few biscuits as payment of their eight miles' stage, and return to Balaclava perfectly satisfied.[503]

Meanwhile, Ömer Pasha was planning to occupy Bessarabia in November 1854 but in December he was ordered to go to the Crimea. He was to base himself at Gözleve and not to participate in the siege of Sevastopol. From December 1854 to February 1855, three divisions (one of which was Egyptian) totalling some 35,000 men with horses and artillery were transported from Varna and Süzebolu to Gözleve.

After the indecisive battle of Balaklava, the Russian and allied armies fought again, at Inkerman, on 5 November 1854. Nikolai was getting nervous; he sent his two sons, Grand Dukes Mikhail and Nikolai to the Crimea to urge Menshikov to action. Meanwhile, Menshikov had received further reinforcements and now commanded 107,000 men inside and outside Sevastopol, excluding the sailors, while the allies had about 70,000 men. For action on 5 November, Menshikov had detached 57,000 troops. He gave the overall command of the operation to General Dannenberg, who had come from Bessarabia and had no knowledge of the terrain. On the day of the battle of Inkerman, the morning weather was foggy and the combat occurred in great confusion for both sides. Overall, the battle ended with a great victory for the allies. This was an infantry battle or a "soldiers' battle", as it came to be called later, because the soldiers had fought without much direction from their officers. The Russian massed bayonet attacks proved useless against the longer-range Minié rifles, for which the Russians muskets were no match.[504] Russian losses were enormous: about 11,000 in dead and wounded, while the Allied losses were around 4,500 dead and wounded.

Shortly after Inkerman, a terrible gale broke out on 14 November. The Allies lost about 30 ships, including two frigates from the Ottoman

---

[503] James Henry Skene, *With Lord Stratford in the Crimean War*, London: Richard Bentley and Son, 1883, pp. 40–41.
[504] Baumgart, op. cit., pp. 137–138.

fleet. Human losses were around 500 and thus its effect was almost comparable to that of a lost battle. It became clear that during this winter neither could the allies take Sevastopol nor could the Russians drive them away from it. War had begun in earnest. The ensuing bitter winter brought all the deficiencies of the Allied armies to the fore. The *Times* correspondent William Howard Russell delivered detailed reports on the disorganization and misery of the British army. These reports were read by a concerned public. This had a revolutionary effect in Britain, and Lord Raglan, his commissariat officials and government ministers were blamed. Soon Lord Aberdeen's government gave way to Lord Palmerston. Both Marx and Engels wrote in the NYDT on the mismanagement of the British war system.[505]

The Russians too had supply and reinforcement problems because there were no railways south of Moscow. The Russians could not resolve these difficulties before the end of the war. In the end, they played a major role in their defeat, because they ran out of supplies and could not replenish them easily. The French were the best organized army, while nothing equalled the misery of the Ottoman troops.

The concentration of large Ottoman forces at Gözleve menaced the Russian supply lines traversing Or Kapusu (Perekop). Emperor Nikolai I ordered an attack on these forces. Prince Menshikov gave the task to General Stepan Khrulev, who attacked the Ottomans with an army of 29,000 infantry and 4,000 cavalry with 80 guns on 17 February 1855.[506] Assisted by gunfire from Allied warships, the Ottoman forces commanded by Ömer Pasha repulsed the Russians, who lost about 700 men.[507] Ottoman losses (including some French and civilians) were 103 dead and 296 wounded. Ferik Selim Pasha and Miralay Rüstem Bey from the Egyptian troops were among the dead. Lord Raglan reported the battle to the Duke of Newcastle (copied to Lord Stratford), praising the "gallant and determined conduct" of the Ottoman troops and testi-

---

[505] "British Disaster in the Crimea – The British War System", anonymous leading article, NYDT, January 22, 1855. See Marx, op. cit., pp. 506–512.

[506] See the *Takvim-i Vekayi*, 11 Receb 1271 (30 March 1855). Yapıcı, op. cit., p. 73. Baumgart (op. cit., p. 145) however gives the total number of Khrulev's forces at 19,000.

[507] Cevdet Pasha argues that the Russians attacked with more than 40,000 men and lost more than 3,000 dead and as many wounded. See *Tezâkir 1-12*, p. 29. This seems an exaggerated account.

fying to the "serious nature of the attack which was made upon them".[508] After this unsuccessful attack Nikolai removed Menshikov from his post and appointed General Gorchakov as Commander-in-Chief in the Crimea. Emperor Nikolai I died soon afterwards on 2 March 1855 and his son Aleksandr II ascended the throne.[509]

The death of Nikolai increased hopes for a diplomatic solution. In mid-March 1855, a new conference for peace among the ambassadors of France (Bourqueney), Britain (Lord Westmoreland), the Porte (Arif Efendi), Russia (Prince Aleksandr Gorchakov) and foreign minister Count Buol of Austria was opened in Vienna. Russia had accepted negotiations on the basis of the "four points". Since Arif Efendi did not know French, Rıza Bey from the Tercüme Odası was later sent to Vienna.[510] Ali Fuat Türkgeldi is highly critical of the Porte's conduct in keeping such an ambassador in Vienna and allowing him to be present at the conference but not to speak, "as if the negotiations concerned not us but China". He also asks why Âli Pasha was not sent immediately. He attributes this to the manipulations of Stratford Canning. However, Türkgeldi is mistaken. Stratford does not seem responsible for this. The problem was that, at the beginning of the Vienna conference, the Porte did not know what to do regarding the four points, especially the fourth point, which dealt with the question of the rights and privileges of non-Muslim subjects of the Porte. This question was discussed among 21 Ottoman statesmen in a *Meclis-i Meşveret* which was held on 24–26 March 1855. Türkgeldi does not mention this important meeting and its resolution (*mazbata*), although it is mentioned as an attachment to Âli Pasha's instructions, published by Türkgeldi.[511] We will take up this issue in Chapter 5.

Towards the end of March 1855, Foreign Minister Âli Pasha was appointed as an extraordinary delegate to the Vienna conference and he first participated in the conference together with the French for-

---

[508] Lord Raglan to the Duke of Newcastle. Before Sevastopol, 20 February 1855. BOA. HR. SYS. 1190/32 enc. 35. Copy to Lord Stratford, enc. 34.
[509] Tarle, op. cit., vol. 2, pp. 519–520. Cevdet Pasha (ibid) writes that Nikolai was much distressed by the news of the defeat and died thereafter. General Süer (op. cit., p. 151) argues that Nikolai committed suicide upon the news of the defeat of the Russian army by the Ottoman army in Gözleve on 17 February 1855. Nikolai did not commit suicide, but took a near suicidal action: he inspected some troops in cold weather while he was ill.
[510] Türkgeldi, op. cit., vol. I, p. 45.
[511] See Instructions to Ali Pasha, delegate to the Vienna Conference. Türkgeldi, op. cit., vol. I, p. 347.

Illus. 16 Ottoman soldiers and Tatar children at Gözleve. *ILN*, 3 March 1855.

eign minister Drouyn de Lhuys on 9 April 1855.[512] The British had sent Lord John Russell to the conference. After Reşid Pasha's resignation, Âli Pasha became the new *sadrazam* while he was in Vienna in May 1855. Fuad Pasha became the new foreign minister. The conference negotiations were stopped (or officially speaking, deferred) at the beginning of June. The conference could not reach an agreement mainly because of the third point, which dealt with the Straits regime and the constraints on the Russian navy in the Black Sea. During the conference, Âli Pasha proposed the following important formulation on 19 April 1855:

> The Contracting Powers, wishing to demonstrate the importance they attach to assuring that the Ottoman Empire participate in the advantages of the concert established by public law among the different European States, declare that they henceforth consider that empire as an integral part of the concert and engage themselves to respect its territorial integrity and its independence as an essential condition of the general balance of power.[513]

This formulation would later be re-formulated into Article 7 of the Treaty of Paris, without, however, reference to the European balance of power.

The allies continued with the siege and bombardment of Sevastopol and Piedmont-Sardinia joined the allies with 15,000 troops. In April 20,000 Ottoman troops came from Gözleve to take positions outside the siege works. Then began a second duel of artillery. The allied forces had a clear superiority in firepower. During 9 to 19 April, the allies fired 165,000 rounds, while the Russian responded with only 89,000.[514] Meanwhile the allied fleets took an expedition to Kerch and occupied it along with Kefe and Yenikale, later destroying vast Russian supplies round the Sea of Azov. By June the allies totaled 224,000 men. Ottoman forces in the Crimea reached 55,000, stationed at Gözleve, Sevastopol and Yenikale. The French forces amounted to 120,000, the British 32,000. The allies now reached a degree of unprecedented fire concentration in a siege war. They could fire 75,000 rounds per day, whereas the Russians had to economize on ammunition and could reply with

---

[512] Türkgeldi, op. cit., vol. I, p. 55.
[513] Adanır, "Turkey's entry into the Concert of Europe", *European Review* 13(3), London, 2005, p. 408.
[514] Aleksandr Svechin, *Evolyutsiya Voennogo Iskusstva*, vol. II, Moscow-Leningrad: Voengiz, 1928, p. 66.

only a quarter of that number.⁵¹⁵ In the end, the result of the siege was determined by the Allied preponderance in guns and ammunition. Russia simply could not produce and deliver to its troops as much ammunition as did the allies.

On 8 September 1855, after an infernal bombardment of three days in which both British and French troops took part, the French finally took the Malakoff. The fire density of the bombardment was truly unprecedented. Indeed, as early as January 1855, General Canrobert had written to Serasker Rıza Pasha that they would open "a fire perhaps unequalled in the history of siege warfare".⁵¹⁶ The Russian forces were obliged to evacuate the southern part of the city and passed over the harbour to the north side. The allies occupied the city on 12 September. The casualties on both sides were heavy; the Russian side lost about 13,000 and the allies about 10,000 men. The Ottoman troops were not among the storming troops; they were stationed on the Chernaya (Karasu) river. Ömer Pasha had by then left the Crimea for his Caucasian campaign, without appointing a deputy for himself. He was criticised for having caused the Ottomans' non-participation in the final victory in Sevastopol. Cevdet Pasha wrote that Ömer Pasha had quarrelled with the French Commander-in-Chief General Pelissier, and when he came to Istanbul in July 1855, he had said that "Malakoff cannot be taken this year... Sevastopol can be taken in two or three years. The allies may even be defeated. But they have their ships to pull out their troops and may abandon us there".⁵¹⁷ Cevdet Pasha also criticises Ömer Pasha's behaviour in Istanbul, arguing that he debased himself in the eyes of the elite and the common people by using his influence to bring Damad Mehmed Ali Pasha back to the fore (meaning the latter's appointment as Kapudan Pasha) and also appearing in public parades and having relations with some women of ill-repute.

In fact Cevdet Pasha finds fault in Ömer Pasha's command of the Rumelian army as well. He argues that Ömer Pasha could not manage the *başıbozuks* and caused their dispersal, which led to their being forced to pillage. When the Russians crossed the Danube in an extended line, being vulnerable to attack at any point, he did not have courage to mount an attack on them. Cevdet Pasha even argues that Ömer

---

⁵¹⁵ Baumgart, op. cit., p. 159.
⁵¹⁶ BOA. HR. SYS. 1336/31, 29 January 1855. "... nous pourrons ouvrir contre Sebastopol un feu peut-être sans exemple dans les annales des guerres de siège".
⁵¹⁷ Cevdet Pasha, op. cit., p. 57.

Pasha was about to surrender Silistria to the Russians, but the local population led by İbrahim Ağa organized the defence. In the Crimea, he passed his days idly in Gözleve instead of participating in the siege and storm of Sevastopol. Then, according to Cevdet Pasha, Pelissier had told him to wait for one more day and promised to offer the entire fleet for the transport of Ömer Pasha's troops to Anatolia, but Ömer Pasha had not accepted. Instead of marching directly from Batum via Ardahan, he preferred a far away route, leaving Kars to fall into the hands of the Russians.[518]

The Crimean War was not confined to the Crimea and the territory of the Ottoman Empire. The allies also sent a fleet to the Baltic Sea and the British to the White Sea and to Petropavlovsk on the Kamchatka peninsula. The battles fought there were not decisive or at least they did not affect Ottoman troops and do not require attention for the present study.[519]

After the capture of the southern part of Sevastopol, there arose a conflict in overall aims between France and Britain. Napoleon III was basically content with having won a victory in the Crimea and now did not want to continue the war. The British on the other hand were not equally satisfied. The Russian army had not been beaten yet. Britain also had plans for the independence of Circassia. But there was little to do in the Crimea. The allied armies did not want to go into Russian territory, away from the coast. The French were then persuaded into an expedition against the fortress of Kılburun. The allied fleets bombarded the fortress and it surrendered quickly. As we have noted previously, here for the first time ironclad floating batteries were used.

As we have seen, the number of Ottoman troops fluctuated during the progress of the war. However, what was the highest number of Ottoman regular troops involved in the conflict? What is probably the most accurate figure is recorded in a financial report, prepared in October 1855 to be submitted to the loan control commission (more on this will be said in Chapter 4). According to this report, the total effective number of Ottoman land troops (infantry, guards, cavalry, fortress and field artillery) was 199,152 men, excluding the 10,000 men of the "Turkish Contingent" in the pay of the British government, the 23,931

---

[518] Cevdet Pasha, *Tezâkir 13-20*, pp. 34-35.
[519] Andrew Lambert and Stephen Badsey (op. cit., p. 275), however, argue that "in so far as allied military pressure had any bearing on the Russian decision to accept peace terms, that pressure came from the Royal Navy in the Baltic".

Illus. 17 Ferik İsmail Pasha, commander of the Egyptian troops in the Crimea. Photo by Roger Fenton, 1855.

men of the Egyptian army, 2,000 Ottoman Cossacks and 485 Tatar cavalry.[520] If we add them up, then the figure reaches 235,568 men, of which approximately half were *redif* soldiers. Furthermore, according to this report, 77 per cent of the Ottoman troops were infantry and the rest were cavalry and artillery. As for the navy, it must have amounted to several thousands.

The End of the War and the Treaty of Paris

While the allied and the Russian armies watched each other from the two sides of Sevastopol, on 28 December 1855 the Austrian ambassador at St Petersburg, Esterhazy, submitted an ultimatum to Russia to accept peace negotiations on the basis of the "four points". Otherwise,

---

[520] *Le Moniteur Universel*, Paris, 8 January 1856. BOA. HR. SYS. 1355/3 lef3.

Austria would join the allies. Meanwhile Sweden made a defensive agreement with the allies. The King of Prussia too appealed to his nephew to make peace.[521] After some hesitation, Emperor Aleksandr II accepted the terms in January 1856.

The formal peace negotiations began in February 1856 in Paris. The Ottoman Empire was represented by grand vizier Âli Pasha and Mehmed Cemil Bey, (ambassador in Paris and Sardinia), a son of Reşid Pasha. France was represented by Count Alexandre Colonna-Walewski, the new foreign minister, and Baron François-Adolphe de Bourqueney, ambassador in Vienna. Russia sent Count Aleksey Orlov and Baron Filip de Brunnov, the former ambassador in London. The British representatives were Lord Clarendon the foreign minister and Baron Henry Richard Charles Cowley, the ambassador in Paris. The Austrian representatives were Prime Minister Charles-Ferdinand Buol-Schauenstein and their Paris ambassador Baron Joseph-Alexandre de Hübner. The kingdom of Piedmont-Sardinia was represented by the prime minister Count Camille Benso Cavour and de Villamarina. Finally Prussia was represented by Baron Othon de Manteuffel, prime minister and foreign minister and Count de Hatzfeldt, ambassador in Paris.

The war was ended but this was more at the desire of France than of Britain, because for Britain (and for Stratford) it was an unfinished war. Britain had spent much money for the "Turkish Contingent" and the "Osmanli irregular cavalry" yet just when they were ready to do service, the war had ended. The victory in Sevastopol was generally seen as a French victory, so the British needed another campaign to gain victory for itself and to destroy Russian military might. Lord Palmerston had rigorously strengthened Britain's navy and army since he became prime minister in early 1855, replacing Lord Aberdeen. However, Palmerston could not do much because France and Austria had agreed to put an end to the war.

Napoleon III, on the other hand, had already gained what he hoped for from the war: prestige and glory to his dynasty and to France and the disruption of the Russian-Austrian-Prussian bloc. Why should he fight further? French public opinion also favoured an end to the war because it had now come to be seen as more in the interests of Britain. Therefore, the policy of France was now very mild towards Russia,

---

[521] W. E. Mosse, "How Russia Made Peace September 1855 to April 1856", *Cambridge Historical Journal* 11(3), 1955, pp. 305–307.

considering that France would need Russian support in the future. In fact the Paris Congress marked the beginning of a Franco-Russian rapprochement.[522] It also marked the end of the Russian-Austrian-Prussian alliance in European politics. While Austria lost the friendship of both Russia and Britain and even of France, Prussia benefited most from the new balance of power in Europe. Prussia was to defeat France in 1871 and this would eventually encourage Russia to renounce the neutrality of the Black Sea. The other powers finally accepted that new situation.

Before the congress, Abdülmecid issued his Edict of Reforms (*Islahat Fermanı*) on 18 February 1856. The edict promised equality before law for all the subjects of the Porte, reform of the police, taxation, etc. We will deal with it in Chapter 5.

The Treaty of Paris provided for the independence and territorial integrity of the Ottoman Empire and placed it under the guarantee of the great powers. The allies and Russia returned to each other all captured cities and territory, except for some Russian territory in south Bessarabia (Budjak) that went to Moldavia. Thus Russia was removed from a position of control at the mouth of the Danube. The Principalities of Moldavia and Wallachia were to remain under the suzerainty of the Porte. None of the powers would exercise exclusive protection over these principalities. All prisoners of war were to be returned. The Black Sea was declared neutral and free of any war ships except for a limited number of small ships. No fortifications were to be built or held on its coasts. It would be open to merchants ships of all nations. All commercial navigation on the Danube was also opened to all nations. The Russian protectorate over the Danubian principalites was abolished. The principalities, together with Serbia, would be under the sovereignty of the Ottoman Empire and the collective guarantee of the great powers. Serbia would continue to be free in its internal affairs but the Porte would have a garrison in Belgrade as before. While Britian wanted to press for the independence or autonomy of the Circassians, even the Porte did not seem enthusiastic about this project. Therefore the congress did not address the situation of Circassia.

For the Sublime Porte, the most important result was the inclusion of the Ottoman Empire into the Concert of Europe. On the ques-

---

[522] L. S. Stavrianos, *The Balkans since 1453*, London: Hurst & Company, 2000, p. 336.

tion of the rights of the Christian subjects of the Ottoman Empire, Âli Pasha and the Porte tried hard to prevent any article that could be used for interference in the internal affairs of the Porte. First they did not want the *Islahat Fermanı* to be mentioned in the treaty. When they could not prevent it, the Porte objected to the expression that the contracting powers "take note" (*prendre acte*) of it, because the ministers looked the phrase up in dictionaries and found out that the word "*acte*" meant "*sened*"! For the Porte, this would mean that the firman was accepted as a binding convention.[523] Finally Âli Pasha was able to reach an agreement on the expression "the contracting Powers note the high value of this communication" (*Les Puissances constatent la haute valeur de cette communication*). The same article (Article 9) also stated that the firman would not be used as an excuse for the Great Powers either collectively or separately to interfere with the relations of the Sultan with his subjects.

During the Paris congress and afterwards, Napoleon III ardently espoused the "nationality principle". The most immediate and urgent manifestation of this principle was the cause of the unification of the Danubian principalities. Napoleon III had reason to oppose the 1815 settlement which disregarded nationalities. Therefore he urged for a united Rumania under a foreign prince. Piedmont-Sardinia naturally supported the nationality principle. Austria was against it, fearing that a united Rumania would be attractive to her own Rumanian subjects. The Porte was naturally against it because it rightly considered such a unification as a step towards full independence. Britain wavered, while Russia was Napoleon's chief ally in this question. Russia wanted to gain the goodwill of the Rumanian people and to widen the rift between France and Britain. Eventually, the principalities were united in 1859 under Colonel Alexander Cuza.

---

[523] Roderic Davison, op. cit. (1999), p. 435.

CHAPTER FOUR

FINANCING THE WAR

Ottoman Financial Crisis before the War

Even in the middle of the nineteenth century, the Ottoman bureaucracy did not possess any economic theory or idea going beyond the immediate necessities of financing the state apparatus. There were no independent economists and very few works on economics in general, even in translated form.[1] The only concern of the bureaucracy was the collection of taxes and, as long as they continued to receive their salaries, they did not care about increasing the national product and the tax revenues of the country. Stratford Canning, the British ambassador at the Porte, wrote to Lord Palmerston in October 1851, reporting a conversation about finance with Reşid Pasha, that "the Grand Vizier...disclaims all knowledge of the subject himself". Likewise, according to Canning, Abdurrahman Nafiz Pasha (?–1853), the finance minister (his fifth term in office was from August 1851 to November 1852),[2] although "able and honest", was "altogether destitute of European knowledge". Similarly, the British *charge d'affaires* in Istanbul, Colonel Hugh Rose, commented in October 1852: "Only two Turks, Fuad Effendi and Safetti [Safveti] Pasha, know even the commonest European details as to banks, funds, bills etc and no Pasha

---

[1] According to İlber Ortaylı the first Ottoman book on economics is a manuscript titled *Risale-i Tedbir-i Ümran-ı Mülkî*, written some time before 1833. According to Mehmed Cavid Bey, the first economics book is Sehak Abru Efendi's translation of J. B. Say's *Catéchisme de Economie Politique* under the title of *İlm-i Tedbir-i Menzil* in 1851–1852. According to Z. F. Fındıklıoğlu, the first book is Serendi Arşizen's translation of L. Rossi's book under the title of *Tasarrufat-ı Mülkiye*, published before 1852. See Ahmed Güner Sayar, *Osmanlı İktisat Düşüncesinin Çağdaşlaşması*, Istanbul: Der Yayınları, 1986, pp. 277–279.

[2] See Mehmet Zeki Pakalın, *Maliye Teşkilatı Tarihi (1442–1930)*, vol. 3, Ankara: Maliye Bakanlığı Tetkik Kurulu Yayını, 1978, p. 6. Quoting some official documents by Nafiz Pasha, Pakalın also portrays him as an able and sparing finance minister. However, Nafiz Pasha had been among the first Ottoman high bureaucrats who were tried on charges of corruption after the promulgation of the 1840 Tanzimat Criminal Code. Nafiz Pasha was then the governor of Edirne. He was convicted but pardoned a few years later and became finance minister many times. See Cengiz Kırlı, "Yolsuzluğun İcadı: 1840 Ceza Kanunu, İktidar ve Bürokrasi", *Tarih ve Toplum. Yeni Yaklaşımlar* 4 (244), Güz 2006, pp. 45–199.

keeps an account book, or knows his own accounts".³ There is a certain exaggeration here, because the pashas had their *kethüdas* (stewards) who kept an account book, nevertheless, it is generally true that they were not much informed or interested in financial affairs.

The tithe on agricultural products (*aşar* or *öşür*) still formed the biggest item among all tax revenues of the Porte (about one fourth of total revenues).⁴ This implied that a bad harvest meant a serious decrease in tax revenues. Another important source of revenue was internal and external customs duties, but those, especially the import duties, were very low. In fact, it was here that the strangest economic policy in the world showed itself, for the Ottomans charged more duties on exports than on imports, contrary to the practise of such industrialising countries as the USA, the German Confederation, and Russia that protected their domestic industries.⁵

The Anglo-Ottoman Commercial Treaty of 16 August 1838 (Treaty of Balta Limanı) had set import duty at 5 per cent, while export duty and internal customs duty were 12 per cent *ad valorem* for all goods. These rates were not to be changed even in time of war. For comparison, import duties averaged about 20 per cent in Britain.⁶ The treaty also removed the system of state appointed monopolies (*yed-i vahit*) on export and import. After this, other great powers concluded similar treaties with the Porte. Thus a British merchant (or any merchant who claimed protection from any one of the great powers) could sell his goods in all the provinces of the empire after paying the 5 per cent tax, whereas the Ottoman merchant had to pay 12 per cent internal customs duty within the empire.⁷ Referring to Reşat Kasaba, Gülten

---

³ Christopher Clay. *Gold for the Sultan. Western Bankers and Ottoman Finance 1856–1881*, London, New York: I. B. Tauris, 2000, p. 15.

⁴ Tevfik Güran, *Tanzimat Döneminde Osmanlı Maliyesi: Bütçeler ve Hazine Hesapları (1841–1861)*, Ankara: TTK, 1989, p. 21. Also see: Şevket Pamuk, op. cit. (1994), p. 15. A. [Jean Henri Abdolonyme] Ubicini, *La Turquie Actuelle*, Paris: Librairie de L. Hachette et Cie, 1855, p. XVII. Shaw and Shaw, op. cit., vol. II, p. 99. Charles Morawitz, *Türkiye Maliyesi*, Ankara: Maliye Bakanlığı Tetkik Kurulu Yayını, 1979, p. 17.

⁵ See Gülten Kazgan, *Tanzimat'tan 21. Yüzyıla Türkiye Ekonomisi*, Istanbul: İstanbul Bilgi Üniversitesi Yayınları, 2002, p. 20.

⁶ Nassau William Senior, *A Journal Kept in Turkey and Greece in the Autumn of 1857 and the Beginning of 1858*, London: Longman, Brown, Green, Longmans and Roberts, 1859, p. 185.

⁷ For more information see Mübahat Kütükoğlu, "The Ottoman-British Commercial Treaty of 1838", in William Hale and Ali İhsan Bağış (eds.), *Four Centuries of Turco-British Relations*, North Humberside, UK: The Eothen Press, 1984, pp. 53–61. Also see Puryear, op. cit. (1935), Pamuk, op. cit. (1994), pp. 17–22.

Kazgan writes that the terms of the 1842 Treaty of Nanjing, dictated by Britain to China after the First Opium War, were not as comprehensive as the terms of the Balta Limanı Treaty. This policy was imposed upon the Ottoman Empire first by Britain and then other powers partly to suppress the insurgent Mehmed Ali Pasha of Egypt by taking away a large source of his revenues.[8] However, it fitted the Ottoman bureaucracy as well, for in its opinion export goods should be taxed heavier, because exports raised the price of goods to the detriment of the chief internal buyer, the government.[9]

That Britain became the champion of free trade (especially after the repeal of the Corn Laws in 1846) by the time of the Crimean War is quite understandable, because it had excess manufactured goods and sought new markets for its products, but the fact that the Ottoman Empire was probably the most liberal country in the world in terms of customs duties is less easily explainable. In addition to a very unfavourable balance of trade with the West, the Ottoman state also faced the problems of a debased coinage and currency inflation.[10] Constant wars with Russia and internal troubles from 1768 to 1840 had greatly weakened the treasury. The heavy indemnity to be paid to Russia by the Treaty of Edirne of 1829 and the costs of the war against Mehmed Ali Pasha of Egypt in the 1830s had also undermined the finances of the Ottoman Empire. Furthermore, reform meant additional financial burdens for the treasury. First of all, the establishment and maintenance of a modernized army was expensive. The expanded size of the central and provincial bureaucracy, the new judicial system, educational institutions, public works, the services of foreign experts, etc were all new sources of expense, while the state revenues did not rise to meet them.

It was a commonly shared conviction among European contemporary observers that peculation and corruption in the Ottoman bureaucracy was the rule, honesty being the exception. It was indeed difficult

---

[8] Kazgan, op. cit., p. 19.
[9] Mehmet Genç calls this Ottoman economic policy the principle of provisionalism (*iaşe ilkesi*). He also maintains that the two other economic principles of the Ottoman bureaucracy were fiscalism (endeavouring to increase state revenues and maintaining them at high levels) and traditionalism. See Genç, *Osmanlı İmparatorluğu'nda Devlet ve Ekonomi*, Istanbul: Ötüken Neşriyat, 2000, pp. 45–51 and 59–66.
[10] Frederick S. Rodkey, "Ottoman Concern about Western Economic Penetration in the Levant, 1849–1856", *The Journal of Modern History* 30 (4), December 1958, p. 348.

for an honest person to rise to high rank or to maintain his position without getting involved in the general system of bribery. According to Cevdet Pasha, the great reformer Mustafa Reşid Pasha was, at least before the 1850's, personally not involved in the corrupt practises of the pashas, thanks to Sultan Abdülmecid's monetary rewards. Nevertheless, Mustafa Reşid Pasha did not or could not prevent those around him from doing so. On the other hand, Ottoman pashas received very high salaries and rations, which also formed an important burden on the treasury. Those pashas who held the rank of vizier received each 60,000 to 100,000 piastres monthly in salary and provisions.[11] This was equal to 545 to 909 pounds sterling, which at the present time approximately corresponds to 33,000 to 55,000 pounds sterling.

Taxes were numerous, irregular and unequal, despite the *Tanzimat* principles of standardization, regularization and simplification.[12] In addition to regular taxes, some extraordinary taxes were imposed on the population (like the *iane-i umumiye*)[13] and these taxes in time became permanent. The rich paid relatively less taxes while the poor peasants bore the brunt of the tax burden. The rich could also bribe corrupt government officials to avoid some taxes or obligations including military conscription. For example, when some units of the Anatolian army were quartered in villages around Erzurum, the richer villages paid bribes and the troops were quartered in the houses of the poorer villages.[14] The population of Istanbul was exempt from many taxes and from military conscription. Furthermore, in Anatolia, some Kurdish tribes exacted various tributes from non-Muslim villages, mainly the Armenians. The *iltizam* system (farming out of tax revenues) meant that a large portion of the taxes went to intermediaries and pashas before ever reaching the state budget. Furthermore, the high bureaucrats received enormous commissions from the sale of these *iltizam* tenders. The *mültezims* borrowed from the *sarrafs*, who also reaped their profits in the form of interest. The Ottoman chronicler Cevdet

---

[11] Cevdet Pasha, *Tezâkir 1-12*, yayınlayan Cavid Baysun, Ankara: TTK, 1991, p. 18.

[12] See Stanford J. Shaw and Ezel Kural Shaw, op. cit., pp. 95–105. The authors, however, argue (op. cit., p. 96) that the new taxes of the *Tanzimat* protected the peasants from injustice far more than before.

[13] On *iane-i umumiye* see Ali Akyıldız, *Osmanlı Finans Sisteminde Dönüm Noktası. Kağıt Para ve Sosyo-Ekonomik Etkileri*, Istanbul: Eren Yayıncılık, 1996, pp. 51–64. Shaw and Shaw (op. cit., p. 97) present the *iane-i umumiye* as government "bonds". They seem to have confused it with the *esham-ı umumiye* that were issued later.

[14] Sandwith, op. cit., p. 97.

Pasha writes that while Reşid Pasha and his followers claimed to be working for the prevention of corruption and progress in civilization and education, their practise of selling the tenders caused a change in public opinion about them.[15]

After the *Tanzimat* Edict of 1839, the state tried to collect the taxes by its own officials (*muhassıl*) but this system encountered great resistance and was abandoned. In this, as in all reform moves, Abdülmecid was not firm. Budget deficits became chronic in the 1840s. These deficits were being covered by government borrowing in various forms, mainly from the Galata bankers or *sarrafs*. These bankers, mainly Greeks, Armenians, Jews and Europeans, had direct links with foreign banking houses in Paris, London and elsewhere.[16]

On 22 August 1850, being aware of the financial difficulties of the Porte, the British ambassador Stratford Canning personally submitted to the Sultan a long memorandum on reform.[17] He suggested a foreign loan of five to six million pounds sterling, which, he argued, could be secured at four per cent interest, repayable over a period of 25 years. This was not accepted. Many Ottoman bureaucrats were reluctant to apply for foreign loans, fearing that they would fall into the trap of never-ending loans and thus Europe would control them tightly. Abdülmecid's attitude towards foreign loans was negative in general, at times he said it was better to curb expenditures than to borrow from abroad.[18] Yet as usual he contradicted himself and continued his own luxury expenditures.

The Ottoman treasury finally went bankrupt in 1851. The last two years had seen poor harvests and the insurrection in Bosnia had increased military spending. In April 1851, Lord Stratford reported that in the previous year expenditure had exceeded income by 1 million pounds sterling or 1.1 million Ottoman pounds and a deficit of 770,000 Ottoman pounds was expected in the current year. He believed that the government needed about 7.5 million pounds or 8.25 million Ottoman pounds to clear its financial obligations completely. This amount was, as he observed, more than a year's average income of the Porte. Stratford re-emphasized that the only solution was a long-term

---

[15] Cevdet Pasha, op. cit., p. 20.
[16] Clay, op. cit., p. 19.
[17] Rodkey, ibid.
[18] Cevdet Pasha, *Tezâkir 1–12*, p. 22; also see his *Ma'rûzât*, Istanbul: Çağrı Yayınları, 1980, p. 7.

foreign loan. Stratford feared that the financial crisis might ruin the reform movement.[19]

When the finance minister Nafiz Pasha told the Divan that next month's salaries would be delayed, all ministers were shocked. In fact, for the ministers, the financial crisis had come so suddenly that there was not even a counterpart in Ottoman Turkish of the French word *crise*. Cevdet Pasha tells how they finally agreed upon the word *buhran* as an equivalent for it.[20]

Although the first foreign loan was made in 1854, the idea had been expressed first in 1783, when Russia occupied the Crimea and war seemed inevitable.[21] During Abdülmecid's reign, the first attempt had come in 1841, with a proposal to set up a national bank as well. This did not work because the Ottomans did not want to give guarantees and immunities under either an Anglo-Ottoman treaty or a treaty between all the great powers and the Ottoman Empire. At that time this had an important role in the swing of the Porte toward reaction.[22] Some time later, in 1849, the *Dersaadet Bankası* (Bank of Constantinople) was set up by foreign merchants. The duty of this "bank" was to provide for the stability of the Ottoman currency against European currencies, especially sterling.

The Abortive Loan of 1852

In March 1852, the Dersaadet Bankası and the Porte sent Monsieur Couturier, an Izmir merchant, to Paris to find credit for the repayment of the debt of the bank to European markets. In August 1852, Couturier was empowered together with Paris ambassador Kalimaki Bey or London ambassador Kostaki Bey to sign a contract for 40 million francs repayable in 10 years at 6 per cent interest with a 2 per cent commission fee. The Porte presented as lien the tributes of Egypt, Serbia, Wallachia and Moldavia. On 7 September 1852, a contract for a loan of 50 million francs (equal to 2 million pounds sterling) was signed in Paris for 23 years at 6 per cent interest with a 2 per cent commission fee.[23] Afterwards, bonds for 20 million francs were sold.

---

[19] Clay, op. cit., pp. 21–22.
[20] Cevdet Pasha, op. cit., p. 21.
[21] Şevket Akar and Hüseyin Al, op. cit., p. 3.
[22] Rodkey, op. cit., p. 349.
[23] See Akar and Al, "Dersaadet Bankası'nın tasfiyesi ve 1852 borçlanması", *Tarih ve Toplum. Yeni Yaklaşımlar* 4 (244), Istanbul, Güz 2006, p. 162. A. du Velay gives

However, Sultan Abdülmecid had given his consent, although reluctantly, for a term of ten years at most. The grand vizier Mehmed Emin Âli Pasha did not bother to tell Abdülmecid the terms of the loan. Âli Pasha's rival Damad Mehmed Ali Pasha learned of the terms and then informed Abdülmecid. Mehmed Ali succeeded in persuading the Sultan to reject the loan, arguing that his father had never accepted a foreign loan. Abdülmecid was reluctant because he feared foreign intervention in case of any default in repayments.

Abdülmecid dismissed Âli Pasha and replaced him with Mehmed Ali at the beginning of October 1852. Paris ambassador Kalimaki Bey was also dismissed and replaced by Veli (Veliyüddin) Pasha. The ministers had to collect among themselves an indemnity of 2.1 million francs to be paid to the creditors. As Olive Anderson remarked, this was a "disastrous début" for the Ottoman Empire in the Western money market. This cancelled transaction made it "almost impossible for her to borrow on her own credit alone".[24]

Ottoman War Expenses

Ottoman military expenses in the period from 1841 to 1853 consumed on the average approximately 40 per cent of the state "budget". During the Crimean War, this proportion went up to 67 per cent of all actual state expenditures.[25] Most of the ammunition and weapons was being imported but military imports were not confined to steam ships and weapons and ammunition such as Minié rifles and Paixhans shells. Even such items as sabres, harnesses (saddles, etc.) and boots had to be imported from Britain and France.[26]

According to a military report, the total salary and rations of the regular land troops (*asakir-i nizamiye*) for the financial (Julian) year 1266 (13 March 1850 to 12 March 1851) amounted to 129,231,778 piastres.[27] This is roughly equal to 1.12 million pounds sterling at the exchange

---

the amount as 55 million francs, payback period 27 years, and the year as 1850. See his *Türkiye Mali Tarihi*, Ankara: Maliye Bakanlığı Yayınları, 1978, p. 80. Rodkey gives the amount as 50 million francs; the other terms are as above. See Rodkey, op. cit., p. 350.

[24] Olive Anderson, op. cit., p. 48.
[25] Güran, op. cit., p. 24, 37.
[26] See for example BOA. İ. HR. 109/5332, dated 1 May 1854 on the purchase of 50,000 Paixhans shells. BOA. İ. HR. 110/5409, dated 22 April 1854 on harnesses to be imported from France.
[27] BOA. C. AS. 7517, dated 10 April 1850.

rate of 110 piastres per pound, prevalent at that time. In that year the muster-roll was 77,096 for the five armies. We can conclude that during the war the annual salaries and rations alone of the army should have cost almost three times as much, since the army (excluding the *başıbozuks*) had reached around 200,000 men towards the end of 1855, as stated in a report by the Ottoman finance ministry submitted to the loan control commission in October 1855. This report was also published in the French official newspaper *Le Moniteur Universel* on 8 January 1856.[28] According to the report, the total war expenses of the three departments of army, navy, and artillery of the Ottoman Empire for the period from 27 May 1853 to 27 September 1855 (28 months) amounted to 3,015,588 purses, that is, 1,507,794,000 piastres or 11.16 million pounds sterling, the exchange rate now being 135 piastres per pound. This gives us a yearly average total military expense of 4.8 million pounds, which seems rather small when we consider that the pay and rations alone of the soldiers and officers must have constituted at least 3.36 million pounds, as shown above. According to the same report, the total budget deficit during this period reached 5.8 million pounds.

This figure seems in line with Dr. Tevfik Güran's study based on Ottoman fiscal documents from the BOA, provided we take into account the length of the period, because the war lasted more than two years (almost three years including war preparations) for the Ottoman Empire. Tevfik Güran's study gives us a total of actual military expenditures of 1,782,737,764 piastres for the fiscal (Julian) years 1269 to 1271, corresponding to the period from 13 March 1853 to 12 March 1856, that is, a period of three years (see Table 1). If we divide this amount by an average exchange rate of 125 piastres per pound, then we get an approximate amount of 14.26 million pounds sterling for this period.[29]

---

[28] Available at BOA. HR. SYS. 1355/3. Actually the report was sent by the Ottoman foreign minister to Paris to be published in the above newspaper. Upon publication, Reşid Pasha's son Mehmed Cemil Bey, ambassador to Paris, immediately sent a copy of the newspaper to Istanbul. The document is titled "Rapport du Ministre des Finances a la Commission de Contrôle". A. du Velay also refers to this report without mentioning its source. See A. du Velay, *Türkiye Mali Tarihi*, Ankara: Maliye Bakanlığı Yayınları, 1978, p. 82.

[29] Approximately equal to 855 million pounds of today. The exchange rate of pound vacillated between 110 piastres at the beginning and 140 piastres towards the end of the war. Other exchange rates were as follows: 1 pound sterling = 25 francs = 6 silver roubles = 24 marks = 12 florins.

Table 1. Distribution of state payments among various expense items
(thousand piastres)[30]

Fiscal year	Military spending	Sultan's spending	Salaries	Admin. spending	Transfer payments	Total
1269/1853–4	430,372.7	147,485.8	119,180.9	116,437.1	135,416.0	948,892.3
1270/1854–5	601,744.1	57,138.6	119,759.9	90,330.5	31,324.6	900,298.0
1271/1855–6	750,620.8	72,279.1	115,404.7	129,721.7	53,740.8	1,121,767.3
Total	1,782,737.7	276,903.5	354,345.5	336,489.3	220,481.4	2,970,957.6

These numbers become more meaningful in comparison with actual state revenues including budgetary and non-budgetary revenues for the same period. These revenues amount to 2,970,960,465 piastres, roughly equal to 22.8 million pounds for the period or 7.6 million pounds per year on the average (see Table 2). During this period non-budgetary or extra-budgetary revenues and their share in total revenues increased considerably. The extra-budgetary revenues consisted of internal borrowing from the Galata bankers and merchants, issue of paper money (*kaime*, in plural *kavaim*), and of bonds (*esham*), special taxes in the form of donations (*iane-i harbiyye*) and finally the two foreign loans of 1854 and 1855. The Galata *sarrafs* lent money at the annual interest rate of 12 per cent, while it was around 4 to 6 per cent in Europe.[31] While such extra-budget revenues formed one-digit percentages of total revenues before the war, they increased up to 51.5 per cent during the war.[32] Among the extra-budget revenues of the period, foreign loans make up roughly 7.5 million pounds sterling. Of this sum, 2.4 millions come from the first loan of 1854 (nominal value 3 millions) and 5.1 millions from the second loan of 1855 (nominal value 5 millions). Internal borrowing during the war on the other hand, according to Ali Akyıldız, reached 5,129,790 Ottoman pounds or 4,706,229 pounds sterling at the official exchange rate of 109 piastres per pound sterling.[33]

---

[30] Güran, op. cit., p. 36, Table 8 A. I have made some necessary calculations and simplifications.
[31] Ali Akyıldız, "Osmanlı Devleti'nin Kırım Savaşı'nı Finansmanı: İç ve Dış Borçlanmalar", symposium paper in *Savaştan Barışa*, 2007, p. 14.
[32] Güran, ibid., p. 30.
[33] Akyıldız, op. cit. (2007), p. 18.

Table 2. Distribution of state revenues (thousand piastres)[34]

Fiscal year	Budget revenues	(%)	Non-budget revenues	(%)	Total revenues
1269/1853–54	799,490.7	84.3	149,279.1	15.7	948,769.8
1270/1854–55	487,522.3	54.1	412,966.9	45.9	900,489.3
1271/1855–56	543,988.6	48.5	577,712.6	51.5	1,121,701.2
Total	1,831,001.7		1,139,958.7		2,970,960.4

If we accept the above mentioned figure of 14.26 million pounds as total war expenses, then we must conclude that approximately half of the actual Ottoman war expenditures was financed by foreign loans.

Paul Kennedy, in his table of military expenditures of the warring states, for the Ottoman Empire ("Turkey") gives only the figures of 2.8 million pounds for 1852 and 3 million pounds for the year 1855, putting a question mark for 1853, 1854 and 1856.[35] The 3 million pounds here seem to have been reckoned from the first Ottoman loan of 1854, yet Kennedy should have discounted this amount by the issue price of 80 per cent (which reduced the actual amount received to 2.4 millions) and added at least the second Ottoman loan of 1855, amounting to 5.1 million pounds. Of course, these two loans did not cover the whole amount of the Ottoman war spending. In any case, as seen from Table 3, the military spending of the Ottoman Empire was very modest in comparison with any of the three great powers. Nevertheless, if we take into consideration the revenues of the Ottoman Empire, it seems that it felt the financial burden of the war more acutely than other states.

---

[34] Güran, ibid., p. 30.
[35] Paul Kennedy. *The Rise and Fall of the Great Powers. Economic Change and Military Conflict from 1500 to 2000*. New York: Vintage, 1989, p. 176.

Table 3. Military expenditures of the warring states (million pounds sterling)[36]

	1853	1854	1855	1856	Total
Russia[37]	19.9	31.3	39.8	37.9	128.9
France	17.5	30.3	43.8	36.3	127.9
Britain	9.1	76.3	36.5	32.3	154.2
Ottoman Empire	3.5?	4.6?	6.0?	3.2?	17.3
Sardinia	1.4	1.4	2.2	2.5	7.5

The Ottoman official chronicler of the period Ahmed Lutfi Efendi gives the figure of 7 million Ottoman pounds or pounds sterling (*liret*) as the total extraordinary war expenses of the Ottoman Empire for the 28 months of war. Of this amount, he writes, 3 millions came from foreign loans and the remaining 4 millions were obtained through internal borrowing, issue of paper money and the *iane-i cihadiye*.[38] Yet obviously (and as another proof of his incompetence for his task), he omits the 1855 loan of 5 million pounds. In any case, his figure is an underestimation.

While the war meant expenses for the state and new taxes for its subjects, it brought some benefits as well, especially for the shopkeepers and merchants. The allies also spent significant sums for the provisions of their armies and navies. They had their agents sent everywhere in Anatolia and Rumelia to buy food, horses, fodder and other items. It seems that due to the lack of proper roads and railways in the Ottoman Empire, these purchases were made mainly from coastal areas close to ports to facilitate the transport of goods by sea. According to the British economist Nassau William Senior (1790–1864), who visited Kıbrıslı Mehmed Emin Pasha at his mansion in Istanbul on 4 October 1857, the pasha told him that although the late war was "enormously expensive" to the government, because it raised 300,000 men, it had

---

[36] Figures are from Paul Kennedy, except those for the Ottoman Empire, which I prepared from Güran's study with some modifications.

[37] The Russian total expenditure figure here comes close to a Russian estimate of 796 million rubles (132 million pounds) by Ivan Bliokh, cited by Pokrovskiy, op. cit. p. 66. Alexis Troubetzkoy on the other hand gives the total Russian war expenditure as 142 million pounds sterling, "a mere 15 per cent less than France and Britain together". However, he does not cite any source. See Troubetzkoy, *A Brief History of the Crimean War*, New York: Carroll & Graf, 2006, p. 300.

[38] Lütfi Efendi, op. cit., p. 117. *Liret* appears rather strange here. Most probably it is *lira*, meaning Ottoman pounds. But it could be pounds sterling as well.

also profited and "Turkey" was the only country that did so. Mehmed Pasha added that 30 millions sterling or more were spent in Istanbul and if they had had "the means of transport" (meaning roads) they could have sold twice or three times as much to the allies. Cevdet Pasha has also written that the shopkeepers of Istanbul made enormous profits from sales to the British and the French.[39]

Conspicuous Consumption by Palace Women

Conspicuous consumption by palace women seems to have played some role in the Ottoman financial crisis. Cevdet Pasha has written in some detail about the extravagance of such women and seems to put the main blame on them for the deficits in state budget. He argues that the palace women came under the influence of Europeans and Egyptian ladies and started spending enormous sums for luxury items like jewellery, furniture and clothing. They also borrowed from the *sarrafs* of Galata at very high interest rates, going up to 45 per cent.[40] While there may be a certain element of exaggeration in the figures given by Cevdet Pasha, they are, in any case, impressive. These ladies, mainly the sisters, daughters and harem favourites of the Sultan are said to have incurred in the year 1855 a debt of 288,000 purses (approximately 1.15 million pounds sterling); of which, Serfiraz Hanım, one of the favourites of the Sultan, alone was responsible for 125,000 purses (approximately 500,000 pounds sterling).[41] For comparison, Cevdet Pasha writes that during the reign of Sultan Mahmud II, the expenses of the whole palace did not exceed 1,000 purses while under Sultan Abdülmecid it had reached 20,000 purses.[42]

Melek Hanım, the Christian wife of Sadrazam Kıbrıslı Mehmed Emin Pasha wrote that "the Sultan's love for his wives... was ruining the country".

> Covered with diamonds, and attended by numerous slaves, almost as sumptuously attired as their mistresses, they drove out in carriages, each of which, with its equipments, cost about 900,000 piastres (£8000). Their

---

[39] Senior, op. cit., pp. 39–40. Cevdet Pasha, op. cit. (1980), p. 8.
[40] See Ali Akyıldız, *Mümin ve Müsrif Bir Padişah Kızı: Refia Sultan*, Istanbul: Tarih Vakfı Yurt Yayınları, 1998, pp. 1–5, 67–74.
[41] Cevdet Pasha, *Tezâkir* 13–20, p. 4. Cevdet Pasha gives this amount as 120,000 purses elsewhere in the same book (p. 8).
[42] Cevdet Pasha, op. cit., p. 8.

apartments were constantly replenished with new furniture. In the space of two years the seraglio was furnished about four times over... Frequently the favors of one of the Sultan's wives, or odalisques, were attended with bounties and presents big enough to make the fortune of him who received it. In fact, these women were utterly regardless of the costliness of what they bestowed; it was a regular case of pillage.[43]

When Abdülmecid's daughter Refia Sultan's debts reached 60,000 purses (240,000 pounds sterling), her *kethüda* (chamberlain) Eşref Efendi was dismissed and put under house arrest in August 1858.[44] These sums must be compared with the deficit of the state budget for 1851, which was around one million pounds.[45] A commission consisting of Mehmet, Şekib, Safveti and Rıfat Pashas calculated the deficit of 1853 as 300,000 purses (nearly 1.38 million pounds). When war broke out, the Ottoman treasury first tried to borrow from the *sarrafs* of Galata and from internal merchants in general. Yet only 20,000 purses (roughly 92,000 pounds) out of the planned sum of 30,000 purses could be borrowed from them, secured on the Egyptian tribute for the Muslim fiscal year 1271 (March 1855–March 1856).[46]

The Mission of Namık Pasha

The beginning of the war changed the position of the Sultan on borrowing from Europe. When internal borrowing became impossible, international borrowing became a necessity. At the beginning of October 1853 or some time earlier, the Ottoman council of ministers, by the approval of the Sultan, decided to send the Minister of Commerce and Public Works Mehmed Namık Pasha (1804–1892) to Paris and London to contract a loan.[47] Reşid Pasha wrote on 5 October 1853 to Mr Rothschild, the well-known banker of Paris and London, requesting

---

[43] Melek Hanım, *Thirty Years in the Harem*, NJ: Gorgias Press, 2005, p. 41.
[44] Akyıldız, op. cit. (1998), p. 67.
[45] Frederick Stanley Rodkey, "Ottoman Concern about Western Economic Penetration in the Levant, 1849–1856", *Journal of Modern History* 30(4), December 1958, p. 3.
[46] Cezmi Karasu, op. cit., p. 120.
[47] Lütfi, op. cit., pp. 214–215. The firman is dated *Evail-i Cemaziyelevvel* 1270, that is, beginning of February 1854. Namık Pasha gives the same date in his autobiography. See Ahmet Nuri Sinaplı, *Şeyhül Vüzera Serasker Mehmet Namık Paşa*, Istanbul: Yenilik Basımevi, 1987, p. 280. However, this firman was issued as a matter of formality when Namık Pasha was already in London. Sinaplı (op. cit., p. 159) erroneously gives the date of the firman as the date of Namık Pasha's travel to Paris and London.

him to assist Namık Pasha.[48] Namık Pasha's instructions were prepared towards the end of October. His son Major Halil Bey was also appointed to his mission as first secretary and Mustafa Fahreddin Bey from the foreign ministry as second secretary.[49]

Namık Pasha's instructions were to contract a loan for 500,000 *kese* (2.5 million Ottoman pounds or around 2.27 million pounds sterling) in favourable terms. In his memorandum, the grand vizier stated that the securities for the loan should not be in the form of a monopoly and should not appear as a kind of *rehin* (pledge or pawn or mortgage lien) in the opinion of the foreigners. The tribute of Egypt and the customs revenues of Syria and Izmir were to be avoided assignment as security. The *aşar* on the olive oil and the revenue of the province of Hudavendigar (Bursa) could be safely deposited as security. The loan money would be insured for safe arrival at Istanbul. Exchange bills, drafts and notes were not to be accepted; only gold and silver money was to be accepted. For the secrecy of telegraph communications, ciphers would be given to the secretaries.[50] Finally the grand vizier added that instructions on the terms of the loan should be kept very secret and would be given separately in a secret instruction.[51]

Soon a confidential letter of instructions or regulations was also prepared and given to Namık Pasha. It was kept secret from the extended council of ministers and was known only among the six trusted members of the inner circle of the grand vizier who sealed it. The reason for this secrecy was to prevent the limits of the loan terms from being known to the Galata bankers and through them to the European bankers, who might then use this information in their interests. The first item to be decided was the interest rate. It was stated that according to news from Paris, an interest rate of four to four and a half per cent was the going market rate. Namık Pasha was allowed up to six per cent. The second item was the payback period. Namık Pasha was instructed to try to keep it at 10 years, and at most 15 years. Third and last, the issue price should not be lower than 95 per cent, allowing a maximum five per cent discount. The document was sealed by Musa Safveti Pasha

---

[48] However, Rothschild replied only on 25 February 1854. BOA. İ. HR. 332/21357 enc. 2.
[49] BOA. İ. HR. 103/5028, 24 October 1853.
[50] Telegraph lines in the Ottoman Empire at that time were available only in Belgrade. From Belgrade the telegraph was sent to Istanbul via the Danube. In 1855 a telegraph line was built from Sevastopol to Varna and Istanbul.
[51] *Tezkire-i Samiye müsveddesi*. BOA. A. AMD. 49/90, 27 October 1853.

(finance minister), Sadık Rifat Pasha (President of the MVL), Damad Ali Fethi Pasha (superintendent of the Imperial Arsenal, *Tophane-i Amire Müşiri*), Damad Mehmed Ali Pasha (*Serasker*), Mustafa Reşid Pasha (foreign minister), Ahmed Arif Efendi (the *şeyhülislam*) and the grand vizier Giritli Mustafa Naili Pasha.[52]

Thus in the middle of November 1853 Namık Pasha set out for Paris. After 15 days' travel, he arrived there somewhat late on 27 November.[53] The Ottoman ambassador in Paris was Veliyüddin Rifat Pasha, known as Veli Pasha, son of the Grand Vizier Giritli Mustafa Naili Pasha. On the day of his arrival, Namık and Veli Pasha went to visit the French foreign minister Drouyn de Lhuys. Namık Pasha asked for assistance in concluding a loan agreement. Namık also told him that the Porte did not want war, but Russia had again put its expansion plan into action. The Ottoman Empire was not equal to Russia in force, therefore if (God forbid) the Russians occupied their country, then Europe would inherit the problems of the Porte. Drouyn de Lhuys replied that he also thought so but his companions did not agree with him. Then he suggested that they should talk to the emperor as well. On the question of the loan, he promised that he would urge bankers for the loan.[54]

Namık Pasha talked with Mr Rothschild and some other bankers in Paris. They replied that they could give an answer in seven to eight days after consulting their partners. Namık Pasha comments that this delay was due to their anticipation of a peaceful outcome of diplomatic efforts by European cabinets. The bankers had also said that due to the current situation the market rate of interest was 6 per cent and a discount of 10 per cent in the issue price. Namık Pasha had also written to Kostaki Musurus, the Ottoman ambassador in London.

A few days later Namık and Veli Pashas were invited to the Tuileries Palace to be received by Napoleon III.[55] The Emperor however, neither rejected nor approved of Namık's words. On 2 December Namık

---

[52] Instructions to Namık Pasha. Attachment to the petition of the grand vizier to the Sultan. BOA. İ. HR. 103/5039 enc. 1, 31 October 1853 and BOA. A. DVN. MHM. 10/89–2, 6 November 1853.
[53] Namık Pasha to foreign minister Reşid Pasha, 29 November 1853. BOA. İ. HR. 333/21335 enc. 1.
[54] Lütfi Efendi, op. cit., p. 216.
[55] Veli Pasha to Reşid Pasha the foreign minister. BOA. HR. MKT. 68/21, 9 December 1853. Namık Pasha calls the French emperor as Napoleon the Second. See Lütfi Efendi, ibid., p. 216.

and Veli revisited Drouyn de Lhuys. In his report dated 10 December, Namık Pasha first pointed out that Musurus had replied that the London bankers were not inclined positively to the Ottoman loan and even some Russian intrigues were involved. Then he described his second meeting with Drouyn de Lhuys.

When de Lhuys asked about the loan, Namık replied that up to then some petty bankers and commissioners had come to him and made some "excessive and cold" offers like eight to nine per cent interest rate and 80 per cent issue price for the bonds. Having started this operation here in Paris, added Namık, we must conclude it here, otherwise if we go to London then there they will say that we could not achieve anything here and therefore they will create more problems. For this reason Namık asked for the help of the French foreign minister. Thereupon Drouyn de Lhuys said that the revenue of France was just equal to its expenses and he did not have the right to tell the bankers where to invest their money, since it was their money. Then he asked whether the Pasha had any instructions or authority to ask for a guarantee from the French government. To this Namık replied categorically that he did not have any such permission either for a guarantee or for a direct loan from the French government. He added that as friends and allies of the Ottoman Empire, France and Britain should assist it in obtaining the loan at reasonable conditions. The loan issue had been subjected to the intrigues of Russia and the avarice of the bankers, he said. Drouyn de Lhuys promised to talk to the Emperor to find a solution.[56] On 5 December Drouyn de Lhuys also wrote to Baron Bourqueney, the French ambassador in Vienna, that Namık Pasha was in Paris to negotiate a loan of 57 million francs (equal to 2.28 million pounds sterling), and that they hoped for his success. "We believe that a sign of confidence given to Turkey in the current circumstances would be very proper to discourage those who speculate in advance on the fall of the Empire", he added.[57]

Napoleon III then urged his finance minister, who in his turn urged both Rothschild and his arch rival, the *Crédit mobilier* and a third group of bankers to sign a three-sided contract with a reasonable interest rate. Namık Pasha also reported that the news of Ottoman

---

[56] Namık Pasha to Mustafa Naili Pasha, Paris, 10 December 1853. BOA. İ. HR. 333/21335 enc. 4.
[57] AGKK, IV/1, ed. Winfried Baumgart, Munich: Oldenbourg, 2003, p. 674.

victories had also been received well as regards the facility of the loan. Remarkably, he did not mention the news of the destruction of the Ottoman squadron in Sinop, which should have reached Paris by then. The bankers at first had an eye on the tribute of Egypt as a guarantee, but they gave up the idea. They had also agreed on the duration of the loan. However, the interest rate and the commission were not yet determined. While Namık offered 5 per cent, the French finance minister said a 7 per cent interest should be seen normal. Nevertheless, Namık Pasha reported that they were still trying to include other bankers to increase competition and to decrease the interest rate. From this report, it appeared that everything was normal and that the loan would soon be concluded at a normal price. However, this was not to be the case, because at this time diplomatic negotiations had been resumed and it was not certain whether the war would be continued or not. The bankers did not want to commit themselves without having first ascertained the result of these talks.

The reports of Namık and Veli Pashas were discussed at the council of ministers on 28 December 1853. Nevertheless, the ministers could not come up with a solution or clear instructions. Namık Pasha was expected to somehow finish contracting the loan without parting from his original instructions. The grand vizier Giritli Mustafa Naili Pasha reported the decision of the council to the Sultan next day.[58]

In the meantime the Porte was very hard pressed for want of money. It had almost exhausted all ways of borrowing other than the foreign loan. The amount of the loan was increased up to five million pounds sterling. Thus Namık Pasha was to negotiate a loan of five million pounds sterling in Paris and London. Since money was needed urgently, the French and British governments were also asked to advance 10 million francs each (equal to 400,000 pounds sterling) to be paid back together with interest out of the loan.[59]

The Ottoman official chronicler Ahmed Lütfi Efendi applied to Namık Pasha in 1892, or some time before, asking him to give information on his mission. The aged Şeyh ül Vüzera, in his reply, written

---

[58] BOA. İ. HR. 333/21335 enc. 5. Sultan's approval is on 30 December 1853.

[59] Anderson also writes that "after Sinope, France advanced 10 million francs" (op. cit., p. 48), however, France advanced only 5 million francs in instalments, the first of which, 1 million francs, was received in January 1854 and the last towards October 1854. See BOA. A. AMD. 50/50, dated 14 January 1854 and BOA. İ. HR. 114/5469, dated 9 October 1854. This amount of 5 million francs was paid back from the loan money together with its five per cent interest.

years after the event, with the hindsight of the experience of the *Düyun-ı Umumiye İdaresi* (Public Debt Administration), which from 1881 onwards controlled the collection of many of the Ottoman taxes for the repayment of the Ottoman debt, emphasised his unwillingness at that time to sign a foreign loan. Yet we must allow that his story could be genuine, because fear of a foreign loan was really dominant among some parts of the bureaucracy at that time. Apparently Namık Pasha's "heart did not wish to be the instrument of the first foreign loan, for until then the Sublime State (*Devlet-i Aliyye*) did not owe an *akçe* to the foreigners."[60]

In his *layiha* given to Lütfi Efendi, Namık Pasha further added that since he did not think that the Russians could be stopped by money alone, he asked the council of ministers for permission to invite the British and the French governments to an alliance, trying to persuade them by explaining the dangers to Europe in the case of a Russian victory. According to him, the Ottoman council of ministers gave him this authority without much hope of gaining the support of the European great powers.

From Paris, Namık Pasha went to London on 17 December 1853.[61] This was his third visit to London. Namık Pasha had first been to London in 1832 during Sultan Mahmud II's reign as special envoy to seek help against Mehmed Ali Pasha of Egypt. His second embassy to London was in 1834, therefore he knew some of the ministers. The British public was well disposed towards the Ottomans and hostile to Russia. Namık relates how he and the Ottoman ambassador Kostaki Musurus were greeted by people shouting "Brave Turks! Don't worry over Sinop!" on their way to the parliament to hear the inaugural speech of the Queen.[62] Together with Musurus, he went to Lord Palmerston, whom he had met before. Palmerston was known for his anti-Russian stand. From the 1830's onwards the defence of the Ottoman Empire against Russia had become an important policy objective for him.[63] Accordingly, Palmerston received Namık well, and said he agreed

---

[60] For Namık Pasha's report (*layiha*) on his mission see Lütfi, op. cit., numara 18, pp. 215–217. Translations are mine.
[61] BOA. İ. HR. 114/5554-08, 24 December 1853. Cf. Ahmet Nuri Sinaplı, op. cit., p. 159. Sinaplı gives the date as Rebiyyülahir, instead of Rebiyyülevvel.
[62] Namık Pasha to Reşid Pasha. BOA. HR. SYS. 905/1 enc. 86, 31 January 1854.
[63] Rodkey, "Lord Palmerston and the Rejuvenation of Turkey, 1830–41", Part I, *The Journal of Modern History* 1 (4), December 1929, pp. 570–593; Part II, *The Journal of Modern History* 2 (2), June 1930, pp. 193–225.

with him on the necessity of checking Russian expansion, but the Prime Minister Lord Aberdeen and the Chancellor of the Exchequer (Finance Minister) William Gladstone (1809–1898) were opposed to him. Namık Pasha also reported that the British Prime Minister Lord Aberdeen quite rudely stated: "Besides spending its money, should Britain shed its blood as well for you?"[64]

In his letter to Reşid Pasha, dated 21 February 1854, Namık Pasha confirmed his receipt of the instructions from Reşid Pasha dated 29 January 1854 and the attached firman of the Sultan, in reply to his letter dated 28 December 1853. Apparently he had asked for permission to make the contract on an agency basis with a fixed commission, and this was not accepted, because it was argued that this way the Porte would incur a permanent risk while the bankers would safely receive their commission. Namık Pasha stated that up to that time he could not find any banker who would undertake the loan at his own risk, at a fixed price. Even on an agency basis, no banker was willing to contract the loan within the limits of Namık Pasha's instructions. Then he argued against Reşid Pasha that if the loan was contracted to a banker on an agency basis and the desired amount was received, then the Sublime Porte would not incur any losses or profits from the sale and purchase of the loan bonds among the bankers. The risk or drawback in this case would be that the banker would not advance money from his own pocket if the bonds were not sold.[65]

Namık Pasha added that the British cabinet was making some efforts and the banker Rothschild was visiting him, making, however, such an "exorbitant" offer as 70 per cent issue price and 5 percent interest rate, while Namık offered at 90 percent and 5 percent interest. The British secretary of state for foreign affairs Lord Clarendon and the home secretary Lord Palmerston on the other hand insisted to Namık Pasha that since his government needed money urgently

---

[64] Lütfi, op. cit., pp. 216–217. Cf. Sinaplı, pp. 169–170, where Namık says he was friendly with Palmerston, who was expected to become the prime minister. Namık Pasha's memory fails him, for he makes Lord Palmerston foreign minister, while Palmerston was home secretary at that time. Sinaplı also quotes an interview of Namık Pasha to a French journalist in 1883, where Namık mentions Lord "Alberti" (Aberdeen) as foreign minister (Sinaplı, ibid., p. 171). At that time the foreign minister was Lord Clarendon. In the interview Namık also says that Palmerston had expressed his inability to help him, while the French emperor and ministers were willing to help.

[65] Namık Pasha to Reşid Pasha, London, 21 February 1854. BOA. İ. HR. 332/21357 enc. 4.

he should not look at the price but try to get the money as soon as possible. To these words Namık replied that his instructions do not allow such an excessive price and he would not accept it even if it was allowed. Then they advised him to consult the "Minister for Indian affairs" Sir Charles Wood (1800-1885), who was competent in these affairs and could assist him informally. Palmerston had given Namık Pasha a note in French, in which he urged him to conclude the loan and argued that "it was a nonsense to want to fix in Constantinople the price at which the capitalists of London and Paris would like to lend their money".⁶⁶ Namık Pasha attached this note to his letter, adding that he had not yet received an answer from Sir Charles. He concluded by saying that since it was not possible to find money within the conditions of his instructions, he would rather return to Istanbul than stay there in vain.

In another letter of the same date, Namık Pasha reported to Reşid Pasha on the political situation. He stated that, since the Russian emperor gave a negative answer to the open letter from the French emperor, France and Britain no longer find it possible to come to a peaceful agreement with Russia and war now seems imminent. Prussia and Austria were also now closer to France and Britain than to Russia. Lord Palmerston told him that Russia should be driven further north from the mouth of the Danube and that Georgia and Circassia should belong to the Ottoman Empire. Palmerston also told him that all treaties with Russia must be annulled and new ones serving the independence and prosperity of the Porte must be instituted instead. Namık Pasha commented that while the British public in general seemed to favour the Porte, most of the people were influenced by religious fanaticism, they were also opposed to it in some ways and therefore should not be seen as reliable. The situation was, according to Namık Pasha, getting closer to turning into a "general war".⁶⁷

Lord Stratford and the British ministers accused Namık Pasha of delaying the loan by insisting on unrealistic conditions. Clarendon wrote to Stratford on 13 March 1854 that "any man of ordinary experience or capacity would have got the money long ago, but he has insisted on having the same terms as England might make a loan in

---

⁶⁶ Lord Palmerston to Namık Pasha, London, 19 February 1854. BOA. İ. HR. 332/21357 enc. 3. "C'était une absurdité que de vouloir fixer à Constantinople le Prix auquel les Capitalistes de Londres et de Paris voudraient prêter leur Argent."
⁶⁷ Namık Pasha to Reşid Pasha, 21 February 1854. BOA. İ. HR. 108/5293 enc. 8.

times of profound peace!" Anderson is also of the opinion that Namık Pasha "was ill-chosen for such a mission, and he insisted on abiding by his quite unrealistic instructions not to borrow below an issue price of 95." Lord Stratford de Redcliffe wrote privately from Istanbul to Lord Clarendon that the Sultan had told him that he had consented to a foreign loan in time of war to stand out in time of peace. The "Great Elchi" added, "In this, as in other matters, necessity is the only effective lever against Islamism".[68]

The testimony of Namık Pasha, however, confirmed by the correspondence of Musurus, indicates that he did not quite stick to his instructions and on 24 March 1854 he did sign a contract for five million pounds with the London banking house of Rothschild at 6 per cent interest rate and at the issue price of 85 per cent.[69] These were indeed relatively good conditions for the loan, because Rothschild had gone down to 60 per cent in his offers and the loan was finally contracted at 80 per cent.

Accordingly, on the London and Paris stock exchanges, Ottoman six per cent bonds were issued at 85 per cent issue price, with a two-percent brokerage fee including expenses. The loan was to be collected in four months and to be paid back in 15 years. But the problem was that the demand for them was low due to the bad memories of the cancelled loan of 1852 and due to a general lack of confidence in the Porte's financial and administrative affairs. Only 1.1 million pounds were subscribed to in London, while the amount of subscription in Paris is not known.[70]

On 23 March (the same day as the date of Namık Pasha's despatch), Musurus also wrote to Reşid Pasha that Aberdeen said that he and the other ministers found the price of 75 per cent and the interest rate of

---

[68] Anderson, op. cit., p. 48.
[69] Namık Pasha to the foreign minister, 23 March 1854. BOA. İ. HR. 107/5283 enc. 1. Musurus to the foreign minister, 23 March 1854. BOA. HR. TO. 52/50. Namık Pasha telegraphed the news of the agreement on 24 March 1854 to Belgrad to be transferred from there to the Sublime Porte. BOA. İ. HR. 107/5272 enc. 3. Akar and Al (op. cit., p. 4) give the date of the agreement with Rothschild as of 8 April, which is not true. On the other hand, in his *layiha* to the chronicler Lütfi Efendi, written about 1892, Namık Pasha remembers the conditions as four per cent interest and one per cent sinking fund, which is also not true. See Lütfi, op. cit., p. 217.
[70] Namık Pasha to Reşid Pasha, London, 23 March 1854. BOA. İ. HR. 107/5283, enc. 1. Sinaplı (op. cit, pp. 160–162) gives a simplified transliteration (with many mistakes) of this letter. Cf. Akar and Al, op. cit. (2003), p. 5. Akar and Al do not mention Sinaplı's work at all.

5 per cent offered previously by Rothschild agreeable and recommended them to sign it. However, he and Namık Pasha had negotiated with Mr Goldsmid and Mr Palmer and then Rothschild had agreed to an 85 per cent issue price with 6 per cent interest. Musurus wrote that the terms of the loan were similar to those of the 1852 abortive loan, even better because it had a 23 years' term while the new one was only for 15 years. The terms could have been better if it had been contracted several months ago. But still these were good conditions because the prices of all other loans were higher. Musurus was certain that the business of the loan was over now.[71]

However, within a week, on 29 March 1854, Great Britain and France declared war against Russia, and this changed the market conditions drastically.[72] The issue prices of all loans went down. Upon this development, Rothschild gave up the loan, and his obligation was returned without demanding any indemnity as a result of "imperial generosity on behalf of the Sublime State". Namık Pasha later boasted that he had told Rothschild "Thank God, you are dealing with a Turk" (*işiniz elhamdülillah bir Türk iledir*) upon which Rothschild had become much satisfied and pleased. It would be interesting to know whether Namık actually told him that he was a Turk or he used the term Ottoman or Muslim.

Meanwhile, the Porte resorted to another way of financing the war expenses by issuing bonds or share certificates (*esham-ı mümtaze*) on the customs revenues of Istanbul. The *esham* were preferred to the *kavaim* because the value of *kavaim* had fallen much. It was a temporary measure until the receipt of the foreign loan. In February 1854, *esham* at the value of 60,000 *kese* were issued at 10 per cent interest for three years.[73]

On 3 April 1854, Musurus wrote to the Ottoman foreign minister Reşid Pasha that the British parliament approved the declaration of war on Russia on 31 March. On the question of the 10 million franc advance money, Musurus had again pressed Lord Clarendon, who said that the cabinet did not approve of it. He explained that according to

---

[71] Musurus to Reşid Pasha, dated 23 March 1854. BOA. HR. TO. 52/50.
[72] Namık Pasha in his interview again errs in some details. He says that people protested against Prime Minister Aberdeen by breaking the window glasses of his house and upon this Lord Aberdeen resigned and Lord Palmerston replaced him and then war was declared. In reality, Aberdeen was replaced by Palmerston nearly one year later on 29 January 1855.
[73] Akyıldız, op. cit. (1996), p. 46.

the constitution ("*konstitüsyon*") of Great Britain such advances must be approved by the parliament and there the opposition members of the government would bring it down. He added that the cabinet was of the opinion that the Ottoman bonds should be issued at a lower price than that contracted with Rothschild. Rothschild himself told Musurus that the ministers did not want to give the 10 million franc advance money or a guarantee for the "Turkish loan". The only way for the Ottoman government to raise money was to offer the loan bonds to the public on favourable conditions. On the question of the guarantee, Musurus made the following remark:

> Although I did not make even an allusion to any guarantee for our loan, the abstention of the British cabinet from this guarantee is, in my humble opinion, not to be regretted. On the contrary, it would be regrettable if (God forbid) the Sublime Empire were compelled to apply to foreign states in order to contract a loan in Europe. Because in that case the reputation and credibility of the Sublime State would be reduced to the degree of states like Greece…[74] [My translation]

Indeed the Porte was soon forced to ask for foreign guarantees. Musurus added that two or three months ago he believed they could have gained the loan on better conditions than those later agreed upon with Rothschild, and now, although they (he and Namık) did not achieve this goal, he was still hopeful to do it with Rothschild at the first opportunity on the same or more convenient conditions without any foreign guarantees. Musurus then argued against the British cabinet, trying to refute their argument that the conditions of the "Turkish loan" were not acceptable to the public and therefore that its price should be reduced. He wrote that if this had been so, then their bonds would not have attracted customers to the amount of 1.1 million pounds on the day of its announcement and the price would not have gone up by two per cent and finally Mr. Rothschild, being an expert in these affairs, would not have taken upon himself the brokerage of the loan.

The change in the attitude of the public to the Ottoman loan occurred within one day after the news of the tsar's refusal to accept the British and French ultimatum, which led to the declaration of war by France and Britain on 29 March 1854. Had this news reached them

---

[74] Official translation (from French into Ottoman Turkish) of the despatch of Ambassador Musurus to Reşid Pasha, the foreign minister. BOA. HR. TO. 52/60, 3 April 1854.

five days later, or had they signed the contract with Rothschild five days earlier, argues Musurus, they would have succeeded in getting the loan, which was more favourable to the public than the bonds of other states. The real reason for the failure of the loan was the decrease in the price of all government bonds due to the declaration of war. Since the capital of the public was invested in these bonds, in order to buy the Ottoman bonds they needed to sell their holdings in other bonds but, those being now devalued, they faced incurring serious losses. Thus Britain's declaration of war in defence of the Ottoman Empire ironically worked against the Ottoman loan.

Namık Pasha, on the other hand, in his letter to Reşid Pasha, the day after the despatch of Musurus, wrote that in his earlier letter he had already pointed out the necessity of British and French assistance, because the loan brokered by Rothschild had stuck at the amount of only 1.1 million pounds of subscription in London. Furthermore most of those who subscribed to the loan in London were not financially solvent. Therefore Rothschild had expressed his conviction to the British foreign minister and the French ambassador that the loan was impossible without the guarantee of the British and the French governments. Namık Pasha continued that he had no authority to demand a guarantee, whose disadvantages were obvious, and that he went to Clarendon simply to ask for help in getting the loan and in urgently sending the advance money of ten million francs, because the Sublime Porte had an acute need for cash in the ongoing war. To this Clarendon is said to have replied as follows:

> You have dragged the loan along for so long and even now you asked such a high price that nobody wanted to buy. Now that we are at war, we have incurred countless costs and we have increased people's taxes. You spend money in so many inappropriate ways and if we were to submit to parliament such matters as giving taxpayers' money to you or giving guarantees on your behalf, they will not accept it in any way and we will be unable to answer their questions. We can give neither money nor guarantee. Do as you think best.[75] [My translation]

Namık Pasha tried to argue that the price of the Ottoman bonds was very low for the public and very expensive for the Ottoman government, that people indeed wanted to buy them, but they could not sell

---

[75] Namık Pasha to Reşid Pasha. BOA. İ. HR. 108/5309, 4 April 1854, quoted by Akar and Al, op. cit. (2003), p. 5.

their existing bonds, that the Porte needed money in this war and that the help of the allies was essential in this matter as well. Nevertheless, he was not successful in persuading Clarendon. Upon this Namık said that he must therefore go to Paris and, if unsuccessful there as well, return to Istanbul. Clarendon agreed with him. Meanwhile Lord Palmerston also entered Clarendon's house and agreed with his words on this question. Despite all this, the two obstinate Ottomans went to Palmerston as well on the following day. However, Palmerston spoke in even more accusing and humiliating tones:

> When all the people of Britain knows that you collect taxes in a corrupt way and squander the money on so many needless things, it is impossible for us to give the money collected from them to you or to act as your guarantor. Even crossing the stormy sea is easier. If you need money, then go to the public, they may want to lend their money at the price of fifty to sixty, with seven to eight per cent interest. Try to persuade them as best as you can...[76] [My translation]

Meanwhile the French ambassador in London stated that they were ready to give a guarantee for the Porte's loan, if Britain agreed as well. The British and the French also recommended assigning the tribute of Egypt as security, but Namık replied that he had no authority to dispose of the tribute of Egypt. Having been unable to get the loan from London, poor Namık Pasha concluded at the end of his letter that if nothing comes out of Paris as well, then the only solution would be rather to issue paper money than to take on such an expensive loan. He then suggested waiting for a better moment to borrow from Europe under better conditions and then to remove the *kavaim* from the market.

Namık Pasha and Musurus were disappointed when the British cabinet did not use its influence in the City. Gladstone argued that "the wishes of the Ministry weigh exactly nothing in regard to a question of lending money to a Foreign State".[77] Furthermore he was following at the time a policy of financing the war by taxation and not loans.

Having attained no results in London, Namık Pasha returned to Paris. There he went again to the French foreign minister together with Veli Pasha. He explained to the minister the situation. When the

---

[76] Ibid. In the original, there is the expression "*yelli denizi içmek*", which does not make sense, there must be an error here, logically it must be "*yelli denizi geçmek*".
[77] Anderson, ibid.

minister asked him whether he was authorised to contract the loan at a higher price than that with Rothschild and to assign the tribute of Egypt for the loan and (finally) to ask for the guarantee of the allied governments, Namık Pasha said that he had already taken the responsibility upon himself of signing a contract at a price beyond his authority, yet still he was not successful. He could not go down from the issue price of 85 per cent and up from the interest rate of six per cent. He had no authority on the Egyptian tribute. Finally, in Istanbul there had not been any discussion of foreign guarantees because it had not occurred to them that they might be necessary. Drouyn de Lhuys answered that the question would be discussed by the cabinet under the supervision of Napoleon III. After that, when Namık and Veli Pasha again visited the minister, he told them that the decision was that they could not give guarantee unilaterally – without Britain. If the Porte accepted the assignment of the tribute of Egypt as security for the loan and if it accepted whatever price was available in the market, then the French cabinet would do its best to assist the contracting of the loan.[78]

Drouyn de Lhuys also wrote to the Ottoman foreign ministry that he regretted Namık Pasha's not having attained the desired result in the loan affair. He suggested that the reason was not the inherent difficulties of the business, but the strictness of the instructions given to Namık Pasha. Therefore he urged his Ottoman colleague to give sufficient independence and licence to the person who would be authorized to negotiate the loan.[79]

Eventually Namık Pasha abandoned further hopes and left Paris for Istanbul towards the end of April. Meanwhile Veli Pasha wrote from Paris to his father the grand vizier, who would soon lose his office, confirming that Namık Pasha could not have attained the loan in conformity with his instructions. Veli Pasha saw two alternatives for the contracting of the loan; either a guarantee from the allied governments or putting the Egyptian tribute as security for the loan. He declared that he would execute whichever of the alternatives would be assigned to him. He also wrote that Rothschild had told that the Galata bank-

---

[78] Namık Pasha to Reşid Pasha. BOA. İ. HR. 5348, 9 May 1854. Cf. Sinaplı, op. cit., pp. 167–169.
[79] Drouyn de Lhuys to Reşid Pasha, 28 April 1854. BOA. İ. DH. 299/18893 enc. 3.

ers Baltazzi and Alleon were intriguing through their partners in Paris and London.[80]

Namık Pasha arrived at Istanbul on 13 May 1854. He was received by the Sultan on 16 May.[81] We do not know what passed between them, although Namık Pasha later argued that Abdülmecid was glad that he did not strive for the loan. Namık Pasha ended his *layiha* to the chronicler Lutfi Efendi by saying that on his return, Abdülmecid Han approved of his not concluding the loan agreement and despite this the loan was contracted through Veliyüddin Rifat and Kostaki Musurus. He boasted that Abdülmecid told him "if it were another person, he would give importance to the loan. But you have proved that you are the right and honourable man as I have known you since my childhood".[82] Namık Pasha's account, given in his very old age, however, is not clear enough, and cannot be taken for granted. He did not give the details, and even if he had wanted to, his memory would most probably be inaccurate as he had already made some mistakes. He was furthermore an interested party in the actual question at the time of his writing; therefore his evidence cannot be objective. It must be verified by other sources; above all with his own reports in the BOA that are certainly more reliable.

Namık Pasha's narrative of his role in the alliance of France and Britain with the Porte is of course exaggerated. He did not and could not have a role here. British and French policies were determined by their cabinets, parliaments and to a considerable degree, the public opinion. In fact the British and French governments did not discuss political matters with the Ottoman ambassadors or envoys in London and Paris, rightly thinking that this was a waste of time.[83] They had their ambassadors in Istanbul, who also thought it was a waste of time to discuss important political matters with the foreign minister, and sometimes even with the grand vizier. At that time, the Ottoman

---

[80] Veli Pasha to Mustafa Naili Pasha, 29 April 1854. BOA. İ. DH. 299/18893 enc. 2. Theodore Baltazzi, alias Baltacı Todoraki (1788–1860) belonged to the prominent Levantine family of Baltazzi, bankers to the Sultan. In 1847, together with the French banker Jacques Alleon, he had founded the *Bank-ı Dersaadet* (Bank de Constantinople) which was forced to close in 1852.

[81] BOA. İ. DH. 300/18966, 16 May 1854.

[82] Lütfi Efendi, op. cit., p. 217.

[83] Sinan Kuneralp refers to Lord Salisbury on this point. See Kuneralp, "Bir Osmanlı Diplomatı Kostaki Musurus Paşa 1807–1891", *Belleten* XXXIV/135, July 1970, p. 422.

ambassadors in European capitals in many cases would first hear the decision of their government from foreigners.

It had become very clear that the Porte would not be able to borrow without the guarantees of the allied governments. Thus it was rather the Porte's instructions, the international conjuncture, problems with the credibility of the Porte and attitudes of the British ministers that had really prevented the loan's materialization than Namık Pasha's "amateurishness" and unwillingness. Under such conditions, anyone in his place might be equally unsuccessful.

On the day after Namık Pasha's visit to the Sultan, the finance minister Musa Safveti Pasha gave his report on the financial situation of the Ottoman Empire to the grand vizier Mustafa Naili Pasha. He wrote that from the beginning of the current question, an amount of more than 300,000 purses (1.5 million Ottoman pounds or around 1.36 million pounds sterling) was assigned to extraordinary expenses until October 1853. After that *kavaim-i nakdiye* at the amount of 100,000 purses (500,000 Ottoman pounds) were also assigned to the extraordinary (war) expenses. The revenues of the new financial year beginning from 13 March 1854 hardly made up for the debts. The treasury had borrowed 320,000 Ottoman pounds secured against the tribute of Egypt for the fiscal year 1270 from some merchants and bankers, plus 100,000 Ottoman pounds from Baltacı Todoraki. Furthermore *esham* bonds at 10 per cent interest rate to the amount of 300,000 Ottoman pounds were being issued. Nevertheless, the needs of the armies were increasing day by day and the revenues of the provinces were directed to these armies. The provinces of Yanya and Tırhala needed assistance from the centre. Now that Namık Pasha had also returned "empty handed" from Europe, it was necessary to take urgent measures, because the treasury could only survive two months more. The finance minister ended his report by warning that he had stated the facts and disclaimed all responsibility in advance.[84] Money was needed urgently from Europe.

The Mission of Black and Durand and the First Foreign Loan of 1854

Since the Porte needed money urgently, this time it sent off two foreign merchant bankers of Galata, Messrs J. N. Black and François

---

[84] Musa Safveti Pasha to Mustafa Naili Pasha, 17 May 1854. BOA. İ. DH. 299/18893 enc. 1.

Louis Justin Durand (1789–1889) in June 1854. The first was close to the British and the second to the French embassy. Now they were prepared to pay the market price. Furthermore they were authorised to offer as securities the Egyptian tribute and the customs revenues of Izmir (Smyrna) and Syria, which were sold to a banker company for a yearly amount of 30 million piastres or 270,000 pounds sterling for 4 years. Although not mentioned in the instructions, Olive Anderson also cites as a security the deposit of the firman for the loan at the Bank of England.[85] Black and Durand still had instructions not to ask for the guarantee of the allied governments unless all independent efforts utterly failed.[86] Their commission fees were to depend on the terms of the loan – the better the terms, the more the commission.[87] Meanwhile the French government suggested to the British that only by a guarantee could the allies control the spending of the loan. According to Lord Cowley, the British ambassador in Paris, the aim of the French was to interfere with the revenues of Egypt. Gladstone thought that Britain's "immense" war efforts gave her the right to interfere anyway.[88] Yet the discussion between the allies about how to control the expenditure of the loan leaked out, and the Ottomans were naturally indignant. However, by the end of July 1854, they agreed to any controls by the allies in return for their guarantee. On 8 August 1854, the companies of two London bankers, Baron Sir Isaac Lyon Goldsmid and John Horsley Palmer offered to raise a 6-per cent loan of three million pounds sterling at the issue price of 80, with a payback period of 33 years, on the condition that Clarendon certified the full authority of the negotiators and the honouring of the terms. The British cabinet was averse to guarantees, but the French were interested and tried to block the loan unless their guarantee was accepted. Finally the London firm became the sole contractors for the loan and subscriptions opened. The Egyptian tribute was deposited as security. Reşid Pasha approved the loan with the right of reserving the 2 millions[89] out of the five at the Porte's discretion. However, time had been lost and the issue of the Sultan's firman approving the loan was delayed, which dealt another blow to Ottoman credibility.

---

[85] Anderson, op. cit., p. 50.
[86] Instructions to Black and Durand, BOA. HR. MKT. 78/51, 6 June 1854.
[87] BOA. HR. TO. 418/259, 6 June 1854.
[88] Anderson, op. cit., p. 50.
[89] Anderson gives this amount as three millions (op. cit., p. 52) but this must be an error.

Stratford de Redcliffe was anxious to have a mixed control commission for the expenditures of the loan. With Clarendon's support he set out to form a committee of three Ottomans, one Briton and one Frenchman to pay out the loan money and to superintend its application. The Ottoman view would prevail in this committee but it would be independent of the Ottoman government. The Ottoman representatives were Mehmed Nazif Bey (member of the MVL), Kabuli Efendi (the president) and Reşid Bey (controller of the finance ministry). Later Mehmed Nazif Bey was replaced by Kâni Pasha. The British representative was Demetrius Revelaky and the French nominated David Glavany. The Ottomans did not like the idea of a loan commission and accepted it rather grudgingly.

The distribution of the loan money can be seen in Table 4. The effective interest rate is 7.5 per cent excluding costs and commissions. The first problem of the loan commission was the exchange rate of pound to piastres, which was officially 110 piastres per pound, but the market rate was 125 piastres in September 1854 and 137 piastres in January 1855. The commission chose to apply the existing market rates at the time of actual payments. Thus the average rate of exchange for the all transactions until February 1855 was 130.

After preliminary deductions and payments, there remained little more than 2 million pounds, as can be seen from Table 4. More than half of the balance of the loan money remained in London at the Bank of England for bills of exchange drawn on European banks or persons. Only 829,000 pounds were received in cash, equal to 109,199,000 piastres. However, after a net currency exchange loss, only 104,751,000 piastres[90] actually entered the Ottoman treasury.

Up to 20 February 1855, a total of 239,463,000 piastres was demanded for the needs of the Ottoman armies and the loan control commission released 205,053,000 piastres from that amount. In the work of the commission up to 20 February 1855, the biggest reduced item (and the most outstanding enigma) was the salaries of the Anatolian army which were 15 months in arrears. The commission approved only 7.5 million piastres out of the proposed 21.6 million piastres.[91] Next came the reduction in the allocation of the Batum army, from 12.5 million to 5 million piastres. It would be interesting to know

---

[90] Akar and Al, op. cit. (2003), p. 17.
[91] Op. cit., Ek 3, p. 35.

Table 4. Distribution of the Loan of 1854 (pounds sterling)[92]

Amount of the loan	3,000,000
Deduction of 20 per cent because of the issue price of 80 per cent	600,000
Brokerage fee of Goldsmid and Palmer (2 per cent of 2,400,000)	48,000
Commission fee of Black and Durand[93]	18,800
Insurance and other costs payable to the Bank of England	8,088
Six months interest payment to the Bank of England (half of the 6 per cent of 3,000,000)	90,000
Payment to Mr [Charles] Hanson for the purchase of gunpowder	20,000
Return of the advance (5 million francs) from the French Govt. with 5 per cent interest	205,439
Balance	2,009,673

on what basis these amounts were reduced, because the commission was supposed to make sure the loan went to the needs of the army, especially the soldiers. This was most probably due to the reports of Colonel (General) Williams, who found out that the payroll of the Anatolian army was greatly swollen by the pashas for purposes of embezzlement, as we have seen in Chapter 3.

The İane-i Harbiye

As we have seen above, one of the methods of financing the war expenses was the *iane-i harbiye* or *iane-i cihadiye* or *iane-i seferiye* (war assistance or donation or benevolence), which was not truly a voluntary donation but rather a compulsory tax. It is not to be mixed with the *iane-i umumiye*, which was another extraordinary tax and was being collected before the war. While there was a certain element of enthusiasm at the beginning of the war, especially in the provinces, it must have waned in time because there are reports of *iane* arrears even after the war. These arrears seem to have been prosecuted like ordinary tax arrears. Even a cursory look at the list of these "donations" reveals

---

[92] BOA. HR. MKT. 92/78, 21 November 1854. Cf. Akar and Al (op. cit., 2003, p. 16), who refer to another document, BOA. İ. MM. 133, dated 20 February 1855.

[93] Akar and Al give the commission fee of Black and Durand as £9,628, however, this is only the amount paid in London. Their full commission is £18,800 by contract. The rest they had already received in Istanbul. See the contract, BOA. HR. TO. 418/259, 6 June 1854. Also see the documents submitted to Âli Pasha by Black and Durand, BOA. HR. TO. 419/31, 23 May 1857.

surprising similarities among the amounts given by governors and *kaimmakams* or provinces and districts so far away from each other. It is clear that these amounts were predetermined from the centre. Yet some governors may have slightly exceeded their quota.

While Namık Pasha was negotiating a loan in London and Paris, the extended council of 121 statesmen under Grand Vizier Mustafa Naili Pasha discussed on 27 March 1854 the question of raising the *iane-i harbiye*. It was decided that all dignitaries and persons of power should contribute a certain amount of money to the war efforts, since the holy duty of *jihad* could be fulfilled bodily or financially. Despite this Islamic discourse, however, not only Muslims but also non-Muslims paid the *iane*.

The highest officials set the example by paying predetermined sums according to rank. These "donations" began to be published in the official newspaper *Takvim-i Vekayi* on 19 April 1854.[94] Thus the grand vizier, the foreign minister (Reşid Pasha), and the former Seraskier Mehmed Ali Pasha gave 300,000 piastres each, while the others gave sums in descending order. The chronicler Lütfi however asks the question: Were these sums all paid out? His answer is that it is only known to the financial records. He seems to imply that not all of these sums were paid out.[95]

It is indeed very interesting to look at the lists of "donations" by persons and by provinces because they are really good indicators of their economic power and wealth, though not without exceptions. While the governor of Tunis, Ahmed Pasha (1806–1855) gave the biggest amount (5.7 million piastres), the governor of Egypt, Abbas Pasha (1813–1854), being equal in rank to the grand vizier and his son İlhami Pasha gave 4 million piastres and 1 million piastres respectively, reaching together 50,000 Ottoman pounds.[96]

It is not surprising that the Egyptian governor or his son alone contributed more than the total sum collected from all the bureaucrats

---

[94] Besim Özcan. *Kırım Savaşı'nda Mali Durum ve Teb'anın Harb Siyaseti (1853–1856)*. Erzurum: Atatürk Üniversitesi Yayınları, 1997, p. 34. Özcan, however, argues that the *iane* was really a donation.

[95] Lütfi, op. cit., p. 94.

[96] Lütfi writes that Abbas Pasha donated 8,000 kese and his son İlhami Pasha 12,000 kese *akçe*, which totalled 50,000 Ottoman pounds. İlhami Pasha was given the hand of Abdülmecid's daughter Münire Sultan and their wedding took place in the Baltalimanı *sahilhane* on 10 August 1854. Abdülmecid married his other daughters likewise to the sons of his pashas (op. cit., p. 98).

and traders (*esnaf*) of Istanbul until October 1854, which was only 3,944,242 piastres.[97] If we take into consideration the salary of the *şeyhülislam* (around 100,000 piastres), which was close to that of the grand vizier, it comes a bit surprising that the ex-*şeyhülislam* Arif Hikmet Beyefendi and the recently appointed Arif Efendi gave such small amounts (30,000 piastres and 20,000 piastres respectively) in comparison with other grandees. That the new *şeyhülislam* paid less than the former one seems normal because the change in office took place only on 11 March 1854, therefore the newcomer could not have amassed enough wealth. We must also take into account the fact that at that time the high bureaucrats were not receiving their salaries in full, but only two thirds or four fifths. Among the provincial governors, after Tunis and Egypt, the governor of Baghdad Reşid Pasha paid the highest amount at 147,000 piastres. He was followed by Asfer Ali Pasha, the governor of Damascus (100,000 piastres) and Mehmed Pasha, the governor of Crete (98,000 piastres).

Adolphus Slade wrote the following on this subject:

> A council of Ulema and dignitaries was convened for the purpose of raising a "benevolence" from the civil, military, and naval authorities of the state above the rank of colonel, and from the wealthy denizens of the capital. Hitherto Constantinople had escaped this test of patriotism, while warmly applauding provincial liberality. Although termed voluntary, the gifts were often involuntary. Lists of names were circulated by authority, and no one ventured to signalize himself by writing down less than the expected sum; which, in the case of officers and employees, amounted to about ten days' pay...Certain districts, remiss in responding to the appeal, were long afterwards invited to pay up arrears. Gradually, as enthusiasm waned, benevolence degenerated into requisition.[98]

According to Besim Özcan's calculations, total cash "donations" from all state officials and other taxpayers of the Empire reached 44,074,742 piastres.[99] This is equal to around 352,598 pounds at the average exchange rate of 125 piastres per pound during the war. If we compare this amount with the alleged debt of Serfiraz Hanım (500,000 pounds) it becomes an insignificant sum. It is remarkable that the

---

[97] Özcan, p. 46. Özcan gives this information but makes no comments on it.
[98] Adolphus Slade, op. cit., p. 197. Turkish translation (1943), p. 122. Özcan (p. 37) quotes from Slade on the enthusiasm of the provinces for war efforts, but ignores this passage.
[99] Özcan, op. cit., p. 86.

three Ottoman Arab dependencies of Tunis, Egypt and West Tripoli accounted for more than half of the total *iane*. It is also remarkable that the province of Tunis contributed more than Egypt, which was certainly more prosperous. On the other hand, "donations" in kind and services are not so easily calculable but they must also constitute a considerable sum, as much as the cash contribution.

Özcan gives the cash "donations" of the non-Muslims at 1,477,734 piastres (11,821 pounds), although it is not clear whether this sum is included in the former sum. Slade in his turn writes that during 1854–55, "the inhabitants of a part of Turkey" gave about 1.5 million pounds in money and an equal amount in kind, as supplies to the army, "under the head of *iani umoumie*".[100]

The Guaranteed Loan of 1855

By the spring of 1855, little remained of the loan of 1854, yet the needs of the Ottoman armies were still growing. It was necessary to claim the remaining two millions of the first loan. By this time it was also clear to the allies that the capture of Sevastopol was not going to be as quick as they thought. In Britain the cabinet of Lord Aberdeen resigned on 29 January 1855 and Lord Palmerston set up a new cabinet, which was determined to win the war at any cost. On 5 April 1855 the Ottoman ambassadors asked the French and the British governments to guarantee one million sterling each. The British government was still reluctant. Clarendon wrote to Stratford on 9 April 1855 that "we, or rather the House of Commons, object to all guarantees and subsidies", but then added "the Cabinet will I suppose agree to it if it *must* be".[101] Meanwhile the peace negotiations at Vienna had collapsed. War was the order of the day everywhere. On 2 May 1855, Âli Pasha and Fuad Pasha took over the government from Reşid Pasha, Âli becoming the grand vizier and Fuad receiving the foreign ministry. They now demanded a totally new loan at the amount of five million pounds sterling. This time it was indisputable that the loan was impossible without a guarantee from the British and French governments. While the French wanted a joint guarantee, the British wanted separate guar-

---

[100] Slade, ibid. Slade seems to have used the word *iane-i umumiye* instead of *iane-i harbiye*.
[101] Anderson, op. cit., p. 54. Italics in the original.

antees for each government. The British government also wanted to include an article on the control of the expenditures of the loan, to which Musurus objected because it would "touch upon the dignity of the state".[102]

Finally the French view was accepted. On 27 June 1855 an agreement was signed between France and Britain (subject to approval by their parliaments) on the guarantee of the payment of the interest of the five million pound loan to the Porte. While the French parliament approved the agreement without a problem, the British parliament passed the resolution only with a very slight majority on 20 July 1855. There were heated debates against the guarantee. According to Olive Anderson, these were the result of "dominance inside Parliament of ancient prejudices, financial, constitutional and diplomatic".[103] Indeed, British public opinion was more inclined towards the guarantee and towards continuing the war than the House of Commons. Although Stratford again did not want to miss the opportunity to control Ottoman war finance affairs by means of a loan control commission, the Ottomans again dragged their feet, using the conflicts between the British and the French. This was so obvious that the regulations of the new control commission were accepted only in January 1856, when war was practically ended.

The loan of 5 million pounds sterling at four per cent interest was negotiated with the London house of the N. M. Rothschild & Sons. In addition to the interest of four per cent, a sinking fund of one per cent was to be applied as well. Thus in practise the loan's interest rate was five per cent. Article 4 of the Agreement between His Excellency C. Musurus Bey on behalf of the Ottoman Government and Messrs. N. M. Rothschild & Sons as contractors, dated 15 August 1855, was as follows:

> The interest and sinking fund are made a charge on the whole tribute of Egypt which remains over and above the part thereof already appropriated to the loan of £3,000,000 negotiated on the 24th August 1854 and moreover on the Customs of Smyrna and Syria.[104]

---

[102] Kostaki Musurus to Fuad Pasha, 23 June 1855, BOA. İ. HR. 122/6055. Also see Akar and Al, op. cit. (2003), p. 11.
[103] Anderson, ibid, p. 56.
[104] Agreement as to Ottoman Loan of 1855, 15 August 1855, The Rothschild Archive (London), reference no. 401b015.

This time the guarantee of the British and French governments on the interest of the loan greatly increased the issue price of the loan, which became 102.62 per cent. Thus the terms of the 1855 loan were very advantageous and much better than the previous one.[105] The actual proceeds from the loan were 5,131,250 pounds sterling.

For the sake of comparison, let us also mention Russian foreign loans during the war. Despite international isolation, the Russian government managed to contract two foreign loans through the St Petersburg banking house of Baron Schtiglitz with the participation of Bering Brothers from London, Mendelson & Co. from Berlin and Hope & Co. from Amsterdam. The first loan was contracted in June 1854 for the nominal sum of 50 million silver roubles (8.33 million pounds sterling) at 5 per cent interest and 89.76 per cent issue price. The second loan was concluded in November 1855 for the same amount and at the same interest rate with 91.36 per cent issue price. Total budget deficit in Russia for the period 1852–1857 reached 772.5 million roubles (129.25 million pounds sterling).[106] While the Ottoman and Russian loans were conducted under very similar conditions, the Sublime Porte financed nearly half of its budget deficit through foreign loans while Russia covered only a small part of its budget deficit through foreing loans.

The Loan Control Commission of 1855

Although this time the allies were more seriously intent on controlling the spending of the loan, they could not get a detailed plan of control simultaneously with the guarantee. Stratford was anxious over this omission. He tried to press for a new three-party commission with more powers but the Ottoman government resisted. Meanwhile both governments appointed official loan control commissioners to Istanbul. For Clarendon, this was a chance for the Ottomans "to learn how to introduce something like order and regularity into Turkish finance".[107]

---

[105] Edhem Eldem considers both loans contracted at favourable conditions. See his article, "Ottoman financial integration with Europe: foreign loans, the Ottoman Bank and the Ottoman public debt", *European Review* 13 (3), 2005, p. 434.

[106] Valeriy Stepanov, "Krymskaya Voina i ekonomika Rossii", unpublished paper submitted to the conference on the Crimean War, organized by the Polish Academy of Sciences, Institute of History, Warsaw, 3–4 October 2007.

[107] Anderson, op. cit., p. 58.

The British loan commissioner Sir Edmund Grimani Hornby (1825–1896) arrived at Istanbul on 8 September 1855 together with his wife, who wrote afterwards her memoirs of Istanbul. The French had sent Mr. A. Cadrossi.[108] The Ottoman side was to be represented by Kâni Pasha. Instructions for the work of the control commission prepared by the French and British embassies were not accepted by the Ottoman government, saying that it contained articles contrary to the dignity of the Sublime State. Then began a long process of negotiations. The Ottoman side resented and resisted the work of the commission for reasons of "pocket and pride".[109] A draft instruction (constitution) of 12 articles was prepared on 10 December 1855.[110] Finally a compromise was reached on 17 January[111] 1856, when the war was practically over.

One of the biggest issues was the tenders for military purchases. While the foreign commissioners wanted to control all big purchases, the Ottoman government argued that this would cause delays that might jeopardize the armies. The sides agreed on subjecting purchases worth more than 600,000 piastres to the approval of the commission.[112] In any case the ministry of finance was to submit monthly reports of the use of the loan funds.

The practical result of the inability to get the commission working was delay in the release of the loan money. Thus the Ottoman armies were again without money when they needed it most. According to Akar and Al's excerpts from Ottoman fiscal records, the first instalment of 500,000 pounds came only on 3 December 1855 and second one of 400,000 pounds reached the treasury at the end of January 1856.[113] Thus by the beginning of February 1856 only 900,000 pounds in cash had been received and no bills had yet been drawn on the Bank of England. However, Anderson refers to a British document according to which, by 6 February, £1,891,919.6 of the loan had been sent

---

[108] BOA. İ. HR. 6390, 3 December 1855. Also see Sir Edmund Hornby, *An Autobiography*, London: Constable & Co. Ltd., 1929, pp. 75–81. A. du Velay and many others quoting from him send instead Lord Hobart on the British side and Marquis de Ploeuc on the French side. In fact, these gentlemen came later. Anderson, Akar and Al are correct on this point.
[109] Anderson, op. cit., p. 60.
[110] BOA. İ. HR. 6356, 10 December 1855.
[111] Anderson (op. cit., p. 58) gives 14 January 1856.
[112] Akar and Al, op. cit. (2003), p. 19.
[113] Akar and Al, op. cit. (2003), Ek 5, Ek 6, pp. 42–45.

out. This large difference is not easily explainable. Lady Hornby, in her letter, dated 10 November 1855, writes that an English merchant speaking Turkish, told them that

> there is a great feeling of anger among the Turks about the Commission; that they are bent (three or four of them especially, who are furious at the idea of not being able to finger some thousands for their own private purse) on getting the whole of the loan into their own hands; that they declare they will never consent to disgrace the Ottoman government by asking foreign Commissioners' consent to their spending their own money, and that they are resolved to tire their patience out. How all this will end remains to be seen. Of course they well know that it was only on the solemn agreement that England and France should direct the disburse-ment of the money, that is was lent. There are five millions here in gold now. Edmund is going to send a dispatch begging that that no more instalments should be sent out...[114]

Lady Hornby was not right on the question of the "solemn agreement". There was no such binding written agreement. That there were five millions (either in pounds sterling or Ottoman pounds) in November 1855 in Istanbul is also doubtful. In any case, this money had not yet been disbursed, because the loan control commission had not yet started working. It seems that the Porte took an advance payment of 600,000 pounds sterling from the Rothschilds.[115] On the other hand, it was highly likely that without some kind of foreign control, part of the loan money would have gone into private pockets.

Thus most of the loan money was still lying at the Bank of England in London and this was sure to cause indignation even in London. On 4 January, Clarendon wrote to Stratford that "some of the Tory and Radical papers are already crying out about the injustice done to the Turks and are attributing the fall of Kars solely to our withholding from the Turks the means necessary for relieving the place".[116]

Until 12 June 1856, a total of 4,666,976 pounds sterling was spent from the loan. Of this amount 3,705,000 pounds were paid in cash and the remaining 592,025 was drafted on the Bank of England. The exchange rate fluctuated between 116 and 144.5 piastres per pound.

---

[114] Lady [Emilia Bithynia] Hornby. *Constantinople during the Crimean War*. London: Richard Bentley, 1863, p. 91.

[115] See the financial report mentioned above. *Le Moniteur Universel*, 8 janvier 1856.

[116] Anderson, op. cit., p. 69.

The average exchange rate was 128 piastres during this time.[117] Of the 3,705,000 pounds cash payment to the treasury, 2,113,137 pounds were spent on the regular army, 721,332 pounds on the navy yards, 197,958 on the arsenal and 672,575 pounds by the finance ministry.[118] By September 1856 all loan money was spent and the Commission finished its work.

Sir Edmund Hornby gives some information about the work of the loan commission in his autobiography written in old age. According to him, corruption was rampant in the Ottoman army among officers above the rank of major:

> It soon became evident that "pay lists", commissariat lists, etc., whether receipted or not, or even vouched for by the War Department, were not to be depended on. It was necessary to count the corps and ask the rank and file if they had been paid and find out what pay was in arrears. Clothing, provisions, ammunition had to be similarly checked. The officers were not to be trusted either in the field or out of it, and not once, but dozens of times, I had to get officers of rank suspended for embezzlement and malversation.
>
> From this censure I except the "Uzbashis and Bim-bashis," what we should call non-commissioned officers. These were really splendid fellows, selected from the ranks for their courage and knowledge of regimental duty.[119]

On one occasion, some Ottoman officers had sold the fresh vegetables sent to save the Ottoman soldiers from scurvy to the French and bagged the cash. Nevertheless, Hornby argued that, of the loan money of five million pounds sterling, "not more than half a million was misapplied". Some part of this "misapplied" money was simply stolen. Hornby remembered that on one occasion one of the cash bags at the treasury, which ought to have held £20,000 in gold sovereigns, was found full of copper coins. The thief was not found out. When the Sultan conferred upon Hornby the order of the *Mecidiye* and a snuff-box in brilliants, he thought that he did not deserve it, because he "had only kept him [the Sultan] from squandering his own money". Hornby then remarked that had they been led by temptation, he and his French colleague could have made a small fortune out of the loan money. "All we had to do was to shut our eyes a little to what the real

---

[117] Calculated from data given by Akar and Al, ibid., p. 25.
[118] Akar and Al, op. cit. (2003), p. 44.
[119] Hornby, op. cit., pp. 75–76.

owners of the money wanted to do with it".[120] Hornby also recollects the incident of the Armenian banker Theodore "Batazzi" [Baltazzi] trying to give him and Cadrossi a cheque for £1,250 each as commission for the business they brought to him. Hornby refused. His French colleague, on learning of the incident from him, had also felt himself terribly insulted. But for Baltazzi it was business as usual.

After these two first foreign loans, what some Ottoman bureaucrats had much feared all along about the foreign loans became true: The Porte got used to foreign loans and finally they reached uncontrollable amounts, leading thus to direct foreign control over Ottoman tax revenues. Damad Ali Fethi Pasha's prophetic remark in 1852 had become true: "But I know that, if this state borrows five piastres, it will go bankrupt. For if once it gets used to borrowing, then there will be no end to it. It will be drowned in debts".[121]

The Ottoman loans of 1854 and 1855 were later collectively referred to as the tribute loans (with reference to the Egyptian tribute), while that of 1855 was also called the guaranteed loan. When the Ottoman government defaulted on the interest payments on its, by then, huge foreign debt in October 1875, the guarantee of the British and French governments caused much trouble. As it is well known, the final result of the Ottoman financial crisis was the establishment of the Public Debt Administration (*Düyun-ı Umumiye İdaresi*) in 1881. This was the clearest sign of the semi-colonial status of the Ottoman Empire. While this was the culminating point, the seeds were sown by the loans of the Crimean War period.

---

[120] Hornby, op. cit., p. 77.
[121] Cevdet Pasha, *Tezâkir 1–12*, p. 22.

CHAPTER FIVE

THE IMPACT OF THE WAR ON OTTOMAN SOCIAL AND POLITICAL LIFE

Contacts with the Europeans

One of the arguments of this study is that the Crimean War played an important part in Ottoman modernization. The war introduced many social novelties and practices, first into Istanbul high society and then society at large. While these changes are not always concrete or quantifiable, they can still be perceived. In this chapter I shall attempt to assess the social and political impact of the war on Ottoman state and society.

The first practical impact of the war was an increase in the number of visitors to Istanbul and in the contacts between Europeans and Ottomans at all levels. During the war years, many people came to Istanbul from Europe: soldiers, officers, nuns, diplomats and their families, traders, tourists, engineers, etc. The Ottoman Empire and Istanbul also received wide coverage in European newspapers. The appearance of British, French and Sardinian soldiers and officers in Istanbul as allies had a mixed impact on the minds of ordinary people. For example, thousands of British soldiers, officers and their wives lived for a while in Üsküdar. This left some impressions on the local people. On the one hand, for the first time people saw the "giaour" soldiers as real allies who had come to shed their blood for the security of the Ottoman Empire. They were suffering and dying for the security and integrity of the Ottoman state and its people, who were able to see this for themselves.

On the other hand, it would be wrong to assume that the Europeans produced an altogether positive impression upon the inhabitants of Istanbul. In fact, soon they began to worry, wondering why the allied troops remained so long in the capital and why they did not advance to Varna and Silistria. Many houses on the Bosphorus were commandeered for allied officers, the owners being forced to evacuate their homes. While in most cases the Porte paid the rent, there were cases when the owners did not get rent at all.¹ The Allies, especially the French, had also occupied many public buildings, including military, naval, and medical schools for barracks and hospitals, leaving only two buildings to the Ottomans. The French were quartered in the barracks of Davutpaşa, Maltepe, Ramizçiftlik, Taşkışla, Gümüşsuyu and Gülhane, and in the Russian embassy in the centre of Pera.² Furthermore they encamped at Maslak and also settled in the quarter of St. Sophia. The British were quartered at the Selimiye barracks in Üsküdar.

Adolphus Slade's observations of Istanbul towards the end of 1854 are worth quoting at full length here:

> The Turks, in stupor, were drinking the bitter waters of humiliation, were expiating the sins of their ancestors. Frank soldiers lounged in the mosques during prayers, ogled licentiously veiled ladies, poisoned the street dogs, part and parcel of the desultory bizarre existence of the East, shot the gulls in the harbour and the pigeons in the streets,..., mocked the *muezzins* chanting *ezzan* from the minarets, and jocosely broke up carved tombstones for pavement...The Turks had heard of civilization: they now saw it, as they thought, with amazement. Robbery, drunkenness, gambling, and prostitution revelled under the glare of an eastern sun, or did mild penance in the shadow of a dozen legations: to each of whom the withdrawal of a rascal from the station-house was a duty, the shielding of a miscreant from punishment was a triumph. The Sultan still sat in his palace but his power was in abeyance...The Allies' troops had possession of the capital, the English on the Asiatic the French on the European side of the Bosphorus; and their guards patrolled Pera and Galata – sanctuary for hybrid swarm from all parts of the Mediterranean, whose avocations the police were cautious in interfering with, for fear of drawing on themselves the wrath of some legation, by confounding an Ionian with a Hellenist, a Genoese with Sicilian, or a Javanese with a Hindoo.³

Slade then went on to criticise the capitulations. He argued that the capitulations, instituted in the 16th century for the protection of a few European traders, responsible for the conduct of their servants, had

---

¹ For example, Halil Efendi's waterside mansion (*sahilhane*) in Fındıklı was rented by the Porte for Admiral Boxer. Its monthly rent (3,000 piastres or 24 pounds sterling, equivalent of 1,440 pounds at current prices). See BOA. İ. HR. 114/5607, 7 November 1854. In another case, 91,100 piastres were paid by the Porte for six months' rent for eight houses in Üsküdar rented for British officers. See BOA. HR. SYS. 1337/7, 12 April 1855. The owners of storehouses in Varna had also demanded rent for their stores occupied by the Allied troops. See BOA. HR. SYS. 1356/8, 12 January 1855.
² Besbelli, op. cit., p. 77.
³ Slade, op. cit., pp. 355–356.

now become a shield for murderers and unscrupulous profit seekers, as its strict enforcement in favour of 50,000 Europeans of various nationalities and professions in Istanbul, and twice as many in the provinces, was a disgrace to "Turkey" and a reproach to Europe. He even argued that "probed to their source, the occasional outbreaks in Turkey, called fanatical would be seen to be the natural reaction against the overbearings and insolence of foreigners and protected natives".

Frank Leward from the British army in his letters to his friend Charles Bampton had an altogether different opinion:

> Of all the low greedy stupid lot in the world commend me to the Turk to beat them all. They will rob you and abuse you and havn't the slightest gratitude to us for coming to help them. Better let the Russians or any one else have the place than these Turks... They were beastly impertinent too at first, used to spit on the ground when any of us went by and wouldn't let us go into their mosques and places but were knocking all that out of them pretty fast. I don't think they care much about our coming now to tell you the truth. One old Pasha said the other day he'd like the Russians to come or any one else if they could only get rid of the English and French.[4]

There are some records of friction between the allied troops and the local people. For example, French soldiers who were quartered in the Davudpaşa barracks came and went from the French centre in Galata and sometimes, especially at night, they lost their way and entered Muslim quarters, making noise and other drunken demonstrations. It was decided then to put warning signs in French and Turkish on the roads. There were also cases of drunken allied soldiers attacking Ottoman police officers, and fights occurred between Egyptian and French troops in Galata. Some shopkeepers also complained of the behaviour of the French soldiers. In another case local people did not want to rent their houses even to French doctors, who were billeted in their houses nonetheless. Most of these events seem to have been more or less isolated outbreaks and the Ottoman participants in these rows also seem to be rather non-Turkish, such as Albanians, Croats, Egyptians and Tunisians. There were also other events of a social and religious character related to the behaviour of some of the allied soldiers. For example, as early as May 1854, it was decided to prepare a

---

[4] Frank Leward, Letter to Bampton, from Misseries Hotel, Constantinople, 1854, in *Memorials*, Charles Bampton (ed.), London: Kegan Paul, Trench & Co., 1884, p. 209.

warning in French to prevent French soldiers from entering mosques with shoes on.[5]

Economically, the impact of the Westerners was to boost the prices of many items in Istanbul. For example, the price of Yenice tobacco went from sixty piastres to three hundred piastres. House rents soared and it became very difficult to find a house in the Bosphorus for rental.[6] The shopkeepers of Istanbul were in general happy with the rise in their sales volume.

The best-known English-Turkish dictionary, that of Sir James Redhouse, was also a product of the Crimean War. First published in the spring of 1855 under the title of "Vade-mecum of Ottoman Colloquial Language", it was intended for the use of the British army and navy.[7] Fifty copies of the dictionary were bought for the Sublime Porte, army headquarters and the Translation Office. The author was given a gift box worth ten thousand piastres, equal to about eighty to ninety pounds sterling at that time.[8]

The personality of the Sultan himself played an important role in the transformations. Sultan Abdülmecid was probably not an efficient political or military ruler, but he was quite open to novelties. His character was, in the words of Stratford de Redcliffe, "gentle, understanding, responsible, modest and humane". Sultan Abdülmecid introduced many novelties into Ottoman social life. Increased contacts with Europe also meant changes in the attitudes of the Sultan and state officials towards European diplomats. These changes in Ottoman diplomacy that began with the Tanzimat now accelerated. Before Sultan Abdülmecid, the Ottoman sultan and the grand vizier did not discuss political matters with foreign ambassadors. The *şeyhülislam*, head of the Islamic clergy, did not meet them at all. During the Crimean War, we witness for the first time the reception of foreign ambassadors by the *şeyhülislam* and the reception of foreign orders by the sultan.

The French ambassador Edouard-Antoine de Thouvenel first succeeded in having Abdülmecid accept the order of *Legion d'Honneur*. Other ambassadors had also offered orders to the sultan but he had

---

[5] BOA. HR. SYS. 1336/5, 21 May 1854.
[6] Cevdet Pasha, *Ma'rûzât*, Istanbul: Çağrı Yayınevi, 1980, pp. 8–9.
[7] See Sir James W. Redhouse. *A Turkish and English Lexicon*. Preface. Constantinople, 1890. New Edition. Beirut: Librairie du Liban, 1996.
[8] BOA. İ. HR. 139/7219, 4 January 1857. 80 pounds sterling of 1857 are worth more than 4,800 pounds today.

refused them. After the French award, Lord Stratford lost no time in offering the Order of the Garter. However, negotiations on the details of the ceremony took much of Lord Stratford's time because the sultan feared a loss of dignity in receiving an order from a Christian. He also had an aversion to being touched. Stanley Lane-Poole gives a lively description of Abdülmecid's reception of the order:

> Sultan Abdu-l-Mejid was invested by Lord Stratford, as the Queen's representative, with the most exclusive order of knighthood in the world. Assisted by the King of Arms, the Elchi made his Majesty a Knight of the Garter. Did the Sultan know what the stately ambassador was saying, as he placed the George and Riband round his neck?...When a Sultan submits to be enjoined to emulate the career of a Martyr and Soldier of Christ, who shall say that the fanaticism of Islam is inextinguishable?[9]

In February 1856, after the end of the war, Sultan Abdülmecid honoured two balls with his presence within three days, appearing first at the British embassy on 2 February and then at the French Embassy on the fourth.[10] The first ball at the British embassy was given by Lady Stratford de Redcliffe. The sultan came to the costume ball wearing his Order of the Garter. Lady Emilia Hornby, the wife of Sir Edmund Hornby, the British loan commissioner, gives a detailed description:

> The Sultan had, with very good taste, left his own Guard at the Galata Serai, and was escorted thence to the palace by a company of English Lancers, every other man carrying a torch. Lord Stratford and his Staff, of course, met him at the carriage-door, and as he alighted, a communication by means of galvanic wires was made to the fleet, who saluted him with prolonged salvoes of cannon. Lady Stratford and her daughters received him at the head of the staircase...It would take me a day to enumerate half the costumes. But everyone who had been to the Queen's *bals costumés* agreed that they did not approach this one in magnificence; for besides the gathering of French, Sardinian and English officers, the people of the country appeared in their own superb and varied costumes; and the groups were beyond all description beautiful. The Greek Patriarch, the American Archbishop, the Jewish High Priest, were there in their robes of state. *Real* Persians, Albanians, Kourds, Servians,

---

[9] Stanley Lane-Poole, *The Life of the Right Honourable Stratford Canning*. London: Longmans, Green, and Co., 1888, vol. II, p. 444. Cf. Necdet Sakaoğlu, Nuri Akbayar. *A Milestone on Turkey's Path of Westernization. Sultan Abdülmecid*. Istanbul: Creative Yayıncılık, 2002, p. 99. This is in fact a back translation from the Turkish translation into English.

[10] Cezmi Karasu mentions only the French ball as the first appearance of the Sultan in a ball. However, this is not true. See Karasu, op. cit. (1998), p. 184.

> Armenians, Greeks, Turks, Austrians, Sardinians, Italians, and Spaniards were there in their different dresses, and many wore their jewelled arms. There were...and Turkish ladies without their veils...Abdul Medjid quietly walked up the ball-room with Lord and Lady Stratford, their daughters, and a gorgeous array of Pashas in the rear. He paused with evident delight and pleasure at the really beautiful scene before him, bowing on both sides, and smiling as he went...Pashas...drink vast quantities of champagne, of which they pretend not to know the exact genus, and slyly call it "eau gazeuse".[11]

Stanley Lane Poole's biography of Stratford Canning also describes the incident as a great success of the British ambassador and as the first ball of Abdülmecid, but it does not give the exact date of the ball in February 1856:

> One evening the ambassador and his staff are standing in front of the embassy. It is the month of February, in year 1856. Over the entrance, the names of Abdülmecid and Victoria are written by colored light bulbs. Then the British lancer riders move towards the outer gate to meet the Sultan. As the Sultan steps over the threshold, through an electrical wire tied to the guns, the British Navy salutes the sultan with forty-one cannon shots. In the meantime, the Embassy band is playing 'God Save the Queen'. For the first time in the history of the Ottoman Empire, a Sultan becomes a guest to a Christian ambassador. Lady Stratford is holding a costume ball and the Sultan is honouring this ball with his presence.... The Sultan enjoyed his first ball very much and as the ambassador took him by the hand to lead him to the armchair prepared for the Sultan among the British officers, the onlookers knew that the barriers around the Sultan had been knocked down and that a Moslem and a Christian could meet in equal conditions. If there was an initiator in this event, that was Ambassador Lord Stratford.[12]

On the other hand, the official Ottoman historian of the time and a member of the councils of the *Tanzimat* and of Education, Ahmet Cevdet Pasha, who was among the invited, confirms this event in his *Tezakir* but his tone is rather disapproving of such practices. He gives a first-hand account of the confusion created by the invitation of the British embassy. The şeyhülislam did not accept it and offered his apologies. When Cevdet Pasha asked the grand vizier whether he should go to the ball or not, he said: "Ask the şeyhülislam!" But the şeyhülislam

---

[11] Lady Hornby, *Constantinople during the Crimean War*, London: Richard Bentley, 1863, pp. 205–208.
[12] Lane-Poole, op. cit., p. 99. For the Turkish translation by Can Yücel, see *Lord Stratford Canning'in Türkiye Anıları*. Istanbul: Tarih Vakfı Yurt Yayınları, 1999, p. 196.

told him: "The grand vizier knows best". Thus Cevdet Pasha could not get an answer to his question and decided not to go.[13] He tells us that before this event, even grand viziers did not visit foreign embassies, however, since the previous year they had begun visiting embassies and now the Sultan himself made such visits. Cevdet Pasha gives us the date of the ball as 2 February 1856. Interestingly, however, Cevdet Pasha does not record the ball at the French embassy.

The Islahat Fermanı *and the Question of the Equality of Muslims and Non-Muslims*

As we have already seen, the question of the rights and privileges of the non-Muslim subjects of the Ottoman Empire had been one of the important questions in the diplomatic efforts to end the war. The fourth point of the famous "four points" concerned this issue. Because of the war, Ottoman statesmen were now in an especially vulnerable position with respect to reform demands and pressure from the European great powers. The allies helped the Porte in its war against Russia, but they too demanded some improvements for the non-Muslim subjects of the Porte. While this process resulted in the famous Reform Edict (*Islahat Fermanı*) of 18 February 1856, the Ottomans had already tackled this question one year before, at the beginning of the Vienna Conference in March 1855.

On 24 and 26 March 1855, about one week after the opening of the Vienna Conference, a council of 21 ministers and some other bureaucrats (*Meclis-i Meşveret*) was convened to discuss the instructions to be given to the Ottoman delegate to the conference.[14] The council focused on the fourth point, which it defined as "the complete removal of the empty claim of Russia concerning the protection of the Greek Orthodox subjects of the Ottoman Empire and the repeal of all former treaties, especially of the treaty of Kaynarca, whose misinterpretation caused war, as well as entrusting the reforms desired by Europe for all the Christian subjects of the Sublime State to the grace of the Sultan".[15]

---

[13] Cevdet Pasha, *Tezâkir 1-12*, pp. 61–62.
[14] Mehmet Yıldız, "1856 Islahat Fermanına Giden Yolda Meşruiyet Arayışları (Uluslararası Baskılar ve Cizye Sorununa Bulunan Çözümün İslami Temelleri)", *Türk Kültürü İncelemeleri Dergisi* 7, Istanbul, Güz 2002, pp. 75–114. The *mazbata* of the meclis is on pp. 100–108.
[15] Yıldız, op. cit. (2002), p. 100.

Illus. 18 Sultan Abdülmecid at British fancy-dress ball, Pera. *ILN*, 1 March 1856.

Interestingly, throughout the document, only Christians are mentioned, omitting Jews. For practical purposes however, Christian subjects can be considered to cover all non-Muslim subjects here. The *mazbata* of the *meclis* then recorded that, while Britain and France joined the war as allies of the Porte, because they were Christian states, they had also promised their subjects and other states to recommend to the Porte measures for the well-being of the Christian subjects of the Porte, long desired by Europe. Furthermore, it stated that a somewhat adverse treatment of Christian subjects was offensive to Europe and there had been remonstrations long before. Until now, such demands had been diverted, sometimes by temporizing and sometimes by yielding a little bit. However, times had changed and, if Europe was not satisfied, then the Porte would be subject to their persistent pressure; this was dangerous because it could lead them to demand further measures.

The *mazbata* argued that while Europe's disappointment with the Ottoman Empire would be a great danger for the Porte, taking measures at the behest of European powers and allowing them to become a condition of a treaty was also very dangerous, because in that case the Christian subjects would be grateful to Europe and not to the Porte. Russia on the other hand, might consider itself as morally victorious for serving the Christian cause even if it lost much by conceding the first three of the four points. The Ottoman ambassador had written from London that Lord Palmerston had stated that if the Porte granted some rights to its Christian subjects, it would do a great service both to the allies and itself. Otherwise, the great powers would have to compel the Porte to act. While some improvements had already been made, and not all of these were known in Europe, there remained some issues of adverse treatment. Therefore the ministers thought that if they could remedy the deficiencies to some extent and "sell them sweetly" to Europe, saying "this and that has been done by the Porte for its subjects", then Europe would be satisfied.[16]

The question of the non-admission of Christian evidence against Muslims in courts was also a "thorn in the eye of Europe", said the *mazbata*, but internal and external objections had now been eliminated by setting up commissions of investigation (*tahkik meclisleri*). These commissions were now to be further improved and incorporated into the new laws. It was also recommended to employ more Christians in state

---

[16] Yıldız, ibid., p. 103.

service and even in the land army. It was noted that although some ranks were being given to Christian subjects they were not addressed according to their rank. For example, if addressing a Christian as "*saadetlu efendim*" or "*izzetlu beyefendi*" was considered unbecoming in the eyes of Muslims, then general titles and forms of address could be found to suit all subjects. It was further recommended that it could be announced to Europe that in principle Christian subjects could rise up to the rank of *ûlâ*, but there was no need to announce this inside the country. It was necessary also to show that Christian subjects were already being employed in embassies. As for the question of military service, this was not a matter pertaining only to the satisfaction of Europeans or Christian subjects, but was an important issue for the state, because Muslims alone carried the brunt of war and therefore their population was decreasing while the population of Christians was increasing. At present, Christian subjects were being employed in the navy and it was necessary to find ways to employ them in the army as well. It would be wise to announce to Europe that Christian subjects would be taken into the army and that they could rise up to the rank of colonel.

The *mazbata* mentioned the question of the freedom of restoration and building of churches for Christian subjects as well. Since Christian subjects sometimes used caves in mountains as churches because they did not have a place for religious rituals, it was considered expedient to allow them to some extent to build some new churches. Finally the poll-tax (*cizye*) paid by the non-Muslim subjects of the Porte was considered an insult to Christians and it was now impossible to evade Europe's persistence on this point. Therefore it was necessary to find a way forward. For some time, *cizye* had been collected on a *millet* basis instead of by direct collection and this had gained some time for the Porte, but what Europe wanted was to remove the *cizye* terminology. Although collection of the *cizye* from Christians was a necessity demanded by the sharia, it was a great danger to oppose the 250 million-strong Christian nations. At this point the meeting was adjourned for the *şeyhülislam* to study the matter.

On 26 March the council met again. In the meantime the *şeyhülislam* had searched for a solution in Islamic law. The only example was that of Caliph Ömer's agreement with the Christian Arabic tribe of Beni Tağlib. The latter had expressed their readiness to pay double the tax, provided that it would not be termed *cizye*, since they found it unacceptable. Ömer had accepted this, saying it was cizye whatever others might call it. Another possibility for a *fetva* was to refer to a kind of *force majeure* or necessity in Islamic law. But such a *fetva* would effectively proclaim the weakness of the Ottoman Empire to friend and foe. Therefore it was better to collect the cizye under the name of *iane-i askeriyye* than to issue such a *fetva*. The British ambassador (Stratford de Redcliffe) had reportedly told the grand vizier: "If the Porte does not do what is required by Europe now, it certainly will be subject to many bad things and great dangers". He had even said "the Porte will do these things by force of treaty". The Vienna embassy too had reported Lord John Russell as saying "if the Porte had done what was recommended before on behalf of Christians, then it would have been possible to ward off these issues in this conference by saying 'these have already been done'". Such words from the representative of Britain appeared to be the beginning of what the Ottomans feared so much. The ambassador had also reported that one day the representatives had met without the Ottoman ambassador and, when the latter complained, they had brushed aside his concerns by saying the meeting concerned the general affairs of Europe. He went on to say that despite this claim, it was possible they had signed an agreement among themselves regarding the conditions of Christian subjects of the Porte, and would perhaps reveal it later. In view of these and other reports from embassies and the negotiations in Vienna, it was therefore decided unanimously to ward off (*savuşturmak*) this issue by turning the name of *cizye* into *iane-i askeriyye*. If some unaware ulema were to object, they would be informed confidentially about the situation. If some people still continued speaking out against this measure, they would be reprimanded and punished, because speaking out of turn showed their lack of "patriotism and religious honour".[17]

Whenever the Ottoman bureaucracy was squeezed between the sharia and European pressure, it chose a pragmatic way out of the situation, as in the case of the slave trade discussions, which began earlier and which we will also discuss in this chapter. The pragmatism of the Ottoman bureaucracy is best expressed in the two verbs of *oyalamak* (to temporize) and *savuşturmak* (to ward off) that were used in official documents. Thus *cizye* came to be known as *iane-i askeriyye* or *bedel-i askeriyye*. The fact that a tax was called *iane* confirms our view that the *iane-i harbiyye* which we discussed in Chapter 4 was a tax as well.

---

[17] Yıldız, op. cit. (2002), p. 108.

Actually we have reason to think that non-Muslims in general (except for the poorest of them) would also have preferred paying the tax to serving in the Ottoman army. However, as we have seen in the above *mazbata*, it is certain that even if they had shown much eagerness to serve in the army, the Porte would not have accepted this. Because then they would not have paid the *iane-i askeriyye*, equivalent to the *cizye*, and this was contrary to the sharia. Nevertheless, Mehmet Yıldız has argued that the decision on the conscription of non-Muslims into the army was not applied because non-Muslims themselves did not want to serve.[18]

Recruitment of non-Muslims into the army continued to be a serious problem long after the Crimean War. There were very practical considerations working against any movement towards a mixed Ottoman army. Cevdet Pasha was a member of a commission set up to solve this problem in the early 1860s, arguing against the inclusion of non-Muslims. He told the commission that if non-Muslims were to be admitted, every battalion would need a priest as well as an imam. If there were only one priest, there would be no problem, he said. However, there were Orthodox, Catholic, Armenian, Protestant and other confessions. Furthermore, even Orthodox Bulgarians would not accept Orthodox Greek priests. These confessions would all demand different priests. The Jews in turn would want their rabbis. Thus a battalion would need numerous religious personnel. Furthermore, the Muslims and non-Muslims having different fasts, it would be difficult to administer such a mixed body. Finally Cevdet Pasha touched upon the most important question. He wrote that an Ottoman commander used religious feelings and martyrdom for Islam to encourage his soldiers into action. What would the major of a mixed battalion say to urge on his soldiers? The Europeans, Cevdet Pasha added, used patriotism (*gayret-i vataniyye*). However, he argued, *vatan* meant for the Ottoman soldiers only some squares in their villages. It could not replace religious motivation. Furthermore, Muslim soldiers endured all hardships while the non-Muslims would not. Therefore the state could be subjected to European interference, if non-Muslim soldiers complained of not receiving their pay or rations.[19]

---

[18] Yıldız, op. cit. (2003), p. 320.
[19] Cevdet Pasha, *Ma'rûzât*, pp. 113–115.

While the Ottoman council of ministers thus tried to "ward off" the issues related to Christian subjects by making some improvements, we see that the British government increased its pressure for reforms. During the Vienna conference, on 24 April 1855, Lord Clarendon sent a despatch to the British ambassador in Vienna the Earl of Westmoreland, instructing him to give a copy to Âli Pasha as well. This despatch contains very important demands and they are not limited to the questions of non-Muslim military service and the admissibility of Christian evidence. Lord Clarendon asserted that although Christian evidence was admitted in criminal courts, the judges were still "exclusively" Muslims, the only mixed tribunals being the commercial courts. He maintained that Christian evidence was still inadmissible in civil cases and since civil injuries like robbery perpetrated against Christians were more frequent than murder, the inadmissibility of Christian evidence in civil cases was a "severe and daily felt grievance". Therefore he wrote that there ought to be an equal number of Muslim and Christian judges in both criminal and civil cases. Furthermore, Clarendon wrote that all the local authorities in the provinces were Muslims and this led to "endless oppression and injustice committed and connived at towards Christians". Therefore, he concluded, there ought to be a Christian officer of suitable rank attached to each governor and this officer should have the right to appeal to Istanbul on behalf of injured Christians.[20]

Clarendon then argued that "Christians ought to be allowed to rise to any rank in the military and civil services, and their advancement should not form an exception to the rule by which they are excluded from the higher ranks of their profession". The British foreign secretary then suggested a reform of schools by establishing mixed primary schools throughout the empire for Muslim and Christian children. Finally the secretary expressed his government's confidence in the "enlightened views and benevolent intentions" of the Sultan, blaming the bureaucrats for not being "animated by his [the Sultan's] spirit".

About this time, Sadık Pasha, commander of the Ottoman Cossack regiment, was ordered by the Porte to prepare a study regarding the possibility of conscription of Christians into military service. The report Sadık Pasha submitted to the grand vizier discussed places where Christian volunteers could be recruited for the army. He wrote

---

[20] BOA. HR. SYS. 1030/4 enc. 65.

that cavalry troops could be recruited from Tırnova, Niş, Yeni Pazar and Saraybosna and infantry could be recruited from Mostar, İşkodra, Janina, and Salonica.[21] Sadık Pasha wrote in his memoirs that the Sultan wanted the project to be discussed with the representatives of the European great powers.[22] However, according to Sadık Pasha, they did not like the idea. Lord Stratford de Redcliffe even told him that this should not be allowed because within a few years the Christian subjects of the Ottoman Empire would have a full army, well trained and capable of fighting. "This is not our aim", Lord Stratford allegedly told him.[23] Austria was of the same opinion fearing the appearance of a military spirit among the Ottoman Slavs. Thus according to Sadık Pasha, the Porte met opposition from all sides and eventually the Western powers did not permit it to undertake this reform.

The decision to enrol non-Muslim subjects as soldiers was proclaimed in the *Takvim-i Vekayi* in May 1855. *Cizye* was abolished and all male subjects would now serve in the army. Those who could not serve in the army would pay the *iane-i askeriyye* in return.[24] Nevertheless, it was not easy to apply this decision in practice. Attempts to levy troops from the non-Muslim areas of Rumeli led to the dispersal of population to the mountains and neighbouring countries.[25] In the province of Trabzon, governor Hafız Pasha mustered troops from Muslims and non-Muslims for the aid of Erzurum in the summer of 1855. However, the administrators (*müdir*) of districts (*kaza*) abused this decision leading to mistreatment of both Muslims and non-Muslims. They also collected a lot of money as *iane-i askeriyye* and embezzled most of it. The Porte sent Kabuli Efendi to investigate these affairs.[26] On his return from Trabzon, Kabuli Efendi submitted his report to the MVL. The mazbata of the MVL stated that the governor had left the task of recruitment to "men who were used to oppressing poor, com-

---

[21] Mehmed Sadık Pasha to the Grand Vizier, 19 April 1855. BOA. HR. TO. 420/5 enc. 2.
[22] "Zametki i vospominaniya Mikhaila Chaikovskago (Sadyk-pashi)", *Russkaya Starina* XXXV/12, St. Petersburg, December 1904, p. 573.
[23] Lord Stratford's words are quoted by Tarle, op. cit., vol. 1, p. 62.
[24] Ufuk Gülsoy, *Osmanlı Gayrımüslimlerinin Askerlik Serüveni*, Istanbul: Simurg, 2000, pp. 57–59.
[25] Yıldız, op. cit. (2003), p. 170.
[26] Gülsoy, op. cit., p. 56.

mon people as they pleased before the introduction of the procedure of justice of the auspicious *Tanzimat* into the province".[27]

The question of the transformation of *cizye* into *iane-i askeriyye* and military service of the non-Muslims was discussed in the *Meclis-i Âli-i Tanzimat* as well in November 1855. (This time the document used the expression "non-Muslim subjects", as opposed to the *mazbata* of the *meclis* of 26 March 1855). Afterwards, a special council discussed the resolution of the said *meclis*.[28] The council determined the amount of the *iane* as 50 gold liras (5,000 piastres). About this time a commission including Foreign Minister Fuad Pasha, Şeyhülislam Arif Efendi and some of the Western ambassadors was set up to work out a new formula.[29] At that time Âli Pasha was the *sadrazam* and Fuad Pasha the foreign minister. Reşid Pasha had been deposed and did not hold any office, although his influence was still considerable. The Reform Edict of 18 February 1856 was the work of this commission.

While the 1839 Gülhane Edict of *Tanzimat* was an important step for the guarantees of subjects against the arbitrariness of the Sultan, it had not clearly stipulated equality of Muslim and non-Muslim subjects of the Ottoman Empire. The firman of 18 February 1856, however, specifically declared them equal. At the popular level, this was understood as "now we will not call the giaours giaours".[30] In fact, there are signs that the Ottoman government tried to eliminate the word "gavur" from all official terminology. Thus we see that as early as February 1854, even the name of a mountain, the *Gavur Dağı* (Giaour Mountain) in the *sancak* of Maraş was changed into *Bereket Dağı* by an *irade* from the Sultan at the suggestion of the MVL.[31] Christians would no longer be degraded in official parlance. For example, the Pope would no longer be called a pig. Since the grand vizier Âli Pasha had departed for Paris to participate in the peace congress, Kıbrıslı Mehmed Emin Pasha was the acting grand vizier during the proclamation of the firman, although tradition required the foreign minister Fuad Pasha to

---

[27] *Mazbata* of the MVL, 10 October 1855. BOA. İ. MMS. 6/213, enc. 1. Gülsoy (op. cit., p. 56) briefly mentions this document but does not make any quotation from it.
[28] BOA. İ. MMS. 132/5650, 16 November 1855.
[29] Cevdet Pasha, *Tezâkir 1-12*, p. 67.
[30] Abdurrahman Şeref, *Tarih Söyleşileri (Müsahabe-i Tarihiye)*. Sadeleştiren Mübeccel Nami Duru. Istanbul: Sucuoğlu Matbaası, 1980, p. 63.
[31] BOA. İ. DH. 290/18239, 5 February 1854.

be his *kaimmakam*. According to Cevdet Pasha, Kıbrıslı was chosen because he was not known as a westernizer and therefore he might be a shield against the threat of Muslim reaction.[32]

There is no doubt that Lord Stratford put more pressure on the Porte than the other ambassadors for reforms affecting non-Muslim subjects of the Porte. Lord Palmerston told Parliament on 1 May 1856 that, when the government changed in 1846, Lord Stratford had accepted the Istanbul embassy on one condition:

> It was, that he should be supported by government at home,...to obtain that equality between Christians and Mahomedans, which has at last (1856) crowned the efforts of his life. It was that honourable ambition which induced Sir Stratford Canning to continue so long in a post which, under other circumstances, perhaps, he would have been reluctant to occupy.[33]

However, by the end of the war both Britain's and Lord Stratford's influence had decreased somewhat, while that of France increased. At the beginning of January 1856, Clarendon wrote to Stratford that the "Turkish" government had asked three times for Stratford's recall:

> They did full justice of course to your eminent talents and goodwill towards Turkey, but declared they could no longer get on with you, as you required, that your influence should be so paramount and notorious that they were lowered in the eyes of the people, and that you would not allow the Sultan to *corégner* with you (that was Aali's expression).[34]

Yet as we have seen the Sultan honoured Stratford's ball first. In fact Stratford would still hold out for some time, and he continued to affect the discussions on the package of reforms. On 25 January 1856, he sent the Porte a new memorandum and an official note on administrative reforms and religious persecutions, together with his instructions to his head dragoman Mr Pisani, to be submitted to the foreign minister Fuad Pasha and grand vizier Âli Pasha. He advised the admission of "all classes" into state service and councils (*meclises*), arguing that in the current state of things, it was the "union alone of the classes" which could return to the Empire the force which it lacked "in the interior",

---

[32] Cevdet Pasha, op. cit., p. 66. Cf. Roderic Davison, *Reform in the Ottoman Empire 1856–1876*, New York: Gordian Press, 1973, p. 103.
[33] Harold Temperley, "The Last Phase of Stratford de Redcliffe", *The English Historical Review* 47(186), April 1932, pp. 216–217.
[34] Temperley, op. cit., p. 218.

and without this measure any real union was an impossibility. As for the foreigners, Stratford asserted that while he was supposed to attach less importance than the representatives of France and of Austria to the question of foreigners' rights to possess (purchase) real estate in the Ottoman Empire, this assumption was completely erroneous. He was convinced, on the contrary, that the "cordial rapprochement" of "Turkey" with Europe was essential for the well-being and the maintenance of the Ottoman Empire, and that the most effective measure in this direction would not be other than the assured right of foreigners to possess any kind of real estate there.[35]

Cevdet Pasha's treatment of the question of equality of non-Muslim Ottoman subjects is interesting. He seems to try to conceal his feelings, and gives the opinions for and against, but he does not make a clearly binding statement for himself. He was also the member of a commission (together with Fuad Pasha and Afif Bey) set up to change the forms of address (*elkab*) of the firmans. He wrote that Fuad Pasha was fond of creating such novelties, however, since the proclamation of the *Islahat Fermanı* would already offend Muslims, it was not appropriate at that time to be engaged in changing the *elkab* of firmans. Then he noted that according to the firman,

> Muslim and non-Muslim subjects were now to be equal in all rights. But this significantly offended the Muslims. Previously, one of the four points that was accepted as the base of negotiations was the question of the privileges of Christians, provided that sovereignty was not sacrificed. But now the question of privileges was left behind, non-Muslim subjects were considered equal to Muslims in all rights of government.[36] [My translation]

According to Cevdet Pasha, the non-Muslim subjects rejoiced at the reading of the firman. Not all of them, however, were pleased. For example the Greek patriarchate was not happy with being equal to the Jews, while before the *Islahat Fermanı* they used to come before all other non-Muslim *millets*.

Cevdet Pasha concludes that Muslims were discontented with the *Islahat Fermanı* and reproached the ministers for this. According to him, the *şeyhülislam* also lost favour. He also claimed that people started saying that if Reşid Pasha and the former şeyhülislam Arif

---

[35] BOA. HR. TO. 222/30 enc. 2.
[36] Cevdet Pasha, *Tezâkir 1–12*, pp. 67–68.

Hikmet Beyefendi had been in office, the result would have been different. Since Stratford de Redcliffe had striven to effect the equality of the Christian subjects more than any other diplomat, he and Britain also lost favour. Cevdet Pasha wrote that the French were happy with this result. The French ambassador even said that the Ottoman government had given in too much, and he would have helped if they had resisted Stratford a little. But Cevdet considered these words calculated to further vilify the British embassy. Reşid Pasha then seized the opportunity to criticise his rivals and gain the confidence of the pro-Islamic circles. Therefore he took a stand against the *Islahat Fermanı*. He even wrote a *layiha* to the Sultan stating his reasons.[37]

Shortly after the treaty of Paris, the Ottoman Greeks Kostaki Musurus Bey and Kalimaki Bey were promoted to the rank of ambassador extraordinary and plenipotentiary (*büyükelçi*).[38] Musurus had been envoy extraordinary and minister plenipotentiary (*ortaelçi*) in London, whereas his colleague in Paris, the Ottoman ambassador Veliyüddin Rifat Pasha (Veli Pasha), son of grand vizier Giritli Mustafa Naili Pasha, bore the title of full ambassador.

Except for the Greek insurrection in Thessaly and Epirus, the non-Muslim subjects of the Ottoman Empire in general supported the war effort of the state. As we have already seen, some Armenians, Bulgarians and Greeks even applied to the government for permission to serve in the army. Nevertheless, there were still some fanatical Muslim attacks on non-Muslims in some places such as Damascus.

One of the visible signs of the improved status of non-Muslims was an increase in the number of their churches and synagogues. During the war and just afterwards (from 1853 to the end of 1857), many churches and synagogues were repaired and some new ones were built. We must note that the building of new churches and synagogues and the repair of existing ones in the Ottoman Empire required the Sultan's license (*ruhsat*). During the war, there was a noticeable increase in the number of such licenses. For example, Greek churches in Midilli, İzmit, Büyükada, Mihalıç, Salonica, Vidin, Niş, Tırnova and other cities, towns and villages were repaired.[39] Three villages in Filibe (Plovdiv) and one village in Yenice also received licenses to build churches, while

---

[37] Cevdet Pasha, op. cit., pp. 76–82.
[38] Cevdet Pasha, op. cit., p. 84.
[39] BOA. İ. HR. 130/6608, 130/6667, 131/6694, 136/7012, 137/7099, 138/7133.

the rebuilding of the church of the town of Vize was approved.⁴⁰ New Greek churches were built in Jerusalem, Erzurum, Filibe and other places.⁴¹ Armenian churches in Kasımpaşa, Rumeli Hisarı, Harput, Erzurum, Van, Muş, Diyarbekir, Trabzon and some other places were allowed to be repaired and new ones were permitted in Diyarbekir, Karahisar-ı Şarki, Muş, Harput, Erzurum, Sivas and other places (in cities, towns and villages).⁴² Construction of new Catholic churches was approved in Varna, Rusçuk, Drac, İşkodra, Samatya, Büyükada (Prinkipo), Erzurum and other places.⁴³ For the repair of the Catholic church in Sinop, burned during the battle of Sinop, the government sent 15,000 piastres.⁴⁴ Two Catholic churches in the districts of İşkodra were repaired. Repairs to synagogues in Salonica and Ruse (Rusçuk) were permitted. Construction of a new Protestant church was allowed in Ortaköy, and another was built in the Bahçecik village in İzmit, while a land allotment near the *Mekteb-i Tıbbiye* was given to the British embassy for building a church. Various churches were also built and repaired in Sophia, Erdek, Limni, İzmir, Mostar, Ereğli, Salonica, Vidin, Larissa (Yenişehr-i Fener), Hersek and other places.⁴⁵

The Reform Edict of 1856 (*Islahat Fermanı*), among other things, stipulated equal opportunity for all Ottoman subjects for admission into civil and military schools and also recognized the right of every religious community, admittedly under state supervision, to establish their own schools. Armenians, Bulgarians and Greeks made good use of this point and opened many schools. This in turn urged the Sublime Porte to develop an all-Ottoman, empire-wide public school system more rapidly. In 1856 a new educational body, the Mixed Council of Education, (*Meclis-i Muhtelit-i Maarif*) was established in order to coordinate Muslim and non-Muslim schools. Its six members consisted of

---

⁴⁰ Özcan, op. cit. (1997), p. 153.
⁴¹ BOA. İ. HR. 135/6965, 135/6984.
⁴² BOA. İ. HR. 114/5570, 126/6311, 136/7007, 137/7060, 138/7164, 142/7481, 143/7534, 144/7563. Cf. Özcan, op. cit., p. 153. Özcan refers to some other documents from the BOA and writes that 8 Armenian churches were allowed to be repaired and 6 churches to be built again.
⁴³ BOA. HR. SYS. 1353/61, İ. HR. 130/6592, 132/6768, 137/7109, 138/7175. Özcan (op. cit., p. 154) mentions only Büyükada, Drac and Rusçuk.
⁴⁴ BOA. A. AMD. 73/41, quoted by Özcan, op. cit. (1997), p. 155. Also see OBKS, p. 298.
⁴⁵ BOA. İ. HR. 131/6726, 128/6487, 130/6597, 130/6635, 131/6690, 134/6938, 132/6743, 132/6781, 132/6784, 132/6790, 134/6901, 135/6946, 136/7007, 136/7047, 137/7085, 137/7128, 138/7142, 138/7153.

Muslim, Greek-Orthodox, Gregorian Armenian, Catholic, Protestant and Jewish representatives. This council had the authority to determine the quality and curricula of the schools and the selection of teachers.[46] Education was at three levels. At the primary level (*sıbyan mektebleri*), the language of instruction was determined by each religious community separately. At the secondary level (*rüşdiye* schools) education was in Ottoman Turkish, because the graduates of these schools were counted as potential civil servants. At the third level, that is, in the professional schools, the language of instruction was in conformity with the art or science taught. Schools at the secondary and higher levels offered mixed-language education.

The quality of education was also enhanced by including natural sciences in the curricula of secondary and higher schools. Students had to wear uniforms, which also contributed to the process of secularization. This policy of mixed education for Muslims and non-Muslims confirmed the intent of the government to include non-Muslims in government services. After one year, the council of public education and the mixed council of education were merged to form the ministry of public education (*Maarif-i Umumiye Nezareti*) in 1857. The new ministry had more authority and a more autonomous structure. The former directorate of public schools was formed into an undersecretariat (*müsteşarlık*) of the new ministry. Thus the Sublime Porte proved its serious intentions towards the modernization of the educational system.

The Prohibition of the Black Sea White Slave Trade

Slavery was an issue of controversy between the Ottomans and the European states and even Russia during the Crimean War. By the time of the Crimean War, slavery and the slave trade were already illegal in Europe. However, slavery still had legal status as a recognized Ottoman institution and as such it was never abolished in the Ottoman Empire.[47] The most important source of white slaves for the Ottoman Empire

---

[46] Selçuk Akşin Somel, *The Modernization of Public Education in the Ottoman Empire, 1839–1908*. Leiden, Boston, Köln: Brill, 2001, p. 43.
[47] Y. Hakan Erdem, *Slavery in the Ottoman Empire and Its Demise 1800–1909*. London & NY: Macmillan Press, St. Martin's Press, 1996, pp. 94–124.

was the Circassian coast of the Black Sea.[48] Secondly, Sub-Saharan Africa provided black slaves. There was a demand for beautiful boys and girls as domestic servants for the households (*konaks*) of high-ranking bureaucrats and in the Sultan's palace. Until 1846 these slaves were sold openly and the most famous slave market in Çemberlitaş near the grand bazaar was closed down in this year by Abdülmecid. We do not know whether he did it on his own initiative or upon the remonstrations of foreigners (especially Stratford de Redcliffe). However, it seems likely that the initiative was his own. In any case this did not indicate the prohibition of the slave trade, but only that public purchase of slaves was brought to an end.

Russia was also trying to prevent the slave trade from Circassia, which was given to Russia by the treaty of Edirne in 1829. However, Russian rule was nominal in Circassia, where local rulers continued to have a significant autonomy. Nor were the Circassian tribes easy to control. These tribes had a caste system whereby a part of the society consisted of slaves. The sale of these slaves was a lucrative business for the Circassian nobles and notables. There was also a contraband slave trade from the Georgian coasts by Ottoman subjects.

When Prince Menshikov appeared in Istanbul in the spring of 1853, one of his demands concerned the prohibition of this trade from the Georgian and Circassian coasts. In his instructions to Argyropoulo, the head dragoman of the Russian embassy, Menshikov stated on 18 April 1853 that a certain Hurşid Reis from Arhavi was engaged in the Georgian and Circassian slave trade. The Russian consulate in Trabzon had reported that more than a hundred boys and girls from Georgia had been brought to Giresun. Around twenty of these, under the guidance of two Georgians or Circassians, being Russian subjects, were brought to Trabzon secretly at night to embark on the Ottoman steamer *Vasıta-i Ticaret* going to Istanbul via Giresun and Samsun, where Hurşid Reis would then take other slaves on board. Sarım Pasha the governor of Trabzon was also accused of being involved in this trade.[49]

The Ottomans were ready to suppress the slave trade to save face with the Europeans, but not to abolish slavery as an institution. When France and Britain became indispensable allies of the Porte in the war

---

[48] Ehud Toledano, *The Ottoman Slave Trade and Its Suppression*. NJ: Princeton University Press, 1982, pp. 14–48.
[49] BOA. HR. SYS. 1345/10.

against Russia, they acquired substantial bargaining power. The influential British ambassador had been putting pressure upon the Ottoman government to abolish the slave trade, but the Sublime Porte was rather unwilling to completely abolish the white slave trade in the Black Sea because the Ottoman elite used slaves as domestic servants, and also frequently chose their wives from among slave women. Thus they were dependent upon the supply of slaves, especially white slaves. On the other hand, they had to appease their allies somehow.[50]

Towards the end of August 1854 the allies decided to take action to prevent the slave trade from the Georgian and Circassian coasts. The British ambassador Stratford de Redcliffe and the French *chargé d'affaires* Vincent Benedetti gave official notes to the Porte through their dragomans, demanding the prohibition of the slave trade from Georgian and Circassian coasts and the sale of these slaves in the Ottoman Empire.[51] Lord Stratford's note, dated 29 August 1854, stated that enslavement of Christian Georgians was offensive to the allies, and enslavement of Muslim Circassians was not legal from an Islamic point of view. He had received authentic information that Georgian children were brought to Constantinople as slaves on an Austrian steamer, and submitted to "a person high in the Turkish employment". Stratford warned that the allies, "without whose cooperation the very existence of the Turkish Empire would be endangered", could in no way be expected to assist such "outrages" and "atrocities". Such "barbarous practices" were incredible,

> when viewed as public transactions occurring at Constantinople under the reign of so benevolent a Sovereign as the present Sultan. Brought to notice at a time when Christian Powers have sent their armies and squadrons into Turkey for its defence, and when those armies and squadrons composed of Christians, are fighting side by side with Mussulmans, and confounding all differences of religion in the common cause of humanity and national independence, they set at nought every calculation and excite the most unqualified disgust.[52]

---

[50] Erdem, "Kırım Savaşı'nda Karadeniz Beyaz Köle Ticareti", symposium paper in *Savaştan Barışa*, 2007, pp. 86–87.
[51] Toledano, op. cit., p. 117. Erdem, op. cit. (1996), p. 102.
[52] Lord Stratford's instructions to head dragoman Stephen Pisani, 29 August 1854, cited by Erdem, op. cit. (2007), pp. 87–94. Erdem compares the original with the official Ottoman Turkish translation and points out that the translation is somewhat simplified. The same document is also available at BOA. HR. TO. 220/45.

Stratford then admitted that slavery in the Ottoman Empire was different from African-American slavery. Nevertheless, he argued, the vices of slavery were still there. Stratford went on to say that a "total relaxation" of the enthusiasm for the Sultan's cause could be produced "throughout Christian Europe", if the Ottoman authorities did not stop this trade. He did not forget to add that a move against slavery would definitely increase the popularity of the Sultan in Europe:

> Such being the case, it is not too much to expect that in its own interest, as well as from consideration for its allies, the Porte will exert itself to check the barbarous and shameful practise which I have described. Let preventive measures be applied to three stages of the traffic, to *purchase*, to *conveyance*, and to *sale*. Let a firman declare the Sultan's pleasure in these respects. Let peremptory instructions prohibiting the purchase of slaves be sent to the commanders of His Majesty's forces. Let the conveyance of slaves be treated as contraband on the responsibility of all concerned. Let their sale within the Sultan's dominions be strictly prevented by the police, and every transgression be visited with punishment on buyer and seller alike.
>
> So long as the trade is permitted or connived at, so long as preventive measures, capable of enforcement, are loosely or not at all, employed, the Turkish authorities will justly be opened to censure, and incur, to their peril, the charge of acting upon principles inconsistent in spirit and effect with the existing alliances. Let them beware of producing throughout Christian Europe a total relaxation of that enthusiasm for the Sultan's cause, which has hitherto saved his empire from the grasp of Russia.[53]
> [Italics are underlined in the original]

The Ottoman council of ministers discussed the issue on 18 September 1854. According to the report of the Grand Vizier Kıbrıslı Mehmed Emin Pasha to the Sultan, there was certainly an increase in the volume of the Black Sea white slave trade. The grand vizier pointed out that the total prohibition of Georgian and Circassian slave trade was not desirable, but the government could not afford to leave the gate wholly open to the traders. If they ignored the question, that too would cause problems. Consequently, it was necessary to take some measures which would limit slavery to its low pre-war level and it seemed possible to ward off this issue by making such measures public. If they did nothing, then things would compel them to abolish the white slave trade totally. Thus, they had to find a solution by which they would demonstrate, with new proofs, to the two allies that the Ottoman Empire abided by

---

[53] Ibid. The last paragraph has been quoted by Toledano, op. cit., p. 117.

the principles of humanity and in this way they would be able to secure their goodwill as well as that of the Georgian people.⁵⁴

For the Porte, the problem was not the slave trade *per se*, but the explicit way in which it was conducted. The grand vizier further remarked in his petition to the Sultan that slaves were sold and bought openly even in Galata and Beyoğlu (the districts of Istanbul where the Europeans mainly lived). This was not a good scene before the eyes of the "civilized world". Therefore it was essential to reduce the slave trade to its pre-war state of seclusion, slaves should be bought and sold only in homes. The Grand Vizier proposed to send two orders to Mustafa Pasha the commander of Batum, prohibiting the Georgian and Circassian slave trade from the Ottoman Black Sea posts. The embassies would be informed. The police and the customs authorities were also to be instructed to push the slave trade into secrecy, away from the eyes of the foreigners.⁵⁵

Consequently, Abdülmecid issued two firmans in October 1854 to Müşir Mustafa Pasha, the Commander of the Imperial Army at Batum, one for the Georgians (to be announced in Batum and Çürüksu) and the other to be publicized in Circassia. Since Christian Georgians and Muslim Circassians were treated differently, the wording of the two firmans also differed. The Circassians, who were an independent-minded Muslim people fighting against the Russians, were to be admonished that selling relatives into slavery was not humane, whereas the Georgian slave trade was prohibited outright; for while the Circassians sold their relatives themselves, the Georgians did not engage in such trade, their children being kidnapped by slave dealers.⁵⁶

The Porte notified the French and British embassies that the enslavement of Georgian women and children had never been endorsed by the Ottoman government. Orders had been sent before but regrettably violated. The Georgians who had been brought in as slaves would be immediately manumitted and sent to their families if they wished. But there was no mention of the Circassians. Orders were also issued to

---

⁵⁴ Grand Vizier Kıbrıslı Mehmed Emin Pasha to Sultan Abdülmecid. BOA. İ. HR. 114/5553, 21 September 1854, cited in Erdem, op. cit. (1996), pp. 102–103 and op. cit. (2007), pp. 94–98. Abdullah Saydam has also cited this document but for some reason he has converted the above *Hicrî* date into 21 April 1856 and has also mistransliterated several words (such as *rakkiyet* instead of *rıkkiyet*). See Abdullah Saydam, *Kırım ve Kafkas Göçleri (1856–1876)*, Ankara: TTK, 1997, p. 195.

⁵⁵ Saydam, op. cit., p. 196. Erdem, op. cit. (2007), p. 98.

⁵⁶ Erdem, op. cit. (1996), pp. 104–105.

the police and the customs authorities to prevent the open trade of slaves. On the same day orders were sent to the governors of Trabzon, Lazistan and Canik prohibiting the Georgian slave trade. The Austrian embassy was also notified that Lloyd company ships should be warned not to accept slaves on board.[57]

In December 1854 new orders were sent to the *müşir* of Batum and the governor of Trabzon, reminding them of the presence of the British and French fleets in the Black Sea and of their duty to prevent the slave trade; the commander and the governor were to assist the allies in all relevant efforts.

At the beginning of December 1854, the commander of the Batum army and the governor of Trabzon were instructed to prevent the export of slaves from Georgia and the Circassians' sale of their own children, relatives and servants.[58] Towards the end of December 1854, Grand Vizier Reşid Pasha sent new instructions to the governors of Trabzon, Erzurum and Lazistan and to the commanders of the armies of Batum and Anatolia. They were reminded that during the battles of last year near Şekvetil and Ahıska, some children were kidnapped and sold into slavery and also that some young men who came to Ottoman territory to become Ottoman subjects were somehow enslaved. It was pointed out that some officials and officers were engaged in this "inhuman" trade and that this had become a great resource for Russian propaganda, alienating the population from the Ottoman state and causing damaging rumours about the whole Ottoman *millet*. Therefore all such slaves were to be returned. Those boys who accepted Islam and who were willing could be taken into military service. Those boys who had not yet been circumcised and wanted to go home should be sent home. Children should be turned over to trustworthy parties for return to their families. Girls of appropriate age who accepted Islam could be married off.[59]

When the head of police Hayreddin Pasha was sent by the Porte as inspector to the Anatolian and Batum armies in January 1854, one of the questions he directed to the military *meclis* in Erzurum concerned the slave trading, in which, as he had heard, the commander

---

[57] Toledano, op. cit., pp. 119–121. Saydam, op. cit., p. 196. Erdem, op. cit. (2007), pp. 99–103.
[58] BOA. HR. MKT. 93/93, 1 December 1854.
[59] BOA. A. MKT. MHM. 63/41 and HR. MKT. 96/99 and 97/16, 26 December 1854.

in Ahıska, Ferik Ali Rıza Pasha was involved. It was rumoured that the latter had acquired some slaves, distributing some and retaining others. The *meclis* did not confirm this information and replied that Ali Rıza Pasha only had bought three Georgian slaves (two girls and one boy) from Selim Bey the *müdir* of Şavşat (near Batum) and his brother Şakir Bey. Ali Rıza Pasha himself also denied having taken slaves, but admitted that three months before the beginning of the war he had bought one Circassian boy and one Circassian girl, acquired as children and raised by the said brothers.

As late as February 1855, the slave trade apparently was still being practised by the officers of the Kars army. An extract from a report of the British consulate in Erzurum, probably written by General Williams or by one of the British officers in his staff, was given to the Ottoman foreign ministry:

> The buying and selling of slaves by the officers of the Kars army is as notorious as any other malpractices on their part. Boys are preferred by these brutes, and the girls are sent as bribes to Constantinople; and until the allied consuls are authorized to demand the restitution of these victims to Turkish Sensuality, and are provided with funds to send them back to their families in Georgia; and until the Porte is bound by treaty to send the culprits so detected to the galleys for a certain specified time, this infamous traffic will flourish, and all which has been said or may be written about abolitionary firmans simply adds mockery to crime and woe.[60]

Furthermore, the Sultan's firman on the prohibition of the slave trade had not yet reached Sohum by the end of December 1854. Lord John Hay from the British navy reported on his visit to Sohum(kale) and Çürüksu:

> On the 28 December 1854 I visited the Mushir at Choorooksou: having expressed my surprise that the Pacha at Soukoumkale had not received orders relative to the suppression of the Slave Trade, the Mushir informed me that he was most anxious to give effect to the Sultan's Firman, but although he had received the Firman 6 weeks previously, no opportunity had as yet presented itself of communicating with Soukoumkale. Indeed the country boats passing were liable to capture by the enemy's gun boats out of the rivers at Poti and Anakria, and the only steamer at his disposal was merely sufficient to bring provisions from Trebisonde for the use of the army. Proceeded to and arrived at Trebisonde on 29th Dec. 1854. The Pacha was absent when I visited him. I however learnt from Mr. Stevens,

---

[60] BOA. HR. TO. 221/6, 6 February 1855.

Vice Consul, that Two Boats laden with Circassian slaves had arrived at this Port a few days previous. The Pacha did not clearly see how he could give effect to the Firman of the Sultan not knowing how to define whether the people were slaves or not.

I recommended that Mr Stevens' advice should be acted on and that the Boats and people should be detained on suspicion.

Altogether I think there does not appear to exist among the Turkish officials any excessive anxiety to put a stop to the Circassian and Georgian Slave Trade.[61]

About this time, Clarendon was giving clear instructions to Stratford to request the Porte to take effective measures to prevent the Black Sea slave trade:

The Turkish authorities in the Porte of the Black Sea have shewn no willingness to give effect to the Sultan's Firman prohibiting the traffic in Circassian and Georgian slaves; and that when two boats laden with Circassian slaves arrived at Trebizond about the 26 of December last, the Pasha's excuse for not detaining them was that he could not define whether they were slaves or not.

I have to instruct Your Excellency to communicate the enclosed extract to the Ottoman Govt and to request that clear and stringent Instructions may be sent to the proper authorities in the Ports of the Black Sea, pointing out to them that there can be no difficulty in ascertaining whether or not the Circassians and Georgians brought to those ports are intended for sale; and that the Pashas must be held strictly responsible for the punctual execution of the Sultan's order declaring that this traffic is to cease.[62]

The Ottoman statesmen also tried to convince the Europeans that the conditions of slavery in Turkey were somewhat different from others and that Ottoman slavery was idiosyncratic. Let us give an anecdotal example. In 1856, Fuad Pasha invited Mme Thouvenel and Marie de Melfort to his harem. There he introduced a young lady and said: "this lady is my daughter-in-law. Originally she was a Circassian. We bought and brought her up to marry our son. You see, our conception of slavery is different from yours".[63] When urged again by the British to end the white slave trade in 1857, the Foreign Minister Âli Pasha also

---

[61] Extract of a dispatch from Lord John Hay to Sir Edmund Lyons dated 8 January 1855, enclosed in a letter from Admiralty dated January 29th 1855. BOA. HR. TO. 221/13 enc. 2.
[62] Clarendon to Stratford, date unknown, translated on 16 March 1855. BOA. HR. TO. 221/13 enc. 4.
[63] Baronne Durand de Fontmagne, op. cit. (1977), p. 255.

replied that "the so-called slaves are no slaves as most of them come to Constantinople of their own accord".[64]

Throughout the Ottoman Empire, the most violent reaction to the prohibitions on the slave trade came (as could be expected) from a religious and highly sensitive area. This was Hijaz, which included the two holy cities of Islam and which was ruled semi-autonomously by *emirs*, appointed by the Sultan from among the descendants of the prophet Muhammad (sharifs). Although Hijaz was excluded from the prohibition of the black slave trade, the religious notables of Arabia were disturbed. Sharif Abdulmuttalib Efendi, the *emir* of Mecca, was not on good terms with Kamil Pasha the governor of Jeddah. Fearing his deposition, Abdulmuttalib seems to have wanted to use the discontent of the notables of Jeddah, Mecca and Medina to get rid of Ottoman supremacy. Therefore he urged some notables of Jeddah to write a letter to some sharifs and *ulema* of Mecca. They wrote it on 1 April 1855, criticising what they saw as the recent concessions given to the Europeans. They argued that besides prohibiting the slave trade, the Porte had sent orders to governors permitting non-Muslims to build any edifices in the Arab peninsula, allowing non-Muslim men to marry Muslim women, and prohibiting interference with women's dress, etc. The Jeddah notables urged them to petition the *emir* of Mecca to petition the Sultan.

Meanwhile the Porte had already been suspicious of Abdulmuttalib's behaviour and in August 1855 sent Ferik Raşid Pasha with confidential orders to depose Abdulmuttalib and appoint Sharif Muhammed bin Avn if necessary. Cevdet Pasha wrote that by that time, orders from the grand vizier prohibiting the black slave trade had been sent to governors in order to feign friendship (*müdara*) to European states.[65] In any case, these comments implied the temporary character of the orders due to the necessities of war.

Cevdet Pasha claimed that Ferik Raşid Pasha was able to establish that the letter of the notables of Jeddah was the product of a secret order from Abdulmuttalib, who was at that time in Taif. According to Cevdet Pasha, Abdulmuttalib then invited Sheikh Cemal Efendi, the head of the ulema (reis-ül ulema) from Mecca to Taif and made the following statement:

---

[64] Erdem, op. cit. (1996), p. 51.
[65] Cevdet Pasha, *Tezâkir* 1–12, p. 102.

The consequences of the present war will be grave for the Sublime State. It cannot overcome this [disaster]. Even if this war were to end in some way, it cannot survive its debt and it will be crushed. What is more, the Turks have become apostates and though they are concealing their apostasy for the time being, obviously they will declare it later. This time of war is an opportunity for us. We can obtain the power of government which was our right from old times, and the prohibition of slavery can serve as an excuse. Although it has not come here yet, it has been exercised elsewhere. Soon it will be executed here as well. We must wait until the season of pilgrimage passes, for during pilgrimage there will be many troops around. Thereafter we must take care of our affairs. However, it is already necessary to take measures.[66] [My translation]

The governor Kamil Pasha tried to carry out the orders of the central government to stop the importation and sale of slaves. In Jeddah he ordered the public reading of the order on the prohibition of the slave trade, while the Mecca *ulema*, supported by Sharif Abdulmuttalib, declared the order contrary to the *sharia*. Widespread rioting broke out. Houses belonging to French and English protégés were looted. The *ulema* and the rioting mobs demanded the complete expulsion of all Christians (including consuls) from the Hijaz.[67]

Raşid Pasha reached Jeddah on 28 October 1855. On 15 November 1855, the order appointing Sharif Muhammed ibn Avn as the new *emir* was proclaimed. But Abdulmuttalib refused to accept his deposition. He tried to urge the Bedouin chiefs of the desert Arabs (*urban*) to rebellion as well. 600–700 *urban* led by some sharifs sent by Abdulmuttalib attacked Ottoman troops in Bahre, between Jeddah and Mecca, but they were repulsed. After a few days, Abdulmuttalib sent another 2,000 *urban* against the Ottoman forces in Bahre but these were also repulsed.[68] While there were riots in Mecca and Jeddah, Medina was relatively quiet.[69]

While Abdulmuttalib continued to revolt and fight, Şeyhülislam Arif Efendi sent a letter on 11 January 1856 to all the religious dignitaries of Mecca, trying to explain that the rules of the sharia were not

---

[66] Cevdet Pasha, op. cit., p. 103. "Prohibition of slavery" must be understood here as "prohibition of the slave trade".
[67] William Ochsenwald, "Muslim-European Conflict in the Hijaz: The Slave Trade Controversy, 1840–1895", *Middle Eastern Studies* 16, 1980, p. 119. Reprinted in *Religion, Economy, and State in Ottoman-Arab History*, Istanbul: The ISIS Press, 1998, p. 83.
[68] Cevdet Pasha, op. cit., p. 122.
[69] Ochsenwald, op. cit. (1998), p. 84.

being violated. Among such rules, he cited the sale of slaves, giving women the right to seek a divorce and the acceptance of help from non-Muslims as well. Defending the rightfulness of receiving help from non-Muslims, the *şeyhülislam* gave the example of the Prophet Muhammad's asking the Jews of Beni Kaynaka for help against the tribe of Beni Kureyza. The *şeyhülislam* further argued that the Ottoman caliphs were always guided by the sharia and they would not abolish the rights to legitimate possessions belonging to Muslims. By these possessions he meant slaves.[70] The revolt of Abdulmuttalib ended in 1856 when he was captured and brought to Istanbul. He was not punished, however, but simply required to live in Istanbul. Yet the tensions between the Hijaz notables, dignitaries and owners of slaves on the one hand and the European consuls and the Porte on the other continued, which led to a massacre of consuls in Jeddah in 1858.

We can conclude that European pressure did not bring significant change to the Circassian slave trade. However, the Ottoman government took a decisive step in 1857 when the black slave trade was totally prohibited by a *firman* of the Sultan. Again it was not black slavery *per se* that was prohibited but rather the import and export of black slaves: the existing slaves would not be freed. Nevertheless, this was an important decision for the Ottoman Empire, even if it was not applied for a long time. As argued by Erdem, in practical terms, the Porte could ban the slave trade, and prevent new slaves fro entering the empire, but it could not challenge the legal status of a category sanctioned by Islamic law. Even the Sultan could not do it, because he would need a religious edict (*fetva*) from the *şeyhülislam*; and this he was not likely to obtain.

After the war and the prohibition of the black slave trade, Ottoman officials were no longer interested in preventing the Circassian white slave trade in the Black Sea. Âli Pasha told the British dragoman Simmons in August 1857 that "had Circassia been given over to Turkey [in the Paris Peace Congress] they would have managed to alter things".[71] But these words come strangely from Âli Pasha, because according to Cevdet Pasha, he did not want to do anything for Circassia during the peace congress in March 1856. Cevdet Pasha recorded that he heard that Lord Clarendon and the British ambassador in Paris (Lord Cow-

---

[70] Cevdet Pasha, op. cit., p. 136. Cf. Ochsenwald, op. cit. (1998), p. 84.
[71] Erdem, op. cit. (1996), p. 107.

ley) had asked Âli Pasha to jointly present to the congress a motion for a new arrangement for Caucasus, but Âli Pasha had replied: "For us those places are not so important, we have only a disputed area around Çürüksu; we will be content with saving that area".[72] Again according to Cevdet Pasha, the British representatives were surprised and Lord Clarendon later said: "I cannot be more Turkish than a Turk". Therefore, either what Cevdet Pasha reported was wrong, or Âli Pasha forgot in August 1857 (or rather did not want to remember) what he had said during the Paris Congress.

Law and Order in the Provinces

During the Crimean War revolts broke out in various parts of the Ottoman Empire. These were either directly related to the causes of the war, as with the revolt of the Greeks in Thessaly and Epirus, or else indirectly resulted from the general lack of authority in the provinces due to the concentration of troops on the fronts, the revolt of the Kurdish beys being a case in point. Then there were those revolts which also expressed a reaction to the alliance of the caliph with Christian powers, as we have seen, the revolt of the Arabs in Hijaz fell into that category. The disturbances in Damascus were also a reaction of some Muslims to the proclaimed legal equality of the Christian subjects of the Ottoman Empire.

After the declaration of war, some fanatical Muslims had attacked Christian subjects of the Porte and foreigners. Therefore Grand Vizier Mustafa Naili Pasha sent an order to the governors of Damascus and Jerusalem in December 1853 to prevent such treatment of the Christians. He wrote that the Christian subjects of the Sublime State were heart and soul together with Muslims in the current war against Russia. It was very unbecoming to look with suspicion and hostility at such loyal subjects who had been showing their loyalty and righteousness. The perpetrators of such acts of violence against them were "certain fanatics and feather-brains, who cannot distinguish between good and evil and who cannot tell friends from enemies".[73]

Apart from the revolts, the most disturbing internal source of disorder was the infamous bands of irregular soldiers, the so called *başıbozuks*.

---

[72] Cevdet Pasha, *Tezâkir 1-12*, p. 101.
[73] BOA. A. MKT. UM. 149/7, 8 December 1853.

These volunteers proved more of a burden than a help to the war effort of the Ottoman state. While they attacked and robbed both Muslims and non-Muslims on their way, the chief victims were nevertheless the non-Muslim subjects of the empire. Meanwhile, banditry in general also increased. Some nomadic Kurdish tribes in Anatolia were engaged in robbing non-Muslim villages, caravans and merchants. Nomadic Arab sheikhs (*urban meşayihi*) also warred among themselves. We will analyse here in some detail the revolt of the Kurdish emirs or *bey*s in Kurdistan and the problems related to the actions of the *başıbozuks*.

The Revolt of Yezdanşêr

Towards the middle of the nineteenth century, Kurdistan was one of the places where central authority of the Porte was weakest and that of the local lords highest. Kurdistan was the name of a region from Diyarbekir to Van and to Mosul where mostly Kurds lived. From 1847 to 1867, it was also the official name of an Ottoman province (*eyalet*) centred in Harput, and then in Diyarbekir. Şemseddin Sami, author of the *Kamus ül A'lam*, the first encyclopaedia in Turkish, defined Kurdistan as follows:

> A big country [*memleket*] in West Asia with its larger portion in the Ottoman Empire and another portion subject to Iran. It has been named after the Kurdish people [*kavm*] that forms the majority of the population.[74] [My translation]

Although Sultan Mahmud II had done a lot to reduce the power of these local notables, in remote and traditionally autonomous areas like Kurdistan, local *bey*s, emirs, and khans, still held sway. Especially due to the turmoil caused by Mehmed Ali Pasha of Egypt in Anatolia during the 1830s, Kurdish beys tried to develop their power bases. They did not want to share their power with the Sultan, though recognizing him as the caliph of all the Sunnite Muslims. In particular they did not want to share taxes and allow military recruitment. Indeed, the Prussian military adviser Helmuth von Moltke, who served in Mahmud's army in its campaign against the Egyptian forces in 1838–1839, wrote

---

[74] Şemseddin Sami, *Kamus ül A'lam*, vol. 5, Istanbul: Mihran Matbaası, 1896, p. 3840. For a modern Turkish translation see M. Emin Bozarslan, *Tarihteki İlk Türkçe Ansiklopedide Kürdistan ve Kürdler*, Istanbul: Deng Yayınları, 2001, p. 45.

in his letters that the two biggest problems for the people were taxes and military conscription. Taxes were very arbitrary and the military service too long, fifteen years in theory, but almost lifelong in practice. If only these were reformed, he advised, the state would enjoy the support of the local people.[75] However, reform was not easy because it was harmful to so many vested interests. Corrupt pashas and governors paid bribes to get appointed to their provinces and then, knowing that their term of office would be short, tried hard to squeeze out the amount they had paid, often borrowed at high rates of interest from the *sarraf*s of Istanbul. Other pashas engaged in all kinds of intrigues in Istanbul against the current governors, who therefore avoided embarking upon any long term projects.

On the other hand, the local *bey*s, while equally corrupt and tyrannous, were still better for the local people because they saw the provinces as their permanent home, as hereditary property, and cared – albeit within limits – more for the local people. One of these Kurdish dignitaries, Bedirhan Bey, bearing the traditional title of the *emir* of Botan (Bohtan) and the Ottoman title of *mütesellim* (deputy of a *sancak* or *kaza* governor) of Cizre, became the actual ruler of this area in the beginning of the 1840s, subduing all other Kurdish and Armenian notables in the region. Moltke noted that Bedirhan participated in the war against Ibrahim Pasha of Egypt (son of Mehmed Ali) and he was given the rank of colonel. According to some Kurdish authors, Bedirhan Bey struck coins in his own name, sent students to Europe for education, and established the manufacture of gunpowder and weapons.[76] However, this is not confirmed by other sources and seems doubtful. Bedirhan had first served in the Ottoman army's campaign against some rebel Kurdish chiefs in 1838, and then had become a powerful chief himself, revolting against the Ottomans. According to the Soviet Kurdish historian Naftula Halfin, Bedirhan Bey had become the de facto ruler of a vast area extending from Lake Van to Diyarbekir and south to Baghdad, though these provinces belonged to the Ottoman Empire in theory.[77]

---

[75] See *Moltke'nin Türkiye Mektupları*, İstanbul: Remzi Kitabevi, 1999, p. 238.

[76] See for example Celile Celil, *XIX. Yüzyıl Osmanlı İmparatorluğu'nda Kürtler*, Istanbul: Özge Yayınları, 1992, pp. 127–135. Kemal Burkay, *Geçmişten Bugüne Kürtler ve Kürdistan*, Cilt 1, Istanbul: Deng Yayınları, 1997, p. 355.

[77] *Bor'ba za Kurdistan. (Kurdskiy vopros v mejdunarodnyh otnosheniyakh XIX veka)*. Moscow, 1963. Turkish translation: *19. Yüzyılda Kürdistan Üzerine Mücadele*. Ankara: Komal Yay., 1976, pp. 62–63.

While Halfin and some other Kurdish writers consider the revolt of Bedirhan as a national movement, it seems rather a power conflict between the local feudal notables and the modernizing central authorities, without an apparent nationalist ideology.[78] Bedirhan was finally besieged by Ottoman troops in the castle of Evreh in 1847.[79] While he still held out, Yezdanşêr,[80] who was the grandson of Bedirhan's uncle and his left wing commander, betrayed him and joined the Ottoman forces in return for a promise of rank and position. Bedirhan Bey was forced to surrender, and was then brought to Istanbul and later exiled to Crete (to the fortress of Kandiye) together with his retinue and with some other insurgent Kurdish *beys*.[81] Thus Ottoman authorities were able to abolish autonomous Kurdish *beylik*s and started ruling the area directly.

After the suppression of the revolt of Bedirhan, Kurdistan was in a way "conquered anew" in 1847, in the words of the then grand vizier Mustafa Reşid Pasha.[82] A new *eyalet* (province) of Kurdistan was cre-

---

[78] For example, Kemal Burkay considers Bedirhan's movement a "national movement". Burkay has also written that Bedirhan was not an Ottoman pasha. See Burkay, op. cit., p. 306. However, it is well known that Bedirhan Bey was later pardoned and the title of pasha together with the order of Mecidiye was conferred upon him for his services in Crete where he tried to reconcile Muslims and Christians. He died in Damascus.

[79] See Malmîsanij, *Cizira Botanlı Bedirhaniler*. Istanbul: Avesta Yayınevi, 2000, p. 57. Malmîsanij gives the alternative spelling of Ewrex. As he has pointed out, Nazmi Sevgen and İbrahim Alaattin Gövsa have misread this fortress as "Orak" or "Oruh". Cf. Nazmi Sevgen, *Doğu ve Güneydoğu Anadolu'da Türk Beylikleri. Osmanlı Belgeleri ile Kürt Türkleri Tarihi*. Ankara: Türk Kültürünü Araştırma Enstitüsü, 1982, p. 99, p. 104. İbrahim Alaettin Gövsa, *Türk Meşhurları Ansiklopedisi*, vol. 1, Istanbul: Yedigün Neşriyat, undated, pp. 67–68. Sinan Hakan on the other hand writes that the castle is called "Erwex" in Kurdish. See Hakan, *Osmanlı Arşiv Belgelerinde Kürtler ve Kürt Direnişleri (1817–1867)*, Istanbul: Doz Yayıncılık, 2007, p. 226.

[80] Yezdanşêr's name passes as "İzzeddin Şir" in Ottoman official documents. British documents mention his name as "Ezdeen shir". Sinan Hakan uses the alternative modern Kurdish spelling of "Êzdin Şêr".

[81] Sevgen, op. cit., p. 103. Many times Sevgen or his editors have supplied wrong dates. It seems that he thinks (or they think) that Hicri years fully coincide with Gregorian years. Thus for example, they have equated the Muslim year 1263 with the Gregorian year 1846.

[82] Sevgen, op. cit., p. 106. Hakan, op. cit., pp. 253–258. Sevgen or his editors again give a wrong Gregorian year. They indicate the date of Reşid Pasha's petition as "20 Cemaziyelevvel 1263 (1846)". However, in reality this date corresponds to 6 May 1847. As the title of his work suggests, Sevgen considers Kurds as Turks. He even takes issue with the Porte, arguing that "by a very wrong understanding and expression", a certain "territory" [arazi] in the "East" was officially called Kurdistan. Then he argues that "in reality there is not and there cannot be such a region and such a division" [My translation]. See Sevgen, op. cit., p. 105.

ated, including the *eyalet* of Diyarbekir, the *sancak*s of Van, Muş and Hakkâri; and the *kaza*s of Cizre, Botan and Mardin. Here and elsewhere, we see the most favoured tactic or method of the Porte in dealing with local insurgents. It consisted in appealing to some leaders or their relatives, promising good office, title and pay. Thus the revolt would be suppressed with help from inside. Another method was to provide amnesty for the leader(s) and thus deprive the revolt of leadership.

A study of the archival documents concerning the Kurdish revolt of the time of Bedirhan and Yezdanşêr reveals some formulas frequently used in official discourse. Many documents depict the Kurds as "those ill-natured (*bednihad*) Kurds who have long been well-known for insurgence and rebellion".[83] It was necessary to bring them into the "circle of obedience" (*daire-i itaat*). They were to be both frightened by force and assured by pledges of good treatment after submission (*te'min ve terhib*). Promises of rank and pay could be given provided that these should be taken back at the first opportunity.

For his services in the suppression of Bedirhan Bey, Yezdanşêr was first given Bedirhan's title of the *mütesellim* of Cizre with a salary of 3,500 piastres, but soon he was dismissed.[84] Cizre was now to be administered by an Ottoman *kaimmakam*, named Mustafa Pasha. Nevertheless, the Porte did not dare to reduce Yezdanşêr's salary or to completely alienate him. He was given secondary jobs and was fed with promises. Thus we read in a petition of the grand vizier to the Sultan that Yezdanşêr should not be alienated from the state, although he was quite useless for any official position because he did not understand the workings of the Ottoman government.[85] Thus he was first sent to Istanbul in March 1849 and then back to Mosul in the same year. He was not allowed to return to Cizre.[86] He must have resented this treatment, for he revolted at the first opportunity during the Crimean War.

---

[83] See for example BOA. İ. MSM. 69/2015 enc. 2 or A. AMD. 49/76, quoted in my symposium paper "Kırım Savaşı Sırasında İsyanlar ve Asayiş Sorunları (1853–1856)", in *Savaştan Barışa*, p. 289.

[84] Hakan, op. cit., pp. 283–285. Quoting from Kendal [Kendal Nezan?], James Reid (op. cit., p. 299) has written that Yezdanşêr became the "governor of Hakkâri province" after the fall of Bedirhan. This is not true.

[85] BOA. A. AMD. 13/79, dated 1265 (1848–49), quoted in my paper in *Savaştan Barışa*, p. 300. Sinan Hakan (op. cit., p. 283) refers to a *mazbata* of the MVL on this point.

[86] Hakan, op. cit., p. 285.

Meanwhile, the *Tanzimat* had begun to be applied in earnest in Kurdistan. The state started collecting military levies and taxes. An example of the new taxes was the *iane-i umumiye* which was a kind of temporary tax instituted in 1852. According to the table of allocations, for example, the *sancak* of Diyarbekir was to pay 19,093 purses and 460 piastres, Dersim 554 purses and 60 piastres, Muş 1,363 purses and 100 piastres, Hakkâri 415 purses, Cizre 458 purses and 240 piastres, etc.[87] However, these amounts must have been reduced later, because in a resolution of the MVL, dated 31 July 1853, we read that only 6,000 purses (300,000 piastres) out of the 12,400 purses (620,000 piastres) allocated to the province (*eyalet*) of Kurdistan were collectible. The province of Kurdistan at that time included the *sancak*s of Diyarbekir, Dersim, Siirt and Muş. The local authorities had petitioned that if the remaining part were also collected, the impoverished population would scatter. Therefore they asked for a significant reduction. The council stated that the population of the region had just been saved from the oppressions to which they had previously been subjected, and they were really in dire straits. However, the council decided that since outright cancellation would serve as a bad example for populations in a similar position and since the amount was recorded as revenue in the budget, it could only be deferred for some time. The Sultan endorsed this decision.[88] On the other hand, İsmail Kâmil Pasha the *kaimmakam* of Hakkâri had visited the districts and villages of the *sancak* and explained the temporary character of the tax. He had also distributed gifts to sheikhs and other local notables. He had been able to register an additional male population of 12,418 persons, thus raising the total *iane* of the *sancak* up to 911 purses 360 piastres. The difference stemmed from unregistered nomadic tribes who frequently crossed the Iranian border. As we have seen in Chapter 4, another extraordinary tax (*iane-i harbiye* or *iane-i cihadiye*) was also levied during the Crimean War.

We have seen in Chapter 3 that in the autumn of 1853 several confrontations took place between the Ottoman and Russian armies near Kars. Although the Ottomans won one of these battles, they faced a heavy defeat in the Battle of Başgedikler in December 1853. In this battle there were around 15,000 to 16,000 Kurdish irregular cavalry.

---

[87] Akyıldız, op. cit. (1996), p. 54.
[88] BOA. İ. MVL. 280/10958 enc. 1, 9 August 1853. Cf. Akyıldız, op. cit. (1996), p. 57. Akyıldız mentions the *mazbata* but does not quote from it.

But they dispersed very soon after the first shots. From then on Kurdish *başıbozuks* were not eager to go to war against Russian regular forces. In fact most of these irregulars came from borderline Kurdish nomadic tribes who were inclined towards plunder and robbery even in peacetime. Even before the war, they had engaged in plundering and even slave trade from Russian territory, and on account of these intrusions, the Russian embassy had handed the Ottoman government numerous protest notes.[89]

The British consul in Erzurum, in a letter to the British embassy in Istanbul, dated 25 June 1853, wrote that "in every part of the country the Koords are actively engaged in robbing, both on the high roads and in the villages". He stated that if the country was left "at the mercy of the Koords", then "incalculable injury to the cultivator" would ensue. He further stated:

> The militia has been called out, and altogether the forces to be collected here will, it is said, amount to about 40,000 disciplined troops. I hope that with such an imposing force the Porte and the General may not be tempted to make an attack on Georgia, as from the want of skill in the Turkish officers, there would not be much hope of success. But if Russia were to meet with reverses in Europe, so as to disable her from succouring Georgia, and if an [sic] European force were landed in that country to cooperate with the Turkish force, then indeed a forward movement, combined with an attack on the part of the Caucasian tribes would not fail to drive the Russians out of Georgia, for they would find few friends among the natives, were they to experience a reverse.[90]

We must add that the Russians too had their own *başıbozuks* (*militsiya*) from their Kurds and also some Ottoman Kurds who joined them. These Kurds formed two cavalry regiments of 1,500 men each, one under the command of Ahmet Ağa and the other under Cafer Ağa.[91] While both Ottomans and Russians tried to attract these Kurds from the borderlands to their own side, the tribesmen in general were not devoted to any one side, trying to appease both of them. Typically they tried to ascertain who would be the victor and to side with that party to avoid the results of having joined the wrong side. Furthermore

---

[89] Dr. Hasan Şahin, "Kırım Harbi (1853–1856) öncesinde Erzurum vilayetinde ve Doğu Anadolu Kafkas sınırında meydana gelen karışıklıklar", *Atatürk Üniversitesi Türkiyat Araştırmaları Enstitüsü Dergisi* 9, Erzurum, 1998, pp. 159–164.

[90] BOA. HR. SYS. 1191/1 enc. 8, 25 June 1853. From the British consulate in Erzurum.

[91] Ibragimbeyli, op. cit., p. 280.

they were more of a nuisance to any side than a real help because they were given to all the vices of the *başıbozuk*s in general. They did not even hesitate to plunder their own army quarters in the event of a defeat or retreat, and also robbed Armenian villages and caravans coming from Iran.

After the Battle of Başgedikler in December 1853, some fourteen Kurdish chiefs from the borderlands went to the Russian quarters at Gümrü (Aleksandropol) to reach an agreement with the Russian army. The task of developing relations with the Kurds was given to Colonel Loris-Melikov. Loris-Melikov also met Ahmet Ağa of the Zilanlı tribe (*aşiret*) in March 1854. Then in November he succeeded in gaining for the Russian side the allegiance of the powerful Kurdish chief Kasım Khan or Kasım Ağa who held the rank of kapucubaşı in the Ottoman service. Kasım Ağa was given the rank of colonel and the corresponding salary. Other chiefs also received valuable gifts; according to Colonel Williams, Kasım Ağa's 300 Kurds were accorded 6 silver roubles each.[92] If we compare this amount (equal to about 1 pound or 125 piastres) with the monthly pay of the Ottoman soldier (20 piastres, irregularly paid) and of the *başıbozuk* cavalry (80 piastres including rations), it becomes clear that the Russians paid better.

Nevertheless, these Kurds were not yet entirely out of Ottoman control. Thus Kasım Ağa had to obey the order of Zarif Mustafa Pasha, the governor of Erzurum and commander of the Anatolian army, to provide a cavalry force for the Sultan's army. But Kasım Ağa supplied only 200 men. According to the Russian military intelligence officer Pyotr Averyanov, although the Kurds could not openly abandon the Ottomans, every day their chiefs visited the Russian camp near Gümrü, promising that they would join the tsar's forces at the first retreat of the Turks towards Kars and that at the first Russian victory they would openly renounce their allegiance to the Turkish government.[93] In April 1855, General Muravyov reported to Russian war minister Prince Dolgorukov that Prince General Bebutov had reported his relations with the Kurdish chieftains. Bebutov had sent a Cossack regiment and the regiment of Colonel Loris-Melikov to the village of Kızıl Kilise in Kağızman. Loris-Melikov's tasks were to meet Kasım Khan and to

---

[92] Colonel Williams to the Earl of Clarendon. Erzurum, 7 December 1854. PRMA, No. 79, p. 74.

[93] Averyanov, op. cit. (1900), p. 93. Turkish translation is at Averyanov, op. cit. (1995), p. 54.

force him to make his position known, to meet the heads of the eleven Armenian and Karapapak villages on the frontier and to see how many irregular cavalry could be recruited from the Kurds.[94]

Thus those Kurds who had hoped for easy plunder by joining the Ottoman army at the beginning of the war were now very cautious of going against the Russians. They deserted from the Ottoman army. In fact at the battle of Kürekdere on 5 August 1854 their number fell to about five hundred. This battle proved devastating for the Ottoman war effort: an 18,000-strong Russian army had utterly defeated the 40,000-strong Ottoman army in an open field battle. From then on, few Kurds fought against the Russians in the Crimean War. The commander of the Russian forces in Erivan, Colonel Tsumpfort sent a letter dated 20 August (1 September) 1854 to Yezdanşêr.[95] In his letter the Russian commander warned Yezdanşêr not to participate in the Russo-Ottoman war.

At this time the situation was indeed very conducive to a revolt in Kurdistan. Ottoman forces were concentrated in Erzurum and Kars against the Russian army. Few regular troops remained in the countryside. For this reason some Kurdish tribes were now pillaging villages. For example, the Kurdish tribes of Abbas Uşağı and Pilvenkli in the sancak of Dersim belonging to the province of Harput had revolted and they were involved in banditry due to the lack of troops to hold them in check. The governor of Harput reported in July 1854 that the revolt of the "ill-natured Kurds" had been subdued.[96]

Yezdanşêr was ordered to recruit Kurdish infantry and cavalry for the Ottoman army from Cizre and Botan. He came to Cizre from Mosul with 200 cavalry and recruited 900 men. However, he soon came into conflict with Ottoman pashas over the amount of money due to him for his recruitment activities.[97] In the autumn of 1854, Yezdanşêr gave his first signs of disobedience. While it is not clear exactly at what point in time and how he rebelled, we might date the beginning to November 1854, because his salary was cut as of the end of the financial month of *Teşrin-i Evvel* 1270, which corresponds to 11 November

---

[94] General Muravyov to Prince Dolgorukov, 21 Mart/2 April 1855. AKAK, vol. XI, Tiflis, 1888, p. 79.
[95] Averyanov, op. cit., 109. An Ottoman Turkish translation of this letter is at BOA. İ. MVL. 353/15435, translated into modern Turkish by Hakan, op. cit., p. 287, p. 379.
[96] Governor of Harput to the grand vizier. BOA. A. MKT. UM. 163/35, 19 July 1854, the full transcription is in my paper in *Savaştan Barışa*, pp. 305–306.
[97] Hakan, op. cit., p. 286.

1854.⁹⁸ Lieutenant-Colonel Salih Bey from the Anatolian army was sent to him for negotiations. There are some petitions from Yezdanşêr in the BOA, probably sent through Salih Bey, written at various dates from November 1854 to January 1855. In these petitions, Yezdanşêr complains of the wrongdoings of some local officials (especially Osman Pasha, the *kaimmakam* of Mardin) towards him, trying to excuse himself, maintaining that his actions were not intended for a revolt. Nevertheless, there are other letters as well, by him and his brother Mansur Bey to some administrators of small districts (*kaza*), written in Arabic and Persian and captured by the Ottomans, wherein they urged these administrators (*müdirs*) to join them. These *müdirs* were most probably Kurdish notables themselves, who were given such little titles in return for their hereditary fiefs (*yurtluk* and *ocaklık*). Therefore the Porte did not, of course, accept Yezdanşêr's claims of innocence.⁹⁹

In one of his letters, dated 17 November 1854, Yezdanşêr wrote that Hacı Süleyman Ağa and Molla Sadık were engaged in conspiracy against him, and that the *kaimmakam* of Mardin, Osman Pasha, did not deliver to him the rations for the one thousand infantry and two hundred cavalry troops that he had mustered. Angered by this, he reported seizing these two conspirators and punishing them in some unspecified manner. Then he argued that if he had intentions of rebellion, he would have brought his family to his side, and as a further proof of his obedience he offered to send his son or his *kethüda* (steward) as hostage.¹⁰⁰

Yezdanşêr offered his terms for dispersing his troops and surrendering in a letter from Siirt, dated 7 January 1855. Firstly, his family in Mosul should be allowed to come to Cizre. Secondly, the districts of Cizre and Botan should be given to him and the district of Hacı Behram to his brother Mansur Bey. Both should be issued orders of amnesty (*rey ve aman buyruldusu*). Thirdly, Said Bey of Şirvan, holding the rank of *kapucubaşı*, should be made the *müdir* of Şirvan and should receive an amnesty. As a fourth point, troops garrisoned at Garzan and Midyat were to be removed, while Yezdanşêr's men, who were prisoners of war in Garzan, Midyat and Cizre were to be released. He still argued that he had come to Siirt on orders to levy 1,500 soldiers to

---

⁹⁸ Finance minister to the grand vizier, 9 August 1855. BOA. İ. DH. 21234.
⁹⁹ See the tezkire of the grand vizier, 21 February 1855. BOA. İ. MMS. 4/135 enc. 75.
¹⁰⁰ BOA. İ. MMS. 4/135 enc. 62.

join the Anatolian army in the spring. He stated his apprehension due to the plots of certain persons and indicated that he would continue to render good service if these plots and conspiracies against him were terminated.[101]

Despite what he wrote in his letters, Yezdanşêr captured Bitlis with a force of two thousand horsemen in January or February 1855. Then in the middle of February 1855, he attacked the town of Midyat and plundered it. The British consul in Diyarbekir reported this event as follows:

> Ezdeen shir Bey has lately attacked the district of Mediat which he has plundered and almost totally ruined. The Government troops, consisting solely of Bashi Bozuk, under a certain Abdullah Bey made little or no resistance, a portion returned to Mardin, and Abdullah Bey with the rest retired to his native village Sour between Mediat and Mardin, plundering all the villages on his way. He then tendered his resignation of his command which was accepted by Osman Pasha, Caimakam of Mardin without any kind of enquiry into his conduct…Troops, sent from Baghdad to Mosul to the amount of about three thousand regulars and four thousands bashi bozuk, are now said to be on their march towards Jezireh. His movement has caused Ezdeen shir Bey to withdraw from Mediat towards that place, and has prevented a threatened attack on Mardin.[102]

It was also reported that Yezdanşêr had developed friendly relations with the Arabs in the vicinity of Mardin by sending them rich presents. His successes had greatly encouraged him, and it was believed that if he could disperse the government troops now on their way to Cizre, the Arabs would unite with him to attack and pillage Mosul. Yezdanşêr would then control Mosul, Siirt and Van. Meanwhile the rebellion grew in size. Apart from Kurds, many Arabs, Nasturians and Greeks joined his forces.

While Averyanov and some Kurdish historians write that the number of rebel forces reached 60,000 or even 100,000, these figures are obviously very much exaggerated.[103] Nevertheless, the number of participants in this rebellion was probably higher than those who had followed Bedirhan. Some Ottoman sources also confirmed that the

---

[101] BOA. İ. MMS. 4/135 enc. 67, 7 January 1855. For the full-text transcription of this document, see my paper in *Savaştan Barışa*, pp. 309–311.

[102] BOA. HR. TO. 221/14, 15 February 1855. This report was sent to the British embassy in Constantinople and from there it was forwarded to the Ottoman foreign ministry. See my paper in *Savaştan Barışa*, pp. 311–312.

[103] Averyanov, op. cit., 1900, p. 149. Celile Celil (op. cit., p. 164) agrees with him.

revolt of İzzeddin Şir was a greater problem. For example, the *kaimmakam* of the *sancak* of Zaho (that included Cizre, Hacı Behram and Bohtan as well) reported that the rebellion was by far larger than that of Bedirhan, with a union and cohesion among the Kurds unheard of since the time of the conquest of Kurdistan by the Ottomans, and with unequaled violent battles.[104] However, these expressions must also be viewed with caution because the *kaimmakam* of Zaho was interested in exaggerating the number of insurgents so that his services would be better appreciated.

Yezdanşêr had also written letters to the Russian army command proposing a joint operation. He thought the Russian army to be in Bayezid, but it had retreated to Erivan to spend the winter. Thus his letters most probably did not reach the Russian command.[105] It is doubtful whether the Russian army would have taken steps even if the letters had arrived, because at that time Prince Bebutov was behaving very cautiously or had received orders not to move too far beyond Erivan.

British Interference and the Suppression of the Rebellion

Meanwhile the allies of the Ottoman Empire, in other words Britain and France began to worry about the growth of this rebellion and the consequent weakening of the eastern front. Britain especially was anxious to prevent the revolt from spreading and becoming more serious; as a result, the British consul in Mosul was given the task of negotiating between Yezdanşêr and Ottoman authorities. On the other hand, the British military commissioner with the Anatolian army, General Williams had met Yezdanşêr in Cizre in 1849, then as Lieutenant-Colonel Williams, British representative in a commission for the resolution of a border issue between the Porte and Iran.[106] Williams had decided at that time to give Yezdanşêr a guarantee on his life and property if he would take refuge in the British consulate at Mosul. According to Adolphus Slade, Williams "had been led to believe him [Yezdanşêr] an

---

[104] *Mahzar* (memorial or petition) of the *sancak* of Zaho, 15 January 1854. BOA. A. MKT. UM. 150/86.
[105] Averyanov, op. cit., 1900, p. 109. Halfin, op. cit., p. 59. Celil, op. cit., p. 165.
[106] The commission included Ferik Derviş Pasha from the Ottoman side, Mirza Cafer Han from Iran and Russian Colonel E. I. Chirikov as well. See Celile Celil, op. cit., pp. 152–153.

oppressed man".[107] Williams had, in his report to Clarendon, dated 12 December 1854, interpreted the news of the revolt as follows:

> Sinister rumours of the insurrection of the Koords at Sert [Siirt], and in the direction of Bitlis, have reached me: this is the natural result of the robbery of the Bashi-Bozouks' pay by Zarif Mustafa Pasha, and Hassan Yaziji of Damascus. These men returned to their camps full of discontent and vengeance against those who, instead of robbing them, should have led them against the enemy…[108]

General Williams did not want any detachments from the Anatolian army to be sent to suppress the revolt, because he was worried that this would weaken its position against the Russians. Therefore he wrote to Lord Stratford to urge the Porte not to use any part of the Anatolian army against this revolt.[109] Lord Stratford accordingly advised the Porte not to send a detachment from the army at Kars against Yezdanşêr, but instead to use troops from Constantinople, joined by others from Syria (Aleppo). Apparently the Porte accepted this proposal and decided to use troops from Baghdad as well. Nevertheless, Williams reported to Stratford that upon orders from Istanbul, Şükrü ("Shukri") Pasha, the acting commander-in-chief of the Anatolian army, had ordered a regiment of infantry, a regiment of cavalry and a battery of six guns to leave Toprakkale to advance upon Siirt and Cizre. Therefore Lord Stratford gave a written instruction to the head dragoman Stephen Pisani, to be read to Grand Vizier Reşid Pasha, which reads in part as follows:

> Besides the contradiction which is thus shown to exist between fact and assurance, it appears that, Toprak-Kaleh is the most important outpost of the Kars army, that the detachment could never reach its destination, owing to the deep snow and intense cold, and finally, that so hazardous a measure as the one in question was adopted without reference to the opinion of the British commissioner and by orders transmitted from Constantinople.
> You will read what precedes to Reshid Pasha, and you will express the deep concern with which I contemplate this inconsistency of conduct on the part of Government, over which he presides. You will prepare him for the impression which will be made in England by a knowledge of the circumstances, and you will observe how impossible it is for the allies to

---
[107] Slade, op. cit., pp. 423–24.
[108] Colonel Williams to the Earl of Clarendon. Erzeroom, December 12, 1854. PRMA, p. 68.
[109] Lord Stratford de Redcliffe to the Earl of Clarendon, 19 February 1855. PRMA, p. 130.

act with any confidence of success, or to provide for their own responsibility, if the principal functionaries of the Porte exhibit so lamentable a want of fair dealing and common prudence.[110]

According to Pisani's report, Reşid Pasha did not accept "the charge of having dealt inconsistently and unfairly with Her Majesty's Embassy". He said that the order to Şükrü Pasha was made long before Stratford's representation to the Porte. Upon Stratford's suggestions, the *serasker* had sent a counter-order to abstain from detaching any of the troops under his command, informing him that the Porte had adopted other measures to quell the disturbances. Pisani also reported the Reşid Pasha had given verbal instructions to the new commander-in-chief (Vasıf Pasha), two days prior to his departure, to prevent any of the troops of the army at Kars or Erzurum leaving their posts. As to the non-reference to the opinion of the British Commissioner, Reşid Pasha

> observed that Shukri Pasha was not bound to do so, because the orders he received from his superiors were peremptory, and consequently could on no account disregard them without swerving from his duty. The British Commissioner, added he, has a right to be consulted on matters immediately connected with the army in general, but not to interfere with orders issued direct from the Porte to its own officers on internal questions.[111]

Lord Stratford sent to the Earl of Clarendon, the British foreign minister, copies of his instruction to Pisani and Pisani's report of Reşid Pasha's reply, expressing his regret in a highly patronizing tone:

> It is a matter of regret that Reshid Pasha allowed so important a step as the withdrawal of a portion, however comparatively small, of the army at Kars from the defensive positions which it occupies, to be taken without the knowledge of Her Majesty's Embassy, and I intend to apprize him in becoming language of my opinion in that respect.[112]

Meanwhile Williams decided to act on his own and he sent a messenger to Yezdanşêr; this was a certain Major Mahmud Ağa or Mahmud Efendi, a Polish convert enrolled in the Anatolian army in Kars, who had come to Erzurum on duty. According to the reports of three pashas,

---

[110] Lord Stratford de Redcliffe to M. E. Pisani, 17 February 1855. PRMA, p. 131.
[111] M. E. Pisani to Lord Stratford de Redcliffe, Pera, 18 February 1855. PRMA, p. 131.
[112] Stratford to Clarendon, 19 February 1855. PRMA, No. 136, p. 130.

namely Hamdi Pasha, ex-governor of Diyarbekir[113] and now governor of Kastamonu, *kaimmakam* Osman Pasha of Mardin and *kaimmakam* Kenan Pasha of Siirt, this Mahmud Ağa went directly to Yezdanşêr, without ever visiting the commander of the Ottoman forces surrounding the rebellious dignitary.[114] In his letter to Yezdanşêr, dated 28 January 1855, Williams told him that the authorities were aware of his correspondence with Kurdish chiefs in Van, Bitlis and Muş. In his capacity as the special commissioner of Her Britannic Majesty, holding the rank of *ferik* from the Sultan, Williams warned Yezdanşêr not to go against three states. Williams guaranteed life and property to Yezdanşêr on behalf of Britain and France, if he surrendered on his own.[115]

On the other hand, the British doctor Humphry Sandwith, the medical inspector in the Anatolian army under General Williams, writes in his memoirs that Mahmud Efendi visited first the Ottoman commander Kavaklı Mehmed Pasha, who on learning Mahmud's mission arrested him, believing that he was about to capture Yezdanşêr. However, for fear of the influence of General Williams, Mehmed Pasha later released Mahmud, who went to Yezdanşêr, giving him the letters with which he had been entrusted.[116] Yezdanşêr accepted Williams' offer of terms and promised to go to the British consulate in Mosul to surrender together with his brother Mansur Bey and his retinue. Mahmud believed in the promises of Yezdanşêr and wrote to Ferik Veli Pasha of the Anatolian army that there was no need for his coming. Finally Yezdanşêr, his brother Mansur Bey, Şirvanlı Said Bey and Ibrahim Bey, son of Said Bey of Hacı Behram went to Mosul together with Major Mahmud and took refuge in the British consulate. Sandwith fully endorsed the initiative of Williams as a "bold and prompt measure", that "effected in a few

---

[113] Although that province (*eyalet*) was formally known as the province of Kurdistan at that time, we see in grand vizier Reşid Pasha's petition to Sultan Abdülmecid the expression of "*Diyarbekir eyaleti*" as well. This suggests that both names were being used interchangeably.

[114] BOA. İ. DH. 20545. March 1855. See my paper in *Savaştan Barışa*, pp. 313–314. Sinan Hakan (op. cit., pp. 296–299) seems to be unaware that this Mahmud Efendi and Mahmud Ağa are the same person. Hakan guesses that Mahmud Efendi was probably the famous "Mele Mahmud-i Bazidi", which is not correct. Hakan also mentions the "King" of Britain (*İngiliz Kralı*) twice as guarantor, being unaware that at that time Queen Victoria sat on the British throne.

[115] BOA. İ. MVL. 353/15435, quoted in simplified form by Hakan, op. cit., pp. 295–296.

[116] Humphry Sandwith. *A Narrative of the Siege of Kars*. London: John Murray, 1856, 3rd edition, p. 213.

days what it would have taken a larger Turkish army than that under Mehemed Cavakli Pasha as many months to accomplish". Arguing that Williams probably saved the southern half of Turkey in Asia, Sandwith writes in arrogant, unmistakably Orientalist tones:

> The word of an Englishman has such magic power in the East, that this rebel, when he had ascertained the validity of Mahmoud Effendi's mission, at once chose rather to deliver himself up to the safekeeping of the Consul at Mosul, than run the risk of a hazardous mountain campaign, with followers difficult to manage, and ready to desert their colours on the least reverse. Not all the promises of all the viziers and pashas of the Turkish Empire could have enticed this wary chief into their power, since he well knew the faithlessness of such men.[117]

Comparing the accounts by Sandwith and Williams with those of Hamdi, Osman and Kenan Pashas, it is not easy to establish the truth. If Williams had not interfered, would Yezdanşêr still have been captured or forced to surrender by the forces of Kavaklı Mehmed Pasha? We can only speculate on this question. Williams, on the other hand, defending his action in his reply to Ambassador Stratford de Redcliffe, stated that he had obtained the consent of the Ottoman pashas and that he had not assumed a right or an authority to make proposals to the rebel chief, but he had "entirely thrown himself on the favourable interpretation of Her Majesty's Government", and also on that of His Excellency (the Ambassador). He begged to remark:

1. That Mahmoud Effendi the officer in question was desired by Kherim Pasha, the officer in command at Kars to wait on me to put into my hands the letters of the traitor's correspondence with the enemy and to follow my directions. I therefore inclosed those letters to Your Excellency, and detained Mahmoud Effendi to fulfill the mission to the rebel Kurdish chief.
2. Before drawing up these letters, I consulted with the Governor General of this province, and also with Shukri Pasha, who pronounced the project as one worthy of being tried to save the flames of rebellion from spreading throughout Kurdistan.
3. The Governor's secretary wrote these letters for me, by the permission of His Excellency.

---

[117] Ibid., pp. 214–215.

4. The Defterdar of the Army supplied Mahmoud Effendi with the necessary funds for prosecuting his journey; and the Governor General gave that officer orders for horses etc.
5. My having made the personal acquaintance of the rebel at Jezireh in 1849, induced us all to hope that he would not turn a deaf ear to my appeal.[118]

If these points are correct, it becomes evident that Williams did not act on his own. Nevertheless, this may also show the helplessness of the pashas in Erzurum against him. When Major Mahmud and the Kurdish chiefs arrived in Mosul, the Ottoman pasha residing there tried to get them into his control. Nevertheless, the French consul did not turn them over even in the absence of the British consul. So Yezdanşêr and his associates in rebellion remained in Mosul until September 1855 and were then sent to Constantinople via Diyarbekir under heavy guard.

The rebel forces dispersed very quickly after the surrender of Yezdanşêr, his brother Mansur and some other chiefs. On the other hand, during the entire period of Yezdanşêr's revolt, the Russian army remained too cautious and lost a most favourable opportunity to catch the Ottoman army between two fires by coordinating their actions with those of the Kurdish rebels. Averyanov also argued in the same manner that, had Yezdanşêr postponed his revolt until spring, when the newly appointed Russian commander and Caucasian Viceroy General Nikolai Muravyov arrived, he could have received help from the Russians. But Prince Bebutov, the commander of the Russian army in Erivan, opposed all proposals to attack Van and to join the Kurds.[119]

Yezdanşêr, Mansur and their retinue were imprisoned in Istanbul, where they remained until April 1856 when they were subsequently exiled to Vidin. In the meantime the MVL had tried him and found him guilty of killing sixty civilians, in addition to his crimes against the state. Nevertheless, on learning of the exile of Yezdanşêr and his retinue to Vidin without prior agreement with him, Stratford de Redcliffe protested in an official note to Foreign Minister Fuad Pasha on 17 April 1856. Stratford reminded Fuad Pasha that while he (Stratford)

---

[118] BOA. HR. TO. 221/18, 4 March 1855. An extract from Williams' letter to Stratford was presented to the Ottoman foreign ministry, bearing the title of "Excuses for and explanations of his reason for sending Mahmoud Effendi to Yez-di-sheer Bey". See my paper in *Savaştan Barışa*, p. 312.
[119] Averyanov, op. cit., p. 87.

was "unwilling to interfere in a matter of internal concern", nevertheless, Yezdanşêr and his retinue had surrendered to a British Officer and he (Stratford) had handed them over to the authority of the Porte provided that "their lives and properties being spared, they should be tried by the Supreme Council, and on conviction be disposed of according to what should be agreed upon between the Porte and Her Majesty's Embassy". Stratford maintained that "the offenders" remained at the department of the *serasker* several months without trial. Stratford then wrote that, three days ago, his

> attention was drawn to the unexpected circumstance of their having been sent away from Constantinople without any previous communication of the proceedings instituted against them, or any preconcerted arrangement for their ultimate disposal. This negligence is the more to be regretted as questions of property were at issue, and Her Majesty's Government in sanctioning the promise given to Yez-di-sheer Bey, that his property as well as his life should be spared did not lose sight of the circumstances which throw a suspicion on his manner of acquiring that property, and give a presumptive claim upon part of it, at least, to those whom his violence and cruelty had despoiled.
>
> The Undersigned remembers that when he had the honor of being received in private by Fuad Pasha more than a fortnight since, His Excellency spoke incidentally of the Porte's inclination to send the above mentioned rebels into exile, to which he could have seen no objection, if the concerted engagements had been previously fulfilled, and his Government duly apprized of the intended decision.
>
> On learning the real state of the case from Mr. Pisani, the Undersigned conveyed to Fuad Pasha his expectation that the rebels, who had surrendered to a British officer, and been transferred under agreement to the Porte, should be brought back to Constantinople as the only effective way of correcting the error which had been committed, and enabling the Porte to redeem the pledge which it had previously given to Her Majesty's Embassy.
>
> The Undersigned formed an additional cause of surprise in learning from His Excellency that the required measure would be deemed a disparagement of the Sovereign's dignity. Surely no movements, however inconvenient to himself, of a rebel in custody of the Porte's officers, could have such an effect. The only point of view, in which the interpretation can be admitted, is that of the change being occasioned by foreign interference. But in the present case there was a previous agreement, founded on very peculiar circumstances, between the Porte and the Embassy, and,

if there were really any question of disparagement, it could only result from the neglect of that agreement.[120]

Upon this note, Fuad Pasha replied first verbally that the matter had already been agreed upon between them and then in an official, carefully worded note, explained how the Sublime Porte amnestied a savage criminal, deserving capital punishment under any law, simply out of respect for its ally; he enclosed a list of the crimes committed by the rebel against the population.[121]

Yezdanşêr and his associates fled to Bosnia in January 1858, but they were captured and returned to their exile in Vidin in April 1858.[122] A year later his family was allowed to join him in exile. Furthermore, his due receipts from some Kurdish notables were collected and sent to him. In 1865 the brothers applied for an appointment in state service. In reply, it was said that they were now free within the *vilayet* of *Tuna* (the Danube), but they still had to wait for some time to get appointed to state service. Finally Yezdanşêr was appointed as the administrator of the district of Adliye within the province of *Tuna*, and then in 1868 became the *mutasarrıf* of Janina.[123] He died probably in this post, in the 1870s.[124]

Desertions and the Başıbozuk *Troops as a Source of Disorder*

During the Crimean War, Ottoman recruits were caught in their villages, by way of arresting anyone who happened to be eligible, without subjecting them to the formal draft. This was especially true where the Anatolian Egyptian levies were concerned. As a result, desertions from the Ottoman army were numerous, having began even before the war. Especially the reserve troops (*redif*), who were middle-aged, married men with families to feed, tended to desert at the first opportunity. For

---

[120] Stratford de Redcliffe to Fuad Pasha, 17 April 1856. BOA. HR. TO. 222/59. Official translation into Turkish is in BOA. İ. HR. 131/6698 enc. 1, 3 June 1856. See my paper in *Savaştan Barışa*, pp. 317–320.

[121] BOA. İ. HR. 131/6698 enc. 2. See my paper in *Savaştan Barışa*, pp. 321–323.

[122] BOA. A. MKT. MHM. 130/74. Cf. Hakan, op. cit., pp. 304–305. Hakan refers to another document from the BOA.

[123] BOA. A. MKT. UM. 374/53, A. MKT. UM. 387/29, A. MKT. UM. 396/68, İ. MVL. 535/24032, A. MKT. MHM. 407/76.

[124] Mehmed Süreyya, op. cit., vol. 3, p. 845.

example, in August 1853, five hundred *redif* soldiers on their way to Erzurum deserted in the vicinity of Sivas and Tokat, becoming outlaws and robbing caravans and passengers. They had also killed a Greek on the way to Amasya.[125] According to Ferik Ali Rıza Pasha, thirty *redif* soldiers deserted on their way from Kars to Ardahan in October 1853.[126] According to Doctor Sandwith, early in 1855, "desertions had become so numerous that it was well-known the province of Sivas alone contained 10,000 men who had left their colours".[127]

Some of the soldiers who deserted from the Kars army during the siege of Kars in 1855 were taken prisoner by the Russians and returned during the exchange of prisoners after the end of the war. Upon their return to Istanbul by ships, these deserters were tried at the military court (*Divan-ı Harb*) presided by Ferik Hafız Pasha. Thus we have the opportunity to "hear" soldiers' voices as recorded in the court records. One of them, Sergeant Said of Muş, from the 8th company of the 3rd battalion of the 4th regular infantry regiment of the Anatolian army said during his interrogation that although he had been proposed for promotion to the rank of lieutenant, he received only a sergeant's salary for two years during his service in Kars and he became indebted. His children in his home-town were left starving. Said then stated that he decided to go to Erzurum and told the doctor (Tabip Ahmed Efendi) about his intention, whereupon the doctor urged him to take his (the doctor's) horse as well. He fled during the night and was caught by the Russians. Said repeatedly indicated that the reasons for his desertion were debt and hunger. Nevertheless he had re-married in Kars. To the question of why he left his wife in Kars, he answered that his wife's father could take care of her and he fled because "one's own life is dearer than everything".[128]

Another deserter, Sergeant Osman of Istanbul, from the 7th company of the 1st battalion of the 2nd regular infantry regiment of the Anatolian army also answered that his desertion was due to hunger.

---

[125] Grand vizier to the serasker, 30 August 1853. BOA. A. MKT. NZD. 88/46. For the transcription of this document, see my paper in *Savaştan Barışa*, 2007, p. 301.

[126] Ali Rıza Pasha's statement. BOA. İ. MMS. 3/107 enc. 4. On desertions from the Anatolian army before and during the war, also see BOA. A. MKT. UM. 162/53, 9 August 1854, from the governor of Sivas on desertions after the battle of İncedere (Kürekdere). Also see Colonel Atwell Lake, *A Narrative of the Defence of Kars*. London: Richard Bentley, 1857, p. 132.

[127] Sandwith, op. cit., p. 229.

[128] *Mazbata* of the *Divan-ı Harb*, BOA. İ. DH. 362/23964, 12 October 1856.

When asked whether he received less rations than others, he said that they all received equal rations but he could not endure hunger any more. In his own words, Sergeant Osman had deserted forty-five days after the Battle of Tahmas, meaning the Battle of Kars on 29 September 1855; Tahmas was one of the bastions of Kars. He thus had left the Ottoman army seven days before the fall of Kars. The interrogators also questioned Corporal Halil and Captain Ibrahim Ağa about Osman's desertion. Captain Ibrahim said that there were five soldiers together with Sergeant Osman who all deserted during their night duty. Corporal Halil reported that Sergeant Osman had taken him and Corporal Hasan for duty. They told him that they would desert and asked him to go with them. However, Halil did not accept, while the other two deserted.

The *başıbozuk* or the *asakir-i muvazzafa* as they were called officially, had always been a source of trouble.[129] They robbed and killed civilians wherever they stayed or happened to pass through. While they committed crimes against all populations, the non-Muslims were affected more because, being unarmed, they were more vulnerable. During the Crimean War the *başıbozuk*s continued their atrocities and plunder. However, this time the Ottoman authorities reacted more energetically due to the presence of allied officers. Now that the British and French embassies were in an excellent position to dictate policy, they pressurized the Porte to control the *başıbozuk* and to prevent their atrocities. In this respect Stratford de Redcliffe really stands out: apparently he submitted more official notes to the Porte than all other ambassadors put together. Aided by the network of British consuls spread out all over the Ottoman Empire, the British ambassador was well-informed of many events even before Ottoman ministers heard of them and he energetically pressed for measures.

The Ottoman foreign ministry political section (HR. SYS) collections of the BOA contain many extracts from British consular reports submitted to the Sublime Porte. These reports include complaints about *başıbozuk*s and also about the pashas who were supposed to control the *başıbozuk*s. Similar complaints about local officials were also sent by individuals and local *meclises*, but those councils were in most cases in

---

[129] James Reid (op. cit., p. 270) argued that they were also called *muâvine asker* (auxiliary troops), probably referring to Mahmud Nedim Pasha during his governorship of Beirut. My research in the BOA has shown that in the context of the Crimean War the words *asakir-i muâvine* meant the allied troops.

Illus. 19 Başıbozuks coming into Shumla from Machin. *ILN*, 13 May 1854.

the hands of the governor who dictated his will. Certainly, non-Muslim members of these local councils, the primates (*kocabaşı*) were not in a position to influence its decisions. It is even doubtful that they fully understood what was written in the *mazbata* (council resolutions) to which they put their seals.

The mobilization of the *başıbozuk* troops started in the summer of 1853 and the reports from British consulates started to come in at this time as well. The first reports seem to have come from places like Amasya, Thessaly, Salonica and Damascus, where Muslims and Christians lived close to each other. Thessaly and Salonica were sensitive areas of Greek nationalism and later insurgence, where some Albanian and other *başıbozuk* troops were concentrated. As early as 15 June 1853, a British consular report probably from Trabzon stated that the *redif* troops had committed "excesses" towards Christians in Amasya.[130] Lord Stratford immediately sent a note to Reşid Pasha, protesting the "insults and offences" against "persons under British protection".[131] This suggests that these Christians were probably Protestants. Then we have the following report in July 1853 from the British consulate in Salonica:

> By the last accounts up to the 19th instant, which I have received from Volo and Larissa, the alarm still continues both in consequence of the conduct of the irregular troops and the number of other Albanians in that vicinity, who have come to Thessaly in the hopes of being employed by the several chiefs. The irregulars are also clamorous for the pay which is due to them...
>
> The Archbishop of Salonica has received intelligence of the Greek monastery on Mount Olympus having been plundered of every thing, and that the monks were afterwards tormented in the, I may say, now usual Thessalian way; viz., with drops of boiling oil upon their chests, because they did not confess where the money of the monastery was secreted. There is also advice that another monastery in the vicinity Cosnia has been plundered and the monks tormented in the same way with drops of boiling oil. These sacrileges are supposed to have been committed by the disbanded Derbent troops of Haggi Hussein Pasha. There can be no doubt but that the Christians will suffer in certain districts during the passage of the irregular troops to their homes, in the event of present differences being arranged, without coming to hostilities, unless indeed the Porte provide for the safety of the people either by the escort of each

---

[130] Extrait d'une lettre d'Amasia. BOA. HR. SYS. 1190/1 enc. 3, 15 June 1853.
[131] Stratford to Monsieur Etienne Pisani. BOA. HR. SYS. 1190/1 enc. 1, 22 June 1853.

corps of irregulars by a troop of cavalry, or conveying them by steamers to the coast of Albania. These irregulars enlist more for plunder than patriotism.[132]

The consul also suggested that an "active military man of rank" with some troops should be appointed to command all irregular chiefs from his head quarters in Larissa.[133]

Another report from the British consulate in Damascus at about the same time stated that a certain Resul Ağa's "300 Koordish irregular horsemen" had robbed and killed 12 persons at Raşiye (Rasheya).[134]

The grand vizier wrote orders to the commander of the Rumeli army Ömer Lütfi Pasha and to the governor of Tırhala on 29 October 1853. In the instructions to Ömer Pasha, the translation of a report submitted to the Sublime Porte on the disorders of the *başıbozuk* troops in some places, is said to have been attached. (This is most probably another British or French consular report). The grand vizier wrote that needless to say, it was necessary in those troublesome days to satisfy all subjects of the state more than ever and not to offend them in any way, and to protect their property and honour. However, the grand vizier stated, the *başıbozuk* troops were perpetrating all kinds of cruel and indecent treatment towards some wretched people and other subjects. The grand vizier then referred to the recently issued imperial order and those sent to all the commanders from his own office, demanding the prevention of such actions.[135]

The order to the governor of Tırhala also mentioned an enclosure, a letter from Yenişehir-i Fenar, whose author has not been indicated, concerning the atrocities of the *başıbozuks* employed in that region. As the central authorities pointed out, such actions were very harmful and caused all kinds of evil especially at the current and most critical time. The governor was accordingly ordered to prevent these atrocities.

We have seen that *başıbozuk* troops committed excesses in Şekvetil, Ahıska and around Gümrü, particularly in Armenian villages. They also decapitated some enemy troops or even civilians in order to receive cash rewards. At Bayındır, the irregular cavalry brought about one hundred severed heads to Ahmed Pasha who gave 50 piastres each to the men who handed them over, officially registering their names.

---

[132] BOA. HR. SYS. 1928/14 enc. 2.
[133] Salonica, July 11, 1853. BOA. HR. SYS. 1928/14 enc. 1.
[134] BOA. HR. TO. 219/50, 16 July and 1 August 1853.
[135] BOA. HR. SYS. 1345/41, 29 October 1853.

Then he had the severed heads loaded into carts and sent to Kars to the *müşir*.[136] Ahmed Pasha had also sent the *müdir* of the *kaza* of Şüregel Meded Bey together with some chiefs of Kurdish tribes such as Kasım Ağa of the Zilanlı tribe, Beto (Tebo?) and Hasan Beys of the Kaskan tribe, Serhenk Ağa of the Cemedanlı tribe and the like to a Cossack village called Tuhaber (?) on the Russian side. They had plundered the village and taken some prisoners as slaves. The military *meclis* in Erzurum stated that they heard that Ahmed Pasha had taken one of the slave girls as odalisque for himself, but Abdi Pasha had made him release her. Other slaves had remained in the hands of the Kurdish chiefs.

Inspector Hayreddin Pasha also asked the *meclis* about 10,200 cattle and horses, 29,838 sheep, 2,760 *somar*s (about 550 tons) of barley and 3,280 *somar*s (about 650 tons) of wheat that was said to have been plundered from some ten villages. The Erzurum *meclis* stated that such acts of plunder were committed by the local tribes and voluntary troops with the approval of Ahmed Pasha but no regular and irregular troops were sent to villages for plunder. Abdi Pasha replied that it was rumoured that the "Revan tribe" had plundered some Russian villages and returned to Ottoman territory and probably this news had been distorted. Sergerde Hasan Yazıcı on the other hand, during his interrogation after the war, said that he had not been to the battle of Gümrü (Bayındır) under Ahmed Pasha, but he had heard that "a lot of things were taken". Before the battle of Kürekdere, he had raided Bayındır under the command of İsmail Pasha (General Kmety). There, he said, troops took some oxen and buffaloes as booty (*iğtinam*) but this was a "trifling" amount and he brought 27 of those oxen to the army, while the rest, being sheep, were eaten up by the troops.[137]

At the beginning of March 1854, the Armenian Patriarch and the *meclis* of the Armenian *millet* applied to the grand vizier, complaining about the atrocities and plundering of the *başıbozuk* volunteers on their way to the Anatolian army (to Erzurum and Kars). According to the petition of the Armenian patriarch and the *meclis*, these *başıbozuk*s had collected by force 5,000 to 10,000 piastres each for their chiefs (*başbuğ*) and 40 to 50 piastres for each *başıbozuk*. They also had collected horses from the reaya in the districts of Eğin, Arapkir, Kuruçay,

---

[136] BOA. İ. MMS. 3/107 enc. 3, question 15.
[137] Interrogation of Hasan Yazıcı, 15 May 1856. BOA. A. M...15/18 enc. 1.

Çemişkezek and Divriği in the provinces of Harput and Sivas. They had severely beaten those who could not pay the amounts demanded, entered houses, demanded food and even dishonoured women. They had also closed churches during Easter for fifteen days in some places. Therefore the patriarch and the *meclis* asked for orders to be sent to the administrators of the region to prevent these outrages.[138] The grand vizier sent appropriate orders to the governors of Harput and Sivas and to other governors and *mutasarrıfs*.[139]

In March 1854, the British consuls in Varna, Edirne and Erzurum also reported on pillaging and other disorders caused by the *başıbozuks*. The British consul at Varna reported to Lord Stratford on 12 March 1854 on the outrages and disorders perpetrated by "Turkish irregular troops" in the vicinity of Rahova (Rassova) on the Danube. According to him,

> A party of Mokans (Transylvanian shepherds) driven by the concentration of Russian troops in Wallachia, sought refuge with their flocks on an island situated opposite Rassova. The Turkish irregular troops appear to have gone over to the island and although the Mokans stated that they were Austrian subjects and occupied the island for no hostile purpose and urged in proof of this statement that they were unarmed thirty of their number were decapitated on the spot and six or seven thousand sheep were carried off by the Bashi Bozuks. One of the Mokans who escaped has arrived in Varna, and the depositions he has made upon this event form the subject of a report which the Austrian Vice-Consul here has addressed by this occasion to the Internuncio.[140]

The consul added that similar and still greater atrocities had been committed by the *başıbozuks* upon the inhabitants of the village of Keserler, five hours distant from Rahova. The women were dishonoured and many of the men and children killed. Those who managed to escape had fled to the woods.

Thanks to regular steamship mails between Varna and Istanbul, the report reached Istanbul quickly and Stratford lost no time in remonstrating with the Porte, although the shepherds were Austrian subjects. The tone of his instructions to his head dragoman, to be read to Reşid Pasha, was indignant and even vehement:

---

[138] BOA. HR. SYS. 1347/18 enc. 1, 2 March 1854.
[139] BOA. HR. SYS. 1347/18 enc. 2.
[140] Lt. Col. Edward St. John Neale to Stratford de Redcliffe, 12 March 1854. BOA. HR. SYS. 904/1 enc. 125.

Not many days have elapsed since I reported the crimes which had been perpetrated by the Bashi-Bosooks at Eski-Zaara and other places in that neighbourhood and the Turkish minister promised to redress by adequate measures the wrongs of which I complained.

The steamer from Varna has brought in this morning a fresh catalogue of crimes perpetrated by the same people. I inclose Consul Neale's dispatch describing the disorderly and atrocious acts which he so justly reprobates. The places where these acts occurred are an island *on the Danube near Russova* and *Kesserler* five hours distant from that place. The decapitation of thirty shepherds and the plunder of their numerous flocks are circumstances which, standing in connection with each other exhibit at once the sanguinary character of the *Bashi-Boosooks* and motive of their cold blooded cruelty. Such outrages on humanity are a dishonor to the country where they occur and to the army which allows their perpetrators to cooperate with it. Measures must be adopted to check them, or it will ultimately be found impossible for Christian Powers to act in concert with the Turkish Authorities…

There is no excuse to be found for this shameful indifference either in religion or in policy. True religion cannot possibly warrant such horrors. The professors of a religion acting with such barbarous inhumanity would deserve to be treated as the enemies of mankind. As for policy, the true policy of the Porte is to obtain the sympathies of Christendom and to maintain discipline in its armies. The Bashi-Boozooks are notorious cowards in presence of the enemy. All their prowess is exhausted in ravaging their Sovereign's country, and slaughtering his peaceful subjects. They are worse than useless. Their disorders unsettle the regular army; their example disheartens the good soldier.

I repeat that means must be found to put down so intolerable a scandal, and I call upon the Porte to acquaint me with its intentions in this respect.[141] [Italics are underlined in the original]

Within a few days the consul in Erzurum also wrote on the plundering of the helpless peasants in the neighbouring villages by the *başıbozuk* troops. He added that he heard that the infamous *başıbozuk* chief Hasan Yazıcı had been arrested by Selim Pasha in Bayezid.[142] Another consular report from Edirne stated that the *başıbozuks* from Maraş and Ankara had committed atrocities on their way to Şumnu.[143] Another British consular report stated that the Muslim and non-Muslim notables of Yenişehir-i Fenar were demanding that regular troops be sent to disperse the *başıbozuks*. These inhabitants also stated that if the Sublime

---

[141] BOA. HR. SYS. 904/1 enc. 130–131, 14 March 1854.
[142] BOA. HR. SYS. 1347/21 and HR. TO. 220/18, 16 March 1854.
[143] BOA. HR. TO. 220/16, 16 March 1854.

Porte did not send troops, then they would apply to the insurgents who were already offering their services to free the people from the tyranny of the *başıbozuks*.[144]

British chief engineer General Sir John Burgoyne wrote from Varna to Lord Stratford that some inhabitants of villages around Şumnu and Varna complained to him about the insults that the *başıbozuk* had perpetrated against them and especially against their wives and daughters. According to this letter, the inhabitants were ready to provide residences, provisions and horse fodder and even to spend money on the *başıbozuk*; but they asked only for personal protection for themselves and their families. Burgoyne suggested to have small detachments of regular cavalry troops or mounted gendarmes, who would go round the villages, obtain the necessary information, and have the authority to punish culprits in a summary way.[145] At the beginning of April 1854 Stratford again applied to the Porte about the disorders of the Albanian *başıbozuks* under the command of Nureddin Ağa.[146] Another complaint regarding the irregular troops came from the Prussian embassy, which stated that the oppressions of Christian subjects at the hands of these quite worthless irregular troops could turn European public opinion against the Porte.[147]

The British officer George Palmer Evelyn noted that the *başıbozuk* cavalry in Ömer Pasha's army committed "great ravages and atrocities, violating and murdering women, and burning villages" during the retreat of the Ottoman army from Maçin in April 1854.[148]

On 18 April 1854 Sultan Abdülmecid issued a firman ordering the punishment of the unlawful acts of the *başıbozuks*.[149] The firman was published on 7 May 1854 in the *Takvim-i Vekayi*.[150] It declared that some persons belonging to the *asakir-i muvazzafa*, known by the name of *başıbozuk*, who were unable to distinguish between good and evil, perpetrated acts of violence and plunder against the life, property and

---

[144] BOA. HR. SYS. 1347/28 enc. 2, 21 March 1854.
[145] BOA. HR. SYS. 904/1 enc. 142, 23 March 1854. A translation of this letter into Ottoman Turkish is in BOA. HR. SYS. 1347/28 enc. 1. The translator indicates the date of the original letter as 3 March but this must be a scribal error.
[146] BOA. HR. SYS. 904/1 enc. 170, 9 April 1954.
[147] BOA. HR. SYS. 1336/3 enc. 1, 19 April 1854.
[148] George Palmer Evelyn, *A Diary of the Crimea*, London, 1954, p. 54, quoted by Reid, op. cit., p. 246.
[149] BOA. İ. DH. 296/18680.
[150] *Takvim-i Vekayi*, 9 Şaban 1270. For its transliteration, see Yapıcı, op. cit., pp. 40–44.

honour of the Muslim and non-Muslim subjects of the empire. Such actions and behaviour were to be punished severely. The perpetrators were to be arrested and sent to army commanders, whose military courts were authorized to pass capital punishment on the perpetrators. However, this firman and other orders from the Porte seem to have had little effect. Reports and complaints from various parts of the empire and from British and French consuls continued to come in.

The Greek insurgence in Thessaly and Epirus increased complaints of the conduct of the *başıbozuks*. For example, the British Acting Consul in Salonica Henry Razy reported the following on 9 May 1854 to the British ambassador Lord Stratford:

> A body of the insurgents who landed at "Seikia" proceeded to "Poleiros" and endeavoured to excite the inhabitants to rise. Their efforts were ineffectual, the Primates on the 14/26 April sent off intelligence to Galatesta, about 5 hours distant, where Hassan Aga and Mahmut Bey were at the head of 800 Bashee-Bozouks entreating them to come to their assistance and drive out the invaders who were only 200 strong and tormented them. The Bashee-Bozouks of 4 times that force, however, hesitated and it was only after repeated requests personally made by the Primates that they at last consented to set out. This was on the 20/2 May. While on the march and near "Votenia" they encountered a poor woodcutter about 55 years of age upon whom they alleged to have found papers proving a connection with the insurgents, him they beheaded instantly. This was but the preliminary to more horrible excesses. Arrived within about 10 minutes walk of Poleiros, they were met by two of the Primates and conducted to the outskirts of the village where the rest of the Primates 23 in number received them with all cordiality; the 200 insurgents having some days previously decamped. For a few minutes the best understanding seemed to be established between the leaders of the Bashee-Bozooks and the Primates, and it is even said that the customary cup of coffee had been served, when the former exclaimed pointing to the mountains, "who are these people approaching", nothing was visible but some flocks of goats and the Primates replied, of course, in that sense. Presently a Bashee-Bozook was dispatched as if to reconnoitre. In a few minutes, a pre-concerted signal was heard, a shot was given [?] by the vidette [?], the chiefs of the irregulars at once exclaimed "cut them down" an order you may well supposed promptly responded to by their followers. The work of slaughter commenced and the 23 primates soon succumbed under the edge of the yatagan, nor were their lifeless corpses unmolested, but were hacked and mutilated in such a manner as to become unrecognisable – nor was this all. 4 or 5 of the Kirajis actually employed by the troops in carrying their ammunition were at the same time indiscriminately massacred.
>
> ...

> All these victims were personally and well known to Hassan Aga and Mahmut Bey, what may have been their motive, it not easy to divine! Let the cause be what it may the effects stand before us as an incontestable fact and while it makes our best feelings revolt and cause the blood of Christian men to boil with indignation, it must ever stamp all concerned in the diabolical atrocity and most of all the Master fiends Hassan Aga and Mahmut Bey with undying infamy.[151]

Upon receiving this report Lord Stratford again applied to Grand Vizier Reşid Pasha to demand justice in very strong words:

> His Highness will find in Mr. Razy's dispatch an ample confirmation of the massacre previously denounced to him. The discrepancies of detail are few and unimportant. We have in both reports the butchery without provocation or resistance, of about thirty Christians, more than twenty of whom were primates of district, by a band of irregular troops, or *Bashee-Bozooks*, [underlined in the original] summoned from Salonica to protect them against the Hellenic marauders, who had vainly endeavoured to seduce them from allegiance, and acting by command of two Turkish leaders, whose names are given identically in both accounts.
>
> No words of horror and indignation, however natural, no cries for vengeance, however just, can give any additional weight to simple statement of facts like these. We have at once in view of the cruel, cowardly, calculated butchers, together with the innocent, unarmed, unsuspecting victims, – the former betraying the honor of their Sovereign, the latter sacrificed by their submission to his authority. In every heart not rendered callous by brutal passion or senseless fanaticism there is what calls for judgement on the one and sympathy with the other. I will not insult the Turkish Ministers by supposing it otherwise with them. Indeed I am assured by you that they are alive to the requirements of justice in this case, and to the obligation of punishing with exemplary rigour an outrage which is no less treasonable towards the Porte, than disgraceful to humanity, and ruinous to the Empire. It is enough therefore, I hope for me to repeat.[152]

The French ambassador Baraguey d'Hilliers also made a representation to the Porte in June on the atrocities committed by the *başıbozuks* in Thessaly. Baraguey d'Hilliers stated that the government had raised five thousand *başıbozuk*s, but with the consent of the pasha of Larissa their number had risen to more than twenty thousand and they were doing all kinds of repressions against Christians. He maintained that,

---

[151] BOA. HR. SYS. 904/1 enc. 213–214, 9 May 1854.
[152] BOA. HR. SYS. 904/1 enc. 215–216, 14 May 1854.

Thessaly and its inhabitants are treated by them [*başıbozuks*] like a conquered territory and an enemy population. The cries of the Christians, victims of these disorders, will resound soon in all the capitals of Europe, and public opinion, moved, irritated, will accuse the Ottoman government and its allies of improvidence or partiality.[153] [My translation]

Another consular report from Salonica stated that the depredations committed by the Albanians were increasing daily. The *başıbozuk* should be recalled from the interior to Salonica. Mehmet Pasha was weak and timid against them.[154]

After the concentration of French and British troops in Varna, reports started to come from Bulgaria on the disorders there. Towards the end of July 1854, Stratford had "again to perform the painful duty of bringing to the knowledge of the Ottoman secretary of state a barbarous outrage committed by one class of the Sultan's subjects upon another" in the immediate vicinity of the British camp in Bulgaria. Stratford wrote that according to the report of General Sir de Lacy Evans, the Christian inhabitants of a village had been "turned out of their homes by a band of Mussulman strangers", and "forced to seek shelter from worse violence in the neighboring forest".[155] Shortly afterwards on 12 August Stratford again had to complain of the wrongful treatment of Bulgarian peasants in the purchase of provisions for the army.[156]

We have seen in Chapter 3 that the British tried to reinforce their army in the Crimea by hiring regular and irregular Ottoman troops. Thus, in the spring of 1855, British recruitment officers were sent to some provinces for this purpose, including Colonel Walpole who was sent to Damascus. With the help of local authorities Walpole started recruiting irregular cavalry there in March 1855 and the number of his troops reached about five hundred by mid-May. However, according to reports from the governor, the city *meclis* and the chief of staff of the Arabia army Mehmed İzzet Pasha, he recruited his men among

---

[153] "La Thessalie et les habitants sont traités par eux comme une terre conquise et une population ennemie. Les cris des chrétiens, victimes de ces désordres, retentiront avant peu dans toutes les capitales de l'Europe, et l'opinion publique, émue, irritée, accusera le gouvernement ottoman et ses alliés d'imprévoyance ou de partialité." BOA. HR. SYS. 1191/1 enc. 34, 11 June 1854.

[154] BOA. HR. TO. 220/35, 15 June 1854.

[155] Redcliffe to Reşid Pasha, 29 July 1854. BOA. HR. SYS. 1191/1 enc. 42. See my paper in *Savaştan Barışa*, pp. 306-307.

[156] Redcliffe to Reşid Pasha, 12 August 1854. BOA. HR. SYS. 1192/1 enc. 24-25. See my paper in *Savaştan Barışa*, p. 307.

disreputable, ignorant and revengeful people. These levies also started molesting women and the shopkeepers in the city. Colonel Walpole himself had an Ottoman soldier from the second infantry regiment arrested at the gate of the *idadiye* school and taken to his *konak* where he had him beaten, because the soldier had not saluted him.[157] It seems that these levies increased their acts of violence against the population to such an extent that signs of serious mass violence became evident in the city.[158] Therefore the governor Vamık Pasha sent an official note to Colonel Walpole and kindly requested him either to take the troops out of the city or to take measures that they went about unarmed and did not molest anybody.[159]

Next day the *meclis* of Damascus convened and discussed the matter together with all the foreign consuls in the city except for the British consul Mr Wood, who was in Beirut at that time. A *mazbata* (council resolution or "round robin") signed by Governor Vamık Pasha and other members of the council of the province (*eyalet meclisi*), including the representatives of the Greek, Catholic and Jewish communities, was sent to the Porte complaining of the misdeeds of the British officer and his recruits.[160] First it confirmed the receipt of the relevant order from the Porte, dated 17 February 1855, on the recruitment of irregular cavalry for the British army. (The order seems to have reached Damascus rather late, on 7 April 1855). The order was read in the council of the province. The *mazbata* further stated that the British officer sent for the recruitment paid no attention to the Ottoman authorities, did not consult them and recruited around 500 soldiers for cavalry and infantry from among the riff-raff of Damascus. Yet these ruffians (*haşerat*, literally "insects") enjoying the liberties given to them by the British officer, started committing outrages, molesting women and taking revenge on people against whom they had old grievances. The British officer was kindly requested to put a stop to these acts but he apparently did not accept it.

After that the irregular troops of Colonel Walpole became more impudent and increased their violence. The shopkeepers shut up their shops and came to the governor's office to make a complaint. Therefore

---

[157] Mehmed İzzet Pasha to the *serasker*, 17 May 1855. BOA. HR. SYS. 1352/51.
[158] Mehmed İzzet Pasha to the *serasker*, 24 May 1855. BOA. HR. SYS. 1352/61.
[159] Vamık Pasha to Colonel Walpole, 15 May 1855. (Copy). BOA. HR. SYS. 1352/71.
[160] *Mazbata* of the *meclis* of Damascus, 17 May 1855. BOA. HR. SYS. 1352/49.

a special council consisting of the chief of staff and the Defterdar of the Arabistan (Arabia) army, Molla Efendi, as well as some members of the grand council of the province, the consuls of France, Austria, Sardinia and Iran, and the dragomans of the consulates of Britain and Prussia convened and decided that the troops in question should be sent to Hama or to the village of Qibbe (Qiyye?) near Damascus. If this was not acceptable then the troops should be forbidden to go about armed, otherwise there would be no other solution than applying the law against them. Colonel Walpole took offence at these suggestions and moved to the village of Dum (?) with his troops as an act of protest. The *meclis* then sent deputies to invite him back to Damascus.

It seems remarkable that the British military commissioner (Colonel Walpole) apparently defied Ottoman authority by arresting an Ottoman soldier in broad daylight. It seems no less remarkable that the governor or the chief of staff of the Ottoman Arabistan army could do nothing against him beyond applying to the foreign consuls resident in the city. The British commissioner seems to have acted with total disregard for the local authorities.

One of the main problems with the *başıbozuk*s was that they were themselves robbed of their rations by the pashas and secondly, they were in most cases collected from unreliable elements, who looked upon the war as a means of getting booty or who were fanatically anti-Christian. In any case, unable to receive food for themselves and for their horses, they resorted to pillaging the population. Even the regular soldiers did not receive any pay for months or years. General Williams reported that in the Anatolian army in Erzurum there were soldiers who had not received any pay for the last fifteen to twenty-two months.[161] These payments did not reach them even if they were sent. Embezzlement was common in the command of the army, beginning with the *müşir* down to regimental commanders. Nevertheless, even if these pashas were not corrupt, they were under continuous pressure because people who wanted their positions were constantly conspiring against them in Istanbul. During the war, the *müşir* of the Anatolian army was changed five times.

---

[161] Colonel Williams to the Earl of Clarendon. Camp near Kars, September 26, 1854. PRMA, p. 30.

The *Morning Chronicle* correspondent Charles Duncan met a *başıbozuk* chieftain, who admitted their despised situation but complained thus:

> But see how we are treated. We leave our homes with a formal engagement with our government, and we are promised eighty piastres the month (about fourteen shillings), provided we bring our horse, our arms, and that we feed ourselves. Now, look at our condition, and say if we are not rather to be pitied than condemned. Government has not paid us; we have spent the little money we possessed and many have sold their arms; then, when abandoned to starvation, can my men be blamed if they help themselves at the villages they may pass to whatever they may meet?[162]

Abdi Pasha, the former commander of the Anatolian army, who was under arrest together with his successors Ahmed Pasha and Zarif Mustafa Pasha in Istanbul for charges of corruption and mismanagement, during his interrogation was asked why he did not prevent the *başıbozuk* chiefs (*sergerde*s) from unbecoming acts. Abdi Pasha answered that among the *başıbozuk sergerde*s a certain İnce Arab was said to have committed much evil on his way from Damascus to Kars. He was appointed to Bayezid but he committed some mischief there as well and he was imprisoned. Abdi Pasha then gave the following answer to the question of why he did not prevent the Kurdish *başıbozuk*s from plundering villages around Erzurum:

> The *başıbozuk* troops from the neighbouring villages asked for permission to go to their villages in order to complete some affairs of theirs and to get [buy?] food and fodder from the villages and from the bazaar. It is probable that they might have dared to commit such deplorable acts during their trips there and back, but it is also doubtless that it is impossible to prohibit them from behaving in this way.[163] [My translation]

As it is seen from the above, the *müşir* admits his powerlessness in preventing the *başıbozuk* from plundering. The *başıbozuk* cavalry commanders in the Kars army, especially Hasan Yazıcı and İnce Arab from Damascus had also become notorious for their many outrages. They had not appeared on the battlefront and because they did not get paid, they started pillaging. General Williams and the British consulate in Erzurum repeatedly wrote complaints to the British embassy and finally managed to get them arrested. One of these documents was

---

[162] Duncan, op. cit., vol. I, p. 277.
[163] Abdi Pasha's statement. BOA. İ. MMS. 3/107 enc. 6.

sent from Erzurum, dated 4 January 1855 (author not specified). It stated that the *başıbozuk* cavalry under the command of Hasan Yazıcı had not been of any use against the Russians in the last year. This year they were again expected to oppose the *başıbozuk* cavalry of the enemy which had occupied and looted the Ottoman villages in the area between Kars and Gümrü. However, some Ottoman subjects from Kars to Bayezid had also accepted service in the irregular cavalry and infantry of the enemy, who spent much money to recruit spies.

From the British embassy an extract of the letter was given to the grand vizier who responded by writing to the *serasker* instructing him to look into the matter on 14 March 1855. The *serasker* replied on 21 March that the commander in chief of the Anatolian army was instructed to investigate the behaviour of these *sergerdes*.[164]

The irregular Arab, Albanian and other troops recruited for the British army and camped in Kala-i Sultaniye (Çanakkale, the Dardanelles) under the command of General William Beatson were also a constant source of disorder. As noted by Skene and Money, Beatson had been too mild with these *başıbozuk*s and he was unable to discipline them. They looted the bazaar and used all kinds of violence including rape and murder against the population, even wounding an Ottoman officer and attacking French soldiers. When the governor of the province remonstrated to General Beatson, the general either defended his troops or made a feeble effort to stop them.[165] Finally the Ottoman governor gathered all the consuls, and after negotiating they decided to ask for help from Istanbul in July 1855. In response the Porte sent a punitive force of three companies of infantry with artillery from the Hassa army in Istanbul under the command of Miralay Muhiddin Bey.[166] According to Captain Money, this force consisted of 500 infantry, 250 cavalry, 250 artillery troops and 8 field pieces.[167] Only after this show of force did the *başıbozuk*s agree to go unarmed in the town.

---

[164] HR. SYS. 1336/57 enc. 1, 4 January 1855. Translation of an extract from a letter from the British consulate in Erzurum. Enc. 2: From the grand vizier to the *serasker*, 14 March 1855; and the reply of the *serasker*, 21 March 1855.

[165] Money, op. cit., pp. 103–105; Skene, op. cit., pp. 49–50. Cf. Reid, op. cit., pp. 274–276.

[166] BOA. HR. SYS. 1337/35, 19 July 1855, HR. SYS. 1353/33, 26 July 1855 and HR. SYS. 1353/34, 29 July 1855. Also see Skene, op. cit., pp. 48–50; Money, op. cit., pp. 103–106.

[167] Money, op. cit., p. 103.

By September 1855, the Porte decided to send special punitive missions to the Balkans and Thessaly. Thus Midhat Bey, second secretary of the MVL and Selim Pasha the Engineer General (*Mühendishane-i Hümayun Feriki*) were each appointed to special missions, the former to Varna and its environs and the latter to the left (south) side of Rumelia as far as Janina. Their duty was to inspect the administrators and punish the culprits of the atrocities and disorders.

In the instructions to Midhat Bey (the future famous Midhat Pasha) the central authorities stated that the army commanders were naturally too involved in the current affairs of the war to give time to such disorders and the governors were also very busy with other affairs, hence lower-level administrators had neglected their duty to prevent the various oppressions and barbaric treatments of Muslim and Christian subjects alike. The victims were then more specifically described as some helpless Bulgarians. Midhat Bey was empowered with special authority to deal with the issue on the spot, go directly to the locations of atrocities and try to capture the perpetrators, punishing them according to law and regulations. He would also punish indifferent administrators according to the degree of their crimes.[168] Instructions to Selim Pasha were similar: the perpetrators of inhuman actions were to be punished severely.[169] However, we do not have information on how and to what extent these orders were implemented.

Public Opinion and Patriotism

In the introductory chapter, we have seen that there are many *destan*s and *zafername*s on the Crimean War. Only two of these give information of use to the historian: Salih Hayri's *Hayrabat* and Ahmed Rıza Trabzoni's *Manzume-i Sivastopol*; we have already discussed these works in Chapter 3. The remaining *destan*s are rather purely literary works imbued with religious heroism and valour. We have also seen that among the poets who wrote about the war Yusuf Halis Efendi stood out on account of his patriotism. His *Vatan Kasidesi* and *Destan-ı Askeri* exalt love of homeland (*hubb-ül vatan*). The former poem is also remarkable for its Turkish nationalism. Halis Efendi criticised

---

[168] Draft of instructions to Midhat Efendi, second secretary of the MVL. BOA. HR. SYS. 1353/68 1, 12 September 1855.
[169] BOA. HR. SYS. 1353/68 2, 12 September 1855.

the former poets of the Arabs, and of Anatolia and Iran for not being patriotic. He also accused them of cloaking Turkish with Arabic and Persian expressions. The following verses exemplify this:

*Giydirüp maşlahı Urban ü Acem kalpağın
Sanki pek çıplak idi Türkî-i zibây-i vatan
    Mustalahdan kaba Türkçe yolu güç hem dardır
    Zahiren gerçi kolaydır reh-i mecray-ı vatan*[170]

As the writer of these lines was a translator working in the official Translation Bureau (*Tercüme Odası*), he might have been influenced by European concepts of nationality and nationalism.

According to Captain Fevzi Kurtoğlu, during the battle of Oltaniçe (4 November 1853), the Ottoman army band in Tutrakan across the Danube played an army march which included the expression "lion-hearted Turks" in its refrain:

*Başlar kesilüp ser-be-ser dehşetli toplar patlasun,
Arslan yürekli Türkleri görsün de düşmen çatlasun.*

This is very interesting, but unfortunately Kurtoğlu does not indicate his sources, so we can not ascertain the authenticity of this information.[171]

It is well-known that Europeans and Russians called the Ottoman Empire Turkey for short, while the Ottoman official language used other names. In 1855, Sultan Abdülmecid's official title included the word "Türkistan" in the ratification of the agreement on the guarantee of the Ottoman loan by Britain and France (*Biz ki bi-lütfihi teala Türkistan ve Türkistan'ın şâmil olduğu nice memalik ve büldanın padişahı*).[172] This was probably the first time an Ottoman Sultan used the word *Türkistan* (a translation of the French word *Turquie*) in his title. In the ratification of the Treaty of Paris in 1856, Sultan Abdülmecid again defined himself as "by the grace of God, we the *Padişah* of *Türkistan* and the countries and territories which it encompasses".[173]

Ottoman press life was enriched by the Crimean War with the appearance of European newspapers in Istanbul. By the standards of the time these newspapers published very recent news from the theatre of war. As for the Ottoman press, at this time it consisted of the official

---

[170] See Fahrettin Kırzıoğlu, op. cit., p. 54.
[171] Kurtoğlu, op. cit., p. 17–18. Also quoted by Kırzıoğlu, op. cit., p. 53.
[172] OBKS, No. 19, dated 14 July 1855, p. 58.
[173] See Erdem, "Türkistan: Nerede, Ne Zaman?", *Toplumsal Tarih* 10 (58), Istanbul, October 1998, p. 40. Also see OBKS, s. 67.

Takvim-i Vekayi and the semi-official *Ceride-i Havadis*. Ottoman newspapers started quoting from European newspapers. In the 1860s Ottoman press life became further enriched with the appearance of the first independent newspapers such as the *Tercüman-ı Ahval* of Şinasi and Agâh Efendi in 1860 and especially the *Tasvir-i Efkâr* of Şinasi, Ahmet Vefik Pasha and Namık Kemal in 1862. Thereby criticism of the government increased. These years were also the formative years of an Ottoman public opinion.

The notion of public opinion (*efkâr-ı umumiye*) itself was a novelty and it soon became a high-frequency word in the vocabulary of the new intelligentsia that came to be known as the Young Ottomans, such as Şinasi, Namık Kemal, Ziya Pasha, Ali Suavi etc. Şinasi had been excluded from membership of the *Encümen-i Daniş*, the Ottoman "Academy of Sciences" in 1856, because he had shaved his beard, the *ulema* thinking that a learned man of letters should have a beard.[174] On close examination, however, it turned out that he had shaved his beard due to reasons of health.

Muslim reactions to the *Islahat Fermanı* and to the extravagance of the Sultan gave rise to a conspiracy in Istanbul in 1859. The event was later called *Kuleli Vakası* (Kuleli Incident) because the arrested conspirators were tried in the barracks of Kuleli. The leader of the conspiratorial organization or the secret society was a certain Sheikh Ahmed of Süleymaniye, a medrese teacher at the Sultan Bayezid Mosque. Sheikh Ahmed belonged to the Naqshbandi-Khalidi order. He applied to the authorities in spring 1854 to join the Anatolian army together with his alleged 3,000 followers (*mürids*).[175] Prominent members of the organization included Cafer Dem Pasha, Ferik Çerkez Hüseyin Daim Pasha, Major Rasim Bey and Arif Efendi, a secretary of the *Tophane-i Amire*.[176] Şinasi was related to some of the conspirators. The conspiracy was betrayed by an officer in September 1859. The aims of the conspira-

---

[174] BOA. İ. MMS. 8/312, 18 September 1856.

[175] Burak Onaran, "Kuleli Vakası hakkında 'başka' bir araştırma", *Tarih ve Toplum Yeni Yaklaşımlar* 5, Spring 2007, p. 17. Onaran seems certain that Sheikh Ahmed participated in the war with his 3,000 men. However, the archive document he cites (BOA. A. MKT. MHM. 58/60) does not give information about the actual number of men brought to the Anatolian army by Sheikh Ahmed. I have not come across Sheikh Ahmed's name among *başıbozuk* leaders in the Anatolian army. Most probably he mustered less than 3,000 men. I have not seen Onaran's recent PhD dissertation "A bas le Sultan..", EHESS, Paris, 2009.

[176] Uluğ İğdemir, *Kuleli Vakası Hakkında Bir Araştırma*, Ankara: TTK, 1937, p. 11.

tors are not clear and there are two basic approaches among historians. Some consider it as the first constitutional movement. Others find it to be merely an Islamic, anti-Western movement in opposition to Sultan Abdülmecid's way of life. According to Davison, "the basic motif of the conspirators was opposition to westernisation".[177] As Davison has noted, while general dissatisfaction might have arisen from economic difficulties, the excessive spending of the palace, and arrears of pay in the army, it took the shape of a religious fanaticism and hostility to the equality of non-Muslims. However, the religious character of the conspiracy is not surprising. In the Ottoman Empire most reactions to the government usually took on a religious character, probably as a result of the absence of other ideologies. Burak Onaran analysed the participants' newly-found statements in the BOA and came to the conclusion that the motives of the conspirators were complex, contradictory and multi-layered, going beyond the dichotomy of progress versus reaction.

Although only forty-one persons were arrested, it was certain that many members of the *ulema* were involved. The Russian military agent in Istanbul, Captain Frankini, reported the event to St Petersburg as a conspiracy against Sultan Abdülmecid and in favour of Sultan Abdülaziz.[178] Frankini noted that the causes were the dissatisfaction of the people because of financial problems and the carelessness of the Sultan. The report also stated that "the benefits of some foreigners, the luxury and the opulence exhibited by the Turkish dignitaries, the venality of their entourage and the administrators, the sense of complete dependence in which, since the last war, Turkey finds itself with respect to Europe" had caused a major resentment in the Muslim population. Interestingly, the report also noted that Cafer Dem Pasha had been "particularly protected by Lord Redcliffe who had even obtained the rank of the general of division for him". Abdülmecid forgave the organizers and lessened their punishments, commuting their death sentences to life-long imprisonment. This leniency was interpreted by the Russian agent as weakness.

Finally let us note that the first patriotic Ottoman theatre play was inspired by the Crimean War: Namık Kemal's *Vatan yahut Silistre*

---

[177] See Davison, op. cit. (1973), pp. 101.
[178] Staff Captain Frankini to the Russian minister of war, 17 (29) October 1859. RGVIA. *Fond* 450, *opis* 1, *delo* 60, *list* 81–87.

(Homeland or Silistria) took its subject from the defence of Silistria. Namık Kemal seems to have taken the names of his heroes from real people, because the two prominent heroes of his play, Islam Bey and Abdullah Çavuş are the names of an officer and a sergeant who served in the Rumeli army. There is also a Colonel (Miralay) İslam Bey mentioned with praise by Ömer Pasha in the correspondence of the war ministry.[179] Abdullah Çavuş was a sergeant orderly (*emir çavuşu*) serving under the command of İsmail Pasha in the Rumeli army. Together with a certain Süleyman Ağa, he was nominated by İsmail Pasha and then Serasker Rıza Pasha and accordingly decorated with the *Mecidiye* order for his bravery during the battle of Çatana (Cetate).[180] Namık Kemal may have read their names in the medal lists – probably published in the *Takvim-i Vekayi* or *Ceride-i Havadis* – or heard them from people. The play ends with the words "Long live the homeland (*vatan*)! Long live Ottomans!".

The topic of another play (*Akif Bey*) by Namık Kemal is taken from the naval battle of Sinop. The hero of the drama is the commander of a frigate from the Ottoman squadron in Sinop, which was attacked and burnt by a Russian squadron under the command of Vice-Admiral Pavel Nakhimov. Akif Bey survives the battle, is taken prisoner by the Russians, but flees from prison and returns to Batum only to find his wife married to another person. We must also note that Namık Kemal came to Kars when he was 13–14 years old and spent one year in the town (from June 1853 to July 1854) when his grandfather Abdüllatif Pasha served as the local governor (*kaimmakam*). Fahrettin Kırzıoğlu argues that the young Namık Kemal was influenced by the "moral atmosphere" and folk literature traditions of Kars.[181]

Corruption and its Treatment

Until the issue of the penal code of 1840, there was no definition of bribery in the Ottoman legal language. Gifts to officials were a widespread custom. There were myriad names for such gifts from small

---

[179] BOA. İ. DH. 17361, 14 July 1853.
[180] BOA. İ. DH. 302/19167, 7 June 1854.
[181] Kırzıoğlu, "Folk Traditions in Kars during the Last Six Turkish-Russian Wars on the Anatolian Front", *Kars and Eastern Anatolia in the Recent History of Turkey. Symposium and the Excavation*, Ankara: Publication of Governor's Office of Kars and Atatürk University, 1994, p. 152.

officials and ordinary subjects to their "belters". Even the 1840 penal code was vague about what kind of gifts constituted bribery. Although grandees such as Hüsrev Pasha and Nafiz Pasha were soon convicted and sentenced to exile according to the new rules of conduct, there is no doubt that these trials were political; for while almost all pashas engaged in similar practices, only a handful of them were put on trial. The reformist Mustafa Reşid Pasha had used these trials as a leverage against his political rivals.[182] From 1841 onwards gifts from the sultan (*atiyye-i seniyye*) were included in the state budget as a separate item. The idea was to make the ruler more visible and exalted as the ultimate distributor of gifts and favours, and to make the bureaucracy more invisible and homogeneous.[183] Thus the law against bribery was part of a policy of centralization and taming the bureaucrats: a sword of Damocles now hung over their heads.

Remarkably, almost all pashas convicted in 1840 enjoyed a gradual rehabilitation. Most significantly, within two or three years Nafiz Pasha became a member and then the president of the MVL that had tried and convicted him. Furthermore, gifts from provincial governors continued to be accepted. For example, in July 1840 the governor of Tunis Ferik Ahmed Pasha sent very precious jewellery to the grandees of the Porte supposedly to celebrate the accession of Abdülmecid. He repeated this gesture in 1849, this time without any visible reason. Presumably Ferik Ahmed Pasha wanted to smooth his relations with the centre and receive the rank of *müşir*.[184] As described in Chapter 4, he also made the largest "donation" of the *iane-i harbiye* during the war. In fact, despite the ban, many pashas regarded gift exchange as normal and wanted to continue while paying lip service to the new law. Their ideological legitimation came in the form of a *hadis* (word of the Prophet) that encouraged the exchange of gifts. Thus they tried to legitimise their source of revenue. A new penal code issued on 14 July 1851 clarified the type and amount of acceptable gifts. However, gift-giving remained the principal means of getting on well with the central government and obtaining promotion. Even swearing on the

---

[182] Yüksel Çelik, "Tanzimat Devrinde Rüşvet-Hediye İkilemi ve Bu Alandaki Yolsuzlukları Önleme Çabaları", *Türk Kültürü İncelemeleri Dergisi* 15, Istanbul 2006, p. 49. Cengiz Kırlı, op. cit., p. 116.
[183] Kırlı, op. cit., p. 117.
[184] Çelik, op. cit., pp. 38, 52.

Koran that they would refrain from this activity did not deter members of the Ottoman elite from their ingrained habits.

We also observe the gradual rehabilitation of many pashas convicted for mismanagement, abuses and corruption during the Crimean War. In January 1855 a novel regulation on the prevention of corruption (*Men-i İrtikab Nizamnamesi*) was issued by the new legislative body, the Supreme Council of Reforms (*Meclis-i Âli-i Tanzimat*, MAT), the successor of the MVL. The *mazbata* of the MAT stated that corruption was the fundamental cause of all evil and, despite many strict laws enacted until then, it had not been totally prevented. The deficiency of the previous legislation was not in the mildness of the punishments ordained, but rather in its non-application. Furthermore, the *mazbata* stated that the corruption of Turkey had become proverbial in the mouths of friend and foe and the "nation" had therefore lost prestige in the eyes of foreigners.[185] In their *layiha*, the legislators also wrote that since the promulgation of the *Tanzimat*, people were no longer forced to pay bribes in order to protect their lives, honour and property. Now the chief form of bribery aimed at gaining material benefits.

These statements clearly show that the *Tanzimat* leaders were well aware of the low opinion of European observers of the Ottoman Empire with regard to corrupt practices. They also show that *Tanzimat* leaders such as Âli Pasha, who was the president of the MAT at that time and Fuad Pasha, who was an influential member, admitted the existence of widespread corruption in the Ottoman Empire.

The *layiha* described the payment of bribes to obtain state offices and ranks as one of the circumstances that gave rise to corruption. It clearly stated that those who paid bribes to obtain an office hoped to recover their money (and more) during their term of office. The most important reason for such bribes was that many Muslims had become accustomed to earning their livelihoods either by direct state service or by indirectly serving state officials. These people could not think of any other way of living. The *layiha* writers claimed that while the state had for example ten thousand offices at its disposal, there were one hundred thousand applicants. Therefore ninety thousand obviously remained unemployed. For this reason, turnover was high, in other words there were frequent rotations of officials. This created a vicious

---

[185] See Karal, "Rüşvetin Kaldırılması için Yapılan Teşebbüsler", *Tarih Vesikaları* 1, June 1941, p. 57.

circle. Therefore, the *layiha* suggested that the state should open new ways of making a living for people so that not everybody would depend on the treasury for a living. It was also necessary to appoint people to state offices according to their merits and to make them feel secure that they would not lose their posts without reason. However, at the present time, every civil servant was insecure of his future in his post and did not know how long he might remain unemployed. Therefore, he tried to "hoard" as much money as possible as an unemployment insurance by taking bribes and stealing from the state during his term of office, at the same time behaving like a hired worker or daily servant.

The *layiha* then went on to state that another important cause that forced civil servants into either corruption or indebtedness was large retinues of servants and dependants that they needed to maintain. Just as the state could not easily get rid of its many redundant officials, these civil servants could not get rid of their own servants because the latter could not make a living without their patron. Thus many civil servants had to feed a "horde" of people during their term of office and many of these employees remained with their patrons even when the latter were unemployed. Again the main problem was that, for many people, making a living from trade and industry was much harder than making a living in state service.

The new law on corruption stipulated one year of prison or two years of exile together with a fine double the amount of the bribe in question, payable by the bribe giver, taker and any intermediary. The culprits would also lose their offices. Wives giving or taking bribes on behalf of their husbands were also held accountable. The law stipulated sentences for embezzlement and corruption in state tenders and in tax farming (*iltizam*) as well. Thus, in theory, we see that the MAT and the Sublime Porte were all for the prevention of corruption. However, in practice, few pashas ever got punished on charges of corruption. Even if they did, they were soon rehabilitated – as we have noted in the case of Mustafa Zarif Pasha (see Chapter 3).

General Williams' charges against Zarif Mustafa Pasha already have been discussed in detail, but we need to analyse Adolphus Slade's argument against the English general. Slade argued that Williams did not take into consideration the fact that Ottoman rations increased geometrically with rank. This is indeed true; because, depending on their rank, Ottoman officers received rations from two to forty times higher than the rations of the rank and file. Therefore the total number of daily rations had to be larger than the total number of troops and officers, and this fact did not necessarily indicate corruption. However, it does not seem credible that Williams, who had spent some years in the Ottoman Empire working closely with the Sultan's officers, did not know these differences in rations. It is also doubtful whether the troop numbers given to him even included officers. Secondly, even if he did not know about the higher rations accorded to officers, the difference could not have been so large as to justify the huge discrepancies discovered by Williams. Indeed, Slade himself was well aware of the general corruption in the Ottoman army. For example, he wrote that "twenty millions of piastres (180,000*l.*) of the sums sent in 1853–54 to the army of the Danube were never satisfactorily accounted for."[186]

The Crimean War and the Reform Edict of 1856 seem to have had little effect on the course of corruption in the Ottoman Empire. Nevertheless, pashas were now less willing to accept "gifts" publicly. Thus, for example, in 1855 Ferik İsmail Pasha was promoted to the second class of the *Mecidiye* order, because he did not accept gifts from the people during his stay in Bucharest as commander of the reserve troops there. Kamil Pasha, the Governor of Jeddah, did not accept gifts of jewellery from Mehmed Efendi the Sharif of Mecca when he returned to Istanbul at the beginning of 1856. Such acts must have been exceptions rather than the rule. Lord Stratford reported to the Earl of Malmesbury on 22 October 1858 that after two years from the Reform Edict and the Treaty of Paris very little had changed in the Ottoman Empire and that especially bribery remained a widespread disease.[187]

---

[186] Slade, op. cit. (1867), p. 199.
[187] Çelik, op. cit., p. 62.

CONCLUSION

The present study has focused not on the reasons for the outbreak of the war, but rather on the processes it set in motion, particularly where the Ottomans were concerned. In the narrative, I have endeavoured to present a non-biased, balanced and comparative view of the strengths and weaknesses of the warring sides. I have also tried to find out the reasons for the defeats of the Ottoman armies, examining the Ottoman method of waging war and the functioning of the relevant military machine.

From a political point of view, the results of the war were not altogether beneficial for the Ottoman elite. Victory in this war did not bring any significant material gain, not even a war indemnity. On the other hand, the Ottoman treasury was nearly bankrupted due to war expenses solely occasioned by the Russian occupation of the Sultan's territory, without any provocation from the Ottoman side. Nor were there any significant territorial gains except for some areas in Bessarabia. Like many other guarantees and stipulations of the Paris Treaty of 1856, moreover this gain would soon be nullified, because the war gave impetus to the union of the Danubian principalities and ultimately to their independence. In reality, the Ottoman Empire became a European protectorate although in theory it had become a member of the European Concert or the European state system. Although it was on the side of the winners, the Porte also lost the right to have a navy in the Black Sea together with Russia. Put differently, the Empire had become a part of the European Concert, but not an actor in the European balance of power. Thus it was not recognized as a great power that could claim compensation in case of territorial gain by another member of the system. By the beginning of the 1870s, after the defeat of France by Prussia, the European balance of power changed and Russia took advantage of the new situation by declaring void the previously stipulated neutrality of the Black Sea.

The war brought about the *Islahat Fermanı*, which is one of the most important documents of nineteenth century Ottoman history. This firman was meant to prevent European interference in the affairs of the Ottoman Empire on behalf of its Christian subjects. The Porte wanted to make some improvements for its non-Muslim subjects in order to prevent the question from being included in an international treaty. It rightly feared that if rights were given by an international treaty and not by the grace of the Sultan, then the non-Muslim subjects would feel gratitude towards the great powers and not to the Sultan. The Porte did not want the firman even to be mentioned in the treaty but it could not prevent this from happening.

We have seen that some historians consider the alliance of the Porte with France and Britain and the resulting Paris Treaty a success of Ottoman diplomacy. I do not find this position tenable. The alliance was dictated by the interests of the ruling classes of France and Britain and the Ottomans had little input. In other words, the great powers tried to find solutions with little reference to the Porte. On one occasion they even did not forward a note from the Porte to St Petersburg, finding it unacceptable on behalf of Russia. Furthermore Ottoman diplomacy also did not function in an optimal fashion. During the war, Vienna was the centre for diplomatic negotiations and the Ottoman ambassador in this city Arif Efendi did not know French and had limited relations with the *corps diplomatique*. Nevertheless, Reşid Pasha and the Porte were not just passive onlookers. Reşid Pasha showed much diplomatic skill. The Porte even rejected the Vienna Note which all the Great Powers urged the Sultan to accept.

Relations between the Porte and the allies during the war were not harmonious either. Obviously the allies fought not for the sake of the Porte, but for their own ends, namely the containment of Russia. Thus the allies did not want the Porte to gain territory, especially Christian territory: certainly they did not want to place the Christians of Georgia under Ottoman sovereignty. As for the Muslim Circassians, the allies (especially the French) were not much interested in their independence or annexation to the Ottoman Empire. The British former Secretary of State for War, the Duke of Newcastle even remarked that it was "monstrous to see the Turkish flag flying" in Circassia and "to witness attempts to establish Turkish government in the Country". In the summer of 1854, the allies effectively prevented the appearance of an Ottoman fleet with agents and war material on the Circassian coasts. On the other hand, the Porte could not coordinate its actions with Shamil on the Caucasian front and the Ottoman defeats in this area forced Shamil to remain passive. Nevertheless, even his passive stand caused Russia to detach many troops away from the front. Thus it was rather the Ottomans' fault that they had not sought an effective alliance with Shamil. Admittedly Shamil's kidnapping of some women including a French governess greatly harmed his relations with the Porte.

The equality of the non-Muslim subjects with Muslims was imposed upon the Porte and the Islamist or conservative sections of society and the bureaucracy did not like it, although even those statesmen who opposed equality were aware of the necessity of reform. The question was rather about the pace. For some statesmen like Mustafa Reşid Pasha the political equality of non-Muslims happened too fast and was too radical a reform. The war indeed made the Porte very sensitive towards the demands of its allies Britain and France. We have seen that the basic Ottoman approach in the question of reforms involved dissimulation and temporizing. The Ottoman elite was also in a genuine dilemma between religious (şer'i) rules and the necessities of the time, especially where slavery and the *cizye* were at issue: the Porte chose to ward off European objections by issuing many edicts and orders. However, application proceeded very slowly. We also have seen that practical necessity rather than any long-term plan was the real force behind the Ottoman reforms.

The Ottoman elite lost a great opportunity by not seriously integrating non-Muslim subjects into the army. During this war, many non-Muslims did indeed show eagerness to serve their country. If non-Muslims had been accepted into the army, of course not just as rank and file, but also as officers, and if they had been given equal opportunities in other state services, perhaps the eventually failed project of Ottoman citizenship might have had a better chance. Nevertheless, we must not forget that the great powers did not favour Christian conscription, neither did the non-Muslim communities themselves. Realistically speaking, military service was not popular among either Muslims or non-Muslims. People had good reasons for this sentiment, because enlistment lasted too long and the poor soldiers were much abused in every way, without receiving pay for months and being exposed to all kinds of diseases because of malnutrition and ill-treatment. More soldiers died of diseases than of battles in the Crimean War.

In retrospect, Nikolai I seems to have been simply more outspoken than other imperialists in seeking the partition of the Ottoman Empire. However, he began and conducted the war in an indecisive way. As Friedrich Engels noted at the time, he ought to have known that the other European powers would not allow him to destroy or subdue the Ottoman Empire.[1] Engels then argued that once Nikolai decided on war, he should have crossed the Pruth with a much larger force, reaching across the Balkans before the Ottomans gathered their armies. This indeed seems possible. However, Engels did not take into account, that not all of Nikolai's generals, including Field Marshal Paskevich, believed in or favoured such a plan. In fact Nikolai did give orders to act more firmly than his generals actually did. Differently expressed, he had not chosen the right commanders for this task. The best examples are Paskevich, Gorchakov and Menshikov who all proved ineffective. In most of the battles where the Russian army was successful, it did not fully utilize its success by following the Ottoman army and dealing a decisive blow. For example, some time after the battles of Başgedikler and Kürekdere General Bebutov could have captured Kars, had he followed the scattered Ottoman army. Ultimately Muravyov was successful in capturing Kars, but victory came at an enormous cost for Russia. Nevertheless, even if Nikolai had appointed more effective generals and if his armies had taken Edirne as in 1829, it is very doubtful that they could have gone farther or obtained a treaty similar to the Treaty of Edirne. For due to over-extension their supplies would most probably have failed as they did in 1829. The allies would certainly have defended Istanbul and then Russia might have faced a heavier defeat. Yet one is tempted to ask another speculative question: What would have happened if Russia had attacked the Ottoman Empire from the Caucasian frontier only, as Menshikov had once advised, instead of occupying the principalities? Probably Britain would still have been willing to oppose Russian expansion towards India, but would Napoleon III still have been as much interested?

In the end, Russia was not defeated in a strict sense in the Crimea. The Russian army had evacuated the southern part of Sevastopol but it was still in place and ready to fight. The allies could not afford to go deep into Russian territory; rather they had to stick to the shore so as to ensure a constant flow of supplies. On the other hand, Russia had now firmly entrenched itself in the Caucasus: at this point even the alliance of the most powerful naval states with the Porte could not drive it away from this region. Thus within three years after the end of the war, Russia captured Shamil and ended the long Caucasian confrontation. We must also take into account the discontent of many

---

[1] "The Russian Failure", *NYDT*, 11 July 1854, in Marx, op. cit., p. 398.

locals with Shamil's or his naibs' rule, already corrupt at this stage. In fact the new post-Soviet Russian orthodox nationalism considers that Russia was not defeated in the Crimean war, rejecting most of what Tarle and other Soviet historians said on the topic. These "new Russians" do not accept the backwardness of Russia at that time either.[2]

Britain later tacitly accepted the partition of the Ottoman Empire. Around twenty years later in 1878, when Russia again attacked the Ottomans, Britain only took advantage by seizing Cyprus. This time British public opinion was not pro-Ottoman because of the default on Ottoman debts and the "Bulgarian horrors" of 1876. A good example of the change in British attitude can be observed in the person of Doctor Humphry Sandwith, who, as we have seen, was attached to the Anatolian army in Erzurum and Kars during the war and wrote his memoirs afterwards. Sandwith was also one of those few Englishmen who spoke Turkish. In his book on the Crimean War, published in 1856, he mentioned the Ottoman Armenians only negatively. But in 1878 he wrote an article in which he took an extremely anti-Ottoman position.[3] He had also mentioned the atrocities of the *başıbozuk*s before, but now he directly linked the *başıbozuk*s and the plight of the Ottoman Armenians. Actually certain British reports about the disorders of the *başıbozuk*s during the Crimean War can be read as precedents of British attitudes in the 1870s concerning the Ottoman Christians. Later, in World War I, those very allies who fought Russia in the Crimean War in order to prevent Ottoman partition finally reached an agreement with Russia, the Sykes-Picot secret agreement which stipulated dismemberment of the Ottoman Empire.

I have also shown that the Ottomans did not consider their defeat at Sinop as a "massacre". They called it the deplorable (*müteellime*), distressing (*mükeddire*), or heart-rending (*dil-sûz*) event, as if it were a natural disaster, but I did not see any reference to a massacre in the documents that I saw in the BOA. Kostaki Musurus, the Ottoman

---

[2] These arguments were expressed in a conference in Moscow on 7–8 November 2006 under the heading of "The Crimean War in the Cultural Memory of the Peoples of Russia and the World" (*Krymskaya Voina v kul'turnoy pamyati narodov Rossii i mira*), organized by the *Tsentr Natsionalnoy Slavy Rossii* (Centre for the National Glory of Russia, an endowment close to the government). See my news article, "Unutulmuş Bir Hikaye: Kırım Savaşı", *Toplumsal Tarih* 156, Istanbul, December 2006, p. 6.

[3] See James Reid's article in Richard G. Hovannisian (ed.), *Armenian Karin / Erzerum*, Costa Mesa, CA: Mazda Publishers, 2003, pp. 147–187.

ambassador in London, used a similar expression, namely *déplorable événement*.[4]

We have seen that the disorders, atrocities and plunders of the *başıbozuk*s occurred mostly because governors and pashas deprived them of their pay and rations. Unable to feed themselves, the *başıbozuk*s then attacked civilians; and the behaviour of the *başıbozuk* troops during the Crimean War was a major cause of the Armenian question as it emerged in the last quarter of the nineteenth century. For as we have seen by 1876 European and especially British public opinion had turned against the Ottoman Empire largely because of the Bulgarian and Armenian events.

Economically, the war accelerated the process of the entry of the Ottoman Empire into the European financial system. The two foreign debts contracted during the war were followed by others until the Ottoman Empire defaulted on its loans. Actually, the Porte never recovered; for the money entering the treasury was not used for productive ends but rather for consumption and debt servicing. We have also seen that the interests of London financial circles were paramount in British policy. With regard to Namık Pasha's loan mission to Paris and London, I have argued, *pace* Anderson, Akar and Al, that his failure was not a result of his amateurishness, but of the financial conjuncture prevailing at that time. With regard to the *iane-i harbiye*, I have shown that it was not a donation but a war tax.

Culturally, the Crimean War was a period of closer contacts with Europeans and some improvements for non-Muslims along with some fanatical attacks on them. The war also presented material for a kind of Ottoman Muslim patriotism and even Turkish nationalism. Namık Kemal's plays and the *destan*s of Ahmed Rıza, Salih Hayri and many others are good examples of this spirit. Public opinion played a major role during the war, which in turn contributed to the spread of the notion among the Ottoman elite. In this sense, the war also contributed to the formation of the future "Young Ottomans", a major school of political thought in the late Empire.

From a military-technical point of view, the war showed that the Ottoman army did not resemble its modern European counterparts. As the Russian General Prince Mikhail Gorchakov noted, the Otto-

---

[4] Musurus to Reşid Pasha. Londres, le 15 Décembre 1853. BOA. İ. HR. 105/5151 lef 37.

mans had destroyed the old army, but had not yet built a new one in the European sense. Except for a few units, the army was poorly trained, poorly armed and poorly clothed. We have seen that the soldiers' pay was in arrears for many months. There was much corruption in the army and the poor soldiers did not receive proper rations, clothes or shelters. As a letter of the grand vizier shows, the practise of muster-roll fraud in the army was well known to high-level Ottoman dignitaries. But this fraud was not rigorously investigated by the MVL during the trial of the former commanders of the Anatolian army, thus demonstrating the complacency of the military and civil authorities.

As James Reid has pointed out, the Ottoman strategy of piecemeal deployment of troops was among the causes of the defeats suffered on the Caucasian front. However, we must not forget that even the scattered Ottoman forces were in most cases still equal or superior in numbers to the Russian forces that opposed them. Thus the real reasons for the defeat were rather in the low quality of the officer class and the troops' lack of training. Especially the Ottoman regular and irregular cavalry were quite useless. Ottomans had also much difficulty in provisioning their troops. As was common in pre-industrial warfare more soldiers died of diseases, malnutrition, cold and lack of proper housing than of wounds received in battle.

No newspapers were available to relate the deprivations and bravery of Ottoman troops. The latter were unqualified to engage the enemy in the open field due to lack of training and most important of all, lack of confidence in their officers. With few exceptions, high ranking officers proved inefficient. The system of promotion prevented honest and talented candidates from ever being promoted to a rank higher than that of major. The Ottoman army was also paralyzed by personal rivalries and corruption, especially in the Anatolian army. Many foreign and refugee officers from Europe, of Hungarian, Polish, Italian, British, French origins and even from America served in this war in the Ottoman army. Some of these men were really good officers. Yet their use was also limited and often nullified because of rivalries and jealousies.

Very few of the guilty officers were ever punished. In fact many of the accused pashas soon were rehabilitated. The most notorious is Mustafa Zarif Pasha who was made a member of the MAT just two years after his dismissal. Other commanders of the Anatolian army also returned to official posts. On the other hand, the British military commissioner Williams Pasha's accusations against Zarif Pasha are a mixture of right and wrong. For example, he accused Zarif Pasha of ordering an open field attack upon the Russian army in Kürekdere. However, as we have seen, Zarif Pasha himself accused Guyon and other generals, pashas and staff officers on this account. Williams also made false accusations of disrespect by some Ottoman officers towards himself, when he had in fact been respected more than was necessitated by his rank. However, such faults of Williams, and even his Orientalist views on the Ottomans do not necessarily refute his concrete accusations of corruption.

The Marxist notion of "uneven and combined development" during the age of imperialism refers to the coexistence of the most modern modes of production with pre-capitalist modes in underdeveloped countries. It also describes regional or sectoral inequalities or irregularities of the capitalist mode of production. I think this model can be applied to Ottoman military reform in the nineteenth century. The Ottoman army during the Crimean War is an interesting case in point as well. On the one hand, some of its units, such as the artillery or the *chasseurs* had the most modern weapons of the time such as rifle carbines or Minié rifles. These units were also recognized by many European observers as worthy of the best armies in Europe. On the other hand, the Ottoman army had ignorant and even illiterate commanders, including even an army chief of staff. The war effort was also bedevilled by irregular troops with archaic weapons and tactics, archaic methods of provisions and archaic systems of fortifications. The Rumelian army in general was better organized than its Anatolian counterpart. Within these armies some regiments or battalions were better than others. Overall, however, the backward side of the army was decisive. The Ottoman generals did not demonstrate a sufficient understanding of European warfare.

The military contributions of Egypt and Tunis were important. We have seen that these dependencies were still part of the Ottoman Empire and accordingly sent troops. In the case of Egypt, some sort of bargaining involved the Porte and the governors of Egypt, Abbas Pasha and later Said Pasha. These governors were trying to conclude a contract with the French on the Suez Canal project and another contract with the British for a railway line. In both cases, the Porte asserted its right of approval for such plans, while the Egyptian pashas thought it was their internal affair. By sending troops, they planned to secure the approval of the Porte for their enterprises. Another subject for bargaining concerned the expenses of the Egyptian troops in Istanbul and the Crimea. In the end, the Porte agreed to pay.

Ottoman high officers, ministers and governors did not want to take personal responsibility. Even in battle operations, a single hierarchical line of authority and responsibility was not favoured. If anything went wrong, everybody put the blame on others, while the commander-in-chief did not take responsibility either. All pashas had their representatives and their enemies in the capital. In the provinces they had to take the local notables into consideration. Then there were the numerous councils in the capital and provinces (*meclis*), a novelty of the *Tanzimat*. Although these institutions were intended to prevent personal arbitrariness, for the most part they did not function properly. They took away personal responsibility from many officials but did not produce results in turn.

To many observers Abdülmecid seemed to be a weak Sultan. Within the period covered by this study, there is hardly any original sentence, important decision, or thought that can be attributed to him. He mainly indulged in women and drinking. Nevertheless, he was believed by some Western diplomats to be holding some "enlightened" views about topics such as slavery and the rights of Christian subjects. Whether he really held these views or was engaged in dissimulation and temporizing like his subordinates is difficult to answer. But one thing is certain: he was mild in character and did not like bloodshed. He even pardoned those who plotted to assassinate him in 1859.

There was little unity among Ottoman statesmen at the top. Many pashas were jealous of their superiors and waited for an opportunity to replace them. The system of promotion in the bureaucracy was not based upon merit at all. Damad Mehmed Ali Pasha, Reşid Pasha, Ali Pasha and Kıbrıslı Mehmed Emin Pasha all had their grudges against one another. The *serasker* Hasan Rıza Pasha and generalissimus Ömer Lütfi Pasha did not get along well. A harmful side effect of the reforms and Westernization was that the Ottoman ruling class lost its dignity, as admitted by Cevdet Pasha: they were forced to swallow many insults and slights from the allies.

On the other hand, the xenophobic discourse that claims that the Ottoman Empire or Turkey had no friends is also problematic. For in this war almost the whole of Europe was behind the Ottoman Empire. True, the allies had their own interests, but this does not change the fact that they were allies and defended the independence of the Porte on the battlefield. Such a discourse cannot take – and does not want to take – lessons from history, because it too readily assigns the role of the injured party to the Porte in every case, even when the opposite was true.

I have also argued that there is no clear-cut, permanent dichotomy among Ottoman statesmen. It makes little sense to categorically oppose "reformers" and "conservatives". Most Ottoman statesmen were pragmatists. Their positions and views on many issues depended upon their being in office or else deposed. As for Reşid Pasha, he had lost much of his previous influence and reforming energy, despite his last two terms of grand vizierskip. As we have seen, he opposed the reform edict and the political equality of the non-Muslim subjects of the empire.

While some aspects of our problematic require further research, the present study has hopefully presented a fair view of the Crimean War as conducted and suffered by the Ottoman elite and its subjects.

BIBLIOGRAPHY

This is not a bibliography of the Crimean War; it includes only works cited in the book.

Archives

Turkey

Başbakanlık Osmanlı Arşivi, Istanbul (BOA).
A. AMD., A. DVN. MHM., A. M..., A. MKT. NZD., A. MKT. UM., HR. MKT., HR. SFR. 4, HR. SYS., HR. TO., İ. DH., İ. HR., İ. MMS., İ. MSM., İ. MTZ.5, İ. MVL.

Russia

Rossiyskiy Gosudarstvenny Voenno-Istoricheskiy Arkhiv, Moscow (RGVIA).
Fond 450 (Turtsiya), Fond 481 (Voina 1853–1856 gg.), Fond 482 (Kavkaz), Fond 846 (Voenno-Ucheny Arkhiv).

Britain

The National Archives (TNA), London. (Formerly the Public Record Office, PRO). FO 195.
The Rothschild Archive, London. Documents related to the 1855 Turkish Loan contracted by Rothschild.

Manuscripts

Arif Efendi. (Düyun-u Umumiye Başmüdürü). *1270 Rus Seferi*. İstanbul, Marmara Üniversitesi Fen Ed. Fak. Kütüphanesi, Yazma Eserler 11.
Kırım Harbi Hakkında Ruzname. Ankara, TTK Kütüphanesi, Yazma Eserler 119.

Published Documents

Adamov, E. and L. Kutakov. "Iz istorii proiskov inostrannoy agentury vo vremya Kavkazskikh voyn", *Voprosy Istorii* 11, Moscow, November 1950, pp. 101–125.
Akarlı, Engin. *Belgelerle Tanzimat: Osmanlı Sadrazamlarından Ali ve Fuad Paşaların Siyasi Vasiyyetnameleri*. Istanbul: Boğaziçi Üniversitesi, 1978.
Akten zur Geschichte des Krimkriegs (AGKK), (ed.) Winfried Baumgart, Munich, Vienna: Oldenbourg Verlag, 1988–2006.
Akty, Sobrannye Kavkazkoyu Arkheograficheskoyu Komissieyu. (AKAK). Arkhiv Kantselyarii Glavnonachalstvuyuschago. 12 vols. Tiflis: Tipografiya Kantselyarii Glavnonachalstvuyuschago grazhdanskoyu chast'yu na Kavkaze, 1866–1906.
Omarov, Khalat A. (ed.). *100 pisem Shamilya*. Mahachkala: Dagestanskiy Nauchny Tsentr Rossiyskoi Akademii Nauk, 1997.
Osmanlı Belgelerinde Kırım Savaşı 1853–1856. (OBKS). Ankara: BOA Yayın Nu. 84, 2006 [appeared in print in February 2007].
Papers relative to Military Affairs in Asiatic Turkey and the Defence and Capitulation of Kars. Presented to Both Houses of Parliament by Command of Her Majesty.

(PRMA). London: Harrison and Sons, 1856. With a supplement (*Supplementary papers relative to...*).
Shamil' - Stavlennik Sultanskoy Turtsii i Angliyskikh Kolonizatorov. Sbornik dokumental'nykh materialov. Pod redaktsiey Sh. V. Tsagareyshvili. Tbilisi: Arkhivnoe Upravlenie MVD Gruzinskoi SSR, Gosizdat Gruzinskoi SSR, 1953.
Şeyh Şamil'in 100 Mektubu. Mektuplar ve açıklama notları: DAM RBA [sic]. Çeviren: Dr. Fikret Efe. Istanbul: Şule Yayınları, Mayıs 2002.
Türkgeldi, Ali Fuat (1867-1935). *Mesâil-i Mühimme-i Siyâsiyye*. I. Cilt. Yay. Haz. Bekir Sıtkı Baykal. Ankara: Türk Tarih Kurumu, 1960. Second edition 1987.
Zayonchkovskiy, Andrey Medardovich (1862-1926). *Vostochnaya Voina 1853-1856 gg v svyazi s sovremennoy ey politicheskoy obstanovkoy. Prilozheniya*. St. Petersburg, 1908.

Periodicals

Ceride-i Havadis. Istanbul. (CH)
Daily News. London.
The Globe. London.
The Illustrated London Times. London. (ILN)
Journal de Constantinople. Istanbul.
Kavkaz. Official newspaper of the viceroyalty of the Caucasus. Tiflis. (twice a week)
Kavkazskiy Sbornik. Tiflis. Journal published by the commander in chief of the Caucasian army.
Morning Advertiser. London.
Morning Chronicle. London.
Morning Herald. London.
Observer. London.
Russkaya Starina. St. Petersburg, monthly journal. 1870-1918.
The Sun. London.
Takvim-i Vekayi. Istanbul, official Ottoman newspaper.
The Times. London. Daily newspaper.
Voenny Sbornik. St. Petersburg, monthly journal.

Memoirs, Diaries, Chronicles, Newspaper Articles, War Reportage, Epic Poems and Other Primary Sources

Ahmed Lütfi (Lutfi) Efendi. See Lütfi.
Ahmed Rıza Trabzoni. *Manzume-i Sivastopol*. Hazırlayan Veysel Usta. Ankara: Kültür Bakanlığı Yayınları, 2000.
Bentley, Nicolas (ed.). *Russell's Despatches from the Crimea 1854-1856*. London: Panther Books, 1970.
Blokada Karsa. Pis'ma ochevidtsev o pokhode 1855 goda v Aziatskuyu Turtsiyu. Tiflis: Tipografiya kantselyarii namestnika Kavkazskago, 1856.
Blunt, John Elijah (1832-1915). *"Blunt Speaking". The Crimean War Reminiscences of John Elijah Blunt, Civilian Interpreter*. Ed. Dr Douglas J Austin. UK: Crimean War Research Society, Special Publication 33, 2007.
Borozdin, Korniliy Aleksandrovich (1828-1896). *Omer-pasha v Mingrelii. Iz vospominaniy o Vostochnoy voine 1853-1856 godov*. St Petersburg, 1873.
Buzzard, Thomas. *With the Turkish Army in the Crimea and Asia Minor. A Personal Narrative*. London: John Murray, 1915.
[Calthorpe, Colonel Somerset]. *Letters from Head-Quarters, or the Realities of the War in the Crimea. By an Officer on the Staff*. Two vols. Vol. I. London: John Murray, 1856.

Cevdet Paşa (1822–1895). *Ma'rûzât*. Ed. Yusuf Halaçoğlu. Istanbul: Çağrı Yayınevi, 1980.
——. *Tezâkir*. Ed. Cavid Baysun. 4 vols. Ankara: TTK, 1991. First Edition 1953.
Czajkowski, Michal (Mehmed Sadyk Pasha) (1804–1886). "Zametki i vospominaniya Mikhaila Chaykovskago (Sadyk-pashi)", *Russkaya Starina* 12, St. Petersburg, December 1904, pp. 558–594.
——. *Moje Wspomnienia o Wojnie 1854 Roku*. Warsaw: Wydawnicstwo Ministerstwa Obrony Narodowej, 1962.
Duncan, Charles. *A Campaign with the Turks in Asia*. London: Smith, Elder and Co., 1855. 2 vols.
Durand de Fontmagne, Baronne. *Kırım Harbi Sonrasında İstanbul*. Translated by Gülçiçek Soytürk. Istanbul: Tercüman 1001 Temel Eser, 1977.
Hornby, Mrs. Edmund [Emelia Bithynia Maceroni Hornby]. *In and Around Stamboul*. Philadelphia: James Challen & Son, [1858?]. Reprinted by Michigan University Library.
—— (Lady Hornby). *Constantinople during the Crimean War*. London: Richard Bentley, 1863.
Hornby, Sir Edmund. *An Autobiography*. London: Constable & Co. Ltd., 1929.
Klapka, George. *The War in the East: From the Year 1853 till July 1855*. Translated by A. Mednyanszky. London: Chapman and Hall, 1855.
Kovalevskiy, Yegor Petrovich (Eg. Kowalewski). *Der Krieg Russlands mit der Türkei in den Jahren 1853 und 1854 und der Bruch mit den Westmächten*. Leipzig: Verlag von Bernard Schlicke, 1869.
Lake, Henry Atwell (Colonel). *Kars and Our Captivity in Russia*. London: Richard Bentley, 1856.
——. *A Narrative of the Defence of Kars*. London: Richard Bentley, 1857.
Lane-Poole, Stanley. *The Life of the Right Honourable Stratford Canning: Viscount Stratford de Redcliffe*. 2 vols. London & New York: Longmans, Green, and Co., 1888.
——. *Lord Stratford Canning'in Türkiye Anıları*. Çev. Can Yücel. Ankara: Türkiye İş Bankası Yayınları, 1959. Ankara: Yurt Yayınları, 1988. Istanbul: Tarih Vakfı Yurt Yayınları, 1999.
Leward, Frank. *Memorials*. Ed. Charles Bampton. London: Kegan Paul, Trench & Co., 1884.
Likhutin, Mihail D. (?–1882). *Russkie v Aziatskoy Turtsii v 1854 i 1855 godakh*. St. Petersburg: Tipografiya tovarischestva "Obschestvennaya Pol'za", 1863.
Lütfi Efendi. *Vak'a-nüvis Ahmed Lütfi Efendi Tarihi. C. IX*. Yayınlayan Prof. Dr. Münir Aktepe. Istanbul: İstanbul Üniversitesi Edebiyat Fakültesi Yayınları, 1984.
Marx, Karl. *The Eastern Question. A reprint of letters written 1853–1856 dealing with the events of the Crimean War*. Edited by Eleanor Marx Aveling and Edward Aveling. New York: B. Franklin, 1968. London: Frank Cass, 1969. First edition London, 1897.
Melek Hanım. Wife of H. H. Kibrizli-Mehemet-Pasha. *Thirty Years in the Harem*. London, 1872. New edition: NJ: Gorgias Press, 2005. Introduced by Irwin C. Schick.
——. *Haremden Mahrem Hatıralar*. Fransızca'dan çeviren: İsmail Yerguz. Istanbul: Oğlak Yayınları, 1999.
Millingen, Frederick. See Osman Bey.
Moltke, Helmuth von. *Moltke'nin Türkiye Mektupları*. İstanbul: Remzi Kitabevi, 1999.
Money, Edward. *Twelve Months with the Bashi-Bazouks*. London: Chapman and Hall, 1857. Reprinted by Adamant Media Corporation, (Elibron Classsics), 2005.
Muravyov, Nikolay Nikolayevich. *Voina za Kavkazom v 1855 godu*. 2 vols. St. Petersburg: Tipografiya tovarischestva "Obschestvennaya pol'za", 1877.
Mustafa Zarif Paşa. See Zarifi Mustafa Paşa.

Nafiz Efendi. *Silistre Muhasarası*. İstanbul: Teodor Kasap Matbaası, 1290 [1873-74].
———. "Krepost' Silistriya v 1854 godu", *Voenny Sbornik* 106(12), 1875, pp. 488-502 (translation from Ottoman Turkish).
Oliphant, Laurence. *The Trans-Caucasian Campaign of the Turkish Army under Omer Pasha. A Personal Narrative*. Edinburgh and London: William Blackwood and Sons, 1856.
Osman Bey (Major). "Vospominaniya o 1855 gode", *Kavkazskiy Sbornik*, t. 2, 1877, pp. 143-214.
Öztelli, Cahit. *Uyan Padişahım*. Istanbul: Milliyet Yayınları, 1976.
Petrov, General Andrey Nikolayevich. *Voina Rossii s Turtsiey. Dunayskaya kampaniya 1853 i 1854 gg*. Vol. I. St. Petersburg, 1890.
Russell, William Howard (*The Times* correspondent). *The British Expedition to the Crimea*. Revised Edition. London: G. Routledge & Co., 1858.
———. *Despatches from the Crimea 1854-1856*. London: Deutsch, 1966. Also see Bentley, Nicolas.
Salname-i Devlet-i Aliyye 1268-1273.
Sandwith, Humphry. *A Narrative of the Siege of Kars*. London: John Murray, 1856.
Senior, Nassau William. *A Journal Kept in Turkey and Greece in the Autumn of 1857 and the Beginning of 1858*. London: Longman, Brown, Green, Longmans and Roberts, 1859.
Skene, James Henry. *With Lord Stratford in the Crimean War*. London: Richard Bentley and Son, 1883. Reprinted by Elibron Classics, 2005.
Slade, Adolphus [Mushaver Pasha] (1804-1877). *Turkey and the Crimean War. A Narrative of Historical Events*. London: Smith, Elder and Co., 1867.
———. *Türkiye ve Kırım Harbi*. Translated by Ali Rıza Seyfi (officer of the Turkish general staff). Istanbul: Genelkurmay X. Ş., 1943.
Zarifi Mustafa Paşa. Enver Ziya Karal (ed.). "Zarif Paşa'nın Hatıratı 1816-1862", *Belleten* IV, Ankara, 1940, pp. 442-494.

Secondary Sources

General Reference Sources, Bibliographies

Bol'shaya Sovetskaya Entsiklopediya. Article "Krymskaya Voina" by I. V. Bestuzhev-Lada.
Cliff, David. *A Crimean War Bibliography*. West Yorkshire: Crimean War Research Society, 1987.
Devellioğlu, Ferit. *Osmanlıca-Türkçe Ansiklopedik Lûgat*. Ankara: Aydın Kitabevi, 2002.
Encyclopedia Britannica. Article "Crimean War".
Katalog Knig o Krymskoi (Vostochnoy) Voine v fondakh nauchnoy biblioteki "Tavrika" im. A. Kh. Stevena. Krymskiy respublikanskiy kraevedcheskiy muzey. Krymskiy tsentr gumanitarnykh issledovaniy. Sostavitel' N. N. Kolesnikova. Simferopol: Krymskiy Arkhiv, 2005.
Kuneralp, Sinan. *Son Dönem Osmanlı Erkan ve Ricali (1839-1922)*. Istanbul: The Isis Press, 1999.
Mehmed Süreyya. *Sicill-i Osmani*. 6 vols. Istanbul: Tarih Vakfı Yurt Yayınları, 1996.
Redhouse, Sir James W. *A Turkish and English Lexicon*. Istanbul, 1890. Beirut: Librairie du Liban, 1996.
Şemsettin Sami. *Kamus ül A'lam*. Vol. 5. Istanbul: Mihran Matbaası, 1896.
——— and M. Emin Bozarslan (Osmanlıcadan çeviren). *Tarihteki İlk Türkçe Ansiklopedide Kürdistan ve Kürdler*, Istanbul: Deng Yayınları, 2001.
Sovetskaya Istoricheskaya Entsiklopediya. "Krymskaya voina", vol. 8, Moscow, 1965, pp. 196-203.

The Turks (Encyclopedia). Vol. 4. Ankara: Yeni Türkiye, 2002.
Zayonchkovskiy, Pyotr Andreyevich (ed.). *Istoriya dorevolyutsionnoy Rossii v dnevnikakh i vospominaniyakh. Tom 2. Chast' 1. 1801-1856*. Moscow: Izdatel'stvo "Kniga", 1977.

Books, Articles, Reviews, Symposium Papers

Abdurrahman Şeref. *Tarih Söyleşileri (Müsahabe-i Tarihiye)*. Sadeleştiren Mübeccel Nami Duru. İstanbul: Sucuoğlu Matbaası, 1980.
Abu-Manneh, Butrus. *Studies on Islam and the Ottoman Empire in the 19th Century (1826-1876)*. Istanbul: The Isis Press, 2001.
Acar, Kezban. *Resimlerle Rusya, Savaşlar ve Türkler*. Ankara: Nobel Yayınları, 2004.
Açba, Sait. *Osmanlı Devletinin Dış Borçlanması (1854-1915)*. Afyon: Afyon Kocatepe Üniversitesi İktisadi ve İdari Bilimler Fakültesi Yayınları, 1995.
Adanır, Fikret. "Der Krimkrieg von 1853-1856", in *Handbuch der Geschichte Russlands, Band 2*, Stuttgart: Anton Hiersemann Verlag, 2001, pp. 1189-1250.
———. "Turkey's entry into the Concert of Europe", *European Review* 13(3), London, 2005, pp. 395-417.
Akar, Şevket K. and Hüseyin Al. *Osmanlı Dış Borçları ve Gözetim Komisyonları 1854-1856*. Istanbul: Osmanlı Bankası Arşiv ve Araştırma Merkezi, Kasım 2003.
———. "Dersaadet Bankası'nın tasfiyesi ve 1852 borçlanması", *Tarih ve Toplum. Yeni Yaklaşımlar* 4(244), Istanbul, Güz 2006, pp. 149-207.
Aksan, Virginia. *Ottoman Wars 1700-1870: An Empire Besieged*. London, NY: Pearson Longman, 2007.
Akün, Ömer Faruk. "Eski Bir Şeyh Şamil Destanı", in *Atsız Armağanı*, Erol Güngör et al (eds.), Istanbul: Ötüken Yayınevi, 1976, pp. 17-59.
Akyıldız, Ali. *Osmanlı Finans Sisteminde Dönüm Noktası. Kağıt Para ve Sosyo-Ekonomik Etkileri*. Istanbul: Eren Yayıncılık, 1996.
———. *Mümin ve Müsrif Bir Padişah Kızı: Refia Sultan*. Istanbul: Tarih Vakfı Yurt Yayınları, 1998.
———. "Osmanlı Devleti'nin Kırım Savaşı'nı Finansmanı: İç ve Dış Borçlanmalar", symposium paper in *Savaştan Barışa*, 2007, pp. 11-18.
Ali Haydar Emir [Alpagot]. "Kırım Harbinin Safahat-ı Bahriyesine Müteallik Vesaik-ı Resmiye", *Risale-i Mevkute-i Bahriye*, cilt 4, numero 11-12, Eylül - Teşrin-i Evvel 1334 [Sept.-Nov. 1918], pp. 529-545.
Ali Rıza Seyfi. "Serdar-ı Ekrem Ömer Paşa'nın Mavera-i Kafkas Seferi ve Kars Niçün Sükut Etti?", *Donanma Mecmuası*, 1327-1328, pp. 2017-2022, 139-142.
Allen, W. E. D. and Paul Muratoff. *Caucasian Battlefields. A History of the Wars on the Turco-Caucasian Border, 1828-1921*. Cambridge: Cambridge University Press, 1953. Nashville: The Battery Press, 1999.
Anderson, M. S. *The Great Powers and the Near East (1774-1923)*. Great Britain: Robert Cunningham and Sons Ltd., 1970.
Anderson, Olive. "Economic Warfare in the Crimean War", *The Economic History Review*, New Series, 14(1), 1961, pp. 34-47.
———. "Great Britain and the Beginnings of the Ottoman Public Debt, 1854-55", *The Historical Journal* 7(1), 1964, pp. 47-63.
———. *A Liberal State at War: English Politics and Economics during the Crimean War*. New York: St. Martin's Press, 1967.
Andıç, Fuat and Süphan Andıç. *Kırım Savaşı. Ali Paşa ve Paris Antlaşması*. Istanbul: Eren Yayıncılık, 2002.
Averyanov, Pyotr Ivanovich (1867-1937). *Kurdy v voinakh Rossii s Persiey i Turtsiey v techenie XIX stoletiya*. Tiflis: Tipografiya Shtaba Kavkazskago voennago okruga, 1900.
———. Avyarov [sic]. *Osmanlı-Rus ve İran Savaşları'nda Kürtler 1801-1900*. Osmanlıcadan tercüme eden: Muhammed (Hoko) Varlı (Xani). Ankara: Sipan Yayıncılık, 1995.

Badem, Candan. "The Treatment of the Crimean War in Turkish Historiography", *Vostochnaya (Krymskaya) Voina 1853-1856 godov: Novye materialy i novoe osmyslenie*, vol. 1, Simferopol: Krymskiy Arkhiv, 2005, pp. 24-35.
——. "Rus ve Sovyet Tarih Yazımında Kırım Savaşı", *Toplumsal Tarih* 155, Istanbul, November 2006, pp. 16-23.
——. "Başbakanlık Osmanlı Arşivi'nden *Osmanlı Belgelerinde Kırım Savaşı* Derlemesi", review article, *Toplumsal Tarih* 160, Istanbul, April 2007, pp. 92-94.
——. "Kırım Savaşı Sırasında İsyanlar ve Asayiş Sorunları (1853-1856)", symposium paper in *Savaştan Barışa*, Istanbul: İ. Ü. Ed. Fak. Tarih Araştırmaları Merkezi, 2007, pp. 285-327.
——. *The Ottomans and the Crimean War*, PhD dissertation, Sabancı University, 2007.
——. "Kırım Savaşı Esnasında Namık Paşa'nın Avrupa'da Borç Arayışı (1853-54)", *Toplumsal Tarih* 186, Istanbul, June 2009, pp. 68-75.
Bailey, Frank Edgar. "The Economics of British Foreign Policy, 1825-50", *The Journal of Modern History* XII/4, December 1940, pp. 449-484.
——. *British Policy and the Turkish Reform Movement*, Cambridge (Massachusetts), London: Harvard University Press, 1942.
Baumgart, Winfried. *The Crimean War, 1853-1856*. London: Arnold; New York: Oxford University Press, 1999.
Baykal, Bekir Sıtkı. "Makamat-ı Mübareke Meselesi ve Babıali", *Belleten* XXIII (90), Ankara, April 1959, pp. 240-266.
Berkok, İsmail. *Tarihte Kafkasya*. Istanbul: İstanbul Matbaası, 1958.
Besbelli, Saim [Retired Naval Colonel]. *1853-1856 Osmanlı-Rus ve Kırım Savaşı (Deniz Harekâtı)*. Ankara: Genelkurmay Harp Tarihi Yayınları, 1977.
Bestuzhev, Igor Vasilyevich. *Krymskaya Voina 1853-56*. Moscow: Izdatel'stvo AN SSSR, 1956.
Blanch, Lesley. *The Sabres of Paradise*. NY: Carroll & Graf Publishers, 1995.
Bogdanovich, Modest Ivanovich. *Vostochnaya Voina 1853-1856 godov*. St. Petersburg: Tip. M. Stasiulievicha, 1877.
Budak, Mustafa. "1853-1856 Kırım Harbi Başlarında Doğu Anadolu-Kafkas Cephesi ve Şeyh Şamil". *Kafkas Araştırmaları* 1, 1988, pp. 52-58, 132-137, 236-243.
——. "1853-1856 Kırım Savaşı'nda Osmanlı Devleti ile Şeyh Şamil Arasındaki İlişkiler". *Tarih Boyunca Balkanlardan Kafkaslara Türk Dünyası Semineri, 29-31 Mayıs 1995. Bildiriler*. Istanbul: İ. Ü. Edebiyat Fakültesi Basımevi, 1996, pp. 79-92.
Burchuladze, Yermolay Yevseyevich. "Krushenie Anglo-Turetskikh Zakhvatnicheskikh Planov v Gruzii v 1855-1856 godakh". *Voprosy Istorii* 4, Moscow 1952, pp. 10-24.
Burkay, Kemal. *Geçmişten Bugüne Kürtler ve Kürdistan*. Cilt 1. Istanbul: Deng Yayınları, 1992. İkinci baskı, 1997.
Celil, Celile. *XIX. Yüzyıl Osmanlı İmparatorluğunda Kürtler*. Rusça'dan çeviren Mehmet Demir. Ankara: Öz-Ge Yayınları, 1992.
Chernyshevskiy, N. G. "Rasskaz o Krymskoi Voyne (po Kingleku)", *Polnoe sobranie sochineniy*, t. X, Moscow: Gospolitizdat, 1951, pp. 193-440. Written 26 October 1863.
Clay, Christopher. *Gold for the Sultan. Western Bankers and Ottoman Finance 1856-1881*. London, New York: I. B. Tauris Publishers, 2000.
Curtiss, John Shelton. "The Army of Nicholas I. Its Role and Character", *The American Historical Review* 63(4), July 1958, pp. 880-889.
——. *The Russian Army under Nicholas I, 1825-1855*. Durham, N.C.: Duke University Press, 1965.
Curzon, Robert. *Armenia: A Year at Erzeroom, and on the Frontiers of Russia, Turkey, and Persia*. New York: Harper & Brothers, 1854.
Çavlı, Emin Ali. *Kırım Harbi (Paris Muahedesi 1956)*. Istanbul: Hilmi Kitabevi, 1957.
Çelik, Yüksel. "Tanzimat Devrinde Rüşvet-Hediye İkilemi ve Bu Alandaki Yolsuzlukları Önleme Çabaları", *Türk Kültürü İncelemeleri Dergisi* 15, Istanbul 2006, pp. 25-64.

Davison, Roderic. *Reform in the Ottoman Empire, 1856-1876*. Princeton, N.J.: Princeton University Press, 1963. New York: Gordian Press, 1973. Turkish translation: *Osmanlı İmparatorluğu'nda Reform, 1856-1876*. Translated from the English by Osman Akınhay. Istanbul: Papirus, 1997.
——. *Essays in Ottoman and Turkish History, 1774-1923: The Impact of the West*. Austin: University of Texas, 1990. London: Saqi Books, 1990.
——. *Nineteenth Century Ottoman Diplomacy and Reforms*. Istanbul: Isis Press, 1999.
Druzhinin, N. M. "Spornye voprosy Krymskoi voiny". Pis'ma v redaktsiyu. (Reply to Tarle). *Istoricheskiy Zhurnal* 4/140, Institut Istorii AN SSSR, Moscow 1945, pp. 113-120.
Dubrovin, Nikolai Fyodorovich. *Istoriya Krymskoi voiny i oborony Sevastopolya*. 3 vols. St. Petersburg: Tipografiya tovarischestva "Obschestvennaya Pol'za", 1900.
Edgerton, Robert B. *Death or Glory: The Legacy of the Crimean War*. Boulder, CO: Westview Press, 1999.
Eldem, Edhem. "Ottoman financial integration with Europe: Foreign loans, the Ottoman Bank and the Ottoman public debt", *European Review* 13 (3), Cambridge University Press, 2005, pp. 431-445.
Engelhardt, Edouard. *Türkiye ve Tanzimat Hareketleri*. Türkçesi Ayla Düz. Istanbul: Milliyet Yayınları, 1976.
Erdem, Y. Hakan. *Slavery in the Ottoman Empire and Its Demise 1800-1909*. Houndmills, Basingstoke, Hampshire: Macmillan Press; New York: St. Martin's Press, 1996.
——. "Kırım Savaşı'nda Karadeniz Beyaz Köle Ticareti", symposium paper in *Savaştan Barışa*, 2007, pp. 85-118.
Fevzi. See Kurtoğlu, Fevzi.
Fortescue, John William. *A History of the British Army*. Vol. XIII (1852-1870). London: MacMillan, 1929. London: Naval & Military Press, 2004.
Gammer, Moshe. *Muslim Resistance to the Tsar: Shamil and the Conquest of Chechnia and Daghestan*. London: Frank Cass, 1994.
——. "Shamil and the Ottomans: A Preliminary Overview", *V. Milletlerarası Türkiye Sosyal ve İktisat Tarihi Kongresi. Tebliğler. İstanbul 21-25 Ağustos 1989*. Ankara: TTK, 1990, pp. 387-394.
Genelkurmay Harp Tarihi Başkanlığı. *Türk Silahlı Kuvvetleri Tarihi. III. Cilt. 5. Kısım. 1793-1908*. Ankara: Genelkurmay Basımevi, 1978. See pp. 450-466 for the Crimean War.
—— and Genelkurmay Askeri Tarih ve Stratejik Etüt Başkanlığı. *Selçuklular Döneminde Anadolu'ya Yapılan Akınlar - 1799-1802 Osmanlı-Fransız Harbinde Akka Kalesi Savunması - 1853-1856 Osmanlı - Rus Kırım Harbi Kafkas Cephesi*. Ankara: Kültür Bakanlığı Yayınları, 1981.
Gencer, Mustafa. "Alman Basınında Kırım Savaşı", symposium paper in *Savaştan Barışa*, 2007, pp. 151-172.
Genç, Mehmet. *Osmanlı İmparatorluğu'nda Devlet ve Ekonomi*. Istanbul: Ötüken Neşriyat, 2000.
Geyrot, Aleksandr Fedorovich. *Opisanie Vostochnoy Voiny 1853-1856 gg*. St. Petersburg: Tipografiya Eduarda Goppe, 1872.
Goldfrank, David. "The Ottoman Empire and the Origin of the Crimean War: Sources and Strategies", *The Turks*, vol. 4, Ankara: Yeni Türkiye Yayınları, 2002, pp. 233-245.
Göçen, Hayreddin Nedim. See Hayreddin Bey.
Gövsa, İbrahim Alaettin. *Türk Meşhurları Ansiklopedisi*. Vol. 1. [Istanbul]: Yedigün Neşriyat, undated.
Grigoryants, Vladimir Yervandovich. "Vostochnaya (Krymskaya) voina i armyane", *Istoricheskoe Nasledie Kryma* 6-7, Simferopol, 2004.

Gülsoy, Ufuk. *Osmanlı Gayrimüslimlerinin Askerlik Serüveni*. Istanbul: Simurg Yayınları, 2000.
Güran, Tevfik. "Tanzimat Döneminde Osmanlı Maliyesi, Bütçeler ve Hazine Hesapları 1841-1861", Türk Tarih Kurumu, *Belgeler* XIII (17), Ankara 1988, pp. 213-364. Ayrıbasım: Ankara: TTK, 1989.
Gürel, A. Tevfik (Kur. Yzb). *1853-55 Türk-Rus ve Müttefiklerin Kırım Savaşı*. Istanbul: Askeri Matbaa, 1935.
Hakan, Sinan. *Osmanlı Arşiv Belgelerinde Kürtler ve Kürt Direnişleri (1817-1867)*. Istanbul: Doz Yayıncılık, 2007.
Hale, William and Ali İhsan Bağış (eds.). *Four Centuries of Turco-British Relations*. North Humberside, UK: The Eothen Press, 1984.
Halicz, Emanuel. *Danish Neutrality during the Crimean War (1853-1856): Denmark between the Hammer and the Anvil*. Odense: University Press of Southern Denmark, 1977.
Hayreddin Bey. *1270 Kırım Muharebesinin Tarih-i Siyasiyesi*. Istanbul: Ahmed İhsan Matbaası, 1326 [1910]. New simplified edition: *Kırım Harbi*. [Hazırlayan: Şemseddin Kutlu]. Istanbul: Tercüman Gazetesi 1001 Temel Eser, 1976.
Heinzelmann, Tobias. *Heiliger Kampf oder Landesverteidigung? Die Diskussion um die Einführung der allgemeinen Militärpflicht im Osmanischen Reich 1826-1856*. Frankfurt am Main: Peter Lang, 2004.
Henderson, Gavin B. "The Diplomatic Revolution of 1854: I The Four Points", *The American Historical Review* 43(1), October 1937, pp. 22-50.
Hüseyin Hüsnü. *Saika-i Zafer*. Istanbul: Maarif Vekaleti, 1292 [1876].
Ibragimbeyli, Khadji Murat. *Kavkaz v Krymskoi Voine 1853-1856 gg. i Mezhdunarodnye Otnosheniya*. Moscow: Nauka, 1971.
İğdemir, Uluğ. *Kuleli Vakası Hakkında Bir Araştırma*. Ankara: TTK, 1937.
İlgürel, Mücteba. "Rus Donanmasının Sinop Baskını", *Birinci Tarih Boyunca Karadeniz Kongresi Bildirileri (13-17 Ekim 1986)*, Samsun 1988, s. 163-177.
İnal, İbnülemin Mahmut Kemal. *Son Sadrazamlar*. 1. Cilt. Istanbul: Dergah Yayınları, 1981?
İnalcık, Halil; Quataert, Donald (eds.). *An Economic and Social History of the Ottoman Empire*. Vol. II. Cambridge: Cambridge University Press, 1997.
Jorga, Nicolae. *Osmanlı İmparatorluğu Tarihi*, cilt 5. Çeviri: Nilüfer Epçeli. Istanbul: Yeditepe Yayınevi, 2005.
Karal, Enver Ziya. "Rüşvetin Kaldırılması için Yapılan Teşebbüsler", *Tarih Vesikaları* 1, June 1941, pp. 45-65.
——. *Osmanlı Tarihi* V. Ankara: TTK, 1995.
Karasu, Cezmi. "Kırım Savaşı'nda Kontenjan Askeri", Yedinci Askeri Tarih Semineri Bildirileri I, Ankara: Genelkurmay ATASE Yayınları, 2000, pp. 15-27.
Kaylan, Aziz [Derleyen]. *(Tarihimizin Unutulan Olayı) Kırım Savaşı (1853-1856)*. Istanbul: Milliyet Yayın Ltd. Şti. Yayınları, 1975.
Kaynar, Reşat. *Mustafa Reşit Paşa ve Tanzimat*. Ankara: TTK, 1991.
Kazgan, Gülten. *Tanzimat'tan 21. Yüzyıla Türkiye Ekonomisi*. Istanbul: İstanbul Bilgi Üniversitesi Yayınları, 2002.
Kennedy, Paul. *The Rise and Fall of The Great Powers. Economic Change and Military Conflict from 1500 to 2000*. New York: Vintage, 1989.
——. *Büyük Güçlerin Yükseliş ve Çöküşleri*. Çeviren: Birtane Karanakçı. Ankara: İş Bankası Yayınları, 1990.
Khalfin, Naftula Aronovich. *Bor'ba za Kurdistan. (Kurdskiy vopros v mezhdunarodnyh otnosheniyah XIX veka)*. Moscow, 1963.
—— (Halfin). *XIX. Yüzyılda Kürdistan Üzerinde Mücadeleler*. Ankara: Komal, 1976. Istanbul: Komal, 1992.
Kırım Savaşı'nın 150nci Yılı / 150th Anniversary of the Crimean War. Istanbul: Vehbi Koç Vakfı Sadberk Hanım Müzesi, December 2006.

Kırımlı, Hakan. "The Crimean Tatar Units in the Ottoman Army during the Crimean War", unpublished symposium paper presented at the French Institute of Anatolian Studies (IFEA) in Istanbul on 27 November 2004.
Kırlı, Cengiz. "Yolsuzluğun İcadı: 1840 Ceza Kanunu, İktidar ve Bürokrasi", *Tarih ve Toplum. Yeni Yaklaşımlar* 4 (244), Güz 2006, pp. 45-199.
Kırzıoğlu, Fahrettin. *100. Yıldönümü Dolayısıyla 1855 Kars Zaferi*. Istanbul: Işıl Matbaası, 1955.
——. "Folk Traditions in Kars during the Last Six Turkish-Russian Wars on the Anatolian Front", *Kars and Eastern Anatolia in the Recent History of Turkey. Symposium and the Excavation*. Ankara: Publication of Governor's Office of Kars and Ataturk University, 1994, pp. 147-162.
Kızıltoprak, Süleyman. "Egyptian troops in the Crimean War (1853-1856)", *Vostochnaya (Krymskaya) Voina 1853-1856 godov: Novye materialy i novoe osmyslenie*. Tom 1, Simferopol: Krymskiy Arkhiv, 2005, pp. 48-55.
Kinglake, Alexander W. *The Invasion of the Crimea: Its Origin, and an Account of its Progress Down to the Death of Lord Raglan*. 6 vols. New York, London: Harper, 1863-87.
Kundukh, Aytek. *Kafkasya Müridizmi: Gazavat Tarihi*. Haz. Tarık Cemal Kutlu. Istanbul: Gözde Kitaplar Yayınevi, 1987.
Kuneralp, Sinan. "Bir Osmanlı Diplomatı Kostaki Musurus Paşa 1807-1891", *Belleten* XXXIV/135, Temmuz 1970, pp. 421-435.
Kurat, Akdes Nimet. *Türkiye ve Rusya: XVIII. Yüzyıl Sonundan Kurtuluş Savaşına Kadar Türk-Rus İlişkileri (1798-1919)*. Ankara: Ankara Üniversitesi Dil ve Tarih-Coğrafya Fakültesi Yayınları, 1970.
[Kurtoğlu], Fevzi (Yüzbaşı, Bahriye mektebi muallimlerinden). *1853-1855 Türk-Rus Harbi ve Kırım Seferi*. Istanbul: Devlet Matbaası, 1927.
Kütükoğlu, Mübahat. *XX. Asra Erişen İstanbul Medreseleri*. Ankara: TTK, 2000.
Lambert, Andrew. *The Crimean War: British Grand Strategy against Russia, 1853-56*. Manchester: Manchester University Press, 1991.
Lambert, Andrew and Stephen Badsey. *The War Correspondents. The Crimean War*. Gloucestershire: Alan Sutton, 1994.
Levy, Avigdor. "The Officer Corps in Sultan Mahmud II's New Ottoman Army, 1826-39", *International Journal of Middle East Studies* 2, 1971, pp. 21-39.
——. "Formalization of Cossack Service under Ottoman Rule", in Gunther Rothenberg, Bela Kiraly and Peter Sugar (eds.), *East Central European Society and War in the Pre-Revolutionary Eighteenth Century*, NY: Columbia University Press, 1982, pp. 491-505.
Lewis, Bernard. "Slade on the Turkish Navy", *Journal of Turkish Studies / Türklük Bilgisi Araştırmaları*, vol. 11, Harvard University, 1987, pp. 1-10.
Malmîsanij, [Mehemed]. *Cızira Botanlı Bedirhaniler*. Istanbul: Avesta Yayınevi, 2000.
Mardin, Şerif. *Yeni Osmanlı Düşüncesinin Doğuşu*. Istanbul: İletişim Yayınları, 1998.
Mawson, Michael Hargreave. *The True Heroes of Balaclava*. Kent, Bedford, London: Crimean War Research Society Publications, spiral-bound printout, 1996.
Morawitz, Charles. *Türkiye Maliyesi*. Ankara: Maliye Bakanlığı Tetkik Kurulu Yayını, 1979.
Mordvinov, R. N. *Sinopskiy Boy*. Leningrad: Obschchestvo po rasprostraneniyu politicheskikh i nauchnykh znaniy, 1953. Stenogramma publichnoy lektsii.
Mosse, Werner E. "How Russia Made Peace September 1855 to April 1856", *Cambridge Historical Journal* 11(3), 1955, pp. 297-316.
Ochsenwald, William. "Muslim-European Conflict in the Hijaz: The Slave Trade Controversy, 1840-1895", *Middle Eastern Studies* 16, 1980, pp. 115-126.
——. *Religion, Economy, and State in Ottoman-Arab History*. Istanbul: The ISIS Press, 1998.

Onaran, Burak. "Kuleli Vakası hakkında 'başka' bir araştırma", *Tarih ve Toplum Yeni Yaklaşımlar* 5, Spring 2007, p. 17.
Ortaylı, İlber. *İmparatorluğun En Uzun Yüzyılı*. Istanbul: İletişim Yayınları, 2001.
Osman Bey, Major. "Vospominaniya o 1855 gode", *Kavkazskiy Sbornik*, vol. 2, 1877, pp. 143-214.
Özcan, Besim. *Kırım Savaşı'nda Mali Durum ve Teb'anın Harb Siyaseti (1853-1856)*. Erzurum: Atatürk Üniversitesi Yayınları, 1997.
Pakalın, Mehmet Zeki. *Maliye Teşkilatı Tarihi (1442-1930)*. Vol. 3. Ankara: Maliye Bakanlığı Tetkik Kurulu Yayını, 1978.
Palmer, Alan W. *Kırım Savaşı ve Modern Avrupa'nın Doğuşu*. Translated by Meral Gaspıralı. Istanbul: Sabah Yayınları, 1999.
Pamuk, Şevket. *Osmanlı Ekonomisi ve Dünya Kapitalizmi (1820-1913)*. Ankara: Yurt Yayınları, 1984. Revised edition: *Osmanlı Ekonomisinde Bağımlılık ve Büyüme 1820-1913*. Istanbul: Tarih Vakfı Yurt Yayınları, 1994.
Pokrovskiy, Mikhail N. (?-1932). *Istoriya Rossii v XIX veke*, tom III, chast' 2-ya, otd. 1. Moscow: Br. A. i I Granat i Ko., 1908. Moscow: Izdatel'stvo "Tsentrpoligraf", 2001.
——. *Diplomatiya i Voiny Tsarskoy Rossii v XIX Stoletii. Sbornik Statey*. Moscow: Krasnaya Nov', 1923.
Ponting, Clive. *The Crimean War. The Truth Behind the Myth*. London: Chatto & Windus, 2004; Pimlico, 2005.
Puryear, Vernon John. "New Light on the Origins of the Crimean War", *The Journal of Modern History* 3(2), June 1931, pp. 219-234.
——. *England, Russia, and the Straits Question, 1844-1856*. Berkeley: University of California Publications in History, 1931. Reprinted, Hamden: Archon Books, 1965.
——. *International Economics and Diplomacy in the Near East: A Study of British Commercial Policy in the Levant, 1834-1853*. Stanford University Press; London: H. Milford, Oxford University Press, 1935. Reprinted, Hamden: Archon Books, 1969.
Quataert, Donald. *Ottoman Manufacturing in the Age of the Industrial Revolution*, Cambridge & New York: Cambridge University Press, 1993.
Ralston, David B. *Importing the European Army*. Chicago & London: The University of Chicago Press, 1990.
Reid, James J. *Crisis of the Ottoman Empire. Prelude to Collapse 1839-1878*. Stuttgart: Franz Steiner Verlag, 2000.
——. "'How the Turks Rule Armenia'", in Richard G. Hovannisian (ed.), *Armenian Karin / Erzerum*, Costa Mesa, CA: Mazda Publishers, 2003, pp. 147-187.
Riasanovsky, Nicholas V. *A History of Russia*. Oxford: Oxford University Press, 2000.
Rodkey, Frederick Stanley. "Lord Palmerston and the Rejuvenation of Turkey, 1830-41", Part I, *The Journal of Modern History* 1 (4), December 1929, pp. 570-593; Part II, *The Journal of Modern History* 2 (2), June 1930, pp. 193-225.
——. "Ottoman Concern about Western Economic Penetration in the Levant, 1849-1856", *Journal of Modern History* 30(4), December 1958, pp. 348-353.
Rosenthal, Steven. "Foreigners and Municipal Reform in Istanbul: 1855-1865", *International Journal of Middle East Studies* 11(2), April 1980, pp. 227-245.
Royle, Trevor. *Crimea. The Great Crimean War 1854-1856*. London: Little, Brown and Company, 1999. Second edition: London: Abacus, 2000.
Rudnytsky, Ivan Lysiak. "Michał Czajkowski's Cossack Project During the Crimean War: An Analysis of Ideas", in P. L. Rudnytsky (ed.), *Essays in Modern Ukrainian History*, Edmonton, Alberta: Canadian Institute of Ukrainian Studies, 1987, pp. 173-186.
Saab, Ann Pottinger. *The Origins of the Crimean Alliance*. Charlottesville: University Press of Virginia, 1977.

Sakaoğlu, Necdet; Akbayar, Nuri. *Sultan Abdülmecid. A Milestone on Turkey's Path of Westernization.* Istanbul: Denizbank Publications (Creative Yayıncılık Ltd), January 2002.
Salih Hayri. *Kırım Zafernamesi - Hayrabat.* Hazırlayan Necat Birinci. Ankara: Kültür ve Turizm Bakanlığı Yayınları, 1988.
Savaştan Barışa: 150. Yıldönümünde Kırım Savaşı ve Paris Antlaşması (1853-1856). 22-23 Mayıs 2006. Bildiriler. Istanbul: İ. Ü. Ed. Fak. Tarih Araştırma Merkezi, 2007.
Sayar, Ahmed Güner. *Osmanlı İktisat Düşüncesinin Çağdaşlaşması.* Istanbul: Der Yayınları, 1986.
Saydam, Abdullah. *Kırım ve Kafkas Göçleri (1856-1876).* Ankara: TTK, 1997.
Seaton, Albert. *The Crimean War. A Russian Chronicle.* London: B. T. Batsford Ltd, 1977.
Semenov, L. S.; Sheremet, V. I. "Vneshneekonomicheskie svyazi Turtsii epokhi Krymskoi voiny", *Vestnik Leningradskogo Universiteta* 14, vypusk 3, 1973, pp. 44-49.
Sevgen, Nazmi. *Doğu ve Güneydoğu Anadolu'da Türk Beylikleri. Osmanlı Belgeleri ile Kürt Türkleri Tarihi.* Yayına hazırlayanlar: Şükrü Kaya Sertoğlu - Halil Kemal Türközü [Erdal İlter]. Ankara: Türk Kültürünü Araştırma Enstitüsü, 1982.
Seyitdanlıoğlu, Mehmet; İnalcık, Halil (eds.). *Tanzimat.* Ankara: Phoenix, 2006.
Sezer, Hamiyet. "Ferhat Paşa'nın Kırım Savaşı Sırasında Kafkas Cephesindeki Osmanlı Ordusuna Dair Düşünceleri", *Sekizinci Askeri Tarih Semineri Bildirileri*, I, Ankara: Genelkurmay Basımevi, 2003, pp. 75-85.
Shaw, Stanford J.; Shaw, Ezel Kural. *History of the Ottoman Empire and Modern Turkey.* Vol. II. Cambridge, UK: Cambridge University Press, 1977.
Sheremet, Vitaliy Ivanovich. (co-author L. S. Semenov), "Vneshneekonomicheskie svyazi Turtsii epokhi Krymskoy voiny", *Vestnik Leningradskogo Universiteta* 14, vypusk 3, 1973, pp. 44-49.
—— (co-author Khadji Murat Ibragimbeyli), "Sovremennaya Turetskaya Istoriografiya Vostochnoy (Krymskoy) Voiny", *Voprosy Istorii* 4, Moscow, April 1977, pp. 45-57.
Shkedya, Oleg P. "Turetskaya armiya v Krymskoy kampanii", *Vostochnaya (Krymskaya) Voina 1853-1856 godov: Novye materialy i novoe osmyslenie*, vol. 1, Simferopol: Krymskiy Arkhiv, 2005, pp. 78-90.
Sinaplı, Ahmet Nuri. *Şeyhül Vüzera, Serasker Mehmet Namık Paşa.* Istanbul: Yenilik Basımevi, 1987.
Somel, Selçuk Akşin. *The Modernization of Public Education in the Ottoman Empire 1839-1908.* Leiden, Boston, Köln: Brill, 2001.
Sondhaus, Lawrence. *Naval Warfare, 1815-1914.* London & NY: Routledge, 2001.
Stavrianos, L. S. *The Balkans since 1453.* London: Hurst & Company, 2000.
Stepanov, Valeriy. "Krymskaya Voina i ekonomika Rossii", paper submitted to the conference on the Crimean War, organized by the Polish Academy of Sciences, Institute of History, Warsaw, 3-4 October 2007.
Süer, Hikmet. *Türk Silahlı Kuvvetleri Tarihi. Osmanlı devri. Osmanlı-Rus Kırım Harbi Kafkas Cephesi Harekatı (1853-1856).* Ankara: Genelkurmay Askeri Tarih ve Stratejik Etüt Başkanlığı Yayınları, 1986.
Svechin, Aleksandr Andreyevich. *Evolyutsiya Voennogo Iskusstva.* 2 vols. Moscow-Leningrad: Voengiz, 1928.
Şahin, Hasan. "Kırım Harbi (1853-1856) öncesinde Erzurum vilayetinde ve Doğu Anadolu Kafkas sınırında meydana gelen karışıklıklar", *Atatürk Üniversitesi Türkiyat Araştırmaları Enstitüsü Dergisi* 9, Erzurum, 1998, pp. 159-164.
Şener, Abdüllatif. *Tanzimat Dönemi Osmanlı Vergi Sistemi.* Ankara: İşaret, 1990.
Şimşir, Bilal. "Kırım Savaşı Arifesinde Mustafa Reşid Paşa'nın Yazışmaları". *Mustafa Reşid Paşa ve Dönemi Semineri. Bildiriler. Ankara, 13-14 Mart 1985*, Ankara: Türk Tarih Kurumu, 1987, pp. 77-91.

Tansel, Fevziye Abdullah. "Yardıma Koşan Manevi Ordu ve Kırım Harbi (1853-56)". *Kubbealtı Akademi Mecmuası* 16(3), Temmuz 1987, pp. 25-41.
——. "1853-1856 Kırım Harbi'yle İlgili Destanlar", *X. Türk Tarih Kongresi. Ankara: 22-26 Eylül 1986. Kongreye Sunulan Bildiriler*, V. Cilt, Ankara: TTK, 1994, pp. 1977-2009.
Tarle, Yevgeny Viktorovich. *Krymskaya Voina*. 2 vols. Moscow: Izdatel'stvo AN, 1943, 1950. Moscow: Izografus & Eksmo, 2003.
Temperley, Harold. "The Last Phase of Stratford de Redcliffe", *The English Historical Review* 47(186), April 1932, pp. 216-259.
——. "Stratford de Redcliffe and the Origins of the Crimean War", Part I, *The English Historical Review* 48(192), October 1933, pp. 601-621. Part II, ibid., April 1934, pp. 265-298.
——. *England and the Near East: the Crimea*. London: Longmans, Green and Co. Ltd., 1936. London: Frank Cass, 1964.
Timm, Vasily (Georg Wilhelm). *Russkiy Khudozhestvenny Listok*. St. Petersburg, 1853, 1854, 1855, 1856.
Toledano, Ehud. *The Ottoman Slave Trade and Its Suppression*. NJ: Princeton University Press, 1982.
Tozlu, Selahattin. "Kırım Harbi'nde Kars'ı Anlatan Kayıp Bir Eser: Muzaffer-Name", *Akademik Araştırmalar* 1(2), Erzurum, Güz 1996, pp. 123-144.
Troubetzkoy, Alexis. *A Brief History of the Crimean War*. New York: Carroll & Graf, 2006.
Turgay, A. Üner. "İane-i Cihadiyye: A Multi-Ethnic, Multi-Religious Contribution to Ottoman War Effort", *Studia Islamica* LXIV, pp. 115-124.
Türkgeldi, Ali Fuat (1867-1935). *Mesâil-i Mühimme-i Siyâsiyye*. 3 vols. Yay. Haz. Bekir Sıtkı Baykal. Ankara: Türk Tarih Kurumu, 1957-60. Second edition 1987.
Ubicini, A. [Jean Henri Abdolonyme]. *La Turquie Actuelle*. Paris: Librairie de L. Hachette et Cie, 1855.
Urquhart, David. *Turkey and Its Resources: Its Municipal Organization,...Prospects of English Commerce in the East, etc*. London, 1833.
Velay, A. du. *Türkiye Mali Tarihi*. Ankara: Maliye Bakanlığı Yayınları, 1978.
Vernadsky, George. *A History of Russia*. Yale: Yale University Press, 1969.
Wason, David. *Battlefield Detectives: What Really Happened on the World's Most Famous Battlefields*. London: Granada Television Production, 2003.
Yamauchi, Masayuki. "Sheikh Shamil and the Ottoman Empire in the Period of the Crimean War. Enlightened by the ATASE Archives in Ankara", *Orient* XXII, Tokio, 1986, pp. 143-158.
Yavuz, Celalettin (Dr. Dz. Kur. Kd. Albay). *Osmanlı Bahriyesi'nde Yabancı Misyonlar*. Kasımpaşa, Istanbul: İst. Dz. İk. Grp. K.'lığı Basımevi Müdürlüğü, [2000?].
Yıldız, Mehmet. "1856 Islahat Fermanına Giden Yolda Meşruiyet Arayışları (Uluslararası Baskılar ve Cizye Sorununa Bulunan Çözümün İslami Temelleri)", *Türk Kültürü İncelemeleri Dergisi* 7, Istanbul, Güz 2002, pp. 75-114.
Yıldız, Netice. "İngiliz Basını ve Arşiv Belgeleri Işığında Kırım Savaşı ile İlgili Bazı Sosyal Etkinlikler", *Tarih ve Toplum* 103, Temmuz 1992, pp. 24-29.
Zaklitschine, S. de. *Kars et le Général Williams. Réponse au Livre Bleu*. Malta, 1856.
Zayonchkovskiy, Andrey Medardovich. *Vostochnaya Voina 1853-1856 gg v svyazi s sovremennoy ey politicheskoy obstanovkoy*. Tom I-II. St. Petersburg, 1908-1913. 4 vols. St. Petersburg: Poligon, 2002. 2 vols., vol. II in two parts. Simferopol: Krymskiy Arkhiv, 2005. 2 vols.

Unpublished Doctoral Dissertations and MA Theses

Akyüz, Fatih. *Kırım Savaşı'nın Lojistiğinde İstanbul'un Yeri*. MA Thesis. Marmara University, 2006. Supervisor: Zekeriya Kurşun.

Budak, Mustafa. *1853-1856 Kırım Savaşı'nda Kafkas Cephesi*. Doctoral Dissertation. Istanbul University, 1993. Supervisor: Mehmet Saray.
Kantarcı, Şenol. *Kars Tabyalarının İnşası*. MA Thesis. Atatürk University, Erzurum 1997. Supervisor: Muammer Demirel.
Karasu, Cezmi. *Kırım Savaşı Sırasında Osmanlı Diplomasisi (1853-1856)*. Doctoral Dissertation. Ankara University, 1998. Supervisor: Yavuz Ercan.
Köremezli, İbrahim. *The Place of the Ottoman Empire in the Russo-Circassian War (1830-1864)*. MA Thesis. Bilkent University, Department of International Relations, Ankara, 2004.
Özcan, Besim. *Rus Donanmasının Sinop Baskını (30 Kasım 1853)*. Doctoral Dissertation. Atatürk University, Erzurum, 1990. Supervisor: Enver Konukçu.
Şahin, Hasan. *1855 Erzurum Harekatı*. Doctoral Dissertation. Atatürk University, Erzurum, 1995. Supervisor: Enver Konukçu.
Şimşek, Veysel. *Ottoman Military Recruitment and the Recruit: 1826-1853*. MA Thesis. Bilkent University, Department of History, Ankara, 2005.
Taşkın, Figen. *Kırım Savaşı'nın Osmanlı İmparatorluğu'na Ekonomik Etkileri ve İaşe Sorunu*. Doctoral Dissertation. Istanbul University, 2007. Supervisor: Toktamış Ateş.
Türk, İ. Caner. *1853-56 Kırım Harbi Sırasında Osmanlı-İran İlişkileri, Osmanlı Devletine Karşı Rus-İran Gizli Antlaşması*. MA Thesis. Atatürk University, Erzurum, 2000. Supervisor: Hasan Şahin.
Yapıcı, Hakkı. *Takvim-i Vekayi'de Kırım Harbi (1853-1856)*. MA Thesis. Supervisor: Besim Özcan. Atatürk University, Erzurum, 1999.
Yıldız, Mehmet. *1856 Islahat Fermanının Tatbiki ve Tepkiler*. Doctoral Dissertation. Supervisor: Kemal Beydilli. Istanbul University, 2003.

INDEX

Abbas Pasha, 320
Abdi Pasha, Çırpanlı (Müşir Abdülkerim Nadir Pasha), 13, 36, 49, 143, 146, 157, 160, 162, 392
Abdulmuttalib Efendi (Emir of Mecca), 356-358
Abdurrahman Pasha, Mirliva, 219, 223, 224
Abdülmecid, Sultan, 46-49, 51, 72, 77, 78, 86, 98, 101, 130, 131, 134, 140, 315, 320, 322, 332, 336, 349, 352, 386, 395, 397, 399, 411
    firmans on Georgian and Circassian slave trade, 352
    honouring balls at the British and French embassies, 333-335
Aberdeen, Lord, 307
Abu Manneh, Butrus, on Abdülmecid, 47
Ahmed Pasha, Bahriye Feriki, Kayserili, 112, 131, 133, 197
Ahmed Pasha, governor of Tunis, 320
Ahmed Pasha, Ferik, Tacirli, 143, 146, 157, 160, 171
Ahmed Pasha, Mirliva, 236
Ahmed Pasha, Nazır, 103
Ahmed Rıza Trabzoni, 10, 121, 124, 146, 170, 255, 256, 394
Ahmet Cevdet Pasha, see Cevdet Pasha
Ahısha (Ahıska), battle of, 157, 162, 163
Aivasovskiy, Ivan, 126
Aleksandr, Prince of Serbia, 81
Aleksandr II, Emperor of Russia, 286
Ali Mahir Bey, Miralay, 123
Âli Pasha, Mehmed Emin, 9, 18, 47, 86, 87, 282, 286, 288, 295, 322, 341, 343, 344, 355, 358, 359, 400
Ali Pasha, Mirliva, 161, 162
Ali Fethi Pasha, 328
Ali Rıza Pasha, Ferik, 144, 162, 163, 164
allied fleets, 115, 129, 136, 137, 142, 183, 187, 194, 195, 197, 199, 201, 202, 282, 284
Andronikov, General Prince, 161
Anglo-Ottoman commercial treaty of 1838, 58
Anrep, General Count, 107, 177

Ardahan, 156, 157
Arif Efendi, Sheikhulislam, 97
Arif Hikmet Bey Efendi, Sheikhulislam, 98
Aristarchi, Nikolaos, Greek logothete, 78
Arnaud, Marshal Saint, 85, 185
asakir-i muvazzafa, see *başıbozuks*
Averyanov, General Pyotr I., review of his book, 28

Balaklava, battle of, 270-275
Baltazzi, Theodore, 315, 328
Başgedikler, battle of, 168, 169
başıbozuks, 52, 103, 147, 154, 155, 163, 165, 167, 194, 220, 257, 261, 263, 283, 296, 359, 360, 365, 366, 377-380, 382-388, 391, 396, 407, 408
    and decapitation, 161
    at the battle of Kürekdere, 220
    Kurdish başıbozuks, 170, 367
Bayezid, occupied by the Russians, 213
Bayındır, battle of, 159, 160
Beatson, Colonel, 261
Bebutov, General Prince Osip, 159
Bedirhan Bey (Pasha), 28, 44, 171, 361-363, 369, 370
Behcet Efendi (Behcet Pasha), 152, 202
Benedetti, Vincent, 74, 201, 214, 226, 350
Black, Mr J. N. (Galata banker), 316, 317
Blunt, John, 35, 270, 271, 275, 276
Boyacıköy, convention of, 186
Brant, James, 152
British, consulate in Alexandria, 81
    consul(ate) in Damascus, 382, 390
    consul in Edirne, 384, 385
    consul(ate) in Erzurum, 152, 172, 174, 226, 227, 233, 252, 365, 384, 392
    consul in Salonica, 387
    consul in Varna, 384
    declaration of war, 180
    interference in the revolt of Yezdanşêr, 370-377
Budak, Mustafa, review of his dissertation, 22
Buol, Count, 181

Canning, Stratford, see Lord Stratford de Redcliffe
Caucasian front, 143, 190
Cetate, see Çatana
Cevdet Pasha, 6, 41, 42, 45, 86, 283, 284, 292, 294, 300, 334, 335, 340, 344–346, 356, 411
  on Shamil and Circassians, 211
  on Âli Pasha's attitude towards Circassia during the peace congress, 358–359
Champoiseau, Charles, 208
cholera, 188, 189
churches, repair and building of, 346, 347
Circassians, 21, 31, 36, 51, 85, 113, 135, 149, 195, 197, 198, 225, 253, 287, 349, 350, 352, 353, 355, 404
cizye, 50, 338, 342, 343
Clarendon, Lord, 41, 78, 84, 94, 216, 355, 358, 371, 372
corruption and embezzlement, 172, 226–228, 231, 234–236, 238, 289, 291, 293, 327, 392, 398–402
  muster roll fraud, 168, 230, 231, 319, 409
Crimea, 268, 274, 277, 278, 280–285, 291, 294, 295, 299, 389, 406
Czajkowski, Michal (Sadık Pasha), 39, 50, 103, 147, 185, 217, 238, 243
  report on conscription of Christians, 341, 342
Czartoryski, Adam, 51
Çatana, battle of, 177, 178

Dannenberg, General Pyotr, 107
Danubian front, 101, 102, 177
desertions, 164, 171, 176, 178, 194, 222, 230, 245, 252, 254, 267, 367, 377–379
destans (epic poems), 9
dissertations and theses in Turkish, 22
Divan-ı Harb, 378
Dundas, Admiral, 74, 197, 199
Durand, François (Galata banker), 317

Egyptian fleet, 112
Engels, Friedrich, 34, 125, 165
esnan, 189
equality for Ottoman non-Muslims, 347
Ethem Bey, Kaimmakam, 123
export bans, 59

favouritism in the Ottoman army, 49
four points, 181

France, declaration of war, 180
French consul in Batum, 203
  consul(ate) in Erzurum, 163, 164, 170, 224
  consul in Mosul, 375
  consul in Trabzon, 224
Fuad Efendi (Pasha), 9, 31, 37, 48, 73, 74, 282, 289, 322, 343, 355, 375–377, 400

Galata bankers, 293, 297, 300, 302, 314, 316
Georgian militia, 254, 255
Ghyka, Prince, Hospodar of Moldavia, 81
Giaour Mountain, 343
Goldsmid, Baron Sir Isaac Lyon, 310, 317, 319
Gorchakov, General Mikhail, 99
Gözleve, 15, 24, 85, 249, 266, 268, 278–284
  Russian attack on, 279–280
Greek Church and Patriarchate, 75–80, 90, 333, 345
Greek insurgence, 68, 183, 346, 359, 387
Gromonosets, 73
guerre d'Orient, 4
Guyon, General Richard (Hurşid Pasha), 173, 174, 215, 219
  on the defeats of the Anatolian army, 175, 176
  trial at the MVL, 223
Gürel, Tevfik, 13

Halil Efendi, Mülazım, 123
Hamelin, Admiral, 116, 199
Hamid Bey (Mikhail Shervashidze), 206, 207, 209
Hasan Bey, Binbaşı Yalovalı, 123
Hasan Pasha, Egyptian, Mirliva, 112
Hasan Pasha, Mirliva, 219, 221
Hasan Rıza Pasha, Serasker, 131, 185, 191
Hasan Yazıcı, 167, 168, 170, 371
Hayreddin Bey, 11
Hayreddin Pasha, Zaptiye Müşiri Mehmed, 162, 172, 190, 232, 353, 383
d'Hilliers, General Louis-Achille Baraguey, 101, 128, 137, 388
holy places, dispute over, 64
Hornby, Lady, 326
Hornby, Sir Edmund Grimany, 325, 327
Hungarian officers in the Ottoman army, 147, 148, 215

Hurşid Pasha, see Guyon
Hurşid Reis of Arhavi, 349
Hüseyin Avni Pasha, 103
Hüseyin Pasha, 233
Hüseyin Pasha, Riyale, 113, 117

iane-i askeriyye, 50, 339, 340, 342
iane-i harbiye, 319–322
Ingur, battle of, 253, 254
Inkerman, battle of, 278
Iran, frontier with the Ottoman Empire, 67
Islahat Fermanı, 335, 343, 344
İsmail Pasha, Ferik Çerkes, 103, 107, 177
İsmail Rahmi Pasha, governor of Aleppo, 264
İzzeddin Şir, see Yezdanşêr

Kabuli Efendi, 318, 342
Kamil Pasha, 364, 402
Kapudan Pasha, 197
Karal, Enver Ziya, review of his work *Osmanlı Tarihi*, 15
Karapapak irregular cavalry, 159
Kars, siege and fall of, 245, 251, 256
  medal of, 252
Kasım Ağa, 229, 366, 383
Kerim Pasha, Müşir (Baba Kerim), 8, 10, 157, 166, 214, 219, 223, 233, 251, 256, 257
Kırzıoğlu, Fahrettin, review of his work *1855 Kars Zaferi*, 15
Klapka, General, 148, 225, 226
Kmety, General György (Ismail Pasha), 147, 214
Kornilov, Vice Admiral, 118
Koszta, Martin, affair of, 86
Kozma, 231, 232
Kuleli Incident, 396
Kurat, Akdes Nimet, review of his book, 16
Kurdistan, 46, 102, 149, 360, 361, 364, 367, 370, 373, 374
  defined by Şemseddin Sami, 360
Kurds, 28, 105, 159, 167, 168, 170, 173, 229, 292, 359–363, 365–370, 375
  Kurdish notables, 359–362, 366, 368, 377
Kurtoğlu, Fevzi, 12
Küçük Kaynarca, treaty of, 75
Kürekdere, battle of, 220–222

Lacour, Edmond de, French ambassador in Istanbul, 94
Légion Polonaise, 51, 147

Leward, Frank, 331
Lhuys, Edouard Drouyn de, 94, 282, 303, 304, 314
line-of-battle ships, 110, 111, 113, 115–117, 119, 126, 138, 187, 197, 200, 201, 270
loan control commission, 18, 112, 284, 296, 318, 323, 324, 326
Longworth, John, 208
Loris-Melikov, Colonel Mikhail, 218, 366
Lyons, Rear Admiral Edmund, 200
Lütfi Efendi, as official chronicler, 6, 305

Mahmud II, reforms, 49
Mahmud Pasha, Kapudan, 97, 110, 113, 126, 131, 134, 135
Mansur Bey, 368, 373, 375
Marx, Karl, review of his war reportage, 34
  on Anatolian army, 173
Meclis-i Âli-i Tanzimat, 343
Meclis-i Bahriye (Naval Council), 133
Meclis-i Mahsus, 134
Meclis-i Umumi, 95
Meffray, Colonel Count Charles de, 215, 217, 219, 222, 224, 225
Mehmed Ali Pasha, Serasker, Damad, 73, 98, 177
Mehmed Pasha, Kavaklı, 13, 373, 374
Mehmed Emin Pasha, Kıbrıslı, 7, 51, 130, 131, 191, 204, 230, 231, 299, 300, 343, 344, 351, 411
Mehmed Pasha, Vanlı, 224
Mehmed Reşid Pasha, governor of Baghdad, 264, 265
Melek Hanım, 300
Menshikov, Aleksandr Sergeyevich, name spelled as *Mençikof*, 4
  mission to Istanbul, 71
  ultimatum to the Porte, 77
Mesud Giray, 85
Meyendorff, Baron, 181
Mingrelia, 254, 255
Minié rifles, 229, 230, 251, 253, 269, 278, 295, 410
Muhammed Emin, 151, 196, 197, 206, 210
Muravyov, General Nikolay N., 26, 27, 238, 243, 244, 251, 255, 258, 366, 375, 406
Musa Hulusi Pasha, Ferik, 183
Musa Safveti Pasha, 289, 301, 302, 316

Mustafa Naili Pasha, Giritli, the grandvizier, 93, 130, 150
Mustafa Pasha, Bahriye Feriki, İngiliz, 112, 117, 131, 132, 135
Mustafa Pasha, Müşir Alyanak, 203, 206
Mustafa Raşid Pasha, Mirliva, 216, 219
Mustafa Zarif Pasha, see Zarif Mustafa Pasha
muster roll fraud, see corruption
Musurus, Kostaki, 78, 88, 90, 137, 138, 142, 180, 303, 306, 309-312, 315, 323, 346, 407

Nakhimov, Vice Admiral, 118, 120
Namık Kemal, 7, 10, 11, 396-398, 408
Namık Pasha, Mehmed, 17, 18, 30, 41, 130, 301-316, 320, 396, 408
Napoleon III, 29, 30, 35, 65-67, 74, 101, 126, 141, 142, 304, 314, 406
Nesselrode, Count Karl, 68, 71, 72, 80, 186
Newcastle, Duke of, 210
Nikolai I, 16, 27-30, 33, 49, 55, 58, 60, 101, 106, 129, 280, 405, 406
Novosilskiy, Rear Admiral, 119

Odessa, bombardment of, 182
"Old Turkish" party, 47, 70
Oltenitsa, battle of, 108
Orbeliani, General Prince, 159
Osman Bey, Major, 8
Osman Pasha, Patrona, 113, 117, 123
Osman, Sergeant, of Istanbul, 378, 379
Osten-Sacken, Colonel, report on Ömer Pasha, 57
 report on Ali Rıza Pasha and Selim Pasha, 144
Osten-Sacken, Count, governor of Odessa, 182
Ottoman and Turkish sources, 5
Ottoman army
 Anatolian army, 8, 13, 14, 24, 38, 49, 58, 93, 124, 143, 146, 214, 383, 391-393, 396, 407, 409
 animosity between the educated and the uneducated, 146, 232
 artillery, 160, 170
 at Başgedikler, 167
 Batum army, 8, 13, 41, 93, 143, 153, 155, 191, 203, 206, 252, 253, 318, 353
 bayoneting live prisoners, 177, 178
 deaths from diseases, 190, 191, 195
 deprivations suffered in the Crimea, 276-278
 expedition to Circassia, 201, 202
 fleet, 111, 112, 115, 122, 129, 136, 137, 187, 197-202, 270, 404
 number of regular troops, 284
 Rumeli(an) army, 14, 49, 57, 81, 93, 99, 102-104, 143, 146, 147, 171, 179, 206, 226, 233, 283, 382, 398, 410
 weakness of, 145
Ottoman financial crisis, 289, 316
 loans of 1854 and 1855, 316-319, 322-324
 military expenditure, 299
 revenues and budget, 298
 taxes, 292
 war expenses, 295
Ottoman-Turkish historiography, 5
Ömer Lütfi Pasha, 8, 12, 15, 31, 36, 38, 49, 57, 81, 93, 99, 100, 103, 108, 171, 177-179, 185, 248-256, 264, 266, 267, 273, 278, 283, 311, 321, 338, 382, 386, 398, 411

palace women, 300, 301
Palmerston, Lord, 29, 87, 142, 216, 279, 286, 289, 306-308, 313, 322, 337, 344
Paris, Treaty of, 285-288
Paskevich, Field Marshal Ivan, 104, 106, 184, 186
Pélissier, General, 247, 250, 251, 271, 283
Pokrovskiy, Mikhail, review of his work, 29
 on Nikolai's demand, 84
Polish officers in the Ottoman army, 147, 148, 215, 217
Porte, the Sublime, see Sublime Porte
public opinion, 87, 141

Raglan, Lord, 185
Rauf Bey, 95
Redcliffe, Lord Stratford de, 76, 95, 115, 116, 136, 138, 203, 240, 293
 on Ottoman slavery, 351
Redhouse, James, 237, 332
redif troops, 55, 163, 189, 245
Reid, James, review of his book, 42
reform in the Ottoman army, 49
Reşid Pasha, Mustafa, 6, 9, 31, 46, 48, 97, 100, 129, 362, 371, 372, 381, 384, 388, 399, 404, 405, 411, 412
 against the *Islahat Fermanı*, 346
Reşid Pasha, governor of Baghdad, 321
Rifat Pasha, 74
Rıza Efendi, Müsteşar, 157

Rose, Colonel Hugh, 74
Rothschild, 301, 303, 304, 307, 309, 310, 312, 323, 326
Russell, Lord John, 69, 70, 282, 339
Russell, William Howard, 34, 44, 272–275, 279
Russian, appeal to the population, 244
  armies cross the Pruth, 81
  Caucasus army, 62, 218
  fleet, 112, 115, 117, 126, 187, 191, 199, 201, 202
  foreign loans, 324
  military agents, reports of, 55
  occupation of the principalities, 16, 79, 82, 88, 106, 141, 183, 184, 403
  sources, review of, 25
  trade with Britain, 63
Ruzname-i Ceride-i Havadis, 6

Sadık Pasha, see Czajkowski
Sandwith, Dr Humphry, 7, 15, 24, 35, 44, 145, 171, 191, 217, 229, 231, 232, 373, 378, 407
sarrafs, 292, 293, 297, 300, 301, 361
Sefer Bey (Pasha) Zanuko, 152, 197, 202
Selim Pasha, Ferik, 144, 213
Selim Pasha, Haseki Mehmed Selim, Hassa Müşiri, 112, 154, 252
Serfiraz Hanım, 300
Sevastopol, siege of, 268–270, 273, 278, 280, 282–286, 322, 406
Seymour, Sir Hamilton, conversation with Nikolai I, 68
Shamil, Sheikh, 31, 113, 149, 150, 153, 195, 196, 202
  kidnapping of women, 203, 205
Shamuil, see Shamil
Shervashidze, see Hamid Bey
"sick man of Europe", 68
Silistria, siege of, 184
Sinop, battle of, 109
  "massacre of", 143
Slade, Vice Admiral Adolphus (Mushaver Pasha), 7, 20, 21, 24, 37, 38, 43, 44, 83, 90, 109, 113, 114, 116, 121–123, 126, 128, 130, 138, 182, 198, 199, 242, 248–250, 255, 260, 269, 272, 275–277, 321, 322, 330, 370, 401
slavery and slave trade, 22, 54, 154, 165, 211, 238, 254, 339, 348–358, 365, 383, 405, 411
  at the Kars army, 354
softas, 84, 91, 139
soldiers' pay, 52–55

Stein, General Maximilian (Ferhad Pasha), 148, 215
Stirbey, Prince, Hospodar of Wallachia, 81
Straits Convention of 1841, 80
Sublime Porte, protest against the occupation of the principalities, 82
  declaration of war, 99
Şahin, Hasan, review of his doctoral dissertation, 24
Şekvetil, battle of, 154
şeşhane, şeşhaneci (chasseurs), 108, 160, 218, 229, 253
şeyhülislam, 93, 94, 97, 303, 321, 332, 334, 338, 343, 345, 357, 358
Şükrü Pasha, Mirliva, 214, 222, 223, 233, 236, 237, 371, 372

Taif, the steamship, 121, 136
Tanzimat, 14, 149, 193, 289, 292, 293, 332, 334, 343, 364, 400, 411
Tarle, Yevgeniy, 30, 124
Takvim-i Vekayi, 6, 142, 143, 272, 320, 342
The Times, 142, 221, 272
Thouvenel, Edouard-Antoine de, 332
Totleben, Eduard, Colonel, 183
Translation Bureau, 48
Tunis army, 42, 81, 155, 230, 246, 410
Turkish, Contingent, 24, 52, 245, 246, 247, 249, 257, 259–263, 265
  nationalism, 394, 395, 408
  official military history, review of, 19
Ultimatum, 82
Türkgeldi, Ali Fuat, 12
Türkistan, 395
typhus, 190

ulema, 5, 23, 79, 84, 91, 92, 94–98, 139, 218, 321, 339, 356, 357, 396, 397
Urquhart, David, 58

Varna, on fire, 188
Vasıf Pasha, Müşir Mehmed, 8, 192, 234, 238, 243, 245, 252, 255, 256, 265, 372
Veli (Veliyüddün) Pasha, Ottoman ambassador in Paris, 78, 303, 305, 313, 314, 315, 346
Veli Pasha, Ferik, 158, 219
Vienna Conference, March 1855, 335
Vivian, General, 246, 247, 249, 260, 263, 265, 266, 267
Vorontsov, General Prince, 148
vostochnaya voina, 4

Walpole, Colonel, 263, 264, 389–391
Williams, Colonel (General) William, 14, 34, 35, 38, 205, 226–256, 267, 319, 354, 366, 370–375, 391, 401, 409, 410
Wysocki, General, 147

Yahya Bey, Captain, 124
Yezdanşêr, 28, 44, 170, 360, 362, 363, 367–377
Yıldız, Mehmet, review of his dissertation, 23
Yusuf Halis Efendi, 10

Zaim Feyzullah Pasha, 192
Zakavkaz'e, 4
Zamoyski, Count Wladislaw, 103
Zarif Mustafa Pasha, 13, 150, 153, 157, 162, 191, 192, 219
   memoirs, 192, 193, 194
   charges against, 234

www.ingramcontent.com/pod-product-compliance
Lightning Source LLC
Chambersburg PA
CBHW081145290426
44108CB00018B/2447